McGraw-Hill's dynamic new PowerWeb completes the online offering with access to current full-text articles, quizzing and assessment, validated links to relevant material, interactive glossaries, weekly updates, and interactive web exercises. PowerWeb is organized by course area, ensuring that you and your students receive only the most pertinent and topical information. *http://www.dushkin.com/powerweb*

Instructors in the new economy space continually confront the problem of staying current. Securing fresh materials and cases in the classroom, and more generally, being at the cutting edge of practice and theory are among the most important—and time-consuming—of the Instructor's duties. The marketspaceU.com site solves these problems by offering key features for the Instructor: (1) Dashboards that update cases every 60 days, (2) a newsfeed that announces developments related to the case, (3) recommended video "snippets" (5–10 minute videos) that support the lecture/case discussion, (4) recommended case mixes, and (5) e-mail support from our in-house e-commerce faculty team. *http://www.marketspaceu.com*

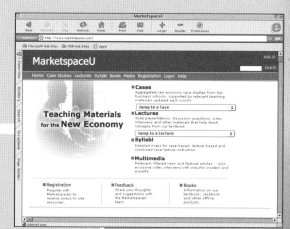

e-Commerce strategy formulation entails basic choices about how a given firm will win in the new economy. These choices include questions such as: Where does the firm play (market-opportunity analysis)? How does it win (business model)? and What is the firm worth (valuation)?

The strategy formulation framework identifies seven choice areas that confront the firm and three "market forces" that provide context for these choices. The seven choices involve:
- market opportunity analysis,
- business model selection,
- design of the customer interface,
- branding and communications,
- implementation and evaluation (including both valuation and metrics)

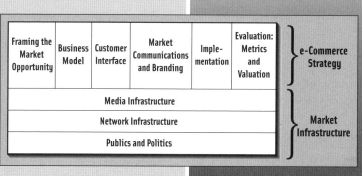

The three market forces involved are network infrastructure, the convergence of traditional (e.g., broadcast television, radio, magazines, newspapers) and new media (e.g., the Web, Interactive CDs), and the public policy issues that are central to sustainability of the Internet (e.g., privacy, taxes, community).

Cases in
e-Commerce

Jeffrey F. Rayport
CEO of Marketspace, a Monitor Group Company

Bernard J. Jaworski
Marketspace, a Monitor Group Company

McGraw-Hill/Irwin
marketspaceU

Boston   Burr Ridge, IL   Dubuque, IA   Madison, WI   New York   San Francisco   St. Louis
Bangkok   Bogotá   Caracas   Kuala Lumpur   Lisbon   London   Madrid   Mexico City
Milan   Montreal   New Delhi   Santiago   Seoul   Singapore   Sydney   Taipei   Toronto

McGraw-Hill Higher Education

A Division of The McGraw-Hill Companies

CASES IN E-COMMERCE
Published by McGraw-Hill/Irwin/marketspaceU, an imprint of The McGraw-Hill
Companies, Inc. 1221 Avenue of the Americas, New York, NY 10020. Copyright © 2002 by
Rayport and Jaworski. All rights reserved. No part of this publication may be reproduced or
distributed in any form or by any means, or stored in a data base or retrieval system, without the prior written consent of Rayport and Jaworski, including, but not limited to, in any
network or other electronic storage or transmission, or broadcast for distance learning.
Some ancillaries, including electronic and print components, may not be available to customers outside the United States.

Case material of the Harvard Graduate School of Business Administration is made possible
by the cooperation of business firms and other organizations which may wish to remain
anonymous by having names, quantities, and other identifying details disguised while maintaining basic relationships. Cases are prepared as the basis for class discussion rather than to
illustrate either effective or ineffective handling of an administrative situation.

This book is printed on acid-free paper.

1 2 3 4 5 6 7 8 9 0 CCW / CCW 0 9 8 7 6 5 4 3 2 1

ISBN 0-07-250095-6

Publisher: *John E. Biernat*
Executive Editor: *Gary L. Bauer*
Developmental Editor: *Christine Parker*
Marketing Manager: *Kimberly Kanakes Szum*
Project Manager: *Christine A. Vaughan*
Lead Production Supervisor: *Heather D. Burbridge*
Media Producer: *Todd Labak*
Designer: *Artemio Ortiz*
Cover Design: *Proof Positive/Farrowlyne Associates, Inc.*
Interior Design: *Proof Positive/Farrowlyne Associates, Inc.*
Printer: *Courier-Westford*
Typeface: *10/12 Minion*
Compositor: *Black Dot Composition/Proof Positive/Farrowlyne Associates, Inc.*

Library of Congress Card Number: 2001087307

www.mhhe.com

PREFACE

To say the Internet changes everything is, in some high-technology circles, almost a cliché. But the case studies contained in this volume collectively make a strong argument for the truth of that now-familiar phrase. Or, put differently, the application of new media and information technology to business—which, of course, includes the Internet and the World Wide Web—has not only changed what we know about management, strategy, and business design but also has assured us of a continuing and unfolding impact on what managers do and how businesses operate in the foreseeable future. All hype aside, there is truly a revolution here, and we have little choice but to embrace it.

With this collection of cases on businesses that are enabled by the Internet and powered by new media, we aim to equip present and future executives, managers, and strategists in becoming successful at this time of sweeping change. This book is an entry point into a learning system that includes this casebook, a separate but closely related textbook, video interviews, and integrated Web support. The result is a state-of-the-art, integrated system for teaching e-commerce business practice and theory.

The most succinct way of characterizing the business revolution unfolding today is to understand that we are operating in what some call the new economy. While there are many definitions of this concept, new economy businesses all exhibit signal attributes that identify them as such. Successful new economy firms must be able to accomplish each of the following tasks:

- Create value largely or exclusively through the gathering, synthesizing, and distribution of information. Success is predicated on creating value by tapping the power of electronic information networks and new media interfaces.
- Formulate strategy in ways that make managing the enterprise and the technology converge.
- Compete in real time rather than in "cycle time" and operate in a constantly responsive dialogue with customers and markets.
- Operate in a world characterized by low entry barriers, near-zero variable costs of operation, and, as a result, intense, constantly shifting competition.
- Organize resources around the demand side—e.g., customers, markets, trends, and needs—rather than around the supply side, as businesses have done in the past.
- Manage relationships with customers and markets through "screen-to-face" channels and interfaces, meaning that in addition to traditional face-to-face or people-mediated interfaces, technology also manages these relationships.
- Use technology-mediated channels, which means that ongoing operations are subject to measurement and tracking in unprecedented and accountable ways.

Taking these themes together does more than furnish a rigorous understanding of what business managers and pundits alike mean when they talk about doing business in the new economy. Each of these statements implies significant changes in how new economy practitioners determine strategy, deploy resources, manage firms, craft relationships with their markets, and measure results. This does not mean that everything we know about business up to this point has become irrelevant and obsolete, but it does mean that significant changes in the environment of business justify—indeed, demand—radically new approaches to thinking about strategy and management.

As a result, as the cases in this volume illustrate, we strongly believe that the revolution in business is, in fact, larger than any one particular technology, including the Internet, and that it is more profound than any one innovation, including the World Wide Web. We are entering a world in which a new array of considerations—issues that were once peripheral to management or completely outside its scope—have now taken center stage. These include technology, interface design, real-time performance, and market metrics, along with deep understanding of customer attitudes and behavior. For anyone who is considering a career in business of any kind that impinges on these new economy realities, understanding the complexity of these themes is essential to business success, if not business survival.

In this sense, we have developed this set of cases (and related materials) to focus not only on technology but also on a world of business activity enabled by technology. Increasingly, the new economy is built of businesses that at their core, exploit a variety of technological innovations. These innovations have proven necessary, but not sufficient, in the creation of a viable business proposition. Rather, they have created a flood of new entrants in every sector of the economy, most with some kind of technology-enabled approach to changing the way traditional industries work; this trend, in turn, has resulted in a flood of venture capital and private equity into the new economy sector that has further fueled the pace of innovation and competition.

The decline of the technology sector in the world's financial markets in mid-2000 has not wiped out the venture capital allocated to fueling this revolution, nor will the revolution necessarily slow. Instead, capital flows have slowed because investors have become more considered in their funding decisions. The result of that action is nothing but good: we will simply see better, more rigorous business plans completing their funding rounds—and more profoundly innovative business models emerge throughout the economy.

It would, however, be a mistake to interpret these developments—both the hype surrounding digital technology and its more recent deflation in the estimation of our capital markets—as a sign that technology is the new competitive weapon for business. Rather, it is part of the new definition of the minimum entry price—or what gamblers would call "table stakes"—of doing business. Put differently, technology is no longer the scarce resource. Indeed, it is as ubiquitous in the new economy as, until recently, was capital. The scarce resources are the talented individuals with management, strategy, and executive skills tailored to doing business in the new economy. And it is to those talented managers, present and future, that we dedicate these cases.

Equipping managers today and tomorrow constitutes the goal of the learning system that includes this casebook. Again, we are here to provide tools to present and future executives, managers, and strategists in becoming successful creators of value in the new economy. While this success involves a solid grasp of relevant technology and new media forms, it demands just as solid a grasp of how the functions of the manager and executive have changed in this new world.

It is no coincidence that today in Silicon Valley—easily "ground zero" of the Internet business revolution—there are hundreds of CEO positions open with few if any candidates to fill them. The Valley is a place rife with ideas, entrepreneurs, and capital; it is a place where the idea of a shortage in *anything* seems almost a contradiction in terms. Yet there is truly a shortage of one critical skill set, and it is the ability to manage effectively at the highest levels in the world that the new economy has wrought.

You, the reader, are the person with the potential to develop such skills—and this is an exciting notion. There could not be a better time in the history of business to have such skills. We believe that one highly effective way of acquiring those skills is through the detailed study of what other managers, entrepreneurs, and businesses have done as they grapple with their own strategic exigencies. A detailed snapshot into real businesses facing real challenges is what case studies are all about.

Indeed, every one of the cases in this book represents a capsule of our experiences visiting the companies; talking to managers, customers, suppliers, and competitors; figuring out what issues kept the CEOs up at night; and ultimately framing those issues as managerial choices for students in classrooms at Harvard Business School (HBS). Almost without exception, our classes that used these cases were blessed by the CEOs of the companies themselves, who came to HBS to tap into the high-octane blend of analytic insight, focus-group feedback, and future talent that the classrooms at the top business schools represent. Also without exception, the reactions of those CEOs and their top managers to those case discussions drove our revision of the cases, in order to highlight key details and to ensure that we got the dynamics of their businesses right. This volume is the fruit of that process. Each case truly constitutes a piece of business reality at a time of enormous, dramatic, exciting change—and at a time when managers throughout the world were truly inventing the future of business as we will know it in the digital era.

With these case studies at your fingertips—and therefore the combined managerial experience contained therein—the world will truly be your oyster—a high-technology one.

Background on Case Development

The majority of the case studies in this volume were developed at HBS to support instruction in a course that originated in the 1994–1995 academic year called "Managing in the Marketspace." The course was created by Jeffrey F. Rayport, a member of the HBS faculty in the Service Management Unit, and John J. Sviokla, a colleague in the HBS Management Information Systems Unit. Rayport and Sviokla coined the term "marketspace" at a time when it was clear that commercial activities were taking place increasingly in the information world rather than the physical one. Indeed, it was while teaching first year marketing at HBS that this insight first became apparent. Old models such as the marketing mix (product, price, promotion, and distribution) seemed instructive but limited in a world where customer relationships and economic transactions created maximum value in technology-based information environments or through technology-mediated information channels. This conviction took the form of a simple observation—namely, that businesses were increasingly competing not in one but in two worlds, one made of physical reality (marketplace) and the other of information (marketspace).

The earliest version of the course—the first e-commerce course offered at a top-tier business school in the world—bore little resemblance to the cases in this book, in that it contained very few cases involving the Internet. After all, in 1994, Mosaic had barely seen the light of day, and the Web, therefore, was immature in every sense, especially as a platform or arena for commerce. Instead, the course focused on case studies dealing with management of customers and markets using other kinds of network-enabled technology platforms, such as catalogs using call centers, TV-home shopping such as QVC and Home Shopping Network, auto auctions using proprietary satellite link-ups such as AUCNET in Japan, commercial dial-up services such as Prodigy and Compuserve, and, of course, all manner of CD-ROM businesses for reference materials and data retreival. Only near the time of the second iteration of the course, in 1996, did the Web emerge to dominate all other e-commerce platforms and define the digital revolution for business. At this point, our case development shifted primarily to Web-enabled businesses (although not exclusively), and the course became a staple of the second-year curriculum at HBS.

Indeed, a fundamental tenet of our work continues to be that the revolution at hand is only exemplified by, and certainly not limited to, the Internet. Anywhere we find technology managing relationships between companies and their customers and markets—where technology rather than people drives the "front-office" interface—in that place, we can say with confidence, another aspect of this revolution is unfolding. The cases in this book reflect that bias.

The marketspace course went on at HBS to be taught successfully by a number of our colleagues, including Professor Leonard A. Schlesinger, now an executive at The Limited, and Tom Eisenmann, who remains at HBS. Meanwhile, beginning in 1997, Bernie Jaworski began using cases from the course to establish the first required curriculum e-commerce course in the United States at the University of Southern California's Marshall School of Business. Jaworski's teaching helped further to refine these materials and broaden their appeal as vehicles for understanding Internet businesses.

In developing and revising these cases, we are indebted to the entrepreneurs who made their time available to travel to HBS to see students there discuss the cases on their companies. The cooperation of these entrepreneurs in allowing us access to their companiers and their insights as they reacted to class discussions proved invaluable to the creation of these materials. The individuals include Jeff Bezos, founder and CEO of Amazon.com; Martin Nisenholtz, founder and CEO of nytimes.com; Robert Rodin, former CEO of Marshall Industries, Inc. (the company is now part of the merged entity Avnet Marshall); Andrew Heyward, President of CBS News; Larry Kramer, founder, Chairman, and CEO of CBS.Market-Watch.com; Jeff Taylor, founder and CEO of Monster.com (a unit of TMP Worldwide); Carl Rosendorf, a top executive at BarnesandNoble.com; Stuart Spiegel, former Vice President and General Manager of iQVC; Darlene Daggett, Executive Vice President of Merchandising/Sales and Product Planning at QVC, Inc.; Kevin Newman, former CEO of first direct; Tim DeMello, founder and CEO of now defunct Streamline; Robert Olson, cofounder and former CEO of what was Virtual Vineyards (now Wine.com); Jim Griffin, now CEO of Cherry Lane Digital and formerly chief technology officer at Geffen Records; and Jack Rovner and Bob Jamieson, who together run the RCA Records label at BMG Entertainment.

Every one of these individuals worked with us on case studies concerning their businesses and joined us in one or more class discussion. We are truly the beneficiaries of their innovation and inspiration.

Approach

This casebook is written for present and future business practitioners in the new economy. As such, it provides both best of breed case studies and a preview of core concepts of new economy management and strategy. The casebook is informed and structured according to the major topics examined in our e-commerce textbook. We take this approach for a variety of reasons.

As we go to press with these cases, new economy management and strategy are, of necessity, subject to invention in real time. Every marketspace business we have studied—and our work is based on more than 100 case studies completed at the Harvard Business School over the last six years—has been engaged in the often wholesale creation of "new science" for doing business. Whether an enterprise is pioneering new forms of transactional commerce or mining customer information in new ways, thanks to the entrepreneurs building the new economy, entirely new areas of management science are unfolding around the world. We believe that researchers can only generate real insights for practice through deep observation of both new and established businesses as they wrestle to redefine business in light of these new economy challenges. Thus, we take a militantly field-based and practitioner-focused perspective on this work. This is not to say that management theory is irrelevant. Existing concepts and theories such as "network effects" and "increasing returns to scale" do apply. However, in general, we remain convinced that practice is far ahead of theory at this time in history.

Cases in e-Commerce provides 25 case studies that examine a broad range of business structures and core activities—from offline companies adding an online component to their business to pure "dot-com" companies attacking established players. Most of these cases represent materials developed through work at HBS; a small number are drawn from our colleagues engaged in field-based study of e-commerce at other top-flight business schools. Taken together, this case collection not only covers online renditions of retail and wholesale businesses but also provides insight into the business choices facing infrastructure, financial service, and media companies.

In this book, a collection of the freshest and most relevant case studies are presented within a structure of rigorous concepts, frameworks, and approaches that represent an entire applications suite of tools for doing business in the new economy. Observation of business practices, while often fascinating and instructive, is really just the beginning. We have taken our knowledge of practice, as developed through these case studies, and followed through with conceptualization. This collection of cases, along with our "wrap-around" conceptual structure, provides instructor and student alike with a broad, comprehensive, and rigorous survey of the challenges new economy managers must currently face, along with approaches to address them.

Content and Organization

Cases in e-Commerce is organized around the decision-making process we propose for formulating new economy enterprise strategy. There are six interrelated, sequential decisions to this strategy—market-opportunity analysis, business model, customer interface, market communications and branding, implementation, and evaluation. These decisions are made in the context of a changing market-level infrastructure. As we define it, infrastructure includes factors related to network infrastructure and media convergence.

As such, the sequence and topics of chapters reflect the intellectual architecture of our approach to managing in this field. Chapters are organized to reflect the framework sequence of the decision-making process.

- **Chapter 1–Overview:** Many students and clients ask us what is different about managing in the new economy. In this chapter, we present Amazon.com and BarnesandNoble.com as cases of quintessential new economy companies, then set forth the differences as seen through lenses of their business challenges. Through these cases we attempt to frame the unique attributes of the new economy and the implications for managers and strategists. We present a working definition and framework for the study and practice of e-commerce.

- **Chapter 2–Framing the Market Opportunity:** In this chapter, we revisit the basics for any business to construct an original new economy approach to formulating business strategy. We provide PlanetAll and CarPoint.com as examples for discussion of the process. We focus on the players who make up the dynamics of any business—customers, competitors, and strategic partners. The goal here is to understand what market analysis becomes in this new world, introducing a process for not only understanding the market but also identifying those portions of the market that are unserved or underserved.

- **Chapter 3–Business Models:** A business-model definition is essential to competition in this new space. Here we introduce the four components of the marketspace business model: (1) the value proposition or cluster, (2) the product offering that we call a marketspace offering, (3) the resource system that the firm selects to deliver the offering, and (4) a financial model that enables the business to generate revenues, cash flows, and, ultimately, profit margins or valuation potential. We introduce Egghead.com, Virtual Vineyards, Weather Services Corporation, Streamline, ChemUnity, and Independer as examples to consider when discussing these four key choices that consitute the foundation of strategy decisions.

- **Chapter 4–The Customer Interface:** The visible presence of most e-commerce businesses is a digital or rich media interface. While new economy businesses may make substantial use of traditional offline interfaces—such as retail points of sale, printed catalogs, stand-alone kiosks, and call centers—they rely primarily on a virtual storefront located on the Web and enabled by the Internet. These elements include content, context, community, commerce, customization, communications, and connection. Here we present iVillage, first direct, QVC, Inc., and Frontgate Catalog as examples for discussing the various customer interfaces that managers must consider when building online and/or offline businesses.

- **Chapter 5–Market Communications and Branding:** In the demand-oriented world of the new economy, there is nothing more valuable than mindshare or the ability to attract and hold the attention of markets and customers. The traditional tools of attention management are marketing communications and promotion. Many believed that the Web would create a world of downward price pressure and rapid margin erosion for goods and services, wherein everything sold would almost instaneously become a commodity. But the truth is very different. In fact, differentiation of products, services, and offering is not only possible on the Web, but also enormously attractive in commercial terms, if done effectively. At the same time, brands are more important than ever—some would argue that, at least in business-to-consumer ventures, they are essential to success. We provide Monster.com and E-LOAN as examples for this discussion.

- *Chapter 6–Implementation:* If strategy is about "what to do," implementation is about "how to do it." Because most management texts focus on strategy, implementation is often left to the last chapter. Indeed, in the management literature, implementation has constituted a "poor cousin" of fashion-forward fields such as strategy, marketing, and finance. Doing business in the new economy demands a different approach. Because technology-enabled businesses operate in constant and dynamic dialogue with their markets, it is difficult—and unproductive—to approach strategy and implementation in a linear, sequential fashion. Rather, they are two elements in a real-time cycle, wherein each set of decisions pertaining to strategy and implementation must constantly be reevaluated, based on new data passsed from one activity to the other. In this chapter, we consider both the "delivery system" and role of practice-based innovation in strategy implementation. Here iQVC and Marshall Industries serve as examples for discussing the importance of implementation in business strategy.

- *Chapter 7–Metrics and Valuation:* One of the more provocative aspects of the e-commerce revolution has been the extraordinary valuations that Web-based businesses achieved at the height of dot-com mania in capital markets around the world. These range from Yahoo!, the Web's leading search engine, which on good days is worth more than General Motors, to America Online, which achieved a valuation so high that it was able to acquire Time Warner, the world's largest media conglomerate. Examples also include phenomenal valuations outside the United States, such as the Hong Kong–based Pacific Century CyberWorks, a holding company of Internet business investments, which at one point achieved a valuation so rich that the company succcessfully acquired Hong Kong's national telecommunications giant and the India-based Wipro, an Internet services firm that, after an IPO on India's national stock exchange, became the most highly valued company in the nation's history. We attempt to cut through the hype that once surrounded such valuations with the aid of one of the world's leading experts on corporate valuation, Tom Copeland. We think the Tom.com case will enable a class to discuss the challenges of determining or projecting the valuation of an e-commerce business.

- *Chapter 8–Network Infrastructure:* In the new economy, the infrastructure of economic activity—primarily oriented around the processing and shipment of information—is both less visible and less familiar than, for example, traditional channels of distribution. In this chapter, we examine the market-level dynamics that operate outside the formal boundaries of the organization to provide the infrastructure for traditional and new business approaches. The cases "Nortel Networks: Internet Point of Presence" and "MindSpring" are good examples for discussing components of the "railroad" enabling the new economy.

- **Chapter 9–Media Convergence:** What rides on the "rails" of this new infrastructure is a wide variety of content and media. In this chapter, we examine media undergoing transformation from analog to digital and the consequences of value migration from old media to new media, media megamergers, and synergies. We provide *The New York Times* Electronic Media Company, CBS Evening News, CBS.MarketWatch.com, and RCA Records: The Digital Revolution as points for discussing the cross-over and combining of old and new media.

Supporting Materials

For Faculty

The changes taking place in real time in the new economy have both energized the classroom and brought a new set of challenges. Students have unprecedented access to sources of information and data, they have had a greater range of experiences—from investments in new economy companies to their own startup battle scars—and support for teachers in the classroom has advanced from a blackboard or two to a multimedia tool kit designed to make lessons more immediate.

These developments make the job of staying on top of the new economy and of effectively conveying its lessons more difficult. Given the speed of change, how can we prevent being blindsided by late-breaking developments? Because the "old warhorse" cases often no longer work, what *can* we repurpose, and where do we turn for new frameworks? In an effort to assist instructors, we have developed a comprehensive support package that includes materials available on the Web.

- ***e-Commerce* textbook:** Available separately for purchase, *e-Commerce* complements our casebook and charts an educational course through the key practical and theoretical issues in the new economy business landscape. The textbook is a collection of rigorous concepts, frameworks, and approaches that represent an entire applications suite of tools for doing business in the new economy. Observations of business practices, while often fascinating and instructive, are not enough. We have taken our knowledge of practice as developed through case studies and followed through with conceptualization.

Qualified adopters of *e-Commerce* or *Cases in e-Commerce* will also have access to two unique supporting websites, McGraw-Hill's Online Learning Center (OLC) and Marketspace's *www.marketspaceu.com*. Also available is a wide variety of additional materials to support the text.

- **McGraw-Hill/Irwin OLC:** McGraw-Hill/Irwin continues its leading role in providing excellent support to instructors and students in higher education. Instructors using this casebook to teach an e-commerce course or module are able to access the McGraw-Hill/Irwin OLC at *www.mhhe.com/marketspace* to obtain a print copy of the Teaching Notes for *Cases in e-Commerce*, find out about other McGraw-Hill/Irwin/Marketspace titles, and connect to *www.marketspaceu.com* for faculty support. Students can also utilize the self-assessment material that supports the companion textbook *e-Commerce*

1e and connect to *www.tnbt.com* for up-to-the-minute news on the new economy.

- **Teaching Notes:** Concise teaching notes help instructors understand the cases and teaching themes and also provide several helpful resources. Each teaching note offers a case synopsis, case teaching objectives, several case-analysis questions (and answers), warnings about potential problems with teaching the case, an endnote that provides a general update on what has happened to the company since the case was written, and several suggestions on how to organize the classroom boards when teaching a case.

- **Instructor's Manual:** Available directly from the McGraw-Hill OLC at *www.mhhe.com/marketspace,* the instructor's manual is designed and written to help faculty using the *e-Commerce* textbook. The manual offers a concise summary of each chapter's key themes, classroom questions (and answers) that highlight those themes and spur lively classroom debates, and relevant student project assignments (and answers) designed to reinforce key learning points in each chapter. For each chapter the instructor's manual provides teaching tips and suggestions, suggested test/discussion questions, and suggested exercises and associated websites that illustrate each chapter's content.

- **MarketspaceU Multimedia Materials:** We draw upon the extensive professional media capabilities of the Marketspace media group and of our sister website at *www.tnbt.com* to let the new economy speak for itself.

The MarketspaceU media archives contain over 100 focused broadcast-quality interviews with leading CEOs, investors, inventors, and implementers. All of the interviews were conducted at leading new economy conferences around the world. Streaming video excerpts are available on the website at *http://www.marketspaceu.com*, and full interviews are available on videotape for purchase.

MarketspaceU.com has captured Professors Rayport and Jaworski in a series of "dot-com debates" on live and lively issues in the new economy. Does profit matter? Do the valuations make sense? Who has it better, dot-com startups or dot-coms backed by brick-and-mortar giants? Does segmentation matter on the Web? Tune in by visiting us at *http://www.marketspaceu.com*, as Dr. Rayport and Dr. Jaworski provide an educational—and entertaining—Point-Counterpoint discussion.

- **Case Dashboard™ and Lecture Dashboard™:** For each case and lecture we offer an online dashboard, an enhanced multimedia teaching note to keep instructors informed about the cases and lecture topics and in control in the classroom. Each dashboard provides a quick summary of the case or lecture, key articles, teaching aids (e.g., a timeline of company developments), discussion questions and focused Point-Counterpoint debates, and real-time updates powered by our sister site, *www.tnbt.com.* Designed by our unique combination of academics and practitioners, briefing books provide confidence in the classroom. They focus and enhance preparation time, reduce the chance for blindside surprises, and direct discussion to the most recent issues.

Lecture Dashboards™ include an expanded PowerPoint presentation designed to capture key chapter themes and insights. These slide decks offer visual aids. Instructors can also incorporate these slides into PowerPoint presentations on various new economy topics.

- **Syllabi:** Also available are three types of suggested syllabi (all-case format, all-lecture format, combination case/lecture format):

  - *All-Case Teaching Format:* For instructors using an all-case format, we offer a syllabus that outlines a 13-week course structure and specifies suggested course timing, class-session summaries, recommended cases that illustrate important e-commerce themes, and class-preparation questions.

  - *All-Lecture Teaching Format:* For instructors using an all-lecture format, we offer a syllabus that outlines a 13-week course structure and specifies suggested course timing, class-session summaries, and class-preparation questions.

  - *Combination Case/Lecture Format:* For instructors using a combination case/lecture format, we offer a syllabus that outlines a 13-week course structure and specifies suggested course timing, class-session summaries, recommended cases to augment textbook-based lectures, and class-preparation questions.

For Students

You are riding the wave of a technological revolution that is changing the way that economy operates. Businesses, entrepreneurs, governments, academic institutions, nonprofit organizations—all are scrambling to hire students who understand, can operate in, and can lead in the new economy. MarketspaceU provides you with the knowledge to harness, drive, and benefit from the opportunities brought on by the new economy.

- *e-Commerce* provides a strong knowledge foundation of information about the new economy.
- *Cases in e-Commerce* show how new economy knowledge is applied in the business world.
- **Articles and forums** provide in-depth insight on what academic and new economy business leaders are thinking and doing.
- And every day **our sister site, *www.tnbt.com,*** provides new economy news updates—knowledge to keep you on the cutting edge of the new economy.

BRIEF CONTENTS

CONTENTS

Overview of
e-Commerce Framework

1

OVERVIEW OF e-COMMERCE FRAMEWORK

In the past few years, a great deal has been written about e-commerce. These writings have appeared in a variety of sources including the new wave of business periodicals such as *Business 2.0*, the *Industry Standard*, and *Upside*. They also have appeared in such age-old standards as the *Wall Street Journal, Business Week*, and *Fortune*. Articles on e-commerce now regularly appear in the business section of leading American newspapers, including the *Los Angeles Times*, the *New York Times*, and *USA Today*. In addition to print media, e-commerce dialogue has expanded to every media format possible, including the Internet, radio, television, and the corner drugstore. In short, e-commerce has not only taken over Wall Street, it has taken over Main Street.

Despite the term *e-commerce* entering into the vernacular, there are precious few case studies of what works in the New Economy. Case studies—long used in clinical psychology and medical and in business school programs—are designed to facilitate a dialogue, or more appropriately, a *healthy debate* on the alternative solutions to a particular problem. The interesting challenge in crafting cases on New Economy firms is that the "solution" seems to be changing as rapidly as the practitioner is able to diagnose the problem. We use the term *seems* since we believe there are some basic strategy principles that do stand the test of time. Our intent in providing the following set of case studies is to challenge your thinking—and your classroom debate—about the lasting principles that emerge in the New Economy.

In a general sense, the purpose of this book is to provide a series of case studies that will assist present and future managers in crafting and implementing e-commerce strategy. In particular, this chapter provides an overview of the framework that organizes the managerial decision-making process for e-commerce strategy (see Exhibit 1-1). The strategy process is comprised of five parts: framing the market opportunity, developing a sustainable business model, designing a customer interface, implementing the strategy, and evaluating the results. This strategy process rests on two key platforms: the network infrastructure that makes the Internet possible; and the convergence of alternative forms of media, such as radio, TV, magazines, and newspapers.

Electronic commerce can be formally defined as *technology-mediated exchanges between parties (individuals or organizations) as well as the electronically based intra- or interorganizational activities that facilitate the exchanges*. The focus of e-commerce is evolving away from simply technology-enabled to technology-mediated exchanges. Increasingly, transactions are managed or mediated largely by technology, and so is the relationship with the customer.

Exhibit 1-1 A Framework for e-Commerce

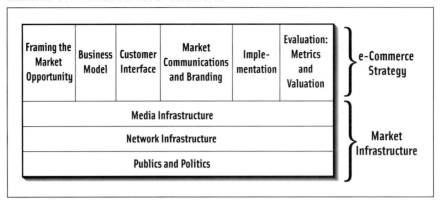

Four distinct categories of electronic commerce can be identified: business-to-business, business-to-consumer, consumer-to-consumer, and consumer-to-business. Business-to-business refers to the full spectrum of e-commerce that occurs between two organizations. Many of the same activities that occur in business-to-business also occur in the business-to-consumer context, except transactions relating to the "back office" of the customer that are often not tracked electronically. Consumer-to-consumer activities include auction-exchanges, classified ads, games, bulletin boards, and personal services. Consumers can also band together to form buyer groups in a consumer-to-business relationship (see Table 1-1).

While many authors and pundits have argued that there is nothing new about the New Economy, we believe e-commerce—in its purest form—is unique in several respects:

- Core strategic decisions are technology-based. Technology has been an increasing part of business strategy; in the New Economy, it is interlinked with strategy decisions as opposed to being a secondary, support activity.
- There is real-time competitive responsiveness. Competitors are easy to find, track, and compare. This transparency of activity leads to unprecedented speed in competitive responses.
- The store is always open. It is not necessary to retool the factory or close down for a quarterly inventory assessment.
- The customer interface shifts from a traditional, face-to-face interaction to a screen-to-face interaction.
- The customer controls the interaction. Certainly the online business attempts to shift and influence consumer behavior, but the consumer has increasing control of the interaction.
- On the firm side, e-businesses are able to track behavior to an unprecedented level—noting where the consumer visited, how long he or she stayed, and so on.
- Businesses benefit from network effects. Namely, the value of the service increases as the number of other users use the service. But network effects place increased burdens on online firms to become the "standard" for the category.
- e-commerce uses nontraditional evaluation metrics and emergent valuation models. Cash flow will continue to be the single most important indicator of the value of a business, but the logic of valuation has become more complex (i.e., real options theory). Moreover, the "scorecard" that one uses to judge the progress of a business is also changing.

Table 1-1 Four Categories of e-Commerce

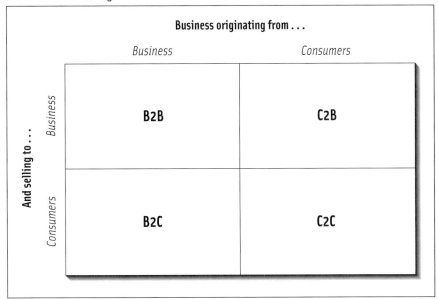

The combination of screen-to-customer interfaces, network effects, real-time competitive responses, and one-to-one customization leads to "value increases" for both the customer and the firm. Both parties have increased access to unique, heretofore inaccessible information—the customer benefits from increased availability, convenience, ease of use, and full information, while the firm obtains objective behavioral data on customers and competitors. This combination leads to a new, highly dynamic, competitive marketplace.

SYNOPSES OF CHAPTER CASES

AMAZON.COM (A)

Case Overview

Billed as the "Earth's Biggest Bookstore," Seattle-based Amazon.com lacked the espresso bars and comfortable sofas of the mega-chain bookstores, but it did offer highly integrated management systems that enabled its customers to search for books and receive e-mail notification of upcoming titles. The company founder, Chairman and CEO Jeffrey Bezos, believed these systems would ultimately allow Amazon.com to provide each customer with his or her own customized bookstore.

A key philosophy was to keep a small inventory of books on hand and order books directly from book distributors or publishers as needed, when orders were placed through the website. In addition, Amazon.com emphasized convenience, selection, price, and customer service—which Bezos believed to be even more important online than in the physical world. "Online, if you make a customer unhappy," he noted, "they won't tell six friends, they'll tell six thousand friends—e-mail lists, newsgroups, and so on. . . . But on the other hand, if you do everything that you say you'll do, if you treat your customers well, serve them in the ways you've promised, then you will have the opposite effect."

In response to the mega-bookstore challenge, Amazon.com also developed "communities of interest" through its Associates program, and its personalized search and notification services *Eyes* and *Editors*. Bezos explains, "Our goal is to redefine what a 'store' means." Despite the enormous success, Bezos did not believe his new Web retailer represented a threat to traditional bookstores: "Good bookstores have become the community centers of the late twentieth century. That's the basis on which they are going to compete." Physical and Internet bookstores simply serve different buying occasions, he contended. How would Amazon.com continue to dominate bookselling on the Internet? And how would it maximize its advantages over physical booksellers?

AMAZON.COM (B)

Case Overview

In January 1998, Jeff Bezos recalled the frenzied activity of the previous 12 months. Amazon.com was now a public company; it had raised $50.2 million in an initial public offering (IPO) in May 1997. It was, however, engaged in a fierce competitive battle with the Web-based subsidiary of Barnes & Noble, the largest bookseller in the United States, over domination of the online bookselling market.

During 1997, the war of electronic bookselling was fought between the two retail giants along seven dimensions. These were pricing policy, customer acquisition, associates and affiliates programs, personalization, customer service, user navigation, and legal challenges.

By the end of 1997, Amazon.com had developed a customer base of 1.5 million individuals, but its average gross margin on books sold had slipped. While Wall Street analysts did not expect Amazon.com to record a profit until 1999, Amazon.com's market valuation at year-end 1997 was approximately $1.4 billion, with its stock price at $60.25 per share as compared to an IPO price of $18 per share. By comparison, BarnesandNoble.com was expected to record $14 million in sales for its first nine months of operation in 1997.

Which business model would best serve Amazon's goal of being the "Earth's Biggest Bookstore"? Should Amazon.com match BarnesandNoble.com tit for tat with respect to pricing, marketing, and so on? Or should Amazon.com focus on attracting and retaining the growing market of mainstream users? What hybrid strategy would enable the company to keep its edge?

Amazon.com (A) and (B) Preparation Questions

1. Evaluate the Amazon.com website. What aspects of interface design, features, and functionality represent key strengths or weaknesses?

2. How would you account for Amazon.com's success in becoming the Web's most prominent retail site and one of its best known brands?

3. How is customer information captured on the Amazon.com site? How does Amazon.com use that information to create value for users?

4. How important is Amazon.com's homepage and site as opposed to its associates' sites? Should Amazon.com aim to realize sales primarily through its own site or through those of its associates?

5. What role do virtual communities play in enhancing users' experiences at Amazon.com? Are virtual communities central or peripheral to the site's efficiency and effectiveness as an online retailer?

6. Given the market entry of BarnesandNoble.com and Bertelsmann's BookCentral, what are the key moves Amazon.com should make to defend its franchise and sustain its revenue growth?

AMAZON.COM (C)

Case Overview

This case reviews Amazon.com's activities during 1998 and follows Amazon.com (A) and Amazon.com (B). At the beginning of 1999, Jeff Bezos, Amazon.com founder and CEO, is pondering the company's expansion into other product categories beyond books, music, and movies. Where should he expand the company's product line, and how should he maintain the company's focus on doing a few things well instead of several things just adequately? Bezos has benefited from Amazon.com's dominance over BarnesandNoble.com in the online bookselling category and a surging stock price, which allows him to build marketshare quickly. Still, critics of Amazon.com question Bezos's strategy of pursuing marketshare instead of profits, and others wonder how far the Amazon.com brand can be stretched.

Preparation Questions

1. Can the Amazon.com brand be extended beyond books, music, and movies?

2. Where should Amazon.com extend its product line next?

3. Do you agree with Bezos's strategy to "get big fast" over "get profitable fast"?

AMAZON.COM (D)

Case Overview

This case reviews Amazon.com's activities during 1999 and follows Amazon.com (A), Amazon.com (B), and Amazon.com (C). At the end of 1999, Jeff Bezos, Amazon.com founder and CEO, and his newly appointed president and COO, Joe Galli, are pondering the company's future, having added new categories over the past year for auction items, home improvement goods, toys, and Z-shops. How far can the Amazon.com brand be stretched? Amazon.com had been the dominant online retailer during the 1999 Christmas season, having expanded its infrastructure to fulfill 99% of the holiday orders on time and having increased its customer base from 6.2 million to 16.9 million. Still, critics of Amazon.com question Bezos's long-term strategy of pursuing marketshare instead of profits, and others wonder if the company has overextended itself in the pursuit of growth opportunities. With the stock value of the company at $45 per share in January 2000, after reaching a high of $106 per share in November 1999, some think Amazon.com's quick ride to the top is beginning to rapidly fade. At the end of 1999, the company had yet to make a profit.

Preparation Questions

1. Do you agree with Bezos's strategy to "get big fast" over "get profitable fast"?

2. Do you agree that Amazon.com should have expanded into auctions, household tools, toys, Z-shops, electronics, and software in 1999? Which categories should it have avoided?

3. Evaluate Amazon.com's business model. How can it leverage its customer base and strategic partnerships to create new revenue streams?

BARNESANDNOBLE.COM (A)

Case Overview

Barnes & Noble and its prime competitor, Ann Arbor–based Borders Inc., were the two largest retail booksellers in the United States, dominating the nation's $26 billion retail bookselling market. Despite the closing of many small independent bookstores in the face of the onslaught of new superstores, the senior management of both Barnes & Noble and Borders Inc. had confronted new, upstart bookselling competitors of a different kind—approximately 500 websites selling books over the Internet. The most prominent of these was Seattle-based Amazon.com, which had begun selling books online in Summer 1995.

While Amazon.com matched the large physical booksellers in price discounts, it offered added benefits of convenience and selection to its customers—being open for business 24 hours a day on the Web and offering an inventory of 2.5 million books. In response, in 1997 Barnes & Noble launched its AOL Bookstore site and its separate proprietary website, BarnesandNoble.com, each managed as separate business units. Throughout 1997, BarnesandNoble.com and Amazon.com developed parallel strategies in a fierce battle for customers involving price-cutting, partnership agreements, and signing up affiliates—or third party websites—to drive traffic to their respective storefronts in exchange for a commission on resulting book sales.

With Borders expected to launch its online storefront during the first quarter of 1998, Barnes & Noble Vice Chairman Steve Riggio had to determine the best way for the bookseller to fight back on the Internet over the next year to extend its franchise in cyberspace, and to increase the public's awareness without cannibalizing sales in its physical retail franchise. How could the bookseller use its 484 superstores effectively to promote its online subsidiary? Should BarnesandNoble.com consider selling other media products such as video, music, and software?

Preparation Questions

1. Evaluate the BarnesandNoble.com website. How compelling is the site as an online retail environment?

2. What attributes, features, and functions does BarnesandNoble.com offer that differentiate it from Amazon.com?

3. In what ways might BarnesandNoble.com derive competitive advantage from its superstores and mall stores? From its existing distribution infrastructure? From its physical-world brand name?

4. In what ways might these same assets become competitive disadvantages for BarnesandNoble.com?

BARNESANDNOBLE.COM (B)

Case Overview

Jonathan Bulkeley, the newly appointed CEO of BarnesandNoble.com, contemplated the company's steps to solidify its claim as being the "World's Largest Bookseller Online." Already, since its launch in May 1997, BarnesandNoble.com had grown to serve 1.4 million customers at year-end 1998. Despite these successes, Amazon was still number one with 6.2 million customers for the same period.

With the pricing policies for both BarnesandNoble.com and Amazon.com remaining largely unchanged—30% off most hardbacks and 40% off selected titles—during 1998, BarnesandNoble.com attempted to differentiate itself from Amazon.com in three key areas: selection, service, and scope. BarnesandNoble.com already offered 8 million titles, exceeding Amazon's claim to 4.7 million. To increase its edge in service, Barnes & Noble added two new distribution centers, anticipating shorter delivery times. A new joint-venture agreement with European conglomerate Bertelsmann AG allowed BarnesandNoble.com to increase the scope of its offering to include more foreign titles than any competitor.

"The biggest piece of the market is still ahead of us," observed Barnes & Noble's Vice Chairman Stephen Riggio. Indeed, Forrester Research predicted online bookselling would grow to $3 billion in 2003. What steps should the joint online bookselling venture of Barnes & Noble and Bertelsmann AG pursue next in its ongoing battle with Amazon.com?

Preparation Questions

1. How can BarnesandNoble.com leverage off the assets of its two partners, Bertelsmann and Barnes & Noble, to build marketshare against Amazon.com?

2. Should BarnesandNoble.com stay focused on only selling media products online—pursuing a vertical strategy instead of Amazon.com's horizontal strategy?

BARNESANDNOBLE.COM (C)

Case Overview

This case reviews BarnesandNoble.com's activities during the year of 1999 and follows cases BarnesandNoble.com (A) and BarnesandNoble.com (B). Steve Riggio, BarnesandNoble.com's newly appointed chairman and acting president, wonders what he needs to do to jump start BarnesandNoble.com—which raised $55 million in an IPO in Spring 1999—ahead of Amazon.com, which is the current leading online bookseller but has now expanded in retail categories beyond media products. What can Riggio do to leverage the resources of Barnes & Noble and its partnership with AOL in order to exploit the weaknesses of Amazon.com and make BarnesandNoble.com the leading online bookseller in the world?

Preparation Questions

1. How can BarnesandNoble.com exploit the Amazon.com brand to dominate the online book space as Amazon expands into other product categories?

2. How can BarnesandNoble.com use its physical bookstores and its partnership with AOL to reinforce its brand online as the premier bookseller?

INTEGRATIVE STUDY QUESTIONS

As you consider the entire set of questions in the first chapter, you should also reflect on the following integrative questions:

1. What are the advantages and disadvantages of starting out as a "pure" dot-com versus a pure brick-and-mortar firm? Which type of firm would you rather be? Why?

2. Are speedy decisions and quick implementation more important than rigorous strategy analysis?

3. Is first-mover advantage critical, or simply a necessary but not sufficient input? How does a second mover overcome the advantages of the first mover?

4. How important is online/offline integration for firms in this space?

5. Is business strategy in the online environment truly unique? Or can we simply repurpose much of what we know in the brick-and-mortar world into the New Economy environment?

SUMMARY

The purpose of this chapter was to introduce a basic framework for e-commerce strategy formulation and implementation. Each of the steps in the strategy framework can be applied to both Amazon and BarnesandNoble. In particular, the Amazon and BarnesandNoble competition is generally regarded as the classic confrontation of a pure dot-com versus the brick-and-mortar, Old Economy stalwart. The case studies reveal a number of basic lessons related to market opportunity assessment, the business model, customer interface, and other components of the framework.

AMAZON.COM (A)

www.amazon.com

Billed as the "Earth's Biggest Bookstore," Seattle-based Amazon.com ostensibly lacked the comforts of the typical mega-chain bookstores. While Barnes & Noble or Borders superstores featured espresso bars and cafe lattés, comfortable armchairs and sofas, and autograph signings with famous authors, Amazon.com offered none of these. Instead, the world's dominant Internet-based bookseller offered the simple convenience of ordering books any time of day or night, a selection of 1.1 million titles, and discount prices on many volumes ranging from 10% to 30% off list price.

Looking out his office window in a renovated office building in downtown Seattle, Jeffrey Bezos, Amazon.com Founder and Chief Executive Officer, was pleased with the success of the electronic bookseller so far. Only 18 months old, Amazon.com had been doubling its revenues almost every 11 weeks—with sales growing at a rate of 20% to 30% per month—since its inception in summer 1995. It was considered one of the best-known sites on the Internet for electronic commerce, and was widely noted as one of the most innovative retailing businesses on the Web.

But Bezos and his management team knew other challenges lay ahead. The most serious was the launch of mega-chain bookstores on the Internet. Sitting on Bezos' desk that January morning was a copy of a *Wall Street Journal* article[1] reporting that Barnes & Noble was planning to launch its first on-line bookselling venture with America Online within the next month. Both Barnes & Noble and its prime competitor, Borders, were planning to establish bookselling sites of their own on the Web. In addition to increased competition, Amazon.com faced other challenges common to many start-ups: how best to serve its growing customer base, how to create an infrastructure to handle the rapid expansion in sales, and how to create a nurturing company culture.

The History of Amazon.com

"Books are for nothing but to inspire."
—Ralph Waldo Emerson,
The American Scholar, 1837

Amazon.com began operating in July 1995—nine months after the first Netscape Web browser appeared on the market—out of the garage of Bezos' rented house in Bellevue, Washington. Bezos, a 32-year-old electrical engineering and computer science graduate of Princeton and a former Senior Vice President at D.E. Shaw and Co., a Wall Street brokerage house, realized the potential of electronic commerce on the Internet early. As he recalled:

> In spring 1994, I came across a statistic that the growth rate of Web usage was 2,300% a year. And that was a time, remember, when nobody had any idea how many people were on the Web. It turned out that, though you couldn't measure the baseline usage, you could measure growth rate. And things rarely grow that quickly. If something's growing that fast, unless

---

[1]Patrick Reilly, "Booksellers Ready for Battle on Net's World," *Wall Street Journal*, January 28, 1997.

the baseline is incredibly small, then it's going to be ubiquitous very quickly. Just anecdotally, I could tell that the baseline was non-trivial. And therefore it looked like the Web was going to get very big very fast.

Bezos concluded, for these reasons, that interactive retailing would become a "killer application" on the Internet. In deciding what product categories would work best, Bezos first made an analysis of 20 product groups and weighed the pros and cons of each one. He quickly narrowed his choices down to two—books and music—and settled on books because of the category's larger size, greater diversity, and lower risk of possible influence by a handful of distributors. While there were over 200,000 active music CDs in print at any given time, there were over 1.5 million English book titles in print around the world. Furthermore, the music industry had six major companies that owned most of the big labels, which Bezos saw as a concentration of power that could easily freeze out an upstart. In the book industry this was much less a risk, given that there were over 20,000 publishers in the United States alone. The two largest booksellers in the United States, Barnes & Noble and Borders, together accounted for less than 25% of total sales. "There aren't any 800-pound gorillas in bookselling," said Bezos.[2]

Bezos also believed that the large number of book titles available made book selling an aptly-suited retail business on the Internet. Many book buyers, Bezos observed, were already comfortable with the concept of searching for books on computers. Added Bezos:

> At the time, I made the observation that books was one of the few—maybe the only—category where computers have already been very helpful in selling the product. For a long time, bookstores have had information desks, where you walk up and somebody uses a computer to help you find what you're looking for. Computers were already helpful in selling books. You could see how with a large number of products, the sorting and searching could help. But that wasn't the main thing. The main thing was that you could build a bookstore on the Web that simply couldn't exist any other way. The Web is an infant technology. If you want to be successful in the short-to-medium term, you can only do things that offer incredibly strong value propositions to customers relative to the value of doing things in more traditional ways. This basically means that, right now, you should only do

on-line what you cannot do any other way. The largest physical bookstores only carry 170,000 titles. There are only three that big. We have 1.1 million titles in our catalogue. And if we printed our catalogue, it would be the size of seven New York City phone books.

As a result of these insights, Bezos decided to quit his job at D.E. Shaw in June 1994, and moved west to start a bookselling operation over the Internet. Bezos wrote the business plan for Amazon.com on his laptop computer while he and his wife drove to the Pacific Northwest; he had chosen Seattle as the ultimate destination because of its proximity to computer industry talent and several large book distributors. The original name for the company was "Cadabra," under which it was incorporated, but many test consumers wound up confusing it with "Cadaver," which seemed unpropitious, so Bezos selected the name "Amazon.com" instead. Bezos felt that future consumers would have an easy enough time remembering the world's biggest river as the name for the world's biggest bookstore.

Amazon.com was established with a small number of private investors who put up a few million dollars; an additional $8 million was later invested, in 1996, by venture capital firm Kleiner Perkins Caufield & Byers. The business opened to the public in July 1995, operating out of a small office with a tiny staff. Recalled Bezos about the first days of business:

> The day before we opened the store to the public in July 1995, we looked at the miniature warehouse we had made ready. It was only 500 square feet. One of our senior developers looked at the small size and said, "I don't know if this is hopelessly pathetic or incredibly optimistic." It turned out to be hopelessly pathetic.
>
> Fortunately, though the physical warehouse was in many ways a toy, the software we had built to manage our almost-in-time inventory system was not. We had put a lot of work into the system in advance, and it paid off. We were able to scale very quickly as our volume grew. On the day we first opened the store, we programmed the system so that every time we received an order it rang a bell on every employee's terminal and simultaneously put up a little line on the screen describing the sale. This quickly became tedious, so we eliminated the bell.
>
> Even without the bell, the single line of sales info forcing its way onto our screens quickly became disruptive, so we changed to a little real time program

[2] G. Bruce Knecht, "How Wall Street Whiz Found a Niche Selling Books on the Internet," *The Wall Street Journal*, May 16, 1996.

anyone could run on demand to check sales over any desired period of time. We still use that program and its successors today.

On the fulfillment side, we were immediately understaffed and every person in our company had to spend long hours each day packing and shipping books, in addition to doing their "real" jobs. The warehouse didn't even have proper packing tables, so we had to pack on the floor on hands and knees. Within a couple of weeks, we had properly sized packing tables, and I remember thinking, "Hey this is nice!"

By Labor Day 1995, six weeks later, word had spread about Amazon.com on the Internet and Bezos moved the company to a 2,000-square-foot warehouse. There, ever conscious of keeping a tight lid on costs, Bezos designed a packing table for Amazon.com's particular book handling activities, and the company's staff then built numerous replicas in-house. Six months later, in March 1995, the firm's operations moved to a third home, a 17,000-square-foot building. And five months after that, by Thanksgiving Day 1996, the business had moved into its fourth and current home, a 45,000-square-foot warehouse located south of downtown Seattle. Reflecting this phenomenal growth—as the number of daily visits to Amazon.com's site grew from 2,200 in December 1995 to approximately 80,000 in spring 1997—Amazon.com's workforce grew four-fold over a seven-month period—from 33 employees in May 1996, to 100 in September 1996, to 160 in December 1996.

Unlike the traditional bookstores, Amazon.com kept a small inventory of books on hand—usually the best-selling items—and ordered books directly from book distributors or publishing houses when orders were placed by customers using its Web site. This business model, unlike that of brick-and-mortar booksellers, allowed Amazon.com to achieve inventory turns equivalent to 70 per year, as opposed to an industry average among traditional booksellers of approximately 2.7. At the same time, the lack of physical retail space eliminated the need for expensive furniture and sales people, and allowed Bezos to keep the "doors" open 24 hours a day. Initially, Bezos had been concerned about meeting the minimum order quantities that book distributors

required; most book distributors were unwilling to ship orders of less than ten books at the normal discount to channels.[3] For orders of less than ten books, Bezos had planned to reach the distributor's minimum by adding either fast-moving or out-of-print titles. (He assumed fast-moving titles would be easy to sell, and out-of-print titles would be counted by the distributor toward the minimum quantity, but never shipped or charged.) The nearly immediate demand from the market, however, made it possible for Amazon.com to do business with practically any national distributor without padding orders.

By late 1996, customers from over 125 countries had purchased books from Amazon.com, ranging from U.S. Army soldiers in Bosnia to a cleric in Germany. Recalled Laurel Canan, Manager of Operations and Fulfillment:

> The story I like to tell—the one that I really like because my degree is in English Literature—is that I remember a customer who wanted eight scholarly books on James Joyce's "Finnegan's Wake." These were the kind of university press books that are cloth-bound and really nicely printed. High quality books—I'm not sure how good the scholarship was—but I'm guessing that there probably isn't a library in the country that had all eight of those books on hand. And here we are, the one source that has all eight. You don't have to go to the library; you can actually own them. I don't remember where the customer lived, but it wouldn't make much difference if the customer lived in New York City or if the customer lived in the farther reaches of Africa. The person can still order those eight books and get them easily from us.

Despite its rapid revenue growth, similar to that of many Internet start-ups, Amazon.com was not yet profitable at year end 1996, showing a net loss of $5.8 million on net sales of $15.8 million for 1996 (see Exhibit 1).[4] "We are taking what may be the profits and reinvesting them in the future of the business," said Bezos. "It would literally be the stupidest decision of any management team to make Amazon.com profitable right now."[5]

Book Retailing in the United States

"Wear the old coat and buy the new book."
—Austin Phelps,
The Theory of Preaching, Lectures on Homiletics, 1861

By 1996, the bookselling industry in the United States had grown to revenues of $26.1 billion as compared with

[3]G. Bruce Knecht, "How Wall Street Whiz Found a Niche Selling Books on the Internet," *The Wall Street Journal*, May 16, 1996.
[4]Form S-1, Amazon.com, Securities and Exchanges Commission, May 15, 1997.
[5]Seth Schiesel, "Payoff Still Elusive in Internet Gold Rush," *The New York Times*, January 3, 1997.

$14.7 billion in 1987.[6] Included in this amount were institutional sales of approximately $2.2 billion through book clubs, mail order catalogs, and subscriptions; and revenues of $5.8 billion from elementary, high school, and college textbook sales. In geographic terms, the top ten book markets in the United States were Los Angeles, New York, Chicago, Boston, Washington D.C., Philadelphia, San Francisco, Seattle, San Jose, and San Diego (see Exhibit 2).

Industry experts believed that there were several factors driving the growth of book sales. First, a large percentage of books were increasingly sold at discounted prices through stand-alone superstores—such as Barnes & Noble, Borders, and Bookstar—which had become community centers within neighborhoods, offering consumers a menu of media selections. The "category killers" of the book world sold more than just books; they also stocked magazines, audio-books, music CDs, and multimedia software and games, complemented by comfortable reading areas, in-store cafes, and periodic literary talks and author book signings. The average size of a superstore was approximately 30,000 square-feet— more than triple the size of an average mall bookstore. Each had on average 128,000 book titles and 57,000 CDs and cassettes.[7]

The concept for the book superstore emerged in the 1970s, when several major-city independent bookstores, such as the Tattered Cover in Denver, established themselves as important gathering places in their communities. The largest book retailer in the United States, Barnes & Noble, adapted this retail format with the opening of superstores in downtown New York City and Boston. Barnes & Noble replicated the superstore concept in suburban markets with a test of four such stores in 1987.[8] These proved a success: by end of fiscal year 1996, Barnes & Noble operated 431 superstores (including those under the Bookstar and Bookstop names) in urban and suburban markets across the country. The second largest book retailer, Borders, showed a similar increase in superstores, growing to 159 superstores at the end of fiscal year 1996 from 41 superstores at the end of fiscal year 1993. Superstores accounted for 50% to 76% of each company's annual sales (see Exhibit 3).

As both Barnes & Noble and Borders sought to increase the numbers of superstores nationwide, they simultaneously scaled back the number of mall bookstores under ownership. Barnes & Noble owned the Doubleday, Scribner's, and B. Dalton chains, while Borders owned Waldenbooks. Because of increased competition from rival superstores and softening demand from reduced mall traffic, each bookseller sought to consolidate their mall outlets in 1995. The increase in the number of superstores also had an impact on several independent bookstores nationwide. For example, the American Booksellers Association estimated that the annual sales growth for independent bookstores had declined by 52% between 1994 and 1995, from 8.4% to 5.2%; in 1996 alone, 50 to 60 independent bookstores had closed their doors.[9]

With more resources for promotion, staffing, and information systems to acquire and retain customers, the superstores could afford to engage in what the industry had begun to call "entertainment retailing" and customized inventories at a much deeper level than any neighborhood bookstore could do. Entertainment retailing was used to make each superstore a social gathering place by hosting book signings, artistic performances, and lectures. "The motivation behind entertainment retailing in bookstores," observed one industry expert, "was, very simply, to increase the amount of time a customer spent in a bookstore. Research showed that the more time an individual spent in a store, the more money he or she spent."[10] The two dominant book retailers also took advantage of their scale to "customize" inventory at the store level. Customization was achieved through sophisticated inventory management systems, whereby each store could tailor single-store inventories based on local sales patterns.[11]

Another factor driving growth in retail book sales was strong demand in the two largest categories of consumer books—trade books and mass market paperbacks—and the increased sales of textbooks. Trade books (adult and juvenile) and mass market paperbacks, respectively, accounted for approximately one-half and one-quarter of all consumer book sales nationwide (see Exhibit 4). Between 1987 and 1996, sales of trade books more than doubled, from $4.5 billion in 1987 to $9.5 billion in 1996. During the same period, retail sales of mass market paperbacks increased from $1.4 billion to $2.3 billion, reflecting the continued popularity of paperbacks—a trend that began gathering momentum in the 1960s. As for non-consumer books, half of all adults between the ages of 35 and 54 had enrolled in some kind of adult

[6]"Book Industry Trends," Book Industry Study Group, Inc., 1997.
[7]Borders, Inc. 1995 Annual Report.
[8]Barnes & Noble, 1995 Annual Report.
[9]Dinitia Smith, "Epilogue for Another Bookstore," New York Times, January 18, 1997.
[10]Also see Malcolm Gladwell, "The Science of Shopping," The New Yorker, November 4, 1996.
[11]Borders, Inc., 1996 Annual Report

education course in 1995, contributing to the increase in textbook sales, which rose by an estimated 61% between 1987 and 1996, from $3.6 billion to $5.8 billion, respectively.[12]

Book buyers were traditionally an upscale audience. In 1995, approximately one-quarter of books sold were purchased by households with annual incomes of $75,000 or greater (over twice the national average of $31,428). Households earning between $30,000 and $75,000 purchased 42% of all books (see Exhibit 5). A 1996 survey showed that 28% of all book buyers—almost twice the national average of 17%—were likely to use on-line technology some of the time. For those under the age of 50, the likelihood of using on-line technology was almost double—approximately 50 percent of the book buying population in that age band (see Exhibit 6).

Electronic Commerce on the Internet

"Books are the treasured wealth of the world and fit inheritance of generations and nations."
—Henry David Thoreau, "Reading" *Walden*, 1854

Estimates for retail revenues occurring over the Internet—an alternate retail channel to physical outlets and catalog shopping—was approximately $230 million in 1995, which was less than 1% of all retail sales for the same year. Though small in number—8% of consumers had made a purchase through the Internet in 1995—the purchase rate was double that for the segment of the population that was 18 to 35 years old. Estimates for on-line commerce were projected to increase to almost $7 billion by the year 2000 (see Exhibit 7), as the number of Web users worldwide was expected to increase almost seven-fold to 152 million in 2000 from 23 million in 1996 (see Exhibit 8). Corresponding to the increasing number of Web users was the rising percentage of personal computer users with access to the Web, which was expected to grow to over 67% in 2000 from 15% in 1996.

By year end 1996, several start-up companies had established a presence in on-line retailing. Advantages to consumers for making purchases on-line included 24-hour retail access, a large inventory selection, and an abundance of product information and related services on demand. Increased security for credit card transactions over the Internet, enabled by security features build

into new releases of Netscape and Microsoft browsers, eased consumer concerns regarding on-line credit card purchases. In addition to Amazon.com, the most prominent retailers on-line included:

CD Now! *(www.cdnow.com).* This Web site allowed visitors to browse through a large collection of over 150,000 CD titles, ranging from Broadway musicals, to Madonna, to soft jazz. Open 24 hours a day, the Penllyn, Pennsylvania-based retailer gave potential customers a chance to find the bestselling CDs on the charts and to read the latest reviews on its Web page.

Internet Shopping Network *(www.isn.com).* An on-line computer retailer purchased by the Home Shopping Network in 1994, this company, located in Palo Alto, California, competed with over 200 other computer shops on the Net. Visitors to this site could search for computer accessories by category (drives, memory, and multimedia hardware), read product reviews from the trade weekly, *InfoWorld*, or download the latest versions of Microsoft's Word, Excel, and PowerPoint software.

Travelocity *(www.travelocity.com).* This Web site, owned by American Airlines parent company, AMR, provided busy travelers with the capability to book their own travel itinerary, to read about travel destinations, and to check the weather forecast in various cities.

Virtual Vineyards *(www.virtualvin.com).* This Web site provided visitors the capability to choose from an inventory of California wines over the Internet. If visitors were unsure of the type of wine that they needed for a special occasion, an e-mail message to the "Cork Dork" yielded a personalized response.

Other examples of on-line retailing included AOL Marketplace, operated by America Online, which provided links to merchants, such as Lands' End, JC Penney, Starbucks Coffee, Godiva, and the Nature Company, for over 150,000 of its members daily as well as The Internet Mall (www.internetmall.com) which had links to over 20,000 stores, including Macy's and the Disney Store Online. Other prominent merchants joining on-line marketplace included the electronic home shopping channel QVC (www.qvc.com) and Wal-Mart, the mass discount store, who had announced plans for an Internet joint venture with Microsoft. By the end of 1996, it was estimated that 14% of all U.S. retailers had Web sites or planned to, compared to only 4% a year earlier.[13]

---

[12]"Book Industry Trends," Book Industry Study Group, Inc., 1997.
[13]*San Francisco Chronicle*, December 25, 1996.

Value Proposition at Amazon.com

"I cannot live without books."
—Thomas Jefferson,
letter to John Adams, June 10, 1815

Bezos believed that convenience, selection, price, and customer service were the key elements of Amazon.com's value proposition for consumers buying books on the Internet. Even Bill Gates, Co-Founder, Chairman, and Chief Executive Officer of software powerhouse Microsoft, located just miles away from Amazon.com's downtown headquarters, was a customer of the on-line bookseller, mentioning Amazon.com's convenience, selection, and service in an interview. Added Bezos:

> Those are three of our four core value propositions: convenience, selection, service. The only one Gates left out is price: we are the broadest discounters in the world in any product category. But maybe price isn't so important to Bill Gates.
>
> These value propositions are interrelated, and they all relate to the Web. We have the widest selection because we operate in a virtual world. We discount because we have a lower cost structure than physical stores do.[14]

Convenience. Like many Web-based businesses, Amazon.com offered customers the opportunity to place orders at any time of the day, seven days a week. A visit to Amazon.com's home page (see Exhibit 9)—which could be downloaded easily and quickly because it lacked fancy graphics and Java applications—provided customers with hyperlinks to several daily features that readers could browse: The Book of the Day, Featured Books, Hot This Week, and Titles in the News. Another feature, Amazon.com Notes, listed the birthdays of both noted and obscure authors, from horror writer Stephen King to Spanish essayist and novelist Angel Ganivet y Garcia, each day.

Selection. Visitors could browse through Amazon.com's 1.1 million title catalog by searching for a particular book by author, title, subject, or keyword (see Exhibit 10). The entire inventory was seven times the inventory of the world's largest mega-bookstore and 30 times the size of an average mall bookstore. (However, several versions of the same title, such as hardcover and paperback editions, were counted as separate inventory items or stock-keeping units, making the actual number of unique titles smaller than the stated 1.1 million SKUs.) Observed Bezos:

> For some books, like Tom Clancy's *The Hunt For Red October,* you might have something like 20 editions. You'll have the mass market paperback, the regular paperback, the hardcover edition, the large print edition, the unabridged audio book, the abridged audio book. You'll have the music soundtrack on CD. You'll have the videotape of the movie. And we even have the Braille edition of the book for a best-selling book like that.

This diversity of titles and SKUs translated into outstanding value for customers searching for less recognized titles. Far from winning business simply as a discounter, Amazon.com delivered customer value by streamlining the customer's search and decision-making process. Noted Susan Stenberg, a California-based media executive and a frequent Amazon.com customer:

> I was looking for a book that I wasn't able to find in Crown or Barnes & Noble and several of my colleagues recommended that I try Amazon.com. I tried it and found the book right away. After that, my first choice is to go through Amazon.com when I need a book, unless I'm already planning to go to a mall or other location with a bookstore immediately.[15]

There were 39 categories of books that visitors could "browse," ranging from Art and Architecture, to Mystery, to Romance, to Business. For both entertainment and promotional purposes, Amazon.com staffers compiled a weekly list of the 20 most obscure titles on order. Examples included such volumes as *How to Start Your Own Country, Training Goldfish Using Dolphin Training Techniques,* and *Life Without Friends.*[16]

Judy Dugan, an editor at the *Los Angeles Times,* was a reluctant Amazon.com fan. What brought her into Amazon's customer franchise was this kind of broad selection:

> I first heard about Amazon.com through news reports, probably beginning in early 1996. At first I ignored Amazon, for two reasons: I like to handle a book, to flip through it, before buying, and I try as much as possible to support a local independent bookstore. However, my husband is sight-impaired and can read only large-print books. No bookstore in

---

[14]William C. Taylor, "Who's Writing the Book on Web Business?," *Fast Company,* October/November 1996.
[15]Interview with case writer
[16]*The Wall Street Journal,* May 16, 1996.

Los Angeles stocks a decent selection, so we decided to try Amazon.[17]

Price.

Approximately one-third of Amazon.com's book inventory was available at 10% off suggested retail prices—virtually equivalent to the discount offered by the large bookstore chains. Bestsellers were available at 30% off. Noted Jennifer Cast, Acting Vice President of Marketing:

> We're actually the most discounted bookstore in the world. Of our one million titles, approximately 300,000 of them are discounted at 10%. And we discount bestsellers 30%. Any book reviewed by the *New York Times* is discounted 30%. And then we feature 100 or more titles that are discounted between 20% and 30%.

Although customers living outside of Washington state did not pay sales taxes on books purchased through Amazon.com, they did pay service charges for shipping, which was usually $3.95 per order. The books were shipped through a variety of carriers, including two-day Priority Mail via the United States Postal Service, UPS Ground Service, or DHL. For an additional charge of $2 per order, Amazon.com also gift-wrapped books, and customers could use a Web page to select the wrapping paper they wished Amazon to use.

"Price is a factor," said Stenberg, "the shipping charge is a bit high, but they discount their books. To me, the shipping charge is usually worth the convenience of not having to go to the bookstore and search for a book."

Service.

Customers wishing to order books for the first time from Amazon.com followed a simple 12-step procedure that involved providing name, mailing address, e-mail address, and credit card information (see Exhibit 11). Customers then typed in a password so that future transactions would not require reentering this information unless the order was to be sent to a different address. Customers had the choice of transmitting their credit card information directly on-line or by telephone. An on-line profile of the book informed the site's users about inventory status. Most requests took two to three days to fulfill. Said Canan:

> We have an availability status for each book. There are different categories. The best availability is zero waiting, and that means that we actually have that book

here, in house, right now at this time. Then we also have two to three day availability status, where we think we have good information about where we can source a particular book. And if we can get it from a distributor, then we're saying two to three days. Then there's a one-to-three week category and a four-to-six week category. The one-to-three week category is from distributors on the east coast or those that are going to take a little bit longer to get to us. The four-to-six week category is special order items, requiring direct order with publishers. We're confident that we can't get such items from the distributors themselves.

Once an order was completed, customers received, on-line, an itemized list of the books ordered and their cost (see Exhibit 12). Before the order could be finalized, the customer had to confirm the order twice while on-line. After an order went through, the customer received a subsequent e-mail confirming its receipt by Amazon.com. The e-mail listed the order number, the books ordered, the total price, the shipping method, the customer's shipping address, e-mail address, and phone number (Exhibit 13). Questions on a particular order could be e-mailed to orders@amazon.com.

To Bezos, delivering the books ordered within the time frame promised was crucial to Amazon.com's reputation. He remarked:

> Good customer service means that if you order a book from us, we ship the book in the time-frame that we say we'll ship the book. If it's two or three days, then we should ship the book within two to three days. If we say four to six weeks, we should ship the book within four to six weeks. Likewise if you send us an e-mail message asking about your order, we ought to respond to that e-mail message in a reasonable period of time. Good customer service is fulfilling the promises you make to your customers.

Bezos felt that this follow-through on customer service was more important in the digital world than in the traditional retail world, because of the increased impact of on-line communications:

> Customer service is probably the most important thing in retail, no matter what form the business takes. But on-line it's even more important than in the physical world. And the reason is that on-line, if you make a customer unhappy, they won't tell six friends, they'll tell six thousand friends—e-mail lists, newsgroups, and so on. People have a very powerful voice on-line, and you know that everybody can have

---

[17]Interview with case writer.

a megaphone on-line. But on the other hand, if you do everything that you say you'll do, if you treat your customers well, serve them in the ways you've promised, then you will have the opposite effect. You'll have powerful word of mouth from each of your customers. These guys will go on-line and tell people—not just six friends but six thousand people—to "Come try Amazon.com."

After an order was received by Amazon.com, the Order Department requested the books directly from distributors or publishing houses. The books were then sent to the Amazon.com warehouse for shipment to the customer.

When books arrived at Amazon's warehouse, staffers matched the customer's order with a packing slip (see Exhibit 14) and prepared it for shipping, while the bar code on the package's shipping label was scanned. Upon scanning, another e-mail went out to the customer notifying him or her that the order had been sent, with details confirming the carrier used and total price charged (see Exhibit 15).

Customers could return a book for a full refund (except for shipping charges) within 15 days of receipt. The number of books returned by Amazon customers was quite low—less than one percent compared to an industry bookselling average of almost 30% (which represents returns from booksellers to publishers). This was due, in part, to the high quality of service Amazon.com delivered to its customers. Remarked Dugan, "the service is just fine. The ordering process lets you know right away how long it will take to get any item, and the company confirms the order's status by e-mail. The books arrived as promised, when promised."

Bezos believed that the advantages of operating an on-line store as opposed to a traditional bookstore were significant:

Look at the advantages that an on-line bookstore has: first, you can have a much larger selection. You have infinite shelf space on-line. Second, it's very easy to under-price physical bookstores, because we don't have to spend 10% of our sales for rent, for example. That alone is a huge, huge cost advantage. The third thing that you have is the ability to redecorate the store for each and every customer who walks in. Physical stores have to be laid out for the mythic average customer. In the virtual world, every store should be different. Your store should be optimized for you. And my store should be optimized for me, based upon my stated preferences.

Customer Acquisition and Retention

"Some books are so familiar reading them is like being home again."
—Louisa May Alcott, *Little Women*, 1868

During Amazon.com's first year in business, most of its on-line traffic was generated through word of mouth and press reports. Beginning in mid-1996, Amazon.com placed ads on-line, using the home pages of Four11 Directory, Festivalfinder.com, and CNN Interactive, and in print media (see Exhibit 16), using publications such as *The New York Times Book Review* and *The Los Angeles Times Book Review*.

As Cast remarked:

On-line advertising is very measurable. We have a weekly report which shows us how successful each on-line advertisement is for us. It shows how many people viewed the ad, how many people clicked through to our home page, how many people made a purchase, and how much revenue was generated. With this we can eliminate ineffective ads or Web sites or compare the effectiveness of two on-line ads on the same Web page.

Amazon.com used another tactic to generate traffic in its Associates program, which represented an attempt to gain leverage from the formation of "communities of interest" on the Internet.[18] Associates referred prospective book-buying customers to Amazon.com's home page from their personal home pages, through hyperlinks; for these referrals, Associates received commissions of 8% on any books subsequently sold on click-throughs from their home pages. Cast estimated that Amazon.com had signed on more than 5,000 Associates by year-end 1996.

Customers were also prompted to visit the site through two personalized search and notification services: *Eyes* and *Editors*. *Eyes* provided customers with e-mail notification of new books by selected authors or on selected subjects. *Editors* provided customers with e-mail alerts when recommended books arrived in selected categories. Amazon.com had 29 editors, headed by its Vice President of Editorial, Rick Ayre, formerly Executive Editor of *PC Magazine*; its editors reviewed books on a continuous basis in 50 different categories. An example of e-mail notification by *Eyes* appears below:

---

[18]Michael H. Martin, "The Next Big Thing: A Bookstore?" *Fortune*, December 9, 1996.

Subj: Books whose authors(s) include "Walter Cronkite"

Date: January 9, 1997

From: eyes@amazon.com

To: grubear@mba1997.hbs.edu

Hi, as per your request, we at Amazon.com Books are notifying you of new books matching the following criteria:

Author(s) include "Walter Cronkite"

The new books are listed at the end of this message. If you're interested in any of these books you can order them on-line at *http://www.amazon.com/*

Your most humble automated search agent,

Eyes, Amazon.com Books

And an e-mail from *Editors* which recommended books by categories of reader interest. For example, a sample of recommended business books from Howard Rothman, Amazon.com's business editor, appears below:

Date: Wed, Jan 15, 1997 7:54 AM EDT

From: business-editor@amazon.com

Sender: business-editor@amazon.com

Reply-to: business-editor@amazon.com

To: business-editors-subscribers@amazon.com

Thanks for signing up for Amazon.com Books business e-mail message. We're pleased to introduce you to our business editor, Howard Rothman. Howard is the author of "RX Inc.: The Small Business Handbook for Building a Healthier Workforce" and other books. He currently publishes an on-line newsletter for small business owners and operators, The Rothman Report. From his first job in high school—which involved operating a mechanical device that counted and wrapped coins—Howard has had his eye on the bottom line.

Here's his first dispatch. We hope you'll enjoy it as much as we did. In fact, we want to be sure you do. Please let us know what you think of this e-mail. We've included information on giving us feedback at the end of this message. We look forward to hearing from you!

—Rick Ayre, Executive Editor, Amazon.com Books

****

Males in my family have always run their own businesses. My dad, both grandfathers, four uncles—all of them operated retail or service enterprises that they had either founded or inherited. Since none had a formal business education, all found themselves constantly struggling to reinvent the corporate wheel. Thanks to today's explosion in business books, though, we don't have to rely on trial-and-error like they did.

Russ Wild's "Business Briefs: 165 Guiding Principles from the World's Sharpest Minds" offers a snappy compendium of general tips from experts both expected and surprising. "Cyberwriting: How to Promote Your Product or Service Online (without being flamed)" by Joe Vitale concentrates on the cultivation of business on the Internet. "Coaching Knock Your Socks Off Service" by Ron Zemke and Kristin Anderson spotlights delivery of top-notch customer service.

The ins and outs of fiscal management—always a concern to business owners—are clearly addressed by Herbert T. Spiro in "Finance for the Non-Financial Manager." And help with the unique fiscal problems encountered by the business world's fastest growing segment is the focus of "Business Capital for Women" by Emily Card and Adam Miller. Perhaps, with assistance like that, my daughters can finally plunge into this family business thing, too.

—Howard Rothman

You'll find Howard's favorite business books on the shelves of Amazon.com Books http://*www.amazon.com/business*.

A Bill of Rights (see Exhibit 17), posted on-line by Amazon.com, safeguarded the privacy of customers who might feel concerned about the amount and detail of information Amazon.com collected about them, based on their expressed preferences and actual buying patterns with respect to books. The Bill articulated three major planks: first, that personal notifications services of *Eyes* and *Editors* would be provided free of charge and obligation; second, that customers could unsubscribe at any time; and, third, that Amazon.com's list of customers—their shopping habits and their preferences—would not be sold or rented to outside merchants or other third parties.

In addition to personal notification by Amazon.com of upcoming books and reviews by the company's own editorial staff, customers could also browse through reviews of books written on-line by readers (see Exhibit 18); they could also interview book authors on selected titles and occasions (see Exhibit 19). Bezos believed that providing value-added content and "product" information on-line was critical to retaining customers in the digital world. After all, he believed, Amazon.com's greatest disadvantage was the obvious fact that his customers could not touch or browse through books as they would in a physical bookstore.

What are the areas where physical bookstores have an advantage over Amazon.com? At the very beginning, 18 months ago when we launched, we had only bare bones bibliographical information. It was author, title, publisher, and publication date. And now we have 170,000 titles with at least a synopsis, some third-party reviews, and [some of our own reviews]. In the future, we will have the texts of first chapters, pictures, tables of contents, excerpts, and cover art for all million books. Ultimately, we can offer much more information about a book on-line than you could ever offer in a physical store. What is a disadvantage for us now will become an advantage. We could have five third-party reviews for each and every book in our catalogue; in a physical bookstore, it's hard to organize reviews, let alone make them available to customers.

Cast noted that one of the functions Amazon.com's catalogue department served was "to obtain as much valuable content about books as possible." For example, Cast noted, books on *The New York Times Book Review* Bestseller List always appeared with excerpts or synopses, and that Amazon.com was working, Cast remarked, "with a lot of different organizations that have information about books—publishers themselves—to license that content. And we encourage customers—if you liked or hated a book—to help each other learn about books and to review books." Customers could use an Amazon.com-proprietary of one to ten to rate books they have read or purchased from the service.

In addition to value-added content, Bezos wanted to make Amazon.com a highly entertaining place to visit—just as the major bricks-and-mortar chains used super bookstores to create entertainment experiences in their retail spaces. Bezos focused on doing this by constantly refining the site's customer interfaces. As he observed:

Many people, including myself, like to spend two hours on a Sunday afternoon just strolling around in a bookstore. It's a fun way to spend an afternoon. It's entertainment. And it's important for us to recognize

that and to focus on making Amazon.com an enjoyable, fun place to be. If you consider the recent history of physical bookstores, they recognized the importance of this experience a long time ago and responded with softer sofas and tastier lattés. We'll be doing the exact same things but without the sofas and the lattés. We'll be able to offer other things that are every bit as compelling, but quite different. A lot of those things revolve around customer-to-customer interaction and customer-to-author interaction, which actually work better on-line than in physical store environments.

Cast echoed Bezos' commitment to making Amazon.com a fun place to be on the Web:

Our goal is to redefine what a "store" means. And you know that there's been a lot of press about Barnes & Noble being a place people hang out and buy lattés. What we want is to have our Web-based store be a different kind of retail experience entirely. We want people to have fun in the store site. We want to have author interviews. We want to have access to a lot of content. We want to have a lot of opportunities for community. We want people to have their book groups and have relationships with other book groups. And we want Amazon.com book groups that use our space to congregate on a regular basis. At some point, we'll have reading lists. For example, "Here are Harvard University's American History course reading lists that Amazon.com has tracked down for you."

Approximately 44% of customers who had ordered a book from Amazon.com became repeat purchasers. Cast believed that Amazon.com was not cannibalizing demand for books sold in physical bookstores. Rather, she believed that customers were simply expanding their reading lists:

People on the Internet right now are more highly educated, more affluent. After all, they're already on the Internet. They're buying computers. They're buying Internet software. And because they are more highly educated, they're more likely to buy books. But what we're finding is that because these customers value the convenience, lower prices, and better selection, they're buying more books right now from vendors like us. I would guess that a lot of these people are buying some books at Amazon.com that they would have bought in the physical world, but they're also buying more books overall.

In addition to Amazon.com, other on-line and start-up booksellers included Cleveland-based Book Stacks (www.books.com) with 425,000 titles, which offered on-line ordering at substantial discounts and hosted a variety of book clubs, including discussion of Oprah Winfrey's book club selections. In addition, Britain's Internet Bookshop (www.bookshop.co.uk), which claimed to be the "largest on-line bookshop in the world" with 912,000 titles, offered reader reviews, images of book covers, and a top 100 list.[19] A few traditional bookstore operators had also entered the on-line world. Borders had established a Web site (www.borders.com) which allowed users to locate stores near them, view snapshots of store employees, and search for books; the site did not, however, make it possible for users to purchase books on-line. Crown Books, by contrast, made on-line book ordering available with standard 10% discounts on its site (www.crownbooks.com), but offered little in the way of related content about stores or merchandise. Meanwhile, Barnes & Noble announced plans in winter 1997 to launch an on-line bookselling service on America Online, but had not yet established a presence on the Web.

Building the Culture

"Five years from now, you're the same person except for the people you've met and the books you've read."
—John Wooden, former UCLA basketball coach

Another one of the challenges facing Bezos was how to create Amazon.com's culture as an organization. In building the company at a rapid pace, Bezos noted that he had hired people more on the basis of attitude and ability than skills or prior experience. Many of Amazon.com's senior managers had logged stints in entrepreneurship ranging from companies such as Federal Express to a wide variety of Silicon Valley start-ups. As Bezos commented:

We are really focused here on recruiting for intensity and raw talent. We want to have a culture that's intense and friendly as opposed to intense and combative. Intensity is incredibly important. In fact, if someone convinced me you had to be internally combative in order to get intensity, I would be promoting combativeness. But, in fact, I don't think it's necessary. I would put an intense and friendly company

side by side against an intense and combative company any day, and I think the intense and friendly company would come out the victor every time.

Among the companies that Bezos admired were Federal Express, Starbucks, and Wal-Mart. He admired each of these firms for different reasons. Observed Bezos:

I have lots of models that we look at. I look at FedEx as a company that experienced hyper-growth and still had an extraordinary need to deliver perfect customer service during the hyper-growth period. I look at Starbucks for a model of how they've used guerrilla marketing on a large scale. Also, Starbucks has done some extraordinarily smart things in their marketing. I can't walk into a *Fortune* 500 company cafeteria without seeing a sign in the cafeteria that says, "We proudly serve Starbucks coffee." And I look at Wal-Mart as an example of a company that really focused on developing a cost advantage over its competitors—a substantial cost advantage. When you look at K-Mart versus Wal-Mart in the 1980s, K-Mart spent a lot of money on advertising. But Wal-Mart spent a lot of money on building ten super distribution centers across the country and developing information technology systems to control inventory. It's clear who won that battle!

Conclusion

The highly integrated management systems at Amazon.com had already enabled its customers to search for books and receive e-mail notification of upcoming titles. These systems, Bezos believed, would ultimately allow Amazon.com to provide each customer with his or her own "customized" bookstore. In the longer term, he was certain that this would prove to be the key competitive advantage over present and future competitors—including the large, well-funded, national bookstore chains. His programmers had created the entire system in-house, rather than seeking a ready-made or shrink-wrapped solution. Noted Bezos:

We've been working on our IT systems for two-and-a-half years. It is now a big advantage. It was a huge amount of work. There is simply no off-the-shelf inventory control system that can do what our system does. We have five different availability categories. Things can be in stock, and usually shipped within 24 hours. They can be shipped within two to three days. They can ship in one or two weeks. They can ship in

[19]Roy Rivenburg, "Let Your Fingers Do Your Book Shopping," *Los Angeles Times*, December 11, 1996.

four to six weeks. And they can be not yet published, and shipped when available. That's an example of a complicating factor. Our system has to support tracking and control of more than a million different items. And it is fully integrated with all of the various e-mail messages we send to customers.

Still, despite the enormous amount of attention Amazon.com had received during 1996 and the high levels of user satisfaction and loyalty, Bezos did not believe his new Web retailer represented a threat to traditional bookstores:

Amazon.com is not going to put bookstores out of business, any more than TV put the movies out of business. Barnes & Noble is opening a new superstore currently every four days. Borders is opening a new superstore every nine days. Personally, I still buy half my books at bookstores. Sometimes I want the book right now, not tomorrow. Good bookstores have become the community centers of the late 20th century. That's the basis on which they are going to compete. There's plenty of room for everyone.

Customer Dugan appeared to agree with Bezos' sentiments. Physical and Internet bookstores simply served different buying occasions. As Dugan observed, "Internet ordering is not a substitute for visiting any kind of bookstore. But, when it comes to a specialized need, it's a great boon." As a result, several questions remained in Bezos' mind: How would Amazon.com continue to dominate bookselling on the Internet? And how would it maximize its advantages over physical booksellers?

Exhibit 1 Amazon.com Income Statement

Amazon.com Income Statement				
12 months ending December 31, 1996 and 1995				
	In Thousands of Dollars		As % of Revenue	
Revenue	**1996**	**1995**	**1996**	**1995**
Net sales	$15,746	$511	100.0%	100.0%
Expenses				
Cost of sales	12,287	409	78.0%	80.0%
Gross Margin	3,459	102	22.0%	20.0%
Operating Expenses				
Marketing and sales	6,090	200	38.7%	39.1%
Product development	2,313	171	14.7%	33.5%
General and administrative	1,035	35	6.6%	6.8%
Total operating expenses	9,438	406	59.9%	79.5%
Earnings (Loss) from Operations	(5,979)	(304)	−38.0%	−59.5%
Interest Income	202	1	1.3%	0.2%
Net Loss	($5,777)	($303)	−36.7%	−59.3%

Source: Amazon.com, Securities and Exchange Commission, S-1 Filing, 1997

Exhibit 2 Top 20 Book Markets in the United States

	Establishments	Sales ($ Thousands)
1 Los Angeles-Long Beach, CA	454	$383,902
2 New York, NY	363	359,716
3 Chicago, IL	366	271,867
4 Boston, MA-New Hampshire	249	238,116
5 Washington, DC-Maryland-Virginia-West Virginia	296	234,586
6 Philadelphia, PA-New Jersey	268	161,735
7 San Francisco, CA	167	138,875
8 Seattle-Bellevue-Everett, WA	176	131,679
9 San Jose, CA	99	125,015
10 San Diego, CA	175	115,419
11 Detroit, MI	171	115,319
12 Atlanta, GA	171	108,449
13 Oakland, CA	137	108,453
14 Houston, TX	143	108,449
15 Dallas, TX	146	106,771
16 Nassau-Suffolk, NY	127	90,976
17 Minneapolis-St. Paul-Wisconsin	134	89,720
18 Denver, Colorado	130	87,284
19 Orange County, CA	134	85,547
20 Phoenix-Mesa, AZ	128	78,626

Source: Adaptation of data from American Booksellers Association, based on 1992 sales.

Exhibit 3 Barnes & Noble and Borders Group, Inc. Financial Statements

Barnes & Noble Income Statement	In Thousand of Dollars			As Percentage of Revenue		
Revenue	**1996**	**1995**	**1994**	**1996**	**1995**	**1994**
Superstores	$1,861,177	$1,349,830	$ 952,697	76.0%	68.3%	58.7%
Mall bookstores	564,926	603,204	646,876	23.1%	30.5%	39.9%
Other	22,021	23,866	23,158	0.9%	1.2%	1.4%
Total Revenue	$2,448,124	$1,976,900	$1,622,731	100.0%	100.0%	100.0%
Expenses						
Cost of sales, buying and occupancy	1,569,448	1,269,001	1,050,011	64.1%	64.2%	64.7%
Gross Margin	878,676	707,899	572,720	35.9%	35.8%	35.3%
Selling and administrative	456,181	376,773	311,344	18.6%	19.1%	19.2%
Rental expenses	225,450	182,473	147,225	9.2%	9.2%	9.1%
Depreciation and amortization	59,806	47,881	36,167	2.5%	2.4%	2.2%
Pre-opening expenses	17,571	12,160	9,021	0.7%	0.6%	0.6%
Restructuring charges	0	123,768	0	0.0%	6.3%	0.0%
Operating Earnings (loss)	119,668	(35,156)	68,963	4.9%	−1.8%	4.2%
Net interest expense	38,286	28,142	22,995	1.6%	1.4%	1.4%
Earnings (Loss) before income tax	81,382	(63,298)	45,968	3.3%	−3.2%	2.8%
Provision (benefit) for income tax	30,157	(10,322)	20,085	1.2%	−0.5%	1.2%
Net Earnings (loss)	51,225	(52,976)	25,883	2.1%	−2.7%	1.6%
Preferred stock redemption premium	0	0	0	0.0%	0.0%	0.0%
Net Earnings (loss) After Preferred Stock Redemption Premium	$ 51,225	$ (52,976)	$ 25,883	2.1%	−2.7%	1.6%

Borders Group Income Statement	In Thousand of Dollars			As Percentage of Revenue		
Revenue	**1996**	**1995**	**1994**	**1996**	**1995**	**1994**
Superstores	$ 979,100	$ 717,500	$ 425,500	50.0%	41.0%	28.2%
Mall bookstores	979,700	1,031,500	1,085,500	50.0%	59.0%	71.8%
Total Revenue	$1,958,800	$1,749,000	$1,511,000	100.0%	100.0%	100.0%
Expenses						
Cost of sales, buying and occupancy	1,437,800	1,302,300	1,127,100	73.4%	74.5%	74.6%
Gross Margin	521,000	446,700	383,900	26.6%	25.5%	25.4%
Selling and administrative	409,600	374,500	333,300	20.9%	21.4%	22.0%
Pre-opening expenses	7,200	7,300	5,700	0.4%	0.4%	0.4%
Goodwill amortization and writedowns	1,100	205,500	7,400	0.0%	11.7%	0.5%
FAS 121 impairment	0	63,100	0	0.0%	3.6%	0.0%
Operating losses of stores identified for closure	0	(3,300)	(12,700)	0.0%	-0.2%	-0.8%
Restructuring charges	0	0	6,400	0.0%	0.0%	0.4%
Operating Earnings (loss)	103,100	(200,400)	43,800	5.3%	−11.4%	2.9%
Net interest expense	7,000	4,600	1,000	0.4%	0.3%	0.1%
Earnings (loss) before Income Tax	96,100	(205,000)	42,800	4.9%	−11.7%	2.8%
Provision (benefit) for income tax	38,200	6,100	21,900	1.9%	0.4%	1.4%
Net Earnings (loss)	57,900	(211,100)	20,900	3.0%	−12.1%	1.4%
Effect of accounting changes, net of income tax	0	0	0	0.0%	0.0%	0.0%
Net earnings (loss) after net effect of accounting changes	$ 57,900	$ (211,100)	$ 20,900	3.0%	−12.1%	1.4%

Barnes & Noble: Number of Stores						
Superstores	431	358	268			
Mall stores	577	639	698			
Total	1,008	997	966			

Borders Group Inc.: Number of Stores						
Superstores	157	116	75			
Mall stores	961	992	1,102			
Total	1,118	1,108	1,177			

Note: Both companies have fiscal years ending January 31; e.g., FY1996 ended January 31, 1997.
Sources: Barnes & Noble 1995 and 1996 Annual Reports, Borders Group Inc. 1995 and 1996 Annual Reports

Exhibit 4 Book Market by Major Categories

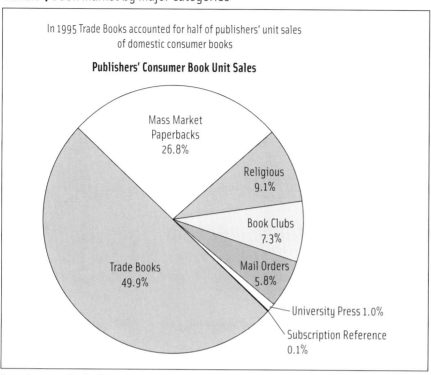

In 1995 Trade Books accounted for half of publishers' unit sales of domestic consumer books

Publishers' Consumer Book Unit Sales

- Mass Market Paperbacks 26.8%
- Religious 9.1%
- Book Clubs 7.3%
- Mail Orders 5.8%
- University Press 1.0%
- Subscription Reference 0.1%
- Trade Books 49.9%

Note: Consumer book sales exclude textbook sales, which is approximately one-fourth the size of consumer book sales.
Sources: Adaptation of data from The Veronis, Suhler & Associates Communications Industry Forecast 1996; ABA Research Dept.

Exhibit 5 Book Buying Patterns by Household Income Level

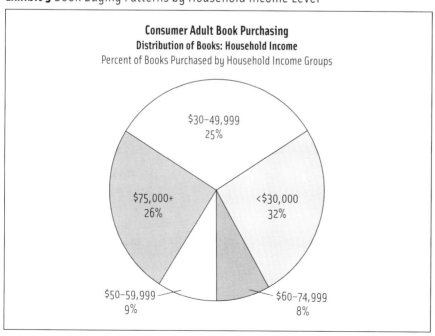

Consumer Adult Book Purchasing
Distribution of Books: Household Income
Percent of Books Purchased by Household Income Groups

- $30–49,999 25%
- <$30,000 32%
- $75,000+ 26%
- $50–59,999 9%
- $60–74,999 8%

Sources: Adaptation of data from 1995 Consumer Research Study on Book Purchasing; ABA Research Dept.

Exhibit 6 Usage of Technology by Book-Buying Consumers

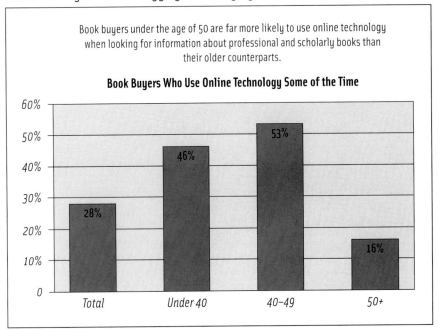

Book buyers under the age of 50 are far more likely to use online technology when looking for information about professional and scholarly books than their older counterparts.

Book Buyers Who Use Online Technology Some of the Time

	Total	Under 40	40–49	50+
	28%	46%	53%	16%

Sources: Adaptation of data prepared by Wirthlin Worldwide for ABA-PSP Professional & Scholarly Book Buying Study; ABA Research Dept.

Exhibit 7 Projections of On-Line Commerce, 1996–2000

Segment	1996	1997	1998	1999	2000
Computer products	$ 140	$ 323	$ 701	$1,228	$2,105
Travel	126	276	572	961	1,579
Entertainment	85	194	420	733	1,250
Apparel	46	89	163	234	322
Gifts/flowers	45	103	222	386	658
Food/drink	39	78	149	227	336
Other	37	75	144	221	329
Total ($M)	$ 518	$ 1,138	$ 2,371	$ 3,990	$ 6,579

Source: Adaptation of data from Forrester Research.

Exhibit 8 Projections of World Wide Web Usage, 1995–2000

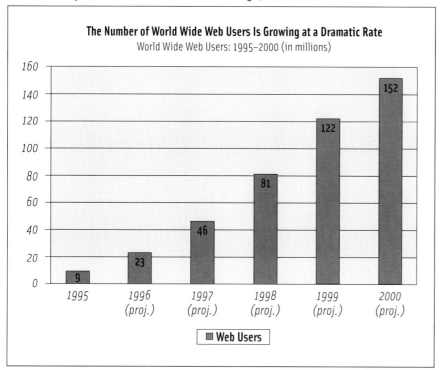

The Number of World Wide Web Users Is Growing at a Dramatic Rate
World Wide Web Users: 1995–2000 (in millions)

Source: Adaptation of data from "The Internet Report," 1996, Morgan Stanley (NY); SIMBA Information Inc.

Exhibit 9 Amazon.com Home Page

Exhibit 10 Amazon.com Search Page

Exhibit 11 Amazon.com Order Page

Finalizing Your Order is Easy

You can place your order online without transmitting your credit card over the Internet! However, you must first complete the online ordering forms. If you have questions about this form, please scroll down the page for more information, along with our toll-free number.

1. What is your e-mail address?

> **Note: One small typo here, and we won't be able to communicate with you about your order.**

> My e-mail address is [   ]

> **Please check your e-mail address carefully!**

2. What method of payment do you intend to use?

> ○ Credit Card (Visa, MasterCard, Discover, or American Express only) (why this is safe)
> ○ Check or Money Order (why this takes longer)

3. Is this your first order from Amazon.com Books?

> ○ I am a first-time customer (or I have forgotten my password.)
> ○ I am a returning customer, and my password is [   ]

4. Is this order a gift?(if not you can skip to step 5)

> For gift orders we will not include prices on the packing slip. You can include a personalized gift message in your order. These services are free of charge.

> We also offer gift wrapping, for which we charge $2.00 per order.

> ◉ This order is **not a gift**.
> ○ This order is a gift, but I prefer **no gift wrapping**.

Otherwise please select one of the following giftwraps:

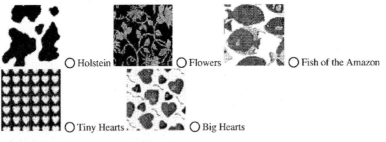

○ Holstein   ○ Flowers   ○ Fish of the Amazon

○ Tiny Hearts   ○ Big Hearts

We usually use the giftwrap you choose, but sometimes we have to make substitutions.

Your gift message, to be printed on the packing slip (maximum 500 characters):

[   ]

5. Press [this button to continue] **to the next page. You will still have a chance to cancel or change your order.**

Exhibit 12 Amazon.com Confirmation Page

Amazon.com Books

Items in your shopping basket:

Quantity:

....

Available in 2-3 days:

1 *Microsoft Secrets : How the World's Most Powerful Software Company Creates Technology, Shapes Markets, and Manages People*;
Michael A. Cusumano, Richard W. Selby; Hardcover;

     List: $30.00 -- **Amazon.com Price: $27.00 -- You Save: $3.00(10%)**

....

Please press this button if you [CHANGED QUANTITIES] of any items in your shopping basket. If you don't press it,
your changes won't "stick." You can set the quantity to 0 (zero) to delete an item from your basket.

....

Go to <u>Author, Title, Subject Search</u> now.

[**BUY ITEMS NOW** | VIEW YOUR SHOPPING BASKET]

[**Home** | **Search** | **Browse** | **Eyes** | **Editors** | **Customer Service** | **Send Us E-Mail** | **FAQ**]

<u>Copyright</u> © 1996, 1997 Amazon.com, Inc.
Send us e-mail

Exhibit 13 Amazon.com Confirmation E-Mail

```
Subj:  Your Order with Amazon.com Books (#3953-0356948-603185)
Date:  Sun, Jan 5, 1997 12:03 AM EDT
From:  orders@amazon.com
To:        dlouie@hbs.edu

Thank you for your order!

Your order information is appended below.  If you need to
get in touch with us about your order, send an e-mail message to
orders@amazon.com (or just reply to this message).

        -- Amazon.com Customer Service

---------------------------------------------------------
Amazon.com Books
One million titles, consistently low prices.
info@amazon.com          http://www.amazon.com/
---------------------------------------------------------


Your order reads as follows:

E-mail Address:        dlouie@hbs.edu

Ship Via:  Standard Domestic Shipping

Ship to:   Dickson L. Louie
                209 Main St.
                Los Angeles
                CA
                90201
tel:            310-555-1212



---------------------------------------------------------
1 copy of "Microsoft Secrets : How the World's Most Powerful Software Company Creates Technology, Shapes Markets, and
Manages People"
            Richard W. Selby, Michael A. Cusumano; Hardcover; @ $27.00 each



Books Subtotal:    $ 27.00
Shipping:          $  3.95
Tax:               $  0.00
                   -------
TOTAL DUE:         $ 30.95

---------------------- Headers ---------------------------
From orders@amazon.com  Sat Jan  4 23:03:00 1997
Return-Path: orders@amazon.com
Received: from spica.hbs.edu (spica.hbs.harvard.edu [128.103.120.140]) by emin31.mail.aol.com (8.6.12/8.6.12) with ESMTP id
XAA15821 for <dlouie@aol.com>; Sat, 4 Jan 1997 23:02:59 -0500
From: orders@amazon.com
Received: from bert.amazon.com by spica.hbs.edu (SMI-8.6/SMI-SVR4)
            id XAA09211; Sat, 4 Jan 1997 23:02:54 -0500
Received: from howler.amazon.com (howler.amazon.com [204.177.154.2]) by bert.amazon.com (8.7.6/8.7.3) with ESMTP id
UAA04374 for <dlouie@hbs.edu>; Sat, 4 Jan 1997 20:02:51 -0800 (PST)
Received: (from nobody@localhost) by howler.amazon.com (8.7.6/8.7.3) id TAA29107; Sat, 4 Jan 1997 19:55:18 -0800 (PST)
Date: Sat, 4 Jan 1997 19:55:18 -0800 (PST)
Message-Id: <199701050355.TAA29107@howler.amazon.com>
X-Authentication-Warning: howler.amazon.com: nobody set sender to orders@amazon.com using -f
To: dlouie@hbs.edu
Subject: Your Order with Amazon.com Books (#3953-0356948-603185)
```

Exhibit 14 Amazon.com Packing Slip

http://www.amazon.com
orders@amazon.com

Dickson L. Louie

Amazon.com Books   Toll-Free: (800) 201–7575
549 South Dawson   Voice: +1 (206) 346–2992
P.O. Box 81410   FAX: +1 (206) 346–2950
Seattle, WA 98108–1310
USA

Your order of January 04, 1997 (Order ID 3953–0307948–603199)

Quantity	Title	Author	List Price	Our Price	Total
	Shipped Today				
1	Microsoft Secrets : How the World's Most Powerful Software Company Creates Technology, Shapes Markets, and Manages People (364–5–12)	Richard W. Selby, Michael A. Cusumano	30.00	27.00	27.00
		Books Total			27.00
		Shipping			3.95
		Order Total			30.95
		Paid via Visa			30.95

Thanks for shopping at Amazon.com, and please come again!

519494/1b/1i/2700/std–us/310–478–7888   *1 million titles, consistently low prices*

Exhibit 15 Amazon.com Shipping E-Mail

```
Subj:  Your Amazon.com order (#3953-0307948-603199)
Date:  Tue, Jan 7, 1997 11:03 PM EDT
From:  orders@amazon.com
To:        dlouie@hbs.edu

We thought you'd like to know that the following book has been
shipped to:

           Dickson L. Louie
           209 Main St.
           Los Angeles CA 90201

using UPS Ground shipment.

For your reference, the number you can use to track your package
is 1Z742E220330081956.  You can refer to our web site's customer
service page or

 http://www.amazon.com/exec/obidos/subst/tracking.html/

to access the shipper's site.

Your order #3953-0356948-603185 (received January 04 1997 19:55 PST)
-------------------------------------------------------------------
Ordered  Title                      Price  Shipped  Subtotal
-------------------------------------------------------------------
  1      Microsoft Secrets : How the Wo  27.00    1      27.00
-------------------------------------------------------------------
                             Subtotal:  27.00
                             Shipping:   3.95
                                Total:  30.95
This completes your order.

If you have any questions, please contact us
via e-mail (orders@amazon.com), FAX (1-206-346-2950)
or phone (1-800-201-7575 or 1-206-346-2992).

Thank you for shopping at Amazon.com.

-----------------------------------------------------------
Amazon.com Books
One million titles, consistently low prices.
info@amazon.com           http://www.amazon.com/
-----------------------------------------------------------


----------------------- Headers --------------------------------
From orders@amazon.com Tue Jan  7 22:02:36 1997
Return-Path: orders@amazon.com
Received: from spica.hbs.edu (spica.hbs.harvard.edu [128.103.120.140]) by emin45.mail.aol.com (8.6.12/8.6.12) with ESMTP id
WAA15887 for <dlouie@aol.com>; Tue, 7 Jan 1997 22:02:30 -0500
From: orders@amazon.com
Received: from bert.amazon.com by spica.hbs.edu (SMI-8.6/SMI-SVR4)
          id WAA12247; Tue, 7 Jan 1997 22:02:23 -0500
Received: from stevens.amazon.com (stevens.amazon.com [204.177.154.12]) by bert.amazon.com (8.7.6/8.7.3) with ESMTP id
TAA01076 for <dlouie@hbs.edu>; Tue, 7 Jan 1997 19:02:18 -0800 (PST)
Received: (from faulkner@localhost) by stevens.amazon.com (8.7.4/8.7.3) id TAA27265; Tue, 7 Jan 1997 19:01:56 -0800 (PST)
Date: Tue, 7 Jan 1997 19:01:56 -0800 (PST)
Message-Id: <199701080301.TAA27265@stevens.amazon.com>
X-Authentication-Warning: stevens.amazon.com: faulkner set sender to orders@amazon.com using -f
To: dlouie@hbs.edu
Subject: Your Amazon.com order (#3953-0356948-603185)
```

Exhibit 16 Amazon.com Print Advertisement

Exhibit 17 Amazon.com Customer Bill of Rights

Amazon.com Bill of Rights
1. No obligation   Eyes & Editor Personal Notification Services are provided free of charge, and you are under no obligation to buy anything.
2. Unsubscribing   You can unsubscribe or change your subscriptions at any time.
3. Privacy   We do not sell or rent information about our customers. If you would like to make sure we never sell or rent information about you to third parties, just send a blank e-mail message to *never@amazon.com*.

Exhibit 18 Reviews of Books by Customers on Amazon.com

Amazon.com Books - *Search* Our Million-Title Catalog

Microsoft Secrets : How the World's Most Powerful Software Company Creates Technology, Shapes Markets, and Manages People

by <u>Michael A. Cusumano</u>, <u>Richard W. Selby</u>

Hardcover
List: $30.00 -- **Amazon.com Price: $27.00** -- **You Save: $3.00(10%)**

Published by Free Pr
Publication date: October 1,1995
Dimensions (in inches): 9.57 x 6.57 x 1.67
ISBN: 0028740483

Availability: This item usually shipped within 2-3 days.

[Add This Book to your Shopping Basket] (You can always remove it later...)

You can <u>write your own review of this book</u> and enter it directly into our system.

Amazon.com Books:
This is a "facts ma'am, nothing but the facts" examination of how Microsoft works, both internally, and in the marketplace. Unlike the raft of gossipy Bill-bios or sardonic and shrill pro- or anti-screeds, this book is focused clearly (if sometimes ploddingly) on one central question: the relationship between business strategies and software development. And, as Microsoft becomes increasingly focused on the Internet, it is essential reading not just for software companies, but for all Internet companies as well. Highly Recommended.

David Yofie, Harvard Business School and Intel Board of Directors:
...will become a standard reference for the computer industry.

Synopsis:
Today, Microsoft commands the high ground of the information superhighway by owning the operating systems and basic applications programs that run on the world's 170 million computers. Based on nearly two years of on-site observation at Microsoft headquarters, two eminent scientists now reveal many of Microsoft's innermost secrets. 10 line drawings.

Customer Comments

<u>John P. Delaney IV(jpd4@deltanet.com)</u>, 12/19/96, rating=8:
Reveals Core Strategic Strengths To Be Dealt With
One must wonder if Bill Gates is an ardent fan of Michael Porter as allowing "Microsoft Secrets" to be written looks a lot like one of several communication strategies described in Porter's 1980 vintage "Competitive Strategy". "Microsoft Secrets" effectively communicates the development tools that they use to match the moves of their competitors quickly. These tools are powerful strategic competencies. Every ally or foe of the Microsoft machine needs to understand them. The reading is slow and the structure is a bit repetitive. Not a novel, not another, "Gee whiz look what Bill did", book. However it is well organized and will serve as an excellent reference work for a long time to come. I see it as a must for any serious player in the computing industry.

<u>Synthysys@msn.com</u>, 06/11/96, rating=8:
Excellent R&D portrait of Microsoft; Other Facets Weaker
Most Microsoft books fall into the "kiss and tell" genre with the authors attempting to inject life into an otherwise stale recounting of the history of Microsoft by exploring topics like what Bill Gates eats for breakfast. This book is refreshing in that it is written in a factual style and offers analysis of the best practices within Microsoft that have contributed to its success. It is particuarly strong with respect to all aspects of R&D; weaker when exploring marketing and sales.

Exhibit 19 Interview Page with Authors on Amazon.com

Amazon.com Books - *Search*

Thomas Mallon: Animating the Past

Thomas Mallon--whom John Updike has called "one of the most interesting American novelists at work"--combines a historian's meticulous research with a novelist's storytelling and imaginative gifts. Some reviewers have wondered if his books fit the term "historical fiction" at all. When he stopped by Amazon.com's offices recently, Senior Editor Nicholas H. Allison asked him about this and about how he saw the relationship between the setting and the story in Dewey Defeats Truman.

Thomas Mallon: Well, "historical fiction" is a really elusive term. I've seen some scholars who have actually tried to define it in terms of how far back it has to be in order to be historical as opposed to contemporary. But the last three books I've written have all been about ordinary people--in some cases real ordinary people like Henry and Clara Rathbone, and in other cases fictional historical people, like the people in this book and in Aurora 7--and their relation to a historical event of some magnitude: Lincoln's assassination, the Dewey-Truman election, Scott Carpenter's space flight. To me that's what makes them historical. In some ways I'm writing about bystanders and how the private lives of individuals on the fringes of these events are influenced by the public event that goes into the historical memory.

Amazon.com: Is that something that interests you in contemporary life, too?

Mallon: I think so. I still think I'll get around to writing a novel in the present one of these days.

Amazon.com: Henry and Clara was set around the Civil War, and **Dewey Defeats Truman** is 1946; are you working your way forward now?

Mallon: No, actually I'm going back. I'm back now in 1877. I'm starting a novel set in the old naval observatory in Washington. The naval observatory was located in a swamp--in Foggy Bottom, where the State Department is today. It's a ridiculous place to put an observatory, because the dome was fogged over half the nights of the year and the astronomers suffered from malaria. In 1877 it was riven by various disputes among scientists, like scientific institutions today, and Washington was more than usually embroiled in its own disputes. Hayes had just come in as president in a disputed election; you've got the last of the Indian wars going on out West and the railroad strike in the East--just this big cauldron of stuff. During this period in August of 1877, an astronomer named Asaph Hall discovered the two moons of Mars and named them Demos and Phobos--"anxiety" and "fear." The main action centers on the observatory, with a mixture of half real characters and half made-up characters.

When you're writing fiction, in some ways you're always writing about yourself. But one of the things that appeals to me a lot about historical fiction is the relief from the self. I mean, most novelists' lives are pretty thin when it comes to general material for writing. History provides so many more interesting stories than would spring from one's own life--especially something like **Henry and Clara**. In my own life I don't think I'd ever stumble on a story like that.

Next page of interview

Back to Thomas Mallon feature

Buy Dewey Defeats Truman now for **30% off!**

AMAZON.COM (B)

In January 1998, as Pacific storm clouds moved eastward over Puget Sound, Jeff Bezos, Founder, Chairman, and CEO of Amazon.com, sat in his downtown Seattle office and recalled the frenzied activity of the previous 12 months. Amazon.com was now a public company; it had raised $50.2 million in an initial public offering (IPO) in May 1997. It was, however, engaged in a fierce competitive battle with the Web-based subsidiary of Barnes & Noble, the largest bookseller in the United States, over domination of the on-line bookselling market, which analysts predicted would reach $2.2 billion in sales by 2002.[1]

Since Barnes & Noble opened its bookselling site in the on-line world—first with a site on America Online (AOL) in mid-March 1997 and then with a site on the Web in mid-May 1997—Amazon.com and BarnesandNoble.com went head to head in a fast-paced war of electronic booksellers. Like other duopoly competitions—such as Coca-Cola and Pepsi in soft drinks or Microsoft and Netscape in Web browsers—each player responded almost immediately to every change in the rival firm's strategy and tactics (see Exhibit 1).

The War of the Electronic Booksellers

During 1997, the war of electronic bookselling was fought along seven dimensions. These were pricing policy, customer acquisition, associates/affiliates programs, personalization, customer service, user navigation, and legal challenges.

Pricing Policy. Barnes & Noble took the lead in pricing policy by announcing in January 1997 that it would sell hardcover titles at 30% off list prices on AOL. At the time, Amazon.com was selling hardcovers at 10% to 20% off, with 30% off only on selected hardback titles. On the day prior to the March 18, 1997, launch of Barnes &

Nobles' AOL site, Amazon.com announced that it would offer 40% off selected hardback titles. At the same time, Amazon.com increased the number of book titles available through its Web site from 1.1 million to 2.5 million, with out-of-print books accounting for roughly 400,000 of the additional book titles. On November 20, 1997, BarnesandNoble.com matched Amazon.com with a 40% discount on selected titles and offered 88% off bargain books. Amazon.com countered the next day by offering 89% off its bargain books.[2]

Customer Acquisition. In the area of customer acquisition, Amazon.com took the lead. To drive traffic to its Web site, the start-up entered into strategic alliances with major on-line partners to increase brand awareness and build traffic among potential on-line customers (see Exhibit 2). Amazon.com's partnership agreements included five of the six most-visited sites on the Web: AOL, Yahoo!, Excite, Netscape, and GeoCities.[3]

Reinforcing this initiative, Amazon.com entered into a three-year co-branding agreement, concluded on July 7, 1997, as the exclusive bookseller for AOL's Web site (www.aol.com) and AOL's NetSearch Engine in a deal valued at $19 million. On July 8, for undisclosed amounts, similar agreements were reached with Yahoo! and Excite, the two most widely used Internet search engines in the United States, with an average of 18 million and 11 million unique users a month, respectively.[4] The Yahoo! deal provided search engine users with a list of book titles available from Amazon.com that were pertinent to any search topic. AOL designated Amazon.com the exclusive bookseller on its Web site by providing the Seattle-based company with prominent icon placement near the top of the AOL home page; similarly, Excite served personalized search results to users with a banner that enabled click-throughs directly to the Amazon.com home page. Similar agreements were reached with

---

Research Associate Dickson L. Louie prepared this case, with the assistance of Research Associate Carrie L. Ardito and Holly S. Cameron, CPA, Mdiv., under the supervision of Professor Jeffrey F. Rayport as the basis for class discussion rather than to illustrate either effective or ineffective handling of an administrative situation.

[1]Dan Goodin, "Booksellers: Partner or Perish?" CNET, September 9, 1997.
[2]Press Release, "Amazon.com Announces New Deeper Discounts," Amazon.com, November 21, 1997.
[3]As measured by Media Matrix, the PC Meter Company, November 1997.
[4]Relevant Knowledge, report, November 1997. "Unique Users" refer to visitors who have visited the site at least once during the past reporting period.

Netscape (*www.netscape.com*) in October 1997 and with GeoCities (*www.geocities.com*) in December 1997.

In response, BarnesandNoble.com concluded similar co-branding alliances with *The New York Times* Electronic Media Company for its on-line book section (*www.nytimes.com/books*) in May 1997; with Lycos (*www.lycos.com*), the Web's third leading search engine, in August 1997; and with Microsoft's MSNBC (*www.msnbc.com*), Microsoft Investor (*www.investor.msn.com*), and The Microsoft Expedia (*www.expedia.com*) sites in October 1997. In addition, in December 1997, BarnesandNoble.com signed a four-year, $40-million agreement with AOL to promote its on-line bookselling channels throughout the AOL commercial on-line service. This agreement was concluded in parallel with Amazon.com's three-year, mid-1997 agreement with AOL, which "made Amazon.com the exclusive bookseller on AOL.com and AOL's NetFind Search Engine."[5]

By year-end 1997, the audience reach of both companies had increased substantially among Internet users.[6] In addition, both companies invested in paid media to promote their brand names and URLs. For example, Amazon.com placed ads in upscale mass-market publications such as *The New Yorker* and *The New York Times Book Review* (see Exhibit 3).

Associates/Affiliates Program.

Another tactic Amazon.com pioneered to drive traffic to its Web site was its Associates program, launched in July 1996. Under this program, any Web site, such as a personal home page, could become an "associate" and embed links to Amazon.com. If a link resulted in a book's sale, the associate received a 15% commission—it was originally 8% through June 1997—calculated based on the sale price. In September 1997, Barnes & Noble established a similar program, which it called its affiliates program, offering 7% commissions on *all* books sold when a visitor arrived by click-through from an affiliate site. To capitalize on the bookseller's relationship with *Fortune* 500 companies, Barnes & Noble also announced the creation of its Affiliates Network—a lineup of 40 major commercial Web sites that would act as BarnesandNoble.com resellers, including CNN Interactive (*www.cnn.com*), the *Los Angeles Times* (*www.latimes.com*), and ZiffDavis's ZDNet (*www.ZDNet.com*). In response, Amazon.com

announced on September 8, 1997, that it was increasing commissions on books sold through its top 500 PC Meter Associates from 15% to 22.5% for the ensuing six months.

At year-end 1997, Amazon.com had over 18,000 affiliates, an increase of 200% over the 5,000 Associates at year-end 1996,[7] while BarnesandNoble.com had over 1,300 affiliates.[8] As Nicole Vanderbilt, a senior analyst at Jupiter Communications, observed:

> As the on-line shopping market matures, innovative selling practices, such as affiliates programs, will be crucial in reaching new on-line customers and driving incremental sales. Jupiter believes that by 2002, over 25% of on-line shopping revenues will be realized through purchases that originate at affiliate sites.[9]

Personalization.

The development of one-to-one relationships with Web customers was another tactic that Amazon.com employed to acquire and retain customers. Unlike the physical world, where retail "location" was considered a key driver of sales, Bezos believed that in the virtual world "one-to-one" marketing was the critical factor.[10] To that end, Amazon.com used its "Eyes" and "Editors" services to notify customers by e-mail of book availability according to topic categories pre-selected by customers. To fight back, BarnesandNoble.com announced a licensing relationship with Firefly Network, a software company based in Cambridge, Massachusetts, that sold collaborative filtering technology. Collaborative filtering employed intelligent software agents to generate recommendations in categories such as books and music, by communication across multiple agents within a database that carried different selections but displayed similar preference profiles. In response, Amazon.com created an on-line "Recommendation Center" in September 1997 to furnish personalized recommendations for visitors to the Amazon.com site. One feature of the Recommendation Center, "Instant Recommendation," automatically provided individual customers with a personalized list of suggested titles to buy based on a customer's purchase history with Amazon.com as well as those of other customers with similar profiles (see

[5]Press Release, "Amazon.com Issues Statement Regarding Barnes & Noble AOL Commerce Agreement," Amazon.com, December 18, 1997.
[6]As measured by Media Matrix, the PC Meter Company. Amazon.com's audience reach increased from 3.2% in June 1997 to 6.3% in December 1997; BarnesandNoble.com's audience reach increased from 0.4% to 2.0% between May and November 1997.

[7]See Amazon.com, HBS Case No. 9-897-128.
[8]Press Release, "Amazon.com Announces Financial Results for Fourth Quarter and 1997 Year-End," Amazon.com, January 22, 1998.
[9]Press Release, "BarnesAndNoble.com Launches Affiliate Network," BarnesandNoble.com, September 9, 1997.
[10]Interview with Professor Jeffrey F. Rayport, August 20, 1998, Wescott Communications.

Exhibit 4). Another feature, "BookMatcher," made book recommendations based on the profile of individuals with similar preferences, using software developed by Minneapolis-based NetPerceptions. First time users of BookMatcher (see Exhibit 5) recorded book preferences in four categories—Popular Fiction, Science Fiction and Fantasy, Mystery and Suspense, and Classic Literature—in order to tap into the value of the service.

Customer Service.
With the launch of BarnesandNoble.com, Steve Riggio, President and Chief Operating Officer of Barnes & Noble, believed that same-day shipment of books would provide a competitive advantage for the bookseller in its on-line operations. Riggio believed that Barnes & Noble's infrastructure and book publishing relationships would make this service possible. Indeed, Barnes & Noble had just completed construction of a new book distribution center in New Jersey that would support both traditional retail and Web-based order fulfillment. Noted Riggio:

> Without question, one of the principal assets we bring to the table is the fact that we are extremely good at book distribution, whether it be to our stores or to our customers, whether they be domestic or international, and whether they buy by phone, mail, or the Internet. By the fall [of 1997], our 350,000 square-foot distribution center will have 90% of the books we believe people are going to be buying on-line.[11]

To counter BarnesandNoble.com's strategy for quick delivery of books, Amazon.com established and opened in November 1997 a 200,000-square-foot distribution center in New Castle, Delaware. This would support same-day shipment of books for customers on the East Coast.

Navigation.
In March 1997, Amazon.com redesigned its home page to make it more user friendly in response to feedback from users. The redesign of Amazon.com's home page departmentalized customer activities (see Exhibit 6). A second redesign of the on-line bookseller's home page appeared in September 1997 (see Exhibit 7); a new service offered returning customers the option of using one-click technology to order books on-line as well as access features in the Recommendation Center.

---

[11]Michael Schrage, "The I.Q. Q&A: Steve Riggio—Barnes & Noble Is Betting That the Printed Word Will Be a Best Seller in Cyberspace," *Adweek Interactive Quarterly,* August 18, 1997.
[12]Prospectus on Amazon.com, May 15, 1997, p. 19.
[13]Press Release, "Amazon.com Announces Financial Results for Fourth Quarter and 1997 Year-End," Amazon.com, January 22, 1998.

BarnesandNoble.com was rumored to be planning a major site redesign for completion in spring 1998.

Legal Challenges.
In October 1997, lawsuits between Amazon.com and Barnes & Noble had been settled without either party paying damages. In early 1997, Barnes & Noble had sued Amazon.com for its having billed its site as "Earth's Biggest Bookstore." Attorneys for Barnes & Noble argued that the claim was misleading (they claimed that Amazon.com was not a "store," since it was virtual, and that it was not largest, because it had limited physical inventory) and represented an infringement of Barnes & Noble's long-standing retail claim as "The World's Largest Bookstore." Amazon.com counter-sued in August 1997, charging that Barnes & Noble had failed to pay local sales taxes on on-line sales in states where retail stores were located. With a neutral settlement, the booksellers resolved to compete in the on-line market and not in the courtroom.

1997 Financial and Operational Results

In 1997, Amazon.com sustained an operating loss of approximately $27.6 million on net sales of $147.8 million, compared with a loss of $5.8 million on $15.7 million in sales in 1996 (see Exhibit 8). Despite these losses, Bezos felt Amazon.com was succeeding along the three dimensions of strategy that would position the company for long-term success: extending Amazon.com's brand position in the on-line world; providing outstanding value to users through superior on-line shopping experiences; and achieving significant sales volume to realize economies of scale.[12]

Net sales had increased more than eight-fold in the previous year. Roughly $39 million, or 67% of the company's operating expenses of $58 million, was allocated to marketing and sales. Included in these expenditures were the co-branding payments to third parties such as America Online and Yahoo! Another $12 million, or approximately 20% of operating expenses, went to product development and upgrades to Amazon.com's Web site. Amazon.com reported a gross margin of approximately 20% on net sales before operating expenses for marketing, sales, product development, and administration.[13] The company's customer base—the number of individuals who had purchased from Amazon.com at least once—also grew rapidly in 1997, from 180,000 at year-end 1996 to over 1.5 million at year-end 1997 (see

Exhibit 9). While Wall Street analysts did not expect Amazon.com to record a profit until 1999, Amazon.com's market valuation at year-end 1997 was approximately $1.4 billion, with its stock price at $60.25 per share as compared to an IPO price of $18 per share (see Exhibit 10).[14]

By comparison, BarnesandNoble.com was expected to record $14 million in sales for its first nine months of operation in 1997.[15]

Conclusion

Bezos was wary of his competitor's next moves. While Michael Lymon, Chief Executive of Penguin Putnam, predicted that Amazon.com could be one of the publisher's largest customers in two or three years, Bezos knew that there were no guarantees about Amazon.com's sustaining its currently torrid rate of growth.[16] After all, other players besides Barnes & Noble were entering the market. Borders Group, Inc., was planning to launch its own Web site during the first quarter of 1998. German media giant Bertelsmann also entered the business with a site called Book Central. As a result, the onslaught was only beginning. Bezos wondered: How might Amazon.com maintain a competitive advantage in the fast-changing market on the Web? Lacking the leverage of a physical store network, how might it continue to drive revenue growth to achieve economies of scale?[17] Should Amazon.com match BarnesandNoble.com "tit-for-tat" with respect to pricing and marketing, given that its average gross margin on books sold had slipped from an average of 21.9% in 1996 to 19.5% in 1997? Or should Amazon.com focus on attracting and retaining mainstream users, knowing that the number of Internet users was expected to grow to 152 million worldwide in 2000 from 36 million in 1997?[18]

Bezos also suspected that Amazon.com's future competitive advantage would derive perhaps from no one strategy but rather from capabilities intrinsic to his management team. He had built a top tier of talent in the company which was impressive by any standards (see Exhibit 11). At year-end 1997, it included executives formerly with Wal-Mart, FedEx, PC Magazine, Kraft Foods, Microsoft, and Avid Technology.

---

[14]Dow Jones Newswires, "Nationsbanc Montgomery Securities Target Price is $70-AMZN," January 22, 1998.

[15]Press Release, "BarnesandNoble.com Expects 1988 Sales to Exceed $100 Million," Barnes & Noble, Inc., January 15, 1998.

[16]Doreen Carvajal, "In the Publishing Industry, the High-Technology Plot Thickens," *The New York Times*, January 5, 1998.

[17]Prospectus, Amazon.com, May 15, 1997, p. 29.

[18]Mary Meeker and Chris DuPuy, *The Internet Report* (New York: HarperCollins) 1996.

Exhibit 1 Bookselling Wars

Timeline across: December 1996 | January 1997 | February 1997 | March 1997 | April 1997 | May 1997 | June 1997 | July 1997 | August 1997 | September 1997 | October 1997 | November 1997 | December 1997

Amazon.com

December 31, 1996
- Amazon.com closes its first full fiscal year with a loss of $6.0 million on sales revenue of $15.7 million. Number of daily visits increase to 50,000 at year-end 1996 compared to 2,200 at year-end 1995.

March 17, 1997
- Amazon.com expands inventory to 2.5 million books. Discounts on Top 50 bestsellers.

May 13, 1997
- Amazon.com announces 40% off on Amazon 500 bestsellers.

May 20, 1997
- Amazon.com goes public—raises $50 million in public offering.

June 2, 1997
- Amazon.com increases its commission for Associates from 8% to 15%.

June 10, 1997
- Amazon.com reduces price to 40% off on selected hardback titles.

July 7, 1997
- Amazon.com signs three-year agreement to be exclusive bookseller on AOL Web page and AOL NetSearch for $19 million. Also signs agreement with Excite!

July 8, 1997
- Amazon.com signs deal with Yahoo! linking their home page to search results.

August 25, 1997
- Amazon.com files suit against B&N for noncollection of state sales tax.

September 8, 1997
- Amazon.com increases commissions to 22.5% for top PC Meter 500 associates for six months.

September 24, 1997
- Amazon.com introduces new recommendation center and one-click ordering technology.

October 9, 1997
- Amazon.com signs deal to be Digital Alta Vista's exclusive bookseller.

October 14, 1997
- 1 millionth customer signs up.

October 20, 1997
- Amazon.com becomes exclusive bookseller for Netscape's Net Center.

November 10, 1997
- Amazon.com takes $75 million credit facility.

November 18, 1997
- Amazon.com opens second distribution center in New Castle, Delaware.
- Amazon.com announces Christmas Gift Center and Gift Certificates by mail and e-mail.

November 21, 1997
- Amazon.com announces 89% off bargain books.

December 3, 1997
- Amazon.com signs deal with GeoCities.

BarnesandNoble.com

January 28, 1997
- B&N announces plans for AOL and Web sites to sell books online. All hardbacks are to be sold at 30% off.

March 18, 1997
- B&N launches B&N on AOL (America Online). Exclusive seller on AOL marketplace. Discount of 30% on all hardbacks.

May 13, 1997
- B&N launches B&N.com on the Web; files lawsuit against Amazon for calling itself "earth's biggest book store." B&N announces technological alliances with Hewlett-Packard, Microsoft, and Firefly.

May 20, 1997
- B&N.com becomes exclusive bookseller for *New York Times* on the Web/books.

August 21, 1997
- B&N.com signs three-year agreement to be the exclusive bookseller with Lycos.

September 4, 1997
- B&N launches online book groups on AOL and new features on B&N.com.

September 10, 1997
- B&N.com announces its affiliates network with 40 top Web sites, including CNN.com, LATimes.com, Time Inc. Pathfinder. Signs deal with Be Free to provide affiliates with information of online sales.

September 16, 1997
- B&N.com becomes exclusive bookseller on Webcrawler (2 years). Firefly technology used to provide customized book recommendations.

October 6, 1997
- B&N signs deal with Microsoft to be exclusive bookseller on MSNBC Microsoft Investor and Expedia.

October 21, 1997
- B&N and Amazon.com settle lawsuits. No damages. They both agree to compete only in the marketplace.

October 28, 1997
- B&N.com signs agreement with Compuserve to be the online service's exclusive bookseller.

November 20, 1997
- B&N.com announces holiday gift center and 40% off on selected hardbook titles.
- B&N.com announces 88% off bargain books.

December 11, 1997
- B&N signs agreement to be exclusive bookseller on PointCast.

December 16, 1997
- B&N signs $40 million 4-year agreement with AOL to be the exclusive bookseller on the online service.

Sources: Press Releases; Amazon.com and Barnes & Noble Prospectus; Amazon.com, May 15, 1997

Exhibit 2 Amazon.com Strategic Alliances

Date	Alliance
July 7, 1997	America Online Web Page and Netsearch
July 7, 1997	Excite Inc.
July 8, 1997	Yahoo! Inc.
October 9, 1997	Digital's Alta Vista
October 20, 1997	Netscape Communications
November 10, 1997	@Home Network
December 3, 1997	GeoCities

Source: Amazon.com Company Documents

Exhibit 3 Amazon.com Advertisements in *The New Yorker* and *The New York Times Book Review*

Sources: *The New Yorker,* December 15, 1997; Amazon.com Company Documents

Exhibit 4 Amazon.com Instant Recommendation Page

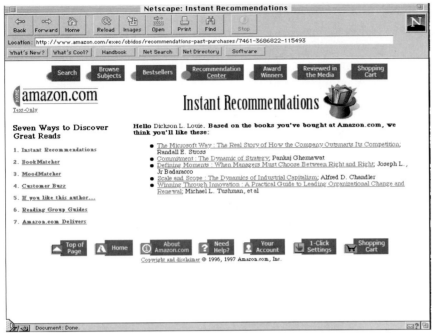

Source: *www.amazon.com*

Exhibit 5 Amazon.com Book Matcher Page

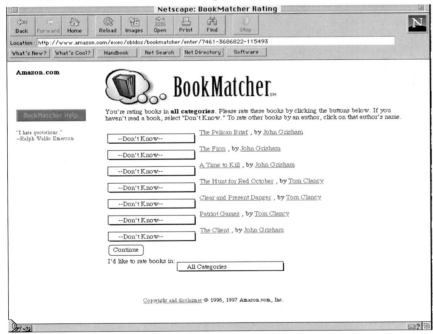

Source: *www.amazon.com*

Exhibit 6 Amazon.com Home Page: March 1997

Source: Amazon.com Company Documents

Exhibit 7 Amazon.com Home Page: September 1997

Source: *www.amazon.com*

Exhibit 8 Amazon.com Profit and Loss Statement, 1995–1997 ($000)

	1997	1996	1995
Net sales	$147,758	$15,746	$511
Cost of goods sold	118,945	12,287	409
Gross Profit	$28,813	$3,459	$102
Operating Expenses			
Marketing and sales	$38,964	$6,090	$200
Product development	12,485	2,313	171
General and administrative	6,573	1,035	35
Total Operating Expenses	$58,022	$9,438	$406
Loss from operations	($29,209)	($5,979)	($304)
Interest income	1,619	202	1
Net Loss	($27,590)	($5,777)	($303)

Sources: Amazon.com Prospectus, May 15, 1997; Amazon.com Press Release, January 22, 1998

As Percent of Net Sales			
	1997	1996	1995
Net sales	100.0%	100.0%	100.0%
Cost of goods sold	80.5%	78.0%	80.0%
Gross Profit	19.5%	22.0%	20.0%
Operating Expenses			
Marketing and sales	26.4%	38.7%	39.1%
Product development	8.4%	14.7%	33.5%
General and administrative	4.4%	6.6%	6.8%
Total Operating Expenses	39.3%	59.9%	79.5%
Loss from Operations	(19.8%)	(38.0%)	(59.5%)

Sources: Amazon.com Prospectus, May 15, 1997; Amazon.com Press Release, January 22, 1998

Exhibit 9 Amazon.com Operating Data, 1997

Customer Accounts	
Date	**Number of Customers**
Dec-96	180,000
Mar-97	340,000
Sep-97	940,000
Dec-97	1,510,000

Audience Reach: At Work Users		Audience Reach: At Home Users	
Date	**Percent of Web Users**	**Date**	**Percent of Web Users**
Dec-96	–	*Dec-96*	2.5%
Jun-97	–	*Jun-97*	3.2%
Sep-97	6.2%	*Sep-97*	4.2%
Dec-97	8.8%	*Dec-97*	6.3%

Sources: Amazon.com Prospectus, May 15, 1997; Press Release, Amazon.com, January 22, 1998; Media Matrix, The PC Meter Company. "At Work" usage was not measured by PC Meter until August 1997; prior to that date, "At Home" usage was combined with "At Work" usage.

Exhibit 10 Stock Price, Amazon.com (AMZN)

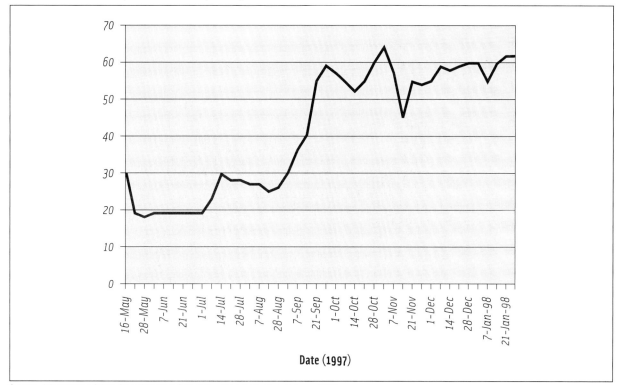

Source: Adaptation of data from *The Wall Street Journal Interactive,* January 1998.

Exhibit 11 Amazon.com Executive and Board Member Biographies

Name	Age	Biography
Jeffrey P. Bezos *President, CEO, and Chairman of the Board*	34	Mr. Bezos has been President and Chairman of the Board of the Company since founding it in 1994, and Chief Executive Officer since May 1996, and served as Treasurer and Secretary from May 1996 to March 1997. From December 1990 to June 1994, Mr. Bezos was employed by D.E. Shaw & Co., a Wall Street investment firm, becoming Senior Vice President in 1992. From April 1988 to December 1990, Mr. Bezos was employed by Bankers Trust Company, becoming Vice President in February 1990. Mr. Bezos received his B.S. in Electrical Engineering and Computer Science, Summa Cum Laude, from Princeton University.
Rick R. Ayre *Vice President and Executive Officer*	48	Mr. Ayre joined the Company in September 1996 as Vice President and Executive Editor. From September 1991 to September 1996, Mr. Ayre served in a number of positions at PC Magazine, most recently as Executive Editor for Technology. From September 1988 to September 1991, Mr. Ayre served as Chief of Information Resources Management of Highland Drive VAMC, a hospital. Mr. Ayre received his B.A. in Sociology from Drury College.
Mark L. Breier *Vice President of Marketing*	38	Mr. Breier joined the Company in January 1997 as Vice President of Marketing. From March 1994 to September 1996, Mr. Breier served as Vice President of Marketing of Cinnabon World Famous Cinnamon Rolls. Mr. Breier was involved in product management and introduction at Dreyer's Grand Ice Cream from October 1988 to March 1994; at Kraft Foods, Inc., a multinational consumer products company, from April 1986 to October 1988; and at Parker Brothers, a worldwide manufacturer of toys and games, from August 1985 to March 1986. Mr. Breier received his B.A. in Economics from Stanford University and his M.B.A. from the Stanford University Graduate School of Business.
Joy D. Covey *CFO, Vice President of Finance and Administration, Treasurer and Secretary*	34	Ms. Covey joined the Company in December 1996 as Chief Financial Officer and Vice President of Finance and Administration, and became Secretary and Treasurer in March 1997. From June 1995 to February 1996, Ms. Covey served as Vice President, Operations of the Broadcast Division of Avid Technology, Inc. ("Avid"), a developer of digital media systems, and from January 1995 to June 1995, Ms. Covey served as Vice President of Business Development for Avid. From July 1991 to January 1995, Ms. Covey served as Chief Financial Officer of Digidesign, Inc., a developer of random access digital audio systems and software. Prior to that, she was an associate at Wasserstein Perella & Co., and a certified public accountant at Arthur Young & Company (now Ernst & Young LLP). Ms. Covey received her B.S. in Business Administration, Summa Cum Laude, from California State University, Fresno; her M.B.A., With High Distinction, from Harvard Business School; and her J.D., Magna Cum Laude, from Harvard Law School. She is a Certified Public Accountant and a member of the California State Bar.
Richard L. Dalzell *Vice President and Chief Information Officer*	39	Mr. Dalzell joined Amazon.com in August 1997, from Wal-Mart Stores, Inc., the world's largest retailer, where he served as Vice President, Information Systems Division since 1994, joined the company in 1990. As Wal-Mart's Information Systems executive responsible for all merchandising and logistics systems, Mr. Dalzell led the development of world-class supply chain systems, set the standard for international retailing and merchandising systems, and was instrumental in establishing the world's largest commercial decision support and data mining systems.
Oswaldo F. Duenas *Vice President of Operations*	51	Mr. Duenas joined the Company in January 1997 as Vice President of Operations. From February 1994 to December 1996, Mr. Duenas served as Vice President of the Latin American division of International Service System, Inc., Latin America's largest integrated service company, where he oversaw sales, marketing, operations and customer relations for the division and managed several thousand employees. From September 1993 to January 1994, Mr. Duenas served as President and Director General of National Vision Associates, a Mexican vision retail business. From 1973 to 1993, Mr. Duenas held various management positions with Federal Express, a worldwide express transportation company.
Mary E. Engstrom *Vice President of Publisher Affairs*	35	Ms. Engstrom joined the Company in February 1997 as Vice President of Publisher Affairs. From December 1996 to February 1997, Ms. Engstrom served as Vice President of Marketing of Symantec Corporation ("Symantec"), a developer of information management and productivity enhancement software, and from February 1996 to February 1997, Ms. Engstrom served as General Manager of the Security Business Unit of Symantec. From July 1989 to September 1994, Ms. Engstrom held several management positions at Microsoft Corporation, including Group Product Manager for Microsoft Access, Group Product Manager for Microsoft Project, and Director of Marketing, Strategic Relations. Ms. Engstrom received her B.A. in Economics from the University of California, Berkeley, and her M.B.A. from the Anderson Graduate School of Management at the University of California, Los Angeles.
Sheldon J. Kaphan *Vice President and Chief Technology Officer*	45	Mr. Kaphan has served as the Company's Vice President and Chief Technology Officer since March 1997. From October 1994 to March 1997, Mr. Kaphan served as Vice President of Research and Development of the Company. From October 1992 to July 1994, Mr. Kaphan served as senior engineer at Kaleida Labs Inc., a multimedia joint venture between Apple Computer Inc. and International Business Machines Corporation. Mr. Kaphan received his B.A. in Mathematics from the University of California, Santa Cruz.

Exhibit 11 Amazon.com Executive and Board Member Biographies (continued)

Name	Age	Biography
Scott E. Lipsky *Vice President of Business Expansion*	33	Mr. Lipsky joined the Company in July 1996 as Vice President of Business Expansion. From March 1994 to July 1996, Mr. Lipsky served as Chief Information Officer of Barnes & Noble, Inc., a national trade bookstore chain, and Chief Technology Officer of Barnes & Noble College Bookstores, Inc., a national college bookstore chain. From September 1991 to January 1994, Mr. Lipsky served as founder and President of Omni Information Group, a consulting, software development and systems integration company serving the retail-chain market. From February 1987 to September 1991, Mr. Lipsky was Vice President of Information Systems at Babbage's, a consumer software retail chain.
John D. Risher *Vice President of Product Development*	32	Mr. Risher joined the Company in February 1997 as Vice President of Product Development. From July 1991 to February 1997, Mr. Risher held a variety of marketing and project management positions at Microsoft Corporation, including Team Manager for Microsoft Access and Founder and Product Unit Manager for MS Investor, Microsoft's Web site for personal investment. Mr. Risher received his B.A. in Comparative Literature, Magna Cum Laude, from Princeton University and his M.B.A. from Harvard Business School.
Joel L. Spiegel *Vice President of Engineering* *Board of Directors*	42	Mr. Spiegel joined the Company in March 1997 as Vice President of Engineering. From March 1995 to March 1997, Mr. Spiegel held several positions with Microsoft Corporation, including Windows 95 Multimedia Development Manager, Windows Multimedia Group Manager and Product Unit Manager, Information Retrieval. From June 1986 to March 1995, he held a variety of positions at Apple Computer Inc., most recently as Senior Manager responsible for new product development in the Apple Business Systems Division. Prior to that, Mr. Spiegel held software product development positions at a number of companies, including Hewlett-Packard and VisiCorp. Mr. Spiegel received his B.A. in Biology with Honors from Grinnell College.
Tom A. Alberg	58	Mr. Alberg has been a director of the Company since June 1996. Mr. Alberg has been a principal in Madrona Investment Group, L.L.C., a private merchant banking firm, since January 1996. From April 1991 to October 1995, he was the President and a director of LIN Broadcasting Corporation, and from July 1990 to October 1995, he was Executive Vice President of McCaw Cellular Communications, Inc.; both companies were providers of cellular telephone services and are now part of AT&T Corp. Prior to 1990, Mr. Alberg was a partner of the law firm Perkins Coie, where he also served as Chairman of the firm's Executive Committee. Mr. Alberg is also a director of Active Voice Corporation, Emeritus Corporation, Mosaix, Inc., Teledesic Corporation and Vision Corporation. Mr. Alberg received his B.A. from Harvard University and his J.D. from Columbia Law School.
Scott D. Cook	45	Mr. Cook has been a director of the Company since January 1997. Mr. Cook co-founded Intuit, Inc., a leading personal finance, tax and accounting software company, in 1983; has served as President of Intuit since that time; and has served as its Chairman of the Board since April 1994. Prior to co-founding Intuit, Mr. Cook was a consultant for Bain & Company, a strategy consulting firm, and a brand manager for Procter & Gamble. Mr. Cook is also a director of Broderbund Software, Inc. and Intuit, Inc. Mr. Cook received his B.A. in Mathematics and Economics from the University of Southern California and his M.B.A. from Harvard Business School.
L. John Doerr	46	Mr. Doerr has been a director of the Company since June 1996. Mr. Doerr has been a general partner of Kleiner Perkins Caufield & Byers, a venture capital firm, since September 1980. Prior to joining Kleiner Perkins Caufield & Byers, Mr. Doerr was employed by Intel Corporation for five years.
Patricia Q. Stonesifer	41	Ms. Stonesifer has been a director of the Company since February 1997. Ms. Stonesifer is an independent management consultant whose clients include DreamWorks SKG. Ms. Stonesifer served as Senior Vice President of the Interactive Media Division of Microsoft Corporation from February 1996 to December 1996, was head of Microsoft's Consumer Division from August 1993 to February 1996 and held a range of positions at Microsoft from 1988 to 1993. While at Microsoft, Ms. Stonesifer managed its investments in new on-line content and service products, including MSN, the Microsoft Network (msn.com); MSNBC, Microsoft's joint venture with NBC; Slate (slate.com); and Expedia (expedia.com), as well as other Internet-based products. Prior to joining Microsoft, Ms. Stonesifer held a number of positions at Que Corporation. Ms. Stonesifer is also a director of Kinko's, Inc. and a member of the Executive Board of the Academy of Interactive Arts and Sciences. Ms. Stonesifer received her B.A. in General Studies from Indiana University.

Source: Company Documents

AMAZON.COM (C)

"Books, Music and More"
Amazon.com promotional tag line, mid-1998

During the Fourth Quarter 1998, Amazon.com's net sales revenue had more than tripled, from $66.1 million for the same quarter in 1997 to $250 million in 1998. The strong finish for 1998 reflected the continuing nation-wide surge in on-line shopping, where an estimated $2.3 billion[1]—or double the amount in 1997—was spent by consumers during the 1998 Holiday Season. Between November 17 and December 31, 1998, Amazon.com had shipped over 7.5 million items, added over one million new members, and had peak shipments of more than $6 million in one day.[2] As a result of the company's strong year-end performance, its 1998 net sales revenue was $610.0 million[3]—a four-fold increase from the company's 1997 revenue of $147.8 million. Despite the company's year-end success, several articles in the business press at the end of 1998 had already begun to note that Jeff Bezos, Amazon.com's 35-year-old founder and CEO, was already thinking about new challenges that lay ahead for the three-year-old startup company.[4] Over the past year, both he and his management team had already taken the first steps to transform Amazon.com from simply being known as the earth's largest online book-seller to achieving its ultimate goal to become one of the world's giant retailers in cyberspace. In June 1998, in its first move to expand its product mix, the company began to sell musical CDs. Five months later, in November 1998, videos and special gift items were added.

Some of the articles on the company speculated about what retail categories Amazon.com should pursue next—toys, consumer electronics, games, software, health supplies, flowers and apparel were all possibilities (see Exhibit 1). A published article noted that Bezos, an avid reader of business history, knew that Amazon.com's successes today could easily become a distant memory

Dickson L. Louie prepared this case under the supervision of Jeffrey F. Rayport, CEO of Marketspace, a Monitor Group Company, written while he was Associate Professor at Harvard Business School. HBS cases are developed solely as the basis for class discussion. Cases are not intended to serve as endorsements, sources of primary data, or illustrations of effective or ineffective management.

tomorrow.[5] The key to Amazon.com's long-term success, Bezos said in published and broadcast interviews, was keeping his management team and his 2,100 employees focused on the few items where the company could gain an advantage against its ever increasing number of online competitors. Recognizing that the company was "at an extremely critical point in its history for category formation,"[6] Amazon.com's goal, Bezos emphasized, would be "to build a valuable and lasting company."[7]

The War of the Electronic Booksellers, 1998

Throughout 1998, Amazon.com continued its "tit-for-tat" battle with BarnesandNoble.com (Exhibit 2). Despite Barnes & Noble's reputation as being the world's largest bookseller, with over 500 superstores located across the United States, BarnesandNoble.com still played second fiddle to Amazon.com in the on-line bookselling market. Net sales revenue for BarnesandNoble.com for fiscal year 1998 was $70.2 million,[8] or $29 million below the $100 million goal projected by Barnes & Noble management early in 1998.[9] In addition, BarnesandNoble.com's customer base at year-end 1998 was 1.4 million or approximately one-fifth of Amazon.com's 6.2 million at year-end 1998.[10] Nevertheless, Barnes & Noble management still felt that it could ultimately win the on-line war with Amazon.com over the long-term, especially with additional resources from Bertelsmann AG,

[1]Leslie Kaufman, "Surge of Shopping in December Gives Merchants a Lift," *The New York Times*, December 28, 1998.
[2]George Anders, "Amazon.com Sales More Than Triple, Boosting Online Bookseller's Shares," *The Wall Street Journal*, January 6, 1999.
[3]Robert D. Hof, Ellen Neuborne, and Heather Green, "Amazon.com: The Wild World of E-Commerce," *Business Week*, December 14, 1998.
[4]Robert D. Hof, Ellen Neuborne, and Heather Green, "Amazon.com: The Wild World of E-Commerce," *Business Week*, December 14, 1998.
[5]Alex Freyer, "Inside Amazon.com," *The Sunday Seattle Times*, July 26, 1998.
[6]Simon, Bob, *60 Minutes II*, CBS News, February 3, 1999.
[7]Bayers, Chip, "The Inner Bezos," *Wired Magazine*, March 1999."
[8]Press Release, "Barnes and Noble Inc. Tops $3 Billion in Fiscal Year 1998," February 24, 1999.
[9]Press Release, "BarnesandNoble.com Expects 1998 Sales to Exceed $100 Million," January 15, 1998.
[10]Press Release, "Amazon.com Announces Financial Results for Fourth Quarter 1998," January 26, 1999.

the German media giant, who had purchased a 50% stake in BarnesandNoble.com in November 1998 for $200 million, and from an expected IPO for Barnes-andNoble.com planned for 1999. Both moves would help increase BarnesandNoble.com's war chest. "The biggest piece of the market is still ahead of us," observed Barnes & Noble's Vice Chairman Stephen Riggio.[11] Forrester Research, a Cambridge, Massachusetts-based research group predicted that the on-line bookselling market would grow from $630 million in 1998 to $3 billion in 2003,[12] an indication that the on-line market for this category still had plenty of room to grow and that it was still too early to declare a dominant player.

In 1998, the battle taking place between Amazon.com and BarnesandNoble.com was fought on four competitive areas: pricing policy, customer service, consumer awareness, and international markets.

Pricing Strategy.
Throughout 1998, both Amazon.com and BarnesandNoble.com continued their pricing strategy of offering up to 40% off on selected book titles. Although the 40% discount was only available on selected titles, many of the hardbacks were sold at 30% off of the retail price. With the addition of CDs, DVDs, and videos, by year-end 1998, Amazon.com had increased the number of media product titles available through its Web site to 4.7 million from the 2.5 million titles available at year-end 1997.

Customer Service.
With the pricing strategy for both Amazon.com and BarnesandNoble.com still unchanged for 1998, shortening the delivery times on the fulfillment of orders was another area where each company sought a competitive advantage. In 1998, Barnes & Noble had added two new distribution centers—one near Atlanta, Georgia, and the other near Reno, Nevada—and boasted in its ads that it carried 750,000 titles, or 450,000 more than Amazon.com had, on hand. In January 1999, Amazon.com announced the opening of its third distribution center in the United States at Fernley, Nevada, which the company's executives believed would shorten delivery of orders to West Coast cities by approximately one day.

Consumer Awareness.
To increase the awareness of the on-line booksellers among the mainstream consumers beginning to buy on the Internet, both Amazon.com and BarnesandNoble.com launched television and radio campaigns in 1998 to promote their sites. Amazon.com launched their first television ads in selected markets in February 1998 while BarnesandNoble.com responded shortly thereafter with television ads featuring noted writers such as military suspense writer Tom Clancy and cartoonist Scott Adams.

International Markets.
With 50% of BarnesandNoble.com purchased by Bertelsmann AG, Amazon.com opened the British version of its on-line store (www.amazon.uk) in September 1998 and its German version (www.amazon.de) in October 1998 (Exhibits 3a and 3b) and by year-end 1998 both sites were the number one on-line booksellers in their respective markets.[13] Both the British and German operations were made possible through stock acquisitions by Amazon.com of Bookpages Ltd. in the United Kingdom and Telebook Inc. in Germany in April 1998.[14]

The on-line bookselling war in 1998 was further complicated by the entry of a third major player into the market, Borders.com, in May 1998 and by Barnes & Noble's proposed acquisition of the Ingram Book Group, the largest supplier of books in the United States, in November 1998. Borders, the second largest bookseller in the United States, estimated that their on-line sales would be $25 million in 1998.

Transforming the Electronic Bookseller into an Electronic Retail Giant

By mid-1998, Amazon.com decided to expand its product line beyond books. In June 1998, the sales of CDs became available through the Web site and five months later in November 1998, videos and selected gift items, such as Palm Pilots and Star Wars toys, were also being sold (Exhibit 4a, 4b, 4c, 4d). A June 1998 survey by Forrester Research indicated that after books, computer hardware, computer software, CDs and videos, travel, and clothing were the five most popular items purchased on the Internet[15] (Exhibit 5). A December 1998 Business Week cover story on Amazon.com observed:

Even though Amazon.com is still a long way from making a profit, its basic economics suggests the upstart will someday look more like a fat-cat software

[11]Robert D. Hof, Ellen Neuborne, and Heather Green, "Amazon.com: The Wild World of E-Commerce," Business Week, December 14, 1998.
[12]Franklin Paul, "How High Can Amazon.com fly?," Reuters News Service, December 18,1998.
[13]Press Release, "Amazon.com Announces Financial Results for Fourth Quarter 1998," January 26, 1999.
[14]Jim Carlton, "Amazon Posts Smaller Loss Than Forecast," The Wall Street Journal, April 28, 1998.
[15]Jonathan Rabinovitz, "E-Commerce Grows Up," San Jose Mercury News, October 25, 1998.

company than a scrambling-for-profits retailer. Once Amazon gets enough customers and sales to pay off its initial marketing and technology investments—and as that technology pays off in falling labor costs—additional revenue falls to the bottom line.[16]

In addition, Amazon.com's high stock price enabled the company to acquire companies to obtain the competencies needed to expand its product line. In anticipation of its expansion into the sale of videocassettes, for example, the company acquired the Internet Movie Database in April 1998, and in preparation for its expansion into other product categories, it acquired Planet All and Junglee in August 1998, respectively, for $90 million and $180 million[17] in stock. The acquisition of Planet All, which provided personal on-line calendars for its users, would enable Amazon.com to remind members to purchase gifts for birthdays, anniversaries, and other important events. This combined with Amazon.com's innovative GiftClick technology, launched in December 1998, that allowed its customers to choose a gift by simply typing in a recipient's e-mail address, would help provide Amazon.com with technological advantages needed for product expansion.

Amazon.com's successful entry into new product categories attracted both the fear and ire of both on-line and mainstream retailers. In the third quarter of 1998, Amazon.com's first full quarter of selling musical compact discs, Amazon.com had already surpassed CDNOW as the category leader with over $14.4 million in sales. By the end of the fourth quarter 1998, total music sales would grow to $33.1 million.[18] In November 1998, a consortium of nine Internet retailers, including CDNOW, reel.com, and eToys, banded together to form a new on-line mall called the Shopper Connection to battle the aggressive expansions by Amazon.com. By teaming up, retailers hoped to attract shoppers from each other's Web sites. "We're allying with other top brands," said Julie Wainwright, CEO of Reel.com. "It's a good way to introduce new customers to our shopping."[19] A month earlier, in October 1998, Wal-Mart, the giant discounter, filed suit in Arkansas against Amazon.com, accusing the on-line retailer of allegedly trying to steal its trade secrets on its inventory and retailing systems through the hiring of key employees.[20]

1998 Financial and Operational Results

During the fiscal year 1998, Amazon.com continued to lose money, sustaining an operating loss of $112.0 million on net sales of $610.0 million, compared with a loss of $32.6 million on net sales of $147.8 million in 1997 (see Exhibit 6). While its gross profit margin had grown from slightly below 20% in 1997 to almost 22% in 1998, Amazon.com's marketing and product development costs had more than tripled from $54.4 million in 1997 to $180 million in 1998 while costs related to mergers and acquisitions added another $50.1 million in operating expenses. Despite these losses, however, Bezos felt that the company was achieving its strategic goal of building Amazon.com over the long term. Bezos explained the company's strategy:

> It's a conscious decision on our part to invest at this time and we will continue to invest at more and more aggressive rates as long as we continue to be successful. It's a formula of success-based investing, we're going to continue to push what works. We'll try to watch the growth rates and be appropriate so if we're not able to get new customers and introduce ourselves to new customers in a cost-effective way, then we'll stop spending such large amounts of investment dollars on marketing expense. So today, we are trying to build an important and lasting company. To do that online in E-commerce, you have to have a scale business. This kind of business isn't going to work in small volumes. We have to level the playing field in terms of purchasing power with the established booksellers and we have to firmly establish our brand name, those are expense things . . . we believe that this is the absolute time when introducing ourselves to customers will be the least expensive it will ever be, so this is when we have to make that big push.[21]

Because of or in spite of Amazon.com's rapid growth over the past year, several Wall Street analysts disagreed about the electronic retailer's market capitalization and future growth. With its stock price at $158 per share at year-end 1998—or 35 times its May 1997 IPO price of

---

[16]Robert D. Hof, Ellen Neuborne, and Heather Green, "Amazon.com: The Wild World of E-Commerce," *Business Week*, December 14, 1998.
[17]George Anders, "Online: Amazon.com Purchases Signal Wider Ambitions," *The Wall Street Journal*, August 5, 1998.
[18]Press Release, "Amazon.com Announces Financial Results for Fourth Quarter 1998," January 26, 1999.
[19]Thomas E. Weber, "Nine Companies Banding Together against Amazon.com," November 23, 1998.
[20]Scott Herold, "Amazon.com in Court," *San Jose Mercury News*, October 17, 1998.
[21]Jeff Bezos, Speech to Commonwealth Club of San Francisco, July 27, 1998.

$3, adjusted for 6-for-1 stock splits—the company was valued at approximately $25 billion, or twice the combined market valuation for both Barnes & Noble and the Borders Group (see Exhibit 7).

Henry Blodget of CIBC Oppenheimer was bullish on Amazon.com's future and noted in a December 1998 report that the stock price of Amazon.com could actually increase to $400 per share within the next year. Blodget wrote:

> Amazon.com is in the early stages of building a global electronic-retailing franchise that could generate $10 billion in revenue and earnings per share of $10 within five years.[22]

Other Wall Street analysts, such as Merill Lynch's Jonathan Cohen, disagreed with Blodget's assessment, noting that Amazon.com's stock price should be valued at only $50 per share. Cohen based his estimate that operating margins for Amazon.com could only be 5 to 7 percent and it was appropriate for Amazon.com to only trade at two times its expected 1999 revenue.[23] Robert Kagle, a venture capitalist with Benchmark Capital who invests in Internet start-ups, also believed that the Amazon.com brand name limited its product line to just media products:

> For one thing, it's unclear that the Amazon.com brand will extend into toys or consumer electronics. I get the combination of books and music and videos. Beyond that, I don't know how far their brand goes.[24]

Despite the talk about Amazon.com market capitalization, Bezos continued to keep his employees focused on the customer. Bezos noted:

> I tell people that if our stock price goes up 30 percent, one of the dangers is that we start to think we're 30 percent smarter. That's just not true. If you think that way, then when the stock price goes down 30 percent, then you'll have to think that you're 30 percent dumber. . . . I ask people around here, think about how do we create real value five years from now, because we can actually affect the stock price five years from now, whereas none of us has any control over what the stock price is tomorrow.[25]

Richard L. Dazell, Amazon.com's senior vice president and chief information officer, emphasized the company's focus-on-the-customer philosophy, where 64% of the company's 6.2 million customers had made repeat buys:

> Underpromise and overdeliver. It's completely what drives us. In this business, the real power is in the hands of the customers. They're always one click away from another store.[26]

Conclusion

Despite Amazon.com's rapid growth during the past three years, Bezos acknowledged that "there are plenty of opportunities to stumble and become a VisiCalc,"[27] referring to the Massachusetts-based software company that was the market leader during the early 1970s in the development of electronic spreadsheets before giving way to the development of Lotus 1-2-3 and Excel, respectively, by the Lotus Development Corporation and Microsoft and then eventually fading away completely. In addition to maintaining a strong customer service focus, Bezos believed that management discipline would be another important key element to Amazon.com's long-term success:

> Not only do you have to avoid the bad ideas, but you have to avoid many of the good ideas for reasons of focus. Ideas are important, but they are relatively easy. What's hard is taking that list of a hundred ideas and ranking them and picking the three that we're actually gonna do. That intellectually one of the most challenging things that happens every day in a company growing this fast, that of brutal triage of ideas.[28]

As for Amazon.com's battle with BarnesandNoble.com to be the world's largest on-line bookseller, Bezos predicted:

> I bet that a year from now that they will not consider us direct competitors. Clearly they do today, but we're on different paths. . . . we're trying to invent the future of e-commerce and they're trying to defend their turf.[29]

[22]Sam Howe Verhovek, "Where a Fingertip Click Meets the Elbow Grease," *The New York Times*, December 23, 1998.
[23]Sam Howe Verhovek, "Where a Fingertip Click Meets the Elbow Grease," *The New York Times*, December 23, 1998.
[24]Robert D. Hof, Ellen Neuborne, and Heather Green, "Amazon.com: The Wild World of E-Commerce," *Business Week*, December 14, 1998.
[25]Alex Freyer, "Inside Amazon.com," *The Sunday Seattle Times*, July 26, 1998.
[26]Sam Howe Verhovek, "Where a Fingertip Click Meets the Elbow Grease," *The New York Times*, December 23, 1998.
[27]Robert D. Hof, Ellen Neuborne, and Heather Green, "Amazon.com: The Wild World of E-Commerce," *Business Week*, December 14, 1998.
[28]Alex Freyer, "Inside Amazon.com," *The Sunday Seattle Times*, July 26, 1998.
[29]Chip Bayers, "The Inner Bezos," *Wired Magazine*, March 1999.

Exhibit 1 Potential Areas of Category Expansion by Amazon.com

Amazon's Growing Universe

NOW
WHERE AMAZON HAS PLUNGED IN

OPPORTUNITY

CHALLENGE

BOOKS
Already the No. 1 online bookseller, with $340 million worth of books sold in the first nine months of this year. That's big—but just a fraction of the $82 billion that will be sold around the world in 1998.

Profit margins are low, even online. Terra firma rivals, such as Barnes & Noble, are beefing up their online presence.

MUSIC

Sales reached $14.4 million in the first three months, outdistancing No. 1 online music seller CDnow. There's room to grow: Music sales amounted to $38.1 billion worldwide last year.

CDnow and N2K, which recently announced they would merge, are already a potent force. On top of that, CDs carry even lower profit margins than books.

VIDEOS
Opened shop this month. Video sales, a $16 billion business worldwide, allow for potent cross-marketing with related books and CDs.

Quick shipments require vast inventory. The shipping delay may keep some buyers in stores.

SOON
WHERE AMAZON IS TESTING THE WATERS

OPPORTUNITY

CHALLENGE

CONSUMER ELECTRONICS
It's a $76 billion market for products such as hand-held game machines, digital cameras, and portable CD players, which have higher average selling prices than books, CDs, and videos.

Sony Walkmen and walkie-talkies are not an obvious fit with books and CDs, discounting is rampant, and rapidly changing product models are tough to compare, even online.

GAMES
Gifts such as Pictionary and Scrabble are likely to appeal to book buyers, too.

Classics are easy to buy, especially for children's gifts, but buyers may take a pass on lesser-known games they can't see and touch.

TOYS
It's a sprawling, $22.6 billion market that offers many tie-ins to books and videos—and it's a natural for quick gifts.

Lack of established wholesale network means toys must be stocked. Dominant retailers, such as Toys 'R' Us, may lock up best terms.

FUTURE
WHERE AMAZON COULD DIVE NEXT

OPPORTUNITY

CHALLENGE

SOFTWARE
Amazon already sells some computer games, and the $5 billion worldwide consumer market fits well with books and CDs.

Software requires lots of post-sale support, so linking with a partner may be more desirable.

HEALTH SUPPLIES
In talks to invest in startup Drugstore.com. Amazon could try to capture a small piece of the $120 billion market for medicines and drugstore products.

Products are nearly ubiquitous in physical stores, and they're often purchased for immediate need.

APPAREL
A $14.3 billion market by mail-order catalog, clothing sales are growing online. Amazon customers are comfortable buying without touching the merchandise.

This is a service-intensive business, and screen resolution can't match paper catalogs; probably best offered through a partner.

FLOWERS
They're an easy sell for holidays and birthdays, and even a sliver of the $15 billion in U.S. sales would be a huge boost in revenues.

With floral networks and online providers such as 1–800-FLOWERS firmly established, this may be practical only through partnerships.

MAGAZINE SUBSCRIPTIONS
A staple in physical bookstores, they're an easy and logical addition to books.

Must take on already established clearinghouses.

TRAVEL ARRANGEMENTS
Travel includes high-ticket items and the potential for higher margins, plus the ability to sell related books and videos.

Requires scads of customer service, and online agencies are firmly established, so linking with a partner seems most likely.

DATA: INDUSTRY ASSOCIATIONS, RESEARCH GROUPS, BUSINESS WEEK

(TOM) PHOTOGRAPH BY DAVID LAWRENCE/STOCK MARKET

Source: *Business Week*, December 14, 1998

Exhibit 2 Bookselling Wars 1998

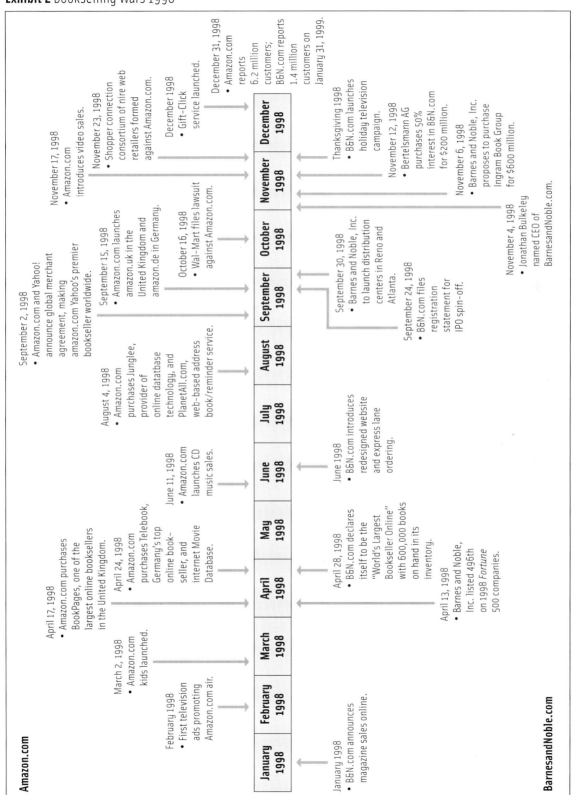

Amazon.com

February 1998
• First television ads promoting Amazon.com air.

March 2, 1998
• Amazon.com kids launched.

April 17, 1998
• Amazon.com purchases BookPages, one of the largest online booksellers in the United Kingdom.

April 24, 1998
• Amazon.com purchases Telebook, Germany's top online bookseller, and internet Movie Database.

June 11, 1998
• Amazon.com launches CD music sales.

August 4, 1998
• Amazon.com purchases Junglee, provider of online database technology, and PlanetAll.com, web-based address book/reminder service.

September 2, 1998
• Amazon.com and Yahoo! announce global merchant agreement, making amazon.com Yahoo's premier bookseller worldwide.

September 15, 1998
• Amazon.com launches amazon.uk in the United Kingdom and amazon.de in Germany.

October 16, 1998
• Wal-Mart files lawsuit against Amazon.com.

November 17, 1998
• Amazon.com introduces video sales.

November 23, 1998
• Shopper connection consortium of nire web retailers formed against Amazon.com.

December 1998
• Gift-Click service launched.

December 31, 1998
• Amazon.com reports 6.2 million customers; B&N.com reports 1.4 million customers on January 31, 1999.

Amazon.com / **BarnesandNoble.com** timeline

January 1998 | February 1998 | March 1998 | April 1998 | May 1998 | June 1998 | July 1998 | August 1998 | September 1998 | October 1998 | November 1998 | December 1998

BarnesandNoble.com

January 1998
• B&N.com announces magazine sales online.

April 13, 1998
• Barnes and Noble, Inc. listed 496th on 1998 Fortune 500 companies.

April 28, 1998
• B&N.com declares itself to be the "World's Largest Bookseller Online" with 600,000 books on hand in its inventory.

June 1998
• B&N.com introduces redesigned website and express lane ordering.

September 24, 1998
• B&N.com files registration statement for IPO spin-off.

September 30, 1998
• Barnes and Noble, Inc. to launch distribution centers in Reno and Atlanta.

November 4, 1998
• Jonathan Bulkeley named CEO of BarnesandNoble.com.

November 6, 1998
• Barnes and Noble, Inc. proposes to purchase Ingram Book Group for $600 million.

November 12, 1998
• Bertelsmann AG purchases 50% interest in B&N.com for $200 million.

Thanksgiving 1998
• B&N.com launches holiday television campaign.

Sources: Press releases, news articles

Exhibit 3a Amazon.uk (United Kingdom) Home Page

Exhibit 3b Amazon.de (German) Home Page

Exhibit 4a Amazon.com Books Home Page

Exhibit 4b Amazon.com Music Home Page

Exhibit 4c Amazon.com Video Home Page

Exhibit 4d Amazon.com Gifts Home Page

Exhibit 5 Projected Net Sales by Category Area

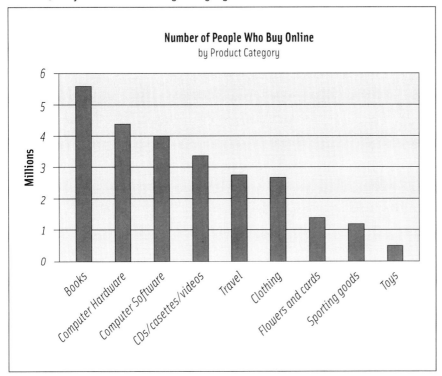

Number of People Who Buy Online
by Product Category

Source: Adaptation of data from Forrester Research, June 1998.

Exhibit 6 Amazon.com Profit and Loss Statement, 1996–1998

	__1998__	__1997__	__1996__
Net sales	$609,996	$147,787	$15,746
Cost of goods sold	476,155	118,969	12,287
Gross Profit	$133,841	$28,818	$3,459
Operating expenses			
Marketing and sales	$133,023	$40,486	$6,090
Product development	46,807	13,916	2,313
General and administrative	15,799	7,011	1,035
Merger & acquisition related costs	50,172	0	0
Total Operating Expenses	$245,801	$61,413	$9,438
Loss from operations	($111,960)	($32,595)	($5,979)
Net interest income (expense)	(12,586)	1,575	202
Net Loss	($124,546)	($31,020)	($5,777)
As Percent of Net Sales	__1998__	__1997__	__1996__
Net sales	100.0%	100.0%	100.0%
Cost of goods sold	78.1%	80.5%	78.0%
Gross Profit	21.9%	19.5%	22.0%
Operating Expenses			
Marketing and sales	21.8%	27.4%	38.7%
Product development	7.7%	9.4%	14.7%
General and administrative	2.6%	4.7%	6.6%
Merger & acquisition related costs	8.2%	0.0%	0.0%
Total Operating Expenses	40.3%	41.6%	59.9%
Loss from Operations	−18.4%	−22.1%	−38.0%

Sources: Amazon.com financial statements and prospectus

Exhibit 7 Stock Price, Amazon.com (AMZN), May 1997–December 1998

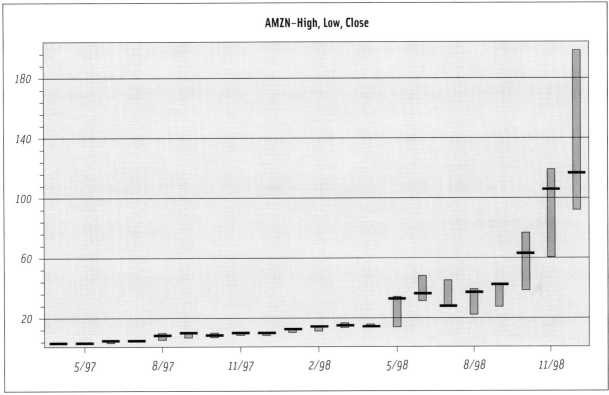

Source: Adaptation of data from Yahoo! Finance Historical Quotes.

AMAZON.COM (D)

"Work Hard, Have Fun, Make History"[1]
—Jeff Bezos, Founder, Chairman and
CEO of Amazon.com

*"Never for me the lowered banner, never the last
endeavor"*[2]
—Sir Ernest Shackleton, legendary Antarctic explorer

By the end of 1999, Amazon.com had completed its first steps toward transforming itself into becoming an online retail superstore. In addition to books, musical CDs, and videos, which Amazon.com was already selling at the end of 1998, the company had now expanded into several new retail categories during 1999, including auction items, electronics, toys, zShops, home improvement, software, and video games (see Exhibit 1 for Amazon.com home page at year-end 1999).[3] To support the company's transformation from an electronic bookseller into a online retail giant, Amazon.com had also increased the number of warehouse locations in the United States from two to seven—funded primarily by the selling of $1.2 billion in convertible, subordinated notes in February 1999—which expanded the company's worldwide distribution capacity from 300,000 square feet to over 5 million square feet[4] in less than 12 months (see Exhibit 2).

The expansion of brick-and-mortar warehouse locations gave Amazon.com control over distribution of most of the products sold through its Web site and what the company had cherished most—providing a unique service experience for its customers. At the end of the Christmas Season 1999, the company had achieved a 99% fulfillment rate on all Holiday orders taken and had seen its customer base increase from 6.2 million at the end of 1998 to 16.9 million at the end of 1999 (see Exhibit 3).[5] Despite the growth in its customer base, the percentage of repeat customers also continued to grow,

from 64% in the fourth quarter of 1998 to 73% in the fourth quarter of 1999.[6] In addition to being the number one online retailer for books—which now accounted for half of its annual sales whereas the category had accounted for almost 100% of the company sales in 1997—Amazon.com was now ranked as the number one retailer for music and toys—displacing CD Now and E-Toys as the category leaders in those respective categories. Approximately 42% of all online Holiday shoppers had said that they had made a purchase at Amazon.com, making it the most visited retail site on the Web (see metrics in Exhibit 4).[7]

Despite the success of the 1999 Christmas season, Amazon.com was not without its critics. With an expanded product line, additional distribution capacity, a workforce of over 7,500 employees,[8] and increased marketing expenditures—$70 million spent alone for the 1999 Christmas season—Amazon.com's reputation for being "famously unprofitable",[9] or having never turned a profit as a public company, became even more pronounced. Despite almost a three-fold increase in revenue from $610 million in 1998 to $1.64 billion in 1999, the company's operating losses increased almost six-fold from $109 million to $605.8 million over the same time period (see Exhibit 5).[10] Critics noted that Amazon.com's gross profit margin in 1999 had decreased from 21.9% in 1998 to 17.7% in 1999, due to increased promotional expenses and inventory write-downs of $39 million in the fourth quarter of 1999.[11] In late January 2000, the company had also announced its first layoffs ever, with the elimination of 150 positions.[12]

[1] Alex Freyer, "Inside Amazon.com," *The Sunday Seattle Times*, July 26, 1998.
[2] As quoted in Alexander, Caroline, "The Endurance," Knopf, 1998.
[3] Amazon.com 1999 Annual Report and 10K
[4] Amazon.com 1999 Annual Report and 10K
[5] Amazon.com 1999 Annual Report and 10K
[6] Amazon.com 1999 Annual Report and 10K
[7] "A Look at the Numbers in Internet Commerce," *The New York Times*, January 2, 2000.
[8] Martinez, Michael, Associated Press, "Amazon.com stock falls amid the layoffs," January 29, 2000.
[9] Sheff, David, "The Playboy Interview," *Playboy*, February 2000.
[10] Amazon.com 1999 Annual l Report and 10K
[11] Amazon.com 1999 Annual l Report and 10K
[12] Martinez, Michael, Associated Press, "Amazon.com stock falls amid the layoffs," January 29, 2000.

Dickson Louie prepared this case under the supervision of Jeffrey F. Rayport, CEO of Marketspace, a Monitor Group Company, written while he was Associate Professor at Harvard Business School. HBS cases are developed solely as a basis for class discussion. Cases are not intended to serve as endorsements, sources of primary data, or illustrations of effective or ineffective management.

Nevertheless, Jeff Bezos—Amazon.com's chairman, founder and CEO—and Joseph Galli—who had been hired in August 1999 from his prior position as president of Black and Decker's Worldwide Power Tools and Accessories Division to be the company's president and chief operating officer—continued to express their optimism about Amazon.com's future in published interviews and statements.[13] With almost 17 million customers, a strong customer-centric focus, innovative software system, and a built-to-suit distribution and customer service infrastructure, both Bezos and Galli believed that Amazon.com had reached a "tipping point" whereby the retailer could launch new e-commerce businesses faster, with a lower incremental cost and higher chance of success than perhaps any other company.[14] And despite the company's overall financial losses, the company's goal was to achieve profitability in its original three categories—books, music and video—in domestic U.S. sales by the end of fiscal year 2000.[15]

Expanding the Franchise, 1999

During 1999, Amazon.com had aggressively expanded its franchise in several ways. These included the addition of new product categories, increased distribution capacity, international growth and strategic partnerships with several key online retailers. An explanation of each follows (see Exhibit 6 for timeline):

Expanded Product Lines

As Amazon.com expanded its retail categories to auction items, electronics, toys, zShops, home improvement, software and video games, Bezos noted that as Amazon.com grew, the complexities of running a business also grew geometrically. He explained:

> We don't think of Amazon.com as a single company. We think of it as a portfolio of self-reinforcing

companies at different stages of development. We have our toy business, we have our tool business, and so on. Everything is less than 18 months old except for U.S. books.[16]

As a result, each individual product category was now managed by a general manager who oversaw a management team responsible for making it profitable over the long-term. The more established product lines, such as books, videos and music, were located at the company's offices on Second Street in downtown Seattle while the less established product lines, such as Z-shops and entertainment goods, were located at Amazon.com's corporate headquarters on Beacon Hill, which allowed easy access to both Bezos and Galli.[17] Bezos added:

> As the company goes through its life cycle, you have to actively manage differently at different stages. You reach different inflection points where you need to focus on different processes.[18]

Increased Distribution Capacity

To support the expanded product categories, Amazon.com increased its distribution capacity to 5 million square feet in what Bezos described in a *New York Times* article as being "the fastest expansion of distribution capacity in peacetime history."[19] At the end of 1999, the company had seven distribution centers—Seattle, Washington; New Castle, Delaware; Coffyville, Kansas; Grand Forks, North Dakota; Campbellsville, Kentucky; Fernley, Nevada; and McDonnough, Georgia. Jeffrey A. Wilke, Vice President and General Manager of Operations, observed:

> In building these distribution centers, we can follow the customer experience from beginning to end and own the data as well as the physical movement of product through the whole process. We think that will deliver a level of customer performance that is unparalleled. The experience is just more consistent.[20]

International Growth

In addition to its U.S operations, Amazon.com's United Kingdom (www.amazon.co.uk) and German (www.amazon.de) sites were also in the top 10 most-visited Web site and leading e-commerce site for each respective county. By year-end 1999, the product categories in both countries had expanded from books to music, auctions and zShops. With products being shipped to over 150 countries, Amazon.com sought to position itself as the leading global e-retailer.[21]

[13]Amazon.com 1999 Annual Report and 10K and Brooker, Katrina, "Amazon vs. Everybody," *Fortune*, November 8, 1999

[14]Amazon.com 1999 Annual Report and 10K

[15]Krantz, Michael, "Cruising Inside Amazon.com," *Time*, December 27, 1999.

[16]Interview with casewriter, January 11, 2000.

[17]Krantz, Michael, "Cruising Inside Amazon," *Time*, December 27, 1999.

[18]Interview with casewriter, January 11, 2000.

[19]Hansell, Jeff, "Amazon's Risky Christmas," *The New York Times*, November 28, 1999, page 1, Money and Business Section.

[20]Hof, Robert D., *Business Week e-biz*, "Question and Answer with Jeffrey Wilke", October 21, 1999.

[21]Amazon.com 1999 Annual Report and 10K

Strategic Partnerships and Alliances

Besides expanding its own operations, Amazon.com took equity interest in several other e-commerce companies as a way to allow its customers to receive a wider range of products and services as well as to generate additional revenue from these companies by helping them sell to the Amazon.com customer base. These companies included Ashford.com, drugstore.com, Home-Grocer, Sothebys.com and Pets.com (see Exhibit 7).[22]

Underlying these milestones were the core values of Amazon.com: customer-obsessed, innovative, ownership, bias for action, high hiring bar and frugality.[23] On being customer-obsessed, Jean Jarvis, Vice President, Investor Relations for a major media company in Los Angeles and an Amazon.com customer, commented on the company's service:

> I did order books over the holidays—stuff for me, stuff for my husband, and was very happy with the responsiveness. In addition, I ordered an e-mail gift certificate for my secretary, who received it promptly and was thrilled, since he's a voracious reader. So I received Amazon gift books from my brother, I ordered and received Amazon gift books for other friends and family, I ordered books I wanted personally and I gave an e-mail gift certificate. I think the service during the holidays was every bit as good as other times throughout the year. Amazon was the first Internet purchase service I ever used, and frankly, I haven't found any other Internet service that I've personally used that has been as good.[24]

1999 Financial and Operational Results

During 1999, Amazon.com's net sales grew from $608.8 million to $1.64 billion and its operating loss grew from $109 million to $606 million. During the Fourth Quarter 1999—the first time sales were broken out by product category—on sales revenue of $676 million, books generated $317 million in sales; toys, $95 million; and music, $78 million.[25] Included in the operating expenses for 1999 were $214.7 million related to the amortization of goodwill and other intangibles and $8 million related to acquisition costs. Marketing and sales expenditures, reflecting Amazon.com strategy to scale up quickly, tripled from $132.7 million in 1998 to $413.2 million in 1999.

Despite Amazon.com's continued customer growth, some wondered if the company was beginning to stretch its brand too thin. Al Riles, a brand management consultant, observed:

> The most powerful brands in the world stand for something simple. Volvo stands for safety. Dell is a personal computer. Now Amazon is going to stand for books and charcoal grills. That makes no sense to me.[26]

Other critics, such as Lehman Brothers debt analyst Ruvi Suria in June 2000, criticized the company for its excessive cash burn rate, noting that Amazon's debt of $2 billion made its "credit extremely weak and deteriorating." Suria also noted that as Amazon evolved from a virtual business into a real world retailer, it has been turning brand value into cash flow but profit per unit sold has been elusive—a criticism that Amazon.com management disagreed with.[27]

In 2000, those who believed in Amazon.com's future and those who did not remained sharply divided. This was not new to Joy Covey, Amazon.com's chief strategic officer and former chief financial officer, who observed, "When it comes to Amazon.com, people fall into two camps. Camp One is 'Ohmygod, they're not profitable!' Camp Two understands what we're trying to build."[28]

Looking Ahead

Despite the short-term pressures to become profitable, Bezos—who was selected by *Time Magazine* to be its Man of the Year for 1999—continued to emphasize in published statements that it was important for the company to take a long-term view toward profitability by building market share first.[29] With increased competition from other retailers, including Barnes & Noble, KB Toys, and Wal-Mart, Bezos reminded shareholders in Amazon.com's 1999 annual report of the note he had

[22]Amazon.com 1999 Annual Report and 10K
[23]Quittner, Joshua, "An Eye on the Future," *Time Magazine*, December 27, 1999, page 59.
[24]E-mail message to casewriter, January 18, 2000.
[25]Francisco, Bambi, "Amazon to focus on Profits," CBS MarketWatch.com, February 3, 2000.
[26]Hof, Robert F., "Can Amazon Make It?" *Business Week*, July 10, 2000.
[27]Jonas, Ilaina, "Amazon.com CEO blasts analyst, sees no cash woes," Reuters, June 28, 2000.
[28]Brooker, Katrina, "Amazon vs. Everybody," *Fortune*, November 8, 1999.
[29]Amazon.com 1999 Annual Report to Stockholders and Sheff, David, "The Playboy Interview," *Playboy*, February 2000.

written in the 1997 annual report about the company's operating game plan:

> We have a window of opportunity as larger players marshal the resources to pursue the online opportunity and as customers, new to purchasing online, are receptive to forming new relationships. The competitive landscape has continued to evolve at a fast pace. Many large players have moved online with credible offerings and have devoted substantial energy and resources to build awareness, traffic and sales. Our goal is to move quickly and extend our current position while we begin to pursue the online commerce opportunities in other areas. We see substantial opportunity in the large markets we are targeting. This strategy is not without risk: it requires serious investment and crisp execution against established franchise leaders.[30]

As for the criticism that Amazon.com was trying to do everything, Bezos commented:

> We're not trying to do everything. Our brand stands for something simple: starting with the customer and working backwards. We can offer many different product categories and be inside our brand.

What we can't do is something ordinary, something without any innovation. So we're not doing physical stores, for example.

Think of a point in a three-dimensional space. Maybe we're a plane in a three-dimensional space, but we're certainly not taking the entire volume. My belief is that you can do more, because you have infinite shelf space and you can personalize the site, but you certainly still have to focus. The question is what do you focus on?

If you're a great physical retailer—and I've said this many times before—and you sell only one category, such as toys, my claim is that it's easier to start a chain of new physical stores selling home improvement hardware, for example, than it is for you to sell toys online because the skills and competencies between running a great chain of toy stores and hardware stores are very similar whereas a set of skills and competencies between being a great e-retailer and great physical retailer are completely different—so where's the focus point?[31]

---

[30]Amazon.com 1999 Annual Report to Stockholders
[31]Interview with casewriter, January 11, 2000

Exhibit 1 Amazon.com Home Page (December 1999)

Exhibit 2 Amazon.com U.S. Distribution Centers (1999)

Seattle, Washington	93,000 square feet
Campbellsville, Kentucky	770,000 square feet
Coffeyville, Kansas	750,000 square feet
Fernley, Nevada	332,650 square feet
Grand Forks, North Dakota	130,000 square feet
McDonough, Georgia	800,000 square feet
New Castle, Delaware	202,000 square feet
Total U.S. distribution capacity	2,984,650 square feet
Total worldwide distribution capacity	5,000,000 square feet

Source: Adaptation of data from Amazon.com and *Time* Magazine, December 27, 1999

Exhibit 3 Amazon.com Number of Customers (at year-end)

1996	180,000 customers
1997	1.5 million customers
1998	6.2 million customers
1999	16.9 million customers

Source: Amazon.com 1999 Annual Report 10-K Statement

Exhibit 4 Amazon.com Key Metrics

	Millions of Visits	Advertising Impressions (in millions)	Buyers	Has Traditional Outlets
DEPARTMENT STORES				
Amazon.com	33.1	683.1	42.1%	
Buy.com	5	145.8	16.1%	
JCPenney.com	4.2	152.7	9.8%	B&M
QVC.com	3.9	None	4.1%	B&M
Quixtar.com	2.7	None	NA	B&M
Sears.com	2.5	234.1	2.8%	B&M
Wal-Mart.com	2.5	None	2.9%	B&M
Shopping.com	2	46.1	NA	
NetMarket.com	1.9	543.8	NA	B&M
ServiceMerchandise.com	1.8	None	NA	B&M
TOYS				
eToys.com	11.1	1032.2	20.3%	
ToysRUs.com	8.9	984.8	19.4%	B&M
KBKids.com	4.9	1631.3	14.3%	B&M
ToyTime.com	2.4	478.7	NA	
toysmart.com	1.5	549.7	NA	B&M
Disney.store.com	1.3	159.1	4.6%	B&M
SmarterKids.com	1.3	132.6	NA	
ELECTRONICS				
BestBuy.com	1.9	0.4	3.7%	B&M
800.com	1.6	360	NA	
CircuitCity.com	1	None	1.6%	B&M
EBWorld.com	0.7	159.5	NA	B&M
hifi.com		138.3	NA	B&M
APPAREL				
Gap.com	2.5	None	2.6%	B&M
landsend.com	2	468.2	5.2%	B&M
VictoriasSecret.com	1.4	None	1.9%	B&M
LLBean.com	1.3	None	3.3%	B&M
jcrew.com	0.9	229.8	0.9%	B&M
EddieBauer.com	0.8	300	2.8%	B&M
Fogdog.com	0.6	120.2	2.8%	
Nordstrom.com	0.3	286.2	1.0%	B&M
Dsports.com		712.9	NA	B&M
OFFICE				
OfficeMax.com	0.7	245.6	2.3%	B&M
OfficeDepot.com	0.5	None	1.2%	B&M
Staples.com	0.3	83.1	1.9%	B&M

	Millions of Visits	Advertising Impressions (in millions)	Buyers	Has Traditional Outlets
ENTERTAINMENT				
barnesandnoble.com	9.2	567.7	16.9%	B&M
CDNow.com	7.8	114.9	14.3%	
BMGmusicservice.com	2.8	None	NA	B&M
ColumbiaHouse.com	2.6	None	4.9%	B&M
Reel.com	1.9	None	4.9%	
bigstar.com	1.1	None	NA	
Borders.com	0.5	None	3.3%	B&M
CheckOut.com	0.2	260.7	NA	B&M
HOME				
MarthaStewart.com	2.9	201.8	NA	B&M
Cooking.com	1.6	614.4	NA	
living.com	0.2	521.4	NA	
Tavolo.com	*	143.1	NA	
COMPUTERS AND SOFTWARE				
egghead.com	5.9	889.3	4.3%	
Beyond.com	2.7	7.2	NA	
Ubid.com	2.6	69.5	1.7%	
Outpost.com	0.8	None	NA	
ECOST.com	0.3	None	NA	
PETS				
PETsMART.com	1.3	539.4	4.9%	B&M
Petopia.com	1.2	478.8	NA	B&M
Pets.com	0.8	636.3	NA	
GIFTS				
Egreetings.com	6.1	356.9	NA	
Hallmark.com	1.9	None	NA	B&M
1800flowers.com	1.4	558.5	3.9%	B&M
Santa.com	1.2	98.4	NA	
gifts.com	*	548.9	NA	
Send.com	*	277.8	NA	
flooz.com	*	225.8	NA	
Ashford.com	*	64.9	40.0%	

Number of visitors (in millions) between November 15 and December 19
Advertising impressions reflect number of network, cable, and local television advertising between November 1 and December 12, 1999 per Nielsen.
Percent of buyers reflect percentage of on-line shoppers who shopped at store per Ernst and Young survey.
B&M indicates that retailer has traditional store outlets.

Source: Adapted from Saul Hansell, "A Look at the Numbers in Internet Commerce" *The New York Times*, January 2, 2000

Exhibit 5 Amazon.com Financial Statements (1995–1999)

INCOME STATEMENT For Years Ended December 31, 1995 to 1999 (in thousands)					
	1999	**1998**	**1997**	**1996**	**1995**
Net sales	$1,639,839	$609,819	$147,787	$15,746	$511
Cost of sales	1,349,194	476,155	118,969	12,287	409
Gross Profit	290,645	133,664	28,818	3,459	102
Operating Expenses					
Marketing and sales	413,150	132,654	40,077	6,081	200
Technology and content	159,722	46,424	13,384	2,377	171
General and administrative	70,144	15,618	6,741	1,408	35
Stock-based compensation	30,618	1,889	1,211	36	0
Amortization of goodwill and intangibles	214,694	42,599	0	0	0
Mergers, acquisition and related costs	8,072	3,535	0	0	0
Total Operating Expenses	896,400	242,719	61,413	9,902	406
Loss from Operations	−605,755	−109,055	−32,595	−6,443	−304
Interest income	45,451	14,053	1,901	202	1
Interest expenses	−84,566	−26,639	−326	−5	0
Other income, net	1,671	0	0	0	0
Net Interest Income (expense)	−37,444	−12,586	1,575	197	1
Loss before equity in losses of equity-method investees	−76,769	−2,905	0	0	0
Net Loss	($719,968)	($124,546)	($31,020)	($6,246)	($303)

Source: Amazon.com 1999 10-K Statement

Exhibit 6 Amazon.com vs. BN.com Timeline

Amazon.com

December 1998	January 1999	February 1999	March 1999	April 1999	May 1999	June 1999	July 1999	August 1999	September 1999	October 1999	November 1999	December 1999	January 2000	February 2000

January 4, 1999
- Walmart sues Amazon.com on hiring away employees.

January 28, 1999
- Amazon.com raises $1.25 billion through convertible notes.

February 24, 1999
- Amazon.com acquires 40% of Drugstore.com.

March 9, 1999
- Amazon.com countersues Walmart on hiring away employees from Walmart.

March 10, 1999
- Amazon.com and Dell announce co-branding deal.

March 29, 1999
- Amazon.com purchases 50% of Pets.com.

March 30, 1999
- Amazon.com launches on-line auction site.

April 12, 1999
- Amazon.com buys LiveOn.com.

April 14, 1999
- Amazon.com announces plan to build its largest distribution center in Coffeyville, Kansas (750,000 sq. feet).

April 26, 1999
- Amazon.com t·ugs trio of backroom companies for $645 million: Exchange.com, Accept.com & Aleva Interne·.

April 27, 1999
- Launches e-card service.

May 17, 1999
- 50% discount on NYT bestsellers.

May 18, 1999
- Acquires 35% equity in NameGames.com.

June 16, 1999
- Amazon.com and Sotheby's launch SothebysAmazon.com. Amazon invests $45 million in Sotheby's.

June 24, 1999
- Black and Decker president Joseph Galli named president and COO of Amazon.com.

July 13, 1999
- Amazon.com announces plans to sell toys and electronics.

July 14, 1999
- Invests in 49% equity of Gear.com.

July 21, 1999
- 2 for 1 stock split announced.

July 22, 1999
- Amazon.com reports 2nd Quarter sales of $314 million, loss of $135 million. 10.7 million customers are registered.

August 25, 1999
- Purchase circles info on Amazon.com.

September 7, 1999
- Amazon.com names Delta Airlines' Warren Jenson CEO.

September 28, 1999
- Amazon.com receives patent for one-click technology.

September 30, 1999
- Amazon.com launches z-shops.

October 4, 1999
- Amazon.com announces wire-less shop anywhere.

October 15, 1999
- Amazon.com to build 2nd data center in Fairfax County, VA.

November 9, 1999
- Home improve-ment, software, video and gift idea open.

November 23, 1999
- Amazon.com daily sales exceed prior year's largest.

November 29, 1999
- Holiday TV ad campaign debuts.

November 30, 1999
- HP to provide Amazon.com servers.

December 1, 1999
- Amazon.com acquires 17% stake in Ashford.com for $10 million.

December 1999
- NextCard Inc. says Amazon.com ranks first in holiday 1999 transactions, averaging $36 per transaction and 44% of all sales.

December 20, 1999
- Jeff Bezos named TIME Magazine Man of the Year.

January 25, 2000
- Amazon.com introduces new logo to focus on customer-centric culture.

February 3, 2000
- Amazon.com says 4th Quarter sales are $678 million and full year sales are $1.64 billion. 4th Quarter book sales are $317 million, music $79 million, toys $95 million. 16.9 million customers and repeat sales are 73% of all sales.

BarnesandNoble.com

December 31, 1998
- Amazon.com reports 6.2 million customers. BarnesandNoble.com reports 1.4 million customers on January 31, 1999.

February 22, 1999
- BarnesandNoble.com 4th Quarter 1999 sales are $31.1 million and full year 1999 sales are $61.8 million.

April 26, 1999
- BarnesandNoble.com announces shorter URL BN.com.

May 17, 1999
- 50% discount on NYT bestsellers.

May 24, 1999
- BN.com launches IPO. Shares go public at $18, rise to almost $23 per share. Raises $421.6 million in capital through public offering (BNBN).

July 7, 1999
- BN.com launches music store.

July 12, 1999
- BN.com and Be Free, Inc. launch MybrLink, allowing user email to generate sales.

July 22, 1999
- BN.com reports 2nd Quarter sales of $39.1 million, loss of $22 million. 2.2 million customers.

October 26, 1999
- BN.com launches prints and posters and e-card service.

November 1999
- Acquires Certani Corp. books.com URL.

December 1, 1999
- BN.com launches On The Go, allowing wireless purchases.

December 1999
- NextCard Inc. says BN.com ranks third in holiday 1999 transactions, averaging $22.16 per transaction.
- Amazon.com wins injunction against BN.com on using one-click technology, due to patent protection.

December 16, 1999
- BN.com acquires 40% equity stake in e-news, largest seller of magazines online.

January 12, 2000
- Steve Riggio named acting CEO.

January 19, 2000
- Co-brand agreement with MBNA credit card $25 million over five years.

February 8, 2000
- BN.com says 4th Quarter 1999 sales of $82.1 million, total 1999 full year sales is $202 million (vs. $61.8 million in 1998). 90% of sales are from books. 4.0 million customers. Repeat sales are 66%. 300,000 affiliate members.

Source: Press Releases, Amazon.com and BarnesandNoble.com

Exhibit 7 Amazon.com Key Strategic Partnerships

Ashford.com	Online retailer of luxury and premium products
Audible	Internet-delivered spoken audio for PC-based listening or playback devices
Della.com	Online service for gift registry, gift advice, and personalized gift suggestions
Drugstore.com	Online retail and information source for health, beauty, wellness, personal care, & pharmacy
Gear.com	Online source for brand-name sporting goods at discount prices
Greenlight.com	Online auto purchasing in partnership with local dealerships
HomeGrocer.com	Online grocery-shopping and home-delivery service
Kozmo.com	Online one-hour delivery service for entertainment and convenience products
Living.com	Online retailer of home products and services
NextCard, Inc.	Online issuer of consumer credit cards
Pets.com	Online source for pet products, information and services
Sothebys	Auction house in cooperation with which we maintain an online auction site devoted to art, antiques and collectibles.

Source: Amazon.com 1999 Annual Report 10-K Statement

BARNESANDNOBLE.COM (A)

www.barnesandnoble.com

It's a fabulous opportunity for us to extend the brand into the marketplace. . . . There's no one in America that knows more about books than Barnes & Noble. The Web simply enables us to broadcast that message on a new channel.[1]

—Steve Riggio, Vice Chairman, Barnes & Noble

On a crisp Monday morning in February 1998, as the time neared 10 a.m., Barnes & Noble's flagship mega-book superstore on New York City's Union Square prepared to open its doors. A small crowd of eager customers milled about the store's main entrance along East 17th Street. Some of the customers were interested in picking up the latest bestseller they had read about over the weekend in *The New York Times Book Review*. Other customers came to purchase a CD or browse for computer games in the bookstore's multimedia section. Still others came to lounge in the bookstore's fourth floor cafe, to sip cappuccino as they looked over out-of-town newspapers and the most recent magazines.

For Barnes & Noble, the first book retailer to roll out the book superstore concept nationwide, the six-story, colonial-style flagship bookstore on Union Square in New York City (see Exhibit 1a) served as an icon for the company. Unlike the original Barnes & Noble bookstore, located just two city blocks away (see Exhibit 1b) and crammed with college textbooks, the flagship had all of the amenities of the modern book superstore. In addition to a multimedia center and cafe, there was a section for children's books, a lecture room for visiting authors and book-signing events, and lounging space for customers to curl up with favorite books. Like Barnes & Noble's 483 other book superstores[2] located throughout the United States (see Exhibit 1c for photo of its book superstore in west Los Angeles), the interior of the Union Square store was decorated in the company's colors of green and gold and adorned with poster-size drawings of some of America's most popular writers, including Patricia Cromwell, John Grisham, Mark Twain, and Alice Walker (see Exhibit 2 for photo of a book superstore interior).

Barnes & Noble and its prime competitor, Ann Arbor-based Borders Inc., were the two largest retail booksellers in the United States, and they dominated the nation's $26 billion retail bookselling market.[3] The combined sales revenue of both companies accounted for approximately 17% of the market nationwide. As the companies raced to increase the number of book superstores nationally, Barnes & Noble and Borders improved operating margins by reducing the number of mall-based bookstores they each owned under the B. Dalton and Waldenbooks names, respectively.

Despite the closing of many small independent bookstores in the face of this onslaught, the senior management of both Barnes & Noble and Borders Inc. had confronted new upstart competitors in the bookselling market of a different kind—approximately 500 Web sites were selling books over the Internet. The most prominent of these was Seattle-based Amazon.com,[4] which had begun selling books on-line during summer 1995. Although Amazon.com had recorded net sales of only $15.7 million for 1996, or less than one percent of Barnes & Noble's total net revenue for the same year, Barnes & Noble senior management—led by vice chairman Steve Riggio—was determined not to let the new company dominate the Internet as a sales channel for books.

With the projected number of World Wide Web users expected to increase seven-fold, from 23 million to 152 million, globally, between 1996 and 2000,[5] and on-line book sales expected to grow to $2.2 billion over the same

---

Research Associate Dickson L. Louie prepared this case, with the assistance of Research Associate Carrie L. Ardito and Holly S. Cameron, CPA, M.Div., under the supervision of Professor Jeffrey F. Rayport as the basis for class discussion rather than to illustrate either effective or ineffective handling of an administrative situation.

[1]Michael Schrage, "The I.Q. Q&A: Steve Riggio—Barnes & Noble Is Betting That the Printed Word Will Be a Best Seller in Cyberspace," *Adweek Interactive Quarterly*, August 18, 1997.

[2]Press Release, Barnes & Noble, Inc., December 1997.

[3]Book Industry Study Group, 1996.

[4]Amazon.com, HBS Case No. 9-897-128.

[5]Mary Meeker and Chris DePuy, *The Internet Report,* New York: Harper Collins, 1996.

[6]Dan Goodin, "Booksellers: Partner or Perish?" CNET, September 9, 1997.

time period,[6] Amazon.com posed a serious, long-term threat. While Amazon.com *matched* the large physical booksellers in price discounts, it offered added benefits of convenience and selection to its customers—being open for business 24 hours a day on the Web and offering an "inventory" of 2.5 million books. Though not yet profitable, having incurred a loss of $27.6 million in 1997, Amazon.com's 1997 net sales had grown over eight-fold to $147.8 million from $15.7 million in 1996.[7]

In January 1998, Barnes & Noble's senior management estimated that its nine-month-old BarnesandNoble.com would record sales of $14 million for fiscal year 1997.[8] Approximately 40%, or $5.6 million, of BarnesandNoble.com's 1997 sales were generated during the nine-week holiday season ended January 3, 1998.[9] Barnes & Noble predicted that its Web-based subsidiary would have sales revenue of $100 million for fiscal year 1998, its first full year of operation.[10] Despite the estimated increase in sales, Wall Street analysts projected that neither Amazon.com nor BarnesandNoble.com would show a profit in 1998.[11]

With Borders expected to launch its on-line storefront during first quarter 1998,[12] Riggio and his team had to determine the best way, over the next year, for the bookseller to fight back on the Internet, to extend its franchise in cyberspace, and to increase the public's awareness of BarnesandNoble.com without cannibalizing sales in its physical retail franchise. One question confronting Barnes & Noble senior management in early 1998 was how to best use the bookseller's 484 superstores to effectively promote its on-line subsidiary. Should the promotion of the site be limited to promoting the URL inside the stores, or should the bookseller take a more aggressive approach by placing kiosks in every superstore so consumers could walk in and order books on-line? Although this question had not yet been resolved, the placing of kiosks in physical stores would force BarnesandNoble.com to charge sales taxes on each book sold on-line, and could make its on-line prices less competi-

tive than Amazon.com, which did not charge sales tax on books sold outside of Washington and Delaware (the site of Amazon.com's new distribution center).

The History of Barnes & Noble

There are several kinds of stories, but only one difficult kind—the humorous . . . .
—Mark Twain

The predecessor retail bookseller, which became Barnes & Noble in 1917, began operations in 1873 in Wheaton, Illinois. The landmark Barnes & Noble bookstore at the corner of Fifth Avenue and East 18th Street in Manhattan opened its doors in 1932, and was sold several decades later in 1971 to Leonard Riggio. Riggio, who had begun his bookselling career as a clerk at New York University's bookstore in the 1960s, founded the independent Student Book Exchange (SBX) in Greenwich Village in 1965 with a focus on staff, selection, and service. With the acquisition of the Barnes & Noble store six years later, Riggio quickly expanded the store's selection to more than 150,000 titles—billing it as the "World's Largest Bookstore"—the Manhattan-based bookstore included complete departments in medical, engineering, and technical books, which made it a model for his company's future book superstores. By the early 1980s, Barnes & Noble had book superstores in New York City and Boston and, by 1987, it had begun testing the book superstore concept in suburban markets.[13]

By year-end 1997, Barnes & Noble had 484 superstores in the United States and was opening new stores at a rate of 70 a year. Rival Borders Inc. had over 200. For many communities, the book superstores—Barnes & Noble, Bookstar (also owned by Barnes & Noble), and Borders—had become neighborhood community centers. Superstores sold, in addition to books, magazines, books-on-tape, and multimedia software and games. The inventory was complemented by comfortable reading areas, in-store cafes, and periodic literary talks and author book signings (see Exhibit 3 for a copy of a monthly store newsletter). The average Barnes & Noble superstore was approximately 30,000 square feet (see Exhibit 4 for floor plan of a typical superstore)—more than triple the size of an average mall bookstore—and had an average of 128,000 book titles. Each superstore—with average sales of $3 million to $4 million (or 120,000 to 160,000 transactions) annually—customized inventory based on individual store sales patterns and consumer demand.[14] Barnes & Noble held 400,000 of the 1.5 mil-

---

[7]Press release, "Amazon.com Announces Financial Results for Fourth Quarter and 1997 Year-End," Amazon.com, January 22, 1998.

[8]Press release, "BarnesandNoble.com Expects 1998 Sales to Exceed $100 Million," Barnes & Noble, Inc., January 15, 1998.

[9]Dow Jones Wires, "Barnes & Noble Web Unit Sees 1999 Above $100M," January 15, 1997.

[10]Dow Jones Wires, "Barnes & Noble Web Unit Sees 1999 Above $100M," January 15, 1997.

[11]Nations Banc Montgomery Securities Report, January 1998, and *ValueLine*, "Barnes & Noble," November 1997.

[12]Press Release, "Borders Group Reports Holiday Sales," Borders Group, Inc., January 15, 1998.

[13]Barnes & Noble, Inc., 1995 Annual Report.

[14]Barnes & Noble, Inc., 1995 Annual Report.

lion in-print titles in its warehouses. Customers could expect to receive, in less than seven days, shipment to a local store on any of these titles. Stephen Johnson, a newspaper executive in Ohio, explained why he liked to visit weekly:

> The selection, the customer service, and the ambiance makes Barnes & Noble an ideal place to visit. You can wander through its books and magazines, sit down with a cup of coffee, and be free of any time constraints. I find Barnes & Noble's casual atmosphere to be a stress-reliever. I try to visit the book superstores as often as I can to see what's new.[15]

In addition to large selection, another attraction bringing customers into Barnes & Noble superstores was price discounting on hardcovers and bestsellers. For example, all hardcover books were discounted 10% off suggested retail prices; all bestsellers on the current list of *The New York Times Book Review* were 30% off; and all bestselling paperbacks on *The Times'* list were 20% off (see Exhibit 5 for newspaper advertisement).

While Barnes & Noble rolled out book superstores in the 1990s, it simultaneously decreased the number of mall bookstores that it owned through the B. Dalton, Doubleday, and Scribner's chains. At year-end 1997, the bookseller had 555 mall-based stores, down from 734 outlets at fiscal year-end 1993, in addition to its 484 book superstores. The roll-back of mall-based bookstores was driven by simple retail economics: store traffic at malls was declining, and sales per square foot in superstores exceeded sales in mall-based chains.

Barnes & Noble also sold books through a direct mail channel, wherein customers could order a selection of discounted reference, historical, and self-help books from a catalog (see Exhibit 6). The catalog was sent monthly to targeted buyers and provided a 24-hour toll-free line (1-800-The Book). Many of the items available through this channel included out-of-print books and publishers' overstocks. In-stock books ordered from the catalog were shipped from a New Jersey warehouse within two to seven days. Analysts estimated annual sales from the catalog at $22 million.[16]

For fiscal year 1996, which ended February 1, 1997, Barnes & Noble had sales of $2.4 billion and an operat-

ing profit of $119.7 million (see Exhibit 7). Approximately 75% of sales were generated through the company's book superstores and 23% from the mall bookstores. Two years earlier, in 1994, Barnes & Noble's first full fiscal year after its initial public offering in September 1993, the bookseller had sales revenue of $1.6 billion and an operating profit of $68.5 million. That year, book superstores accounted for approximately 60% of sales and mall bookstores for 40%. Barnes & Noble's average gross margin on books sold from 1994 through 1997 was approximately 35%.

The Emergence of Electronic Booksellers

What is so wonderful about great literature is that it transforms the man who reads it towards the condition of the man who wrote it.
—E. M. Forster

By mid-1996, there were an estimated 500 sites selling books on the Web.[17] The best-known among these Internet start-up booksellers was Amazon.com (*www.amazon.com*),[18] which first went on-line in July 1995 and was founded by Jeff Bezos, a former senior vice president with the Wall Street brokerage house and hedge fund manager D. E. Shaw. Although Amazon.com was not yet profitable, incurring a net operating loss of $27.6 million on net sales of $147.8 million during 1997, its net sales had increased eight-fold from the previous year. By year-end 1997, over 1.5 million customer accounts had purchased books from Amazon.com, a 739% increase from year-end 1996. In March 1997, Amazon.com had more than doubled its selection of titles from 1.1 million to 2.5 million. Amazon.com's management team believed that the company would succeed if it accomplished three goals: establish the Amazon.com brand name; provide superior service to customers, and drive sales to achieve economies of scale in operations, marketing, and service. Approximately 90% of the $58 million operating expenses incurred by Amazon.com during 1997 were allocated to marketing expenses and product development. Gross margins were approximately 19.5% of net sales.[19]

Other competitors in the on-line book market included Cleveland-based Book Stacks Unlimited (*www.books.com* or *www.bookstacks.com*), which began selling books on-line through a bulletin board service (BBS) in 1992. Owned by CUC International (now Cendant Corp.) and founded by Charles Stacks, Book Stacks launched its Web site in October 1994 and offered a

---

[15]Interview with casewriter, January 17, 1998.
[16]Morgan Stanley, "The Internet Retailing Report," June 1997.
[17]"Online Booksellers: A New Playing Field," CyberTimes, *The New York Times* on the Web, May 31, 1996.
[18]Amazon.com, HBS Case No. 9-897-128.
[19]Press Release, "Amazon.com Announces Financial Results for Fourth Quarter and 1997 Year-End," Amazon.com, January 22, 1998.

Figure A Key Attributes for Bookselling On-Line

Sheer Quantity of Books	Easy to Make Educated Purchase Decision	Industry Dynamics

• Millions of unique:
   Titles
   Authors
   Subjects
 • Physical search is impractical
 • Inventory and warehousing is explosive in general and impossible to this scale
	• Reviews and ratings are easily available
	 • Can test product on computer (e.g. read a chapter)
	 • Don't need to feel/experience a book to make a purchase decision
		• The traditional book retail industry is very fragmented
		   Thousands of physical stores
		   #1 bookseller has only 15% market share
		 • Different model for Web-based Retailing
		   More analogous to publishing and cable models
		   Converge to 2–3 dominant Internet market players

Books Are Text-Based	**Books Are Relatively Cheap**	**Books Are Small**

• Easy to create a database of books (no one liked the Dewey decimal system anyway!)
 • Easy to text-search for titles, authors, subjects, book reviews . . .
	• Inexpensive enough that consumers will part with dollars without touching the product	• Easy to ship
		   Easy to receive
		   May even fit in post office or mail box

Source: Morgan Stanley Research

selection of over 500,000 titles. Unlike other electronic commerce sites on the Web, Book Stacks' maximum discounts of 30% to 40% off list prices were available only to members of its Frequent Buyer Club, who paid an annual membership fee of $29.95. Non-members were allowed to buy books from Book Stacks, but at substantially higher, though still discounted, prices.

Other bookselling sites on the Web included Las Vegas-based Books Now, Inc., (*www.booksnow.com*) with over 400,000 titles; The Cookbook Store (*www.cookbookstore.com*), an on-line extension of the Cookbook Collection catalogue company; and the Sausuga Japanese Bookstore (*www.world.std.com/-sasuga*), which provided publications from Japan to educational institutions.

According to a 1997 report prepared by Morgan Stanley on Internet Retailing,[20] books were well-suited for on-line sales in terms of functionality, purchase decision, and distribution (see Figure A). For example, the sheer quantity of books, with over one million titles in print, made search capabilities on the Internet attractive; the fact that books were relatively inexpensive and did not require a consumer first to inspect the product made the purchase decision on-line easier; and the fact that most books were compact and easy to ship made them straightforward to distribute through a direct channel. Further, the report noted that "the traditional book retail

industry is very fragmented with thousands of physical stores" and over 50,000 publishers. Unlike the traditional book retailing market the report predicted that Web-based book retailing would quickly become a battle among just two or three dominant Internet players with pricing as the key angle of differentiation for consumers:

> Product pricing is likely to be competitive on the Web, in part because of the ease with which consumers will be able to compare prices. Shoppers can compare prices within seconds by switching from Web site to Web site. Provided that shipping costs are equal, in many instances there should be little incentive for customers to order from higher-priced providers.[21]

Background of Barnes and Noble @ AOL and BarnesandNoble.com

Anyone can be an author; the business is to collect money and fame from this state of being.
—A. A. Milne

Under its subsidiary, BarnesandNoble.com, Barnes & Noble entered the on-line book retailing market in early 1997. The giant bookseller's first venture into electronic

---

[20]Morgan Stanley, "The Internet Retailing Report," June 1997.

[21]Morgan Stanley, "The Internet Retailing Report," June 1997.

commerce began in mid-March 1997, when it established a bookselling site on America Online (AOL/keyword: barnesandnoble), almost two years after Amazon.com and Book Stacks first opened for business on the Web. At year-end 1996, AOL had over seven million members worldwide (see Exhibit 8), which made it the largest on-line service in the world; members could access the Internet, send e-mail, or review branded content, such as *The New York Times, George Magazine*, and MTV. Under Barnes & Noble's initial agreement with AOL, the bookselling giant became the exclusive bookseller in AOL's Marketplace, a cybermall for AOL members to shop on-line with many well-known retailers, including Tower Records, The Sharper Image, Starbucks, Hammacher Schlemmer, and The Disney Store. Steve Riggio believed that his company's relationship with AOL would generate prospective customers who might not otherwise shop on-line:

Barnes & Noble's long history and substantial experience as booksellers, coupled with innovations in technology, will enable us to make a quantum leap beyond the current level of on-line selling. We believe that our relationship with AOL will expand our book market and ultimately bring in millions of new customers who prefer to shop on-line.

Leonard Riggio, chairman and CEO of Barnes & Noble and Steve Riggio's older brother, believed that AOL provided the giant bookseller with an opportunity to gain market share at the expense of other on-line booksellers. Noted Leonard Riggio prior to the launch of the Barnes & Noble site:

America Online is the perfect partner for our entry into this business. We intend to dominate the on-line book business with service, selection, and technology, and our exclusive access to AOL's base of seven million members provides us with a means to capture market share immediately.[22]

Two months after the debut of its site on AOL, in May 1997, Barnes & Noble launched its second on-line venture with a site on the Web (*www.barnesandnoble.com*) (see Exhibit 9). Two years earlier, in 1995, Barnes & Noble had launched an Internet site (*www.loci.com*) for College Bookstores, an affiliated company privately owned by the Riggio family. The College Bookstore site provided Barnes & Noble with experience in how to establish, run, and host a commercial Web site by providing college students with a place to chat on-line and order college apparel, posters, and magazines.[23]

John Kristie, Vice President of Information Technology for BarnesandNoble.com, recalled that the development of the on-line subsidiary also benefited from improvements to the information systems supporting Barnes & Noble's physical bookstores, especially those focused on improving in-store search capabilities and real-time inventory checks. Noted Kristie:

A lot of the original Web work came out of store systems. For example, we had a project to expand our database and consolidate multiple products within the stores. Right now, the stores have search capabilities on products, and next to that terminal they also have a "books in print" search tool, which is on a separate PC. It wasn't as comprehensive as we wanted it to be. So one of the goals of the store system was to integrate a title database, so that the bookseller would have a vast amount of information available on its inventory. That's what we tried to do on the Web by creating a powerful database and search engine. The project started six to nine months before the Web project in creating this highly searchable book database for booksellers.

We were also working on a shopping system that would allow us to communicate electronically with wholesalers in a real-time mode—much like a credit card transaction—so we could confirm the availability of product as opposed to the normal method of "I'll get back to you."

Steve Riggio believed that sales made through Barnes & Noble's virtual stores on AOL and the Web complemented sales at the bookseller's physical bookstores. He also felt that physical book superstores and a national advertising campaign would help build brand awareness for the site. Noted Riggio:

I think [the Web site is] complementary in its incremental sales. We have an existing asset—our brand name and stores—that we leverage. We do $15 million of national advertising. If you pick up *The New York Times, The Wall Street Journal, The New Yorker*, or *Entertainment Weekly*, the Web address rides free in these publications. We launched our America Online site in March and our Web site in May. The compounding effect of all that advertising over the next

---

[22]Press Release, "Barnes & Noble, Inc., Announces Initiative to Launch World's Largest Bookseller Online," Barnes & Noble, Inc., January 28, 1997.
[23]Michael Schrage, "The I.Q. Q&A: Steve Riggio—Barnes & Noble Is Betting That the Printed Word Will Be a Best Seller in Cyberspace," *Adweek Interactive Quarterly*, August 18, 1997.

year, we believe, is going to be quite substantial as the Web site becomes ingrained in people's minds.

We will continue to open up 75 to 80 [super]stores a year. We see 300 to 400 Barnes & Noble stores opening up over the next several years. We see tremendous growth opportunity in retail, and we are going forward with that. We see opportunity on-line, and we are going forward with that as well. We believe our on-line business has an opportunity to add incremental sales to our company.[24]

Since March, the pace of the on-line battle between Amazon.com and BarnesandNoble.com had intensified (see Exhibit 11) on several competitive dimensions: service, pricing, customer acquisition, community, and personalization. For 1998, BarnesandNoble.com expected to achieve revenue of over $100 million, up from $14 million projected for 1997.[25] Despite Barnes & Noble's late entry into the on-line marketplace, Carl Rosendorf, Vice President of New Business Development, believed that the bookseller was now setting the standard for the on-line bookselling industry:

> We've only been live since May 1997, but we have led this industry since that time, maybe not in sales, but in terms of pricing and service. Let's talk about pricing. The model for Amazon.com was basically a 10% [discount] model. When we came into the marketplace in May, we came in with discounts of 20% and 30%—20% off paperbacks and 30% off hardbacks. So we set the standard for pricing in this business and our model was the right model, and that's why the competition has matched it. Then, in terms of delivery, we stated from the beginning that we were going to be working toward same-day shipping [books shipped the same day ordered] and we were building our own warehouse. That warehouse opened up in October 1997.

The fast-paced battle with Amazon.com and the prospective entry by Borders.com, placed heavy demands on BarnesandNoble.com's 40-member technology staff. Observed Kristie:

> There are two key challenges in developing an on-line commerce site. One is the tactical nature of producing a site as large as ours. The other, more strategic in

nature, is trying to expand the direction of the site, while everyone is still very focused on what we just put out. We launched a site in March. We launched a site in May. Then we re-did the entire technology infrastructure for the site in September. So we have done three significant launches in a very short period of time, yet we have some concrete ideas about the site and where we want to go.

Establishing the BarnesandNoble.com Bookstore

An honest tale speeds best being plainly told.
—William Shakespeare

Service. On-line customers interested in ordering books from BarnesandNoble.com could search for them by author, title, category, or keyword (see Exhibit 10). A "Fast Delivery" icon on the Search Results page indicated which books were ready for shipment in two to three days from a Barnes & Noble warehouse in Dayton, New Jersey. Over 500,000 (50%) of Barnes & Noble's in-stock titles, were available for fast delivery or ready for shipment in two to three days. Many of these books were shipped to the Dayton location from a central warehouse—where book publishers shipped titles directly to the bookseller, bypassing book distributors—owned by the bookseller in nearby Jamesburg, New Jersey (see Exhibit 12). The Jamesburg facility also served Barnes & Noble superstores. Steve Riggio believed that Barnes & Noble's extensive and long-established backroom operations in book distribution provided a key competitive advantage:

> Without question, one of the principal assets we bring to the table is the fact that we are extremely good at book distribution, whether it be to our stores or to our customers, whether they be domestic or international, and whether they buy by phone, mail, or the Internet. By the fall [of 1997], our 350,000 square-foot distribution center will have 90 percent of the books we believe people are going to be buying on-line.

So it's a core competency that we know how to do this. It's a core competency that we already have existing relationships with 20,000 publishers. It's a core competency that we have the infrastructure to know how to do business with all these folks and all the back-end apparatus of paying publishers, systems,

[24]Michael Schrage, "The I.Q. Q&A: Steve Riggio—Barnes & Noble Is Betting That the Printed Word Will Be a Best Seller in Cyberspace," *Adweek Interactive Quarterly*, August 18, 1997.
[25]Dow Jones Wires "Barnes & Noble Web Unit Sees 1998 Above $100M," January 15, 1997.

and the like. It's all there. The Internet company plugs into it. As a result, our on-line company has been able to hit the ground running without having to invest the extraordinary sums that startups would [need to] in such an operation.[26]

After placing selections in an electronic shopping cart, on-line customers had a choice of three different shipping options for delivery in the United States: standard, second-day air, and next-day air. With standard delivery, books were usually delivered within four to seven business days at a cost of $3 per shipment and 95 cents per book. With second-day air, books were delivered in two to three business days at a cost of $6 per shipment plus $1.95 per book. With next-day air, books were shipped within one to two business days, at a cost of $8 per shipment plus $2.95 per book. An e-mail from Barnes & Noble confirmed the receipt of an order (see Exhibit 13a). A second e-mail confirmed the shipment of an order (see Exhibit 13b). On average, on-line consumers ordered 2.3 books from BarnesandNoble.com in each sales transaction.

Pricing. Book prices at BarnesandNoble.com were usually lower than those found in its physical bookstores. When purchasing books from Barnes & Noble on-line, several of the bestseller hardcover titles were discounted at 40% off. Most of its remaining in-stock hardcover books were available at 30% off the suggested retail price—triple the discount available on all non-bestselling hardback books purchased in a Barnes & Noble physical bookstore. In addition, every in-stock paperback book was available at 20% off when purchased on-line, while all non-bestselling paperbacks were normally sold at list prices in stores. Bargain books, beginning in November 1997, were available at 88% off list price. Amazon.com, however, had matched BarnesandNoble.com's pricing policy on hardcover, paperback, and individual books (see Exhibit 14 for price comparisons across BarnesandNoble.com, Amazon.com, Barnes & Noble, and Borders).

Steve Riggio believed that the differences in discounts for on-line customers and those available for retail store shoppers were justified on the basis of competition with other on-line booksellers and lower distribution costs:

Our on-line pricing is a function of our commitment to compete effectively in the electronic marketplace, and this requires compelling prices. The economics of on-line retailing are very different from those of store retailing—on-line customers complete their own transactions and therefore not only expect to receive, but are entitled to receive, direct-from-warehouse pricing.[27]

Despite differences in pricing policy between on-line as opposed to physical store purchases, Steve Riggio believed that most on-line sales would be incremental— not cannibalization of physical stores, as some critics charged. Explained Riggio:

First, we do not have a Barnes & Noble store in every community in America, nor will we have a store in every community in America over the next five years. There are just too many places where people can't get to a bookstore with a big selection. Our Internet initiative is a way to bring our bookstore to the desktops of potential customers. And because Barnes & Noble has such national brand recognition—it's a name people know and trust—people will buy from us. We are already experiencing that. Second, there are many people today who do not have the time or the affinity to shop retail. The Internet is a way for them to reach us. Third, our international business, or sales of English-language books abroad, is untapped. It's an explosive area for growth. Finally, we believe the concept of having an on-line bookstore on your desktop will cause an explosion of interest in books.[28]

Still, the question of how to use almost 500 superstores to promote BarnesandNoble.com remained. Would the placement of kiosks in the stores cannibalize book sales for Barnes & Noble physical stores? Would consumers be price-sensitive to the inclusion of sales taxes of on-line book purchases compared to Amazon.com which did not charge sales tax outside of Washington and Delaware? Would this promotion increase the awareness of BarnesandNoble.com beyond that of Amazon.com?

Customer Acquisition. An area where BarnesandNoble.com and Amazon.com competed fiercely throughout 1997 was in signing up affiliate—or third party—Web sites to drive traffic to their respective storefronts and acquire new customers. The first of these co-branding agreements in May 1997 made by BarnesandNoble.com was with *The New York Times* Electronic Media Company,

[26]Dow Jones Wires, "Barnes & Noble Web Unit Sees 1998 Above $100M." January 15, 1997.
[27]Press Release, "Barnes & Noble, Inc., Announces Initiative to Launch World's Largest Bookseller Online," Barnes & Noble, Inc., January 28, 1997.
[28]Michael Schrage, "The I.Q. Q&A: Steve Riggio—Barnes & Noble Is Betting That the Printed Word Will Be a Best Seller in Cyberspace," *Adweek Interactive Quarterly*, August 18, 1997.

where visitors to the Book Review section of *The New York Times* on the Web could purchase almost any book noted on the site—from past and current book reviews—directly from BarnesandNoble.com. For referring on-line customers to Barnes & Noble, *The New York Times* received a commission on each book sold. "The reason I chose to partner with BarnesandNoble.com," explained Martin Nisenholtz, president of *The New York Times* Electronic Media Company, "was that it had a great brand name, was based in New York City, and was a major customer of our newspaper [on the print side]."[29]

Building brand awareness on-line was the driving factor behind these co-branding agreements. According to a November 1997 survey conducted by PC Meter, Amazon.com was the top Web shopping site among all Web users, with a reach of 5.7%—a four-fold increase from a reach of 1.4% in October 1996—among active Web users using a personal computer at home. Among those accessing the Web at work, Amazon.com's rating was 8.6% (see Exhibit 15). By comparison, BarnesandNoble.com had a monthly rating for December 1997 of 2.6% at home—six times that from its first month of operation—and 3.1% at work.[30] Jill Yablon, BarnesandNoble.com's Vice President of Marketing, noted that Amazon.com's two-year head start represented a significant competitive advantage over BarnesandNoble.com:

> Amazon.com is a formidable competitor. They're considered the darlings of cyberspace. Amazon was first in the market and most people have heard of Amazon.com. Most people are not yet even aware that Barnes & Noble has a Web site. We have made a lot of improvements to the site since we launched in May. Our goals will be to get people to switch from Amazon, to attract the first-time buyer, to encourage current Barnes & Noble customers to buy on-line, and to retain all of our on-line customers through loyalty and retention programs.

David Palmieri, Director of New Business Development for BarnesandNoble.com, described the frenzied activity among Web booksellers in establishing co-branding agreements:

> The pace is relentless. The principal battleground over the past four months [September to December 1997]has been establishing the affiliate relationships. We went up on AOL in March [1997]. Amazon countered with deals with Yahoo! and Excite around the time we were launching our Web business [in May 1997]. From there it has been an all-out sprint between the two of us to lock up key points of distribution on the Web. If you look at the top sites, the list of those that are not aligned with the booksellers is dwindling, and most of them have chosen to align with either ourselves or with Amazon. Borders being late to the game has really paid a price: so they have paid dearly to be on InfoSeek and CNET. That is the arena where we have seen the most competition, and we run up against Amazon on every single deal.

In September 1997, BarnesandNoble.com expanded the concept of driving traffic through well-known commercial sites with the launch of its Affiliates Network (see Exhibit 16). The Network involved 40 of the most popular sites on the Web, including CNN Interactive (*www.cnn.com*), the *Los Angeles Times* (*www.latimes.com*), and Ziff Davis' ZDNet (*www.zdnet.com*). Affiliates received commissions of up to seven percent on books sold to on-line customers coming through their sites to BarnesandNoble.com. Each affiliate network member provided a link from its site to BarnesandNoble.com for easy click-throughs. In addition, like Amazon.com's Associates program, individual or non-commercial Web sites could join BarnesandNoble.com's Affiliate Network and receive commissions. Unlike Amazon.com's program, however, BarnesandNoble.com paid commissions on *all* books purchased by customers referred on-line to its site, not just on specific titles, and provided updated sales information within 24 hours to all affiliates through a designated Extranet. Palmieri believed that the unique design of the Affiliates program provided it with a competitive advantage over Amazon.com:

> There are two components of support. The first is the Extranet site at affiliate.net, which provides the affiliates with on-line reporting. The second is our account executive. Every affiliate is assigned an account executive. Some of the Affiliate companies that have switched over from Amazon didn't have a point of contact, so people complained that "I didn't have anyone to talk to" or "I kept getting passed off" or "they didn't return my calls." I think it's indicative that [Amazon.com] never intended it to be a true partnership program but only a linking program. We realize that if you work with important media and technology companies, you had better know how to support them and treat them right.

Despite Amazon.com's higher sales commissions of 15% on Associates' book sales, Palmieri noted that the

---

[29]Interview with casewriter, December 11, 1997.
[30]Press release, "BarnesandNoble.com Expects 1998 Sales to Exceed $100 Million," Barnes & Noble, Inc., January 15, 1998.

Seattle-based bookseller paid commissions only on the referred book—not all books—purchased by third parties through Associates. Palmieri compared the commission's policy for Amazon.com's Associate program with that of BarnesandNoble.com's Affiliate program:

Amazon.com's commission structure is great for them and not so great for the Associates, if you really look at how people buy books on-line. You can put out a headline number like 15% commission, or in the case of their PC Meter top 500 accounts, 22.5% commission. They can put numbers like those out there, because they know people won't buy the first book they click on, and—even if they do—they will often buy two or three more books without any commission. The net effect is that our commission pay structures are similar. Our model is based on what we think is sustainable. We went out with a five to seven percent commission structure that we can live with as a business five years from now. We know that if Amazon gave away 15% on every book, they would give away all their margin.

Nicole Vanderbilt, an analyst with Jupiter Communications, projected that the affiliate sites would become a key driver of sales for on-line commerce:

As the on-line shopping market matures, innovative selling practices, such as affiliates programs, will be crucial in reaching new on-line customers and driving incremental sales. Jupiter believes that by 2002, over 25% of on-line shopping revenues will be realized through purchases that originate at Affiliate sites.[31]

Vanderbilt also believed that BarnesandNoble.com's Affiliate program now provided the giant bookseller with a competitive advantage over Amazon.com. In the December 1997 issue of *Online Marketplace*, an industry newsletter, she wrote:

A day on the Internet is really like a year in the physical world. The on-line competition intensifies with every passing second and given that competitors are only a click away, an innovator cannot afford to stop for a breather once the first phase of a product or idea is launched. It is essential to continue enhancing the product in order to keep the competition at bay. After Amazon.com pioneered the idea of affiliate programs, several on-line merchants bought into the

idea. However, recently, BarnesandNoble.com rewrote the compensation structure for the actual sales force and managed to steal some of Amazon.com's important Affiliates. Realizing that an innovator does not a (lasting) premier retailer make, Amazon has had to substantially increase its sales commission in order to keep in stride with its fierce competitor.[32]

While Amazon.com had established co-branding alliances with Yahoo! and Excite, the two largest Internet search engines, to drive traffic to its home page, BarnesandNoble.com entered similar agreements with Lycos, the third largest search engine on the Web, and with Webcrawler, the fifth largest search engine, in summer 1997. Later in the year, it concluded similar agreements with Microsoft's MSNBC, Investor, and Expedia Web sites, and Pointcast. As Palmieri noted, the co-branding agreements with the Affiliate network were critical in building brand loyalty on the Web:

Look at the partners that we have aligned ourselves with: They are big brand names, well-recognized brands from off-line media—CNN, *USA Today*, *The New York Times*—so the next generation of people coming to the Web will find what the early adopters didn't find two years ago. Two years ago you didn't find Barnes & Noble, all your favorite stores, or all your favorite television channels on the Web. Now you do. So, as the next generation of folks come on-line, they will find their familiar brands, and we believe we will build loyalty with them.

In December 1997, BarnesandNoble.com entered into a four-year, $40 million co-branding agreement with AOL to become the exclusive bookseller throughout the commercial on-line service excluding AOL.com and AOL Net Search which had already become exclusive domains of Amazon.com. Under terms of the agreement, AOL, with over ten million members at year-end 1997, agreed to promote BarnesandNoble.com in areas throughout the on-line service and integrate the bookseller with the AOL Greenhouse sites, Digital Cities, and AOL International.

A month later, at the end of January 1998, Barnes & Noble also announced that it would expand its Affiliates program to include non-profit organizations through the Book Benefit Network. With the sponsorship of American Express, the financial services company that had pioneered "cause marketing" through its "Give for Hunger" program, BarnesandNoble.com agreed to donate up to seven percent on book sales generated through non-profit organizations' sites. Among the first

[31]Press release, "BarnesAndNoble.com Launches Affiliate Network," BarnesandNoble.com, September 9, 1997.
[32]*Online Marketplace*, December 1997.

non-profits to join the Affiliates Network were international relief agency CARE (*www.care.org*) and the United Nations Children Fund (*www.unicef.org*).

To date, however, the company had achieved limited awareness of its initiatives. Rosendorf noted that Barnes & Noble did not begin advertising its Web site until August 1997. By year end, advertisements for BarnesandNoble.com appeared in several leading publications, such as *The New Yorker*, in addition to weekly newspaper ads for Barnes & Noble stores which carried the URLs for both BarnesandNoble.com's Web and AOL sites (see Exhibit 5).

Community.

The Barnes & Noble home page on the Web represented an attempt to provide on-line customers with a sense of community similar to that found in a physical Barnes & Noble superstore. The familiar italicized logo headlined the top of each screen in the company's colors of green and gold with the slogan, "World's Largest Bookseller Online." A column on the left side of the screen provided on-line customers with a directory of the virtual bookstore—indicating where visitors could search for books, join an on-line book discussion, obtain personalized book recommendations, and search for features in 19 different book categories, ranging from "Biography" to "History" to "Travel" (see Exhibit 17). The rest of the home page was devoted to promoting special events on the BarnesandNoble.com site—a schedule of upcoming live chats with best-selling authors, on-file interviews with various writers, and excerpts from the hottest-selling books. Steve Riggio commented on the effort to create a community on-line:

> We feel that the stores are warm and cozy and comfortable gathering places where it's easy to buy a book. We wanted to do the same thing on the Web. We felt that in addition to easy checkout, fast shipping, and great prices, we wanted to have a community aspect to our site. From very early on we had the idea of the live author auditoriums and the bulletin board system to be part of the site, and it's been very successful in generating dialogue.[33]

As in the physical superstores, live events with authors played an essential role in Barnes & Noble's on-line bookstore (see Exhibit 18). An "Online Community" page (see Exhibit 19) provided on-line customers with a schedule of upcoming live events with a diverse pool of writers and celebrities, including Scott Adams, Michael Beschloss, Jackie Collins, Patricia Chao, Michael Crich-

ton, Julie Garwood, Doris Kearns Goodwin, Charlton Heston, Andrew Morton, Carol O'Connell, Gabrielle Reece, Danny Seo, and Studs Terkel. At the scheduled date and time, visitors entered the site's Auditorium, submitted inquiries, and awaited authors' answers to these questions posed on-line. Transcripts of past events were available to members in the site's Live Events Archive section. Books with signed bookplates from the authors were usually available directly from BarnesandNoble.com.

For example, the following questions and answers were from a September 3, 1997, on-line session with Howard Schultz, CEO of Starbucks and author of a book called *Pour Your Heart Into It.*

Question: Did you ever imagine this much success for Starbucks?

HSchultz: I guess the answer to that is, we had a big dream for our company and for ourselves. That was to create a national company whose principles became as strong as the quality of our coffee. The success has come more quickly than we thought. After the last 15 years, in which we have worked so hard and with so much passion, the success we have enjoyed and the fact that we enjoyed it with so many people is quite gratifying.

Question: Can you describe the first Starbucks you ever walked into? How does it differ from what we see today?

HSchultz: The first Starbucks store was in the Public Market in Pike Place in Seattle. It opened in 1971, and I visited it for the first time in 1980. The primary difference was that the original stores did not serve any coffee or espresso. The change came after my trip to Italy in 1983, when I saw the connection the Italian people had with the romance of the coffee and a sense of community that existed in all the coffee and espresso bars in Italy. It reminded me of people's front porch, and that was the shift that took place to bring the coffee experience that I discovered in Italy to Starbucks.

Question: Do you think your retail philosophy can be applied to other goods, like clothing or food?

HSchultz: I would say the retail philosophy we execute every day can be applied to other goods. It is important to reiterate what that philosophy is. We live in a society where, in my view, the country is over-

---

[33] *Online Marketplace*, December 1997.

retailed. There are too many stores for not enough people. The result is we are in an environment as merchants that is more competitive than it's been at any other time in retail history. Now, the philosophy we tried to apply can be reduced to a simple formula. That is, our goal at Starbucks is to exceed the expectations that our customers have for us. But in order to do that, the company needs to inspire customers and trust the people who work in our stores that they will apply their belief in what Starbucks is trying to accomplish. Now, obviously in addition to that, we have to provide our customers every single day with a reason to both come to Starbucks and to come back, and we believe we do that by providing high-quality coffee, providing an environment and almost a "third place" between home and work.

Another feature of the BarnesandNoble.com site, "Books In the News," was added in September 1997, and focused on books and authors in the news each week. "What's News" tracked publishing trends and major authors; "Making the Scene" focused on authors and books featured on television, radio, and in print; "Books-in-Brief" provided information on the most talked about titles; and "The Well-Dressed Book" highlighted noted book jackets.[34]

Personalization. An on-line customer at the BarnesandNoble.com bookstore had the option of registering as a member or simply browsing the unrestricted areas of the site as a non-member. Member registration was accomplished through response to seven simple requests: choose an alias name, select a password, provide an e-mail address, and answer questions on country of residence, zip code, date of birth, and gender (see Exhibit 20). Members were then provided, without charge, the benefits of receiving personalized book recommendations and being able to post messages on the site's Book Forum bulletin boards. An on-line customer who chose not to register as a member was still able to shop for books on the site but could not access any of Barnesand-Noble.com's personalization services.

On the site's bulletin boards, which ranged from "The Bible as Literature" to "Tolkien" to "History Lovers" to "Alternate Endings" (see Exhibit 21), members could post reviews of books, participate in book discussions, or read reviews written by other BarnesandNoble.com

members. A sampling of a book review submitted on Walter Mosley's book, *Gone Fishin'*, in the Book Forum on "Contemporary Black Male Writers" is shown below:

I have not read any of the other authors referred to in this forum, but I have read all of Mr. Mosley's books. The latest, *Gone Fishin'* was a terrific read and gives great insight into the origins of Easy Rawlins. The odd relationship between him and Mouse begins to be clarified. Each of the Easy Rawlins novels is not only a good mystery for its own sake, but also an interesting look at another time in American history that does not seem to get explored very often.

Members also received personalized book recommendations. Using collaborative filtering technology licensed from Firefly Network, Inc., a Cambridge, Massachusetts-based software company, BarnesandNoble.com could recommend books to its members based on preferences of other readers with similar interests. Customers interested in using this personalized service were first asked to complete an on-line survey (see Exhibit 22) rating a list of books within a specific subject category on a scale of one ("Hated it") to seven ("The best"). Books purchased by individuals with similar profiles, based on survey ratings, became new book recommendations for the customer. "One of our goals," said Yablon, who was previously Vice President of Content and New Business Development at AOL's Greenhouse Networks, "is to use one-to-one marketing and create the personal bookstore for the customer."

Visiting the Barnes & Noble @ AOL Bookstore

Books we must have though we lack bread.
—Alice Williams Brotherton

Like the BarnesandNoble.com Web site, the Barnes & Noble site on AOL attempted to provide AOL members with the same sense of on-line community and service, but in abbreviated form. For example, while the AOL site provided its on-line customers with live events with noted authors, chat rooms for news groups, and book trivia contests, it did not provide personalized book recommendations as did the Web site. However, when purchasing books through the Barnes & Noble @ AOL site,

---

[34]Press Release, "Barnes & Noble Takes Books 'Off the Shelf' and Puts Them Into Your Hands," Barnes & Noble, Inc., September 3, 1997.

on-line customers ordered from the same directory of over one million titles, enjoyed the same on-line price discounts, and had their orders fulfilled by the same backroom operations. As an added benefit, AOL guaranteed customer satisfaction on any purchases made through Barnes & Noble @ AOL—as AOL did with all its merchants in the Marketplace area.

Barnes & Noble @ AOL was managed by BarnesandNoble.com as a separate business unit. The unit, which reported to Rosendorf, had a staff of eight in early 1998. The potential AOL audience was upscale and purchase-oriented: 63% of all AOL members were college graduates (versus 23% for the general population in the United States), 46% had children in the household (versus 35% for the general U.S. population);[35] and the AOL population spent 15% less time watching television than the general U.S. population.[36] On average, AOL members logged 37 minutes on-line daily during the fourth quarter of 1997 and spent $30 a year on electronic commerce through the on-line service.[37] As Rosendorf noted, however, there were key differences between sales made through Barnes & Noble on AOL as opposed to the Web:

> We have found that consumers buying from us on AOL and on our Web site tend to be different audiences. Because of that, the merchandising, the product offering, and the editorial is tailored to a separate market. Our AOL site is a separate business unit. The type of books that we sell and the time of day when consumers purchase books on AOL varies greatly from that of our Web site. The books sold on AOL are more consumer-oriented versus business- or professional-oriented. The number one category of book sales on our Web site, and probably for Amazon, is computer and technical books. On AOL, the top five books sold are general interest and fiction. You get a different audience. Totally different.

Other Product Line Additions

Some men have only one book in them;
others, a library.
—Sydney Smith

In addition to selling books, BarnesandNoble.com considered selling other media products—video, music, and software—through its Web site in 1998. An agreement to market magazine subscriptions on-line in partnership with Electronic Newsstand (*www.enews.com*) was announced in January 1998. Selling additional categories

would leverage BarnesandNoble.com's distribution infrastructure, and would be competitive with the expected product offerings made by Borders in print, video, and music. Said Palmieri:

> When you do books, you've done a product catalogue of two million SKUs. So you have dealt with the largest number of individual SKUs of any category of information-based products. Music has over 200,000 SKUs. Software—best we can tell—has only about 40,000 SKUs. The complexity and size of the book business is an order of magnitude greater than those two businesses. Incidentally, I would expect Borders to launch with books, music, and video.

Conclusion

In early 1998, Barnes & Noble's senior management was pleased with the progress the company had made in creating two virtual sales channels for the bookseller—Barnes & Noble @ AOL and BarnesandNoble.com. By year-end 1997, BarnesandNoble.com had more than 250,000 customer accounts and over 40% of its business came from repeat buyers.[38] As Steve Riggio commented on Barnes & Noble's efforts:

> We're not building a rocket ship here. It's a way for us to extend our expertise, our passion, and our knowledge of books to the American and global marketplace. And that's good. There is no one in America that knows more about books than Barnes & Noble; the Web simply enables us to broadcast that message on a new channel.[39]

Rosendorf added that expected entry of Borders Inc. in the on-line marketspace would intensify the competition in the on-line marketspace:

> In the minds of people, when you say Barnes & Noble, they tell you books, bookselling. The research is overwhelming. Barnes & Noble stands for books. You ask people to describe Barnes & Noble, and generally it's community, it's safe haven, it's intellectual, it's books.

---

[35]United States Department of Commerce, *Statistical Abstract of the United States*, 1998.
[36]America Online, 1996 Annual Report.
[37]America Online, 1997 Annual Report.
[38]Press release, "BarnesandNoble.com Expects 1998 Sales to Exceed $100 Million," Barnes & Noble, Inc., January 15, 1998.
[39]Michael Schrage, "The I.Q. Q&A: Steve Riggio—Barnes & Noble Is Betting That the Printed Word Will Be a Best Seller in Cyberspace," *Adweek Interactive Quarterly*, August 18, 1997.

Borders doesn't have our scale and doesn't have nearly as strong a history. The name doesn't have the history—although they are a fine company.

Amazon is hip, it's fun. That's true today, but will it be true tomorrow? That remains to be seen. Amazon is now in with this very loyal group of constituents, and they have been able to build a very strong, good little business. It remains to be seen where it moves from this point forward as Borders goes on-line and we are on-line.

The Borders customer today has either had to come to us or they would go to Amazon, and I'm sure they really don't want to do that. Our customer until a few months ago couldn't come to us because we weren't here, and they had to go to Amazon. Now we are here and Borders will be here. So our customers and their customers will have a lot to choose from.

The business is going to be very, very different two years from now.

Exhibit 1 Barnes & Noble Bookstores

1a   Union Square Store
New York City, New York

1b   Original Store
New York City, New York
5th Avenue & 15th Street

1c   Westside Pavilion Store
Los Angeles, CA

Exhibit 2 Interior of a Barnes & Noble Super Bookstore

Exhibit 3 Barnes & Noble Superstore Newsletter

Barnes & Noble Union Square

EVENTS

33 East 17th Street at Union Square · (212) 253-0810

Open 10:00am-10:00pm Seven Days a Week

Writer's Harvest: The National Reading

Share Our Strength and over 1,500 renowned authors for the nation's largest annual series of simultaneous readings to help fight hunger and poverty. On October 23, every Barnes & Noble will support Writers Harvest by donating a percentage of sales to Share Our Strength.

4 OCT., SATURDAY 3:00pm
Our **Saturday Sounds** Program welcomes the contemporary/acoustic duo **Smithline/Manion**.

6 OCT., MONDAY 7:30pm
Meet award-winning actor and comedian **John Leguizamo!** The star of countless movies including *Romeo & Juliet, To Wong Foo: Thanks for Everything! Julie Newmar, Carlito's Way*, and the FOX network show *House of Buggin* signs copies of his new book, *Freak: A Semi-Demi-Quasi-Pseudo Autobiography*.

released in conjunction with the opening of his one-man play on Broadway of the same name.

7 OCT., TUESDAY 7:30pm
Doris Lessing, author of more than thirty books including the critically acclaimed *Under My Skin* returns with volume two of her autobiography, *Walking in the Shade*. This rich and insightful sequel covers the years 1949-1962 and is the fascinating account of the creative process by which her literary masterpiece *The Golden Notebook* was conceived and executed.

8 OCT., WEDNESDAY 7:30pm
Following the critical and commercial success of his Art of the Personal Essay, **Philip Lopate** inaugurates *The Anchor Essay Annual*, a collection of the best prose writing today. Barnes & Noble invites you to join Mr. Lopate and contributors **Vivian Gornick, Lynne Sharon Schwartz, Daniel Harris, Cynthia Ozick** for the launch of this new anthology.

13 OCT., MONDAY 7:30pm
Dorothy Dunnett, author of the acclaimed Francis Crawford of Lymond and the House of Niccolo novels will discuss the

fifth and sixth in the legendary Lymond Chronicles series, The *Ringed Castle* and *Checkmate*. Join us for a delightful evening with the world's greatest writer of historical fiction.

14 OCT., TUESDAY 7:30pm
Join Pulitzer Prize winning author **Doris Kearns Goodwin** for a discussion of her new release *Wait Till Next Year*. Set in the suburbs of New York in the 1950's where neighborhoods were equally divided between Dodger, Giant and Yankee fans, this is a beautiful memoir of a young girl growing up loving her father and baseball.

15 OCT., WEDNESDAY 7:30PM
As part of *The New Yorker Series at Barnes & Noble Union Square*, please join Pulitzer Prize-winning author **David Remnick** for an insightful look into the lives of prominent people and the culture of celebrity as he presents his new work, *The Devil Problem and Other Stories*.

16 OCT., THURSDAY 7:30pm
Barnes & Noble invites you to come meet **Sheri Reynolds**, author of the best-sellerr *The Rapture of Caanan*

as she discusses her eagerly-anticipated new novel, *A Gracious Plenty*.

18 OCT., SATURDAY 10am-2pm
Join acclaimed author **Mimi Sheraton** when she signs copies of her new book, *Food Markets of the World* at the Union Square Greenmarket.

18 OCT., SATURDAY 3:00pm
Our **Saturday Sounds** program welcomes back jazz/folk guitarist **Mark Sganga!**

19 OCT., SUNDAY 2:00pm
Join us for the Barnes & Noble Crossword Puzzle Classic! **Stanley Newman**, *Times Books* Crossword Puzzle and Games editor will host a crossword competition sure to challenge all puzzlers from beginners to expert. Finalists from our event are invited to compete on Sunday, November 17th at Barnes & Noble Union Square for the grand prize. Call (212)352-3690 to register.

DIRECTORY OF SUBJECTS

ALL SUBJECTS ARE ARRANGED ALPHABETICALLY BY AUTHOR UNLESS OTHERWISE NOTED ON SHELF

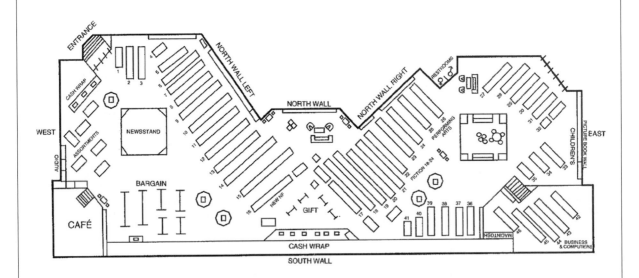

Exhibit 4 Floor Plan of Barnes & Noble Superstore (Jack London Square, Oakland, CA)

98 BROADWAY, OAKLAND, CA 92607 (Broadway & Embarcadero) • (510) 272-0120 • FAX (510) 272-0343
Monday - Sunday 9 AM - 11 PM • Café Hours Monday - Friday 8 AM - 11 PM, Saturday & Sunday 9 AM - 11 PM

Source: Barnes & Noble Company Documents

Exhibit 5 Barnes & Noble Advertisement

Source: *Los Angeles Times Book Review*, September 14, 1997

Exhibit 6 Barnes & Noble Catalog

Barnes & Noble

BOOKS BY MAIL

Thank You For Your Recent Order

Order Toll-Free
1•800•THE BOOK
(1•800•843•2665)
24 hours a day, 7 days a week

Here is our latest catalog where you will find hundreds of exclusive book bargains.
At this time we can only accept orders for books from this catalog by
mail or phone but shortly will provide that ordering option at our web site and on AOL.
As a special 'Thank You,' we'd like to offer you a chance to save on your next order.
When you place an order from this catalog, you may

DEDUCT $10.00

FROM ANY PURCHASE OF $50 OR MORE (not including Shipping & Handling charges.)
This offer cannot be applied toward the purchase of gift certificates.

Defend yourself from verbal violence with this revolutionary book of tactics and tips.
Orig. $12.95
Only from B&N:
$7.98
p. 3

Overcome your fears, meet new people confidently and achieve success at every kind of gathering.
Pub. $9.95
Catalog Price Only:
$7.96
p. 7

A simple system for memorizing 20-digit numbers, lists of names, anything you see, hear, or read—almost instantly.
Orig. $19.95
Only from B&N:
$6.98
p. 2

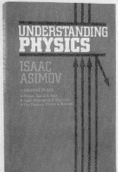

Physics from a gentle genius: Isaac Asimov demystifies a baffling science.
Orig. $24.95
Only from B&N:
$9.98
p. 6

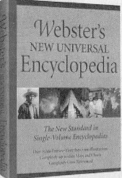

Instant information for the whole family at a price that won't break the budget!
Orig. $75.00
Only from B&N:
$24.98
p. 2

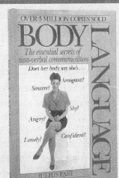

The science of kinesics shows how we reveal the most without saying a word.
Pub. $12.95
SALE
$6.98
p. 4

Exhibit 7 Barnes & Noble Income Statement 1994–1996

	In Thousands of Dollars			As Percentage of Revenue		
	1996	**1995**	**1994**	**1996**	**1995**	**1994**
Revenue						
Superstores	$1,861,177	$1,349,830	$952,697	76.0%	68.3%	58.7%
Mall bookstores	564,926	603,204	646,876	23.1%	30.5%	39.9%
Other	22,021	23,866	23,158	0.9%	1.2%	1.4%
Total Revenue	$2,448,124	$1,976,900	$1,622,731	100.0%	100.0%	100.0%
Expenses						
Cost of sales and buying & occupancy	1,569,448	1,269,001	1,051,011	64.1%	64.2%	64.7%
Gross Margin	878,676	707,899	572,011	35.9%	35.8%	35.3%
Selling and administrative	456,181	376,773	311,344	18.6%	19.1%	19.2%
Rental expenses	225,450	182,473	147,225	9.2%	9.2%	9.1%
Depreciation and amortization	59,806	47,881	36,167	2.4%	2.4%	2.2%
Pre-opening expenses	17,571	12,160	9,021	0.7%	0.6%	0.6%
Restructuring expenses	0	123,768	0	0.0%	6.3%	0.0%
Operating Earnings (Loss)	119,668	(35,156)	68,963	4.9%	−1.8%	4.2%
Net interest expense	38,286	28,142	68,963	1.6%	1.4%	1.4%
Earnings (Loss) Before Income Tax	81,382	(63,298)	22,995	3.3%	−3.2%	2.8%
Provision (benefit) for income tax	30,157	(10,322)	20,085	1.2%	−0.5%	1.2%
Net Earnings (Loss)	$51,225	$(52,976)	$25,883	2.1%	−2.7%	1.6%

Source: Barnes & Noble Annual Reports, 1995 and 1996

Exhibit 8 America Online Membership 1993–1997 (numbers are mid-year, except when noted) (in billions)

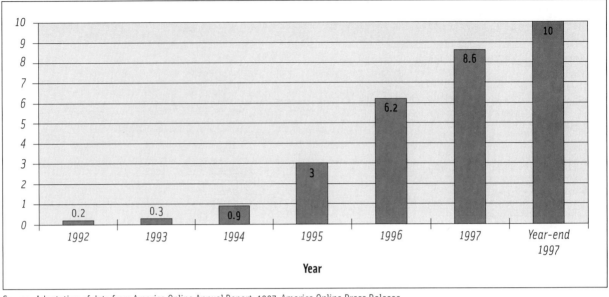

Source: Adaptation of data from America Online Annual Report, 1997, America Online Press Release.

Exhibit 9 BarnesandNoble.com Home Page

Source: *www.BarnesandNoble.com*

Exhibit 10 BarnesandNoble.com Search Page

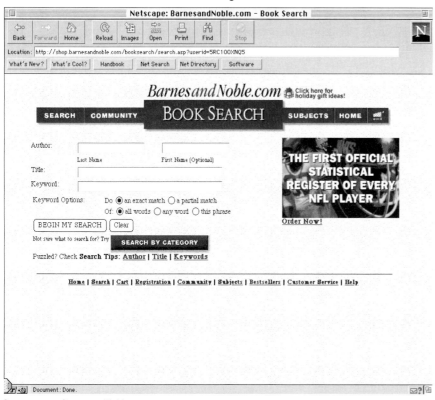

Source: *www.BarnesandNoble.com*

Exhibit 11 1997 Electronic Bookselling War: BarnesandNoble.com Versus Amazon.com

Amazon.com

December 31, 1996
- Amazon.com closes its first full fiscal year with a loss of $6.0 million on sales revenue of $15.7 million. Number of daily visits increase to 50,000 at year-end 1996 compared to 2,200 at year-end 1995.

March 17, 1997
- Amazon.com expands inventory to 2.5 million books. Discounts on Top 50 bestsellers.

May 13, 1997
- Amazon.com announces 40% off on Amazon 500 bestsellers.

May 20, 1997
- Amazon.com goes public—raises $50 million in public offering.

June 2, 1997
- Amazon.com increases its commission for Associates from 8% to 15%.

June 10, 1997
- Amazon.com reduces price to 40% off on selected hardbook titles.

July 7, 1997
- Amazon.com signs three-year agreement to be exclusive bookseller on AOL Web page and AOL NetSearch for $19 million. Also signs agreement with Excite!

July 8, 1997
- Amazon.com signs deal with Yahoo! linking their home page to search results.

August 25, 1997
- Amazon.com files suit against B&N for noncollection of state sales tax.

September 8, 1997
- Amazon.com increases commissions to 22.5% for top PC Meter 500 associates for six months.

September 24, 1997
- Amazon.com introduces new recommendation center and one-click ordering technology.

October 9, 1997
- Amazon.com signs deal to be Digital Alta Vista's exclusive bookseller.

October 14, 1997
- 1 millionth customer signs up.

October 20, 1997
- Amazon.com becomes exclusive bookseller for Netscape's Net Center.

November 10, 1997
- Amazon.com takes $75 million credit facility.

November 18, 1997
- Amazon.com opens second distribution center in New Castle, Delaware.
- Amazon.com announces Christmas Gift Center and Gift Certificates by mail and e-mail.

November 21, 1997
- Amazon.com announces 89% off bargain books.

December 3, 1997
- Amazon.com signs deal with GeoCities.

December 1996	January 1997	February 1997	March 1997	April 1997	May 1997	June 1997	July 1997	August 1997	September 1997	October 1997	November 1997	December 1997

BarnesandNoble.com

January 28, 1997
- B&N announces plans for AOL and Web sites to sell books online. All hardbacks are to be sold at 30% off.

March 18, 1997
- B&N launches B&N on AOL (America Online). Exclusive seller on AOL marketplace. Discount of 30% on all hardbooks.

May 13, 1997
- B&N launches B&N.com on the Web; files lawsuit against Amazon for calling itself "earth's biggest book store."
- B&N announces technological alliances with Hewlett-Packard, Microsoft, and Firefly.

May 20, 1997
- B&N.com becomes exclusive bookseller for New York Times on the Web/books.

August 21, 1997
- B&N.com signs three-year agreement to be the exclusive bookseller with Lycos.

September 4, 1997
- B&N launches online book groups on AOL and new features on B&N.com.

September 10, 1997
- B&N.com announces its affiliates network with 40 top Web sites, including CNN.com, LATimes.com, Time Inc. Pathfinder. Signs deal with Be Free to provide affiliates with information of online sales.

September 16, 1997
- B&N.com becomes exclusive bookseller on Webcrawler (2-years). Firefly technology used to provide customized book recommendations.

October 6, 1997
- B&N signs deal with Microsoft to be exclusive bookseller on MSNBC Microsoft Investor and Expedia.

October 21, 1997
- B&N and Amazon.com settle lawsuits. No damages. They both agree to compete only in the marketplace.

October 28, 1997
- B&N.com signs agreement with Compuserve to be the online service's exclusive bookseller.

November 20, 1997
- B&N.com announces holiday gift center and 40% off on selected hardbook titles.
- B&N.com announces 88% off bargain books.

December 11, 1997
- B&N signs agreement to be exclusive bookseller on PointCast.

December 16, 1997
- B&N signs $40 million 4 year agreement with AOL to be the exclusive bookseller on the online service.

Sources: Press Releases; Amazon.com and Barnes & Noble Prospectus; Amazon.com, May 15, 1997

Exhibit 12 Photos of Barnes & Noble Distribution Center

Exhibit 13a BarnesandNoble.com Confirmation E-Mail

```
From:     service@barnesandnoble.com
To:       dlouie@aol.com
Date: 97-10-16 11:43:07 EDT
Thank you for your order!
We received your order on Oct 16, 1997 11:05 EDT
You ordered:
QTY     PRICE               TITLE
------  -----------         ---------
1     $  13.96              Real Time:  Preparing for The Age of The
      ----------------
      $  13.96    Subtotal
      $   0.00    Sales Tax
      $   3.95    Shipping
      ----------------
      $  17.91    Total
We will notify you by email as soon as your order ships.  If you have any questions
please contact us via email at service@barnesandnoble.com.
Thank you for shopping with BarnesandNoble.com.
BarnesandNoble.com World's Largest Bookseller Online
**********************************************************
Check out our Sweepstakes!
Here's a chance to win a trip to one of four literary destinations:
the Himalayas, the Virgin Islands, Paris & London, or California!
Go to http://www.barnesandnoble.com/destinations/ to enter!
```

Exhibit 13b BarnesandNoble.com Shipping E-Mail

```
From:     service@barnesandnoble.com
To:       dlouie@aol.com
Date: 97-10-19 11:19:23 EDT
Thank you for your order!
We wanted you to know that your order has been shipped.
You ordered:
QTY     PRICE               TITLE
------  -----------         ---------
1     $  13.96              Real Time:  Preparing for The Age of The
      ----------------
      $  13.96    Subtotal
      $   0.00    Sales Tax
      $   3.95    Shipping
      ----------------
      $  17.91    Total
Carrier: UPS 2-Day Air
Tracking Number: 1Zx863w70210338703
If you have any questions, please contact us via email atservice@barnesandnoble.com.
You can track your package at http://www.ups.com.
Thank you for shopping with BarnesandNoble.com.
BarnesandNoble.com
World's Largest Bookseller Online
**********************************************************
Check out our Sweepstakes!
Here's a chance to win a trip to one of four literary destinations:
the Himalayas, the Virgin Islands, Paris & London, or California!
Go to http://www.barnesandnoble.com/destinations/ to enter!
```

Exhibit 14 Prices on Various Hardcover Books and Products on January 20, 1998

Title	Amazon.com	BarnesandNoble.com	Barnes & Noble Superstore	Borders Superstore
Angela's Ashes by Frank McCourt*	$17.50	$17.50	$17.50	$17.50
A Certain Justice by P. D. James*	17.47	17.50	17.50	17.50
Cat and Mouse by James Patterson*	17.47	17.46	17.46	17.47
The Chicago Manual of Style, 14th Edition	28.00	28.00	40.00	36.00
The Christmas Box by Richard Paul Evans*	10.46	9.06	10.46	10.47
Cold Mountain by Charles Frazier*	16.80	16.80	16.80	16.80
Conversations with God, Book 1 by Neale Donald Walsch*	13.97	13.96	13.96	13.97
Competitive Advantage by Michael Porter	26.25	26.25	33.75	33.75
D-Day by Stephen Ambrose	21.00	21.00	27.00	not available
It Takes a Village by Hillary Clinton	14.00	14.00	20.00	not available
The Letter by Richard Paul Evans*	11.16	11.86	11.16	11.17
The Man Who Listens to Horses by Monty Roberts*	16.10	16.10	16.10	16.10
Midnight in the Garden of Good and Evil by John Berendt*	17.50	17.50	17.50	17.50
The Millionaire Next Door by Thomas Stanley*	15.40	15.40	15.40	19.80
Paradise by Toni Morrison	15.00	15.00	22.50	17.50
The Perfect Storm by Sebastian Junger*	16.77	16.76	16.76	16.77
The Service Profit Chain by James Heskett, Len Schlesinger, Earl Sasser	21.00	21.00	not available	27.00
Snoopy: Not Your Average Dog by Charles Schultz	19.95	not available	not available	19.95
Taking Charge: The Johnson White House Tapes by Michael Beschloss	21.00	21.00	27.00	27.00
Truman by David McCullough	22.40	21.00	27.00	16.00
The Winner by David Baldacci*	17.50	17.50	17.50	17.50
The Titanic Soundtrack–Compact Disc	11.89	not available	not available	13.99
7 Habits of Highly Effective People (Audio CD) by Stephen Covey	20.97	20.96	not available	29.95

Sources: Adaptation of data from Amazon.com; barnesandnoble.com; Barnes & Noble Superstore Burlington, MA; and Borders Superstore Chestnut Hill, MA.
* *The New York Times* Bestseller List, Week of January 20, 1998

Exhibit 15 PC Meter Rankings

Top 25 Web Sites—at Home			Top 25 Web Sites—at Work		
Rank	**Web Site**	**Reach**	**Rank**	**Web Site**	**Reach**
1	aol.com	46.0	1	yahoo.com	48.3
2	yahoo.com	39.1	2	netscape.com	41.7
3	netscape.com	26.5	3	aol.com	40.9
4	microsoft.com	23.9	4	microsoft.com	31.1
5	geocities.com	22.2	5	excite.com	25.3
6	excite.com	18.8	6	infoseek.com	23.1
7	infoseek.com	16.6	7	geocities.com	21.9
8	lycos.com	14.5	8	lycos.com	18.9
9	msn.com	10.8	9	digital.com	15.2
10	tripod.com	10.1	10	zdnet.com	15.0
11	switchboard.com	9.7	11	msn.com	12.5
12	digital.com	9.6	12	four11.com	10.2
13	bluemountainarts.com	8.7	13	bluemountainarts.com	9.4
14	zdnet.com	7.9	14	real.com	9.2
15	real.com	7.8	15	switchboard.com	9.1
16	webcrawler.com	7.5	16	amazon.com	8.8
17	four11.com	7.3	17	compuserve.com	8.8
18	disney online	7.0	18	tripod.com	8.0
19	angelfire.com	6.5	19	weather.com	8.0
20	simplenet.com	6.5	20	webcrawler.com	7.8
21	earthlink.com	6.3	21	usatoday.com	7.7
22	amazon.com	6.3	22	cnn.com	7.2
23	pathfinder.com	6.2	23	whowhere.com	6.9
24	att.net	6.1	24	gte.net	6.7
25	hotmail.com	6.1	25	hp.com	6.6
—	BarnesandNoble.com	2.6	—	BarnesandNoble.com	3.1

Source: Adaptation of data from PC Meter, December, 1997.

Exhibit 16 BarnesandNoble.com Major Affiliates

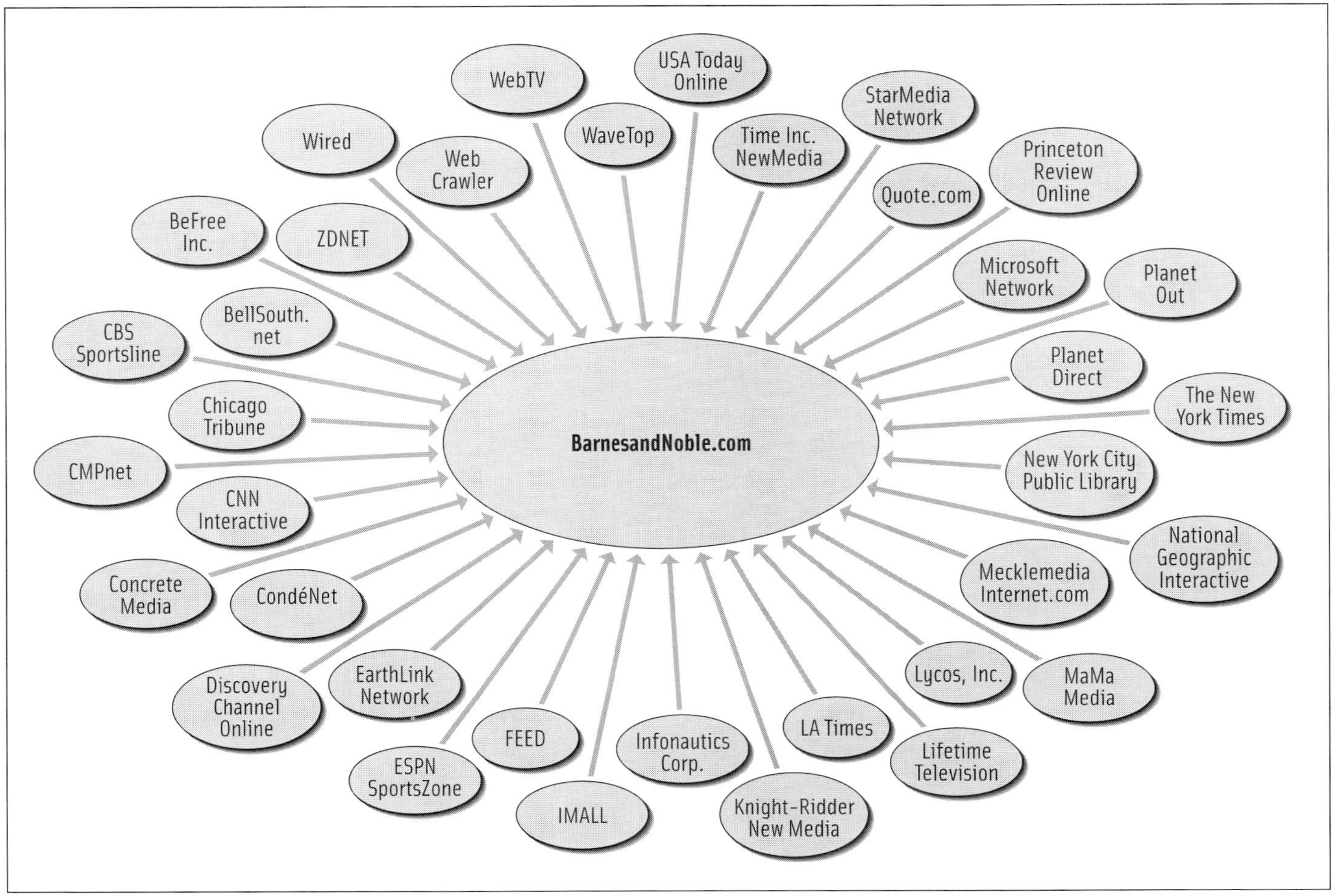

Source: BarnesandNoble.com Company Documents

Exhibit 17 BarnesandNoble.com Subject Page

Source: *www.BarnesandNoble.com*

Exhibit 18 BarnesandNoble.com Schedule of Events

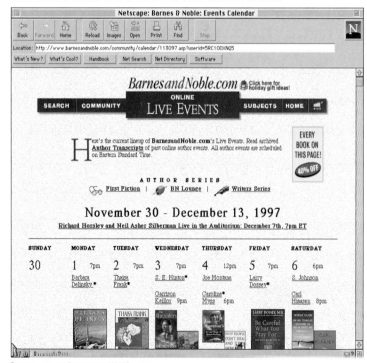

Source: *www.BarnesandNoble.com*

Exhibit 19 BarnesandNoble.com On-line Community Page

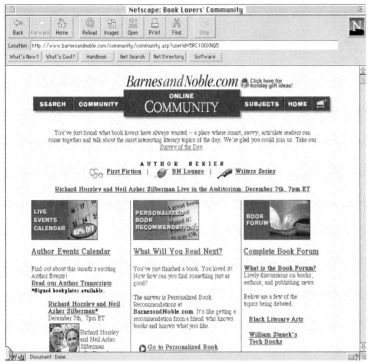

Source: www.BarnesandNoble.com

Exhibit 20 BarnesandNoble.com Registration Page

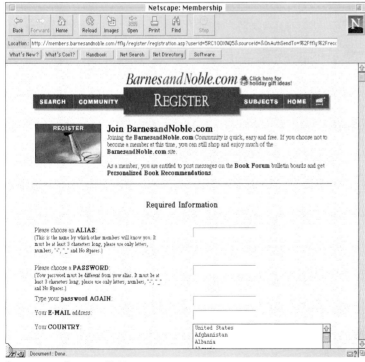

Source: www.BarnesandNoble.com

Exhibit 21 BarnesandNoble.com Book Forum Page

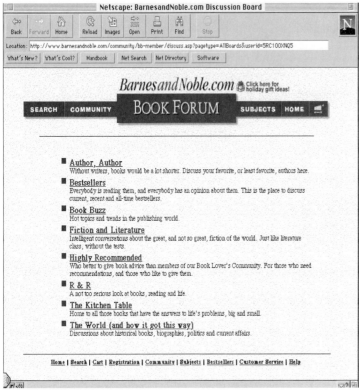

Source: *www.BarnesandNoble.com*

Exhibit 22 BarnesandNoble.com Book Rating Page

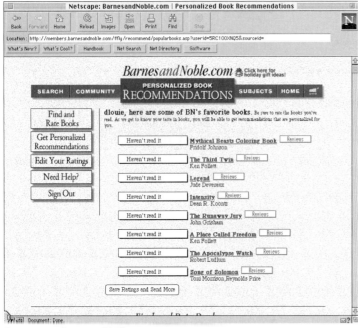

Source: *www.BarnesandNoble.com*

BARNESANDNOBLE.COM (B)

If we don't have your book, nobody does.
—BarnesandNoble.com advertising slogan,
year-end 1998

During 1998—barnesandnoble.com's first full year since the launch of its Web site in May 1997—the company's senior management had taken steps to solidify its claim as being the "World's Largest Bookseller Online." With Barnes & Noble already the world's largest bookseller in the physical world (with over 500 Barnes & Noble Super-stores nationwide at the end of 1998), during the past 12 months, barnesandnoble.com—the joint online bookselling venture of Barnes & Noble and Bertelsmann AG—had increased the number of titles available in its database to 8 million, expanded the number of titles available in its inventory to 750,000 for overnight delivery, and added two new distribution centers to shorten delivery times to customers. These steps, together with a redesigned Web site (see Exhibits 1, 2, and 3) and an aggressive in-print and on-air media campaign, helped increase the number of BarnesandNoble.com customers from 250,000 at year-end 1997 to 1.4 million at year-end 1998—including the addition of 475,000 new customers in the fourth quarter of 1998.[1] Reflecting the five-fold increase in its customer base, Barnesand-Noble.com had moved into the top 25 most-visited sites on the Web, as measured by Media Metrix, after being among the top 250 Web sites during the early part of 1998. Operating revenue for BarnesandNoble.com showed a similar gain, increasing from $14.4 million for 1997 to $61.8 million for 1998.[2]

Despite these successes, however, BarnesandNoble.com still found itself in second place behind Amazon.com, an upstart, Seattle-based rival who continued to dominate this segment of the book-retailing industry at the end of 1998. Continuing its tit-for-tat battle (see Exhibit 4) with BarnesandNoble.com across several fronts in the on-line bookselling wars—in addition to moving into new product categories such as CDs and videocassettes—Amazon.com had 6.2 million customers by year-end 1998 and operating revenue of $610 million, a four-fold increase from the prior year. Despite Amazon.com's early success, executives at Barnes & Noble felt that they would ultimately win the on-line bookselling war. "The biggest piece of the market is still ahead of us," observed Barnes & Noble's Vice Chairman Stephen Riggio.[3] Forrester Research, a Cambridge, Massachusetts-based research group predicted that the on-line bookselling market would grow from $630 million in 1998 to $3 billion in 2003,[4] an indication that the on-line market for this category still had plenty of room to grow and that it was still too early to declare a dominant player.

The Battle of the On-Line Booksellers, 1998

With the pricing policies with both BarnesandNoble.com and Amazon.com remaining largely unchanged—30% off of most hardbacks and 40% off of selected titles—during 1998, BarnesandNoble.com attempted to differentiate itself from Amazon.com in three key areas: selection, service, and scope.

Selection. By the end of 1998, BarnesandNoble.com increased the number of titles available in its database to 8 million and the number of titles available in its inventory to 750,000 (see Exhibit 5, Exhibit 6, and Exhibit 7), which included books from thousands of small independent publishers and university presses.[5] By comparison, Amazon.com reportedly only had 4.7 million titles in its database and 300,000 titles in its inventory at year-end. Steve Riggio, commented on the company's strategy to expand its book selection and on-line inventory:

Dickson L. Louie prepared this case under the supervision of Jeffrey F. Rayport, CEO of Marketspace, a Monitor Group Company, written while he was Associate Professor at Harvard Business School. HBS cases are developed solely as the basis for class discussion. Cases are not intended to serve as endorsements, sources of primary data, or illustrations of effective or ineffective management.

[1]Press releases, Barnes & Noble, "Barnes & Noble Retail Business EPS More than Doubles in Third Quarter," November 19, 1998, and barnesandnoble.com, February 8, 2000.
[2]Reuters, "Barnes & Noble Sees Full Year Below Views," February 22, 1999.
[3]Robert D. Hof, Ellen Neuborne, and Heather Green, "Amazon.com: The Wild World of E-Commerce," *Business Week*, December 14, 1998.
[4]Franklin Paul, "How High Can Amazon.com Fly?," *Reuters News Service*, December 18, 1998.

In little over a year, we have achieved our goal of providing visitors to our site with the largest number of book titles that can be quickly delivered of any online bookseller. Our online inventory continues to grow, almost daily. The unlimited shelf space of our Web site enables us to offer and promote an increasing number of titles that are not widely available. It's truly amazing the kinds of books you can now find on barnesandnoble.com.[6]

With the increased inventory stock, BarnesandNoble.com management believed that it had the ability to ship a wider selection of books to customers within a 24-hour period than any other bookseller, thus providing it with a competitive advantage long-term.

Service. In addition to increasing the number of book titles available on hand, Barnes & Noble also added two new distribution centers in Fall 1998—one in Atlanta, Georgia, and the other in Reno, Nevada. Together with Barnes & Noble's main book distribution center in New Jersey, these two additional centers—350,000 square feet each—would help shorten the delivery time of books to BarnesandNoble.com on-line customers by one to two days as well as servicing Barnes & Noble retail stores in the southeast and western states. Alan Kahn, chief operating officer of Barnes & Noble, observed:

> These new facilities will build upon the success of our present distribution and transportation hub in New Jersey. We expect them to produce additional reductions in the time to market and cost efficiencies in handling the logistical needs of our growing number of retail and e-commerce customers across the country and abroad.[7]

In November 1998, Barnes & Noble also announced the proposed acquisition of the Ingram Book Group, the nation's leading supplier of books, for $600 million–$200 million in cash and $400 million in stock.[8] The vertical integration of Ingram into Barnes & Noble's retail and electronic bookselling operations—which was still under review at year-end 1998 by the United States Department of Justice for anti-trust considerations—would provide the company with direct access to Ingram's 11 distribution centers nationwide and increase the operational efficiencies in the delivery of its book orders, with an estimated 80 percent of Barnes & Noble's on-line and retail customers living within the overnight delivery areas of one of the Ingram distribution centers.[9]

Scope. Finally, in November 1998, BarnesandNoble.com expanded the scope of its operations by selling 50% of the on-line subsidiary to the European media giant, Bertelsmann AG, who owned several publishing houses, including Batam Books, Random House, and Dell. Amy Ryan, an analyst with Prudential Securities observed about the benefits of the joint venture:

> Given its joint venture agreement with Barnes & Noble, Bertelsmann has scrapped its plans to launch BooksOnline in the United States. Instead, BarnesandNoble.com will feature a button for BooksOnline and BooksOnline will feature a button for BarnesandNoble.com in order to make it easy for customers to find and order books in different languages. The sales will go to the respective online company (i.e., a BarnesandNoble.com customer clicking into BooksOnline and placing an order for a German book will be a sale for BooksOnline). Note that Amazon.com currently does not have the capability to offer its customers access to the breadth of foreign books that BarnesandNoble.com and BooksOnline will be able to offer.[10]

Conclusion

Looking ahead to 1999— with the appointment of a new CEO, Jonathan Bulkeley in January 1999—Wall Street analysts were projecting operating revenue for Barnesandnoble.com might increase to $200 million,[11] but other observers felt that with the increased marketing support from Bertelsmann AG, as a result of the joint venture, and with an infusion of cash from barnesandnoble.com's expected initial public offering in the latter part of 1999, barnesandnoble.com would only become a stronger player in its battle with Amazon.com going forward.

---

[5]Press Release, "Barnesandnoble.com Now Offers Online the World's Largest Standing Inventory of Book Titles; 600,000 Titles Available to Be Shipped Within 24 Hours," BarnesandNoble.com, April 28, 1998.
[6]Ibid.
[7]Press Release, "Barnes & Noble Announces Plans to Open Two New Distribution Centers in Reno and Atlanta," Barnes & Noble, September 30, 1998.
[8]Scott Herhold, "The Battle of Shelf Defense," *San Jose Mercury News*, December 13, 1998.
[9]Press Release, "Barnes & Noble, Inc. to Purchase Ingram Book Group," Barnes & Noble, November 6, 1998.
[10]Amy E. Ryan, Barnes & Noble Company Update, Prudential Securities, 1998.
[11]Ibid.

Exhibit 1 Home Page

Source: *BarnesandNoble.com*

Exhibit 2 Magazine Page

Source: *BarnesandNoble.com*

Exhibit 3 Software Page

Source: *BarnesandNoble.com*

Exhibit 4 Amazon.com vs. BN.com Timeline

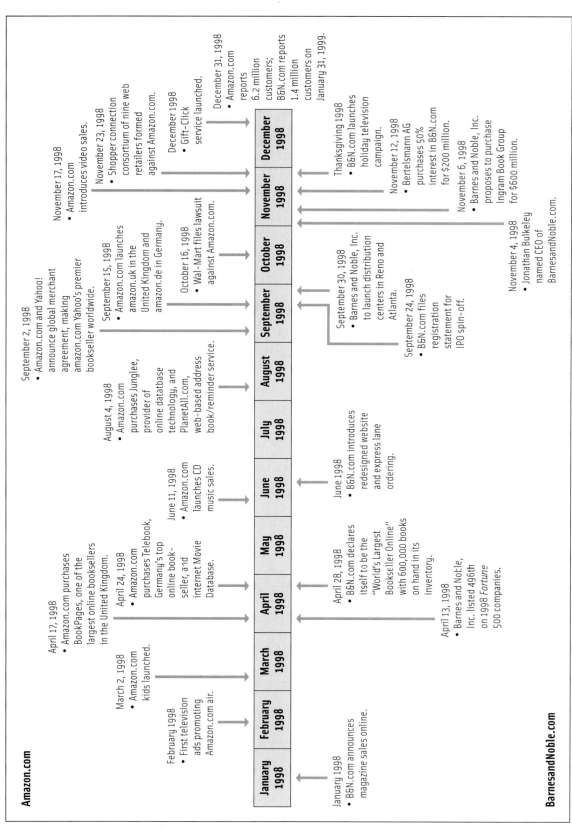

Amazon.com

January 1998	February 1998	March 1998	April 1998	May 1998	June 1998	July 1998	August 1998	September 1998	October 1998	November 1998	December 1998

February 1998
• First television ads promoting Amazon.com air.

March 2, 1998
• Amazon.com kids launched.

April 17, 1998
• Amazon.com purchases BookPages, one of the largest online booksellers in the United Kingdom.

April 24, 1998
• Amazon.com purchases Telebook, Germany's top online book-seller, and Internet Movie Database.

June 11, 1998
• Amazon.com launches CD music sales.

August 4, 1998
• Amazon.com purchases Junglee, provider of online database technology, and PlanetAll.com, web-based address book/reminder service.

September 2, 1998
• Amazon.com and Yahoo! announce global merchant agreement, making amazon.com Yahoo's premier bookseller worldwide.

September 15, 1998
• Amazon.com launches amazon.uk in the United Kingdom and amazon.de in Germany.

October 16, 1998
• Wal-Mart files lawsuit against Amazon.com.

November 17, 1998
• Amazon.com introduces video sales.

November 23, 1998
• Shopper connection consortium of nine web retailers formed against Amazon.com.

December 1998
• Gift-Click service launched.

December 31, 1998
• Amazon.com reports 6.2 million customers; BGN.com reports 1.4 million customers on January 31, 1999.

BarnesandNoble.com

January 1998
• BN.com announces magazine sales online.

April 13, 1998
• Barnes and Noble, Inc. listed 496th on 1998 *Fortune* 500 companies.

April 28, 1998
• BGN.com declares itself to be the "World's Largest Bookseller Online" with 600,000 books on hand in its inventory.

June 1998
• BGN.com introduces redesigned website and express lane ordering.

September 24, 1998
• BGN.com files registration statement for IPO spin-off.

September 30, 1998
• Barnes and Noble, Inc. to launch distribution centers in Reno and Atlanta.

November 4, 1998
• Jonathan Bulkeley named CEO of BarnesandNoble.com.

November 6, 1998
• Barnes and Noble, Inc. proposes to purchase Ingram Book Group for $600 million.

November 12, 1998
• Bertelsmann AG purchases 50% interest in BGN.com for $200 million.

Thanksgiving 1998
• BGN.com launches holiday television campaign.

Source: Press Releases, Amazon.com and BarnesandNoble.com

Exhibit 5 BarnesandNoble.com Advertising

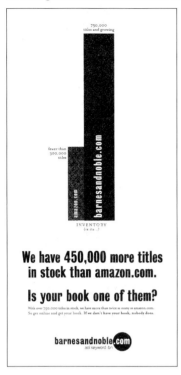

Exhibit 6 BarnesandNoble.com Advertising

Exhibit 7 BarnesandNoble.com Advertising

BARNESANDNOBLE.COM (C)

The Internet is more than anything else, the biggest, the best, and most cost-efficient broadcast channel in the history of retail. It is specific to our demographics; it gets our customers' full attention; and it will create more store traffic.[1]
—Steve Riggio, Vice Chairman and acting CEO, BarnesandNoble.com

During 1999, unlike Amazon.com (BarnesandNoble.com's key competitor in the selling of books online), BarnesandNoble.com had limited its expansion to the selling of books and other media-related products. Whereas Amazon.com had quickly moved into other retail categories such as auction items, electronics, home improvement goods, and toys by the end of 1999, BarnesandNoble.com stuck to its vertical niche strategy of only selling media-related products by limiting its increased consumer offerings to music, prints, posters, and e-cards. In addition, BarnesandNoble.com continued to focus on the basic fundamentals of book selling by carrying a larger number of new titles . . . on hand than Amazon.com and expanding the number of used books available for resale through its site.

As a result of BarnesandNoble.com's continued emphasis on book selling and media-related goods, the company enjoyed strong growth in 1999. During 1999, the company recorded $202 million in net sales, tripling $61.8 million in net sales which BarnesandNoble.com had earned in 1998 (see Exhibit 2). Reflecting the increased sales, the company's customer base increased almost three-fold from 1.3 million to 4.0 million and the number of affiliate sites increased nearly six-fold from 48,000 to 300,000 over the same time period. The percentage of repeat customers increased from 63% in the Third Quarter 1999 to 66% in the Fourth Quarter 1999. By the end of 1999, BarnesandNoble.com was the 24th most visited site on the Web—up from 29th place during the Third Quarter 1999—and the fourth most visited

retailer—but the number one multichannel retailer on the Web[3]—behind Amazon.com, E-Bay, and Bluemountainarts.com.[4]

Despite the increased sales and number of customers, BarnesandNoble.com had lagged behind Amazon.com in marketshare of book sales, by almost a three-toone ratio. During the Fourth Quarter of 1999, when Amazon.com first began to break out its sales figures by category, Amazon.com had recorded $317 million in book sales whereas BarnesandNoble.com had reported $82 million in sales for the same time period. In addition, Amazon.com had now reported 16.9 million customers, an increase of 10.7 million customers from the 6.2 million at the end of 1998.

Nevertheless, Riggio felt good about BarnesandNoble.com's prospects to become the eventual on-line book selling leader. A year earlier BarnesandNoble.com had less than ten percent of all on-line book sales. During 1999, the company had increased its marketshare of book sales to 25% and the sales of media-related products—including books, magazines, and CDs—were expected to almost triple from $3.6 billion in 1999 to $12.4 billion in 2004. In addition, a May 1999 IPO—in which Barnes & Noble and Bertelsmann AG each retained a 40% stake in the company—raised $486 million for BarnesandNoble.com, which left the company debt-free and with almost $450 in cash on hand at the end of 1999. By comparison, Amazon.com carried approximately $2 billion in debt at year-end 1999, largely due to the building of several super warehouses nationwide during 1999 to handle its increased product offerings.

Some industry observers began to wonder whether Amazon.com's expansion into new retail categories would stretch its brand too far[5] and would give BarnesandNoble.com an opportunity to exploit Amazon.com's weakness by making BarnesandNoble.com the premiere

---

Dickson L. Louie prepared this case under the supervision of Jeffrey F. Rayport, CEO of Marketspace, a Monitor Group Company, written while he was Associate Professor at Harvard Business School. HBS cases are developed solely as the basis for class discussion. Cases are not intended to serve as endorsements, sources of primary data, or illustrations of effective or ineffective management.

[1]Barnes & Noble booksellers 1999 annual report.
[2]Riggio had replaced Jonathan Buckeley as the company's acting CEO in January 2000 following Buckeley's resignation.
[3]Barnes & Noble booksellers 1999 annual report
[4]"Top 50 Web sites," *San Francisco Examiner*, March 7, 2000.
[5]Hof, Robert F., "Can Amazon.com Make It?" *Business Week*, July 10, 2000.

"brand" for online book selling, which it had already achieved in the physical, retail world with its 500 locations nationwide.

The On-Line Bookselling Wars, 1999

While BarnesandNoble.com increased the selection of titles which it had available on hand to almost 1 million—with the ultimate goal to stock every known book in print[6]—compared to Amazon.com's 300,000 titles, the on-line book selling wars between Amazon.com and BarnesandNoble.com was primarily fought in four areas during 1999: price, product offerings, patents, and marketing (see Exhibit 3).

Price. With the pricing policies with both BarnesandNoble.com and Amazon.com remaining largely unchanged—30% off of most hardbacks and 40% off of selected titles—during 1998, both companies increased the discount offered on *New York Times* bestsellers from 40% to 50% on May 17, 1999.

Product Offerings. During 1999, BarnesandNoble.com expanded into several media-related product categories. In July 1999, the company announced the launch of its music store, which offered CDs for sale. In October 1999, the company launched its prints, poster, and e-card stores. And in December 1999, BarnesandNoble.com announced that it had acquired a 40% stake in e-news, the leading seller of magazines on-line.

Patents. In September 1999, Amazon.com received a patent for its one-click technology, which enabled consumers to order books and products from its site with a simple click of the mouse, saving consumers downloading time and the necessity of going through several pages to make an on-line order. BarnesandNoble.com had employed a similar technology with the introduction of its Express Lane Ordering in June 1998, after Amazon.-com had introduced a similar feature on its Web site in December 1997. In December 1999, Amazon.com sought an injunction against BarnesandNoble.com to prohibit them from using its Express Lane Ordering to protect its patent for one-click technology.

Marketing. To solidify its position of becoming the dominant bookseller on-line and to simplify the ordering of books through its site, BarnesandNoble.com added two URLs during 1999 that would also access the BarnesandNoble.com site: *www.bn.com* and *www.books.com*. The first URL was added in April 1999 to make it easier for consumers to remember and access the site without keying in the full name. The second URL was purchased from Cedant Corporation in November 1999 to strengthen BarnesandNoble.com's association with books. In addition, during 1999, BarnesandNoble.com began to drive traffic to its site from its 500 physical stores, by offering store visitors coupons to makes purchases on-line. Approximately $6 million of BarnesandNoble.-com's marketing costs were related to these in-store coupons (see Exhibit 4).

Conclusion

As Riggio looked out of his office window, he wondered what should be the next steps that BarnesandNoble.com should take in its battle with Amazon.com. While BarnesandNoble.com had recorded an operating loss of $102 million in 1999, the company was beginning to scale up steadily and was expected to earn a profit in 2001. Nevertheless, BarnesandNoble.com's stock was trading at $14 per share, slightly below its IPO price of $18 per share. Should BarnesandNoble.com stay on its steady course of constant growth or should it attempt to scale up quicker? Also, as Amazon.com continued to expand, what were the downsides of not expanding faster? And how could BarnesandNoble.com exploit the Amazon.com brand as it expanded beyond books?

---

[6]Barnes & Noble, 1999 Annual Report.

Exhibit 1 BarnesandNoble.com Home Page (July 2000)

Source: *BarnesandNoble.com*

Exhibit 2 BarnesandNoble.com Income Statement, 1998 and 1999
(in thousands)

	1999	1998
Net sales	$202,567	$61,834
Cost of sales	159,937	47,569
Gross Profit	42,630	14,265
Operating expenses		
Sales and marketing	111,553	70,423
Product development	21,006	8,532
General and administration	32,714	19,166
Total Operating Expenses	165,273	98,121
Operating loss	(122,643)	(83,856)
Interest income, net	20,238	708
Net Loss	($102,405)	($83,148)

Source: BarnesandNoble.com press release, February 8, 2000

Exhibit 3 On-line Book War Timeline, 1999

Amazon.com

December 1998	January 1999	February 1999	March 1999	April 1999	May 1999	June 1999	July 1999	August 1999	September 1999	October 1999	November 1999	December 1999	January 2000	February 2000

March 9, 1999
- Amazon.com countersues Walmart on hiring away employees from Walmart.

April 12, 1999
- Amazon.com buys LiveOn.com.

April 14, 1999
- Amazon.com announces plan to build its largest distribution center in Coffeyville, Kansas (750,000 sq. feet).

February 24, 1999
- Amazon.com acquires 40% of Drugstore.com.

March 10, 1999
- Amazon.com and Dell announce co-branding deal.

March 29, 1999
- Amazon.com purchases 50% of Pets.com.

March 30, 1999
- Amazon.com launches on-line auction site.

January 4, 1999
- Walmart sues Amazon.com on hiring away employees.

January 28, 1999
- Amazon.com raises $1.25 billion through convertible notes.

April 26, 1999
- Amazon.com buys trio of backroom companies for $645 million: Exchange.com, Accept.com & Aleva Internet.

April 27, 1999
- Launches e-card service.

May 17, 1999
- 50% discount on NYT bestsellers.

May 18, 1999
- Acquires 35% equity in NameGames.com.

June 16, 1999
- Amazon.com and Sotheby's launch SothebysAmazon.com. Amazon invests $45 million in Sotheby's.

June 24, 1999
- Black and Decker president Joseph Galli named president and COO of Amazon.com.

August 25, 1999
- Purchase circles info on Amazon.com.

July 13, 1999
- Amazon.com announces plans to sell toys and electronics.

July 14, 1999
- Invests in 49% equity of Gear.com.

July 21, 1999
- 2 for 1 stock split announced.

July 22, 1999
- Amazon.com reports 2nd Quarter sales of $314 million, loss of $135 million. 10.7 million customers are registered.

September 7, 1999
- Amazon.com names Delta Airlines' Warren Jenson CEO.

September 28, 1999
- Amazon.com receives patent for one-click technology.

September 30, 1999
- Amazon.com launches z-shops.

October 4, 1999
- Amazon.com announces wireless shop anywhere.

November 9, 1999
- Home improvement, software, video and gift idea open.

November 23, 1999
- Amazon.com daily sales exceed prior year's largest.

November 29, 1999
- Holiday TV ad campaign debuts.

November 30, 1999
- HP to provide Amazon.com servers.

October 15, 1999
- Amazon.com to build 2nd data center in Fairfax County, VA.

December 1, 1999
- Amazon.com acquires 17% stake in Ashford.com for $10 million.

December 1999
- NextCard Inc. says Amazon.com ranks first in holiday 1999 transactions, averaging $36 per transaction and 44% of all sales.

December 20, 1999
- Jeff Bezos named TIME Magazine Man of the Year.

January 25, 2000
- Amazon.com introduces new logo to focus on customer-centric culture.

February 3, 2000
- Amazon.com says 4th Quarter sales are $678 million and full year sales are $1.64 billion. 4th Quarter book sales are $317 million, music $79 million, toys $95 million. 16.9 million customers and repeat sales are 73% of all sales.

BarnesandNoble.com

December 31, 1998
- Amazon.com reports 6.2 million customers. BarnesandNoble.com reports 1.4 million customers on January 31, 1999.

February 22, 1999
- BarnesandNoble.com 4th Quarter 1999 sales are $31.1 million and full year 1999 sales are $61.8 million.

April 26, 1999
- BarnesandNoble.com announces shorter URL BN.com.

May 24, 1999
- BN.com launches IPO. Shares go public at $18, rise to almost $23 per share. Raises $421.6 million in capital through public offering (BNBN).

May 17, 1999
- 50% discount on NYT bestsellers.

July 22, 1999
- BN.com reports 2nd Quarter sales of $39.1 million, loss of $22 million. 2.2 million customers.

July 12, 1999
- BN.com and Be Free, Inc. launch MybrLink, allowing user email to generate sales.

July 7, 1999
- BN.com launches music store.

November 1999
- Acquires Certani Corp. books.com URL.

October 26, 1999
- BN.com launches prints and posters and e-card service.

December 16, 1999
- BN.com acquires 40% equity stake in e-news, largest seller of magazines online.

December 1, 1999
- BN.com launches On The Go, allowing wireless purchases.

December 1999
- NextCard Inc. says BN.com ranks third in holiday 1999 transactions, averaging $22.16 per transaction.
- Amazon.com wins injunction against BN.com on using one-click technology, due to patent protection.

February 8, 2000
- BN.com says 4th Quarter 1999 sales of $82.1 million, total 1999 full year sales is $202 million (vs. $61.8 million in 1998). 90% of sales are from books. 4.0 million customers. Repeat sales are 66%. 300,000 affiliate members.

January 19, 2000
- Co-brand agreement with MBNA credit card $25 million over five years.

January 12, 2000
- Steve Riggio named acting CEO.

Source: Amazon.com and BarnesandNoble.com press releases

Exhibit 4 In-Store BarnesandNoble.com Coupon

Source: *BarnesandNoble.com*

Framing the Market Opportunity

2

FRAMING THE MARKET OPPORTUNITY

In the last three years, we have seen an unprecedented launch rate of Internet-related startup companies. While good opportunity analysis will not guarantee the success of a startup, thinking through the conditions that define opportunity attractiveness increases the likelihood of pursuing an attractive idea. Poor or no opportunity analysis increases the probability that a new venture will fail.

Opportunity analysis examines the high-level questions "Where will the business compete?" and "How will it succeed?" Regardless of the reasons a firm seeks online business opportunities, the successful company defines its marketspace (or the digital equivalent of a physical marketplace) early in the business development process.

The market opportunity analysis framework consists of five main **investigative stages**, together with a final assessment of the opportunity, and a final "go/no go" decision. The five stages are (1) define the existing or new value system, (2) identify customers' unmet or underserved need(s), (3) identify the target customer segment(s), (4) assess the company's resource-based opportunity for advantage, and (5) assess competitive, technical, and financial opportunity attractiveness.

Market opportunity analysis for online companies is distinctive in the following ways: (1) competition occurs *across* industry boundaries rather than *within* industry boundaries; (2) competitive developments and responses are occurring at an unprecedented speed; (3) competition occurs between alliances of companies rather than between individual companies; (4) consumer behavior is still in the early stages of being defined, so it is easier to influence and change consumer behavior; and (5) industry value chains or "systems" are rapidly being reconfigured.

An **opportunity story** may be thought of as the first draft of a business plan. The story should articulate the value proposition and the target customers. It should demonstrate the benefits to these customers and the way in which the company will "monetize" the opportunity. It should estimate the magnitude (in financial terms) of the opportunity, identify the key capabilities and resources, and finally discuss the "reasons to believe" the capabilities will create a competitive advantage for the new business in serving its target customers. This opportunity story should be the first of several go/no go gates. If not already defined, the team should describe the criteria necessary to proceed to the next step of the business development process.

SYNOPSES OF CHAPTER CASES

PLANETALL

Case Overview

PlanetAll launched its free, Web-based, "active contact manager" on November 12, 1996. The service collected and stored in a central database member information such as names, addresses, telephone numbers, and e-mail addresses as well as group affiliations such as former and present employers, colleges and universities, fraternities/sororities, and professional groups. In order to succeed in a Web environment crowded with players, PlanetAll had to attract sufficient cross-platform adoption of PlanetAll functionality and achieve critical mass.

Warren Adams, co-founder and president of PlanetAll, explained, "PlanetAll's value to an individual user resides in being able to share and access information with everyone in their network." According to Adams, PlanetAll's objective was simple: "Get big fast. The larger our user base, the more value we're creating for an individual user." Adoption of the technology at that level meant that PlanetAll quickly needed either to become a leading destination site or to establish alliances that would embed its functionality in the major Web services and contact management software and devices.

PlanetAll could remain a destination site but would need to reach a much larger scale, similar to that of Yahoo!, Excite, and Microsoft. Many industry analysts believed that it was already too late to build a major brand on the Web. On the other hand, if PlanetAll decided to position itself as an enabling technology, its value was maximized only if several of the major sites and services—such as Yahoo!, Infoseek, American Online, and Microsoft—participated in adopting their technology. However, each of the major sites appeared to want exclusive deals in order to gain a competitive advantage over the others.

Which strategy—continuing to operate and invest as a branded destination site or becoming primarily an enabling technology—would best serve PlanetAll's value propositions for customers? How would each strategy solve the four primary challenges the company had identified: explaining PlanetAll to customers, user friendliness, privacy and security concerns, and product utility across relevant populations?

Preparation Questions

1. Some industry analysts view PlanetAll as a "virtual community" company, and others see it as a virtual or physical community enabler. What business is PlanetAll really in?

2. Should PlanetAll pursue a branded or an OEM strategy in positioning its service with alliance partners and users? Can it do both at the same time?

3. What factors drive user perceptions of PlanetAll's value? How effective has PlanetAll been in aiding current and potential users to realize that full value?

4. If positioning a firm's value proposition is a combination of segmentation and differentiation, what is the right positioning for PlanetAll in end-user markets? Please prepare a positioning statement of 25 words or less that you believe would aid PlanetAll in communicating key benefits and illustrating the value of its service.

5. What level of investment in PlanetAll business development and positioning is appropriate? What could PlanetAll as a business be worth?

MICROSOFT CARPOINT

Case Overview

Microsoft CarPoint was a late entrant in the online car buying services arena, but in 1998 it was rapidly catching up with the main players in the field. Gideon Rosenblatt, Group Program Manager at CarPoint, was confident that parity with the competition was only months away. A couple of problems, however, were at the forefront of Rosenblatt's attention. To begin with, only 3% of visitors to the website were requesting referrals to dealers for specific cars. CarPoint's main competitors averaged closer to 5%. At the next step in the process, dealers were converting only 20% of CarPoint's referrals into sales. In comparison, CarPoint's strongest competitor was running closer to 30%. If CarPoint could improve these two performance measures to 5% and 30% respectively, their service would generate 2.5 times as many car sales.

CarPoint's mission was to own the largest share of the Internet auto and auto-related transactions by radically improving the consumer and merchant experience in the automotive category. The idea was to capitalize on two trends: consumer dissatisfaction with the automotive purchase process and the rapid proliferation of the Internet as a medium for retail transactions. According to the CarPoint website, "The CarPoint formula is simple. By bringing the efficiency of the Internet to the car buying process, CarPoint saves time, money, and hassle for the consumers and dealers."

The CarPoint teams' strategy for success in this business was clear technological leadership. Their bet was that providing the best software solutions to both the shoppers and the dealers was the way to success. And they intended to take full advantage of Microsoft's biggest asset—excellent software development skills.

Rosenblatt and his team had several initiatives in place for the future, including a revamp of dealer training, more professional management of the dealer channel, and the release of new products. The upcoming launch of MS Start (Microsoft's Internet "portal" site), Rosenblatt felt, would provide another decisive source of competitive advantage. What could Rosenblatt and his team do to create a sustainable competitive advantage going forward?

Preparation Questions

1. Why are consumers so dissatisfied with the face-to-face car buying process?

2. How can online car buying services better meet consumer needs? Are there aspects of the car buying process that cannot be improved through marketspace solutions?

3. How well does CarPoint meet consumer and dealer needs, compared to other online services?

4. What should CarPoint do to create a robust economic model?

INTEGRATIVE QUESTIONS

As you consider the entire set of questions in the second chapter, you should also reflect on the following integrative questions:

1. Are there generic, unmet consumer needs that are best served online?

2. What are the most important elements of strong market opportunity analysis for online? Offline? Both?

3. How are the lessons of CarPoint and PlanetAll similar? Different?

4. Explain the difference between a "large" opportunity for a firm and a "good" opportunity for a firm.

SUMMARY

Market opportunity analysis combines both external market conditions (e.g., Is there an unmet need? Is competition weak? Is the technology "ready"?) and internal firm capabilities (e.g., What assets can we leverage?). In this concrete sense, opportunities can only be judged relative to the capabilities that the firm, or its potential partners, can leverage in the marketplace. Thus, an opportunity is not only out there waiting to be uncovered, but it is also equally a function of the unique ways that the firm can see how it can use or combine its assets in the online environment.

PLANETALL

www.planetall.com

There is nothing more valuable to us than our contacts.
—Jim Savage, CEO, PlanetAll

Warren Adams, co-founder and president of PlanetAll, stared into the mini-fridge in his office in Central Square in Cambridge, Massachusetts. As he searched for some caffeine, his eyes fell upon a half-empty bottle of Jägermeister, the young company's unofficial celebration drink. The bottle was a remnant of PlanetAll's first "birthday" party, celebrated just four months ago.

PlanetAll had launched its free, Web-based, active contact manager on November 12, 1996. The service collected and stored in a central database member information such as names, addresses, telephone numbers, and e-mail addresses as well as group affiliations such as former and present employers, colleges and universities, fraternities/sororities, and professional groups. Users utilized a variety of PlanetAll search functions to identify other PlanetAll users they knew and "link" to them. PlanetAll generated a personalized home page for each individual member that resided on the PlanetAll Web site and contained all relevant contact and group information. This included an "Active Address Book" of all contacts; links to users' groups; access to a personalized planner for making and tracking travel plans, meetings, and events; and access to the PlanetAll search functions for finding potential new contacts who were also users. In addition to storing this information on the PlanetAll Web site, users received periodic "PeopleNews" updates via e-mail.

Members joined PlanetAll through the PlanetAll Web site (*www.planetall.com*) or through one of PlanetAll's co-branded partner sites, including GeoCities' "Geo-Planet," The Monster Board's "People Network," and Infospace's "Personal Address Book," all of which used PlanetAll's functionality and database to provide PlanetAll services as part of their sites. In 15 months the business had acquired nearly one million users and was adding close to 10,000 more each day.

Adams was encouraged by the rapid growth of Planet-All's membership. The company had also attracted the interest of potential strategic partners and investors. However, he felt that ultimate success depended on the timely and widespread adoption of PlanetAll's technology as the premier engine of digital contact management functionality. He explained: "PlanetAll's value to an individual user resides in being able to share and access information with *everyone* in his or her network. This requires us to achieve critical mass so that the vast majority of a person's personal and professional contacts are part of the Active Address Book database." Thus, PlanetAll's overriding objective was simple, according to Adams: "Get big fast. The larger our user base, the more value we're creating for an individual user. Once a member has invested in linking with others, it creates high switching costs. The combination of a large and linked database is essential to our long-term goals as a company."

Adams also believed that within three months Planet-All must have enough momentum—the goal was to add members at a rate of 20,000 a day—to achieve critical mass and thereby stave off competition from other major Web sites.

Given this overriding objective, Adams felt a major decision was whether to continue operating PlanetAll as a branded destination site, or to become primarily an enabling technology provider for other sites and players in the contact management business. Possibly, PlanetAll could attempt some hybrid of the two strategies. In addition, on a more tactical level, Adams and his team faced four fundamental challenges related to member acquisition. First was effectively and quickly communicating the value of PlanetAll to potential members—answering the question "What is it?" Second was increasing the "user-friendliness" of the interface—making it easy and intuitive for users to exploit the full functionality of Planet-All. Third was overcoming user concerns about Web privacy and security related to personal information. And last was making sure PlanetAll had high utility for individual users—meaning there were sufficient

---

Research Associates Michelle Toth and Carrie Ardito prepared this case under the supervision of Professor Jeffrey F. Rayport as the basis for class discussion rather than to illustrate either effective or ineffective handling of an administrative situation.

potential contacts in the PlanetAll database to make membership worthwhile.

The concern that Adams felt regarding these strategic and tactical decisions was compounded by shorter term concerns, such as funding. It was February 26th. In five weeks PlanetAll would run out of cash. Adams glanced at the term sheet sitting on his desk from a prominent venture capital firm interested in making a multi-million dollar investment. The term sheet would expire at, ironically, the exact same time Adams and his partners would make a critical presentation to one of their most important potential partners. As Adams contemplated these decisions and his plan of action, he felt the familiar sense of urgency that had pervaded PlanetAll since its inception.

History of PlanetAll

A social person by nature, Warren Adams had formed a sizable list of friends and contacts by the time he was in college at Colgate University. He realized that his address book was inadequate for managing groups of contacts and their constantly changing addresses and phone numbers. It was then that he first had the idea for a centralized electronic database that automatically updated address books. But at that time, the technology did not exist to facilitate such a concept, and Adams tucked his idea away, imagining that someday the enabling technology would emerge.

Eight years later, following graduation from Harvard Business School's [HBS's] MBA Program in 1995, Adams took a job at Mitchell Madison Group (MMG), a strategy consulting firm in New York City. At MMG, Adams met Brian Robertson, a 22-year-old Massachusetts Institute of Technology (MIT) computer science graduate and former Canadian national barefoot water-skiing champion. Robertson had developed group scheduling and calendaring software with several high-tech and software start-up companies. By summer 1996, Adams and Robertson had left MMG and started working on the PlanetAll idea out of the kitchen of a friend's Peabody Terrace apartment in Cambridge, later moving down the street to a steamy, windowless office in Kendall Square. Robertson, former president of an MIT fraternity, recruited 13 of his tech-savvy fraternity brothers to do programming to help launch the database-driven service; similarly, Adams rallied friends from HBS to develop the business plan. In the early stages, Adams used the working name "Small World," abandoning it after a trademark search uncovered a Russian dating service operating under the Small World name. Instead, the team settled on PlanetAll and by fall 1996, Adams, Robertson, and supporters, convinced that being first to the Web was essential to their long-term success, hastily launched PlanetAll on the Web at *www.planetall.com.*

In its first nine months PlanetAll survived on financing from its founders and a handful of angel investors. In June 1997, the company raised $4 million in venture financing led by CMG@Ventures, a venture capital firm that invested in and integrated advanced Internet, interactive media, and database management technologies. The company's @Ventures investment and development affiliate had a majority interest in Lycos, Blaxxun Interactive (formerly Black Sun Interactive), GeoCities, and significant investments in Ikonic Interactive, Inc., Vicinity Corporation, Silknet Software, Parable, and KOZ, Inc. PlanetAll's other leading investor was Arts Alliance, Ltd., a UK-based investment firm specializing in the Internet. Other Arts Alliance investments included Firefly, Launch, Interactive Investor, and CyberSites.

In December 1997, Jim Savage, who had formerly launched ZDNet, the Web business for computer and trade magazine publisher Ziff-Davis, joined PlanetAll as CEO. Having already launched and served as general manager of a successful Web business—ZDNet had revenues of $30 million when he left—Savage was ready to return to an entrepreneurial environment and "do it all over again." He joined PlanetAll because he felt it was a "killer idea, with the opportunity to be the next big thing."

The PlanetAll Service

The Web Site. Members joined the service through the PlanetAll Web site (*www.planetall.com*) or co-branded sites built for a variety of partners including GeoCities, The Monster Board, and Infospace. Members then used a variety of PlanetAll features to find other PlanetAll members they knew, share contact information with them, and access this information (see Exhibit 1).

Active Address Book. The core service of PlanetAll was the automatically updating Active Address Book which stored all of a person's contact information (see Exhibit 2). The primary means for a member to build his or her address book was to find other members they knew or who shared a common bond such as having graduated from the same college around the same time or worked at the same company at the same time. The member would then request permission to share contact information with these other members and choose how much of his or her own information to make available to each of them (see Exhibit 3 for permission screen). Once there was a reciprocal agreement to share information, each member's record would appear in the other's address book. When one member changed, or added to, his or her own record, the other member's address book was automatically updated. Members could view their private address books through any Web browser.

Another way for members to build their address books was to add contact records themselves. They could either type the information manually or import it into PlanetAll from software running on their personal computers (PCs). Whenever a member added a record to his or her address book, PlanetAll searched for members with matching information so that the record could become self-updating. In January 1998, PlanetAll launched software to allow members to synchronize PlanetAll address books with the address book component of Microsoft Outlook, an e-mail and contact management software program bundled with the Microsoft Office suite of programs. PlanetAll was working on similar software for the Palm Pilot handheld computer and other PC software programs.

On its Web site (and in e-mail messages sent to members), PlanetAll provided timely information about the contacts in a member's address book. This information included notices of addresses or phone number changes, contacts' upcoming birthdays, and overlapping travel plans. In order to help members extend their networks, PlanetAll also notified members of other people with whom he or she might want to share contact information. These included people who had explicitly requested to share contact information with the member, people who had joined the same groups as the member, and people who had a friend in common with the member.

Groups. In the "Groups" area of its Web site, PlanetAll allowed members to join or create groups, administer groups they had created, and post bulletin board messages to other group members.

Friends of Friends. In the "Friends of Friends" area members could find out which of their contacts knew people in a particular group or city.

Planner. In the "Planner" area members entered travel plans in order to determine if any contacts had overlapping plans, set up meetings with contacts, and set up

reminders for themselves (see Exhibit 4). The Planner offered Monthly, Weekly, and List views.

Personal Information. In the "My Info" area members could modify their own contact information for the benefit of their contacts. This included all information previously entered including home and work addresses, telephone numbers, a biographical update, job information, and group information.

E-mail Service. The second component of PlanetAll's service was periodic e-mails. Members chose the frequency—every day, every 3 days, every 7 days, never, or only when contact information changed (see Exhibit 5). The average PlanetAll member received e-mail messages from PlanetAll every four days. The e-mails provided similar information to what the Web site displayed: new contact information, potential contacts, birthday and anniversary reminders (which included advertisements for gifts and cards), summary of travel plans (with advertising for ticket purchase and other travel services), and notification of opportunities to "cross paths" with contacts.[1] Additionally, the e-mail service provided customized news, horoscopes, and jokes. While Adams did not see PlanetAll as being a long-term provider of such information commodities, including this ancillary material helped make e-mails relevant, while members established links that would increase the value of their personalized, periodic e-mails.

The Value Proposition. With this collection of features, PlanetAll was positioned to offer several unique benefits to its members. Most importantly, address book records became self-updating. Additionally, members were able to remain in contact with a greater number of people. They could access contact information for these people from anywhere, either via the Web or their preferred contact management program or device. PlanetAll believed that its contact updates, unlike other Internet content such as news or weather, were entirely personalized and unavailable anywhere else. Because of this personalization and uniqueness, PlanetAll believed that it also enhanced the ability of its business partners to build customer loyalty and of its advertisers to target their messages.

---

[1]If a contact entered travel plans to be within a 25-mile radius of a member's location—whether home base or traveling—PlanetAll would inform contacts that they were "crossing paths" and provide information to facilitate further contact. For example, members could choose to make their hotel names and telephone numbers available to certain contacts.

PlanetAll Database and Technology

The key components of PlanetAll's database that enabled the basic services described above were three "tables," or sets of data fields: a "customer information" table containing contact information for each member, a "relationships" table containing sharing agreements regarding how much contact information would be accessible and to whom, and an "affinities" table tracking the groups to which each member belonged.

The technology used as a platform to develop the PlanetAll database was off-the-shelf—the programming team built the Active Address Book database and other functionality using Microsoft SQL Server and was in the process of moving it to an Oracle database. The database searched for all information relevant to individual members and sent that information out at a rate of 30 to 40 e-mail messages per second. It was also able to embed its software functionality into other contact information providers, including Web sites and personal data managers (handheld devices called Personal Digital Assistants [PDAs] such as the Palm Pilot, and software programs referred to as Personal Information Managers [PIMs] such as Microsoft Outlook).

As PlanetAll's member base grew (see Exhibit 6), speed of access and the ability to support increased traffic became critically important. As potential members navigated the sign-up process, the experience of connecting to the site and searching its 80,000-plus groups had to be fast and easy. Robertson explained, "If a potential member cannot access PlanetAll or if site navigation is slow, he or she may never come back."

In November 1997, Robertson expanded PlanetAll's bandwidth, or connection speed to the Internet, in order to decrease user wait times. PlanetAll previously connected to the Internet from its Central Square headquarters using a single T-1 (1.54 Mbps) connection via Uunet, an Internet service provider. Informed that new bandwidth from Bell Atlantic, the local telephone provider, would entail at least a 45-business-day wait, Robertson decided to move PlanetAll's server farm from its Cambridge headquarters to Navisite, a Web hosting service, in Andover, Massachusetts. Navisite's data center gave PlanetAll servers access to the Internet via four T-3 lines (each T-3 equaled the speed of 16 T-1 lines[2]), an increase in bandwidth of 64 times original capacity.

---

[2]Caulfield, Brian, "Building 10,000 Relationships Each Day," *Internet World*, February 9, 1998.

The move to an off-site server and the increase in bandwidth, Robertson explained, came at precisely the right moment in PlanetAll's history. By early 1998, PlanetAll was sending out 200,000 contact update e-mails each night, a rate that PlanetAll's previous bandwidth could not have sustained. Robertson explained the significance of PlanetAll's engineering efforts:

> The sum of PlanetAll's technical efforts exceeds 15 engineering years, which we've completed in a span of 18 months. It is like an iceberg—all people see is the front-end, the Web site, but an enormous amount of time has gone into the back-end. The database, scalability, site monitoring and maintenance, mail generation, inbound mail forwarding, inbound mail processing and customer service, AutoSync (synchronization with PIM software), and more. Non-Web efforts constitute more than 80% of our engineering investment to date.

Strategic Alliances

As PlanetAll sought to reach critical mass quickly, the company pursued partnerships with large existing organizations, including high-traffic destination Web sites, contact management providers (such as PDAs and PIMs), affinity groups (such as colleges and universities), and telecommunications services providers.

Major Destination Web Sites. PlanetAll formed strategic alliances with various Web services, including GeoCities, WhoWhere?, Infospace, PlanetDirect, and The Monster Board. For example, the agreement with GeoCities provided GeoCities members with membership in a co-branded version of PlanetAll, called GeoPlanet. Upon signing up for GeoCities, users were given the option to join GeoPlanet and get an explanation of its services. Adams felt the next step was to convince the search engines of the value of licensing PlanetAll's Active Address Book technology. So far, one search engine had agreed to do so, and PlanetAll was in serious discussions with other top tier players.

In January 1998, search engines comprised some of the most popular Web sites, with Yahoo!, Infoseek, Excite, and Lycos respectively ranking as the second, sixth, seventh, and eighth most visited sites on the Web for residential users (see Exhibit 7). The search engines, which originally provided users with the means to navigate the Web, were jockeying in 1998 to become "portals" or gateways to the Internet for Web browsers. Each search engine was striking deals with various feature and content providers in order to offer one-stop sites for users. For example, in February 1998, Lycos acquired Tripod, a virtual community with one million members and 2.7 million unique visitors, which offered on-line communities of interests, newsletters, chats, and conferences. Yahoo! invested $5 million in Geo Cities in late 1997 to provide Yahoo! visitors with free personal home pages; and it acquired Four11 to provide directory services and RocketMail free e-mail services. As a result, in addition to Web search services, many of the major search engines provided users with free e-mail accounts, customized news pages, maps, chat, personalized financial advice, contests, telephone directory services, people searches, weather information, shopping, and dating services. (See Exhibit 8 for market value and member information for sample content and feature services.)

Search engines were also migrating toward personalized content. Yahoo!, for example, offered "My Yahoo!," a site which users self-designed to provide only selected information. Users chose for their personal pages specific stock quotes, local weather updates, news topics, and sports scores. (Exhibit 9 shows an example of how PlanetAll might integrate its functionality with that of a search engine.)

Personal Information Managers (PIMs) and Personal Digital Assistants (PDAs)

In 1998, traditional paper-based contact managers, including those made by Daytimer and Franklin, were under attack from electronic contact management solutions. Two categories of electronic solutions were Personal Information Managers (PIMs) and Personal Digital Assistants (PDAs).

PIMs. PIMs were contact management software applications for PCs, such as Microsoft *Outlook*, Lotus *Organizer*, and Now *Contact* and *Up-To-Date*. Advantages of these applications versus traditional non-electronic planners were numerous: electronic tools delivered larger capacity for contact entries, contact search capabilities by name or company, reminders of upcoming events, and integration with e-mail and desktop publishing tools. But these applications did not incorporate Internet features into their programs. As a result, PlanetAll felt there was an opportunity to enhance PIM func-

tionality by linking contact content with PlanetAll's Active Address Book. (See Exhibit 10 for a graphic showing Active Address Book synchronization with *Outlook*.)

PDAs. The second category, PDAs, were handheld digital computers. These portable devices complemented desktop applications by offering convenient contact and word processing file transfer to, and from, Windows 95-based systems. Users could also access e-mail via modem attachments. The value of PDAs lay in portability; they weighed 5 to 14 ounces and could be carried in users' pockets. Smaller devices, lacking keyboards, utilized handwriting recognition software to translate notes "written" on the screen with a special "pen." Costs ranged from a simple model at $299 to $1,000 for a completely loaded machine. Handheld PDAs were beginning to catch on by early 1998; for example, PalmPilot, manufactured by 3Com, had a user base of 2 million. Adams noted:

> [Integration of] PIMs and PDAs [is] important because this is where people who manage their contacts electronically traditionally do it. And while it is easy for Palm Pilot to add new features, it's more of a stretch for them to develop and run a major Web site to facilitate the automatic flow of contact information from the Pilot platform to other platforms. This is where PlanetAll's Active Address Book can be an extension of that functionality, enabling a live, linked data source that is automatically updating. By offering a private label version of our Active Address Book, we allow PIMs and PDAs to market the expanded functionality as part of their product.

Affinity Groups. Recognizing the value to users of staying connected to members of colleges and universities and the institutions themselves, PlanetAll had signed three- to five-year contracts with 70 university sites to provide PlanetAll contact management services for alumni from their home pages. These partnerships, to be rolled out in March 1998, involved a potential user base of 2.2 million alumni.

Telecommunications Services Providers. PlanetAll had already established one partnership to integrate its technology with a major global voice-mail provider. Adams planned to pursue additional opportunities with other telecom services providers, including cellular phone companies and universal messaging services.

Competition

Networking Sites

Adams identified two direct on-line competitors that had developed contact databases: BranchOut, launched by Brainstorm Interactive, a company also begun by a Harvard Business School graduate, and Six Degrees, owned by Macroview Communication Corp. (Exhibit 11 provides a list of PlanetAll's direct and indirect competitors.)

BranchOut (*www.branchout.com*) aimed to create networking opportunities for people with existing common bonds, and had created communities around groups of schools including "Ivy +" (Ivy League and other prestigious universities) and "Jesuit Educated Alumni." BranchOut aimed to generate career and social opportunities for its members through on-line discussion forums, classified advertisements, and job postings. BranchOut, which launched three to four months after PlanetAll, had 5,500 members as of November 1997.[3]

Six Degrees (*www.sixdegrees.com*) was based on the idea that every person was connected to everyone else in the world through a maximum of six other people. Upon sign-up, members registered and identified at least two friends, who were then encouraged to join via e-mail. Each time a person joined who was connected to another member, members were contacted via e-mail and notified of the acquaintance. The goal of the site was to create networking information pertaining to jobs, industries, and interests by connecting members with common contacts. Six Degrees had also introduced a personal bulletin board service for members to post personal information. Bulletin boards were visible to members' first two "degrees"—their friends and people their friends knew. Launched in January 1997, Six Degrees had close to 200,000 members by early 1998.

Major Destination Sites

Adams considered the major Web traffic aggregators to be potential competitors and potential strategic alliances. These included search engines like Yahoo!, Excite, and Infoseek, as well as America Online (AOL) and Microsoft Network.

Search Engines. Adams recognized that the major search engines tended to function like "islands"—each fighting to remain differentiated from others in the emerging "portal" battle. As a result, the likelihood of getting all search engines to "play in the same sandbox" using PlanetAll's functionality for contact management was uncertain. Adams' experience in negotiating with search engine businesses was that such firms preferred, if they did not require, exclusive agreements which conflicted with PlanetAll's open system objectives. Unless PlanetAll could convince the search engines to abandon their exclusive approach to contact management functionality, Adams felt PlanetAll would end up having to take sides.

America Online. America Online (AOL), the most popular Internet service provider with 11 million members, achieved large-scale success by providing members with a community-based gateway to the Internet. Upon dialing into the service, members automatically entered AOL's home page, which was populated with community areas, chat rooms, news, and user resources, such as a children's homework help. Membership to AOL also included an e-mail account and home page. Adams felt that AOL's large member base and resources were a potential threat if AOL chose another means of achieving Active Address Book functionality for its vast population of members.

Microsoft. Adams, like most entrepreneurs, felt Microsoft posed two options for most start-ups—compete and risk elimination or become a partner and risk elimination. Adams believed that PlanetAll services could add value to several of Microsoft's existing applications and Web properties. Users of Outlook and Outlook Express, Expedia, a Web-based travel planner, and Hotmail, a free Web-based e-mail application, could benefit from the Active Address Book's functionality, especially with respect to keeping contact information up-to-date.

Microsoft also ran numerous Web sites, all part of the Microsoft Network, which ranked among the most popular on the Web and were visited by a third of all U.S. Web surfers. Microsoft also provided some of the Web's most sought-after information—travel services (Expedia), stock quotes (Investor), entertainment guides (Sidewalk), comprehensive news (MSN and MSNBC), free e-mail (Hotmail), and on-line games (Zone). In summer 1998, Microsoft planned to launch a site called "Microsoft Start" that combined some of its most

---

[3]Wang, Nelson, "Keep in Touch: New Breed of Site Links People by Common Interest," *Web Week*, November 10, 1997.

popular features into one Web site.[4] Microsoft expected the site to attract enormous amounts of traffic, as Web users made it their starting point for Web visits.

Member Acquisition and Retention

In early 1998, users of the PlanetAll service averaged 37 years of age and were 60% male. At least 69% had attended college or graduate school.[5] Of the nearly one million Active Address Book users, 50% had joined through the PlanetAll Web site, while 50% joined through a partner site. To attract new members, Adams was focused not only on partnerships but also on referrals from existing members, which increased the database and links in the database—an important factor in making the service "work" for new members.

Adams felt that successful referrals, accounting for 25% of growth, were instrumental in retaining, as well as acquiring, members. As members linked each new contact to address books, both the value of the service and users' switching costs increased exponentially. Robertson explained, "People become dependent on other people that they are linked to in their Active Address Book. No other service has this information, and it would take considerable effort to compile [from scratch]." Referrals from members were encouraged through the "Planet-Points" program. PlanetAll awarded members 100 points for each referral, which could be redeemed for Continental and Delta Airlines' frequent flyer miles (one point equaled one mile), charitable donations (1,000 points equaled $10), or a PlanetAll T-shirt.

Adams felt that future member acquisition under a brand-building, destination-site strategy would be vastly different from that of an alliance-driven, enabling-technology strategy. But in both cases the company needed to resolve key marketing and positioning issues.

Product/Marketing Challenges

Regardless of the strategy PlanetAll selected (destination site or enabling technology), the management team had identified four major product/marketing challenges:

Explaining PlanetAll. The first challenge was communications. Few Internet companies had found an effective way to introduce an entirely new concept to Web users that lacked an easily identifiable physical-world counterpart. Frank Levy (HBS '95), PlanetAll's product manager, realized that PlanetAll was a complex service with a value proposition that people did not readily understand. He elaborated:

> Explaining PlanetAll to people is difficult. They understand Amazon.com and books, The Monster Board and jobs. But try explaining a virtual address book where the information changes without them having to do anything and they start to look confused. This is a fundamental problem for us—how to communicate in 30 seconds the idea and the value of PlanetAll. We're not satisfied with our ability to do this yet.

User-Friendliness. The PlanetAll site was complex due to the extensive functionality and enormous amount of information it sought to capture, store, and avail to users, customized and in real time. In light of this complexity, speed and intuitive interface design were areas PlanetAll management sought to improve. Levy estimated that the average time spent in the registration process was three minutes, but members then had to continually use and update the service to reap its benefits. This required an investment of time weekly or even daily to enter additional contact information, encourage friends to join, and find and join groups. Levy remarked, "PlanetAll suffers from 'feature creep.' We have too many bells and whistles, so the core services get obstructed and the process gets confusing. We have been looking at paring down the features and have consulted with outside usability experts. We've done extensive usability testing internally in an effort to continually improve the interface."

Privacy and Security Concerns. The third hurdle was privacy and Web security. Fraudulent use of personal information could be potentially disastrous for individuals. Jim Savage remarked, "The $50 that my credit card charges me in the event of fraud simply does not compare to the problems that may arise from someone walking around with all of my personal information." PlanetAll attempted to alleviate privacy concerns by investing in infrastructure to keep out hackers and requiring the use of a username and password, a five-tier permissions scheme that controlled who saw what information, and a requirement that all links be reciprocal before information was shared.

---

[4]Green, Heather, Himelstein, Linda and Judge, Paul C., "Portal Combat Comes to the Net," *Business Week*, March 2, 1998.
[5]PlanetAll Company Documents.

Product Utility. The fourth hurdle was achieving high levels of usage across relevant populations. For the service to "really work," everyone—or most everyone within an individual's professional and social circles—had to be involved actively. PlanetAll measured product utility by the number of links a member had and segmented users according to three categories: no links, 1–14 links, and over 15 links in their Active Address Book. Adams believed PlanetAll only became truly valuable when members had over 15 links. If an individual lacked sufficient links to other members, not only was the value less but also switching costs were lower.

Economics

The revenue model for PlanetAll was expected to evolve over time. In the near-term, PlanetAll was focused on distribution, leveraging its Web presence and its current and potential partners to facilitate the widespread and efficient distribution of PlanetAll services. In the longer term, PlanetAll's ultimate revenue model would depend on its decision either to develop the PlanetAll Web site as a branded destination or to pursue an enabling technology strategy.

The PlanetAll Web site had two streams of revenue—banner advertisements and electronic commerce. Adams estimated that PlanetAll's Web site displayed 10 million banner ads a month to site visitors. This was referred to as advertising inventory. The factors in determining ad inventory were the number of site visitors, the number of pages each visitor viewed, the number of pages on which advertisements were shown, and whether the ads "refreshed" while a user was viewing a given page. It was customary for Web sites to sell a portion of advertising and to barter (or exchange) advertising space with strategic partners. PlanetAll used some of its advertising inventory for barter to place advertising on other Web sites.

PlanetAll estimated that its average member saw 150 ads per year through the PlanetAll Web site. The average cost-per-thousand or CPM for Web banner advertising was $20 to $25.[6] In terms of e-commerce, PlanetAll had revenue sharing agreements with goods and services providers for purchases made through the PlanetAll site, including travel and gifts. PlanetAll received 10% to 25% commissions on purchases made through its site. Experiments with e-commerce indicated that targeted ads (such as travel services shown when a member was planning a trip and greeting card ads shown at the time of a contact's birthday) had click-through rates of 10 to 20 times the average click-through rate of 1% to 2% for a generic, non-targeted ad. PlanetAll also fueled, and capitalized on, its growth through co-registration revenue deals. PlanetAll received payment by other services when new users registered for these other services while signing up for PlanetAll. Partners in such deals included Cybergold, BonusMail, and MyPoints, companies that rewarded users (with points redeemable for goods and services) for viewing ads, reading commercial e-mails, and/or responding to questions about products. Each paid PlanetAll a flat fee for new registrants acquired through the PlanetAll site.

PlanetAll's e-mail notification service provided another opportunity for placing advertisements. Travel service providers, greeting card companies, and gift sellers in particular could also arrange to target through e-mail PlanetAll users who received birthday reminders for contacts or who entered travel arrangements. Click-throughs for targeted e-mail advertisements were comparable to those of the Web site. PlanetAll estimated that the average member viewed 90 ads in e-mails per year and the total number of e-mail ads exceeded five million per month. The emergence of HTML e-mail allowed PlanetAll to send full-fledged banner advertisements through e-mail rather than simply text-only embedded hyperlinks that readers could click through to get to the advertiser's site. In early 1998, approximately 35% of PlanetAll members used HTML-enabled e-mail programs and therefore received banner ads in their periodic PlanetAll e-mail.

To acquire users directly, PlanetAll paid one to two cents per impression ($10 to $20 CPM) for banner ads placed on other sites on the Web. The click-through rate for these ads was 1% to 2%, and the conversion rate of click-throughs to new members (visitors who actually joined PlanetAll) was 10% to 20%. Once acquired, the estimated total cost to maintain a member's PlanetAll data was approximately $1 per year. As a destination site with its own traffic, PlanetAll kept 100% of revenues generated by advertising and e-commerce that targeted its members on its site.

As an OEM provider, PlanetAll would license its PlanetAll Active Address Book enabling technology and embed its functionality into other sites and services. Adams envisioned this strategy resembling the scenario played out by Spell Checker technology, which came

---

[6]Hamilton, Annette. "What You Don't Know About Web Ads Will Cost You," *ZDNet*, November 10, 1997.

bundled in a variety of word processing applications. PlanetAll approached revenue arrangements with potential partners and customers differently, depending on the business model of the partner service. For example, if a Web site generated revenue from advertising and e-commerce, PlanetAll expected to negotiate a revenue-sharing arrangement that would reflect the incremental revenue generated as a result of PlanetAll being part of the site. If a search engine added the PlanetAll functionality and therefore created more ad inventory, PlanetAll would likely share in incremental advertising revenue. Similarly, if PlanetAll's functionality drove increased purchases of airline tickets, PlanetAll would negotiate to receive a percentage of the incremental commission revenue. The percentage of revenue-sharing would vary by contract (Adams estimated an average of 50%). For PIMs and PDAs, PlanetAll expected the revenue model to be either flat-fee, per-user fee, or licensing arrangement. For telecommunications services providers, revenues were determined by the number of users.

Conclusion

To succeed in a Web environment crowded with players, PlanetAll had to attract sufficient cross-platform adoption of PlanetAll functionality to achieve critical mass. To do this, PlanetAll needed either to fast become a leading destination site or establish alliances that would embed its functionality in the major Web services and contact management software and devices. In addition, Adams knew that PlanetAll had to continue to work to overcome the four marketing hurdles identified—the challenge of explaining PlanetAll to new users, user friendliness, privacy and Web security concerns, and ensuring product utility by having enough potential links in the PlanetAll database for each new member.

PlanetAll could also remain a destination site, but it would need to reach a much larger scale, similar to that of Yahoo!, Excite, and Microsoft. For this model, PlanetAll would need to become a mega-brand and attract considerable traffic, a difficult feat in an increasingly contested Web landscape. PlanetAll would need to begin advertising and promoting the service on a much larger scale than it had to date. Savage noted that advertising banners, which were usually unable to convey a lot of information, would have the difficult task of communicating the depth and significance of the PlanetAll service. Many industry analysts believed that it was already too late to build a major brand on the Web; indeed, Adams estimated that such an endeavor could cost "hundreds of millions of dollars."

If PlanetAll decided to position itself as an enabling technology, its value was maximized only if several of the major sites and services—such as Yahoo!, Infoseek, America Online, and Microsoft—participated in the Active Address Book database. It was not as valuable for users to have friends and contacts using multiple services. In 1998, however, the major sites appeared to want exclusive deals in order to gain a competitive advantage over other sites. Another possible permutation of the enabling technology strategy was to create a corporate Intranet product to serve large corporations with mobile workforces. In fact, PlanetAll had obtained feature requirements from several New York City-based companies that indicated interest and a willingness to pay between $50 and several hundred dollars per user for a system that could meet such requirements. PlanetAll could not currently accommodate these feature requirements but could conceivably build the enhanced functionality into future, specialized versions of the service.

As Adams prepared the final pages of his presentation for the potential alliance partner, and glanced again at the term sheet from the VC firm, he realized that PlanetAll was facing yet another pivotal week. Contemplating the strategic and operational implications of the decisions before him, he reached for more caffeine and prepared for another late night.

Exhibit 1 User Home Section

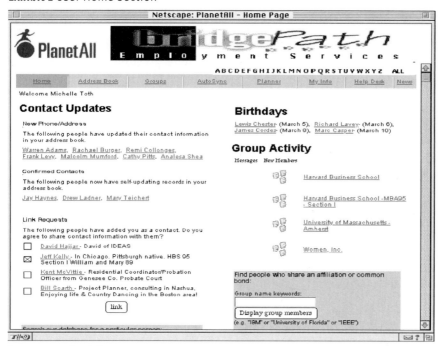

Source: *www.planetall.com*

Exhibit 2 Address Book

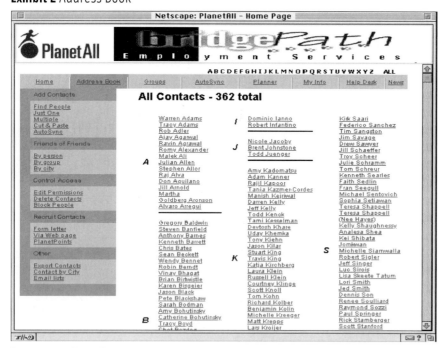

Source: *www.planetall.com*

Exhibit 3 Permission Screen

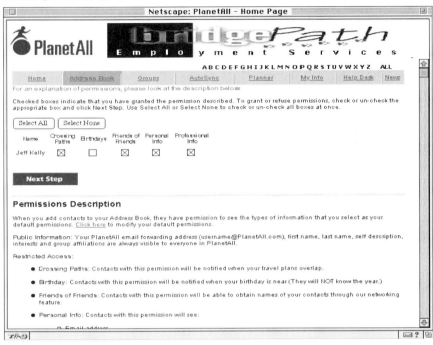

Source: *www.planetall.com*

Exhibit 4 The Planner

Source: *www.planetall.com*

Exhibit 5 Sample PlanetAll E-mail

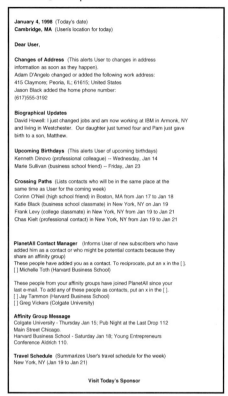

January 4, 1998 (Today's date)
Cambridge, MA (User's location for today)

Dear User,

Changes of Address (This alerts User to changes in address information as soon as they happen).
Adam D'Angelo changed or added the following work address:
415 Claymore; Peoria, IL; 61615; United States
Jason Black added the home phone number:
(617)555-3192

Biographical Updates
David Howell: I just changed jobs and am now working at IBM in Armonk, NY and living in Westchester. Our daughter just turned four and Pam just gave birth to a son, Matthew.

Upcoming Birthdays (This alerts User of upcoming birthdays)
Kenneth Dinovo (professional colleague) -- Wednesday, Jan 14
Marie Sullivan (business school friend) -- Friday, Jan 23

Crossing Paths (Lists contacts who will be in the same place at the same time as User for the coming week)
Corinn O'Neil (high school friend) in Boston, MA from Jan 17 to Jan 18
Katie Black (business school classmate) in New York, NY on Jan 19
Frank Levy (college classmate) in New York, NY from Jan 19 to Jan 21
Chas Kielt (professional contact) in New York, NY from Jan 19 to Jan 21

PlanetAll Contact Manager (Informs User of new subscribers who have added him as a contact or who might be potential contacts because they share an affinity group)
These people have added you as a contact. To reciprocate, put an x in the [ ].
[ ] Michelle Toth (Harvard Business School)

These people from your affinity groups have joined PlanetAll since your last e-mail. To add any of these people as contacts, put an x in the [ ].
[ ] Jay Tammon (Harvard Business School)
[ ] Greg Vickers (Colgate University)

Affinity Group Message
Colgate University - Thursday Jan 15; Pub Night at the Last Drop 112 Main Street Chicago.
Harvard Business School - Saturday Jan 18; Young Entrepreneurs Conference Aldrich 110.

Travel Schedule (Summarizes User's travel schedule for the week)
New York, NY (Jan 19 to Jan 21)

Visit Today's Sponsor

Source: PlanetAll Company Documents

Exhibit 6 PlanetAll Membership Growth

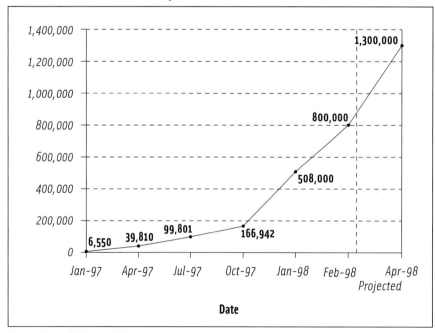

Source: PlanetAll Company Documents

Exhibit 7 Top 25 Web Sites (January 1998)

Top 25 Web Sites at Home			Top 25 Web Sites at Work		
Rank	**Web Site**	**% Reach**	**Rank**	**Web Site**	**% Reach**
1	aol.com	47.7	1	yahoo.com	50.3
2	yahoo.com	39.6	2	netscape.com	44.7
3	netscape.com	27.5	3	aol.com	35.4
4	geocities.com	23.9	4	microsoft.com	28.2
5	microsoft.com	23.4	5	infoseek.com	26.8
6	infoseek.com	19.2	6	excite.com	26.3
7	excite.com	19.0	7	lycos.com	20.4
8	lycos.com	12.9	8	geocities.com	19.7
9	msn.com	11.4	9	digital.com	16.2
10	switchboard.com	11.1	10	zdnet.com	14.7
11	tripod.com	10.1	11	four11.com	11.9
12	digital.com	9.7	12	msn.com	11.9
13	zdnet.com	8.7	13	webcrawler.com	11.5
14	webcrawler.com	8.5	14	switchboard.com	9.9
15	simplenet.com	7.9	15	cnn.com	8.8
16	sony online	7.8	16	amazon.com	8.7
17	angelfire.com	7.5	17	real.com	8.2
18	four11.com	7.4	18	compuserve.com	8.0
19	real.com	7.2	19	tripod.com	7.4
20	amazon.com	6.8	20	ustreas.gov	7.4
21	disney online	6.8	21	weather.com	7.4
22	att.net	6.6	22	cnet.com	7.2
23	pathfinder.com	6.5	23	whowhere.com	7.2
24	hotmail.com	6.2	24	pathfinder.com	6.9
25	compuserve.com	6.1	25	usatoday.com	6.9

Source: Media Metrix—The PC Meter Company

Exhibit 8 Market Value, Membership, and Unique Visitors for Feature Services

Site	Market Value ($ Million)	Members/Accounts	Unique Visitors in January 1998 (Million)
Four11/Rocketmail	$93	2.5 million	27.8 (combined w/Yahoo!)*
GeoCities	$250	1.4 million	10.5
HotMail	$300–400	9.5 million	6.0
WhoWhere	$100	4.2 million	5.1
Tripod	$58	1 million	2.7

Sources: "Top 20 Web Sites," *Interactive Week*, February 10, 1998; Steven Vonder Haar, "Free E-Mailers Ready to Deliver," *Interactive Week*, January 19, 1998; Casewriter's estimates
*"Top 20 Web Sites," *Interactive Week*, February 10, 1998

Exhibit 9 Integration of Lycos and PlanetAll

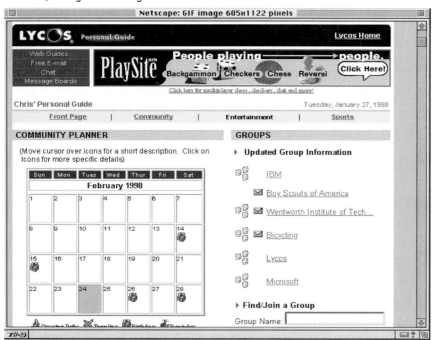

Source: PlanetAll Company Documents

Exhibit 10 Microsoft Outlook and Active Address Book Synchronization

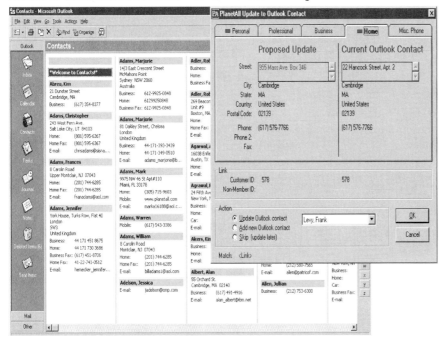

Source: PlanetAll Company Documents

Exhibit 11 PlanetAll Competitors

Current Competitors	Examples
Networking	Six Degrees
	Branch Out
Potential Competitors	
Large web sites	WhoWhere?, MSN/Hotmail Yahoo!/ Four11, Excite, Infoseek
Alumni and college web sites	OurSquare, Main Quad, Reunited
Online Service Providers	AOL, MSN, Prodigy
Groupware vendors and enterprise systems vendors	Netscape, Microsoft, Lotus
PDA/PIM hardware/software vendors	Starfish Sidekick, Symantec Act! Lotus Organizer, MS Outlook Palm Pilot, REX
Instant messaging companies	ICQ People Link

Source: PlanetAll Company Documents

MICROSOFT CARPOINT

Our core competitive advantage is the software that we write and the experience that the software delivers to the customer on the Web site. It allows access to all the information and all the tools they need to buy their next car in an easy to use fashion with very fast presentation. Our competitors are just not able to write that kind of compelling software.
—Alex Simons
Product Manager, Microsoft CarPoint
April 1998

We are going to be a true e-commerce solution—where customers can interact directly with the IT systems in dealerships. Customers will be able to view inventory, to have their financing approved, to sign up for service etc. That is where the software makes a difference and that is an advantage that we have.
—Gideon Rosenblatt
Group Program Manager, Microsoft CarPoint
April 1998

As Gideon Rosenblatt gazed out of his window at another overcast Seattle tableau, he reflected on the state of affairs at Microsoft CarPoint. CarPoint was a late entrant in the online car buying services arena but was rapidly catching up with the main players in the field. Already 1.3 million users were visiting the Web site each month and CarPoint was on track to drive $5.0 million in car sales a day. With Toyota claiming that the Internet was its #1 lead generator and Chrysler forecasting that 25% of its car sales would come from the Internet by the year 2000, Rosenblatt knew that the stakes were high. His management team was confident that parity with the competition was only months away and thus the larger question was what they could do to create a sustainable competitive advantage going forward.

Avnish Bajaj, Steffan Haithcox, and Michael Kadyan (all MBA '98) prepared this case under the supervision of Professor Jeffrey F. Rayport as the basis for class discussion rather than to illustrate either effective or ineffective handling of an administrative situation. Some of the data in this case has been disguised.

Although confidence was prevalent at CarPoint, complacency was not. Rosenblatt stated that "as is typical with any Internet business, we have a whole host of challenges and they keep accelerating in urgency and volume." Indeed, since the first version of CarPoint was shipped in 1996, changes and improvements had been occurring in rapid succession.

A couple of problems were at the forefront of Rosenblatt's attention. They were significantly affecting CarPoint's current performance and needed to be solved to build a strong base for further growth. To begin with, only 3% of visitors to the Web site were requesting referrals to dealers for specific cars. CarPoint's main competitors averaged closer to 5%. At the next step in the process, dealers were converting only 20% of CarPoint's referrals into sales. In comparison, CarPoint's strongest competitor was running closer to 30%. If CarPoint could improve these two performance measures to 5% and 30%, respectively, their service would generate 2.5 times as many car sales.

While working on these immediate concerns, Rosenblatt was also searching for a sustainable long-term competitive advantage—something that would propel CarPoint into the dominant position in the field.

CarPoint's History

Toward the end of 1993, Gideon Rosenblatt was working in Microsoft's burgeoning reference unit—the unit with Bookshelf and Encarta. Rosenblatt began to wonder whether there were other categories besides reference and games that would be important. He soon started to research the question.

> Looking at where people spend their money, a couple of items popped out—housing and automotive. So we asked, "Are there things that we can do in software that would be helpful in these areas?"

Rosenblatt and one part-time marketing employee started what would later become CarPoint. The product concept began as a CD-ROM with online links. The current mantra at CarPoint is "information, decision and action," but at its inception the product was purely informational. It was intended to be sold directly to consumers through traditional retail channels. In September 1994, Rosenblatt presented his idea to Bill Gates and was told to keep pursuing it.

In March 1995, the CD-ROM product was abandoned and the focus shifted entirely to an online model. This turn of events was described by Rosenblatt as one of CarPoint's defining moments.

> We were actually the first online application for Microsoft. It was a big conceptual jump to do an online-only product. It was very difficult to push it through—the business model was substantially different from the models Microsoft was used to.

Seven months later, CarSource (the earlier name of CarPoint) was shipped. Rosenblatt's online emphasis was reinforced in December 1995 on a day known by Microsoft employees as "Pearl Harbor Day." At this time, Gates decided to focus primarily on the Internet. Microsoft's initial plan was to be a player in every area of the Internet, which was eventually changed to focus on a few key services.

The first version of CarPoint was shipped in July 1996. CarPoint was an information product with a link to Auto-By-Tel, an online car buying service. The two partners helped each other in their nascent stages, but were destined to become fierce competitors. In May 1997, CarPoint negotiated a deal with Reynolds and Reynolds (R&R) that eliminated the need for Auto-By-Tel. CarPoint became a content and transaction site with R&R controlling most of the interaction with the dealers—e.g., selling, training and support. R&R needed an online service to complement its product portfolio for auto dealers and thus was willing to strike a better deal than Auto-By-Tel.

CarPoint launched its interactive classifieds product in September 1997. This product was designed to help consumers find, and dealers sell, used cars. According to Rich Glew, business manager for CarPoint:

> In the last two years, when Microsoft went from a many, many title company to making just a few bets, we've always had to fight to remain one of those bets. It was really only when we got the new car buying services up, consumer volume went way up, and the classifieds tool became the best in terms of consumer experience that we solidified ourselves as one of the ISM [interactive services media] bets, along with Sidewalk and Expedia.

Continuing to progress in Internet time, CarPoint version 2.0 was shipped the next month. This version incorporated significant additions, such as auto configuring, richer vehicle information pages, and two-car comparison tools. At this rapid pace, by April 1998 it seemed like CarPoint was due for another upheaval.

The Auto Industry[1]

Over $600 billion were spent on automobiles in 1997 in the United States, 46% on new cars and 54% on used cars (Exhibit 1). This represented about 10% of Americans' disposable income. Another $540 billion were spent on the automobile after-market—service/maintenance, gas/oil, insurance and parts/supplies. After housing, cars were generally a consumer's second largest expense.

Dealers

Dealers were the main distribution channel for the auto industry. Across the country, there were approximately 22,600 franchise dealers in 1997. These dealers were responsible for virtually all of the new car sales and one-third of the used car sales. Another 50% of used car sales happened between private parties, and 15% were sold by independent dealers (Exhibit 2). In total, 46 million automobiles were sold in 1997. New cars represented about 30% of this volume; used cars, 70%.

Approximately $8 billion were spent on local advertising to influence car sales. It is estimated that franchise dealers spent about $400 in total marketing expenditures for each new car sold. For used cars, the figure was closer to $200.

New and used car sales had significantly different characteristics. An average new vehicle cost $22,000 and produced a gross profit of less than 1%. Financing was additive to the 1%. New car sales could be considered a loss-leader to generate financing, service/maintenance, parts and trade-in revenue. On the other hand, an average used automobile cost $12,000 and resulted in a gross profit of 10% (Exhibit 3).

Customers

Americans were known the world over for their love of cars. Almost every household in the United States had at

---

[1]Adapted from CarPoint Internal Strategic Presentation, 1998.

least one automobile. Thus, every American over 16 years old was a potential customer.

Buying Process

Dealers were the point of contact between customers and car manufacturers and formed the epicenter of the car buying process. Consumers generally hated purchasing automobiles[2] due in large part to dissatisfaction with dealers and the traditional car buying process.

A typical car buying experience began with the shopper deciding what type of car they wanted—i.e., new vs. used, two-door vs. four-door, etc. After this step, customers often researched their options through consumer reports magazines and word-of-mouth and made a short list of manufacturers and models. It was from this point onwards that customers detested their experience since they now had to start interacting with dealers—first for test drives and then for the final purchase.

Typically, customers were greeted at the dealership by salespeople who were more interested in short-term commissions than in satisfying their customers. Customers were pressured to make a quick purchase decision even if they were only interested in collecting information or performing a test drive. Once a customer was ready to purchase a particular make and model automobile, s/he had to go through the agony of agreeing on a price with the salesperson. Dealers were notorious for charging customers based on their naiveté and ability to pay, so customers were wary of this step. In addition, car salespeople were known for their skill in haggling and manipulation.

Diligent consumers tried to gain negotiating power by obtaining dealer invoice price information for new cars from consumer magazines or fair market values for used cars from publications like *Kelley Blue Book*. However, even with this information, dealers had plenty of tactics to employ to increase their profits. For example, dealers used financing, warranty sales, and trade-in prices to supplement their income. By the time customers drove away in their new automobiles, they were exhausted and had no idea of whether the price paid was fair. Such interaction at the dealership was particularly puzzling since the dealers made most of their money on new cars from after-sales service and thus it was in their interest to have a happy customer who would continue to return.

The dealers did not serve the auto manufacturers' interests either since customers tended to associate their buying experience with all dealers for that particular manufacturer. Since the dealers provided the only direct contact between the manufacturer and the customer, if a customer had a negative experience it was very hard for the manufacturer to win back loyalty. In an industry where competition was intense and cut-throat, the last thing the manufacturers could afford was to lose a customer despite having a good product. Essentially, the dealer channel victimized the customers while serving the manufacturers poorly. Some auto manufacturers, notably GM with its Saturn line, recognized the extent of the problem and tried to fix it by advertising friendly dealerships with no-haggle pricing. Yet, by the nineties, consumers were fed up. In one survey, 80% of consumers said that minimizing contact with salespeople was very important to their satisfaction. In addition, there was demand for more information about automobiles that was both reliable and user-friendly.

The dealer channel was in trouble by 1998. In addition to the above problems, the total number of dealers had decreased from more than 35,000 a decade ago to the current level of 23,000. Also troubling for traditional dealers was the rise of alternative distribution channels like auto superstores (e.g., CarMax, AutoNation, and Drivers Mart). These were gaining popularity by offering customers what they wanted—no-haggle pricing, quality after-sales service, and a nonthreatening shopping experience.

Online Car Buying Services

Online car buying services were well suited to meet the emerging demands of consumers through an alternate channel which met most of the customer's car buying needs. Online services provided a wealth of information and minimized the hassles of automobile purchasing. A typical Web-based purchase experience began with the customer going to the Web site of one of the online car buying services, which provided links to multiple sources of online data (*Consumer Reports, Kelley Blue Book, Edmunds* etc.) where the customer could perform his or her research very quickly. When a customer requested a dealer referral for a specific car, the online service forwarded the customer's contact information to a network dealer. The dealer was then supposed to call the customer within 24 hours with a price. This price was not negotiable since most online car buying services forbade their dealers from haggling on price. Most online

---

[2]Based on customer interviews.

car buying services also sold insurance, financing, and service packages with the cars and thus provided "everything except a way to kick the tires."[3]

The proliferation of personal computers and the increase in overall online service utilization resulted in steady growth for online car buying services. FIND/SVP estimated that the number of Web users interested in accessing car information jumped from 5.0 to 13.2 million between 1995 and 1996.[4] JD Power estimated that 16% of new car buyers used online services in 1996 and predicted that the percentage would rise to 66% by 2000.[5]

On the dealer side, online car buying services were also gaining popularity. Approximately 5,000 total dealers subscribed to one or more online car buying services in 1997, up from at most 2,000 in 1996. Dealers were searching for less expensive methods of advertising cars and new ways for improving customers' perceptions of the sales process. This contributed to the continued increase in online investment. In 1997, about half of the nation's dealers had their own Web sites, and it was projected that another 20% would add sites within the next half year.[6]

CarPoint's Value Proposition

CarPoint's mission was to own the largest share of the Internet auto and auto-related transactions by radically improving the consumer and merchant experience in the automotive category. The idea was to capitalize on the two trends mentioned earlier—consumer dissatisfaction with the automotive purchase process and the rapid proliferation of the Internet as a medium for retail transactions. According to the CarPoint Web site:

> The CarPoint formula is simple: By bringing the efficiency of the Internet to the car buying process, CarPoint saves time, money and hassle for consumers and dealers.

> Dealers want to participate in the Buying Service because CarPoint customers know exactly what they want to buy and demand a quick and streamlined purchase process. This reduces sales costs to the deal-

er and results in savings that go back to the buyer in the form of lower prices.

Thus, CarPoint presented a compelling value proposition to both its customers—the car shoppers and the dealers.

Shoppers

> *It was very, very simple, a pleasurable experience. It took all the game playing out of buying a car.*
> —Rhona Pearl
> Online Car Buyer[7]

For the shoppers, CarPoint provided a no-hassle, no-intimidation buying service with competitive prices. It minimized contact with dealers and helped generate competitive prices with a minimum investment of time. Not all car shoppers valued the same conveniences equally and CarPoint attempted to cater to individual needs based on its customer research.

Dealers

> *We are getting a different type of customer from CarPoint than we would have gotten otherwise. The customer is more educated. . . . But, I don't think that it has helped short term. I think long-term—six months to a year down the road—is where we're looking for tangible results.*
> —Helena Doyle
> Net Manager, Herb Chambers Honda

> *It has increased our business 40% . . . [It is a] hard process because the consumer is very educated. They know just about everything about the car. They know what they want to spend. They tell you what they want to spend. And you want to be the most competitive person around. . . . [It is] very satisfying for both sides . . . we are getting all these customers that are ready to buy and sometimes they are pre-approved with credit.*
> —Auto-By-Tel Dealer

For the dealers, CarPoint provided a way to reach out to consumers with attractive demographics in a less expensive way than traditional advertising. Since the Internet was currently in an early adopter stage, the average online shopper had very attractive demographics. The ubiquitous nature of the Internet also led shoppers to deals outside their geographic area. Finally, CarPoint gave the dealers an opportunity to win back consumers

---

[3] *Business Week* (March 3, 1998) article "Downloading Their Dream Cars."
[4] Adapted from CarPoint Internal Strategic Presentation, 1998.
[5] Ibid.
[6] Ibid.
[7] Quoted in *Business Week* (March 3, 1998) article "Downloading Their Dream Cars."

who were shopping at the emerging competition—like a car superstore or a no-haggle price dealership.

CarPoint's goal was to generate a car sale for every $100 that the dealer invested. Exhibit 4 shows the dealer profits generated by selling through CarPoint. A comparison with Exhibit 3 shows that selling new cars through CarPoint gave the dealers a chance to dramatically improve their profitability.

Target Customers

Shoppers

This is not a money thing with people. What I am finding with CarPoint clients is this is not about saving $100 (although some of them are). This is about getting [a car] the easiest way possible. This is about a phobia of going into a dealership and having to negotiate and walking out wondering if you've done well enough. This is a time thing and an aggravation thing. I can wrap up the whole thing over the phone in an hour . . . People are not willing to spend that hour sitting in a dealership haggling. This is not about saving $100.
—CarPoint Dealer

In the winter of 1996–1997, CarPoint commissioned JD Power's research arm to conduct a survey in order to help determine CarPoint's target consumer. The survey of about 3,000 computer/Internet users led to the identification of nine customer segments, four of which showed high levels of interest in the CarPoint concept and products/services it intended to provide. These segments represented 41% of all online users. The breakdown was as follows:

Primary Targets

- Intimidated by the process: 10% of users
- Information Seekers: 10%

Secondary Targets

- Price is only one factor: 14%
- Dissatisfied with the process: 7%

Of the remaining 59% of potential users, most exhibited very strong dealership or manufacturer loyalties and were unlikely to use CarPoint. There were some strong underlying characteristics driving customer behavior as outlined in Exhibit 5. Detailed information on each of the four target customer segments is given in Exhibit 6. With an increase in the adoption of the Internet, the customer base was starting to broaden, which brought its own share of problems, as a CarPoint dealer attested:

> The demographics are switching. They are sliding a little bit. I am starting to get the people that I will lose if I can't save them a dollar.

Dealers

CarPoint partnered with Reynolds & Reynolds (R&R)—a supplier of dealer information systems with a huge existing dealer base and a big sales force—to gain scale to reach dealers. Since shoppers preferred big dealers with larger selections, rankings published by manufacturers (CSI rankings) were used to identify the high-quality, big dealers. However, many of the biggest dealerships had already signed up with competitors. In the new areas, the largest dealers with high CSI rankings were targeted by CarPoint.

A dealer was not signed up until there were at least 30 leads in their area.[8] Unlike its competition, CarPoint dealers were not forbidden from signing up with multiple online services since this gave the dealer a chance to try out the service in a low risk environment. CarPoint did offer an added incentive to its dealers by not signing up competing dealers within a certain geographic area until the lead volume built up enough to justify such a move. The dealers were also expected to demonstrate their commitment to this service by appointing at least one dedicated CarPoint person to follow up with Internet generated leads. This person, along with the manager, was also required to attend a one-two day training session which was designed by CarPoint but delivered by R&R. This session provided training in managing Internet leads, increasing close rates, etc. R&R representatives followed up with calls every week for the first month to gauge the dealer's progress and comfort with the new service.

Products and Services

The CarPoint team's strategy for success in this business was clear technological leadership. Their bet was that providing better software solutions to both the shoppers

---

[8]CarPoint determined this number by keeping track of the leads from a particular area that had to be fulfilled by a dealer from outside that area.

and the dealers was the way to success. In order to cater to the needs of the customer segments identified above, CarPoint provided a suite of technologically superior products and services.

At the top level, CarPoint provided two services—a new car buying service and used car classifieds. Exhibit 7 gives an overview of the strategy CarPoint intended to follow to become the leading player for both of these services.

Exhibit 8 explains how the new car buying process works at CarPoint while Exhibit 9 shows the new car purchase request entry screen. Exhibit 10 shows a sample order acknowledgment e-mail that was received by one of the case writers after a purchase request was submitted. The speed with which the dealer responded to a request for a price quote had been shown to have a strong correlation with the close rate. The close rates for dealer response within one, two, and three days were 35%, 25%, and 8% respectively. According to Simons:

> The biggest challenge that dealers face with all these Internet buying services is getting back to the user within 24 hours. Over three days the close rate goes down dramatically.

Since it was in CarPoint's interest to increase the close rates for the dealers, "7 Performance Requirements" were established that dealers had to meet to remain a member of CarPoint (Exhibit 11). In the case of one dealer, the close rate went from 0% to 30% once the performance requirements were adopted. In order to ensure that the dealers were adhering to the requirements, CarPoint representatives contacted the customer by e-mail 48 hours after the referral to check if they had been contacted by the dealer. If not, the dealer was immediately called upon to give an explanation for non-performance. In addition, CarPoint representatives called 600–800 users each month to collect feedback on their new car buying experience with CarPoint. If there were more than 3 complaints about a dealership, it was replaced with one who was better able to meet CarPoint's requirements. Most of the dealers considered the performance requirements basic and easily attainable.

Used car classifieds were different from the new car buying service in that customers preferred to see the car before expressing an interest in purchasing it. Also, these shoppers typically wanted to consider several different used models before focusing on a particular vehicle. Simons:

> It is really hard to decide that you want a particular '93 Acura until you have had a chance to go to the

dealer and see it and know what kind of dents it has and what the interior looks like and whether the baby threw up in the back seat.

Since most shoppers would not fill out the referral request forms without seeing the cars, there was currently no good way to show the dealer measurable results for their classified ads. Defining a strong value proposition in this arena for both the dealer and the shopper was one of the future challenges for Rosenblatt and the CarPoint team.

CarPoint also had a portfolio of products to support the above services. First of all, it was important that the Web interface itself had the right balance of ease-of-use and functionality. Second, the site provided tools for a superior research process (e.g., two-car Compare, Auto-Pricer, etc.) and integration of key content (e.g., *Kelley Blue Book*, Crash Test Ratings, Car Reviews, and links to dealer Web pages). Finally, CarPoint planned to offer convenient ownership services—like membership discounts, evaluation tools (e.g., insurance), roadside & tow services, and hotel reservations. CarPoint was trying to create additional revenue streams with these new products and services in addition to building customer retention. Rich Glew stated:

> The main reason [for these services] is to build consumer retention, get repeat traffic to our site. People on the Web purchase cars 30% more frequently than the average person, but this will shrink as the Web begins to reflect the more typical American. Even with that 30% spike in buying frequency by Web users, people don't buy cars that often—our site tends to be used within a few weeks or even a few days prior to purchase. It's hard for us to get people to come back to the site—in general a strategic objective of ours is to get people to come back post-purchase, which could also be looked at as in-between purchases. Staying on peoples' brains during that interval is an important challenge.

In contrast with its competition, CarPoint had so far made the explicit decision to stay away from financing services due to the conflict it represented with the dealers. In fact, CarPoint hoped to leverage Microsoft's expertise at software development to forge even closer relationships with the dealers by designing software to integrate their Web sites with CarPoint services like service scheduling. One future product—code-named DealerPoint—was designed as a set of Web-based dealer tools that would be password-protected and would enable dealers to go into CarPoint and perform a variety of functions, such as using advertising templates to fine-tune banner ads, performing more specific marketing of used vehicles and providing some differentiation (pop-up ads, better descriptions, unique photos, etc.). Dealer-Point would also enable dealers to receive and act on new car buying leads electronically.

CarPoint management emphasized that they intended to take full advantage of Microsoft's biggest asset—excellent software development skills. While the current products were well received and ahead of the competition, they believed that they could do more.

Promotion

> *We always try to push the Microsoft name because it has a lot of value attached to it. I am not as concerned about "CarPoint" except that it is what you need to type in to get to our Web site.*
> —Alex Simons

The majority of advertising for CarPoint was done through alliances with search engines (Yahoo, Excite, WebCrawler, and HotBot) and other automotive sites (*Kelley Blue Book*, AutoSite). Consistent with the corporate strategy at Microsoft of promoting the Microsoft brand name, 20% of CarPoint's marketing budget was allocated to public relations; that was the second largest portion of the advertising budget. Next came banner advertising on the Internet. Thus far CarPoint had done almost no traditional advertising (e.g., print, radio and TV). As part of its promotional efforts, CarPoint had paid $1.2 million for preferred placement in WebCrawler, $100k for preferred placement on HotBot, had bartered for preferred placement on Yahoo, and had alliances with *Kelley Blue Book* and AutoSite.

By some accounts this strategy was working well. One dealer decided to go with CarPoint because:

> . . . if Microsoft is a player it's going to be okay. Anything that Bill Gates gets his fingers into he does very well with.

Another dealer decided to go with Microsoft because "Microsoft owns the world" and "whatever they do has to be the best." However, this dealer decided to switch to Auto-By-Tel after four months with CarPoint stating:

> Going with Microsoft was a mistake. There was no tech support, a paucity of leads with only 18 last month, and a disappointing level and location of advertising. Microsoft advertises only on the net

and they won't expand. Auto-By-Tel is on TV and Radio . . . when I saw an ad during March Madness [for Auto-By-Tel], that's when I knew I should switch.

Simons emphasized that being a Microsoft property was a big advantage and that the advertising spending numbers did not capture the full effect of this advantage. As a Microsoft property, CarPoint enjoyed exclusive placement on the Microsoft Network home page—msn.com—the 9th largest Web site in the world, and Microsoft.com, the third largest site, in addition to receiving free placement on all other Microsoft Web properties. CarPoint also expected to receive placement on Microsoft's upcoming search engine, Microsoft Start.

Business Model

CarPoint was late to enter the transaction part of the online car buying business. To offset this disadvantage, and in order to rapidly form a dealer network without having to build their own sales force, CarPoint decided to partner with Reynolds & Reynolds (R&R). R&R was an information management company with a strong reputation in the automotive market. R&R, in fact, claimed that they had a presence in over 90 percent of the automotive retailers in North America.[9] CarPoint formed a partnership with R&R wherein R&R would use their 550-person sales force and existing relationships to sign up dealers for CarPoint's network. In return, R&R received 30% of the revenues from dealer subscription fees. This arrangement allowed CarPoint to sign up dealers rapidly and enhanced their ability to electronically tie into dealers' information systems. For example, they used R&R's expertise in the dealers' inventory systems to directly upload car availability information to their Web site. CarPoint's competitors on the other hand relied on dealers to either manually enter information onto their Web site or to fax in inventory data.

While the relationship with R&R definitely had some benefits, it was not without risk. Using a third party's sales force limited CarPoint's ability to directly control the selling process, sales force incentives and compensation, and the message conveyed to customers. CarPoint was also somewhat tied to R&R because CarPoint had entered into some long-term contractual commitments. They traded some of their flexibility and control for speed and access.

---

[9]R&R brochure.

CarPoint had four main sources of revenue—new car sales, used car sales, advertising, and memberships. For new and used car sales, CarPoint followed a subscription model wherein dealers paid a monthly fee. This fee was targeted to be approximately $400/month for a used car dealer and $1,000/month for a new car dealer franchise, on average.[10] Auto-By-Tel charged $750–2,500/month for a used car dealer and $500–1,500/month plus a $4,000 annual fee for a new car dealer. One of CarPoint's competitors, Autoweb.com, was experimenting with transaction based fees, but the CarPoint team decided to go with a flat fee approach for a couple of reasons. First, a subscription model involved less headaches with dealer management. Second, dealers preferred the subscription model because it looked more like advertising wherein the dealers were replacing part of their advertising budget with the CarPoint fees. Simons:

> It is much easier to do a flat fee . . . (it) avoids the huge tracking and management nightmare. There is also less uncertainty for our revenue.
>
> Overall dealers are very resistant to anything that looks like you're getting a percentage or piece of their sales action.

Display advertising on the CarPoint site was another potential source of revenue. Since CarPoint utilized R&R for all of its dealer sales, it decided to focus primarily on the auto manufacturers for its advertising revenue. Advertising by auto manufacturers was a huge market, with $3.7 billion spent in 1995 alone. This roughly translated in $250 per vehicle sold. GM, Chrysler, and Ford were all among the top-10 U.S. advertisers. There was a sense of urgency among the auto manufacturers as they recognized the potential of the Internet. CarPoint intended to charge its advertisers competitive rates of around $30 CPM.[11] CarPoint also intended to have a secondary focus on large national advertisers while leaving the dealers and local advertisers alone. Among its competitors, Auto-By-Tel did not have any display advertising while Autoweb.com had major accounts with auto manufacturers like Saturn and Volvo.

Finally, the introduction of membership based services mentioned earlier was another potential source of revenue. CarPoint planned to charge members a fee of $59/year and was considering strategic alliances which would increase its membership base.

The CarPoint team's goal was to generate revenue of $74 million by FY01. This would be achieved by driving 162,000 new car referrals per month (22% of e-channel; 4% of total U.S. new car market), enlisting 4,250 new car franchises, charging a $1,500 average monthly fee per franchise; and signing up 246,000 (consumer) members at $59/year. Exhibit 12 details the revenue growth and market share projections for CarPoint including a breakdown by the above revenue driver streams.

Competition : Online Car Buying Services

The Number One car sales site . . . Auto-By-Tel generates more business than its two closest competitors—Microsoft's CarPoint and CUC's AutoVantage—combined.[12]
—Wired.com, January 1998

CarPoint faced a number of hurdles as it set off on its goal of becoming the number one or two car buying service site by 1999. It had lagged behind some of its competitors in launching its site and, while traffic to its site had picked up, it was still behind in the number of dealers it had signed up. CarPoint faced competition from three major on-line car buying services: Auto-By-Tel, Autoweb.com, and CUC AutoVantage. While the CarPoint team acknowledged that competition was intense, they were confident that they would become one of the leading players. They felt that they had a good understanding of the drivers of customer and dealer satisfaction in this business. The CarPoint team believed that it was very important to generate a good number of leads for each dealer since this would ultimately affect the customer service that the dealers provided to the shoppers. Simons described this chain effect:

> One legit measure to look at is the number of leads per signed dealer. This gives a very good indicator of the total value being delivered to a dealer. In turn, this is a very strong indicator of the likelihood for a dealer to renew next year, the key variable that all of us live off. It also means that you as a service have more influence with that dealer and can get them to modify their process to your service better.

The CarPoint team was so confident of establishing itself as one of the top three players that it had already started

---

[10]The exact fee varied between dealers and franchises depending upon the size of the market, size of the dealer, etc.

[11]Cost per thousand impressions. For example, if an ad on a CarPoint page cost $1 and was seen by 1,000 unique users, the CPM was $1.

[12]The CarPoint team disputed the data behind this quote. According to their data, Auto-By-Tel was slightly less than twice as big as CarPoint in terms of dealer referral volume and was not as big as CarPoint and AutoVantage combined.

to focus on how it would become the dominant player beyond that stage. Their confidence was supported by the superior quality of their Web site and of the buying experience. Once a customer selected a car, for example, CarPoint's Web site would display all the options that were standard with that particular model and series.

Auto-By-Tel (ABT) www.autobytel.com

Auto-By-Tel (ABT) was the industry leader and CarPoint's most formidable competitor. ABT had already established itself as a leading brand for on-line car buying services and was now focusing on consolidating that position through its channel strategy, advertising, and international growth. In contrast with CarPoint's strategy of using the R&R sales force, ABT had established its own direct sales force to contact dealers and to recruit them to be part of their dealer network.

ABT was the only automotive buying service to require its dealers to sign agreements which restricted them from subscribing to other automotive buying services. In exchange for this commitment from dealers, ABT provided dealers exclusive territories and made investments in initiatives such as a Dealer Real-time System and ABT University to increase dealer adherence to sales practices and retention. With 2,600 paying dealer franchises,[13] ABT was in a strong position with the largest exclusive dealer network (Exhibit 13).

ABT continued to invest in building its brand name by spending over $10 million in marketing and advertising in 1997, as opposed to $2 million for CarPoint. In 1998, this expenditure was expected to increase to $20 million for ABT and $5 million for CarPoint. As part of their marketing effort, ABT formed alliances with search engines and paid $7 million for a three-year exclusive with Excite. ABT also built alliances with other content sites like *Edmunds* and *Kelley Blue Book* to generate traffic, and with AIG and Chase/GE Capital to provide automobile insurance and financing. ABT had a strong relationship with Classifieds 2000 and was Classifieds 2000's main provider of dealer listings. This ability to distribute through one of the Internet's most frequented sites built ABT's brand and dealer appeal. With these alliances and investments it appeared that ABT would continue to be a strong brand in this market and a serious rival for CarPoint.

In order to extend its lead in the U.S. into the international market, ABT had already signed up 100 dealers in Canada and had announced its European roll-out for 1998. Inchcape, a $9 billion global distribution company and a new ABT investor in 1997, was expected to facilitate international expansion. With $13 million of additional financing in 1997, ABT appeared to have the financing and was making the investments that would continue to make it a serious competitor for CarPoint.

Auto Web www.autoweb.com

Auto Web was the number two player in the Internet automotive marketing services business in terms of revenue and the number three player when measured in terms of dealer franchises and user volume. It had grown rapidly and established itself as a major player in the industry by offering a wide array of services through its channels. These services included digital pictures of cars, Web sites for dealers, and free sites with the first year's fee. Auto Web was also testing a new pricing strategy (as of February 1998) where they charged dealers $25 per customer referral. Their dealer network increased from 200 paying franchises in the fourth quarter of 1996 to 1,350 in the fourth quarter of 1997.

Autoweb.com was making investments and taking actions to develop their brand. Although their investment in advertising and marketing was not as high as ABT's $10 million, their $3.5 million budget exceeded CarPoint's investment. Auto Web was expected to stay in the number two position in terms of advertising and marketing spending with their budget of $10 million in 1998. They were also following ABT's lead on the international front and had signed up 61 dealers in Canada.

CUC AutoVantage www.autovantage.com

CUC AutoVantage was the number three player in the Internet automotive marketing services business in terms of revenue. AutoVantage was part of the software division of Cendant, the largest membership services company in the world with more than 66.5 million members and more than 20 consumer-service programs such as Travelers Advantage®, Shoppers Advantage®, Entertainment®, and netMarket®. Cendant was the result of a merger between CUC International, a leading provider of membership-based discount services, and HFS, the world's top hospitality franchiser. Cendant cross-marketed to CUC's and HFS' worldwide clientele.

---

[13]*Business Week* (March 3, 1998) article "Downloading Their Dream Cars."

HFS' real estate (Century 21, Coldwell Banker), relocation, and mortgage services complemented CUC's operations that provided home improvement referrals and other benefits (e.g., mail coupons) to people who had moved. Cendant also enjoyed synergies in travel and hospitality (HFS owned Days Inn, Howard Johnson, Ramada, and Avis brands), vehicle fleet management, and financial services.

AutoVantage's strategy was to leverage Cendant's membership base to acquire customers for online car buying and to invest heavily in customer service. CUC had an existing base of 3 million loyal members and had deep pockets to invest in both online and off-line promotions. They used credit card private label partners as the primary channel for customer acquisition. They also had a strong customer value proposition with a low risk trial membership and a broad range of services. The combination of these strategies had allowed their monthly referral rate to increase to 39,000 per month, second only to ABT.

On the dealer acquisition side, AutoVantage was the number two player with 1,600 franchise dealers.[14] They had followed a nonexclusive dealer network strategy, like CarPoint and Autoweb.com, and used a telesales organization to sign dealers. They also used the telesales organization as the primary means of ensuring quality throughout the dealer organization.

Competition: Other Players

Online car buying services were by no means the only competition facing CarPoint. The entire online car buying industry had to face competition from Internet classified sites like Classifieds 2000; search engines like Excite and Infoseek; content sites like *Edmunds*, *Kelley Blue Book*, and *Consumer Reports*; and from traditional mediums like newspapers. In addition, car superstores and auto manufacturers were also thinking of entering the field.

Classifieds 2000
www.classifieds2000.com[15]

Classifieds 2000's goal was to build the largest classifieds database on the Internet and to develop the most extensive affiliate (distribution) network for that database.

Classifieds 2000 provided listings through its own Web site as well as through its affiliate network which allowed Classifieds 2000 to sell its listings to other sites which had created their own classifieds sections. They did not charge end-users for access to the service and instead generated revenue through advertising and through its affiliate network. Unlike CarPoint, however, they did not develop a dealer franchise network and did not develop a referral system by which customers would be routed to the appropriate dealer in their local area.

They were successful in achieving their goals and built a massive classifieds database with $100 billion in goods and services advertised weekly in the automotive, real estate, employment, personal, and computer categories. They built an extensive distribution network with over 115 affiliate Web sites, providing the greatest distribution of any classifieds database. These affiliates included seven of the top search engines, 12 of the top 20 high traffic Web sites, and CBS affiliates online. And finally, they had turned their own Classifieds 2000 Web site into an established Internet brand.

Search Engines

Search engines posed a long-term challenge to many vertical category sites such as travel, music, automotive, books, etc. They had high customer volume, had repeat customer usage, and were the point of entry—all of which allowed them to maintain superior Internet brands. Search engines took advantage of their position by developing category killer areas on their Web sites like automotive sections. With private labeling of their automotive service components they could also become a major consumer auto destination and pull traffic away from other car buying services.

Search Engines had followed a strategy of outsourcing content and services to keep internal operating costs down. All major search engines except Yahoo (*www.yahoo.com*) were Classifieds 2000 affiliates, which gave them access to Classifieds 2000's massive database. While this strategy did allow them to keep their maintenance costs down, there was little integration between content and decision making support. Search engines were dependent on their alliance partners to provide value to the customer, and there were some questions about whether customers would continue to return to the search engine's automotive section if all the value was in the partner's sites. However, as Excite's purchase of Classifieds 2000 indicated, the search engines had every intention of competing in this area.

---

[14]AutoVantage had originally offered their service to their dealers for free (they lived off the membership revenue from users) and had been able to move only around 600 of their dealers to paying for the service.
[15]Acquired in April 1998 by Excite, Inc.

Content Sites

Content sites like *Edmunds (www.edmunds.com), Kelley Blue Book (www.kbb.com)*, and *Consumer Reports (www.consumerreports.com)* extended their established brands in consumer automotive information to the online audience. They provided hard-hitting pricing and performance data and reviews. Their well-established consumer brands were very popular sources of information, and they were able to successfully leverage this to generate high traffic to their sites. They then directed this highly targeted user base through profitable advertising links to buying services, insurance companies, and financing companies. They did not, however, have any vehicle listings, dealer directories, or other integrated purchase support.

Newspapers

Newspapers enhanced their advertising revenues and consumer services by providing online vehicle listings and information on sites like Cars.com. They leveraged their existing infrastructure and content to protect their core business from the online threat. They had the advantage of already having large automotive classifieds listings and were a recognized source for vehicle information. They were also able to leverage their local sales force to call on dealerships with whom they already had long-term relationships. They did not, however, have electronic access to dealer inventories, which increased the cost of data collection, and they did not have decision making support tied to their listings. Finally, they typically had not invested heavily in the technology on their Web sites, which largely consisted of print content re-purposed in HTML pages.

Auto Manufacturers[16]

For the first time, the customer is going to control the retail system.
—Robert J. Eaton
Chairman, Chrysler Corporation

Even the auto manufacturers were becoming Net-savvy. Both Chrysler and GM were experimenting with their own Web site which linked online shoppers to dealers in a handful of regions. Chrysler was contemplating a plan to go nationwide. Other car makers, including Ford and some Japanese companies, were less aggressive with their Web sites, offering little more than electronic brochures with prices, specs, and a list of local dealers. The car makers were constrained by the fear of a dealer backlash if they got involved in the business of telling shoppers where to get the best price.

Car Superstores

Car superstores were another potential source of competition for CarPoint. These superstores housed large inventories of cars and made the car buying process simpler and more convenient. The largest chain, AutoNation/Republic, had a total of nearly 300 dealerships in the United States. As well as seeing the competitive threat, the CarPoint team saw partnership potential with the superstores. Simons:

> Regarding Superstores, they could turn out to be our best partners or biggest competitors. In terms of partners, they offer the kind of very high quality customer service we need, the no-haggle service our customers want, and they are generally very high-tech/leading edge. However, they could also be competitors if they decided to launch their own services.

Current Business Status

CarPoint had done extremely well in the past year. According to Media Metrix, an authoritative source of Internet traffic ratings, CarPoint was the "Fastest Growing Site in Category." By February 1998, it had signed up 1,300 new car franchises. By January 1998, CarPoint had 1 million unique users which led to a #1 rating for automotive sites in frequency and a #3 rating in reach. Also, according to Media Metrix,[17] CarPoint was the 7th fastest growing site on the Internet.

CarPoint's new car referral rate in January was 3%, which generated 30,000 referrals and was growing at 14% per month. Their dealer close rates were 34% for less than 24-hour response and 18% overall. In February 1998, CarPoint was driving $3.2 million in car sales per day.

---

[16]Sourced from *Business Week* article "Downloading Their Dream Cars."
[17]Report dated 4 November, 1997.

Looking to the Future

We've done really well, but there is a bunch of stuff that we need to do to pull ahead of the competition.
—Gideon Rosenblatt

I know the way to get the market to parity. I am looking for the way to go beyond that point. To get to that point isn't really terribly hard; first we need to get our conversion rate up. I expect that we will have that solved in eight weeks.
—Alex Simons

Rosenblatt and his team had several initiatives in place for the future, including a revamp of dealer training, more professional management of the dealer channel, and the release of new products. The upcoming launch of MS Start (Microsoft's Internet "portal" site), Rosenblatt felt, would provide another decisive source of competitive advantage.

> It is going to get very expensive to distribute your service. It is going to be very expensive for Auto-By-Tel to advertise on Yahoo and other places because they are going to take more and more money over time.

Rosenblatt wondered if these initiatives would prove to be enough to become the dominant player among online car services.

Exhibit 1 Automotive Market (in billions of dollars)[a]

	Car Sales
Finance charges	58
New vehicle purchase	260
Used vehicle purchase	300
Total	618

[a]from Microsoft internal documents

	After-market
Parts/supplies	87
Insurance	134
Gas/oil	141
Service/maintenance	177
Total	539

[a]from Microsoft internal documents

Exhibit 2 Vehicle Distribution[a]

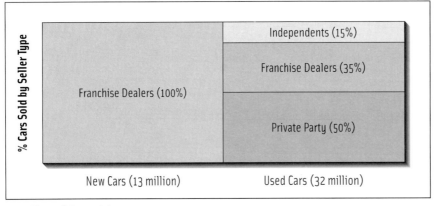

[a]from Microsoft internal documents

Exhibit 3 Franchise Dealer Statistics[a]

	New Cars	Used Cars
Average price/vehicle	$22,000	$12,000
Average gross profit	0–1%	10%
Average marketing expenditure per car sold	$400	$200[b]

[a]from Microsoft internal documents
[b]estimated

Exhibit 4 Dealer Value

Dealer Value—New Cars	Estimated FY 99
Avg. franchise fee	$ 1,000
Leads/franchise	25
Cost/lead	$ 40
Close rate	20%
Cars sold	5
Cost per car sold	$ 200
Profit per CarPoint sale	$ 500
Dealer profit from CarPoint	$ 1,500

Dealer Value—Used Cars	Estimated FY 99
Avg. franchise fee	$ 200
Leads/franchise	30
Cost/lead	$ 7
Close rate	15%
Cars sold	4.5
Cost per car sold	$ 44
Profit per CarPoint sale	$1,300
Dealer profit from CarPoint	$5,650

Source: Microsoft

Exhibit 5 Dominant Customer Characteristics

Brand loyalty

While the degrees differ, all segments have high auto manufacturer brand loyalty. Over 50% indicate they have purchased from the same manufacturer more than once, and over 60% agree with the statement "When I find a brand I like, I generally stick with it."

Price is important

No big surprise when the average automobile sells for $22,000. These segments have different levels of price sensitivity, but they all agree that "Price is one of the most important factors in determining which vehicle I will purchase." Obviously, knowing the general price range for a car is an important piece of information when deciding what to purchase. And everyone wants to get a good deal on the next car they purchase (90%+).

However, this should not be misinterpreted to mean that all segments care about "insider price information" or will go to lengths to find out what the dealer invoice is. Some users won't.

It would be nice to avoid pushy salesman

Most people want to avoid the pushy salespeople if they can (75%+). 50% feel buying a vehicle would be much easier and more enjoyable without the salesperson.

It is important to analyze my finances before I purchase

Over 80% of these folks agree with the statement "I analyze my finances to determine how much I can afford to spend."

I consider both new and used cars.

Over 60% of the target users say they will consider new and used cars when they make their next automobile purchase.

I care about my car's looks and appearance.

I want a vehicle that will last a long time.

I want a vehicle with excellent handling/performance.

I want a vehicle that best meets my needs.

80%+ of the target users agree with these statements.

Source: Microsoft

Exhibit 6 Target Customer Demographics & Characteristics

Primary Targets
Intimidated by the process

This group is unanimous in its dislike for the current automobile purchasing process. They feel like they don't know which car to buy, how to tell if they got a good price, or how to find a dealer they can trust. They also respond very positively to the possibility of avoiding the salesperson or dealership altogether.

Demographics

Average age:	41
Sex:	48% male/52% female
House Income:	$72,000 annually
Education	55% have a college degree or higher
Marital Status:	70% married, 19% single, 11% other

Defining Characteristics

- Feel that the process for purchasing a car today sucks
  1. 49% feel the vehicle buying process is "very intimidating."
  2. 53% are unsatisfied with their current dealer experience.
  3. Only 3% are satisfied with their ability to find a dealership they are comfortable with.
  4. Only 15% feel they can determine if they got a good deal on their last car.
  5. Only 11% feel they are able to determine which vehicle will best meet their needs.
  6. 62% would like to purchase directly from the manufacturer with no dealer involvement.

- Interested in using third party information when purchasing a car
  7. 74% are interested in Blue Book pricing.
  8. 75% want "insider pricing information."
  9. 66% want quality/durability/reliability information.
  10. 63% want articles and reviews on different vehicles.
  11. 60% want satisfaction ratings for local dealerships.

Media Use

They read:
- Consumer magazines like *Consumer Reports* (60%)
- Computer magazines (61%)
- News magazines (55%)
- Household themes magazines (54%)

They don't read:
- Outdoor magazines (20%)
- Adult magazines (16%)
- Men's magazines (12%)

Sentiments

"I would like to avoid pushy salespeople" (89%)

"It is important to me to get a good deal" (96%)

"The vehicle buying process is very intimidating" (49%)

"Buying a vehicle would be much easier and more enjoyable without a salesperson" (68%)

Exhibit 6 Target Customer Demographics & Characteristics (continued)

Information seekers (IS)

The name says it all about this segment. Users in this segment are heavy researchers. They want to know as much information as possible before they buy an automobile. They are the most likely to be attracted to CarPoint.

Demographics

Average age:	38 (25% are under 30)
Sex:	52% male/48% female
House Income:	$66,000 annually
Education:	57% have a college degree or higher
Marital Status:	67% married, 23% single, 10% other

Defining Characteristics

- Place high importance on third party information when preparing to purchase a car
    1. 60% read "consumer guide" magazines.
    2. 66% talk to owners of the cars they are considering.
    3. 66% read the classified section of their newspapers.
    4. 72% say that getting quality/durability/reliability information is extremely important.
    5. 73% say that getting reviews/articles is extremely important.
    6. 74% want "insider pricing information."
    7. 81% say that getting Blue Book pricing is extremely important .

- Enthusiastic computer users
    8. 77% view the Internet as a critical information source.
    9. 62% already use the Internet to obtain product prices and information.

- Much more likely to consider both new and used when purchasing a car (70%)

Media Use

They read:
- Consumer magazines like *Consumer Reports* (71%)
- Computer magazines (65%)
- News magazines (64%)

They don't read:
- Outdoor magazines (25%)
- Adult magazines (23%)
- Men's magazines (13%)

Sentiments

"I like to research before buying a high priced item" (83%)

"I shop for the lowest price before I buy something" (66%)

"I never shop until I know the average purchase price" (79%)

"I always get the dealer's invoice before going to the dealer" (76%)

Exhibit 6 Target Customer Demographics & Characteristics (continued)

Secondary Targets
"Price is only one factor" buyers

This segment is difficult to clearly define. In some ways, they are similar to the IS segment. They think it is important to gather good information prior to purchasing and are enthusiastic computer/Internet users. However, they are older and do not place as high an importance on information.

Users in this segment are better off financially than the other segments, and thus are less urgently concerned with pricing information or "getting the best price." They still want to get a good deal on their next car, but it's not a pressing issue. It is also interesting to note that they are more satisfied with the current process than the other three segments.

Demographics

Average age:	44
Sex:	63% male/37% female
House Income:	$72,000 annually
Education:	57% have a college degree or higher
Marital Status:	72% married, 18% single, 10% other

Defining Characteristics

- Use third party information when preparing to purchase a car
    1. 47% read "consumer guide" magazines.
    2. 58% read the classified section of their newspapers.
    3. 62% say that getting reviews/articles is extremely important.
    4. 61% say that getting quality/durability/reliability information is extremely important.
    5. 67% say that getting Blue Book pricing is extremely important.

- Respond positively to purchasing with limited involvement
    6. 61% would like to purchase direct from the dealer and have a car delivered to their door.
    7. 36% would consider buying a car through a vehicle locator service.
    8. 17% would consider hiring a vehicle broker.

- Less price concerned
    9. Only 63% rank price as one of the most important factors in their choice of automobiles.

Media Use

They read:
- Consumer magazines like *Consumer Reports* (62%)
- Computer magazines (60%)
- News magazines (61%)
- Business/Money magazines (56%)

They don't read:
- Outdoor magazines (22%)
- Adult magazines (24%)
- Men's magazines (14%)

Exhibit 6 Target Customer Demographics & Characteristics (continued)

Sentiments
"I want to find a model that will best meet my needs" (89%)
"It's important to find a vehicle that will last a long time" (85%)
"I analyze my finances to determine how much I can spend" (83%)
"Overall I'm relatively satisfied with the current vehicle buying process" (50%–60%)

Dissatisfied with the process

This group is similar to the Intimidated group in most ways. Their demographics are the same, and their overall dissatisfaction with the process of buying a car is high.

There are three characteristics that set them apart from the Intimidated, however:

- While they are dissatisfied with the process, only 35% find it intimidating
- They are less concerned with price
  1. Only 50% are interested in "insider pricing information."
  2. Only 14% try to find the Blue Book value before going shopping.
  3. Only 5% try to find the dealer invoice price (vs. 50% overall).

- They are less interested in third party information
  4. Only 47% are interested in articles and reviews on different vehicles.
  5. Only 55% are interested in quality/durability/reliability information.
  6. Only 47% are interested in satisfaction ratings for local dealers.

Source: Microsoft

Exhibit 7 CarPoint Strategy

NEW CAR MARKET
• Deliver superior consumer buying experience via content breadth and integration, and dealer proximity and service (scale)
• **Combine best content aggregation and leading edge technology (Surround Video, DynaSpec) to become consumer destination point of choice for Internet new car buying**
• **Leverage industry partnerships (e.g., R&R) to gain channel access and build superior dealer network (quality, breadth)**
• Provide compelling value proposition for dealers to use CarPoint vs. ABT or others (highest close rates)
• Focus on a quality, no-hassle consumer experience
• Add new dealers as lead volume increases
• Maximize close rates through consumer education, dealer training

USED CAR MARKET
• Build the most robust network of franchise dealers
1. Leverage industry partners to build widest dealer & inventory base
2. **Provide compelling value to using CarPoint vs. traditional media and online alternatives**
• Build dealer brand through Web pages, linking and advertising
• Integrate content with high quality dealer network to become the destination point of choice for Internet used car buying
• Focus on developing scale—consumer selection of vehicles
• Pursue most cost effective listings—acquisition strategy (given quality requirements)

Source: Microsoft

Exhibit 8 New Car Buying Process

Source: Microsoft

Exhibit 9 CarPoint–New Car Purchase Request Entry Screen

Source: Microsoft

Exhibit 10 Order acknowledgment e-mail from CarPoint

Dear CarPoint Customer,

This e-mail is in response to your recent CarPoint Purchase Inquiry for a 1998 BMW Z3 2.8.

Your inquiry number is 313717. Please keep this number available for future reference when contacting CarPoint.

Your inquiry has been sent directly to the following CarPoint Qualified Dealership:

Howie Reske/Ed Hohmann

Herb Chambers Honda BMW Saab

1186 Commonwealth Avenue

Boston, MA 02134

617-731-1700

ehohmann@chamberscars.com

You can expect to receive a call from a CarPoint Qualified
Sales Consultant within two business days. If you have not
heard from the dealer within this time period, or if you
are not satisfied with this New-Car Buying Service, please
send e-mail to newcarbuying@rrauto.com. Please include your
inquiry number, listed above, and all relevant details in your message.

If you prefer, you may speak directly to a New-Car Buying Service representative
by calling 1-800-675-3464 (8:00am to 5:00pm Pacific Time, Monday-Friday). To
ensure quick assistance, please have your inquiry number ready when you call.

Once again, our contact information is:

newcarbuying@rrauto.com

1-800-675-3464

Thank you for choosing CarPoint.

CarPoint http://carpoint.msn.com

Source: Microsoft

Exhibit 11 7 Dealer Performance Requirements

- CERTIFIED and TRAINED sales consultants handle every CarPoint lead.

- Answer all leads within ONE business day.

- Quote the price up front, and the price quoted must be the most competitive price you can give. Customers should not have to haggle.

- Tell the customer the status of the vehicle (whether it is on the lot, needs to be ordered, etc).

- Complete as much of the paperwork and processing as possible prior to the customer's arrival at your dealership.

- Provide and maintain a CarPoint sales process. You will develop your own sales process during the training session.

- 100% service response to all inquiries.

Source: Microsoft

Exhibit 12 Revenue Breakdown and Market Share Projections

	FY98	FY99	FY00	FY01
Revenue (% of total)				
New car	77%	76%	75%	74%
Used car	15	4	3	3
Advertising	7	4	7	9
Membership	0	16	15	14
CarPoint gross revenue	100	100	100	100
% Increase over previous year	—	376	84	65
Market share (new cars)				
Total new cars sold	11,300,000	11,300,000	11,300,000	11,300,000
E-Channel share of U.S. new car sales	3%	6%	12%	18%
E-Channel new car sales	339,000	678,000	1,356,000	2,034,000
CarPoint new car sales	38,184	143,678	281,941	465,368
CarPoint share of E-Channel	11%	21%	21%	23%
CarPoint share of total new car market	0.3%	1.3%	2.5%	4.1%

Source: Microsoft

Exhibit 13 Competitive Overview (Numbers are CY1997)

Competitor Benchmark Table—Calendar Year 1997				
	Auto-By-Tel	**Autoweb.com**	**AutoVantage**	**CarPoint**
Revenue	$20 M	$11 M	$5 M	$600 K
Advertising/marketing spending	$10 M	$3.5 M		$2 M
Number of employees	125	100	25 dedicated (plus cust. support org.)	24 (MS)
Management	11	5		2
Advertising/marketing	8	5		6
Sales & sales support	67	46		550 (R&R)
Development/editorial	19	25		27
Administration	20	19		2
Paying franchise dealers EOY 1997	2600	1350	1600	900
Published monthly fee/ franchise	$500–1500 new (+$4K ann. fee) $750–2500 used	$750–900 new $500–700 used	$500–$700 new N/A used	$1400 new $600 used
Est. actual avg. fee 1997	$833	$1,000	$350	$400 (low due to startup price discounting)
Est. purchase requests/ mo.	50K new 5K used	30K new 4K used	39K new (incl. offline)	30K new 4K used
Est. new sales/ mo.	10K	6K	8K	6K
Financing to date	$37 million	$5 million	NA	NA
Strategic partners	GE Capital, AIG, Inchcape, AutoSite, Edmunds, Excite, InfoSeek, Classifieds 2000, CBS GeoCities, Intellichoice, Chase Manhattan, Key Bank, Triad Financial	Car & Driver, KBB, Bank of America, Yahoo, *USA Today*, and ALLData	Microsoft, Classifieds 2000, Consumer Guides, CarFinance	CUC, R&R, Yahoo, KBB, Bank Rate Monitor, AutoSite (AIC), AIS (reliability data partner)

Source: Microsoft

Business Models

3

BUSINESS MODELS

A business model is comprised of four parts: a value proposition, or value cluster, a market-space offering, a unique and defendable resource system, and a financial model. While each component is considered sequentially here, in reality, while developing their model management teams must respond fluidly to the forces unfolding in the marketplace.

The first step in the articulation of the business model is to specify the **value proposition** or **value cluster**. The value cluster approach argues that the customization capabilities now available to online businesses allow them to offer multiple segments of customers a combination of benefits. The value cluster is composed of three parts: the choice of a target customer segment, a particular focal combination of customer-driven benefits, and the rationale for why this firm and its partners can deliver the value cluster significantly better than the competitors.

Once the value proposition has been defined, the next step is to fully articulate the online product, service, and information marketspace **offering.** The senior management team must complete three sequential tasks: identify the scope of the offering, identify the consumer decision process, and map the marketspace offering (product, services, and information) to the consumer decision process.

The **scope** refers to the breadth of products and services that are offered on the site. A firm can choose to focus on one product category—termed a *category killer* in the offline world—or attempt cross-category dominance. The **consumer decision process** can be divided into three stages: pre-purchase, purchase, and post-purchase processes. **Mapping the offering** to the consumer decision process involves walking the consumer through the entire purchase decision cycle, for example, linking the "purchase stage" with the "shopping cart." Ideally, this decision cycle repeats for each of the product categories included on the site.

The **resource system** shows how a company must align its internal systems (and partners) to deliver the benefits of the value cluster. In particular, the company is concerned with matching these capabilities to deliver customer benefits. The **financial model** for a company follows from the resource system. Three strategic models to consider are revenue models, shareholder value or "differentiation" rationale models, and growth strategies.

The most important message to take from this discussion is the need to base all of these decisions on the forces that are unfolding in the marketplace, with each step fundamentally based around the benefits that matter most to customers. Firms that understand both current and future customer needs are likely to be the long-term winners in their respective industries.

SYNOPSES OF CHAPTER CASES

EGGHEAD.COM

Case Overview

At the end of February 1998, George Orban, the new Chairman and CEO of software retailer Egghead, Inc., closed the remaining 80 locations in what was once a 200-branch retail network. Fierce competition in the industry was largely responsible for the move as Egghead struggled to keep up with better positioned players. Some 800 workers were fired—roughly 80% of all employees—and one of Egghead's two distribution centers was shut down. But while driven from the marketplace by its competitors, the company was not going out of business. Instead it was being reborn. Egghead, renamed Egghead.com, had decided to move its entire operations out of bricks-and-mortar and into bits-and-bytes.

Some aspects of the current landscape were less than favorable for Egghead's future. Shopping habits were going to be tough to change, and Internet access was still only available in a quarter of American households. Meanwhile, the competition was fierce and multiplying exponentially. Egghead moved aggressively to lock-in key distribution partnerships. Perhaps most important for Egghead's future prospects was that software lent itself to online distribution through electronic software distribution (ESD), a technology that was already establishing itself prior to Egghead's move.

Because there were no barriers to entry for new online players such as Egghead, software and hardware prices could be driven down very low, leaving few economic profits. The acceptance of electronic software distribution (ESD) might produce an edge for companies that embraced it, reducing costs associated with production, packaging, and shipping. How would Egghead maximize its position as the first significant software retailer to focus strictly online? How could it capture its share of the growing but increasingly competitive market? Was it partnering in the right places? Could it maintain better margins through adjusting its branding strategy?

Preparation Questions

1. As a potential equity investor in Egghead.com, what reasons do you have for optimism about the company's prospects? What concerns do you have that might prevent you from buying stock in the company?

2. Which competitors are likely to present the greatest threat to Egghead.com's efforts to become a leading online retailer of computer hardware and software?

3. Is a presence in "marketplace" channels (in both computer hardware and software stores and mail order) a help or a hindrance when competing in the "marketspace"?

4. By aggressively signing distribution partnerships with Yahoo! and other websites, Egghead.com is pursuing what Jeff Bezos, CEO of Amazon.com, has called a "Get Big Fast" (GBF) strategy. What are the risks and rewards associated with a GBF strategy? Does such a strategy make sense for Egghead.com? Could Egghead.com profitably pursue a less aggressive strategy?

VIRTUAL VINEYARDS

Case Overview

Virtual Vineyards founders Peter Granoff and Robert Olson opened their online wine shop in January of 1995. By November, they were averaging more than 1500 visitors a day, and revenues were increasing 20% per month. Two keys to the company's success were its understanding of the market and a value-added service that compensated for the lack of traditional taste-testing for consumers. Robert Olson, also known on the website as Propeller Head, recognized that the marketplace offered a niche in wine distribution that was currently not being met. Virtual Vineyards (VV) concluded that wine drinkers were more likely to be familiar with the Internet than the population as a whole. Their target audience wanted to spend between $8 and $20 for a good bottle of wine but were not necessarily wine connoisseurs: they needed advice.

Advice was the second key to their service model. Peter Granoff, or the Cork Dork, had an extensive background in wine service, having trained in France and been a *sommelier,* or wine steward, for five years. Granoff's personalized wine recommendations, available on the site and sent by e-mail to individual purchasers, is what VV believed to be the main component of their success.

On the supply side, Virtual Vineyards offered higher percentages to vineyards than traditional distributors. In addition, vineyards trusted Olson and Granoff's expertise to preserve or enhance their reputations.

Olson and Granoff considered additional offerings of specialty foods, fresh produce, and other related products and services. As they moved forward with plans, however, they faced the question of whether to develop brand recognition for individual sites or for the company as a whole. What would be the nature of the service relationship they had established with customers? Would it allow them to extend the sales potential of the firm from wine to related categories? Should they maintain a consistent screen interface or develop a new one for each line of business?

Preparation Questions

1. What are the market conditions that allow VV to provide value to suppliers? To end-users? What end-users does VV target?

2. What is the business model of VV?

3. How has VV established its acknowledged dominance of virtual retailers in this category? What are the resources that VV has used to develop this dominance?

4. What are the attributes of a high quality retail service when it is delivered screen-to-screen rather than face-to-face?

5. What additional actions might VV take to enhance its position in the marketplace?

WEATHER SERVICES CORPORATION

Case Overview

In 1993, when Mike Leavitt returned to his father's Weather Services Corporation (WSC) after ten years as an aviation consultant, he saw tremendous opportunity to build WSC into the leading weather information provider for the digital age. After nearly 50 years of furnishing weather forecasts to a limited market of institutional users on a subscription basis, new technology was creating a limitless distribution channel for WSC direct to consumer homes. But WSC was stretched in terms of cash flow, and all issues demanded immediate attention at this moment, which Leavitt felt was critical to the future of the business.

Through its high-speed data links with the two raw data distributors, WSC received all North American hourly weather data within ten minutes of its receipt by the National Weather Service. Although others in the industry suggested that the forecasting skill of WSC meteorologists and its significant experience in the industry set the firm apart, Leavitt saw its strength as the ability to respond quickly to customers' needs.

Markets for weather information ran the gamut from aviation to local businesses to marine and other specialty markets. The pricing model was tied to the subscriber base. Leavitt explained, "Basically, we grow as they grow." WSC also had a robust business with specialized online services that supplied news, data, and financial statistics to capital markets' trading floors. But the biggest growth market was clearly the online services market, with a 50% jump from 1994 to 1995. In order to compete in the land grab with such major players as The Weather Channel, WSC had to create an integrated strategy. The challenge lay in the complexity of applications for weather information radiating from a single core, the National Weather Service. In addition, the WSC Internet strategy was undetermined.

Preparation Questions

1. Should WSC continue as an information provider, or should it compete head-on with the major online players and offer its own online weather service?

2. How would direct applications via dial-up online or websites potentially threaten existing WSC business relationships?

3. How should the company develop the WSC brand? How could WSC grow the business in vertical markets?

4. Was Leavitt's plan to raise $1 million enough, or should he raise closer to $5 million?

STREAMLINE (A)

Case Overview

Tim DeMello, the 37-year-old founder and CEO of Streamline, believed that his company offered the right solution for suburban family households with a shortage of time. For the past year, his Boston-based company had been experimenting with the concept of direct-to-home delivery services on a test basis in a suburban Boston market. DeMello was convinced that the convergence of changing lifestyles and evolving information technologies would make Streamline's services popular, if not inevitable.

Streamline's business model appeared deceptively simple. Deliveries for groceries, dry cleaning, photo development, and video rentals were to be made once-a-week to each Streamline subscriber household. Weekly orders had to be placed no later than midnight before the designated delivery date. The orders were filled at Streamline's Consumer Resource Center (CRC) and delivered to each household on the designated delivery day.

A major distinction of the Streamline service model was that consumers did not need to be home to receive shipments. Streamline designed a patented delivery receptacle for deliveries and installed it in each customer's garage (or accessible location). Streamline's field service representatives (FSRs) could leave weekly deliveries in the refrigerated unit and thus fulfill the needs of subscribing households without inconveniencing the recipients. Streamline charged a $30 monthly fee for its service, calculating that the average customer made 24 trips per month to stores for grocery and general merchandise. By subscribing to Streamline, DeMello argued, customers saved $60 per trip, or $3120 per year, just in gas consumption, auto maintenance, late fees on videos, and the cost of an individual's time, estimated conservatively at $10 per hour.

What remained was to confirm Streamline's business model as it expanded beyond its test market and opened new markets across the country. What was the best way to replicate the business model so that Streamline could achieve its goal of reaching a base of one million households across the country by 2004?

Preparation Questions

1. Evaluate the Streamline business model. What aspects of the business are easily replicated? What aspects represent key competitive advantages?

2. Which activities does Streamline perform on the physical value chain and which on the virtual value chain? Which value chain has the greater potential for customer value creation?

3. What kinds of information is Streamline likely to collect on its subscriber households? How might Streamline use such information in serving customers? In partnering with brand marketers? In partnering with other local service providers?

4. How should Streamline manage concerns about privacy and customer records?

5. If you were operating a traditional grocery retail business in a Streamline service region, how might you compete with Streamline?

6. Assuming that Streamline will franchise its business model, what are the key conditions it should mandate in the franchising agreement for third-party operation of its business?

STREAMLINE (B)

Case Overview

Streamline grocery home delivery service was doing well in 1998. They were applying state-of-the-art technology to design a highly efficient shopping experience and a physical fulfillment channel to provide the foundation for rapid expansion. The three challenges of scaling the business, according to Kevin Abt, Streamline's Senior Vice President, were systems integration, warehouse management, and merchandising.

A new technology system was deployed that created an integrated end-to-end system linking the customer inquiry database and online shopping interface with the customer service and fulfillment database. To ensure perfect orders, employees wore strapped to their arms a scanning device that connected to the fulfillment database as they packed orders. The wrist appliance immediately checked that items picked and packed for a customer matched the order placed, as well as confirmed that specific customer instructions had been captured. As a result, the efficiency and effectiveness of order fulfillment had improved significantly.

Streamline management enhanced Web ordering by introducing the Don't Run Out automated replenishment program, which allowed families to put regularly purchased items in a

1 to 12 week repurchase cycle. In addition, in February 1998, Streamline announced a deal with Blockbuster Entertainment to provide home delivery of videos to customers.

Preparation Questions

1. What strategic advantages did Streamline create through these new technologies and partnerships?

2. What further online and offline integration would help Streamline maintain its competitive edge over newcomers such as Shoplink and Webvan?

CHEMUNITY.COM

Case Overview

In April 2000, ChemUnity, an electronic marketplace for the chemical industry, was six months old. Though many elements necessary for the western European company's success had come together, Dutch Managing Director Herman Rijks was aware of the challenges that still lay ahead. Rijks and his partner Mark-Jan Terwindt still had to convince the suppliers and the buyers in the marketplace that ChemUnity.com was the place to come when either group needed chemical products. In addition, the business model was untested.

To differentiate from the competition, ChemUnity focused on Western Europe, full truck-load quantities, commodity products, and online-service-based sourcing. The central strength of ChemUnity's business model was that all buyer inquiries were proactively forwarded to all the potential suppliers; the offers were returned to the buyer within 25 hours. Each transaction was binding, and thanks to credit insurance, suppliers were sure they would receive payment. Benefits of the electronic marketplace included increased source-and-supply chain efficiency, lower prices, and access to new markets.

ChemUnity hoped to achieve a considerable share of the transactions in the small segment it targeted. The annual chemicals market in Europe was (Euro) 385 billion, but ChemUnity estimated that it could have 7% of the transactions in the (Euro) 15 billion target segment, or (Euro) 1 billion. In the beginning, ChemUnity charged a 2% transaction fee (more than some exchanges that dealt with petrochemicals or purchases of large quantities of goods), which would translate to annual revenues of (Euro) 20 million in 5 year's time. As the network expanded, advertising and increased financial and transportation services represented additional potential revenues.

Partnerships with Compaq, Computer Science Corporation (CSC), and others were a key element in the start-up phase, with flexible deals for payment for goods and services. Two venture capital companies financed (Euro) 1.5 million in exchange for 27.5% of the company. ChemUnity estimated marketing would take up 60% of the initial costs, leaving approximately 30% to people costs and 10% to IT. Later the share of people costs was expected to increase and that of marketing costs was expected to decrease.

ChemUnity faced both immediate and long-term challenges. The start of trading had been postponed a couple of times due to IT problems. The company still needed to raise awareness of its name and service, especially among suppliers, to make the marketplace effective. A second round of financing to raise another (Euro) 5 to 10 million was planned for a couple of months after the launch of service. Once the concept was proven, ChemUnity had to decide how to expand.

Preparation Questions

1. What is the value proposition for the suppliers and buyers?

2. Would the 2% transaction fee revenue model work?

3. What were the future challenges, and how should ChemUnity anticipate and respond to them?

INDEPENDER.COM

Case Overview

In April 2000 Edmund Hilhorst, Managing Director and cofounder of Independer, a Dutch dot.com start-up in the financial services industry, had to make some fundamental decisions about the company's customer loyalty program. The loyalty program was a key to Independer's future; it would demonstrate that the company offered independent and unbiased advice.

Independer was set up first and foremost to satisfy the needs of financial-product consumers, based on the following key consumer demands: lowest prices, independent advice, convenience, and quality. The Independer revenue model was two-pronged: leads and sales commissions. Independer charged financial product providers a fixed fee per customer request (or lead) it provided. Sales commissions would be generated only when a customer actually purchased the product online via Independer. Independer distinguished itself to consumers by ignoring the incentives that banks and insurance companies traditionally paid to brokers, commissions that were perceived to bias sales. Instead, Independer sales revenues would be set somewhere near the minimum commission level, and commissions beyond that threshold would somehow "belong" to Independer financial service customers.

The immediate issue for Hilhorst was what to do with the "excess commissions." He wanted to use this money to create a loyalty program that he believed would represent the "Independer difference." As he saw it, there were three ways to go: (1) an immediate cash rebate, (2) membership in some kind of consumer club, and (3) the issuance of certificates that would turn into company stocks, which could be sold or kept when Independer went public. Hilhorst was leaning toward the third option, which he felt demonstrated innovation and would entice customers into a long-term relationship with Independer.

Preparation Questions

1. How would the recent plunge in the prices of technology and Internet stocks affect Independer and, in turn, influence the loyalty program's excess-commission policy?

2. Would consumers be interested in stock options as a benefit when the market was so unpredictable?

3. Would Independer now find it harder to raise money from skittish investors, as well as to offer stock options to potential employees, and therefore need to revisit the company's entire strategy? Or, as Hilhorst and his partner Van Embden were convinced, would the "Internet shake-out" reveal the fundamental strengths of the Independer business model to consumers and investors?

INTEGRATIVE QUESTIONS

As you consider the entire set of questions in the third chapter, you should also reflect on the following integrative questions:

1. What are the major problems confronting online firms when they attempt to craft a unique, sustainable business model?

2. How is the online environment unique? Or is it?

3. What are the unique challenges that offline firms confront when they create an online business model?

4. Compare and contrast the pure online strategies of Egghead.com and Virtual Vineyards versus those of Streamline. What advice might Egghead.com give to Weather Service Corporation? Would you agree or disagree with this advice?

SUMMARY

Business models are the essential ingredients of a strong e-commerce strategy. Too frequently, the popular press limits business-model discussions to simply the revenue or profit model of the company. As this overview suggests, there are four parts to the business model: the value cluster, marketspace offering, resource system, and financial model. These components all need to fit tightly together to provide a coherent, mutually reinforcing business model.

EGGHEAD.COM

At the end of February, 1998, software retailer Egghead Inc. closed the remaining 80 locations in what was once a 200-branch retail network. Fierce competition in the industry was largely responsible for the move as Egghead struggled to keep up with better-positioned players. As part of the closures, some 800 workers were fired—roughly 80% of all employees—and one of Egghead's two distribution centers was shut down. But while driven from the marketplace by its competitors, the company was not going out of business. Instead, it was being reborn.

Egghead, renamed Egghead.com, had decided to move its entire operation out of bricks and mortar and transfer it into bits and bytes. From now on the company would sell software as well as hardware through its web site (*www.egghead.com*) and via a toll-free number (1-800-EGGHEAD). It was an unprecedented move. There was no template for its executives to follow, nor was the company's catalog and Web experience to date necessarily enough to help them chart a course. It was somehow both surprising and yet logical that a software retailer would be the first major chain of stores uprooted from the physical world and transplanted online.

As for the 800 jobless workers, at least one ex-employee was following a strategy similar to his erstwhile employer; he was getting out of retail store sales for good. As he explained, "There's not a lot of money in retail, and there is in technology." The former Egghead sales clerk announced his next move would be to return to school, get further training, and then take up a career in high-tech.[1]

Egghead History[2]

Founded by 37-year-old entrepreneur Victor Alhadeff in 1984, Egghead was the product of an unsatisfactory shopping trip. Alhadeff—whose oil and gas tax shelter business had been wiped out by changing tax codes and a hail of investor lawsuits two years earlier—was out looking for software with his son. The experience was less than rewarding: too much jargon from salespeople and too many second-rate stores seemed to greet the pair wherever they went. Alhadeff sensed an opportunity. He opened the first Egghead Discount Software store soon afterwards in Bellevue, Washington.

Key to Alhadeff's strategy was changing the customer experience from the one he and his son had suffered. Staff would be helpful and the stores set up to establish a customer-friendly environment. The company's personification—the Professor Egghead character—was a direct jab at the notion that software was solely the realm of an intellectual, jargon-wielding elite. The goofy Professor was instead promoting bargains for everyone, all too often by means of inane egg-puns. Indeed, the Professor Egghead persona seemed an accurate reflection of the company itself; Alhadeff's secretary, for example, became known as his "eggsecutive assistant."

Alhadeff's efforts to make software shopping less intimidating—aided by the market's general growth—contributed to early successes for the upstart retailer. By the end of FY 1989, Egghead had grown to 112 stores. The founder's ability to raise money did not hurt, either. He had pulled $100 million in just two years for his tax shelter business; he now focused his fundraising talents on his newest creation. Alhadeff raised some $47 million to help fund the expansion of Egghead prior to the company's IPO in 1988.

Fundraising, however, proved only part of what it took to head Egghead's growing business. Just one year after the IPO, Alhadeff resigned as president. Poor inventory management—in particular "shrinkage" due to losses and theft—had taken its toll on the company. Additionally, high turnover among retail personnel hampered the retailers' ability to provide the knowledgeable sales staff originally envisioned as a key to success. It seemed that Egghead's rapid growth might lead to its undoing.

With Alhadeff's departure, a troika of managers took over. They brought inventory under tighter control and

---

Jeremy Dunn (MBA 1998) and Rob Schmults (MBA 1998) prepared this case under the supervision of Professor Jeffrey F. Rayport as the basis for class discussion rather than to illustrate either effective or ineffective handling of an administrative situation.

[1]Suzanne Galante, "Online stores displace workers," CNET News.com, March 2, 1998.
[2]Much of the information in this section was derived from Hoover's Online Company Profile of Egghead.com, Inc.

also rationalized the company's growth by pruning some unprofitable outlets. But it soon became apparent that better internal management alone would not be enough to guarantee continued success. While Egghead stuck to a storefront format, with branches in malls and on main streets, competitors adopted a superstore model that Egghead found increasingly difficult to compete with. Some of Egghead's small-store rivals were driven from the market or forced to reinvent themselves as targeted niche players. Alhadeff's successors lasted until 1992, when another CEO arrived on the scene—and departed within a year. Terence Strom took over as CEO and stayed until early 1997. Strom was replaced by a member of the board, George Orban, who became Chairman and CEO.

Such management turnover mirrored the unsettled competitive landscape facing Egghead and its small-store format. Egghead's struggles in the retail software market, primarily due to strong competition from rivals Computer City and CompUSA, were further compounded by the success of one-stop shops like Wal-Mart, which seemed to threaten almost any small store, regardless of category. As the competition hurt sales, Egghead found itself in increasingly difficult straits. A belated attempt to launch "Super Eggheads" was not enough to redress the balance. In its quarterly earnings report at the end of December 1997, the company revealed that sales had dropped to $99.1 million from $113 million a year earlier. Egghead had a loss of $6.6 million during the quarter, compared with a profit of $1.5 million, or 9¢ a share, a year earlier (see Exhibit 1 for historical company performance).

Egghead finally announced the decision to move out of bricks-and-mortar retail in late January of 1998—just one month before actually shutting down its stores. The 80 stores Egghead was closing were less than half of the 200 stores the company had boasted at its peak. Given the decline, the move seemed to be a last attempt to stave off extinction. "We believe that focusing the management of Egghead on the Internet represents the best opportunity to create long-term value for our shareholders," Egghead Chairman and CEO George Orban said in a release announcing the move. As part of that announcement, the company said it expected substantial operating losses to result over the next two years as it worked to reinvent itself online. Unmentioned was the fact that, while closing Egghead's physical outlets may have moved it out of the path of the superstores, it also erased overnight the source of 70% of the company's revenues.

Still, there were signs for optimism. Even while reporting falling overall sales at the end of 1997, Internet sales for the fourth quarter totaled $11.8 million, $9.3 million more than a year earlier. And visits to the Egghead.com site had exploded from 300,000 in 1996 to some 6 million in 1997.[3] The company's movement onto the Web was thus not a complete leap into the unknown. And Egghead's Web presence had been strengthened by its acquisition of Surplus Direct for $31 million in 1997. Surplus Direct (*www.surplusdirect.com*) was set up to allow manufacturers to liquidate out-of-date hardware and software products and even offered sales via an online auction mechanism. Like its better-known competitor OnSale, Surplus Direct seemed to hold the potential for tapping into a promising vein of e-commerce revenues.

Egghead.com's Online Strategy

One of Egghead's primary justifications for optimism regarding its new focus on online was that it was the first significant software retailer to do so. "I think Egghead, because they have a lot of advantages going in, can quickly jump up the learning curve and make a profitable site in a reasonable amount of time," said Maria LaTour Kadison, a Forrester Research analyst for online retail strategies. "But it is risky."[4] Indeed, being first would only be an advantage if Egghead moved fast and avoided mistakes—mistakes those that followed could learn from and thus avoid.

One of the areas in which Egghead moved most aggressively was in locking in key distribution partnerships. While the company saw name recognition as a possible competitive advantage, it had to get in front of customers first to capitalize on any potential benefit from the Egghead name. And while intimating that it was not yet done in its partnering efforts, by late April 1998 the company had established several relationships that seemed certain to improve its position.

Gateways

Nearly simultaneously with its move out of retail stores, Egghead became a featured software vendor on Yahoo!, one of the Internet's top drawing sites and the start of

---

[3]Thomas W. Haines, Seattle Times.com, Business: Thursday, January 29, 1998.
[4]Jake Batsell, "Egghead.com sees the light." Seattle Times.com, Technology: Wednesday, March 11, 1998.

many a web user's online foray. A button linking users to Egghead sites was prominently positioned on a number of Yahoo!'s computer-related search pages. The deal resembled one put together by Amazon.com, which was paying an estimated $25 million for three years as Yahoo!'s exclusive featured book retailer. While Egghead's placements were less comprehensive across the Yahoo! site, Egghead had plenty of reason for satisfaction over landing Yahoo!, whose power to help funnel customers to vendors was impressive. A survey of Internet commerce found that 14.4% of the purchasers surveyed were referred to vendors from Yahoo! (another 9% were referred from AOL, meaning that these two portals accounted for nearly a quarter of online vendor referrals).[5]

Egghead had already established a similar relationship with another major Web hub. The company had announced in mid-January that it would be featured on GeoCities' home page and throughout GeoCities' 40 online "neighborhoods." Like Yahoo!, GeoCities, a personal web page provider, was frequently listed as one of the top Web destinations by such monitoring services as NetRatings. Egghead's partnership with GeoCities again mirrored that of Amazon.com, as well as online music retailer CDNow, both of which had made similar arrangements to pay GeoCities for customer referrals.

Destinations

In late February, Egghead announced that CNET—one of the leading suppliers of online technology news, as well as the host of such sites as Gamecenter.com, Download.com, and Shareware.com—would be offering links to Egghead.com and Surplus Direct. The financial aspects of the deal were not made public, but like other such relationships, Egghead most likely contracted to pay CNET a substantial flat fee in addition to a percentage of sales generated through CNET's sites.

Two months later, Egghead announced yet another partnership deal, this time with InfoBeat, who provided e-mail delivered content to some 2.6 million subscribers. Egghead was one of the featured vendors in InfoBeat's new marketplace, which offered special deals for InfoBeat subscribers. As part of an incentive program to help boost sales, InfoBeat gave special content bonuses to users who patronized the marketplace's vendors. A similar, non-exclusive arrangement was also established with

the rapidly growing online community The Globe (*www.theglobe.com*). The deal likewise gave Egghead favorable placement in The Globe's online marketplace.

Push

To complete this flurry of partnerships, Egghead announced an alliance with e-mail provider USA.net in early March. Under the terms of the deal, USA.net, the second largest provider of free web-based e-mail, would give Egghead.com banner ads and button placements on USA.net's website. Egghead would also be able to e-mail news, product information, and discounts to USA.net's subscribers. To prevent unwanted "spam" (Internet jargon for unsolicited e-mail, usually considered a grave breach of online etiquette), the e-mails would only go to those users who signed up for the service.

In addition to the USA.net deal, Egghead also initiated a "push" marketing plan of its own. Using e-mail addresses acquired both online and from now-defunct retail outlets, Egghead sent out periodic e-mails containing limited time offers, special deals, and announcements of new products. Again, wary of the charge of "spamming," Egghead was careful to provide recipients an easy way to request that their address be removed from the mailing list.

There seemed to be plenty of reasons for interest in online software vending. Books had been one of the first e-commerce categories to grab popular attention, but from the beginning, industry analysts had pointed to the Internet's potential as a software channel. To begin with, online users were obviously pre-qualified as members of the software-buying public. In addition, the nature of the product lent itself to direct sales: software was well suited to be bought without any physical contact with the purchaser. Generally, the product was at a low enough price point that users could feel comfortable buying direct. Indeed, a spring 1998 survey conducted by International Data Group found that nearly 40% of those people who had made purchases online listed software among the products they bought, while only 22% listed books. Not surprisingly, software was an important component of the rapidly expanding online retail market, and projections looked good for continued fast-paced growth (see Exhibit 2 for online retail projections). Perhaps even more important for future prospects, software was ideal not only for online purchasing, but for online distribution as well. Electronic software distribution (ESD) existed long before Egghead moved online, as the phenomenal success of ID Software's *Doom* and

---

[5]Binary Compass Enterprises, "Fourth quarter Internet shopping report," Spring 1998.

Netscape's browser distribution strategy showed. However, online software distribution had thus far consisted mostly of free products, not software that required payment or was subject to illegal duplication. Payment and intellectual property protection procedures remained uncertain, as did the extent and format of future ESD systems.

Other aspects of the current landscape were less favorable for Egghead's future. Most estimates showed that the percentage of active online users who had bought anything online, while growing, remained around 20%. Ingrained buyer behavior and fears about security still slowed the adoption of online shopping. Forrester analyst Shelley Morrisette, while hardly an opponent of online retailing, nevertheless voiced concerns about the impact such issues, particularly buyer preferences, might have on Egghead:

> The Internet is a channel just like any other channel. Consumers will still be looking for information, personal attention, and sales support. They'll look for "channel synchronization": using different channels for different parts of the transaction. I can understand that the cost of the physical sites was very expensive, but at the same time, customers like the feeling of being able to do things across channels. For example, people like to return things, and the Internet makes that harder. Shopping is very ingrained in people, and it will be tough to change behavior quickly.[6]

Egghead also had to face the fact that, while most estimates showed a personal computer in over 40% of U.S. households, less than a quarter of households were estimated to have Internet access. While Egghead's toll-free telephone number might cover some of the gap, Egghead's concentration on the Internet could well be placing much of its target market out of reach. As a further warning of possible difficulties ahead, the Egghead.com website went down just as Egghead was shuttering its retail stores. It was nearly two days before the site was up and running again.

Competitive Landscape

During the mid- to late-1990s, Egghead faced competition from several different types of companies (see Exhibit 3 for comparables). Many retailers specialized in selling computer hardware, software, and peripherals to home and small business users. Most of these compa-

nies, especially those which concentrated on software, failed to achieve great scale. Of these computer-focused companies, only two—CompUSA, Inc. and Computer City—boasted sales of over $1 billion in 1997.[7] However, during this period, other large American consumer electronics retailers began to concentrate on this market, and sales of computer-related products became increasingly important to their product mix. The two largest players in this sector were Circuit City and Best Buy. Wal-Mart, the nation's largest overall retailer, also attracted attention as it began to move beyond its discount retailing base to compete in the computer hardware and software arena.

Also, new types of competitors were developing business models which did not rely on physical stores to distribute software products to customers, but rather employed commercial sites on the Web to sell products which were delivered to the end user through either package delivery services or electronic means. And, as with Wal-Mart, successful Web-based retailers of other types of products could not be overlooked as potential competitors within the not-too-distant future.

Computer Superstores

CompUSA, Inc. The largest chain of stores devoted solely to computer hardware and software, CompUSA operated about 150 superstores in 70 metropolitan areas in 1997. The chain employed over 10,000 in its stores and corporate offices. The company's top line had increased dramatically in the previous three years; a growth rate of nearly 28% per year had led to sales approaching $6 billion for 1997.[8] CompUSA attempted to be a "one-stop-shop" for consumer and business users. It offered a wide array of products and support services, including repairs, custom system configurations, and technical training in the latest software. In addition to operating its retail stores, CompUSA marketed technology products directly to large corporate, government, and educational institutions.

In early 1998, CompUSA was experiencing softening sales and declining profits, brought on mostly by a steep drop in computer prices; whereas a few years ago, computer systems usually sold for several thousand dollars,

---

[6]Interview with Shelley Morrisette, April 27, 1998.

[7]Ward's Business Directory of U.S. Private and Public Companies, 1998.
[8]"The Power Merchants: Larry Mondry, CompUSA," *Discount Store News*, December 8, 1997.

now a growing portion of computers sold by CompUSA were priced under $1000. Industry analysts praised the company's continuing diversification into software and training as a way to shore up profits over the long term.[9]

The company also operated CompUSA Online, billed as "the virtual computer superstore." Users could find product information, locate the nearest retail location, or purchase products directly from the site.

Computer City. This chain of superstores was owned by the Tandy Corporation of Fort Worth, Texas, which also controlled Radio Shack, a $3 billion electronics retailing concern. With nearly 100 locations and 7,000 employees by the end of 1997, Computer City offered an array of products and services similar to those offered by the larger CompUSA. Recently, Computer City had introduced build-to-order and configure-to-order programs for its PCs, along with a dramatically expanded hardware and software support system. Discussing the new support hotline, David Martella, vice president of retail sales, commented, "The problem in the past has been that most of the calls go to the stores. Handling the programs this way means that the customers get a faster, better answer. Simply put, our stores are not set up to do technical support."[10]

Electronics Superstores

Circuit City. With 549 retail locations and over 40,000 employees, Circuit City was the largest electronics retailer in the U.S., offering consumer electronics, home appliances, personal computers, software, and recorded music. In the fiscal year ending February 1997, Circuit City's revenue was over $7 billion; over the previous three years, the company had experienced top-line growth of over 20%.

Circuit City's retailing empire consisted mostly of superstores, which ranged in size from 18,500 to 43,000 square feet. The company also owned around 50 mall-based Circuit City Express stores, which sold gift items and smaller products in 2,000–3,000 square-foot venues. Other ventures controlled by Circuit City included CarMax, a nationwide chain of used-car dealerships, and Digital Video Express, a new enterprise which planned to market limited-use, disposable video disks.

Sales of "home office" equipment—which included computer hardware and software, in addition to items like fax machines and small copiers—represented the largest sales category for Circuit City in 1997:

Circuit City Sales Breakdown, 1997

Product Category	1997 Sales (% of total)
Home Office	24
Audio	18
Televisions	18
Appliances	15
VCRs/Camcorders	14
Other	11
Total	100

Source: OneSource Information Services, April 1998.

Best Buy. Jockeying from year to year with arch-rival Circuit City for the coveted title of "America's largest electronics retailer," Best Buy also boasted sales of over $7 billion. It operated more than 280 superstores and employed 17,300 people in over 30 states.

Best Buy had been experiencing poor results due to tough competition in both the personal computing and consumer electronics portions of its business. Particularly troubling was its dependence on personal computer sales, which yielded lower profit margins than home appliances. With the advent of under-$1000 PCs, the category was possibly proving even less attractive. Best Buy had been burned by mistakes in the computer area before; in 1996, profits plunged when the company was forced to write-down a large inventory of outdated PCs it could not sell. However, high-margin computer peripherals and services such as hardware upgrades still represented profitable lines of business.

Best Buy Sales Breakdown, 1997

Product Category	1997 Sales (% of total)
Home Office	39
Entertainment (CDs/Videos)	18
Video Equipment	17
Audio Equipment	12
Appliances	9
Other	5
Total	100

Source: OneSource Information Services, April 1998.

[9]Jeff Mamera, "CompUSA latest casualty of falling PC prices," Reuters News Service, April 1, 1998.
[10]Roger Lanctot, "Computer City, Best Buy get aggressive on phone support," *Computer Retail Week*, November 24, 1997.

Wal-Mart. This juggernaut of American retailing, with over 3,400 stores and $118 billion in sales, had shown incredible tenacity over the years in conquering new markets it wished to enter. Whether it was penetrating new geographical areas or starting new retail concepts such as supercenters, competitors found it difficult to ignore Wal-Mart.

As personal computers became more affordable to Wal-Mart's core customer base of middle-income households (see Exhibit 4 for Yearly Income of Web Users), the company had shown more desire to begin a "major push" into software and hardware retailing. The Wal-Mart Online website, which offered an array of products from diapers to consumer electronics, was a major part of plans for moving into technology offerings.

Software Resellers

ENTEX Information Services.
This IT services company represented a different type of business model than that of traditional retailers. ENTEX's lineage can be traced back to Businessland, a retailing chain founded in 1982, focused on computers, software, and other office products. Businessland experienced a moderate level of success, reaching $267 million in sales and posting a small profit in its third year of operations. However, a series of miscues seriously damaged the company's prospects.

The company proved to be a millstone around the neck of JWP, Inc., a conglomerate that purchased Businessland in 1991. JWP, which maintained interests in businesses ranging from computer software to building maintenance to waterworks, lost nearly $500 million in the following two years and declared bankruptcy. An investor group led by Dort Cameron (formerly of Drexel Burnham Lambert) and Businessland management bought the computer side of the business in 1993.

With a new strategic focus and a few key acquisitions, the company, now renamed ENTEX Information Services, proved successful in software sales and systems integration. As more and more medium and large companies outsourced elements of their IT services operations, ENTEX and companies like it stepped in to fill the void. By year-end 1997, the company had 7,500 employees and $2.1 billion in total sales (both software and IT services)[11]; by early 1998, ENTEX managed over 600,000 desktops and boasted clients such as Pacific Bell, Coca-Cola, and American Express.

In the spring of 1998, ENTEX completed beta-testing for an e-commerce system called Order Access-Web. The new system allowed users to pick hardware products and customized bundles of software products from personalized online catalogs. One purchasing agent observed, "[ENTEX's] Web-based electronic commerce is a high productivity booster for us because we give them an order and they act on it immediately." ENTEX had already conducted nearly $200 million in business over electronic interchange platforms in 1997; the new system was predicted to boost that amount dramatically.[12]

Two other large systems integrators followed a strategy similar to that pursued by ENTEX. MicroAge, Inc., with sales of $4.4 billion and 4,400 employees, started as a retailing operation, then grew into one of the nation's largest resellers of software for businesses. It had recently announced that it would separate the integration and reselling aspects of its operations into distinct business units, which might eventually lead to one or more full spin-offs. Software Spectrum of Garland, Texas, also began as a mall-based retailer of computer software products. In May 1996, it purchased Egghead's corporate, government and education sales unit, a major part of an acquisition campaign that led to a doubling of revenues. In 1997, Software Spectrum garnered sales of $824 million from its business-customer base.

Web-Based Resellers

Software.net.
In April 1998, Cybersource Corporation announced that it intended to spin off its online software "superstore," Software.net, so that Cybersource could concentrate on providing electronic commerce sources to a variety of Internet retailers. Software.net marketed over 15,000 software titles from around 600 developers. Many of its products could be downloaded via modem, although most applications required a high-speed Internet connection to download in a reasonable amount of time (for example, downloading a 10-megabyte piece of software with a 28.8 kbps modem would take well over an hour). Previously a traditional mail-order operation, Software.net had initiated electronic delivery in 1995, when it began experimenting with a program that allowed users to download applications free of charge; the software would automatically erase itself from the

---

[11]OneSource Information Services, April 1998.

[12]"Hot Topics: E-commerce, NT migration popular at ENTEX—University Attendees Share Agenda," *Computer Reseller News*, April 6, 1998.

user's computer unless the user provided credit card information online or called the company to arrange payment.

With the spin-off, Amazon.com's former vice president of marketing Mark Breier became CEO of the newly independent Software.net. The company also signed three-year agreements with America Online (a $21 million deal alone) and Excite to be the exclusive software merchant on the popular websites. "We think it's fairly clear that there are going to be just a few major software resellers on the Web," said Bill Holtzman, Software.net's vice president of marketing, "and having placement on the number-one online service and the number-two search engine gives us a way to broaden our presence and reach consumers."[13]

Cendant. Cendant was formed in December 1997, the result of a merger between online merchant CUC and hotel operator HFS. Since its meager beginnings in 1973, CUC had developed into one of the true powerhouses of Web-based commerce, providing shopping, travel, auto, and dining programs through its membership-based system, netMarket.

One of Cendant's largest retailing categories was computer software. In 1996, software represented $375 million of Cendant's $4.5 billion in revenues.[14] In addition to selling through netMarket, Cendant maintained marketing arrangements with many leading software companies. Products ordered from these companies through Cendant could be delivered either by normal package delivery or, sometimes, electronically. Among the companies participating in Cendant's software merchandising program were:

- Davidson and Associates, a publisher of multimedia education and entertainment software;
- Sierra On-Line, a developer of games, interactive entertainment, productivity tools, and educational software;
- Blizzard Entertainment, a maker of games and other software;
- Knowledge Adventure, a publisher of "edutainment" educational software.

In addition to Software.net and Cendant, there were hundreds of other firms that marketed software via the Internet, both as complements to existing bricks-and-

mortar retailers and as totally new start-up operations operating almost entirely in a virtual environment. These resellers often sold a large assortment of hardware and software products, but sometimes chose to limit their offerings to certain product subcategories (e.g., multimedia, education, or games), specialized markets (medical, legal, or retailing), or foreign language editions.

Possible Future Competitors

Amazon.com. One of the early success stories of the World Wide Web, Amazon.com had grown from $511,000 in sales in 1995 to nearly $150 million in 1997. Along the way, it had locked up exclusive partnership agreements with some of the most-trafficked sites on the Web, including Yahoo! and Netscape. The company had created its own sophisticated distribution system, including warehousing and logistical operations, to handle the thousands of books it shipped each day.

After revolutionizing bookselling on the Web, Amazon.com began to move into other products, such as CDs, videos, and audiotapes. CEO Jeff Bezos stated that the company's eventual goal was to offer a large assortment of information-based products and services, including computer software. Amazon.com's capacity and willingness to expand aggressively in order to extend its product line had once again been demonstrated in April 1998, when it acquired the popular Internet Movie Database (*www.imdb.com*), with the intent of using the database's detailed library of movie information to help sell videos. If and when it decided to offer software, Amazon.com would pose a formidable threat to any other online retailers.

Barnes & Noble. Although a latecomer to the world of Web-based retailing, Barnes & Noble's eventual entry into the fray created the marketspace equivalent of the cola wars. The company found itself playing catch-up on the Internet; in 1997, Barnesandnoble.com posted sales of only $14 million, scarcely one-tenth of Amazon.com's sales during the same period. Nevertheless, Barnes & Noble remained a dominant force in bookselling, thanks to its real-world superstores.

While Barnes & Noble's primary online and offline business was bookselling, the company derived quite a bit of its revenue from other sources as well. Most of its superstores possessed sizable music sections, a feature carried over into its online counterpart. Barnes & Noble also had experience retailing computer software: its B. Dalton subsidiary sold many different types of computer

[13]"Cybersource spins out Software.net reseller," *Ziff-Davis Wire Highlights*, April 2, 1998.
[14]OneSource Information Services, April 1998.

products under the name "Software, Etc.," a store-within-a-store concept that was also rolled out as a stand-alone entity in some locations.

Hardware

While software remained the primary focus for Egghead, the company was also attempting to compete more broadly in computer hardware. However, this market was just as crowded as that for software. Many leading software retailers, such as CompUSA, as well as less focused companies, like Wal-Mart and Cendant, also maintained major presences in the hardware market. And, unlike software, hardware retailers faced the powerful force of manufacturers selling directly to end-users. Fierce competitors like Dell Computer and Gateway had made their names by circumventing traditional retailers and relying on fulfilling customer orders over the phone. Not only did they gain a price advantage, they were also able to offer computers manufactured to the customer's exact specifications. Dell, in particular, capitalized on its enormous success in offline direct sales to create a thriving Web-based channel as well. It was commonly reported that Dell was on track to do over $1 billion a year in online sales alone.

Prospects for Egghead.com

One of the authors of a report examining the Information Age's impact on retailing had a mixed view of Egghead's competitive position. Despite the once-popular conventional wisdom that the Internet would cause brands to lose their importance, he felt just the opposite was happening and that Egghead's brand could be one of its biggest assets. Still, there were other issues that gave him pause in evaluating Egghead's situation:

> Right now, there are no barriers to entry for these new online players. The technology is available to everybody. However, the bricks-and-mortar presence makes it so the consumer feels less risk when they make a purchase online. This is extremely important when the product can be complicated, like software; with books, you really don't need technical support.

> Everybody—big guys and small guys—looks the same on the Web; there's no differentiation. Prices can be driven down very low in a situation like this, leaving

very few profits. They could be driven down to nothing. Egghead is in a market which will be very, very tough.[15]

The threat of shrinking margins was a common prediction as intelligent agents and even basic search engines seemed to put pricing power firmly in the hands of consumers. And price was not the only area where predictions of big changes were being made.

"This is the beginning of a trend," said Erica Rugulies, an Internet commerce analyst, commenting on Egghead's reinvention as an online retailer. "This is the first time we've really been able to say, 'Electronic commerce is here.'"[16] However, while Egghead's customer interface was online, most of its distribution remained firmly in the physical world. Order fulfillment still consisted primarily of traditional software packages—cardboard boxes with CD-ROMs or floppy disks—being shipped from Egghead's remaining distribution center. But this too seemed destined to change with the growing possibilities of electronic software distribution.

Electronic Software Distribution (ESD)

Although companies had experimented with delivering retail software products over the Internet for several years, by the late-1990s only a tiny fraction of software was actually delivered to end-users electronically. However, a recent study cited in *Computer Reseller News* had stated that 50% of the software companies responding to a survey on the issue declared that they were working actively to incorporate ESD into their distribution systems.[17]

The benefits of a wider role for ESD were evident. Users could participate in "try before you buy" programs which would allow them to use a demonstration version of a software product to determine if it was what they were looking for. Add-ons such as upgrades, patches, and templates could be more easily distributed to owners of complex software applications. Even the way customers might purchase and use software could be dramatically impacted; some scenarios envisioned pay-per-use or other "rental" structures. For software manufacturers, costs associated with production (copying diskettes or burning CDs), packaging, and shipping

---

[15]Interview with Shelley Morrisette, April 27, 1998.
[16]Stephanie Miles, "Egghead cracks the mold," CNET News.com, February 3, 1998.
[17]Steve Raymund, "Tech Data's Raymund ponders ESD possibilities," *Computer Reseller News*, February 10, 1997.

could be dramatically lowered if not eliminated altogether. And since it was guaranteed that users would have to register at the time of purchase, it was hoped that software piracy could be reduced. Developers could utilize tools such as ZipLock, developed by Portland Software, which authorized programs delivered via ESD to be unlocked only after payment was received by the vendor.

However, any software company asessing the promise of ESD also had to be aware of the barriers to its full implementation, as well as the risks involved in its utilization. Many software packages required a great deal of supporting documentation, but physical operating manuals would obviously still require physical delivery. Some in the industry also worried about safety issues associated with ESD. "If users can download software, they can download trouble," wrote Jesse Berst, editorial director of ZDNet. He suggested the development of gateways through which virus protection, licensing, and payment could be handled centrally. A final concern—one that plagued virtually all aspects of e-commerce, but ESD in particular—was bandwidth. While ESD was viable for corporations and educational institutions with high-bandwidth Internet connections such as T1 lines, it might be a long time before the "pipes" serving the burgeoning home and small-business PC markets could support widespread use of ESD.

Software developers such as Microsoft seemed especially focused on advancing and improving ESD. Martin Tobias, Microsoft's marketing manager for emerging channels, declared that his company's efforts were designed to complement—not bypass—traditional software resellers: "It's the natural evolution of the channel." Resellers, on the other hand, worried that the writing was on the wall: "Online software distribution could be a disintermediation in the channel," commented Pete Rourke of MicroAge. Whatever the motive, ESD offered a potentially powerful means of developing customer relations and profiles within the marketspace.

Conclusion

Wall Street supported Egghead's moves during the spring of 1998: the company's shares rose 66% between late January and the beginning of April. At the same time, a number of Egghead insiders filed to sell portions of their shares, capturing the appreciation in the stock's price. While Egghead spokespeople offered prosaic explanations for the filings, some observers wondered about possible ulterior motives.

The rise of Egghead stock was not the only sign of support for the company's efforts: industry observers expressed favor with Egghead's new focus on the Internet. "What they're recognizing is, if they don't get out there as the big place right now, they're going to be left behind," said John Scott Dixon, director of electronic media for direct-PC marketer Insight. "Retail is going to die. It's on its way out." Dixon and others felt that new technologies like ESD threatened to make traditional software packaging and distribution, not to mention retail formats in general, a thing of the past.

Optimism about the market, though, was tempered with caution about Egghead's chances. "This change in strategy doesn't necessarily mean that they will be successful," commented one analyst. "While the Internet is a very important and viable distribution channel to have, keep in mind that only 18 to 20 percent of households are online."

Still, in its last earnings report, Egghead had claimed that it was generating $1 million a week from online sales. Undoubtedly, many others were watching its continued progress, both as a guide for their own strategy and as a harbinger of the future of retailing.

Exhibit 1 Egghead Historical Financial Information

Selected Egghead Financials: FY 1995–1997			
Income Statement (mil.)	**March 97**	**March 96**	**March 95**
Revenue	$360.7	$403.8	$862.6
COGS	332.1	364.8	769.7
Gross Profit	28.6	39.0	92.9
SG&A	60.6	59.6	90.7
Operating Income	(32.0)	(20.6)	2.2
Nonoperating Income	3.4	2.5	2.4
Income Before Taxes	(44.2)	(18.1)	4.4
Net Income After Taxes	$(49.0)	$(11.1)	$2.7
Balance Sheet (mil.)	**March 97**	**March 96**	**March 95**
Cash	$83.5	$49.6	$42.6
Net Receivables	17.9	24.1	84.5
Inventories	49.1	84.7	102.9
Other Current Assets	4.1	86.1	11.0
Total Current Assets	154.6	244.5	241.0
Net Fixed Assets	19.7	29.5	23.4
Other Noncurrent Assets	1.2	7.6	5.8
Total Assets	$175.5	$281.6	$270.1
Accounts Payable	$43.0	$119.3	$104.4
Short-Term Debt	—	0.3	0.1
Other Current Liabilities	32.0	21.5	17.6
Total Current Liabilities	75.0	141.1	122.3
Long-Term Debt	—	0.3	0.1
Other Noncurrent Liabilities	0.4	0.9	1.3
Total Liabilities	$75.4	$142.3	$123.7
Common Stock	$100.0	$139.3	$146.4
Shares Outstanding	17.6	17.5	17.2
Cash Flow Statement (mil.)	**March 97**	**March 96**	**March 95**
Net Operating Cash Flow	$ (3.8)	$ 20.8	$ 31.0
Net Investing Cash Flow	37.7	(16.9)	(14.1)
Net Financing Cash Flow	—	3.0	—
Net Change in Cash	33.9	7.0	16.9
Depreciation & Amortization	7.1	10.7	10.5
Capital Expenditures	(5.1)	(16.2)	(14.2)

Exhibit 2 Projections for e-Commerce Categories

Online Shopping Revenues by Type (revenue in millions)							
Product Category	**1996**	**1997**	**1998**	**1999**	**2000**	**2001**	**2002**
Travel	$274	$816	$1,841	$3,127	$4,590	$6,301	$8,606
PC Hardware, Consumer Electronics	91	767	1,816	2,953	4,290	5,959	8,219
Grocery	28	85	270	783	1,872	3,889	6,557
PC Software	20	69	173	359	730	1,341	2,315
Books	27	109	216	395	725	1,265	2,199
Clothing & Accessories	6	18	71	192	443	893	1,926
Tickets (e.g., concerts)	2	52	127	277	568	1,071	1,735
Specialty Gifts (e.g., flowers)	14	35	81	174	354	670	1,148
Other	183	519	963	1,293	1,416	2,230	3,409
Total	707	2,594	5,775	9,911	15,574	24,533	37,496
Growth Rate	—	267%	123%	72%	57%	58%	53%

Source: Adaptation of Jupiter Communications, "1998 Online Shopping Report," Spring 1998

Exhibit 3 Selected Company and Industry Performance Data

Egghead and Industry Comparables			
Comparable	**Egghead**	**Industry**	**Market**
Gross Profit Margin	9.50%	12.41%	44.05%
Net Profit Margin	−16.65	0.63	5.60
Return on Assets	−26.40	1.70	2.40
Return on Invested Capital	−43.50	3.60	7.10
Days of Sales Outstanding	11.71	42.63	55.69
Inventory Turnover	3.5	8.1	6.7
Net Receivables Turnover Flow	15.8	9.2	6.6
Current Ratio	1.93	1.53	1.32
Quick Ratio	0.9	0.8	0.8
Leverage Ratio	1.64	3.90	5.37
12-Month Revenue Growth	−16.6	15.5	8.4
36-Month Revenue Growth	−26.9	24.9	9.7

"Market" and "Industry" classification from Media General Financial Services, Inc.
"Market" data refers to 8,000 public companies trading on NYSE, AmEx, and NASDAQ.

Exhibit 4 Yearly Income of Web Users

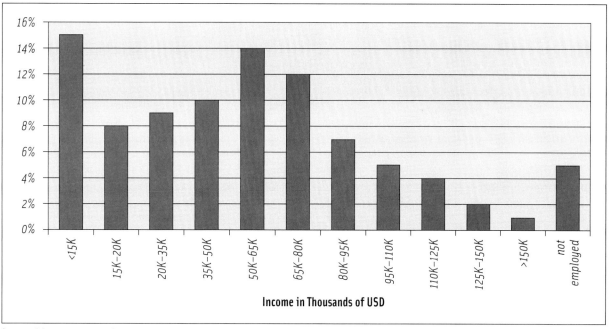

Source: Adaptation of data from Hambrecht & Quist, LinkExchange, "Media Usage and the Internet," Volume 1, Issue 1: March 1998

VIRTUAL VINEYARDS

www.virtualvin.com

If you feel a little bit superior every time the Internet is mentioned—superior because you proudly know nothing at all about it—you have every reason to feel justified. The 'Net is still, in the end, worthless. It is possible to cruise through life without ever getting near the information superhighway. Then again, the same could be said for sailing down the Ganges, bone fishing on some remote shore, or going to hear a Bach chorale in a beautiful old cathedral.

Perhaps, too, your reluctance to go digital was fostered by a suspicion that the vast, interconnected matrix of computer networks was somewhat . . . uncivilized. Well, fret no more. You may be surprised to find that even in cyberspace there are men and women of taste, culture and good breeding, and it can be a place of serendipitous, even urbane, pleasures. On the 'Net you can find a fine cigar or a good pinot noir; you can find up-to-the-minute exchange rates for rubles, or where to get a great deal on a Bugatti.

—William F. Allman, "A Gentleman's Guide to the Internet"[1]

There was no musty smell of old bottles of port in the air, no shop attendant in a burgundy-stained apron behind a counter. In fact, when Virtual Vineyards opened in January 1995, there was no counter at all. Instead, founders Peter Granoff and Robert Olson—otherwise known as the Cork Dork and the Propeller Head—had created one of the most popular wine-buying sites on the Internet. It had neat, simple, and, therefore, quickly downloadable graphics combined with flowering descriptions of wine to replace a real-world retailing environment. Custom-designed tasting charts with ratings of each wine and photographs of vineyards provided an information-based alternative for the traditional customer activity of cradling a bottle or scrutinizing a label.

Virtual Vineyards reported averaging more than 1,500 visitors a day to its World Wide Web site in November 1995, and its revenues increasing 20% per month.[2] The company was devoting millions in investment capital to developing its site, automating order fulfillment, building a database to track Web site usage and orders, and developing its brand through advertising. Although its revenues were growing quickly, Virtual Vineyards had yet to reach profitability, in large part due to heavy investment in automation and technology. (This situation was characteristic of the majority of start-up Internet companies.)

Despite these resource-intensive activities, Olson and Granoff had a greater vision for their new enterprise. Their intentions went as deep as the company name, which officially was Net Contents, Inc. (The company's first Web site was Virtual Vineyards.) Net Contents' technology infrastructure could support a much larger volume of traffic than Virtual Vineyards currently accounted for, and it could do so at a low marginal cost. Olson and Granoff were considering several ways to increase volume, including expanding Net Contents' offerings into specialty foods and fresh produce. As they moved forward with such plans, however, Olson and Granoff faced the question of whether to develop brand recognition for individual sites or for the company as a whole. They also had to assess the nature of the service relationship they had established with customers: would it allow them to extend the sales potential of the firm from wine to related categories? The decision on expansion would have significant impacts on whether the company would maintain a consistent screen interface or develop a new one for each line of business. It would also potentially alter the ways Virtual Vineyards maximized user satisfaction and retention across all its current offerings.

Research Associate Thomas A. Gerace and Doctoral Candidate Lisa R. Klein, MBA '91, prepared this case under the supervision of Professors Jeffrey F. Rayport and Alvin J. Silk as the basis for class discussion rather than to illustrate either effective or ineffective handling of an administrative situation.

[1]William F. Allman, "A Gentleman's Guide to the Internet," (*Forbes FYI*, September 25, 1995) p. 133.
[2]Julie Schmit, "Virtual Stores Set-up Shop," *USA Today* (November 13, 1995), p. 4E.

The Propeller Head

Robert Olson knew computing. After earning a masters in electrical engineering from Stanford University, Olson worked for 21 years in computer systems design, real-time operating systems, software development, engineering management, and marketing with leading technology firms, including Hewlett-Packard and Silicon Graphics, and with a start-up supercomputer company that ultimately failed. Infected by the number of start-ups sprouting up around him in Silicon Valley, Olson left Silicon Graphics in 1994 to found his own company.

The conventional wisdom about Internet-based commerce at the time viewed the Internet as a low cost channel for reaching customers with strong computer skills who enjoyed working and playing on their computers. Consequently, much of the retail development then going on was focused on low-end commodity products. Olson's background was with companies that focused more on quality or value than on price; he came to believe that there was a market for using the Web to retail non-commodity products. As he considered what product to sell on a Web platform, he decided that three criteria should apply in making the selection:

- Customers' buying decisions should be significantly influenced by information at the point of sale.

- The product should not be readily available in all varieties that consumers might want, since there was no point in entering the market to compete primarily on the basis of price from the start.

- There should be a potential to provide enhanced value to customers by bundling the products offered with knowledge provided by an expert who thoroughly understood the product, the industry that created it, and customers' preferences and buying behavior with respect to it.

By May 1994, Olson believed he had identified the perfect product according to these criteria: it was fine California wines. Wine buyers often relied on recommendations and product descriptions at the point of purchase. Rapid mergers in wine distributors had left small vineyards without proper distribution channels; many had tried to sell direct but found the marketing costs too high. Only those retailers with relationships to vineyards producing the best wines were able to get an allotment of wine to sell. Thus, the marketplace seemed to offer a niche in wine distribution that was currently not being met. As luck would have it, Olson's brother-in-law, Peter Granoff, possessed a professional knowledge of wines and was interested in joining Olson's business.

The Cork Dork

When we ask about this wellspring of passion for wine, Peter responds, "I grew up in a rural setting and have a deep attachment to the earth, to the cycle of the seasons, to wild places. Wine and food continue to fascinate me because they are from the soil. They are about farming, and they provide a bridge from those wild places to finer things, like art and culture. Then, of course, wine and food are about pleasure, so they appeal to the senses and the intellect. Additionally, the learning curve is steep in these fields. The more you learn, the more you need to know. Perhaps most importantly, though, wine and food are the vehicles for the coming together of family, friends, and loved ones. I think of the phrase 'breaking bread' and all the traditions and rituals that surround that act." In fact, it was that act that gave rise to Virtual Vineyards, when Peter and brother-in-law and co-founder Robert Olson, were chatting at dinner one night.
—Virtual Vineyards on Peter Granoff

We usually tell people that we made the decision to go into business over a nice dinner and a great bottle of wine; it's more romantic that way. The truth is, though, we got together one morning in my bedroom—which doubles as my home office—and talked it over.
— Robert Olson

Peter Granoff knew food and wine. Growing up in California's coastal Carmel Valley, Granoff remembers when his father once drove 40 miles for fresh cilantro to make a traditional Mexican dish. He recalls how his parents followed European tradition at mealtime, drinking wine or beer as the dish required. "The wine was never very expensive, as money was always an issue when we grew up. My parents rarely took a social drink. Wine and beer were almost always presented in the context of a meal."

Granoff was introduced to fine wines during the winter of 1978, which he spent working as a busboy at a resort in Gstaad, Switzerland. He fell in love with wines and the affair lasted a lifetime. Upon his return to the United States, he received a degree in International Studies from the Monterey Institute. Immediately thereafter, he returned to Europe to work as general manager for the Bombard Society in Burgundy, France. The Bombard Society, a travel company, offered guests hot air balloon rides during the day and fine meals in the evening.

Granoff returned to the United States to employ his expertise in San Francisco as a sommelier, or wine steward, at the Stanford Court Hotel from 1986 to 1991 and at Square One restaurant from 1991 to 1994.[3] He recalled:

> Square One was one of the few restaurants in the country with a dedicated person to focus on their wine program. I was hired to continue building their thriving wine business, maintain their cellar, monitor inventory, train the waitstaff, do promotion, hold events, and work the floor.
>
> It was like a business within a business. Wine accounted for approximately 25% of the restaurant's revenues while I was there. We would hold wine classes twice each month for our more interested customers.
>
> In the evenings, I was always on hand to recommend a bottle of wine to customers who wanted it. With six to eight waiters and only one sommelier, I couldn't hit every table. The waitstaff was trained, however, to know when to suggest that I visit one of our guests.
>
> If our customers knew exactly what they wanted, then the waiter would bring it; I wasn't involved. If the customer, however, had some trepidation about ordering wine, or wanted to try something new, their waiter would signal me and I would stop by the table.
>
> Each table was different. I needed to size up the customer before helping them select a wine. If a customer had a business dinner in progress, I would be in and out quickly, and ask how we might make their evening more productive. If, on the other hand, we had a couple in for a romantic dinner, I might linger a bit to give them the story behind a vineyard or answer their questions about a bottle.
>
> Next, if the customer wanted some guidance, I talked with them about what they usually enjoyed, what food they were having, and make a suggestion or two. Having a sommelier on staff allowed us to offer wines that other restaurants could not, because they needed to be "hand sold."
>
> I love to introduce people to things they've never tried. I especially like to shatter people's preconceived notions about what they do and don't like. I have to tread carefully here, because I come from a family of pontificators. I know that trait can border on obnoxious, especially in the case of wine, which carts so much pompous baggage already. It's why I enjoy taking my wine with a strong dose of humor.

In 1990, after many years in the restaurant business, Granoff was honored with the James Beard Foundation's Sommelier of the Year award. The award inspired him to prepare for and take the Master Sommelier exam in 1991;[4] he passed the exam with the highest aggregate score of any taking the test and thus won the Krug Champagne Cup. By May 1994, Granoff was tired of the restaurant business and looked for a new way to use his talents as a taster. When Olson told him about his new venture, Granoff jumped at the chance to join it.

U.S. Wine Market[5]

An estimated 74.4% of all wine consumed in the United States was made in California, more than 11.1% was made elsewhere in the United States, and the rest was imported. The U.S. industry included hundreds of vineyards, but the top three producers accounted for 63% of sales, with the next seven accounting for another 19%. The wine industry comprised a number of alcoholic beverages, including table wine, wine coolers, champagne and sparkling wine, dessert and fortified wine (e.g., port), and vermouth, all of which were classified as wine because they resulted from the fermentation of grapes.

---

[3]Granoff himself responded to a Virtual Vineyards customer's query, "What is a sommelier, anyway?" as follows: "Sommelier is the French word for wine waiter or wine steward. In many restaurants, hotels and clubs this individual also does the purchasing, writes the wine list, and is responsible for inventories and wine-related staff training. A true sommelier also works in the dining room helping guests select appropriate wines for their meal and budget, and is proficient in all aspects of fine service. A really good sommelier, in my opinion, is not a snob, and endeavors to make wine more fun and understandable. Although long a tradition in fine European restaurants, there are relatively few positions available for sommeliers in American restaurants, clubs and hotels."

[4]The Sommelier credentials program consists of three levels of testing. The first level (Sommelier) requires the candidate pass a written test on wine and other alcoholic beverage service. The second (Advanced Sommelier) has three parts, a blind tasting in which the candidate must describe a wine and explain what the taste of the wine suggested about the grape, region, and winemaking processes, a written component on wine history and theory, and a component dedicated to service. The final level (Master Sommelier) had similar components to the second, but was performed orally—with questions from examiners—and was scored more difficulty.

[5]This section draws significantly from *Jobson's Wine Handbook 1995* (New York: Jobson Publishing Company, 1995) and from Thomas Urban and Ray Goldberg, "Robert Mondavi Corporation," Harvard Business School, Case N9-596-031.

Despite a renewed interest in table wine in the 1990s, the United States represented only 5% of the world's wine consumption in 1995.

Consumers could choose from thousands of different wines from hundreds of vineyards. In 1994, the equivalent of 156,968,000 cases of table wine, each containing twelve 750 milliliter (ml) bottles, were sold in the United States, an increase of 5.6% over 1993. Sales were predicted to grow to 173,500,000 cases by 1999. The most popular bottles of wine retailed for between $4.26 and $10.00, with 65.4% of all sales falling in that range (see Exhibit 1 for the distribution of sales by price).

Virtual Vineyards catered to the upper end of the wine market by giving its customers access to wine from small wineries in California that did not distribute nationally. Most wine sold by Virtual Vineyards cost between $10.00 and $15.00 per bottle. Olson believed that sales of super-premium and ultra-premium table wines—those priced above $7.50 at retail—were growing faster than the table wine market as a whole.[6]

Some statistics were regularly collected on wine purchasers. Consumption was fairly evenly spread across age groups with approximately 24% of adults consuming domestic table wine in any year, with the highest penetration in the 45- to 54-year-old age group. 56.9% of domestic wine drinkers were women. 48.1% of domestic table wine drinkers earned over $50,000 per year, although these consumers comprised only 32.5% of the population. 29.0% of domestic table wine drinkers worked in professional or managerial jobs, even though people in these occupations accounted for just 18.0% of the total U.S. population. Virtual Vineyards therefore believed that wine drinkers were more likely to be familiar with the Internet than the population as a whole. (Exhibits 2 through 15 contain data on wine sales, consumers, and consumption.)

Wine Distribution

In 1994, off-premises sales (that is, sales outside restaurants) accounted for 60% of the money spent on wine and 80% of the wine volume sold. Large producers, such as Ernest & Julio Gallo and Robert Mondavi, dominated wine distribution channels. They had sufficient resources to create a national brand franchise that allowed such companies to charge price premiums for their goods, which, in turn, motivated distributors to carry their products, and secured scarce shelf space in retail wine shops.[7] Many of the hundreds of wineries that produced less than 60,000 bottles per year did not have the scale to develop relationships with retailers and restaurants across the country and were too small to interest distributors. In addition, they lacked the marketing muscle to build nationwide brand recognition. As a result, they sold their wine primarily to restaurants on the West Coast and by mail.

Retail

Vineyards sold the wine they produced to distributors; distributors, in turn, sold it to retailers and restaurants for resale to end-consumers. Vineyards received on average 60% of the price paid by the end consumer, the distributor (wholesaler) took 10% to 25% (covering shipping costs and taxes), and the retailer or restaurant kept the remaining 15% to 30%. Widely divergent state regulatory regimes meant that this split varied considerably depending on the state in which the end consumer purchased the wine.

Retail locations varied significantly in size, offerings, and service. Dan Comerford, owner and manager of the Wine & Cheese Cask, a specialty foods shop in Somerville, Massachusetts, reflected:

> Maybe 70% to 80% of all wine sold in retail locations is sold in supermarkets. People walk in, drop a bottle in their cart, and keep going to the next aisle. Our store isn't like that. Two-fifths of our customers ask for a recommendation about what wine to buy. We have four full-time people who specialize in wine and two part-timers who know a great deal.
>
> If a customer wanted a recommendation, I would first establish the color of the wine they were interested in and their approximate price range. Some people want a $4 bottle and some are looking to spend upwards of $50. Then I'd ask if they preferred wine from a particular country or were going to use it with a specific meal. I'd then suggest a bottle. People tend to follow our suggestions and I guess we must do OK—about 75% to 80% of our sales are to regular customers.

For the Wine & Cheese Cask, as for other specialty wine retailers, providing reliable information concerning what wines to buy proved essential to establishing customer loyalty and capturing repeat business.

---

[6]Super-premium wines were those with retail prices between $7.51 and $10.00 per bottle. Ultra-premium wines sold at retail for $10.01 and more.
[7]Ibid, p. 11.

Direct Mail

The late 1980s saw a rise in direct mail wine distribution. Wine-by-mail began with small vineyards attempting to enlarge the markets for their output by targeting customers beyond their local areas. Vineyards estimated that 25% of the retail price was allocated to shipping and handling, with much of the remainder retained by them.[8] However, many vineyards underestimated the cost of marketing associated with direct mail and eventually closed their direct mail operations after realizing slim to negative profits.

In place of such direct mail programs, however, came catalogs specializing in wine from multiple vineyards. For example, Geerlings and Wade featured descriptions and ratings of selected items, which it sold by the case or half-case. Geerlings, like conventional distributors, had to obtain a distribution license for every state in which it sold wine and charge sales tax on every sale.

New Distribution Channels

With the advent of on-line services and the Internet's World Wide Web, a variety of virtual wine sellers appeared among the hundreds of World Wide Web wine sites. Some virtual sites, like Sam's Wine Warehouse (www.sams-wine.com), were extensions of existing physical retail operations. Sam's offered regular in-stock wines for sale over the Internet, allowed users to read a newsletter about special items, and promoted special services, such as custom labeling of bottles for special occasions. The site did not, however, describe or rate wines beyond those designated as featured selections.

Other sites aimed at direct sale by the vineyards, which found that Internet marketing could be cheap or free if they registered with Internet search engines and catalogues. Kendall-Jackson *(www.kj.com)*, for example, featured descriptions of their vineyard, the wines, and the winemaking processes, as well as information "hot off the presses" about upcoming vintages. As of April 1996, the vineyard did not offer on-line ordering, but its site displayed and described wines and accessories, such as corkscrews and Kendall-Jackson tee-shirts, which could be ordered by calling a toll-free telephone number. The site promised interactive shopping soon.

While many of the online sites did offer virtual shopping, none was as well known as Virtual Vineyards. It also had been a pioneer in the use of encryption protocols to protect customers' credit card information as it was sent over the Internet. The site was widely recognized for ease of use, depth of information about products, and Peter Granoff's wine ratings as well as e-mail responses to customer inquiries.

The Company

To its customers, Virtual Vineyards was a World Wide Web site. Supporting the efforts of Olson and Granoff, however, was an additional staff of 15. The corporate headquarters, a two-room office in Los Altos, California, was packed with people, equipment, and the occasional bottle of wine. An engineering team, intermixed with the first line of order processing, management, marketing, and customer support filled the large outer room. The Virtual Vineyards servers occupied the second room. Storage, order packing, and shipping was contracted through a fulfillment firm located across town.

The Technology

The Virtual Vineyards Web site was designed, built, and maintained largely in-house. The site ran on Pentium-based computer systems and was connected to the Internet through a dedicated, high-speed connection (a T1, or 1.54 megabit per second, line). The site was designed to be attractive, but simple, with few graphics to ensure that it would load quickly when accessed by users with slower connections to the Internet (e.g., using modems rather than Ethernet connections). The company used a standardized format on most pages (see Exhibits 16 through 21 for screen shots of pages from Virtual Vineyards' Web site).

While many competitors required users to jot down a product number or name when browsing, then enter that information on a separate order sheet, Virtual Vineyards recorded customer selections automatically and generated an order form at the click of a button. Customers needed only to fill in quantity information and a "ship to" state and the Virtual Vineyards site would produce a final tally and take ordering information.

Ruth Colombo, vice president of engineering, coordinated the development of technology for the company. "We don't really have titles here, but that's the role I fill," she explained. While most of the staff reported directly to Olson, Colombo coordinated the activities of the four developers and the system administrator. She reflected,

---

[8]See Laura Pochop and Howard Stevenson, "Vintage Directions, Inc.," Harvard Business School, Case 9-393-043.

It's our content—not our technology—that has differentiated Virtual Vineyards from other wine sites. They are not information rich. It's expensive to put that content together and to keep it up to date.

We've developed a lot of tools to automate that process. Today, Peter will review a wine, pop his text into a template, and an HTML [Web] page is automatically generated. Our goal is to have the pages populated dynamically for each individual customer. If a customer likes certain wines, we want to show them similar choices automatically.

Virtual Vineyards had spent approximately $500,000 to develop the Web site; $300,000 to develop relationships with suppliers, arrange contracts with them, and set up its warehouse; and $500,000 to cover marketing and administrative overhead. In early 1996, Colombo and her staff began building a database to enable customer and inventory tracking. The new database and resulting features would require the company to move to a Silicon Graphics platform and invest, Colombo projected, an additional $900,000 during 1996.

Content

Hi,

I hope your holiday season wasn't too frenetic, and that you had the time to linger over a great bottle of wine with family and friends.

Here is a copy of a question that I have received in one form or another many times, along with the answer I have posted in the "Ask the Cork Dork" section of Virtual Vineyards. I thought it might be of interest to everyone on our e-mail list:

Question: I once received a bottle of wine with crystals on the cork and at the bottom of the bottle. What are they? Should I be concerned about them?

Answer: I wanted to address the crystals on the cork you mention, because you might see it someday in one of our wines, too! This is a deposit that sometimes forms in bottles of wine that have been stored for extended periods of time at very cold cellar temperatures. It is known in the wine industry as "tartrates," and is primarily potassium acid tartrate (the potassium salt of tartaric acid), which is naturally occurring in wine. Although cosmetically disturbing, it is not in any way an indication of a bad bottle or inferior

wine. It is, however, an indication that the wine has not been "cold-stabilized," a procedure many artisan producers specifically avoid. To prevent tartrates from forming, a wine must be deeply chilled for several days prior to bottling. The tartrates form and settle in the tank, and the wine is then bottled without them. It is a controversial procedure because some wine makers insist you can't cold stabilize without removing other desirable flavor and aroma elements at the same time. Large producers usually cold-stabilize because they can't afford the risk of thousands of bottles coming back from retailers and consumers who are alarmed in the way that you were. Small producers who take the risk in the interest of better quality, do so with the expectation that their wines are being hand sold by restauranteurs or retailers who are in a position to explain tartrates. Many of the wine producers in the Virtual Vineyards portfolio do not cold-stabilize their wines. I used to actually have some fun with this phenomenon when serving wine to restaurant customers over the years. If they did not appear to be mollified by an explanation of tartrates, I would take a big chunk off the cork and eat it right there at the table—if nothing else it always got a laugh. They are practically tasteless, by the way, and definitely harmless.

Cheers,

Peter Granoff (a.k.a. cork dork) (415) 917 5750 fax (415) 917 5764 URL http://www.virtualvin.com (800) 289 1275 170 State Street, Suite 250 Los Altos, CA 94022

The textual content of the Virtual Vineyards site was provided by Granoff. In addition to the Web site, Virtual Vineyards operated a mailing list in which Granoff would discuss new wines, good wine and food combinations, the state of the current crop, and other items of interest. Granoff recognized that the experience of selling wine on the Web was significantly different from his work at Square One.

The one limitation of the Web is the lack of face-to-face contact. At Square One, I could interact with customers, judge what they needed, and tailor my presentation accordingly. But the Web has its own advantages. The site allows us to present the full story, in perfect language, about every product we have. The customer can read the history of a particular winemaker or vineyard, learn about the specific taste, and receive a complete description of the taste. It's as if I could sit down at every table and spend as much time as our guests would like.

We are also trying, in this medium, to convey the entire story of wine. We discuss its place in society and culture and we talk about the language used to describe wine. We try to demystify or untangle it so that the intimidated customer can learn. I found when teaching wine classes that people would ask their best questions when they came up to me after class. They were embarrassed during class that they would look foolish. With e-mail, there is a comfortable anonymity. People are more likely to ask about new or confusing concepts.

Virtual Vineyards staff believed that Granoff's writing was the primary reason for the company's success. "People believe that Peter is writing a personal letter to them. It's his style," Olson commented. "We once had a customer send Peter a note to let him know she wouldn't be ordering from us for a while. Can you imagine that happening in a local wine store?"

Virtual Vineyards answered every letter and e-mail it received. Peter Granoff bore most of the burden, but in January 1996, Virtual Vineyards hired a second Master Sommelier, Jim Gaiser, to help handle the content-based work and add new wines to Virtual Vineyards' portfolio.

Operations

Louise Holloway was the company's operations manager. Having spent 12 years managing distribution, importing, and exporting in the wine industry, Holloway's primary responsibilities included maintaining relationships with the vineyards that supplied the company and overseeing order fulfillment. At Virtual Vineyards, Holloway explained, fulfillment meant something very different from what it meant in typical retail channels. Virtual Vineyards received wine from its suppliers for storage in its warehouse, marketed it through its Web site at prices agreed upon by itself and the vineyard, and then packed and shipped it to end consumers via overnight mail.[9] The consumers directed payments to Virtual Vineyards; the company passed those payments on to the vineyards after taking a fee for its work marketing the wine and organizing shipment and payment. This fee ranged from 30% to 45% of the retail price and was negotiated in the agreement it reached with each individual vineyard. Vir-

tual Vineyards did not actually sell the wine, because at no point did it own the wine. This was another respect in which the company was "virtual": the only thing Virtual Vineyards owned in the marketing and sales process was the copyright for the images on its Web site.

Holloway explained suppliers' view of the arrangement:

> The vineyards we use would normally sell out [their production run]. We are buying some of the finest wines in the area. They let us have wine on consignment not because they need an additional distribution channel, but because we return a greater percentage of the retail sale price to them.

Granoff explained that his and Holloway's relationships with the vineyards also mattered:

> The wine business [as an industry] is cautious. Reputation is everything to a vineyard, and a vineyard's reputation is developed and maintained partially through positioning. Whose wine lists you appear on, which bottles are next to yours on a shelf or in an advertisement, and what vineyards you are compared with are very important questions for quality vineyards.
>
> Our customers know that I understand the importance of positioning and trust that I won't put them on a Web page with a vineyard that is inappropriate. Compare this to the average Web designer. They rarely understand the industry, charge a fee to develop a customer's site, have little or no concern for the sales that might result, and have every incentive to accept contracts from every willing vineyard.

The addition of a new vineyard did not mark the end of Holloway's work. The back-end customer- and order-tracking database was not in place, so managing order fulfillment was difficult. She explained the process:

> When an order comes in on the system [through the Web site], we first have to validate the order. By that, I mean we have to check to make sure the order looks viable; we've had orders from "Grey Slick"[10] and the like and we don't want to ship wine to a false address. If the order seems normal, we then put it into an electronic file which is picked up by the warehouse. The warehouse ships the order, including gift cards, that day.
>
> On Fridays, we have to hold most orders to avoid storage in bad temperatures. We make sure to advise customers of that delay. They are usually very grateful to be notified and glad we're taking care of their wine.

---

[9]Ground shipping was available in California and other nearby areas, but could not be used for greater distance due to the risk of breakage or damage to the wine due to poor storage conditions en route.
[10]Grace Slick helped found the rock band Jefferson Airplane in the 1960s and was its lead singer.

I have to watch inventory at the same time as I supervise fulfillment. If I see an order coming in for bottles that are in short supply, I yell to Ruth to take it off the system. We don't want to have to tell a customer that we can't send out the order they just placed. Soon, all of this—from order taking to inventory management—will be automated.

Marketing

Defining the Customer

Olson and Granoff believed that their customers were people interested in a good glass of wine with dinner, but not wine connoisseurs. They also believed that Virtual Vineyards provided most value to customers who did not have sophisticated knowledge of wine, since wine enthusiasts would not need Granoff's ratings and commentary to guide their buying decisions. Virtual Vineyards offered wines across a wide price range—$6.50 to $50.00 per bottle—and Olson and Granoff believed that most of their customers were willing to experiment with bottles costing between $8.00 and $20.00. Their ideal target was a woman or man with moderate to high income, who was interested in learning more about wine. However, Virtual Vineyards had done no systematic research on its customers and site visitors, so these opinions were based on casual observation and interactions with individual customers (via e-mail).

As major commercial online services began to offer their customers access to the World Wide Web, Virtual Vineyards' customer base appeared to be shifting and its Web site received many more visits. Traffic ballooned in mid-summer 1995 and weekday fluctuations evened out. As of December 1995, roughly 15% of visitors to the site came from America Online and Prodigy, two of the major online services. These visitors also accounted for approximately 15% of sales.

Finding the Customer through Advertising

Olson and Granoff faced a challenge in creating awareness of the site and attracting customers to visit it. Traditional retail businesses often pursued customers through direct mail advertising, which involved sending information to many people who were believed to be likely patrons. Sophisticated catalog retailers often turned development of such mailing lists into a fine art, estab-

lishing name and address records of heavy users who were characterized by high purchase frequency and volume as well as high retention rates. Based on profiles of those heavy users, catalog merchants targeted mailings for customer acquisition more precisely and thus brought down costs for acquisition by driving response rates up. Even so, direct mail solicitation could represent a scattershot approach, where a response rate of two percent was considered good (i.e., two percent of those who received the direct mail solicitation actually bought something from the catalog) and rates of five to ten percent for retained or current customers was viewed as impressive.

Instead of employing direct mail, Virtual Vineyards advertised on the Web itself, buying advertising space on other Web sites that Olson and Granoff believed were visited by the kinds of people Virtual Vineyards targeted. Their advertisements included "hotlinks" that allowed viewers of the advertisement to click on it and move to Virtual Vineyards' Web site. The company tracked the number of visitors who came through each advertising hotlink and the purchases they made. Many of the links had not brought in customers, but Olson believed that a trial-and-error approach to finding the best advertising sites was necessary. He also suspected that word-of-mouth and reviews from magazines and other Web sites were more effective than advertisements in attracting the right type of customer.

Olson considered marketing to prospective customers through print advertisements and broadcast media spots, but he worried that these advertisements would have to perform two different, though related, functions: first, they would need to interest customers in the site, as Web advertisements did, and, second, they would need to motivate readers to get on-line (while remembering Virtual Vineyards' Web address or URL). Print advertising was also expensive for a small company and difficult to target effectively. Would Virtual Vineyards want to advertise in *Wine Spectator*, with an audience of people interested in wine, or a publication focusing on electronic communication, such as *Wired?* Furthermore, measuring advertisements' effectiveness would be expensive and difficult.

In designing Virtual Vineyards' marketing, Olson spent time studying advertising techniques such as direct mail, catalog retailing, print and broadcast advertising, infomercials, and telemarketing to develop ways of tapping the Web's unique capabilities in the context of the Virtual Vineyards site. The challenge lay in adapting such learning to take advantage of the Web's resources, which included functions that had no parallels in conventional marketing channels. These were hotlinks customers could use to access other sites and sources of related information, as well as the ease with which the Web site could collect information on visitors' activities. As a pioneering retailer on the Web, Olson was, in effect, attempting to reinvent retailing—and, in a larger sense, marketing within his category—for the interactive world.

Communicating with the Customer

From the start, Virtual Vineyards had actively promoted Granoff's expertise as a key source of value. Site visitors were able to put their names on a list to receive information from Virtual Vineyards regularly via e-mail. By early 1996, this list contained nearly 3,000 members. Approximately twice a month they received a note from Granoff describing new selections and making recommendations for wine purchases for upcoming holidays or seasonal events.

In September 1995, Virtual Vineyards implemented a registration process whereby the site could store customers' billing and credit card information to facilitate faster purchasing. Registered users also received access to their own personal "account histories." The registration process surveyed customers with only a few questions about themselves, because Olson believed his target customers were time-constrained and that there were only a limited number of categories of customer information that Virtual Vineyards could use. The experience of other sites suggested that people were hesitant to spend extra time to provide personal information without a strong incentive. (For example, *Hot Wired,* the on-line counterpart of *Wired,* had resorted to making registration optional after receiving negative feedback about the questions it asked in its registration process.) By December 1995, over 1,700 visitors had registered with Virtual Vineyards, and half of those had provided credit card information. Olson was pleased with this response, since the only promotion he had run to encourage registration had been to offer a small discount on orders concurrently with registration.

Tracking the Customer

Survey data represented only a small part of what Virtual Vineyards learned on an ongoing basis about customers using its site. Such information was augmented by automated records on customer behavior within the site, including the number of visits made to each part (or "page"), the Internet address of the computer used by each visitor, the amount of time spent looking at each page, and what pages a user returned to during subsequent visits.

Olson had not had time to analyze thoroughly the data he had. He did know that approximately a third of visits to the site involved visitors' examination of just the first one or two "pages." Another third of the site's visitors dug deeper and visited for five to ten minutes; the rest stayed longer. Certain sections of the site, like the vineyard tours and Granoff's tasting chart, received a large volume of traffic, suggesting to Olson that these were important "stops" on the virtual tour.

Virtual Vineyards was continually improving the tracking capabilities of its server software and Olson planned to hire staff to analyze usage data in greater detail. He was especially interested in discovering what usage patterns correlated with purchasing. For example, he wanted to know if visitors who took a vineyard tour or looked at suggestions of what wines went with particular foods were more likely to make a purchase than others who skipped these items.

Purchase and Repeat Purchase Behavior

From the transaction database, Olson estimated that between 50% and 70% of Virtual Vineyards' sales were to people who had bought from the company before. Beyond these numbers, however, Olson did not know very much about the specific items purchased. He was interested especially in understanding whether customers were experimenting with new wine types or vineyards, based on Granoff's suggestions.

Conclusion: Growing the Business
Enhancing Virtual Vineyards

Even as they implemented basic operations technology, Virtual Vineyards prepared to add new features to create a more interactive, personalized experience. Olson and Granoff's goal was to take advantage fully of the World Wide Web's capabilities as a service delivery vehicle. In early 1996, they were considering adding a number of new features, including:

- A wedding gift registry;
- A feature that would enable users to search for new wines by changing the settings on Granoff's tasting chart and searching a database for wines that matched; and

- A feature that would suggest new wines to users based on their past purchases and their responses to them.

As Olson and Granoff prepared these new features and inclusion of other vineyards, they considered the value of the Virtual Vineyards brand: could this be a retail brand or were the brand names of the wines they sold more important to their customers? They also wanted to learn more about their customers. So far, they knew only their names, addresses, that they were World Wide Web users, and what they did within the Virtual Vineyards site. Olson remarked:

I believe you can always know more about your customers and this knowledge is essential to rapid growth. But the things we want to know are customers' tastes in wines and related products, not demographic items such as income bracket, preferred magazines, and so forth. Those items are the basis for classical mass-marketing approaches to advertising and customer acquisition, but we are trying to develop a more one-to-one approach to customers.

It seemed likely that much of Virtual Vineyards' appeal to customers lay in its friendly, personal interactions with users through an interface that delivered service that was preferred over physical retailing channels. Olson wondered if this might, in fact, matter more than the wine.

New Lines of Business

Olson's and Granoff's growth strategy also called for expanding into new lines of business. Net Contents planned to develop two new virtual stores, featuring gourmet foods and fresh produce. These new enterprises would allow Net Contents to capitalize on economies of scale in technology development. The two founders believed that hiring experts on each kind of food, counterparts to Granoff, would give them important competitive advantages. The two wondered, however, whether they should create these stores as extensions of Virtual Vineyards, with a similar design and interface, or give each a unique personality and "feel." In addition, they wondered if they had solved the puzzle that faced all serious Web retailers—namely, the creation of a series of screen interfaces within a single Web site that could convert fleeting customer visits into long-term customer relationships. Everyone in Web retailing knew that awareness was only half the battle; converting a "clickstream" into purchases was essential to converting free Web content into a revenues generator. Olson and Granoff believed that the key, in conventional retailing, to achieving such results was superior service quality. Yet it remained unclear as to what constituted service quality when service was provided through an automated interface. Extending the brand would only make sense if Olson and Granoff believed that they had achieved such service standards with the flagship Virtual Vineyards site.

Exhibit 1 Distribution of Sales of Wine by Price Class, 1994

Price Class	Price per Bottle (750 ml. equivalent)	Market Share
Lowest	Under $2.75	1.2%
Economy	$2.76–$4.25	8.0
Popular	$4.26–$5.75	40.5
Premium	$5.76–$7.50	24.9
Super-premium	$7.51–$10.00	16.6
Ultra-premium	$10.01 & up	8.8
Total		100.0%

Source: *Jobson's Wine Handbook 1995* (New York: Jobson Publishing Company, 1995).

Exhibit 2 Volume and Per Capita Consumption Trends by Beverage, 1990–1994

Beverage	Volume (millions of gallons)					ACGR[a]	Per Capita (gallons per person)				
	1990	1991	1992[r]	1993[r]	1994	1990–1994	1990	1991	1992[r]	1993[r]	1994
Soft drinks	11,871	12,060	12,240	12,593	12,912	1.7%	46.4%	47.8%	48.8%	48.0%	49.5%
Coffee	6,544	6,712	6,789	7,324	7,687	3.3	26.6	26.6	26.6	28.4	29.5
Milk	6,353	6,426	6,427	6,472	6,508	0.5	25.6	25.5	25.2	25.1	25.0
Beer	5,989	5,857	5,847	5,870	5,893	−0.3	23.4	23.2	22.9	22.8	22.6
Bottled water	2,199	2,210	2,292	2,449	2,588	3.3	8.1	8.8	9.0	9.5	9.9
Tea	1,777	1,786	1,779	1,786	1,798	0.2	6.9	7.1	7.0	6.9	6.9
Juices	1,542	1,614	1,666	1,676	1,680	1.7	6.8	6.4	6.5	6.5	6.4
Powdered drinks	1,318	1,412	1,356	1,341	1,349	0.5	4.8	5.6	5.3	5.2	5.2
Wine	517	479	477	448	458	−2.4	2.1	1.9	1.9	1.7	1.8
Distilled spirits	379	350	352	343	334	−2.5	1.5	1.4	1.4	1.3	1.3

Source: *Jobson's Wine Handbook 1995* (New York: Jobson Publishing Company, 1995).
[a]Annual Compound Growth Rate.

Exhibit 3 National Sales of Wine by Tier, 1993–1994 ($ millions)

	Sales	
Tier	**1993**	**1994**
Vintner/importer	$4,514.1	$4,633.0
Wholesaler	6,711.4	6,889.0
Retailer	11,559.4	11,865.0

Source: *Jobson's Wine Handbook 1995* (New York: Jobson Publishing Company, 1995).
Note: Estimated gross sales.

Exhibit 4 Percentage of Persons Who Drink Wine by Category and Residency

Category	Center City	Suburban	Rural	Total
Domestic table wine	23.3%	27.8%	15.1%	23.7%
Imported table wine	10.8	11.9	5.2	10.1
Coolers	20.5	20.8	18.4	20.2
Champagne & sparkling	18.3	20.3	11.2	17.7
Dessert & fortified	7.8	7.7	4.4	7.0
Vermouth	4.3	3.6	2.4	3.6
Aperitif & specialty	4.5	4.0	2.4	3.8
Adult population (millions of people)	30.8	84.4	38.7	178.1

Source: *Jobson's Wine Handbook 1995* (New York: Jobson Publishing Company, 1995).

Exhibit 5 Percentage of Persons Who Drink Wine by Category and Employment

Category	Professional/ Manager	Technical/ Clerical/Sales	Precision/ Craft	Other Employment
Domestic table wine	38.1%	27.5%	14.9%	16.4%
Imported table wine	18.5	10.7	7.5	6.6
Coolers	21.2	26.6	16.8	22.1
Champagne & sparkling	26.8	22.0	11.6	14.5
Dessert & fortified	8.5	7.2	5.3	5.6
Vermouth	4.6	2.6	2.6	2.7
Aperitif & specialty	5.8	4.5	2.8	2.9
Adult population (millions of people)	32.1	33.7	12.1	32.2

Source: Simmons Market Research Bureau, 1994 Study of Media and Markets
Note: Includes consumers aged 21 and over only.

Exhibit 6 Percentage of Wine Consumers by Category and Gender

Category	Percentage	Category	Percentage
Table Domestic		**Champagne & Sparkling**	
Male	43.1	Male	40.9
Female	56.9	Female	59.1
Table Imported		**Vermouth**	
Male	45.9	Male	54.0
Female	54.1	Female	46.0
Coolers		**Aperitif & Specialty**	
Male	33.8	Male	38.6
Female	66.2	Female	61.4
Dessert & Fortified			
Male	43.7		
Female	56.3		

Source: *Jobson's Wine Handbook 1995* (New York: Jobson Publishing Company, 1995).

Exhibit 7 Age Distribution of Wine Consumers by Category

	Age Groups						
Category	21–24	25–34	35–44	45–54	55–64	65+	Total Consumers
Domestic table wine	6.2%	22.7%	25.4%	19.2%	11.2%	15.3%	100.0%
Imported table wine	5.7	21.9	29.3	20.7	10.4	12.0	100.0
Coolers	13.1	29.3	26.4	15.3	8.0	7.9	100.0
Champagne & sparkling	9.6	24.9	24.5	18.4	10.8	11.9	100.0
Dessert & fortified	5.3	16.2	22.0	22.2	15.0	19.5	100.0
Vermouth	–	26.2[a]	23.5	18.4	12.6	19.3	100.0
Aperitif & specialty	–	30.4[a]	26.6	19.8	10.2	12.9	100.0
Age distribution of U.S. adult population	8.0%	23.3%	22.8%	16.3%	11.9%	17.6%	100.0%

Source: *Jobson's Wine Handbook 1995* (New York: Jobson Publishing Company, 1995).
[a]Includes consumers aged 21–34.

Exhibit 8 Income Distribution of Consumers by Wine Category

Category	$75,000 & Over	$60,000–$74,999	$50,000–$59,999	$40,000–$49,999	$30,000–$39,999	$20,000–$29,999	Under $20,000	Total
Domestic table wine	22.5%	13.2%	12.4%	12.0%	13.8%	12.9%	13.2%	100.0
Imported table wine	25.3	14.7	11.7	11.2	13.2	10.0	13.9	100.0
Coolers	14.5	9.5	10.6	12.1	15.1	15.6	22.6	100.0
Champagne & sparkling	19.7	12.9	12.1	13.0	12.8	14.1	15.5	100.0
Dessert & fortified	18.6	10.8	9.8	11.1	13.3	16.1	20.4	100.0
Vermouth	20.4	9.0	11.2	9.6	12.7	15.2	21.8	100.0
Aperitif & specialty	20.5	11.9	11.3	11.3	13.1	14.2	17.8	100.0
Adult population	13.9%	9.2%	9.4%	11.8%	14.2%	15.7%	25.9%	100.0%

Source: Simmons Market Research Bureau, 1994 Study of Media and Markets
Note: Includes consumers aged 21 and over only.

Exhibit 9 Employment Distribution of Consumers by Wine Category

Category	Professional/ Manager	Technical/ Clerical/Sales	Precision/ Craft	Other Employment	Not Employed	Total Adults
Domestic table wine	29.0%	21.9%	4.3%	12.5%	32.2%	100.0%
Imported table wine	33.1	20.1	5.1	11.8	30.0	100.0
Coolers	18.9	24.9	5.7	19.8	30.7	100.0
Champagne & sparkling	27.3	23.5	4.5	14.8	30.0	100.0
Dessert & fortified	22.0	19.5	5.2	14.4	38.9	100.0
Vermouth	23.4	13.9	5.0	13.7	44.0	100.0
Aperitif & specialty	27.5	22.4	5.0	13.8	31.3	100.0
Adult population	18.0%	18.9%	6.8%	18.1%	38.2%	100.0%

Source: *Jobson's Wine Handbook 1995* (New York: Jobson Publishing Company, 1995).

Exhibit 10 Percentage of Persons Who Drink Wine by Category and Age Group

| | Age Groups | | | | | | |
Category	21–24	25–34	35–44	45–54	55–64	65+	Total Adults
Domestic table wine	18.3%	23.1%	26.3%	27.8%	22.1%	30.3%	23.6%
Imported table wine	7.2	9.5	12.9	12.8	8.8	10.1	10.1
Coolers	32.9	25.4	23.4	18.9	13.5	13.4	20.2
Champagne & sparkling	21.1	18.9	19.0	19.9	16.0	17.6	17.7
Dessert & fortified	4.6	4.9	6.7	9.5	8.8	11.4	7.0
Vermouth	–	3.0[a]	3.7	4.0	3.8	5.8	3.8
Aperitif & specialty	–	3.7[a]	4.4	4.6	3.2	4.1	3.8
Adult population (millions)	14.3	41.5	40.7	29.0	21.3	31.3	178.1

Source: *Jobson's Wine Handbook 1995* (New York: Jobson Publishing Company, 1995).
[a]Includes consumers aged 21–34.

Exhibit 11 Percentage of Persons Who Drink Wine by Category and Education Level

Category	Graduated College	Attended College	Graduated High School	Did Not Graduate High School	Total Adults
Domestic table wine	43.2%	27.1%	18.1%	10.4%	23.7%
Imported table wine	21.0	10.8	6.3	5.0	10.1
Coolers	20.4	22.1	21.0	16.5	20.2
Champagne & sparkling	28.3	20.1	15.5	8.3	17.7
Dessert & fortified	10.9	7.2	5.9	4.9	7.0
Vermouth	6.6	3.1	2.8	2.3	3.6
Aperitif & specialty	6.7	4.2	2.7	2.4	3.8
Adult population (millions)	37.3	36.7	68.7	35.4	178.1

Source: Simmons Market Research Bureau, 1994 Study of Media and Markets.
Note: Includes consumers aged 21 and over only.

Exhibit 12 Last Drink Taken

	1984	1987	1988	1989	1990	1992	1994
Within last 24 hours	39%	38%	39%	32%	29%	26%	34%
1 day to 1 week ago	29	30	25	35	23	25	23
More than 1 week ago	31	31	34	32	47	48	42
No opinion	1	1	2	1	1	1	1

Source: The Gallup Organization

Exhibit 13 Leading Brands of Domestic Table Wine and Sales, 1990–1994 (in thousands of 9-liter cases)

Brand	Supplier	1990	1991	1992	1993	1994
Carlo Rossi	E&J Gallo Winery	17,530	16,000	16,120	15,000	15,430
Gallo Label	E&J Gallo Winery	12,400	11,800	11,900	11,000	12,000
Gallo Reserve Cellars	E&J Gallo Winery	5,800	7,000	8,200	8,900	9,600
Franzia	The Wine Group	5,100	5,300	7,100	7,600	8,100
Inglenook	Canandaigua Wine	7,800	7,200	7,340	7,450	7,450
Almaden Vineyards	Canandaigua Wine	8,100	7,390	7,845	7,750	7,000
Sebastiani	Sebastiani Vineyards	4,865	4,640	4,600	5,200	6,200
Sutter Home	Sutter Home Winery	4,070	4,150	4,800	4,610	4,900
Robert Mondavi	Robert Mondavi Winery	2,650	3,200	3,880	3,960	4,200
Paul Masson	Canandaigua Wine	4,365	4,000	3,975	3,750	3,735
Glen Ellen	Heublein	3,000	3,100	3,380	3,440	3,290
Beringer	Wine World Estates	2,100	2,100	2,300	2,450	2,700
Taylor California Cellars	Canandaigua Wine	2,750	2,575	2,485	2,400	2,450
William Wycliff	E&J Gallo Winery	1,600	1,650	1,720	1,780	1,850
Colony	The Wine Group	1,640	1,665	1,710	1,730	1,800
Fetzer	Brown Forman Beverages	1,380	1,490	1,725	1,740	1,780
Kendall-Jackson	Kendall-Jackson	600	750	1,000	1,250	1,600
Blossom Hill	Heublein	580	880	1,400	1,600	1,500
Napa Ridge	Wine World Estates	900	1,010	1,200	1,270	1,200
Cribari	Canandaigua Wine	1,650	1,000	1,300	1,075	1,050
Manischewitz	Canandaigua Wine	1,100	1,100	1,100	900	900
Total leading brands		89,980	88,000	95,080	94,855	93,735
Others		30,771	31,977	33,278	31,756	33,574
Total domestic table		120,751	119,977	128,358	126,611	132,309

Source: *Jobson's Wine Handbook 1995* (New York: Jobson Publishing Company, 1995).

Exhibit 14 Consumption of Total Wine, 1994 (750 ml bottles per 100 adults)[a]

Alabama	679	Maine	1,247	Pennsylvania	732
Alaska	1,606	Maryland	1,227	Rhode Island	1,670
Arizona	1,334	Massachusetts	1,936	South Carolina	770
Arkansas	457	Michigan	902	South Dakota	559
California	2,119	Minnesota	1,104	Tennessee	639
Colorado	1,589	Mississippi	445	Texas	951
Connecticut	1,682	Missouri	828	Utah	473
Delaware	1,593	Montana	1,127	Vermont	1,902
District of Columbia	3,212	Nebraska	845	Virginia	1,224
Florida	1,505	Nevada	2,579	Washington	1,777
Georgia	940	New Hampshire	2,223	West Virginia	349
Hawaii	1,669	New Jersey	1,875	Wisconsin	1,008
Idaho	1,380	New Mexico	898	Wyoming	770
Illinois	1,531	New York	1,617		
Indiana	881	North Carolina	946	**U.S. Total**	**1,270**
Iowa	476	North Dakota	653		
Kansas	593	Ohio	703		
Kentucky	492	Oklahoma	570		
Louisiana	982	Oregon	1,808		

Source: *Jobson's Wine Handbook 1995* (New York: Jobson Publishing Company, 1995).
[a]Population 21 years and older.

Exhibit 15 On-Premise vs. Off-Premise Case Sales of Wine, 1986–1994 (thousands of cases)

Year	On-Premise (restaurants and bars)		Off-Premise (other, including for home consumption)		Total
	Cases	Share	Cases	Share	
1986	51,062	20.6	196,810	79.4	247,872
1987	51,682	21.2	192,100	78.8	243,782
1988	48,981	21.1	183,156	78.9	232,137
1989	45,478	20.8	173,166	79.2	218,644
1990	44,190	20.3	173,396	79.7	217,586
1991	40,544	20.5	157,626	79.5	198,170
1992	40,753	20.3	160,071	79.7	200,824
1993	38,218	20.3	150,353	79.7	188,571
1994	39,188	20.3	153,858	79.7	193,046

Source: *Jobson's Wine Handbook 1995* (New York: Jobson Publishing Company, 1995).

Exhibit 16 Virtual Vineyards World Wide Web Site: Home Page

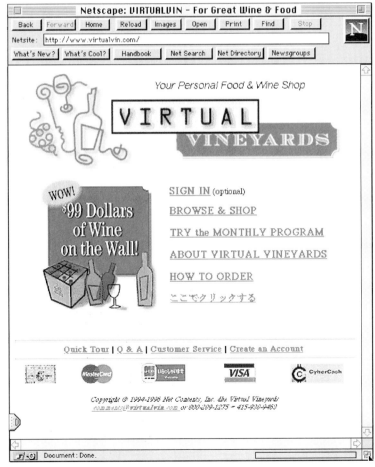

Source: *www.virtualvin.com*

Exhibit 17 Virtual Vineyards World Wide Web Site: Browse and Shop Page

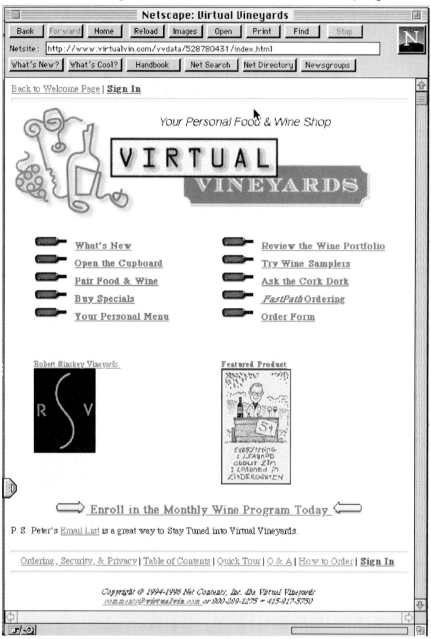

Source: *www.virtualvin.com*

Exhibit 18 Virtual Vineyards World Wide Web Site: Wine Rating by Peter Granoff

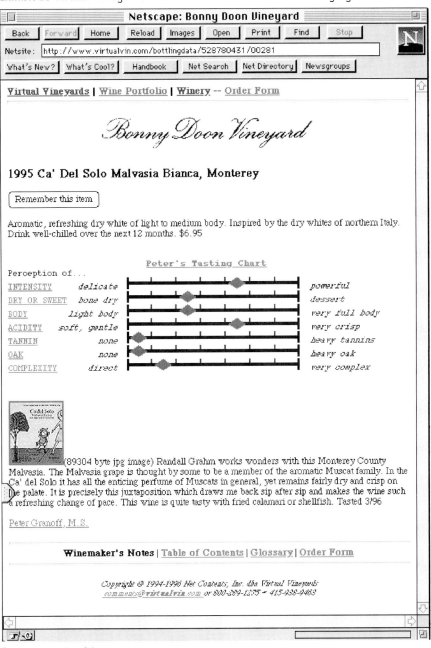

Source: *www.virtualvin.com*

Exhibit 19 Virtual Vineyards World Wide Web Site: Order Form (used once wines were selected)

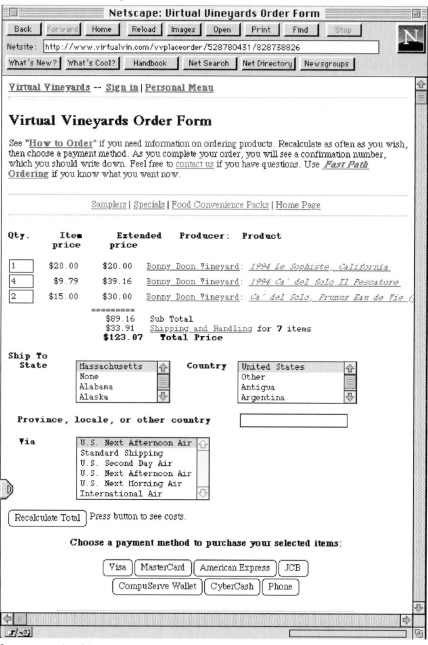

Source: *www.virtualvin.com*

Exhibit 20 Virtual Vineyards World Wide Web Site: What's New Page

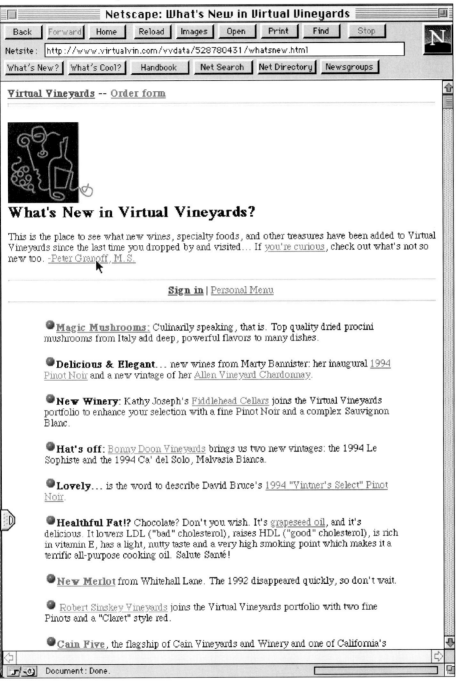

Source: *www.virtualvin.com*

Exhibit 21 Virtual Vineyards World Wide Web Site: Wines Under $15 Page

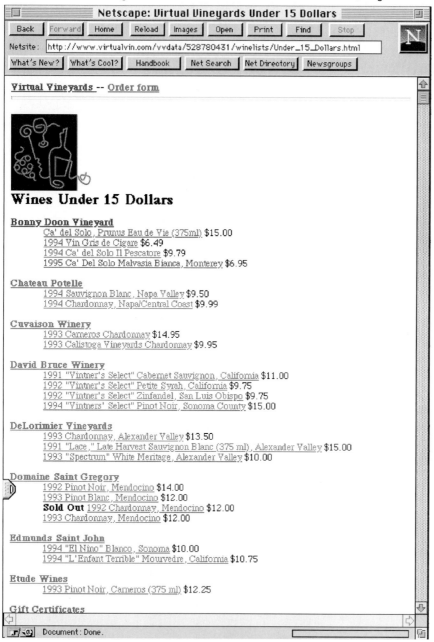

Source: *www.virtualvin.com*

WEATHER SERVICES CORPORATION

Commercial meteorology is the business of producing a product generated from tax-payer-supplied raw materials, and selling it to potential customers who doubt its value, while working in competition with the government. This is a business that simultaneously incorporates the mystique of fortune telling, the rigor of fluid dynamics, and the entertainment value of Saturday morning cartoons.
—A weather industry insider, May 1995

Mike Leavitt stacked up the papers detailing a possible capital raise for his company. The offering would involve a $1 million private placement, scheduled for fall 1995. As he looked out his office window, the sunny New England spring morning had turned to strong winds and dark clouds. He could not help but wonder—was this emblematic of the past two years he had spent running Weather Services Corporation (WSC) or was there a silver lining in those clouds?

Leavitt's father, Peter Leavitt, had been associated with WSC and its predecessor companies since 1957. As a youngster Mike had found his father's "sleepy weather business" interesting but hardly something he wished to pursue in his undergraduate studies at Boston University. Nevertheless, in 1979, he joined his father in forming Weather Services International (WSI), which sought to exploit some of the opportunities in production of computer-generated images for displaying weather data. WSI sourced its weather information from others such as WSC, and sold its value-added graphics services. Meanwhile, WSC continued to focus on the two essential varieties of weather information—forecasting and "nowcasting." Forecasting projected what the weather would be, and nowcasting reported on what the weather actually was. In 1983, the Leavitts and their two partners sold WSI to The Analytic Sciences Corporation (TASC), a subsidiary of Primark Corporation. Mike Leavitt left the

business entirely and became an aviation consultant, while his father continued to run WSC.

Ten years later, Mike Leavitt returned to the weather industry, intrigued by rapid changes in information technology and their potential impact on WSC's business. As the explosion of commercial on-line services in the early 1990s ushered mainstream America into the consumer information age, he saw a tremendous opportunity to build WSC into the leading weather information provider for the digital age. As one of WSC's founders, John Wallace, eased into retirement, Mike Leavitt, with his father Peter's blessing, aggressively pursued the on-line market at WSC. On-line service providers were scrambling for content, and weather information was a hot commodity. After nearly 50 years of furnishing weather forecasts to a defined and limited market of institutional users, new technology was creating a virtually limitless distribution channel for WSC direct to consumer homes.

At the same time, such opportunities raised some pressing questions. Should WSC continue as an information provider, or should it compete head-on with the major on-line players and offer its own on-line weather service? Should it invest in the creation of brand equity around its name—or some other name yet to be determined? Should WSC devote significant resources to marketing its information through a site on the World Wide Web or across other platforms?

As Leavitt wrestled with these issues, WSC was also stretched in terms of cash flow. All issues—from channels to branding to alternate platforms—demanded immediate attention, particularly as growth in the company's new information services businesses continued to exceed even the "stretch" projections. With just over 100 full-time equivalents on the payroll, WSC was arguably larger and more successful than ever. But the moment was critical for the future of the business.

Industry Background: How Weather Became "The Weather"

According to the American Meteorological Society (AMS), a meteorologist was "an individual with specialized education who uses scientific principles to explain,

Research Associate Mary Connor prepared this case, with support from Research Associate Thomas A. Gerace, under the supervision of Professor Jeffrey F. Rayport as the basis for class discussion rather than to illustrate either effective or ineffective handling of an administrative situation.

understand, observe, or forecast the earth's atmospheric phenomena and/or how the atmosphere affects the earth and life on the planet." Notwithstanding this lofty definition, most people in the United States received information about the weather from on-air media personalities; there was no such thing as a "licensed meteorologist." In point of fact, no educational or professional qualifications were required for an individual to become a meteorologist. Anyone could call themselves a meteorologist simply by doing so. Although AMS offered a Certification Program for Consulting Meteorologists and an AMS Seal of Approval for weather broadcasters, neither that organization nor any other had policing authority. Indeed, AMS seals were often used as marketing tools by meteorologists. Of the 70,000 professed meteorologists or scientists in meteorology-related fields (experts, for example, in the ocean or outer atmosphere) in the United States, more than half held university degrees in science-related subjects and only 10,000 belonged to AMS. (AMS certification involved a $250 application fee, and membership, which did not require certification, cost individuals $30 a year.)

Meteorologists worked largely in three sectors of the economy within academic or research institutions (for example, universities and think tanks), organizations in the public sector (such as the National Weather Service), and private industry (companies like WSC). In total, private sector employment represented approximately 30% of the field. The familiar personalities who reported weather in local broadcast markets—media professionals on radio and television—constituted a distinct minority in the field; weather broadcasters numbered around 500 in the nation or less than 10% of industry talent. (The AMS Board, for example, included only one broadcast professional.) Broadcasters played an important role in at least two respects in their metro markets. They often became well-known celebrities in their local areas, because many were skilled at relating weather information to their viewers' day-to-day lives. They also offered valuable re-interpretation of statistical weather data through an understanding, acquired over time by their local presence, of a specific area's topography, microclimates, and historical weather patterns (for example, meteorologists in San Francisco's Bay Area identified 10 microclimates that resulted from the area's varied land masses and consequent development of weather), enabling them to interpret or predict local conditions more accurately than could a nationally averaged, albeit statistically sound, nowcast or forecast.

The Government's Role

The U.S. government first began issuing official weather forecasts in 1870, when President Ulysses S. Grant authorized the establishment of a weather service within the Department of the Army. With the invention of the telegraph, four Army Signal Corps "forecast" professionals began collecting simultaneous weather observations from 22 regional stations around the nation. (In the mid-19th century, however, the United States comprised considerably less territory than today.) Over the next century, the focus shifted to the civilian sector and by 1970, the National Weather Service (NWS), the largest gatherer and supplier of weather information, became an arm of the Department of Commerce. The NWS's primary mission was "the protection of life and property and the enhancement of the national economy." To that end, it provided general national forecasts and warnings of severe weather conditions. Despite occasional public discussion of privatizing the collection of weather data (at one point, Congress nearly did away with it entirely), NWS and its operations had persisted. The reasoning, from a scientific perspective, was obvious: only long-term data records, collected consistently and according to a constant set of standards and measures, would allow interpreters of weather information to gain the historical perspectives required to build the statistical models that supported forecasting. Without a government source to compile such data—in particular, to compile it in consistent fashion across state, county, and municipal lines, since weather respected no borders or boundaries—it was unclear how the nation might otherwise ensure continued access to a highly valued, if sometimes overlooked, information stream.

Of course, weather was only overlooked when it appeared not to exist. Repeated weather-related tragedies—floods, hurricanes, tornadoes, resulting in fatalities, property damage, and disruption of daily life—often kept weather in the news and highlighted its direct, and frequently significant, impacts on people's lives. This real danger to life, limb, and commerce spurred the government to improve its ability to identify and forecast ominous weather patterns. In the 1980s, increased funding allowed NWS to initiate an on-going, $4.5 billion program to modernize weather data collection and forecasting, and to upgrade existing information systems. (For example, the program funded the Next Generation Weather Radar system or NEXRAD, which tracked changes in the atmosphere, and the Automated Weather Information Providers system or AWIPS, which automated observation of weather to enhance performance of NWS surface stations.) In 1990, NWS sought to clarify its role in the weather industry vis-à-vis private-sector weather information companies. In a resulting agreement, NWS agreed that it would continue to supply raw weather data, continue to process the large-scale computer simulation models upon which most forecasts were based, and continue to issue authoritative warnings for potentially life-threatening situations. NWS would not, however, compete on the range of value-added services provided by the private sector. In that sense, the accord was viewed within the industry as something of a public-private partnership to address the nation's needs pertaining to weather information. Since NWS was supported by taxpayer funds, it provided its goods and services free of charge.

NWS's Information Technology

NWS collected weather information through a vast network of data collection centers and contacts throughout the United States. While this flow of information informed, in theory, nearly every weather report encountered by citizens throughout the nation and the world—from the *USA Today* national weather map to the *Farmer's Almanac* five-year prediction to Willard Scott's daily weather overview on NBC's *Today Show*—few people were aware of the vast array of technology and technical tasks that generated the underlying data (see Exhibit 1).

The process began with a network of surface stations for physical observation of local weather by humans and by AWIPS. Every hour from almost 1,000 major airports in the United States and every three hours from nearly 10,000 smaller airports and other locations around the world, NWS received reports on local weather conditions; these included measurements and observations of existing weather, including temperatures, on the ground or "surface" and in the sky or "upper atmosphere." (To predict future surface temperatures, meteorologists needed to know conditions at multiple atmospheric levels or layers, each associated with a specific altitude range in the troposphere, the weather-relevant portion of the atmosphere; the troposphere had a ceiling of approximately 60,000 feet or seven miles—it was somewhat higher at the equator and the poles—as measured from the earth's surface. This integration of weather data was called the "initialization process.") While AWIPS afforded a more comprehensive approach to surface station

observations, the variability of automated observations was, in fact, higher than that for human observations. A human, for example, could easily differentiate between sleet and freezing rain, but a mechanical device could not do so reliably. As a result, quality assurance administered by humans was essential to sound performance of the overall AWIPS system.

Technology-based observations comprised the lion's share of the data, especially in the realm of upper-atmosphere observations, which were made by weather balloons, satellites, and radar. Twice a day, collection stations around the world launched roughly 500 weather balloons carrying measurement instruments linked to radio transmitters to measure the temperature, humidity, air pressure, and wind speed of the atmosphere. Radio transmitters sent collected data to the nearest NWS weather station. Meanwhile, 22,500 miles above the surface of the earth, NWS's Geostationary Operational Environmental Satellite (GEOS), locked in geosynchronous orbit over the equator, measured the temperature at the top of the clouds and received signals from ships and airplanes, unmanned reporting stations, and hourly signals from weather buoys. All of this information was transmitted to the NWS' National Meteorological Center (NMC) in Suitland, Maryland. Finally, the NMC itself collected information about storms and winds through a network of 150 radar scanners and transmitters. These NEXRAD systems provided continuous observation of location, movement, and intensity of precipitation, and they represented a critical component of NWS's tracking of severe weather systems. This high-powered radar network was extremely sensitive, and it tracked the velocity of particles caught in the wind to determine wind vectors to determine wind speed and direction; it could also detect leaves rustling and bugs migrating and thereby map highly local or "mesoscale" weather conditions.

All of this data came together at NMC. There, its Cray YMP-832 supercomputer continuously assimilated real-time data flows into three complex scientific models. As NMC Deputy Director James Howcroft explained, "The different models have a different focus; one may be focused on precipitation, while the other is focused on winds." Capable of making two billion calculations per second, the supercomputer used mathematical equations to process and interpret the raw data. According to Howcroft, "The computer can see even the small-scale features. This has enabled us to steadily improve our ability to forecast events. We do as well now at forecasting events at five days as we used to do at three days." Nonetheless, for any given microclimate, weather predictions were seldom greater than 80% accurate "on the ground" for the region involved, simply because not every point within a region had the same weather at the same time; in other words, even the most detailed nowcasts and forecasts reflected the *dominant* weather conditions in a specified area—and these conditions did not always manifest themselves consistently across even limited portions of time and space.

The computer issued 20,000 general forecasts and 6,000 weather maps each day. The NMC transmitted these forecasts and graphics to the NWS telecommunications gateway, which in turn transmitted the data to local NWS offices and to private weather forecasters throughout the Western Hemisphere. The NWS relied on private industry to provide day-to-day forecasts and data directly to end users.

The Private Weather Industry

While the NWS offered its raw weather data free to anyone who requested it, only a portion of NWS's output represented "finished goods"—in other words, text forecasts that consumers could easily interpret and use. Indeed, the computer-generated statistical data was largely indecipherable to the general public (see Exhibit 2). Except for listeners to the National Oceanic and Atmospheric Administration's weather radio frequency (call letters were simply NOAA), the general public received its weather information mostly from private industry rather than directly from the government. Private sector firms, a large collection of mostly small businesses, acted, in effect, as value-added resellers of NWS information. The only exceptions occurred when weather emergencies were predicted; such warnings were made exclusively by NWS.

Since nearly all firms in the private weather industry were privately held, reliable figures for industry size were not available. Ed Gross, chief of the Industrial Meteorology staff at NWS, estimated total industry revenues in a range of $150 million to $250 million in 1995, and estimated industry sales growth at about 20% a year. Online technology was fueling the rapid growth rate. Prior to 1983, when the government first made weather information available electronically for computer use, the private weather industry consisted of only a handful of firms; by 1995, there were more than 200. (See Exhibit 3 for a list of selected weather information companies and a comparison of their services.)

These private companies fell into two basic categories, which had been established by the 1990 agreement. There were so-called "family of service" (FOS) distributors; such companies collected and distributed government data, functioning simply as channel intermediaries. FOS firms resold data to information providers (IPs), the other basic type of weather business. IPs analyzed the raw data and turned it into forecasts, weather maps, and related graphics. For example, WSI was a FOS company in that it received information—both outputs from NWS statistical models and NWS maps—from the government and resold it to one of its clients, the NBC affiliate in Boston (WHDH, Channel 7), where meteorologists such as Harvey Leonard and Mishelle Michaels then interpreted the quantitative and graphical data as IPs to generate their own reports and forecasts. Some firms, unlike a broadcast station, played both roles, acting as an FOS and an IP firm. For example, the Weather Channel broadcast raw text forecasts from NWS as videotext images.

Family of Service Distributors

In 1995, only 15 FOS distributors had direct connections to NWS computers and enjoyed unfettered access to its raw data. These firms bore the costs of accessing the data, including telecommunications costs, a one-time hookup fee, and an annual fee. Ed Gross at NWS explained the annual fee:

> The annual recurring fee is based on our calculated cost of disseminating the information divided by the number of subscribers. We provide domestic and international data services, high resolution data services, digital facsimile services for maps, and a graphics service. The average annual cost to an FOS distributor per service ranges from about $6,000 to $16,000 [excluding telecommunications hardware and services costs].

For FOS distributors, providing raw information was essentially a commodity business, often used by such firms to attract customers for other value-added offerings. By serving as conduit for government data (which, in its raw form, was a low-margin product), FOS distributors were able to promote their value-added products and services to IPs. Since FOS distributors passed on only a portion of the costs associated with moving the data, it was cheaper for IPs to source data from FOS firms than from NWS directly.

Information Providers. IPs purchased weather information from one or more FOS distributors and then repackaged and customized it for their clients. IPs ranged in size from one employee to several hundred, with activities that spanned forecasting, niche or forensic consulting (for example, wedding day forecasts), and in-depth weather information studies. By 1995, according to industry estimates about 80 firms were engaged in weather forecasting operations. Ten of those were large forecasting firms with revenues in excess of $3 million; 20 were medium-sized firms with revenues between $500,000 and $3 million; and 50 were small firms with revenues below $500,000. There were also five to 10 firms with total revenues of about $50 million, which, in addition to providing forecasts, offered customized graphics, satellite images, radar patterns, and software packages.

Other IPs included consulting meteorologists—typically one-person shops, serving the legal system as expert witnesses—and research and development meteorologists who competed for government and research grants. There were also several "specialty service" firms that focused their marketing efforts on particular niches. Strategic Weather Services, for example, concentrated on retail clients and provided them with long-range weather forecasts. Metro-Weather provided forecasts for movie production companies to help film crews decide where and when to stage their on-location shoots. The absence of any certification requirements and low overhead costs (solo practitioners could "publish" weather information with just a personal computer, a printer, and perhaps a modem) resulted in scores of "mom-and-pop" players who concentrated on a particular market niche or regional area. Other sources of weather information ranged from do-it-yourself to folklore, such as reading the *Farmer's Almanac*, and basing predictions on historical weather data, proverbs, or the view from a window.

Who Buys the Weather?

Markets for weather information ran the gamut from trivial to profound. For many, weather forecasts were simply useful tools for planning what to wear, how to commute, and what to do for recreation. Travelers wanted forecasts for cities on their itineraries, skiers wanted information about the snow conditions on various slopes, and drivers might need reports to decide which car or truck to drive. An inaccurate forecast for such users was largely an inconvenience. For some businesses, however, weather could have tremendous impacts on the bottom line. Restaurant owners, for example, indicated that predictions of snowstorms could result in a 50% reduction in a day's receipts—even if the blizzard never arrived. For other businesses, delays due to snowstorms or icy conditions could cause shortfalls, and even shutdowns. Because of its effect on consumer behavior, for instance, retailers devised advertising strategies and planned inventories around likely occurrences, or predictions, of the weather. Some uses of weather information were more serious still. For airlines flying through treacherous weather systems, shipping lines sailing through the paths of hurricanes, and communities threatened by hurricanes or tornadoes, information about the weather had little to do with convenience, preference, or business economics—it could mean the difference between life and death. As an article in the *Boston Business Journal* summarized it, firms such as WSC and WSI "determine the fate of airline flights, farmers, miners, and numerous other industries and individuals dependent upon the weather."[1]

Aviation

In the aviation industry, knowing about dangerous weather could benefit the bottom line and save lives. Airlines relied on weather data on wind currents and storms to chart flight patterns. These activities represented an essential bulwark of airline safety. Statistics in 1995 indicated that since the 1970s, dangerous weather conditions had led to more deaths in airplane crashes than any other cause. The most recent case in point was the crash of a USAir jet in North Carolina in summer 1994. Investigators determined that the pilots of the plane were surprised by a sudden weather condition known as wind shear, which involved rapid down-drafts of air caused by violent convection currents. Doppler radar, which would have detected the wind shear and provided the warning pilots needed, was scheduled to be installed in a nearby field by the time of the crash. Tragically, the installation had been delayed because the government would not accept the landowner's $2 million asking price for the field.[2] In the end, it cost 37 people their lives. USAir, teetering on the brink of financial collapse, lost millions of dollars in canceled bookings. (The North Carolina incident was the airline's fifth crash in five years.)

[1]Tom Salemi, "Eyes of the Storm: Local Firms Tapping into Growing Demand for Weather Data," *Boston Business Journal*, September 12–18, 1997, pp. 1 and 38.
[2]Cover story, *Newsweek*, April 24, 1995, p. 20.

For safety reasons, the government required airlines to be apprised of weather conditions, and NWS itself provided pilot briefings and aviation-specific forecasts directly to the industry. In truth, no airline could operate safely or economically without such information. Airlines purchased weather information not only from NWS but also from specialized aviation IPs such as Jeppessen (a subsidiary of Times-Mirror), which packaged weather forecasts with customized flight patterns. Such services had high value since these flight plans, integrated with weather data, allowed airlines to take advantage of prevailing winds to burn less fuel and thus lower operating costs. Knowing weather forecasts also helped airlines avoid costs associated with airplane downtime—the likely result, for example, of flying several jets into a hub airport just before a severe winter storm passed through.

Utilities

Electric and gas utilities and energy distributors bought customized weather data, including hourly temperatures, winds, humidity, light intensity, and precipitation. Bill Yardley of Boston Gas explained the utility's need for accurate forecasts: "We buy gas on a daily basis, based on average temperature predictions. If we don't use all that we order or if we use more than we had ordered, we are penalized. We are a major consumer of weather information. It is outrageously critical to our business."[3]

Agribusiness

Agribusinesses purchased daily analyses, short-term forecasts, and longer-term trend analyses of weather conditions throughout commodity production regions and major transportation routes. Weather forecasts were of considerable importance to commodities traders and brokers. Because they determined crop yields, expected weather conditions had a substantial impact on futures prices. Agribusiness spent about $2 million a year on weather forecasting information.

Local Government, Universities, and Local Business

State and local government agencies, schools, and local businesses needed to know about severe weather conditions to determine school closings and to schedule crews

for work, maintenance, and snow removal. This market was estimated at about $2 million a year, but it was declining as a result of cutbacks at federal, state, and local levels.

Media

Newspapers, radio, and television bought weather information from private weather services to deliver to their audiences. Even though newspaper weather information was either very general or very limited and often as much as 15 to 20 hours old when a paper was delivered, its ease of access made it the daily source of weather data to many readers. Newspaper publishers spent an estimated $2.5 million on weather information in 1994. With newspapers increasingly interested in color and graphics, demand for weather information, which could be more easily understood through color graphics than columns of numbers, was increasing. Moreover, running color weather maps could provide other benefits. The high salience of the information to readers combined with the use of color meant that publishers could sell color adjacent display advertising at a premium. (See Exhibit 4 for a positioning map of weather information distribution channels.)

For local television and radio news programs, weather forecasts were one of the main attractions. As Harvey Leonard, chief meteorologist at Boston's WHDH-TV Channel 7, noted:

> Weather is a very important element in the local news mix. Audience research in most markets indicates that weather is either the number one or number two reason that people view television news. When significant or stormy weather threatens or is occurring, [the weather report] is virtually always the number one tune-in factor. Personality is very important, probably the second most important factor—after credibility itself—in establishing authority on weather information. The reason is that people basically want to get their information from someone who is knowledgeable, credible and experienced, but also likeable—that is to say, not a "stuffed shirt." The person must come across and be perceived as a "real" person and not just a science nerd, or much of the audience may be turned off. So it is the combination of, first, credibility, and, second, personality that usually determines the effectiveness of the on-air weather person from the public's point of view.[4]

---

[3]Interview with the author, May 4, 1995.

[4]Interview with Harvey Leonard, chief meteorologist, WHDH-TV Channel 7, July 7, 1997.

Although the trend among TV stations was to hire meteorologists as weather announcers, only about 30% of television weather announcers were certified or trained meteorologists. As Leonard observed, "Meteorological training ranges from important to essential in major metro markets, but there is variability from major market to major market. It's due to the actual weather in a given market—the more changeable, the more training is required—and the lifestyle of people in that market." He illustrated this point with a comparison of the Los Angeles and New York markets: "For example, training is not as important in LA, because the weather doesn't change enough, so news management is more influenced by personality than professional weather training . . . . In NYC, the weather is more changeable, but lifestyles are so fast paced that most people don't have the curiosity to get all the extra touches that a true professional can deliver." As a result, many weather broadcasters were hired according to "show biz," rather than meteorological, criteria. As Bruce Schwoegler, chief meteorologist at Boston's WBZ-TV Channel 4, put it: "Meteorologists study atmospheric physics. Atmospheric physicists have a difficult time communicating with anything other than a slide rule."[5]

Perhaps for that reason, stations without staff meteorologists hired people with on-air talent to read local weather scripts prepared by private vendors. Stations with meteorologists subscribed to private IPs or FOS weather services for hard copy data, satellite feeds, and graphics. The IPs pared down the voluminous data they received from NWS and sent the relevant information to the meteorologists, who used it to make their own forecasts.

Very few radio stations had meteorologists on staff. Instead, they relied heavily on private weather services. Radio stations either hired a private vendor to prepare the script with the radio announcer reading it, or they outsourced the report entirely to a vendor, who provided taped or live weather reports periodically throughout the day. The radio market generated about $3.25 million in revenues for private weather companies.

On-Line Services and the Internet

In 1995, the commercial on-line services market was dominated by three providers, America Online (AOL),

Prodigy, and CompuServe; they had a combined market share of 90% and a subscriber base that was growing at 60% a year. (Total subscribers in mid-1995 were estimated to be seven million in the United States.) Each offered some form of weather information provided by a commercial weather service, which ranged from NWS forecasts, to maps and satellite images, to beach or ski slope reports. While charges and services varied, the on-line pricing models essentially included a flat monthly fee (from $8.95 to $14.95) for on-line usage up to a certain number of hours per month plus an hourly fee (from $2.95 to $5.00) for additional time on-line. Most also offered specialty services or gateways to other databases for additional fees. The Prodigy weather service, for example, furnished subgateways to weather information from Access Atlanta, Newsday, TimesLink, and Tampa Bay Online. Internet users could find a tremendous amount of free weather information. Weather information services, universities, and government agencies had established home pages on the World Wide Web, which gave users access to forecasts for domestic and international cities, surface maps, satellite pictures, radar loops, and jet stream trajectories.

Dial-Up Services

Numerous organizations provided dial-up weather information. Although many 900 and 876 numbers (which charged a per-minute fee) offered such information, they faced severe competition from other fee-based phone services. For the fee-based phone category, 80% of paid minutes were for phone sex, 15% for sports scores, and only 5% for information pertaining to horoscopes, lotteries, and weather. Not surprisingly, consumers vastly preferred free weather information. Local telephone companies offered dial-up weather information services, because these received highly favorable responses from customers—and phone companies could promote their brand names and services to callers before and after weather messages. The NYNEX Boston weather announcement, for example, received an average of 17,000 calls a day, or approximately 6.2 million calls a year. On severe weather days, the announcement might receive more than 70,000 calls in a 24-hour period. NYNEX subcontracted the service to a Boston-area private forecasting firm; meteorologists at the firm dialed into the NYNEX announcement system and recorded the weather four times a day to keep the service up-to-date.

---

[5]Interview with Bruce Schwoegler, chief meteorologist at Boston's WBZ-TV Channel 4, June 2, 1995.

Marine and Other Specialty Markets

Commercial shipping companies tracked ocean weather conditions and the safety of their crews and shipments. The U.S. Coast Guard did likewise. Weather conditions were also a key determinant of shipping routes. Fishermen needed access to marine forecasts and storm warnings for safety reasons, and they checked water temperature information to find out where fish were likely to be swimming. Leisure marine users included individual boaters and crews of specialty racing yachts participating in long-distance or local sailing events such as the Trans-Pac or America's Cup races, respectively. Other specialty clients needing national and international forecasts included sporting event sponsors, retail businesses, and some professional meteorologists.

Weather Services Corporation

In this business, you must always carry a fold-up umbrella: that way, if it rains you can pull out your umbrella and look like a genius.
—Peter Leavitt, Chairman of the Board and CEO, Weather Services Corp.

Founded in 1946, WSC was one of the oldest and most respected providers of weather information in the United States. Before moving to its new corporate offices in Lexington, Massachusetts, in March 1995, WSC had operated for nearly 50 years from a white clapboard farmhouse, packed with hundreds of personal computers, telephones, proprietary workstations, fax machines, and audio and video equipment, in nearby Bedford. Despite the tremendous value of the computing and communications equipment inside the house—located behind a parking lot off the town's main street—there was no lock on the front door. With 500 high-capacity phone lines for audio, video, and data transmission running out of the cramped quarters, Mike Leavitt commented, "We didn't need it. We don't need it. We never close." Mike Leavitt had recently taken over day-to-day operations from his father.

WSC operated seven days a week, 24 hours a day, with at least three, and usually four or five, people working the overnight shifts. Leavitt was a big believer in what he called "redundancy." "We get our raw data from two FOS distributors," he explained, "and we have three computer systems that back each other up. We could get by with less, but since our clients depend on us, especially in bad weather, we have to be there."

WSC was owned by the Leavitts and its 95 employees (who, through an ESOP, controlled 25 percent of the company), 50 of whom were meteorologists (see Exhibit 5 for an organization chart). Despite the long hours, WSC had high levels of satisfaction and loyalty among its employees and a low turnover rate. Leavitt commented on employees' willingness to work 12-hour days and carry beepers at other times: "These are the people who when they were growing up didn't want to be firemen or cowboys; they wanted to be meteorologists. They're among the fortunate few whose vocation is their avocation."

Through its high-speed data links with the two FOS distributors, WSC received all North American hourly weather data within 10 minutes of its receipt by NWS and global data within one hour. With this kind of data flow, WSC knew precise weather conditions in Siberia before most people living in eastern Russia. Indeed, WSC served clients all over the world with weather information about their local markets. For example, one client operated a commodities trading operation in Hong Kong. Most of his calls concerned agricultural conditions around the world; recently, however, he had consulted WSC from Hong Kong about whether a particular Saturday afternoon was suitable to sail his yacht across Hong Kong bay.

Although others in the industry suggested that the forecasting skill of WSC meteorologists and its significant experience in the industry set the firm apart, Mike Leavitt saw its strength as the ability to respond quickly to customers' needs. As he observed, "Our 98% contract renewal rate among clients is undoubtedly in part a reflection of our meteorologists' ability to understand the peculiar nature of weather and to understand the nuances of the NWS computer models. But I believe that it is primarily a result of our willingness to help our customers identify their needs and deliver quality products that meet those needs." Indeed, WSC spent less than $100,000 per year on its "feedstock" or raw FOS weather data; but the ability to turn that raw data into high-quality, customized products allowed WSC to charge a premium for its services. Fees ran from $100 for a one-time "wedding or Bar Mitzvah" forecast to $300,000 a year retainers for comprehensive services.

WSC Customers

WSC products ranged from general forecasts to customized text, graphics, and maps for clients in a variety of industries, including agribusiness, utilities, governments, on-line services, media, and leisure marine (see Exhibit 6). Utilities represented WSC's oldest market and its largest client segment. Over a hundred utilities clients yielded approximately $1.5 million in WSC revenues. WSC was the dominant player in the agribusiness market, which was WSC's second largest revenue-producing industry category, accounting for roughly $750,000 in revenues. With about 50 agribusiness clients, this market represented 20% of WSC's client base.

WSC meteorologists provided daily local drive-time radio weather forecasts to audiences from Florida to Hawaii. Each morning, as people across the country drove to work, they listened to what they believed was the local weather forecast. One voice many of them heard—which they assumed came from their local radio station—was that of Joe Zona, a meteorologist employed by WSC. But rather than sitting in any one local radio station, Zona perched for several hours each day in a soundproof booth at WSC headquarters in Lexington. Since his forecasts and personality were heard in radio markets across the country, he had become a local personality—in hundreds of local communities. Making use of the nation's time zones, Zona could give live, local, drive-time forecasts to listeners in Portland, Maine, and, three hours later, in Portland, Oregon; two hours after that, he was the local broadcaster in Honolulu. People in all these communities knew him as "their" Joe Zona.

One of WSC's largest clients was *USA Today*. Each weekday, WSC produced the newspaper's trademark national weather map, with temperatures and two-day forecasts for major cities across the country and around the world for domestic, European, and Asian editions of the paper (see Exhibit 7 for a description of WSC's newspaper services). The newspaper had recently introduced an on-line weather information service marketed directly to consumers through *USA Today*'s stand-alone dial-up service and via Microsoft Network, using weather information provided by WSC.

Meanwhile, WSC was rapidly becoming one of the two primary providers in its own right of text and graphic weather information to on-line services used by the general public and vertical markets. WSC provided weather information to America Online (AOL), Apple e-World, USA Today Information Network, and AT&T Interchange. Leavitt described the on-line industry pricing model:

> The pricing model is tied to the subscriber base. Basically, we grow as they grow. We crank in a minimum, but we're willing to take a loss at the beginning, with the expectation that in a couple of years, the number of end users will grow substantially. The deal we're get-

ting varies by client and is based on a fee per subscriber or a percentage of the total connect time usage, which can vary from five percent to 50 percent. One year ago, our total revenues from on-line were $1,200 a month; on-line exceeds $75,000 a month today.

WSC also had a robust business with specialized on-line services that supplied news, data, and financial statistics to capital markets trading floors. These services, operated by Reuters, Dow-Jones, and Bloomberg, among others, all carried WSC weather data. Though the structure of each deal was different, these companies generally compensated IPs such as WSC by the number of "screens" on their network. Some of these services offered WSC as a premium information provider whereby a user might pay an additional $10 to $12 a month to have access to WSC information, which compared favorably with the $30,000 a year such an individual might pay to access WSC directly. However, these users did not have direct, live access to WSC's meteorologists, the key angle of differentiation for WSC's premium services.

This market was not limited to either the big three consumer on-line services or the financial information providers; it also included Internet-based information service providers for consumers with access to the World Wide Web. For example, in April 1995, WSC began providing hourly weather updates for a New Jersey Internet news and information service called New Jersey Online. The service's first offering was the *Farmer's Almanac* on-line, and featured the almanac's advice and history as well as WSC-supplied current weather conditions and graphics.

Financial Performance

WSC revenues in 1994 were approximately $3.5 million (see Exhibits 8 and 9). In 1995, nearly half of WSC's revenues came from the utilities and agribusiness markets. But the biggest growth market was clearly the on-line services market, with a 50% jump from 1994 to 1995, and Leavitt believed the growth curve was just at the beginning. Indeed, WSC's annual revenue projections in this category had been exceeded by the end of the second quarter of 1995.

Recent WSC Activities

Branding. The conventional wisdom about branding at WSC seemed counterintuitive. Historically, management had believed that a strong consumer brand would cannibalize the firm's high-end, high-margin business accounts. The theory was that once such accounts became aware of WSC's information services at consumer market prices, they would opt to cut costs and access the information through less expensive channels. Mike Leavitt disagreed. He believed that a strong brand name in the marketplace would attract new high-end accounts to the value-added services that were, in fact, not offered to consumers. These services would, in turn, justify the significantly higher prices that such accounts often paid. As a result, Leavitt considered a move to contradict the strategy, by developing a brand for the company's on-line service products. In addition, as another means to increase WSC's brand awareness, Leavitt had already persuaded such distributors as Reuters, Dow-Jones Telerate, and Bloomberg to replace their private label forecasts with WSC-branded reports.

WxWizard. In 1994, WSC launched the WxWizard, a proprietary desktop system to deliver its color weather forecasting graphics and data. The system used a simple set of eight buttons instead of a keyboard. Users pushed the buttons to select the pages of weather information that they wanted displayed on the 14-inch color monitor (see Exhibit 10). The firm had spent less than $100,000 over a one-year period to develop the new product. It offered WxWizard to WSC subscribers for $1,395 and to non-subscribers for $2,995. (Costs included annual lease of the unit, a satellite dish, and all service/maintenance fees.) Twenty-four hours a day, through a 28-inch satellite dish, WxWizard received updates of the latest WSC color forecast graphics and severe weather storm warnings from NWS. The decision to develop WxWizard was threefold: first, to provide enhanced services for heavy users; second, to establish a visible presence at customer sites; and, third, to deepen key account loyalty. Not only did the WxWizard display make it easier for WSC to describe weather conditions to customers when they called, but it also offered clients more independence. With WxWizard, they could check the system periodically rather than call WSC to get updates. In addition, it offered potential customers a lower priced, entry-level product as an alternative to the company's expensive high-end forecasting services.

One weakness of the WxWizard's proprietary system, however, was the difficulty it presented to any kind of integration with other software and hardware platforms. This, however, was a deliberate strategic decision, Leavitt

claimed, to "own the footprint" on the user site. The objective was to provide WSC's content in a format where it would be continuously displayed on the WxWizard monitor.

Who Sells the Weather?

Private weather companies competed on several dimensions in marketing their weather information. Some of these were skill in forecasting, availability of information, and customer service. Given the fragmented nature of the industry, with small and large companies using a wide range of distribution channels to access various markets, Leavitt saw his competition more as "regional competitors" and "industry competitors," rather than any one "major competitor." Some of the most prominent weather information providers were the following:

Accu-Weather. With roughly 240 employees, including 70 meteorologists, Accu-Weather was both an FOS distributor and an IP. Like WSC, Accu-Weather served a variety of markets and charged premium prices for its services. Founded in 1962 and located in State College, PA, Accu-Weather billed itself as the largest private forecasting company in the weather business, providing nowcasts, forecasts, weather data, graphics, and computer systems for approximately 3,000 clients in radio, television, and other industries. It had successfully branded its product through extensive media exposure—in some radio and TV markets, such as WABC-TV in New York, the weather was presented as the "Accu-Weather Forecast"—and was estimated to have 30% of the radio market. In addition to the company's significant share of the media industry, it had notable sales in utilities, agribusiness, and professional meteorology. With Prodigy and CompuServe as clients, Accu-Weather had about 50% of the on-line services market.

WSI Corporation. After the Leavitts and their partners sold out in 1983, WSI continued to function as WSC's strategic partner in 1995. WSI was one of two FOS distributors from which WSC bought its weather data. (Alden was the other.) WSC also purchased satellite pictures and graphics from WSI. Like Accu-Weather, WSI was both an FOS distributor and an IP, although WSI did not produce any of its own forecasts. The firm, with 135 employees and revenues between $25 million and

$50 million,[6] primarily sold graphics to television stations and claimed to have about 60% of the television market. (WSI focused on production of the computer-generated maps and animated data that appeared on many nightly TV news reports.) It also produced live weather feeds for the Fox Television Network and MSNBC from the company's own studios as well as text reports for NBC network meteorologists. Other clients included American Airlines, Delta, United Airlines, and FedEx. The company recently launched "Weather for Windows," a PC-compatible stand-alone product, and created its own site on the World Wide Web ("INTELLiCast"), offering Internet users access to multimedia weather simulations and other sophisticated graphics.

The Weather Channel (TWC).

Founded in 1982 and owned by Landmark Communications, TWC was a cable-television station specializing in weather information and providing viewers with up-to-date weather reports complemented by on-screen graphics 24 hours a day. In 1992, TWC signed a memorandum of understanding with NWS to standardize formats of forecasts coming from local NWS offices for the industry and to facilitate standardized data processing. The Atlanta-based company had revenues, according to estimates, of $33 million, and it had a staff of 250 employees. In addition to its programming service, TWC had recently launched a Weather Channel Radio Network, providing data to 20 radio stations, a 900-number telephone service, and custom color weather pages for daily newspapers (provided under contract by other commercial weather services through licensing rights for the TWC brand name). TWC also provided on-line weather information to Compuserve subscribers through The Weather Channel Forum; and the Forum provided additional information about TWC meteorologists and the music that accompanied TWC weather reports.

TWC was working on a brand-identification campaign to gain greater leverage from its trademark and to make TWC "*the* brand name for weather." To this end, it had licensed its logo to several third parties. Accord Publishing, for example, had marketed a series of educational products on weather targeting children, including a rain gauge kit, under the TWC logo. TWC had also developed numerous video-documentaries on weather events, including "Forecast for Victory," about the role of weather in World War II; "Sky and Fire," about lightning;

"Dark Days of August," about Hurricane Andrew; and "Danger's Edge," about hurricanes that had overrun the U.S. coastline. The documentaries reportedly sold well, although TWC did not release sales information.

Weather Data.

Weather Data was a WSC competitor in the newspaper industry. Formed in 1981 by meteorologist Mike Smith and based in Wichita, KS, Weather Data had over $1 million in sales from roughly 60 clients. It provided independent commercial weather forecasting services to media clients in print, radio, and television. According to market estimates, 15% of Weather Data's business came from radio and television, and the company had 25% of the newspaper market. Weather Data's strategy was to offer a narrow line of services at moderate prices.

Weather Bank.

Based in Salt Lake City, UT, Weather Bank had $550,000 in estimated sales. With 18 employees, Weather Bank focused on media and utilities, with about 20% of the radio market and 10% of the utilities market. The firm had a focused product line and competed on price.

The Need for an Integrated Strategy

One thing was clear to Mike Leavitt: WSC stood at the crossroads of enormous opportunity. With the explosive growth of commercial on-line services, the diffusion of Internet access, and the blockbuster headlines emerging almost daily from the media business, the world had finally recognized what a focused content provider could do. As Leavitt recalled, "I used to sit with bankers telling them about the potential of this business, and they would look at me wondering what I'd been smoking. Today, they can see it's a rocket ship taking off—and they want to be along for the ride." One aspect of the "ride" was Leavitt's plan to fund the growth in his information services business with a capital raise through a $1-million private placement. While this would address cash flow requirements, the new funds would be applied more immediately to acquiring the kind of human resources that expansion of the on-line services venture required, such as graphic artists, educators, writers, editors, and journalists.

As Leavitt viewed it, the challenge lay in the complexity of applications for weather information radiating out from a single core. Put another way, WSC's core of real-time weather information—including modeling,

[6]Tom Salemi, "Eyes of the Storm: Local Firms Tapping into Growing Demand for Weather Data," *Boston Business Journal*, September 12–18, 1997, pp. 1 and 38.

forecasting, and graphical representation—could serve a multiplicity of vertical markets or information categories defined by usage. "You could talk about our business the way you describe book publishing," Leavitt noted. "For publishers, the marginal cost is just paper and ink; for us, it's faxes and network fees." But the lower incremental costs and greater speed of producing information services electronically gave WSC the kind of flexibility of which publishers could only dream. But the opportunity was one WSC had only begun to exploit.

To date, WSC had responded on two fronts. First, it had successfully entered the on-line market, with a presence across the three major on-line platforms, as well as a new product for AT&T Interchange and a private label role with *USA Today* on the Microsoft Network. Second, it had launched WxWizard as a proprietary platform. As yet, WSC's Internet strategy was undetermined. "The information age is just like Boston weather," Leavitt commented. "It keeps on changing."

One thing, however, was clear. Given WSC's ability to go direct to end users in consumer markets while continuing to extract revenues through its high-margin applications in financial and industrial markets, WSC would need to resolve three areas of pressing concern:

- Moving to direct consumer applications via dial-up on-line or World Wide Web sites sounded like the next logical move. But Leavitt wondered about the issues of pricing in relation to the role of advertising—an issue that every IP faced on the Web. In addition, he wondered about the potential threat of such moves to his existing relationships with firms in both commercial and financial on-line services businesses. He was determined to avoid obvious channel conflict.

- Given the increasing importance of electronic information services to WSC's overall revenues picture, Leavitt knew that WSC was unlikely to extract value as a premier provider of weather information without a clear identity in the minds of its customers. This suggested the importance of developing a brand. Like all marketers, Leavitt wanted to create a name that could become the "Xerox" or "Kleenex" of its category. Unfortunately, many industry insiders believed that one company had already done it—and the name was "Accu-Weather." Leavitt wondered if there might be another brand he could adopt and promote to compete with Accu-Weather's dominance in the consumer market—or whether he should consider building awareness of Weather Services Corporation or "WSC."

- Finally, as he surveyed the company's income statement, Leavitt wondered if there were additional moves to be made in vertical markets. Marine and utility applications were growing revenues at nearly 25 percent a year, indicating that even supposedly mature markets could deliver what Leavitt termed "hockey-stick" growth rates. He believed that there must be new ways to add value for existing key accounts, perhaps without significantly increasing WSC costs. But he wondered about this approach.

As Leavitt considered this array of opportunities, he also wondered about the private placement. Given the potential that he *and* the world now saw in his business, $1 million seemed a small amount to raise. Perhaps WSC could truly outpace its competition with an infusion of $5 million. Leavitt would need to justify the larger amount in terms of specific product lines, services, and market development. And therein lay the challenge.

Exhibit 1 The Weather Information Industry

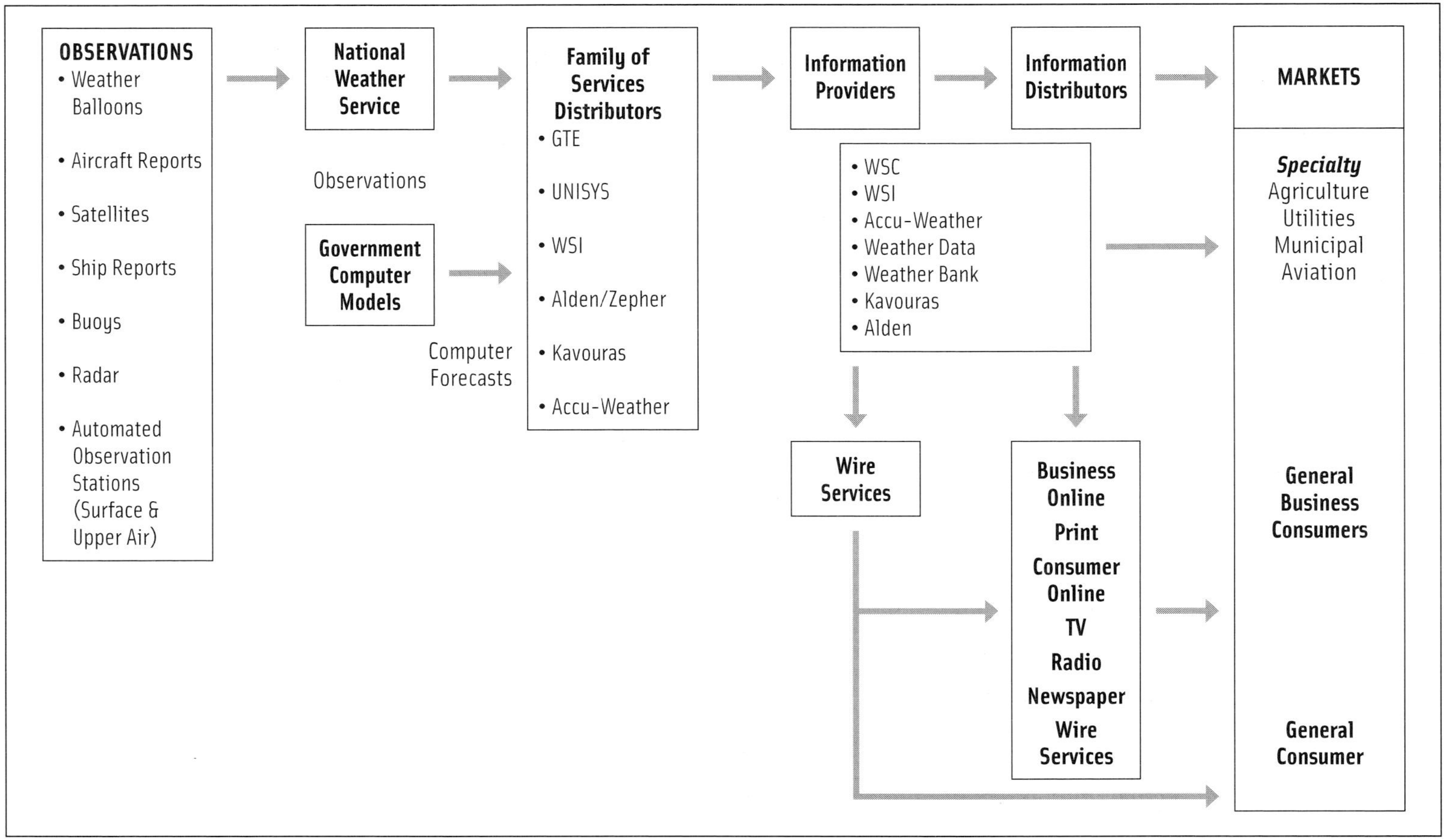

Exhibit 2 Sample Data from the National Weather Service

```
CAR SP 1629 -X M8 OVC 21/2S- 1806/984/S3
HUL SA 1548 E25 OVC 20 140/30/24/2110/991/PRESFR
BGR SA 1548 110 SCT 250 SCT 15 154/40/26/2105/998
AUG SA 1550 100 SCT 180 SCT 15 157/38/23/2010/998
BTV SA 1550 250 -BKN 30 163/44/21/1716/000
MPV SA 1550 100 SCT 30 171/45/19/E2110/000
LEB SA 1545 200 -SCT 20 M/M/E2005/004
PWM SA 1556 AO2A CLR BLO 120 10+ 170/41/23/2209/003/ TNO ZRNO
CON SA 1551 110 SCT 250 -BKN 30 180/47/21/2110/005
MHT SA 1545 200 SCT 25 47/23/2410/009
ORH SP 1628 AMOS 46/22/2319/009 PK WND 25 000
BOS SA 1550 250 -BKN 14 205/49/28/2419G28/014/FEW ACSL SE
BED SA 1545 200 SCT 20 50/24/2420G28/012
RUT SA 1615 AWOS CLR BLO 120 10 46/15/2409G16/004/WND 22V28
HYA SA 1545 200 -BKN 11 55/37/2318G30/020
PVD SA 1551 250 -SCT 15 227/51/29/2514/020
BDL SA 1550 250 -SCT 25 224/48/24/2009G15/018
BAF SA 1545 200 -SCT 15 46/25/2208/019
BDR SA 1550 250 SCT 10 254/49/33/2522G27/028
HVN SA 1545 CLR 20 46/M/2615G22/023
BID SA 1616 AWOS CLR BLO 120 10 49/34/2421G31/025
EWB SA 1545 120 -SCT 15 M/M/2310G20/020
EEN SA 1616 AWOS CLR BLO 120 10 43/22/2012/009
ACK SA 1545 40 SCT 100 -BKN 15 51/36/2420G25/027
BHB SA 1615 AWOS 100 SCT 10 45/28/2313G20/999
LCI SA 1615 AWOS CLR BLO 120 10 42/21/2310/001
DXR SA 1545 250 -SCT 20 46/28/2410G20/022
LEB SA 1545 200 -SCT 20 M/M/E2005/004
MWN SA 1555 40 SCT 30 21/18/2567G76/M
GON SA 1545 CLR 15 47/32/2312G20/028
MVY SA 1545 100 SCT 200 SCT 10 50/32/2415G28/024
BVY SA 1545 200 -SCT 15 2315G23/013/WND 21V28
OWD SA 1545 250 -BKN 7 45/M/2710G15/017
HFD SA 1545 200 SCT 15 M/M/1910/022

+sa bos 12-


BOS SA 1550 250 -BKN 14 205/49/28/2419G28/014/FEW ACSL SE
BOS SA 1450 250 -BKN 12 220/44/28/2420/018/FEW AC/ 722 1071
BOS SA 1350 130 SCT E150 BKN 250 BKN 12 225/41/27/2418/020/FEW LWR
AC
BOS SA 1250 E130 BKN 250 BKN 15 237/39/26/2416/023
BOS SA 1152 95 SCT E130 BKN 200 OVC 15 242/38/26/2212G19/025/BINOVC
S-SW VIRGA E-SE/ 717 1078 33
BOS SA 1050 75 SCT E130 OVC 15 249/38/26/2314/027
BOS SA 0950 E75 BKN 130 OVC 15 256/37/25/2210/029/VIRGA OVHD
BOS SA 0850 95 SCT E130 BKN 15 259/35/23/2211/030/VIRGA OVHD/ 812
1070
BOS SA 0750 E130 BKN 15 266/33/22/2509/032/ 98559
BOS SA 0650 150 SCT 250 -SCT 15 269/33/22/2309/033
BOS SA 0550 E150 BKN 250 BKN 15 271/34/22/2408/033/ 715 1071 44
BOS SA 0450 150 SCT E250 BKN 15 276/35/22/2408/035
BOS SA 0353 150 SCT 250 -SCT 15 278/34/21/2007/035

+uswx bos 12-


    STATION: BOSTON, MA          TODAY'S DATE:  2-DEC-94

 TIME  DATE  TEMP WIND GUST  VIS.          WEATHER
 ==== ===== ==== ==== ==== ======
 ================================
 11PM 1-DEC  34 S  8        15 P CLDY
 12AM 2-DEC  35 SW 9        15 M CLDY
 1AM  2-DEC  34 SW 9        15 M CLDY
 2AM  2-DEC  33 SW10        15 P CLDY
 3AM  2-DEC  33 W 10        15 M CLDY
 4AM  2-DEC  35 SW13        15 M CLDY
 5AM  2-DEC  37 SW12        15 CLOUDY
 6AM  2-DEC  38 SW16        15 CLOUDY
 7AM  2-DEC  38 SW14  22    15 CLOUDY
 8AM  2-DEC  39 SW18        15 M CLDY
 9AM  2-DEC  41 SW21        12 M CLDY
 10AM 2-DEC  44 SW23        12 M CLDY
 11AM 2-DEC  49 SW22  32    14 M CLDY
```

Exhibit 3 Selected Commercial Weather Companies and Their Services

	Agriculture Forecasting	Aviation Meteorology	Commodities Forecasting	Marine Forecasting	Meteorology Database	Newspaper Meteorology	Public Weather Information	Radio/TV Meteorology	Specialized Graphics
Accu-Weather	•	•	•	•	•	•	•	•	•
Compu-Weather	•		•	•	•	•	•	•	•
Fleetweather	•		•	•	•	•	•	•	
Freese-Notis Weather	•		•		•	•		•	•
Knight-Ridder/GWS	•		•	•		•			•
Unisys		•			•		•		
WeatherBank	•		•		•	•	•	•	•
WeatherData	•				•	•	•	•	•
Weathernews	•	•	•	•	•	•	•	•	•
Weather Services Corp.	•	•	•	•	•	•		•	•
WSI		•			•			•	•

Source: Adapted from Commercial Weather Services Association data

Exhibit 4 Positioning Map for Weather Forecast Procedures

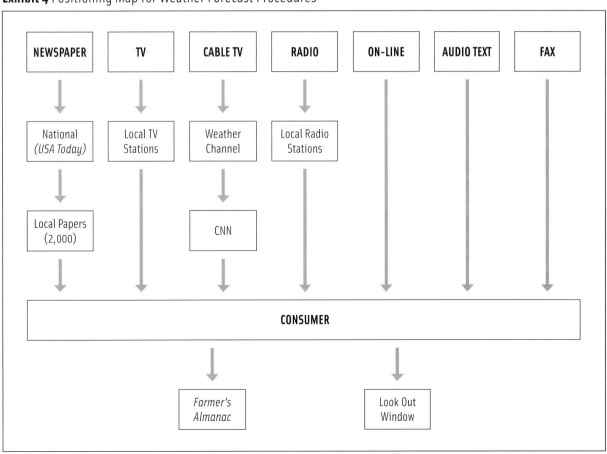

Exhibit 5 WSC Organization Chart

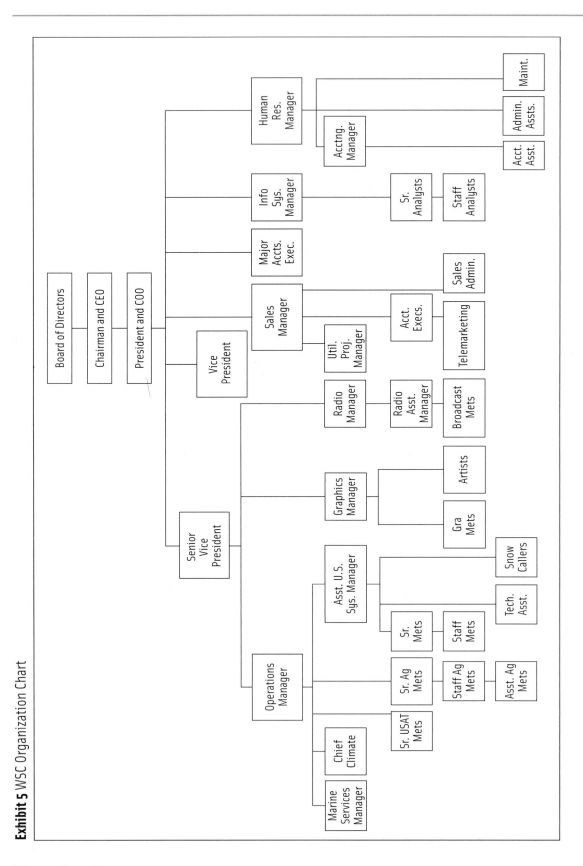

Exhibit 6 WSC Market Segmentation

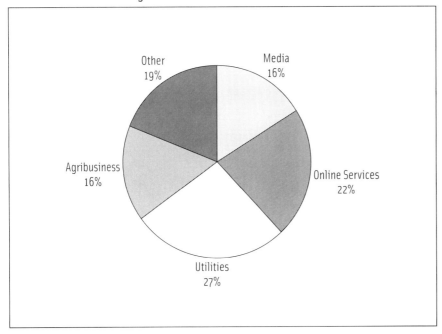

- Other 19%
- Media 16%
- Online Services 22%
- Utilities 27%
- Agribusiness 16%

Exhibit 7 WSC Newspaper Information Services

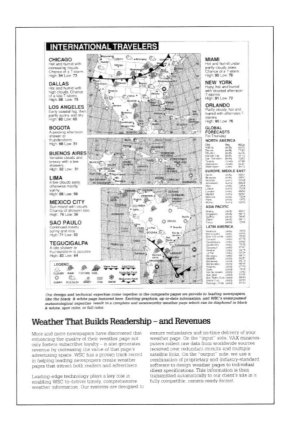

Exhibit 8 Weather Services Corp.—Balance Sheets, December 31, 1995, 1994, and 1993

	1995 (proj)	1994	1993
ASSETS			
Current Assets	866,000	603,000	410,000
Property, Equipment, and Other Assets	1,721,000	1,264,000	1,264,000
Total Assets	2,587,000	1,867,000	1,674,000
LIABILITIES AND STOCKHOLDERS' EQUITY			
Total Current Liabilities	984,000	1,106,000	751,000
Long-Term Debt & Capital Lease Obligations	787,000	643,000	642,000
Total Liabilities	1,771,000	1,749,000	1,393,000
Stockholders' Equity	816,000	118,000	281,000
Total Stockholders' Equity and Liabilities	2,587,000	1,867,000	1,674,000

Exhibit 9 Weather Services Corp.—Income Statements, December 31, 1995, 1994, and 1993

	For the Year Ended December 31, 1995 (projected)	For the Year Ended December 31, 1994	For the Year Ended December 31, 1993
Net Sales	4,304,000	3,342,000	2,562,000
Cost of Goods Sold	115,000	26,000	30,000
Gross Margin	4,189,000	3,316,000	2,532,000
Operating Expenses			
Salaries & Benefits	2,900,000	2,305,000	1,840,000
Communications	480,000	476,000	425,000
Marketing	325,000	220,000	194,000
Depreciation & Amortization	261,000	200,000	165,000
Other Operating Expenses	463,000	291,000	226,000
Total Operating Expenses	4,429,000	3,492,000	2,850,000
Operating Profit/Loss	(240,000)	(176,000)	(318,000)
Other Income/Expense	(109,000)	(65,000)	(69,000)
Profit /Loss Before Income Tax	(349,000)	(241,000)	(387,000)
Allowance for Income Tax	(104,000)	(2,000)	(80,000)
Net Income	(245,000)	(239,000)	(307,000)

Exhibit 10 WxWizard

WSC WxWizard™
The way you look at weather

Weather Services Corporation (WSC), the leader in local and worldwide weather information, introduces WSC WxWizard™. It's the newest and fastest way to display WSC's color weather forecasting graphics and data. WSC WxWizard is a delivery system that instantly brings WSC's vital information to your desktop – and the desktops and homes of everyone in your organization who requires weather information at an unbelievably low price.

STREAMLINE (A)

We're not in the product business; we're not in the service business; we're not in the distribution business. We're in the relationship business. We want to own the relationship with the customer.
—Tim DeMello, Founder, Chairman and CEO, Streamline

Streamline is the future of shopping—a brilliant solution for what we call the '99 lives' phenomenon, having too many responsibilities and too little time.
—Faith Popcorn, Author, *The Popcorn Report*, Director, Streamline

We erase the worry by taking care of the details of your life.
—Streamline direct-marketing brochure

The skit at Streamline's launch party in October 1996 clearly defined the company's mission. The comedy skit, played by three members of the Laughing Stock Comedy Company, showed the frustration of an average American family over an increasing lack of "quality" time on weekends. While the skit poked fun at the miscues of the hypothetical Henderson family—from picking up the wrong dinner item at the grocery store to returning rentals to the wrong video chain outlet—it also underlined the growing desire of many two-income families to take control of their lives. One way to do this, the skit implied, was to reduce the amount of time spent on routine purchasing activities—such as going to the grocery store, the video shop, and the dry cleaners.

Tim DeMello, the 37-year-old founder and CEO of Streamline, believed that his company offered the right solution for such households. For the past year, his Boston-based company had been experimenting with the concept of direct-to-home delivery services on a test basis in a suburban Boston market. The initial test involved more than 100 households, and Streamline

delivered to them groceries, videos, photos, and dry cleaning once a week. The firm calculated that average time saved for each family as a result of its services was approximately three hours a week or over 150 hours a year—the equivalent of almost six full days.

As the skit ended, with the Henderson family signing up to become a Streamline household, DeMello and his management team had already been working out their plan to launch Streamline in affluent suburban markets across the country. DeMello was convinced that the convergence of changing lifestyles and evolving information technologies would make Streamline's services popular, if not inevitable. The key question was determining the best way to replicate the business model so that Streamline could achieve its goal of reaching a base of one million households across the country by 2004.

Streamline History

The concept of Streamline—which summarized the company's goal in consolidating routine household purchasing activities for American families—first formed in DeMello's mind during the early 1980s. DeMello had always aimed to become an entrepreneur. As an undergraduate at Babson College in Massachusetts (where he now served as a trustee), he had known he would pursue a career in business. At year-end 1986, he made a personal vow that he would realize his goal by the first Friday the 13th in the following year. DeMello was ultimately inspired by a chance encounter that became a turning point in his life: he encountered Ray Kroc, the founder of McDonald's. Recalled DeMello:

> I met Ray Kroc when I was a freshman at Babson College. I was impressed by him. From that day on, I wanted to start my own business. Kroc was a person who had figured out how to meet an unmet need for consumers and that was the kind of challenge I wanted to pursue, too.

DeMello's last job as a paid employee was with a Boston investment bank. DeMello's employment ended on the afternoon of Friday, March 13, 1987—missing a self-imposed deadline to resign by noon, to start his own business, by only a few hours.[1] Three days later, DeMello

Research Associate Dickson L. Louie prepared this case, with the assistance of Research Associate Michelle Toth, MBA '95, under the supervision of Professor Jeffrey F. Rayport as the basis for class discussion rather than to illustrate either effective or ineffective handling of an administrative situation.

established a game company, Wall Street Games (later renamed Replica Corporation), that "replicated" the real-world activities of financial markets and professional sports. The business grew to over $5 million in revenues in the next five years. Although DeMello envisioned the concept for Streamline and the "life-style solution" business back in 1987, he didn't have the funds to start the business. In 1992, DeMello sold Replica Corporation and decided it was finally time to launch Streamline.

DeMello believed that the convergence of two major trends in society—the lack of leisure time for two-income families and the increasing use of technology in the household—supported the Streamline concept:

> Any viable business must be supported by larger marketplace trends. Streamline's business builds on two key trends: time and technology. Take the first trend, time. When is the last time you heard someone say they had extra time to do the things they enjoy? Americans today are time-starved. This trend has been exacerbated by the dual-income phenomenon, as more and more women enter the work force and struggle to balance both work and family obligations.

> The second key trend, technology, is a key enabler of our business. In the last few years we have seen a dramatic migration of technology into the home: personal computers, fax machines, PDAs, interactive television; more and more tools are available to assist consumers in managing the information and transactions required to run their households. Streamline is interested in leveraging this technology on the consumer's behalf.

Streamline's business model appeared deceptively simple. Deliveries for groceries, dry cleaning, photo development, and video rentals were to be made once a week to each Streamline subscriber household. Weekly orders had to be placed no later than midnight before the designated delivery date. The orders were filled at Streamline's Consumer Resource Center (CRC) and delivered to each household on the designated delivery day.

One major distinction of the Streamline service model, in contrast to that of many other home delivery services, was elimination of any requirement that consumers be available to receive their shipments. Streamline believed that this need often canceled out the time savings that made such services so compelling. To solve this problem, Streamline designed a patented delivery receptacle for deliveries, allowing Streamline to drop off all items without interaction with household members. This unit was a combination refrigerator, freezer, and storage cabinet, allowing ordered items to be stored in the three temperature zones applicable to household items. By placing the unit in a customer's garage, Streamline's field service representatives (FSRs) could leave weekly deliveries in the unit and thus fulfill the needs of subscribing households without inconveniencing the recipients.

After test marketing the Streamline service with an initial group of 50 households in Westwood, Massachusetts, a suburb outside Boston, DeMello and his colleagues began collecting additional information on how direct delivery of goods might become a solid, profitable business. In short, the service had worked, but the degree of customization required by each household made it difficult to project how the business could be operated at scale or made profitable over time. Recalled DeMello:

> Early on, some of my managers (they are no longer with the company) wanted to give up on the concept for Streamline. There were a lot of financial challenges, and we were spending a lot of time trying to understand and influence consumer expectations. Take our video offering for example. We would use our personal credit cards to rent videos from Blockbuster, and then have to convince our customers to keep the tapes for the entire week. Even though I ended up with the second highest late fees at Blockbuster that year, it was worth it. Today, our customers love the fact that they can rent a video with us for $4 and watch it all week. That sort of learning was invaluable as we went about defining our service offering.

Although DeMello was able to raise $1.7 million from individual investors as "seed money," in addition to the $45,000 he had already personally invested, DeMello was still unable to convince institutional investors of the venture's potential returns. In late 1995, DeMello was able to turn what he did have—first-hand knowledge of consumer behavior in the direct shopping channel—into a valuable asset when Coca-Cola, the giant soft drink company, called and invited him to visit their headquarters in Atlanta. DeMello said:

> One day I got a phone call from Coca-Cola. And Coke said, "I understand you're something of an authority on the subject of direct-to-consumer retailing. Can you come down and tell us what's going on in this whole world?" And I said, sure. So I went to Atlanta with my vice-president of operations, Dave Blakelock.

---

[1]Joshua Macht, "Errand Boy," *Inc.*, November 1996.

We talked to Coke about the potential of this channel; about how we could tell Coke precisely which households were purchasing which products when, and how this information could be used for targeted sampling efforts, or how we could set up consumer repurchase contracts for certain products which we would then deliver automatically to the home. They were very interested.

After presenting a vision of this new marketing channel, DeMello received an unexpected proposition. Coca-Cola executives asked him if he and Streamline could put together a study of the consumer-direct channel. DeMello quickly realized that his knowledge of the subject might translate into a bridge for additional financing; with partners like Coca-Cola he could give Streamline increased credibility. "As we left Atlanta," recalled DeMello, "I told David Blakelock that we had just saved the company."

DeMello then sought out several contacts at Andersen Consulting and proposed that Andersen work with Streamline on a joint study of the consumer-direct business. Andersen then recruited some additional consumer brand marketers as partners in the work. Proctor & Gamble, Kraft, and 14 other manufacturers joined as sponsors of the six-month project, which was now called the Consumer Direct Cooperative. While Andersen provided the industry analysis, DeMello articulated his vision of the model for the project team. DeMello recalled:

> The Consumer Direct Cooperative was a very important milestone for this industry and for Streamline. We ran some marketing tests, we gave our ideas, and we shared. In return, we received half a million dollars and gained credibility. As a start-up, you expend a lot of energy trying to gain credibility. In the end, the study concluded that the industry would be a $60–85 billion dollar opportunity, and that Streamline's business model was the most attractive from both a consumer and financial perspective.

In the meantime, Saul Steinberg, the chairman of Reliance Insurance Company, whose financial analysts had turned DeMello down for financing just a few months earlier, called DeMello in summer 1996 after learning about the formation of the Consumer Direct Cooperative. Now Steinberg was interested and he invited DeMello to visit him in his offices in New York. DeMello recalled:

> I went down to see him, and he said, "Tell me what you've done." I told him, and he said, "Are you looking for money?" Of course, I said, "Yes." He said, "How much?" And I said, "$5 million." And he said, "What will you give me?" And I said, "40%, part-question mark, part-period." And he said, "OK, let's do it." Right on the spot.

Confirming the old adage that "necessity is the mother of invention," DeMello was able to turn around the company's situation, from Streamline as "an idea still waiting to happen" to Streamline as a firm with sufficient resources to create its first Consumer Resource Center. The CRC, a warehouse containing all relevant inventory, served as a model for what DeMello envisioned as the regional hub of Streamline's operations. Streamline completed construction of its first CRC, located in Westwood, Massachusetts, in that same summer. Once in place, the CRC enabled the organization to focus on how to make the Streamline concept work. By March 1997, Streamline had almost 200 subscriber households around the Boston-area hub. Over the next six years, DeMello planned to roll out the Streamline concept nationwide. His goal was to create eight regional operating companies operating 25 CRCs serving over 1 million customers.

In addition, a separate, self-funded Consumer Learning Center was established at Streamline's headquarters in early 1997 to serve as an ongoing research lab for the consumer-direct industry. Through this center, Streamline and its manufacturer partners were privy to the latest consumer research on why and how consumers make their purchase decisions within the home—instead of within the grocery store. The CLC would also explore the role of technology and its influence on in-home shopping behavior. Noted Gina Wilcox, Streamline's director of strategic relations and the head of the Consumer Learning Center:

> Our overall objective with the Consumer Learning Center is to explore how consumers shop in the home today and how they will want to shop in the home tomorrow. By understanding what they buy, how they buy, and when they buy, we can begin to influence purchase decisions in this new shopping environment. We also gain insight into the sorts of technologies which will further enable and enhance the in-home shopping experience.

The Consumer Learning Center supported Streamline's business strategy by providing an ongoing stream of proprietary consumer insight and by strengthening Streamline's relations with key manufacturers. Streamline viewed strategic partnerships as a competitive advantage critical to the company's growth. Noted Frank Britt, Streamline's vice president of marketing and merchandising, about Streamline's strategy to develop and leverage partnerships with blue-chip companies:

> After raising capital, we focused considerable energy on building a portfolio of strategic partners. We believed that to be successful in this business required a diverse set of capabilities. By partnering, we are able to capitalize on the collective strength of companies who are leaders in their fields. In 1997 we are working with these partners to "harden" the Streamline business model, so that in 1998 we can aggressively begin expansion.

Added Wilcox about the importance of developing relationships early:

> The hypothesis here is that strategic alliances can create barriers to entry and greatly accelerate time-to-market. By taking key manufacturer, technology, and financial partners "out of the market," we make it harder for new entrants to successfully acquire the resources necessary to compete. While we have focused on partner acquisition, some of our competitors have focused on customer acquisition. We know that 20% of American households are ready for this service. We believe our partnerships will help us reach those customers faster, and ultimately serve them better.

DeMello compared Streamline's roll-out strategy with McDonald's. "If you want to ramp up to scale in a $60 to $85 billion industry, you don't do it one customer at a time," DeMello said. "You need a strategy to leverage the business; you build the first 'prototype' and then replicate the successful model quickly. You can't replicate quickly unless you have the right business model and right partners in place."

The Grocery Industry[2]

The U.S. grocery industry generated $400 billion in revenues in 1994 through the operation of 131,000 grocery stores, including supermarkets, wholesale clubs, supercenters, convenience stores, and other food outlets.[3] But the highly fragmented,[4] traditionally low-margin (1%–2%), high-fixed cost business was struggling in the 1990s; it had seen real growth of just 0.9% in the preceding decade.[5] Coinciding with this slow growth was intensified competition within and across formats. Supermarkets, the largest sector by sales volume, competed for market share and consumer dollars mostly using pricing innovations and promotional campaigns. The supermarket sector as a whole faced pressure from low-priced, rapidly expanding "alternative store formats" such as warehouse clubs and supercenters, which not only threatened supermarkets' share but created overcapacity in the industry.[6]

One further ill afflicted the industry. The grocery channel, as a whole, engendered exceedingly low levels of consumer satisfaction. Of all Americans, 41% reportedly "hated" grocery shopping,[7] yet a typical family visited a grocery store 86 times a year[8] (see Exhibit 1). In addition to grocery visits, the average consumer visited more than 17 additional retailers for household-related needs each month.[9]

Supermarkets

The supermarket sector included 29,000 grocery stores, each with annual sales of $2 million or more, totaling $301 billion in 1994. This sector excluded warehouse clubs, supercenters, convenience stores, and deep discount drug stores.

The type of store in this sector ranged from independently owned single unit operations to large chains such as Kroger and Safeway. More than one third of sector sales were concentrated in the top ten chains, and the average supermarket carried 20,000 to 30,000 stock-keeping units or SKUs. Smaller conventional stores limited stock to mostly food items, while the larger combination stores and superstores carried food and non-food items, as well.

In the 1990s, to boost earnings, many of the larger stores added higher margin services such as delicatessens, bakeries, food courts, enlarged frozen foods

---

[2]Portions of this section were adapted from "Shopping Alternative Inc.: Home Shopping in the Information Revolution," HBS case No. 796-132.

[3]Progressive Grocer Annual Report, April 1995.

[4]Of the top 107 markets in the United States, 39 markets were considered to be "fragmented" where no dominant grocery chain had achieved a market share of more than 25% and 39 markets were considered to be "highly competitive" with at least two grocery chains having comparable market share. The "fragmented" and "highly competitive" segments represented 47.3 households, or 50% of all households, in the United States. Consumer Direct Cooperative, 1996.

[5]"Food Service 2005: Satisfying America's Changing Appetite," McKinsey & Co., 1996.

[6]Shopping Alternatives, Inc.: Home Shopping in the Information Revolution.

[7]AT&T Electronic Commerce Study, 1996.

[8]A.C. Nielsen Consumer Insights, 1996.

[9]Consumer Direct Cooperative, June 1996.

departments, and specialty produce or other perishable goods areas; some stores added cosmetics counters, video cassette rental services, and banking service desks. However, expansion came at a price: selling space outpaced sales increases by a significant margin. The additions generated higher margins but weekly sales per square foot of selling space declined, falling to $9.18 in 1994 from $9.80 in 1991.[10] Profitability was flat with return on sales of less than 1% and return on assets of 3% in the period from 1989 to 1993. Average order size fell to $17.45 in 1990 from $17.93 in 1994. At the same time, mean family food expenditures in 1995 were approximately $80 a week and consumers made an average of 2.2 supermarket visits weekly.

Volume had shifted in this period from traditional grocers to new grocery or household-related formats. Since 1985, traditional supermarkets lost fully half of consumer purchases to other types of retailers, such as superstores and warehouse clubs. Food eaten outside the home increased dramatically and accounted for all of food industry growth.[11]

Wholesale Clubs

Wholesale clubs were warehouse buildings averaging 100,000 square feet or more and offering a limited selection of grocery and non-food items at low unit prices. The major clubs were Price-Costco, Sam's Club, and BJ's Wholesale Club. By mid-1995, Price-Costco and Sam's Club represented over 90% of the 24 million wholesale club members in the United States; members generally paid annual membership fees ranging from $25 to $35. Consumer members made up two-thirds of wholesale club shoppers but sales to businesses accounted for nearly 70% of this channel's revenues.

Wholesale clubs carried far fewer SKUs than supermarkets, averaging approximately 3,500 per outlet, with a mix of 20% to 30% grocery items and 70% to 80% grocery-related. In 1995, there were 750 clubs generating $20.3 billion in grocery sales, which accounted for 5.1% of the grocery industry total. Clubs took advantage of low operating costs (operating expenses were 7.5% of sales as opposed to 22% for traditional grocery operations); by offering items in bulk, these retailers tended to undersell supermarket prices by an average of 26%.

Clubs continued to grow units and sales, but experts believed their future expansion would be limited due to a less diverse inventory (fewer SKUs) and inconsistent product offerings (SKU selection was sometimes driven by opportunistic buying); in addition, bulk quantities often had a negative impact on consumer convenience and satisfaction. In addition, services offered to consumers were minimal, and stores were often inconveniently located. As a result, it was unclear if consumers would continue to favor lower prices over variety, service, and convenience.

Supercenters

Supercenters, such as Wal-Mart Supercenter or Super K-Mart, offered low prices, regular (not bulk) packaging, and large selections of grocery items and general merchandise in large, low-cost retail outlets. Supercenters were the fastest growing grocery segment with 880 units in 1996, up from 305 in 1993 and 195 stores in 1990.[12] The size of an average superstore was 170,000 square feet (five times that of the average chain supermarket unit); some larger superstores reached 225,000 square feet. The typical merchandise mix was 30% grocery (which accounted for 40% to 45% of store sales); the rest was general merchandise. While supercenters did not always offer the lowest prices, they averaged 9% to 15% below average supermarket prices.

The average supercenter store had $52.5 million in annual revenues. Lower labor, storage, transportation, and promotion costs translated into lower operating expenses of 18.3% as opposed to 22.7% for large supermarkets. Return on invested capital for supercenters was 23.1% as opposed to 20.6% for supermarkets. However, superstores experienced uneven performance by sales category, with high returns on general merchandise but low returns on perishables, which represented a traditionally high-margin category for supermarkets. Most supercenters were located in the Midwest, Northwest, and South Central regions of the United States, but they were beginning to appear in other regions of the country. Grocery-related sales through this channel were expected to increase to $56.4 billion in 2003 from $20.8 billion in 1996, as the number of supercenter stores doubled to 1,790 from 880 in the same period.[13]

[10]Food Marketing Institute, Food Marketing Industry Speaks, 1995.
[11]Food Marketing Institute, Food Marketing Industry Speaks, 1995.

[12]Supercenters and the Future, McKinsey and Company, 1996.
[13]Supercenters and the Future, McKinsey and Company, 1996.

Emerging Industry: Consumer-Direct[14]

For years, selected supermarkets in the United States had been delivering groceries directly to homes, often on a fee or courtesy basis and in a mostly informal manner. But in the 1990s the market for complete direct-to-home delivery operations was still small. Of the $400 billion in grocery sales in 1994, less than 1% came from groceries purchased through direct channels by households. Despite the limited scale, some experts projected substantial growth in this segment. According to Andersen Consulting's contribution to the CDC study, by 2002 the consumer-direct channel—of which home grocery delivery was just one segment—was expected to capture as many as 20 million households (or 21% of 96 million households) in the United States and achieve an 8% to 12% market share, or $60 to $85 billion in sales, of a potential $720 billion market. The growth of the consumer-direct channel was largely attributed to the continued increase in the number of dual-income families and in the number of women entering the workforce (see Exhibit 2). This new channel was expected to exceed the combined revenues of supercenters and warehouse clubs, which had reached maturity in 8 to 12 years from their inception.

DeMello was convinced that consumer-direct's distinctive value proposition of service and convenience could change the landscape of grocery retailing. Put simply, DeMello believed consumer-direct was likely to siphon off the most affluent 15% of consumers who currently shopped in grocery stores. The target households would be suburban, dual-income families, who accounted for most of the profitability in the existing grocery channel. Noted DeMello:

> In the U.S. consumer packaged goods sector, 30% of consumers account for 73% of branded product sales. Some people have said that consumer-direct will only be 15% of the industry. You could say that leaves 85% for grocery stores. That's fine. Grocery can have that 85%—that's not an 85% I'd want. The customers that are attracted to consumer-direct are the industry's best. Those are the customers Streamline is interested in.

According to Andersen, 47% of consumers surveyed wanted groceries delivered at a convenient time; more than 40% wanted to place an order from home using phone, fax, or computer modem. Across demographic categories, consumers regarded grocery shopping as a thankless chore that was best completed as quickly as possible. Consistent with these findings, a 1990 University of Michigan study had asked Americans to rank 22 everyday household tasks in terms of enjoyment; grocery shopping ranked next to last.

By year-end 1996, several companies across the United States were already experimenting with the concept of direct-to-home grocery delivery. These companies included Peapod with services in San Francisco, Chicago, and Columbus, Ohio; Shoppers Express, in Los Angeles, Phoenix, and Dallas; RedWagon, in New York City; HomeRuns, in Boston; and PinkDot, in Los Angeles. Each of these companies employed different business and operational models, ranging from same day delivery to next day delivery and covering a variety of target market segments of consumers (see Exhibit 3).

Streamline's Value Proposition

Streamline offered its customers "lifestyle solutions" that, in fact, went beyond grocery shopping, as compared with many of its competitors, such as Peapod and Shoppers Express. DeMello explained the difference:

> The brands tell you which businesses they're in: Peapod is in the grocery business, HomeRuns is in the delivery business. Streamline is in the lifestyle-solution business; our brand stands for simplicity. Groceries are an important part of the solution we offer consumers, but they are only one part. Everything we do is designed to strengthen our offering and the relationship we have with the consumer.

DeMello foresaw Streamline offering a menu of delivery services—from dry cleaning to video rentals to photo processing—in addition to direct grocery shopping. Streamline management estimated that an average customer made 24 trips per month to stores for grocery and general merchandise products. The average time spent for a single weekend grocery shopping trip usually added up to three hours, including travel to and from stores as well as actual shopping time. The study estimated the average cost of a trip, excluding the retail cost of products and services purchased, was roughly $60 per week or $3,120 per year. These costs included gas consumption, auto maintenance, late fees on videos, and the cost of an individual's time, estimated conservatively at $10 per hour. A household subscribing to Streamline side-

---

[14]Portions of this section were adapted from "Shopping Alternative Inc.: Home Shopping in the Information Revolution," HBS case No. 796-132.

stepped these costs, but incurred a service fee of approximately $7.50 a week, or $30 a month,[15] to have groceries purchased, dry cleaning picked up, and videos returned by Streamline staff.

Busy families (see Exhibit 4), DeMello believed, were the most likely early adopters of this consumer-direct service. Statistics showed that households with children spent more on food consumed in the home than single households or dual households without children. For example, in 1993, single households spent an average of $2,195 annually on food consumed at home. By comparison, married households without children spent $2,896 per year; married households with the oldest child less than six years of age spent $4,452 per year; and married households with the oldest child being between six and 17 years spent $6,404 per year. Annual food expenditures for in-home consumption also varied with household income. Households earning between $30,000 and $40,000 spent an average of $3,736 per year, while households earning more than $70,000 spent in excess of $4,893 per year.[16] DeMello remarked:

Anyone running a business like this wants to get the best customers, and that's what this model attracts: Time-starved busy families that buy major brand names, who aren't overly price-sensitive, and who want good service. So what you're going to start to see as consumer-direct evolves is that people will begin leaving those retail stores, and retailers will begin losing their profitability, because their margins are already very thin and these are the customers who bring them their margins.

Added Britt on the attractiveness of Streamline's "one-service shopping" to consumers:

Streamline believes that the "best" customer is ultimately looking for a package or bundle of products and services vis-à-vis individual pieces. In the long run, consumers, given the appropriate targeted variety, will migrate away from buying "ingredients" toward purchasing "bundled" solutions. This notion is consistent with Streamline's value proposition of convenience, time saving, and stress-reduction. Consumers are not necessarily looking for more choices, just the right choices.

Franklin, Massachusetts, resident and Streamline customer Nancy Wilkie summarized the benefits of Streamline's service to her and her family:

Streamline takes care of my everyday needs, which are time-consuming and often aggravating. I can't begin to estimate how much time and energy Streamline saves me. Just not having to return videos, taking back returnable bottles, and worrying if I'll make it to the dry cleaners before they close, makes the monthly fee seem very small. My time is valuable to me, and Streamline takes care of the chores I don't have time to do. Streamline is much more than a grocery delivery service—it's a lifestyle solution!

In addition to providing consumers with delivery of goods and services, DeMello envisioned that Streamline could become a key "information provider" to its subscriber households. DeMello observed:

Aside from having no other options, why do consumers go to the store? To obtain products and product information. With the help of technology, Streamline can provide consumers with more information on nutrition, pricing, and usage than they are able to get inside the store today.

In addition, Streamline created advantages through information for vendors as well as consumers. For example, manufacturers and brand marketers could obtain more detailed information on consumer buying patterns thanks to Streamline's uncluttered and proprietary access to households. As DeMello noted:

We see ourselves as the purchasing agent for the consumer. We do not sell our customers' names or their purchase data. Instead, we take that information and work with manufacturers to develop targeted offerings on the consumer's behalf. For example, if we see somebody starting to buy diapers, we can approach Gerber or Beech-Nut and say, "Do you want to offer a program to this specific home?" And because the offer is targeted, and is communicated through our proprietary channels, consumer response is generally very high. It's a win for the consumer, and it's a win for the manufacturer.

As marketing consultant and board member Faith Popcorn, observed:

What I love about Streamline is that it is totally connected to the consumer. If you look at the *Popcorn*

---

[15]In 1996, $30 per month was the equivalent of a household's subscription fee to basic cable television.
[16]U.S. Bureau of Census, U.S. Department of Commerce and McKinsey and Company analysis, 1996.

Report,[17] there's a chapter called "The End of Shopping" that identifies "Info-buying" as a trend. I look at the supermarket industry and why it's over. Supermarkets are run by guys and they are insensitive to women. Supermarkets and Department store people are always saying that women like to come here when, in fact, they hate it. They have no other options. You try to go to the supermarket with two kids. Forget it. [DeMello] has created an incredible and viable option which I think will replace the supermarket. It won't replace the food boutique. I think that you might still like to go to a bakery and touch and smell the bread and pastry. And who likes to pick up dry cleaning and video tapes? Nobody. I think Streamline's very on-time—not early—for a trend that's been happening for several years.

Streamline's Business Model

Streamline's business model was based on five key elements: a broad product and service offering; convenient, weekly home delivery; a proprietary home delivery receptacle; a customized shopping experience; and ease of ordering. Streamline's customer experience model—seven "moments of truth" when Streamline interacted with its customers—emphasized the five key elements of the business model (see Figure A).

Customer Selection. Streamline planned to be selective about the customers it drew into its franchise. DeMello described the target consumer:

> We're not interested in the urban or rural markets. We're after the *busy suburban family*. We define family as one child or more. We don't care if it's with nannies, mother-in-laws, one parent, two parents—it really doesn't matter. At least one child is key because children force structure in a family, and our business is about structure and organization.

Added Britt about the demographics of Streamline's target consumers: "Streamline's current customers are suburban homeowners, aged between 30 and 50, with household incomes of $50,000 or more, and an average of two children in the home."

Approximately 89% of Streamline customers served out of the Westwood facility were busy families with the characteristics indicated. The remaining 11% were dual income couples with no children. Streamline expected to establish and maintain a "best" customer ratio of at least 90% in all its markets.

During the company's beta phase, Streamline's 200-household customer base had grown largely through word-of-mouth. As the company grew, Streamline planned to supplement consumer referrals with direct mail (see Exhibit 5) and targeted advertising. However, referrals would continue to play an important role. Noted Dave Blakelock, Streamline's vice president of

Figure A The Customer Experience Model

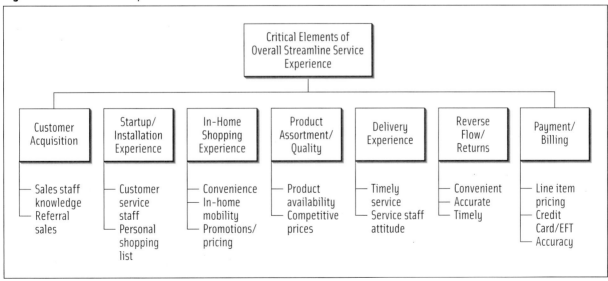

---

[17]Faith Popcorn, *The Popcorn Report*, Doubleday Currency, 1991.

operations, "Our hope is that our next 200,000 consumers look very much like our first 200. We want our consumers to refer families just like theirs, ideally families who live right down the street. That way, we maintain our target customer mix and improve our routing densities." Added Britt:

> The economic benefits of the "best" customer are not limited to operational efficiencies. Busy suburban families spend more than the average shopper, are less transient, and are more brand loyal. We believe they are also more likely to remain loyal to a provider that can meet their household needs.

Start-up/Installation. Customers interested in Streamline's services paid a one-time $39 start-up fee in addition to the ongoing $30 monthly service charge. When a customer signed up with Streamline, Streamline service representatives appeared at the customer's home with hand-held electronic bar-code scanners. Using those devices, they scanned in the household's complete inventory of consumer products—usually 125 unique items in each household—directly into Streamline's database. In addition, the Streamline service receptacle—a combination refrigerator/storage unit (see Exhibit 6)—was installed in the customer's garage.

In-home Shopping Experience. To assure delivery, customers called in orders by midnight the day prior to the designated delivery. Customers could order three ways: phone, fax, or PC (through a Web site at *www.getstreamlined.com*). The Personal Shopping List—five to ten pages in length and based initially on scanned inventory from the home—was used to order goods and helped customize services for specific household needs. For example, customers could indicate what size potatoes they wanted or if they preferred plastic produce bags tied or untied. The Personal Shopping List was included each week with the Streamline Order Packet. Other items in the packet included the weekly order statement, itemizing what had been delivered, a flyer on sale items, and an order sheet for videos. Basic household items, such as soap, detergent, and batteries, were automatically re-ordered (see Exhibit 7); these "replenishment" items were based on initial inventory scans and subsequent ordering indicating consumption rates. Automatic replenishment provided Streamline subscribers with added convenience, but it also delivered other benefits. Noted DeMello:

> Take a program we did with Gillette. Gillette tells us that the average male uses 30 razors a year. So we look

at this. What does this mean? And we tried to understand. If our customer could get automatically get a five-pack of Gillette sensor razors every eight weeks, why not? Why do they need to order that product? To get a fixed price? We'll set it up automatically and we'll send it to them. They have no risk. They can return it to us by just leaving it out [in the receptacle] the following week. We'll give them full credit. Wouldn't you give a $5 credit to someone spending almost $5,000 a year with you?

Streamline used two channels in this way—physical and virtual—to make the customer shopping experience easy (see Figure B). Observed DeMello:

> Streamline has built a business model which is rapidly becoming recognized as the industry's best. The model consists of a physical and virtual channel between Streamline and the customer. The physical channel facilitates the distribution of goods and services, as well as a reverse flow of "processed" products, such as videos, dry cleaning, and film. The virtual channel allows Streamline to communicate product and service information directly into the household, and to receive feedback directly back from the consumer. The virtual channel also allows Streamline to develop a comprehensive database and insights into purchasing patterns and behaviors by household. This data not only builds a tremendous business asset, but also allows Streamline to continually refine its offerings and services to the target customer.

The "physical" channel focused on fulfillment, such as providing consumable and disposable products and services from the CRC to the Streamline service box in the consumer's home.

> Streamline's physical channel provides the company with what may be the lowest operating-cost model in the industry. Our dedicated fulfillment center, or CRC, centralizes all products and services in a facility designed to hold less than a week's worth of inventory. This facility is laid out to maximize picking efficiency, not product facings. Unattended delivery into the service box allows us delivery flexibility and is viewed by consumers as a real benefit since they don't have to be home to receive their order. These advantages are structural, and, consequently, are very difficult for our competitors to imitate.

The "virtual" channel provided product information to the consumer through the two-way ordering process, with targeted sampling and solution selling. When fully

Figure B Streamline's Virtual and Physical Channels

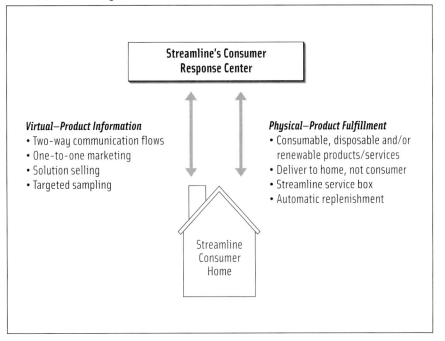

implemented, this channel would include an array of technologies focused on measuring, tracking, and collecting user activities across multiple CRCs and was expected to drive significant electronic commerce volume:

> Home shopping of groceries and related services could drive electronic commerce volume more than any other application. Our business model, which centers on weekly delivery of electronically-placed orders, will steer consumers into the virtual channel, where they will make a $100 purchase at least 47 times a year.

Product Assortment/Quality.
Customer orders were filled at Streamline's CRC, a 56,000-square-foot warehouse holding over 10,500 SKUs. According to Britt, because of the particular needs of the target market, the narrower inventory was not dampening demand—for example, 7.6% of the household and cosmetics brands accounted for 85% of sales. Fewer SKUs helped reduce inventory and operational costs:

> In a typical grocery store of 30,000 SKUs, a 45% reduction in SKU count would result in only a 10% reduction in overall sales. Because we have a very targeted consumer base, we are able to benefit from a very targeted assortment.

Incoming orders were usually taken by a customer service representative (CSR); orders were then hand-picked by an order service representative (OSR). Streamline aimed to stock the top three brands in each category. If a certain product requested was not available, the OSR would then make his or her judgment regarding the best substitute product unless the customer specified otherwise.

Delivery Experience.
Once a week, on the designated delivery day, Streamline FSRs delivered orders to each customer's service box (usually located in the garage). With support from the CSRs and OSRs, field service reps were able to service 30 to 40 homes per day, averaging less than ten minutes per stop.

While customers were not required to be home, occasionally Streamline FSRs would encounter consumers during delivery. Referring to this interaction, Blakelock noted:

> Our FSRs need to be highly efficient, yet personable and professional in nature. If a customer wants to chat, we want them to feel good about the interaction they've just had with our company. We spend a lot of time recruiting the right skill set for this position.

Prior to delivery, Streamline had a CRC ritual that was unusual. Each FSR would read off the names of the families they served on their daily route—including the names of new households served—and Streamline employees were required to provide a news item on each family, such as the "Smiths are having a new baby" or "the Joneses are hosting their grandparents from California for a visit."

Reverse Flows/Returns. Streamline ferried goods to and from its customers each week. If a customer wanted to return a particular product, they put a return label on it, left it in the service receptacle, and Streamline collected and credited it with no questions asked.

Payments and Billing. Bills were summarized for customers on a line-item basis on the weekly order statement and payments were made either by credit card or by electronic funds transfer. Patty Davis, an attorney in Dover, Massachusetts, commented:

> Before I signed up for Streamline, I have to admit I was a bit skeptical. I thought that paying someone else to do your shopping was really decadent. But once I signed up and saw the prices, it didn't seem extravagant at all. The $30 I spend on Streamline's services each month ends up saving me money in the long run, because I don't have to take my kids with me to the grocery store and make impulse purchases. I've been really pleased with the service—it's quick, efficient, and convenient.

Economics of the Streamline Model

As illustrated in Figure C, Streamline's potential profit margin was estimated in November 1996 to be six times greater than that of the typical supermarket, at 6¢ versus 1¢ on the dollar, due to lower operating costs. Using warehouses instead of expensive retail store locations was a key economic driver in Streamline's business model. Noted DeMello:

> Consumer-direct companies fundamentally have lower cost operating structures than their retail competitors. One of the major cost advantages is real estate. Our facility, for example, costs $6.50 per square foot. A Boston grocery retailer might have real estates costs of $18.50 or more per square foot.

A typical Streamline order averaged $110 per week and a Streamline household would typically order 47 times a year (or 90% of available purchase cycles). Monthly service fees contributed an additional $360 per household annually and the average retention rate was projected to be 90%. Fixed costs included overhead expense for the CRC, the service receptacle placed in each household, and customer acquisition costs. Variable costs were limited to the cost of fulfilling an order.

Streamline's business model differed in several ways from Peapod's *(http://www.peapod.com)*, an on-line grocery shopping and delivery service to which it was often compared. Although goods could be ordered and delivered any day of the week through Peapod's proprietary on-line system, the automatic replenishment of basic household items did not occur with Peapod; in addition, Peapod's pricing structure was calculated in a different way. For example, Peapod customers paid a monthly fee of $4.95 and a per-order fee of $6.95 plus 5% of the total order. The typical Peapod order averaged $110, in line with Streamline's; but it would have a per-order charge of $12.45 in addition to the monthly fee. Peapod customers, on average, ordered less often than Streamline customers over the course of a year. As DeMello noted:

Figure C Streamline vs. Supermarkets: More Net per Revenue Dollar

	Typical Supermarket	Streamline
Costs of Goods Sold	$0.75	$0.72
Operating Costs	0.17	0.13
Distribution	0.04	0.06
Corporate Overhead	0.03	0.03
Net Profit	0.01	0.06
	$1.00	$1.00

Source: Joshua Macht, "Errand Boy," *Inc.,* November 1996

With Streamline, you don't have to be home. The assortment is broader. The prices are competitive. We have a different relationship with the customer. The Streamline customer reorders 47 times a year. The Peapod customer reorders 25 to 30 times a year. We're a lifestyle solution business, not a grocery delivery business, and customers are recognizing that.

At year end 1996, the seven-year-old Peapod, Inc.—partially owned by two media companies, Chicago-based Tribune Company and Dallas-based A. H. Belo—served an estimated 35,000 households in four markets across the United States. Peapod provided its on-line service for a grocery chain in each of the markets—Jewel/Osco in Chicago, Safeway in the Bay Area, Kroger in Ohio, and Stop & Shop in New England. Averaging an estimated $2.5 million per week in sales in 1996, Peapod had plans to expand into seven other metropolitan markets by year-end 1997, including Dallas, Houston, and Atlanta. Peapod's stated goal was to become a $1 billion company by 2001.[18]

Rollout of the Streamline Model

To reach Streamline's goal of one million subscriber homes by 2004, DeMello and his management team had segmented the company's growth strategy into three distinct phases. The first phase—proving that the consumer value proposition worked—was complete. Key economic variables of the business model, such as pricing, repeat purchase rates, and average order size in dollars, had been validated. The second phase—designing the processes and infrastructure—was at the company's Westwood-based CRC. What remained was to confirm Streamline's business model as it expanded beyond its test market and opened new markets across the country (see Exhibit 8). DeMello believed that franchising would drive Streamline's growth:

> Our expansion strategy effectively disaggregates the physical and virtual channels; the virtual channel will be managed centrally at a national level, and the physical channel will be managed at the local and regional levels. As the head of a Streamline regional operating company, you will be responsible for building 25 CRCs in your market within a five to seven year time frame. With a total of eight regional operating companies, Streamline can penetrate every major market in the country by 2005.

Britt foresaw Streamline providing all of the necessary financing and marketing support to help the regional companies get started. The centralization of Streamline's marketing functions would also benefit manufacturers. Added Wilcox:

> If as a manufacturer you want to introduce a program or promotion in the consumer-direct channel, you can go to Streamline, Inc. As Kraft General Foods or Nabisco, you don't have to go to every local CRC around the country to sell in your program. It's all handled centrally. Strategic alliances are also better managed under this scenario. We plan to create one central place where ideas are developed and distributed into the marketplace.

> We've spent several years studying this opportunity. We believe that our focus on the consumer has allowed Streamline to build the strongest brand, supported by a robust business model. Our partnerships have accelerated our learning, and will prove valuable as we move toward national roll-out. In the end, it will all come down to execution.

Conclusion

As the Streamline Launch party came to an end, DeMello was buoyed by the events of the evening. Customers, investors, strategic partners, and employees—past and present—had come together in support of the Streamline concept. Having validated the conceptual model, DeMello was prepared for Streamline to tackle the operational, financial, and managerial challenges of the proposed CRC rollout across the country, while building the centralized virtual channel. The question remained: with all the planning, innovating, and excitement generated by Streamline, could the company reach its stated goal of 1 million homes by 2004? As he said goodnight to his departing guests, DeMello felt certain the organization was up to the challenge.

---

[18]Gary Arlen, "Peapod's Agenda Moving Beyond Groceries, Even as Company Adds New Markets," *Information and Interactive Services Report*, November 22, 1996.

Exhibit 1 Annual Trips by Shopping Channel

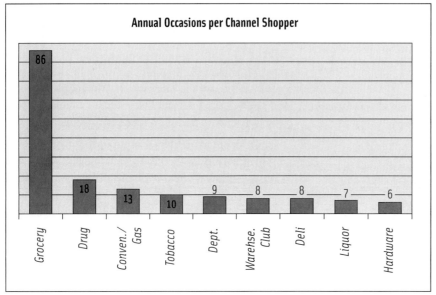

Annual Occasions per Channel Shopper

Source: AC Nielsen

Exhibit 2 Increase in the Number of Working Women and Dual Income Families

Women in the Work Force: Percent Participation

Source: U.S. Bureau of Labor Statistics; U.S. Bureau of the Census

Exhibit 2 Increase in the Number of Working Women and Dual Income Families Continued

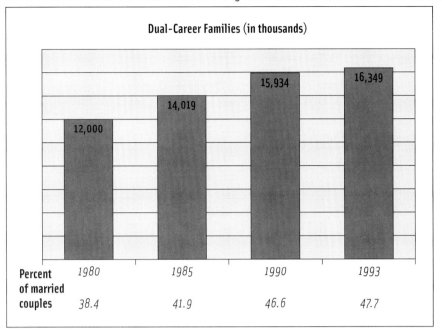

Dual-Career Families (in thousands)

	1980	1985	1990	1993
	12,000	14,019	15,934	16,349
Percent of married couples	38.4	41.9	46.6	47.7

Source: U.S. Bureau of Labor Statistics; U.S. Bureau of the Census

Exhibit 3

Service	URL	Major Markets Served	Monthly Fee	Delivery Cost	Time of Delivery
HomeRuns	www.homeruns.com	Boston	None	Free over orders of $60 Otherwise $10 minimum (minimum order of $30)	Next Day
Peapod	www.peapod.com	Boston, Chicago, Columbus, San Francisco	$4.95/month	$6.95 per order plus 5% of order cost	Same or Next Day
Pink Dot	www.pinkdot.com	Los Angeles	None	$1.99 per order	Same Day (within 30 minutes if between 9 a.m. and 3 a.m.)
Red Wagon	www.redwagon.com	New York City (Manhattan)	None	None (minimum order of $20)	Next Day
Shoppers Express	www.shoppinglink.com	Dallas, Los Angeles, Phoenix	None	10% order cost or minimum fee	Same or Next Day (orders are to be placed six hours in advance)
Streamline	www.getstreamlined.com	Westwood, Massachusetts	$30/month with $39 start-up fee	None	Scheduled Weekly Delivery

Source: Individual services; *The New York Times*, CyberTimes column, September 4, 1996

Exhibit 4 Streamline Checklist

WHY YOU NEED US
Take this test

1. Are you constantly wondering where all of your free time went?
   ❑ Yes   ❑ No

2. Have you paid over $15 in video rental late fees in the past month?
   ❑ Yes   ❑ No

3. Do you dread getting the kids in the car to go shopping?
   ❑ Yes   ❑ No

4. Do you think of Saturday as "Errand Day"?
   ❑ Yes   ❑ No

5. Do you wish you could spend more time just being a family?
   ❑ Yes   ❑ No

6. Is there a gigantic "To Do" list on your fridge right now?
   ❑ Yes   ❑ No

7. Does your family eat take-out once or more each week because you "have no food in the house?"
   ❑ Yes   ❑ No

8. Do you ever come home after spending a lot of time at the office and your kids look at you and ask, "Who are you?"
   ❑ Yes   ❑ No

9. Does your dog look skinnier?
   ❑ Yes   ❑ No

10. Do you ever push two carts through the supermarket at once?
    ❑ Yes   ❑ No

11. Do you make more than two trips to the ATM a week?
    ❑ Yes   ❑ No

12. Is there such an incredible layer of kids' toys and debris in your home that you've actually forgotten the original color of your carpet?
    ❑ Yes   ❑ No

13. Are you currently debating whether or not you actually have time enough to finish taking this test?
    ❑ Yes   ❑ No

14. Is it easier for you to name all of the cashiers at your supermarket than to name the seven dwarves?
    ❑ Yes   ❑ No

15. Have the soles of your shoes ever ignited from excessive friction?
    ❑ Yes   ❑ No

16. Do you have more than two books on the subject of coping with stress or managing your time better?
    ❑ Yes   ❑ No

17. Are you still trying to find time to read those books?
    ❑ Yes   ❑ No

18. Are there Tupperware containers in the back of your fridge that you're afraid to open?
    ❑ Yes   ❑ No

19. If you speak into your cupboard, can you produce an echo?
    ❑ Yes   ❑ No

20. Have your neighbors ever sent you an invoice for the excessive number of times your kids have eaten over at their house?
    ❑ Yes   ❑ No

Exhibit 5 Streamline Direct Mail Pieces

Exhibit 6 Streamline Refrigerator/Storage Unit

Exhibit 7 Streamline Personal Shopping List

John Doe Household, Account #0000

Personal Shopping List

Qty.	Order Unit	Item Description	Comments	Omit from personal list
	EA	Potatoes - Red Bliss - Loose	Med. size, do not tie bag	❑
	EA	Rhubarb - Bunch		❑
	EA	Sprouts - Alfalfa Packaged	Please do not tie bag	❑
		Dairy		
	EA	1% Milk Gallon		❑
	EA	Cabot Salted Butter, 4 quarters 16 oz.		❑
	EA	Columbo Fat Free Yogurt Blueberry 8 oz.		❑
	EA	Columbo Fat Free Yogurt Raspberry 8 oz.		❑
	EA	DiGiorno Shredded Parmesan Cheese 8 oz.		❑
	EA	Eggs Large Brown Dozen		❑
	EA	Homogenized 1/2 Gallon		❑
	EA	Hood Cottage Cheese Small Curd 16 oz.		❑
	EA	Ultra 1/2 & 1/2 Cream Pint		❑
		Bread		
	EA	Pepperidge Farm Crunchy Oat Bread 24 oz.		❑
	EA	Pepperidge Farm Natural Whole Grain Crunchy 24 oz.		❑
		Bakery		
	EA	Bagels - cinnamon raisin		❑
	EA	Bagels - onion		❑
	EA	Bagels - plain		❑
	EA	Mini Bagels - Cinnamon Raisin 10.8 oz.		❑
		Beverages		
	EA	Coca- Cola Diet Caffeine Free 2 liter		❑
	EA	Dole Tropical Fruit Punch 64 oz.		❑
	EA	Florida Natural Premium Orange Juice 1/2 gallon		❑

streamline™

If you have any questions, please call us at (617) 320-1900

Exhibit 8 Streamline Rollout Strategy

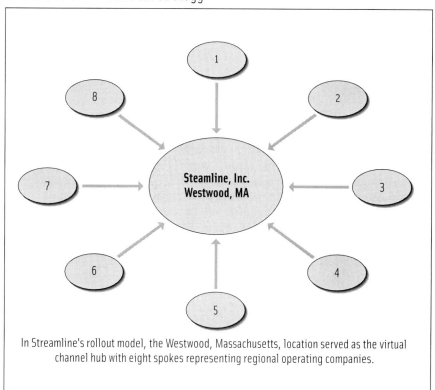

In Streamline's rollout model, the Westwood, Massachusetts, location served as the virtual channel hub with eight spokes representing regional operating companies.

STREAMLINE (B)

As a cool New England winter breeze swept across the quiet suburban neighborhoods of Boston in late December 1999, Tim DeMello, Streamline.com's founder and CEO, sat in his Westwood, Massachusetts, office and reflected upon his company's activities since its October 1996 Launch Party. During the past three years, Streamline.com had focused on refining its business model of providing consumer direct services to busy suburban families in the Boston area. In addition to groceries, videos, and dry cleaning deliveries, Streamline.com now offered a weekly flower service and deliveries of bottled water and prepared meals (see Exhibit 1). Approximately 80 percent of its customer orders were now placed through the Internet—resulting in the company now referring to itself as Streamline.com instead of just Streamline—and it had enhanced its customers' Web ordering by introducing the Don't Run Out™ automatic replenishment program in 1998 (see Exhibit 2 for Streamline.com web site). Having raised $42 million through an IPO on June 18, 1999, DeMello now felt that Streamline.com had the financial resources to begin rolling out its unique "lifestyle solution" concept nationwide. With the added financial resources and the advantages of being a public company, DeMello recruited several senior officers with experience in nationwide rollout of retail startups, opened a second hub site in the Washington, D.C., area, and acquired Scotty's Home Market, a regional consumer direct-based company in the Chicago area, in exchange for Streamline.com stock.

Looking forward to the year 2000, Streamline.com had already announced plans to expand into the Northern New Jersey market by the second quarter. The Northern New Jersey area, which was part of the sprawling New York City metropolitan market, would be the fourth market served by Streamline.com, after the Boston, Washington, D.C., and Chicago markets. By the end of 2004, the company hoped to have 50 distribution centers in twenty markets.

Beyond these markets, DeMello wondered how fast the company should expand. Although Streamline.com had enjoyed success in the Boston market—where it now had 3,600 active customers at the end of the third quarter 1999 and had penetrated up to 5% of households in certain affluent suburbs—other emerging competitors had announced aggressive plans to expand into many of the top 20 U.S. markets. Peapod, one of the first direct-to-consumer grocers, was now in eight markets and was looking to expand into several others. Webvan, the latest entry into the consumer direct field, planned to expand into 26 markets within the next three years. The San Francisco area-based company had financial backing from several Fortune 500 companies and raised over $400 million in its November 1999 IPO.

The Competition[1]

Although about $500 billion was spent on groceries in the United States in 1999, less than 0.1% of this total was related to online grocery expenditures. Nevertheless, Andersen Consulting projected that the percentage for online grocery expenditures could rise as high as 20%—or about $90 billion—by the year 2007, especially with the continued increase in the number of households with Internet access, dual income families, and working women.[2]

In addition to Streamline.com, other significant participants pursuing the consumer direct market included Peapod.com, Home Grocer, and Webvan as well as several regional companies (see Exhibit 3).

Peapod.com

The acknowledged pioneer in on-line grocery sales was Peapod.com, a Skokie, Illinois-based company that had negotiated the turbulent e-commerce market for over ten years. Originally, Peapod's business model relied upon local partnerships with bricks-and-mortar supermarkets; Peapod's employees shopped the supermarket

---

Dickson Louie prepared this case under the supervision of Professor Jeffrey Rayport as the basis for class discussion rather than to illustrate either effective or ineffective handling of an administrative situation. It is a rewritten version of an earlier case, HBS No. 898-178.

---

[1]This section was prepared by Research Associate Gillian Morris.
[2]Barry M. Stouffer, "Internet-Based Consumer Solutions," J.C. Bradford & Company, October 1999.

aisles on a daily basis and then delivered goods within a two-hour window. This strategy, rife with inefficiencies, caused operating costs to consume over 42% of grocery sales by 1997.[3] Mounting losses and new competition in Peapod's primary markets demanded that the company re-evaluate its approach, and by mid-1997, executives called for dedicated warehouses to be tested in Chicago, New York, San Francisco, and Boston, among the eight markets in which Peapod had launched service. Modeled on Streamline.com's approach, this new strategy would decrease operating costs by centralizing order fulfillment, raise product standards, and thus would lower fees to the consumer. In contrast to Streamline.com's model, Peapod executives decided to retain a policy of not charging on orders over $50 and decided to maintain the company's relationships with grocery retailers by using Stop & Shop, for example, to stock its Boston warehouse.

By 1999, this new strategy had won Peapod praise from analysts and consumers. In the Boston market alone, productivity of the packing process doubled, while improvement in delivery logistics yielded productivity gains of over 50 percent. Though still operating at a loss, Peapod projected profitability by 2001, the first online retailer to offer such a concrete deadline. Its consumer base soon topped 100,000, with 1998 sales rising steadily to $69.3 million, four times its 1995 sales. Gross margins also increased to 20%, in keeping with the company's 1999 objectives. Like Streamline.com, Peapod provided demographic research to manufacturers such as Hershey Foods, to very profitable ends. And like Streamline.com, the company also had pursued alliances to further its brand visibility; it had exclusive contracts with Excite and the HomeArts network (the online portal for Hearst magazines such as *Cosmopolitan* and *Good Housekeeping*), as well as a co-marketing agreement with the specialty food e-tailer, GreatFood.com.

With these maneuvers, Peapod positioned itself to meet the challenges of an ever more competitive online market. Its strategy for future growth included offering office supplies and luxury goods such as prepared gourmet meals, as well as opening more dedicated distribution centers in order to maintain its market position. To raise the capital required for growth, industry analysts speculated that Peapod might look to merge with an established bricks-and-mortar grocery company seeking to exploit possibilities on-line.

[3]Forrester Research brief, October 31, 1997.

HomeGrocer

Challenging Peapod's lead was HomeGrocer.com. Based in the Pacific Northwest, this 1998 startup had 10,000 customers in Seattle and Portland as of July 1999. HomeGrocer employed the same warehouse distribution model as Streamline. However, its pricing and delivery policies were more similar to those of Peapod. HomeGrocer offered free delivery for orders over $75 and no monthly service fees; customers choose a 90-minute window for next-day delivery, any day of the week. The company had received financial backing from Amazon.com and Jim Barksdale, former CEO of Netscape and COO of Federal Express. Amazon's initial investment was a 35 percent stake in the company, valued at $42.5 million. Barksdale, after investing $5 million, signed on as chairman of the board of directors. HomeGrocer planned to consolidate its position in the Northwest before extending the brand to the rest of the nation.

Webvan

Another serious competitive challenge to Streamline came from Webvan, a June 1999 startup that had attracted much notice in mid-summer of that year. Founded by Louis Borders, the entrepreneur who built the Borders book chain, Webvan's business strategy was a blend of the no-fee service typified by Peapod and the dedicated warehouse model introduced by Streamline.com. Webvan boasted a much deeper selection of grocery items than Streamline.com, eventually planning to offer over 30,000 SKUs. The company offered free delivery on orders over $50, seven days a week, within a 30-minute window selected by the consumer. Its sophisticated logistical strategy required only five hours between the time the customer placed an order and the time of delivery. In the San Francisco Bay area, the first market targeted by Webvan, the company achieved such service levels by building 14 staging areas in communities surrounding its huge 330,000 square-foot, highly automated central warehouse.

This "dual hub" system was the crux of Webvan's business model. After packing orders in the central warehouse, large trucks shipped them to the outlying staging areas where they were reloaded onto smaller vans. Each staging area was no more than ten miles from the customers it served. According to Webvan management, this strategy allowed greater delivery efficiency and decreased operating costs to such an extent that the company predicted a 10 percentage-point edge in operating margins over traditional bricks-and-mortar supermarkets. Webvan management asserted it could achieve such results while pricing grocery items at parity with, or in some case as much as 5 percent below, supermarket prices. Webvan also planned to exploit its logistical capabilities by providing home delivery services for other Web retailers.

What raised eyebrows was Webvan's July 1999 announcement that it planned to invest $1 billion in 26 new distribution facilities—each averaging 330,000 square feet[4]—designed and built by Bechtel, the eminent engineering and construction company. Such ambitious plans—each warehouse was expected to earn $300 million in revenue—apparently contributed to Webvan's success at raising additional venture capital. Initial investors, including Knight-Ridder, CBS, Yahoo!, and Benchmark Capital, had contributed $122 million at start-up. In July 1999, Webvan sold a 6.5 percent stake to Softbank, Goldman Sachs, and Sequoia Capital for $275 million, thus valuing the startup at an astounding $4 billion.[5] At the same time, the company announced plans to raise an additional $1 billion in high-yield debt—an unusual move for a Web startup. Prior to its November 1999 IPO, Webvan recruited George Shaheen, the chief executive of Andersen Consulting, to be its CEO. Webvan raised an additional $405 million through its IPO, and its market valuation reached $7 billion soon after the initial public offering. Marveling at the scope of Webvan's plans, *The Wall Street Journal* in its April 22, 1999 edition noted: Webvan "could become the biggest consumer company in cyberspace. If it stumbles, it could become the Internet era's equivalent of the movie *Waterworld*, a disaster so epic that it becomes an American legend."

Other Industry Players

Two other notable participants in the online grocery wars were HomeRuns and NetGrocer. HomeRuns was launched in Boston in 1995 by the Northeast supermarket giant Hannaford. As of late 1999, it remained the only bricks-and-mortar supermarket chain with an established online presence. (A few other supermarket chains, including Albertsons of Dallas, were conducting online market trials). Its business philosophy strove to be different from Streamline's focus on BSFs. HomeRuns

was willing to deliver to lower income families in urban areas, where its delivery crews often encountered traffic and parking problems, thus increasing the company's costs. Since its inception, HomeRuns had met with skepticism from some Hannaford investors who watched the division drain capital through a series of management errors, a few freak accidents (one involving a run-in with an errant construction crane), and the unique challenges of the highly competitive Boston market. According to *Wired* (May 1999), Hannaford's CEO acknowledged that the service was too big a drain on the parent company's earnings, and planned to seek outside investors for HomeRuns.

NetGrocer also had rocky beginnings. This startup approached the problems of food and distribution by specializing in dry goods, shipped from its New Jersey warehouse via Federal Express. Due to limited selection and a poorly designed website, NetGrocer undertook a major overhaul of its executive leadership in 1998. The new CEO, Fred Horowitz, focused on a more aggressive marketing strategy as well as alliances with manufacturers in order to offer more products at discounted prices.

The Economics of Consumer Direct[6]

An October 1999 study by Barry Stouffer of J.C. Bradford and Co. focused on economics of the consumer direct market. As illustrated in Exhibit 4, when they reached sufficient volume to efficiently utilize their warehouse and delivery infrastructures, Peapod and Streamline.com were expected achieve variable contribution margins of 9% and 14%, respectively. The average order size for online grocery companies was approximately $115, or almost four times what the typical consumer spent in a bricks-and-mortar grocery store. The contribution margin for online players compared favorably against the average of 4 percent for supermarkets.

Streamline.com earned about $5,000 per year in revenue from each customer, assuming that each customer ordered an average of 42 times per year and paid a monthly service charge of $30 per month. In order to cover the fixed costs for building a warehouse, marketing, and software development, the company would have to scale up in each market entered. "Scalability," observed Stouffer, "is a key question."

[4]Barry M. Stouffer, "Internet-Based Consumer Solutions", J.C. Bradford & Company, October 1999.
[5]Private Equity Week, August 2, 1999.

[6]Information for this section was adapted from Barry M. Stouffer, "Internet-Based Consumer Solutions," J.C. Bradford & Company, October 1999.

Operating Results: First Three Quarters of 1999

Through the third quarter of 1999, all three publicly traded companies in the consumer direct field—Streamline.com, Peapod, and Webvan—incurred losses. Streamline.com had a net operating loss of $12.6 million on revenue of $10.2 million for the first nine months of 1999 (see Exhibit 5). Peapod lost $19.3 million on net sales of $51.5 million over the same period (see Exhibit 6). Peapod's gross margin on the cost of goods sold was 23 percent, slightly higher than Streamline.com's 20 percent. And despite only being in operations for nearly three months in a single market, Webvan had incurred a loss of $95.6 million on net sales of $4.2 million (see Exhibit 7). Webvan's gross margin on the cost of goods sold was approximately 8%.

The Challenges Ahead

Despite the initial losses, the potential to dominate the consumer direct market was too large to ignore. DeMello was optimistic about Streamline.com's future. With the hiring of Ed Albertian as president and chief operating officer in September 1999 and William Paul as vice president of merchandising in October 1999, Streamline added two season retailing executives with experience in national rollouts. Both men had experience in grocery retailing with New England-based Star Markets and with the national rollout of Staples, Inc., the office supply chain. DeMello observed:

Back in 1997, obtaining capital was the big challenge. Since then, Nordstrom became our lead investor in October 1998 by investing almost $23 million, we took the company public on June 11, 1999, and raised another $42 million. Now the challenge will be to convince consumers that this direct service can indeed simplify their lives. It's beginning to come together.

The competitive landscape is a challenge. We are now defined at the industry level. There are now four key players—Streamline.com, Webvan, HomeGrocer and Peapod—in this space. People have seen what Streamline.com has done. Our focus in the past has been to get our model right. We have done a good job in developing our model and now the key to our success will be to roll it out successfully nationwide.[7]

Even with Streamline.com's planned national rollout, DeMello maintained that providing excellent service to its customers would remain a company priority and that its partnership with Nordstrom — J. Daniel Nordstrom, the co-president of Nordstrom's, sat on Streamline's board—would be beneficial in this effort. DeMello commented:

Nordstrom understands the service culture and its importance in a national rollout. We spent a lot of time with them in trying to understand the importance and challenges of replicating a service-oriented culture from one market to another. If our service is not where we want it to be, we can feel it.[8]

[8]Interview with casewriter, October 7, 1999.

[7]Interview with casewriter, October 7, 1999.

Exhibit 1 Streamline.com Products and Services

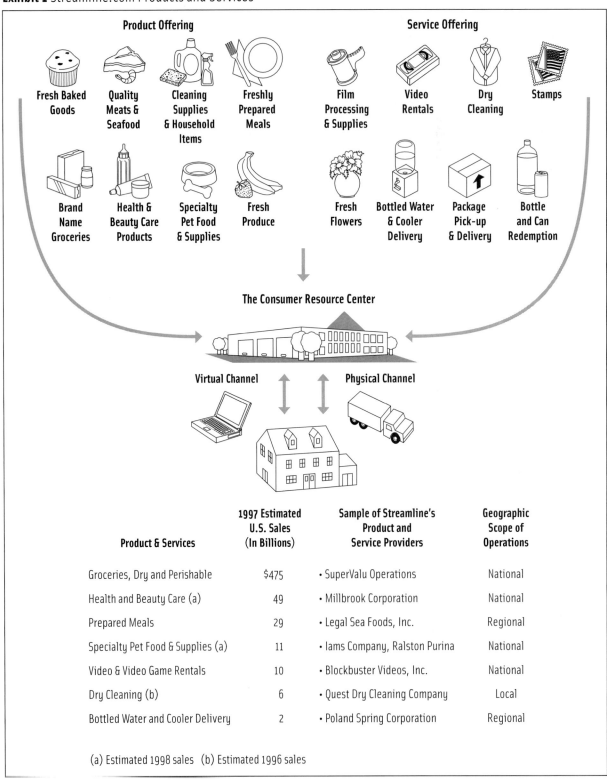

Product & Services	1997 Estimated U.S. Sales (In Billions)	Sample of Streamline's Product and Service Providers	Geographic Scope of Operations
Groceries, Dry and Perishable	$475	• SuperValu Operations	National
Health and Beauty Care (a)	49	• Millbrook Corporation	National
Prepared Meals	29	• Legal Sea Foods, Inc.	Regional
Specialty Pet Food & Supplies (a)	11	• Iams Company, Ralston Purina	National
Video & Video Game Rentals	10	• Blockbuster Videos, Inc.	National
Dry Cleaning (b)	6	• Quest Dry Cleaning Company	Local
Bottled Water and Cooler Delivery	2	• Poland Spring Corporation	Regional

(a) Estimated 1998 sales (b) Estimated 1996 sales

Source: Streamline.com prospectus

Exhibit 2 Navigating Streamline's Web Site

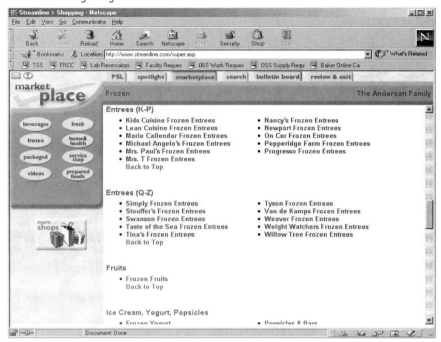

Source: *Streamline.com*

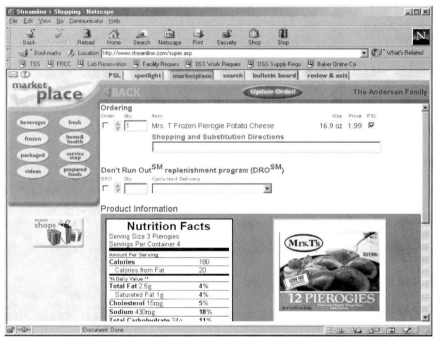

Source: *Streamline.com*

Exhibit 2 Navigating Streamline's Web Site, Continued

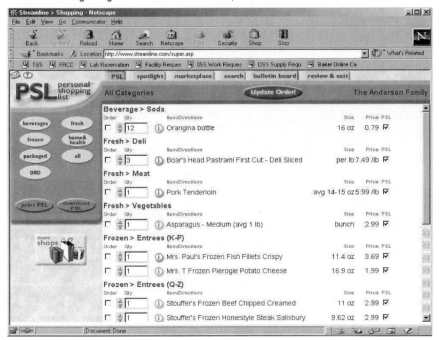

Source: *Streamline.com*

Exhibit 3 Consumer Direct/Online Grocers Competitive Landscape: Winter 2000

Service	URL	Markets Served	Monthly Fee	Delivery Cost	Time of Delivery	Description
HomeGrocer	www.homegrocer.com	Seattle	None	N/A	N/A	Bellevue, Washington-based consumer direct company serves the Seattle area market
HomeRuns	www.homeruns.com	New England region	None	Free on orders over $10. Otherwise $10 minimum	Next Day	Part of the Hannaford food store chain, Homeruns.com serves the New England Market.
NetGrocer	www.netgrocer.com	Nationwide	None	Federal Express charges	1-4 Business Days	Serving the entire United States, NetGrocer fulfills consumer orders of non-perishable items through FedEx
Peapod	www.peapod.com	Chicago, San Francisco, San Jose, Long Island, Dallas, Austin, Columbus, Houston	$4.95	$5 per order	Same or Next Day	Now in eight markets, Peapod is moving away from its original business model of fulfilling orders through local chains and setting up its own warehouse/distribution system.
PinkDot	www.pinkdot.com	Los Angeles	None	$2.99 per order	30 minutes	Serving the Los Angeles market, PinkDot delivers groceries and sandwiches in 30 minutes or less.
Shoplink	www.shoplink.com	Boston	$25	None	Scheduled Weekly	Serving the Boston area, Shoplink delivers dry cleaning, videos, and groceries directly to the home.
Streamline	www.streamline.com	Boston, Washington DC	$30	None	Scheduled Weekly	Serving the Boston and DC areas, Streamline delivers groceries, videos, and drycleaning to the home.
Webvan	www.webvan.com	San Francisco Bay Area	None	$4.95 per order on orders less than $50 (a)	Same or Next Day	Serving the San Francisco Bay Area. Offers delivery within 30-minute windows. Founded by Louis Borders of Borders Books Inc.
YourGrocer	www.yourgrocer.com	Manhattan and NYC counties	None	$5 on $50 minimum order	Next Day	Serving Manhattan borough and selected suburbs of New York City, YourGrocer provides next day delivery.

Sources: *Industry Standard* (3/29/99), online grocer web sites
(a) effective February 1, 2000

Exhibit 4 Theoretical Economics Per Order

	PEAPOD		STREAMLINE	
Product Sales	$115.00	100.0%	$115.00	100.0%
Product Cost	81.99	71.3%	82.80	72.0%
Gross Margin	33.01	28.7%	32.20	28.0%
Order Taking Cost	1.96	1.7%	3.45	3.0%
Picking Cost	7.78	6.8%	6.27	5.5%
Packaging Cost	1.26	1.1%	1.26	1.1%
Delivery Cost	11.28	9.8%	5.23	4.5%
Per-Order Contribution	$10.73	9.3%	$15.99	13.9%

Source: Company estimates and J.C. Bradford & Co.

Exhibit 5 Streamline.com Income Statement (1996–1999) ($ in Thousands)

	Year Ended Dec. 31			Nine Months Ended Sept. 30
	1996	1997	1998	1999
Revenue:				
- Product and Service Revenue, Net	$391	$1,815	$6,026	$8,694
- Subscription Fees	20	99	392	693
- Advertising, Research and Marketing Fees	511	721	529	855
Total Revenue	922	2,635	6,947	10,242
Operating Expenses:				
- Cost of Revenue	$391	$2,098	$4,992	7,016
- Fulfillment Center Operations	916	2,769	4,013	5,978
- Sales and Marketing	440	1,428	1,479	2,595
- Technology Systems and Development	78	1,673	3,003	2,808
- General and Administrative	985	3,167	3,897	5,066
Total Operating Expenses	2,810	11,135	17,384	23,463
Loss from Operations	−1,888	−8,500	−10,437	−13,221

Source: *Streamline.com* prospectus and Streamline.com press release dated October 28, 1999

Exhibit 6 Peapod Income Statement (1996–1999) ($ in thousands)

		Year Ended Dec. 31		Nine Months Ended Sept. 30
	1996	1997	1998	1999
Net Sales	$27,642	$56,943	$69,265	$51,574
Cost of Sales	20,485	40,823	53,903	39,509
Gross Profit	7,157	16,120	15,362	12,065
Operating Expenses:				
- Fulfillment Operations	6,889	14,469	17,196	15,460
- General and Administrative	3,785	5,935	8,029	8,146
- Marketing and Advertising	4,739	7,726	7,545	4,093
- System Development and Maintenance	1,124	1,696	3,386	2,427
- Depreciation and Amortization	651	1,234	3,264	1,603
- Pre-opening Expenses	0	0	0	828
Total Operating Expenses	17,188	31,060	39,420	32,557

Source: Peapod 1998 Annual Report and Peapod Press Release

Exhibit 7 Webvan Income Statement (1997–1999) ($ in thousands)

		Year Ended Dec. 31	Nine Months Ended Sept. 30
	1997 (a)	1998	1999
Net Sales	$0	$0	$4,236
Cost of Goods Sold	0	0	3,910
Gross Profit (Loss)	0	0	326
Software Development Expenses	244	3,010	10,638
General and Administrative Expenses	2,612	8,825	74,379
Amortization of Deferred Stock Compensation	0	1,060	13,543
Total Expenses	2,856	12,895	98,560

(a) Period from December 17, 1996 (Date of Incorporation) to December 31, 1997
Source: Webvan Prospectus and Webvan 10-Q filing with Securities and Exchange Commission

CHEMUNITY.COM

Part 1: Introduction

It was a Monday morning in April 2000, and managing director Herman Rijks was looking back over the past six months. He and his business partner Mark-Jan Terwindt had established a new company, ChemUnity.com, in November 1999 and settled down in Arnhem, a small town in the eastern Netherlands. They had been working hard to get their start-up company up and running. This Monday was the day that the first test trades were to be done. Once ChemUnity, the electronic marketplace for the chemical industry, was operational, Rijks believed that only the sky would be the limit for the expansion.

With all the optimism of their venture, Rijks and Terwindt were still at the beginning of their Internet journey. They had to convince both the suppliers and the buyers in the marketplace that ChemUnity.com was the place to come for the needed products. In addition, the business model was untested. Nobody knew whether it would be profitable. Finally, Rijks and Terwindt knew they would encounter new challenges.

The Beginning of ChemUnity

Herman Rijks telling about the idea:

> The business idea of ChemUnity occurred to me in the summer of 1999 when I was a manager of a chemicals distribution business in Hungary. I observed closely a group of purchasing assistants negotiating non-stop on the prices of 350 different chemicals. They called, mailed and faxed to get quotes and then tried to make sense of which was the most feasible. The pressure was high, and I felt the inefficiency was too. This picture stuck in my mind. With some additional information about the possibilities of the Internet, the idea formed in my head.

Research Associate Petri Lehtivaara prepared this case under the supervision of Professor Carlos Cordon as a basis for class discussion rather than to illustrate either effective or ineffective handling of a business situation.

> The idea I developed was to set up a web site where suppliers and buyers of chemicals could match their interests and agree on trades. I was convinced of the idea and suggested it to my boss. I was even prepared to take personal risk to establish the venture. I offered to cut part of my salary and all the bonuses in exchange for 10% of the shares in the proposed venture. The answer was negative, as it was not a core activity of the company.

> The idea was so good I felt that this opportunity could not be missed. I went to venture capitalists with Mark-Jan Terwindt. We got the first round of financing for the venture and resigned from our previous jobs at the beginning of November 1999. This was the start of ChemUnity.com.

The Founders

Herman Rijks. Rijks was 37 years old, with over ten years experience in the chemicals industry. He had a Master of Science from the Technological University of Delft, Netherlands. He had experience in green-field chemical distribution start-ups in countries like Bolivia and Romania. He also had general management experience in various chemical companies like Inverquim and HCI. He had worked for a long time for HCI over the past three years in Hungary and Romania. Prior to setting up ChemUnity.com in late 1999, he had been part of the HCI corporate e-commerce task force.

Rijks was born in South Yemen and grew up in Africa. He was fluent in Dutch, English, Spanish, and French and had a working knowledge in German. He was married and had two sons, aged five and three years. During his free time, he enjoyed water sports, flying, ball sports, and music.

Mark-Jan Terwindt. Terwindt was 34 years old, with a background in the chemicals industry. After graduating from Nijenrode Business School in the Netherlands, he had worked for eight years in Central and South America in the chemical distribution. His countries of operation had included Ecuador, El Salvador, and Venezuela. After this time, Terwindt went to Prague in the Czech Republic to manage HCI operations. His last position

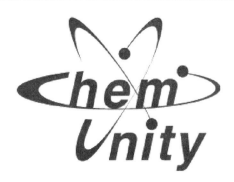

**European
Full-Truck-Load
Chemical Commodity
Sourcing On-line**

before ChemUnity. com had been in South Africa managing the integration of an acquired company.

Terwindt was fluent in Dutch, Spanish, and English, with German as a working language. He was married and had three daughters, aged five, three, and one. His hobbies included sports and travel.

Specific Service Offering

The concept of ChemUnity was to provide an electronic marketplace for the chemicals industry. To differentiate from the competition, ChemUnity had decided to start with a very focused approach. This meant a focus on Western Europe, full truckload quantities, commodity products, and online service based sourcing.

Western Europe was chosen as the geographical region due to the common currency, Euro, as well as for competitive reasons. The Euro became the common currency in eleven Western European countries in 1999. The common currency made cross-border transactions easier and reduced the currency exchange risk. Through the Euro, suppliers and buyers spoke the same monetary language. From the competitive view, Europe had less competing electronic marketplaces. There was still space to become the market leader.

ChemUnity targeted the middle segment of customers in volume sense. In this segment a truckload of goods was a standard volume measure. This volume was still a small part of suppliers' production, but still a reasonable amount for mid-range customers. ChemUnity felt this segment had the most potential to benefit from the service, which provided the large suppliers a possibility of reaching the lesser-known customers. The large strategic buyers were well served by the existing channels. The small volume customers were difficult to manage without a retailer.

An electronic marketplace could operate efficiently only with commodities. Commodities are products of which all variables (grade, concentration, packaging etc.) can be standardised, leaving the price as sole variable element. This also made it possible to trade these products electronically.

The basis of ChemUnity's business model was to make sure that all buyer's inquiries were proactively forwarded to all the potential suppliers and that their offers would be returned to the buyer in a day. In this way, it wanted to make the buying and selling easy. ChemUnity preselected the suppliers per product, to avoid sending them irrelevant requests. This way, the buyer did not have to go through hundreds of pages of product descriptions. Rijks compared ChemUnity to some

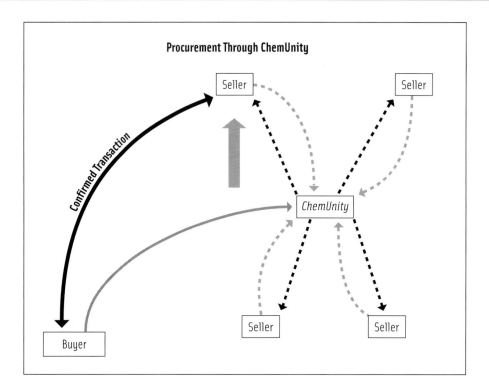

Procurement Through ChemUnity

competitors. "We were not a billboard. Some other sites expected product managers to stroll through lists of irrelevant enquiries."[1]

Trading in ChemUnity

The transaction started with an inquiry posted from the buyer to ChemUnity. This inquiry included the name, grade, concentration, and packaging of the commodity based on a predetermined list, delivery date, geographical region of the buyer, and a price indication. The price indication included both a preferred price and the highest acceptable price. Only the preferred price was transferred to the suppliers.

ChemUnity immediately forwarded this inquiry to the suppliers. Only the potential suppliers received the message. ChemUnity determined these suppliers based on the information it had received when companies registered. In addition, both the buyer and the supplier were able to exclude some parties or regions outside their scope of trading. The contact person in the suppliers' organisation was informed of a new inquiry by e-mail and SMS (Short Message System) to their mobile phone.

The supplier had 25 hours to respond with its bid. The bid for the deal was made only once, which avoided the price erosion effect of auction-like bidding.

ChemUnity compared the bids and informed the supplier who had got the deal.

The buyer was informed of the deal, and the confirmed transaction was managed between the supplier and buyer. The transaction was binding, and thanks to the credit insurance, the supplier could be sure he would always receive the payment. None of the parties had the possibility of withdrawing from the deal. All inquiries were thus serious.

Part 2: Suppliers and Buyers

ChemUnity was one of several electronic marketplaces in the chemical industry. These marketplaces were mushrooming in all industries. The basic concept was to use the possibilities of the Internet to improve the efficiency of buying and selling. The most common arguments in support of these marketplaces were:

- The buyers would be able to source from new companies more efficiently and at lower prices.

---

[1]Chemical Industry B2B Set to Launch, Revolution, 01/03/2000, p. 5.

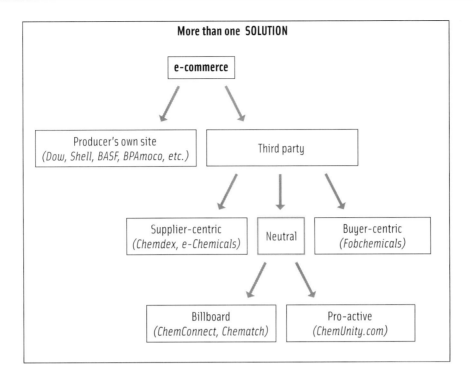

- Suppliers would be able to serve new markets and customers.
- The supply chain would become more efficient.

But the concept of supplier exchanges had not been proven decisively. The companies had not been around long enough to really determine the benefits for the supplier and buyers.

ChemUnity as a Marketplace

ChemUnity's concept turned out to be something different from the other platforms in the electronic commerce market. The whole market could be divided into third party solutions and producer's own sites. Most of the trades would still go through company sites.

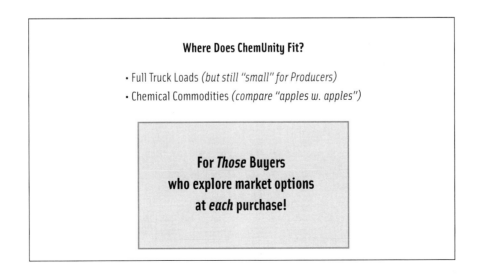

```
┌─────────────────────────────────────────┐
│              ADVANTAGES                   │
│                                           │
│  TIME Efficient  (both for Buyer & Seller)│
│                                           │
│  Pro-Active & Filtered  (no info-overload)│
│                                           │
│  Reach WHOLE Market  (incl. Unknown)      │
│                                           │
│  Cost Efficient  (no unnecessary middlemen)│
│                                           │
│  Usage Is Optional  (react when YOU want!)│
│                                           │
│  Emotion-Free  (No room for confusion)    │
│                                           │
│  Only Approved (serious) Users            │
│                                           │
│  Credit Insurance                         │
│                                           │
│  Profile Reflects "real life"  (Tailor to strategy)│
│                                           │
│  Future Linkage to Your Order Entry       │
│                                           │
│  No Time Zones                            │
│                                           │
│  No Reckless Dumping                      │
│                                           │
│  Clear Legal Framework                    │
└─────────────────────────────────────────┘
```

In the third party solutions, supplier-centric solutions were either owned or run by suppliers. The buyer-centric sites concentrated on aggregating the needs of the buyers.

The middle way was to be neutral. The existing sites were bulletin-boards that passively waited for trades to happen. Alternatively, they could be proactive sites. ChemUnity's proactive approach meant that the site took an active interest in making the trade and informed the suppliers when new requests occurred.

ChemUnity considered it could provide an efficient solution for sellers by targeting the segment that was inefficient to manage in a traditional way. Second, ChemUnity made sure that buyers could compare apples with apples.

Advantages of ChemUnity

ChemUnity took out the need of contacting multiple sellers with each purchase, and allowed quick response to requests.

The supplier only received truly interesting requests. ChemUnity filtered the information based on the profile of the suppliers and the buyers.

The supplier had the possibility of serving the smaller customers directly and reaching customers in new geographical markets.

The middleman that did not add value but only costs to the value chain could be cut out. This made the products cheaper for buyers and margins higher for suppliers.

The supplier was not obliged to provide a bid, although once the bid was made, it was binding.

Many meetings between buyer and supplier were emotional, and often left at least one of the parties unhappy. Here the supplier bid for the price it wanted and the buyer determined the price range it could accept.

All the suppliers and buyers had a good track record. To get into the ChemUnity the parties had to sign a contract. Suppliers needed to have a European base to confirm their ability to deliver goods to European buyers.

Provided the supplier the necessary coverage for the payment, and made credit checks easy. Buyers were provided with credit insurance that covered all purchases through ChemUnity.

The participant had the possibility of tailoring its needs. Parties were allowed to exclude regions or companies for potential suppliers or buyers lists.

ChemUnity had ideas for future expansion to develop linkages to order-entry systems.

Suppliers could do normal business and travel, as long as they could check bids once a day. Suppliers were not bound to working from a certain region. Thanks to the usage of WAP phones, availability of Internet access wasn't even necessary.

All suppliers bid only once. Besides the obvious time-advantages, this meant that price erosion did not occur more than in normal bidding. The suppliers were encouraged not to dump, but to quote a fair price.

The members of ChemUnity signed an agreement outlining their rights and obligations. For example, if a company failed to deliver the goods as promised, the first failure would lead to a warning. After the second failure, the supplier was asked to leave the exchange.

Business-to-Business Marketplaces

With the increased use of the Internet, new opportunities had arisen in the business-to-business market. The emergence of the electronic marketplaces was one of such phenomenon. The electronic marketplaces could be divided roughly into four categories. The first category was the catalogue sites that continuously displayed and updated hundreds of catalogues from competing suppliers for comparison-shopping. The second category was the aggregators, who integrated the needs of a set of companies. After that the aggregator used aggregated buying power to achieve improved deals. The third category included auction sites that let buyers request bids and let sellers bid in return. Finally, the fourth category was the exchanges that let buyers and sellers bid on and auction commodity products.

The early e-commerce marketplaces had taken a wide, horizontal view of the market. These sites had tried to gather suppliers and buyers from different sectors and industries. With the increased number of marketplaces, the shift had moved towards segmentation, especially in late 1999. The sites had gone from horizontal generalisation to vertical specialisation. Industries had started to have their own industry specific trading places. At the time there were about 500 marketplaces, but the projection was that there would be 7,500 to 10,000 vertical marketplaces in 3 to 5 years.

Business-to-business marketplaces often competed with traditional distributors. Electronic marketplaces were said to be a more efficient way to do business, but as ChemUnity pointed out, distributors who could add value to the product had a place in the supply chain.

Competing Exchanges

ChemUnity was not the only player in the electronic marketplace. Already earlier (in the second half of 1999), some marketplaces had established their operations and gathered a customer base. These companies competed for the same customers, although they had a different approach, different product range, different geographic focus and were targeting a different volume segment. According to industry experts, 200 companies were pushing for exchanges, auctions, and catalogue-related business in chemical and natural resources industry, compared to only a handful a year earlier. In addition to third party electronic marketplaces, some chemical companies (e.g., Eastman Chemical, Kingsport) sold their products online. The following were some other companies providing similar services in the chemical industry.

Chemconnect.com was a chemicals and plastics exchange. It provided a venue for manufacturers, buyers, and intermediaries to buy and sell all types of chemicals and plastics products. It had started as an online supplier directory and later added online transactions and exchange functions.

Fobchemicals.com was an Internet-based aggregator of buyers. It aggregated demand and centralised the purchasing of smaller buyers. By doing so, it was able to go to the manufacturers and potentially lower the purchase price. It operated in research-grade, commodity, and traded chemicals.

CheMatch.com operated an online exchange that allowed buyers and sellers of high volume, bulk commodity petrochemicals to trade anonymously. CheMatch targeted the market of the top 25 petrochemical products, as well as polymers and plastics products. This market was estimated at US$400 billion.

e-Chemicals.com provided an online solution for procuring industrial chemicals. This market was estimated at US$250 billion. e-Chemicals allowed users to select a product, get a price, order, and track order status on-line. e-Chemicals had partnered with Yellow Freight for logistics and SunTrust Bank for credit and collections services.

E-Business in the Chemicals Industry

The chemicals industry had been one of the first markets to be hit by the emerging electronic marketplaces. The

---

[2]Forrester Research.

industry was large and global. A distinctive share of the products were commodities. The industry was also highly fragmented on both the supplier and the buyer side. Due to this fragmented nature, the industry was used to intermediaries like traders, brokers, or retailers.

It was estimated that the chemical e-business transactions would account for roughly US$50 billion in sales in 2001, US$100 billion in 2002, and US$300 billion in 2003. By that time, it was estimated that 40% of chemical sales in North America would be conducted over the Internet.[2]

At the time, almost 95% of chemical sales were made directly between producer and consumer. Five percent passed through distributors and 2% were actively traded on the spot market. The prediction was that direct channel would continue to be the largest part, but that the share would go down to 60% to 70%. The distribution part would increase to 10%, and the spot market would increase 5 to 10 times. The spot market was driven by the exchanges.

Question 1

What is the value proposition for the suppliers and buyers?

Part 3: Business Model and Partners

ChemUnity did not target a large segment of the chemicals industry, but hoped to achieve a considerable share of transactions in the segment. In the beginning, ChemUnity charged a 2% transaction fee, more than some exchanges which dealt with petrochemical or purchases of large quantities of goods. The average size of a deal was estimated to be €5,000 to €10,000.

ChemUnity felt that it had a good set of partners. This was an important element of its start-up phase. It had flexible deals with its partners to pay for the services and goods. As the partners had something to gain from the success, the relationship was supportive.

Potential Market Size

ChemUnity estimated in its business plan that the value of the total annual chemicals market in Europe was €385 billion. When the export volume of 15% was excluded, the market volume came down to €330 billion. These estimates included all types of products, from petrochemicals to life sciences.

ChemUnity excluded from its scope the standardised large volume products like petrochemicals. It also excluded the specialty chemicals. With these restrictions the target products accounted for €80 billion.

Finally, ChemUnity did not try to compete with the strategic supplier relationship. It targeted the segment of smaller quantities and less strategic buyer or seller relationships. This market was estimated at €15 billion.

ChemUnity estimated that it could have 7% of the transactions in its segment. This meant €1 billion of transactions agreed through ChemUnity. With the volume, ChemUnity could expect annual revenues of €20 million (based on the 2% transaction fee).

Revenues from Different Sources

Herman Rijks talking:

We estimated that we should be able to have revenue from the transactions of around €20 million in five years' time. This was based on the 2% transaction fee and the transaction volume of €1 billion. We were opposed to membership fees since they would deter potential customers. No smaller company would have committed itself to subscription fees before it had even seen the service. This had represented a barrier to entry. But we saw many other possibilities for revenues.

Selling advertising on our Web site was a possibility. We had a very focused group of customers. They could have been targeted very well. Let's take the example of paint manufacturers buying acetone. They also needed some catalyst for their process. Our Web site was an excellent medium for these catalyst manufacturers to provide targeted advertising. We could not underestimate the fact that 3,000 people with focused needs were visiting our Web site every day.

In addition to advertising, we thought that additional services might bring in more revenues. When the basic business was up and running, we could start providing more financial services, transportation services and the like. These should bring in some revenues. As we had good information from our customers, we could have conducted market research or sold information to marketing agencies.

Costs Related to Marketing, People, and IT

For ChemUnity the costs were mainly related to marketing, people, and IT. Marketing was the largest cost in the beginning. Suppliers' and buyers' awareness of ChemUnity had to be increased. ChemUnity had held a couple of large marketing events at chemical conferences. It had also put advertisements in *ECN* and *Chemical Week*, two major industry magazines. These efforts were aimed at making the brand known and getting the companies to use ChemUnity's services.

People and IT were the two other main cost areas. As a service company, ChemUnity's main assets were people. It recruited product managers and regional managers. ChemUnity wanted to provide good financial terms, including stock options for its employees. This was necessary to attract highly skilled people. The third main cost element was IT. Setting up the software system was relatively expensive, even if ChemUnity could negotiate a good deal with the software developer. Future development and additional services kept the cost of IT as a key cost component.

In the beginning, ChemUnity estimated marketing to take up to 60% of the costs, leaving approximately 30% to people costs and 10% to IT. Later the share of people costs was expected to increase and marketing costs were expected to decrease. Exact cost management was not ChemUnity's main priority at the moment. As Rijks mentioned:

I thought the cash flow bottom was around €10 million.

Partners Willing to Participate

Herman Rijks explaining:

We believed that having good partners was essential to the success of this venture. We also wanted to involve them in our success. We felt that the partners were also eager to participate and learn from the experience. That was why we were able to negotiate unorthodox deals with them.

We had two venture capital companies providing the early financing. They financed ChemUnity with €1.5 million and had a share of 27.5% of the company.

Software was developed together with Computer Sciences Corporation (CSC). Once we had established with them what we wanted, they committed themselves to delivering it. CSC put a lot of effort and additional people on the project to provide the appropriate solution. We had made a deal on a fixed price and agreed that we would pay half of the project cost during the project and half once ChemUnity was successful. This was obviously a new type of deal from their side.

ChemUnity had a special hardware deal with Compaq. The deal was that we would only pay for Compaq if ChemUnity succeeded. Otherwise we would return the equipment.

Credit insurance was a key element of the ChemUnity service. We provided credit insurance in one umbrella for all buyers. This took the difficulty out of organising credits for each transaction. NCM was willing to participate in the venture and bundle this service with us. With this partner, ChemUnity did not have any special deal, and paid for the credit insurance.

Headhunters Egon Zehnder was the final important member of the partner list. As the market for people was scarce and many firms were competing for the good people, ChemUnity felt that it was important to have close connections with headhunters. With Egon Zehnder we had a deal that ChemUnity paid with shares for the services.

Question 2

What is your view of the revenue generation model?

Part 4: Future Challenges

ChemUnity faced both immediate and long-term challenges. The start of trading had been postponed a couple of times mainly because of IT problems. These issues had been mainly sorted out.

ChemUnity still needed to raise the awareness of its name and service, especially among the suppliers. It needed to get the lead suppliers for the products, so that active trading was possible and buyers did not leave ChemUnity empty-handed. Once the concept was proven with a small number of products, ChemUnity had to decide how to expand. This was a longer-term challenge, but just as important for the profitable business.

ChemUnity Was Facing Challenges Immediately

Herman Rijks explaining:

Increasing the awareness, testing the technical business model and recruiting good people were the main challenges at the moment. Increased awareness of ChemUnity was important to attract the buyers and the suppliers to ChemUnity service. IT and business model had to be tested and operational. The third challenge of people was also immediate. People marketed ChemUnity and managed the relationship to suppliers and buyers. ChemUnity had to manage its own IT development, human resources, and marketing. These issues could not be outsourced.

Our main challenge in the near future was to test the concept with a couple of products. This would tell us if we were on the right track. Successful implementation started from marketing. We needed to make the suppliers aware of the exchange and get so-called product leaders. We believed that getting buyers was easier once we had the suppliers onboard. And then once we had suppliers and buyers, we needed to activate them and to get the market liquidity up. Once known in the marketplace for these type of products, we had succeeded in our first challenge.

The second challenge was the human resources issue. We had concluded that we needed people with a chemical industry background. These people had to be able to communicate with chemical suppliers and buyers. Our challenge was to find interesting characters who brought enthusiasm to us and believed in this venture.

The third challenge was IT. The technology needed to work, and we needed to be able to provide flawless execution of our services. At the time, the service was not perfect but we were moving on.

With the experience of ChemUnity, IT and people were the two key problems in setting up a dot com business. If someone had both of these, it was a very attractive company to buy.

Long-Term Challenges Range from Expansion to Financing

Herman Rijks saying the following:

In the longer term, we needed to expand the operations sensibly. We targeted a couple of strategic suppliers and many fragmented buyers in each product. In total we thought we could have 200 to 500 suppliers and up to 10,000 buyers. But we needed to proceed with one product at the time to be able to test the concept and to concentrate our efforts on a focused segment. The challenge was to pick the right products.

Additionally, we could expand our service portfolio. We could start providing more financial services to generate revenues through that channel. Transportation was also a related service. But also in this area we needed to choose the right services, good partners and the right expansion pace.

In the beginning of the operation, our cash flow was negative. So we needed to target for additional financing. A second round of financing was timed for a couple of months after the launch of the service. ChemUnity's target was to raise another €5 million to €10 million from banks, venture capitalists and market players. Market players were included in the financing round to gain credibility in the marketplace.

Question 3

What should ChemUnity do about its future challenges?

INDEPENDER.COM

Edmond Hilhorst enjoyed, and needed, his twenty-minute bicycle ride to work. As managing director and co-founder of Independer, an Internet startup in the financial services industry, he rarely enjoyed a stretch of quiet time in which to think. This particular morning, on 17 April 2000, Hilhorst had a lot on his mind. Not only had the NASDAQ dropped sharply the week before, but he had to make some fundamental decisions about how to structure the company's customer loyalty program. The loyalty program, he knew, was a key to Independer's future: it would be one way to demonstrate that the company offered independent and un-biased advice.

Hilhorst was concerned, but not panicked, about the recent plunge in the prices of technology and Internet shares. On April 14th, the NASDAQ index fell to 3,321, or 7% in one day, to a total decline of about 35% from a record high of more than 5000 on March 10, 2000. There had been talk in the media about the popping of the information-economy bubble, i.e., a long needed "market correction" that would weed out the poorly conceived Internet companies and perhaps restore some realism to the notion of the "new economy," which Hilhorst disdained as "badly over-hyped." On the one hand, Independer would find it harder to raise money from skittish investors, as well as offer stock options to potential employees, who would demand higher wages. In light of this, should Independer revisit the company strategy? On the other hand, Hilhorst wondered if the coming "Internet shakeout," which he had long anticipated, would reveal the fundamental strengths of their business model. Indeed, in many ways, Independer did not even consider itself a dot.com startup, but was rather a financial-services provider that happened to be using a new technology to reach customers.

The immediate issue was, what was to be done with the "excess commissions" that Independer expected to reap. According to the vision of its founders, Independer was set up first and foremost to satisfy the needs of financial-product consumers, not only by providing them with objective comparisons (and personalized advice at a later date), but by ignoring the "incentives" that banks and insurance built into the products they offered. In practical terms, that meant refusing to allow the commissions, which banks and insurance companies offered to their financial-service brokers, to govern the company's advice to Independer customers. It was principally these commissions, in view of the company's founders, that tilted traditional brokers in favor of certain products. Regardless of whether they were in the consumers' interest, brokers tried harder to sell the products that paid them more and hence offered fewer options to their customers. Existing brokers, in the company's view, were "biased."

In the Independer scheme, company sales revenues would be set somewhere near the minimum commission level. Anything beyond that threshold, which could vary by several percentage points of the total sale price—and in the case of a mortgage could represent significant sums of money, would somehow "belong" to Independer's customers, in the form of either cash rebates or the automatic issuance to them as some kind of Independer stock. These excess commissions were to form one of the pillars of the company's loyalty program, contributing both to Independer's positioning as a consumer advocate, and to encouraging customers to come back (Exhibit 1).

As Hilhorst parked his bicycle, he paused outside to think for a few more moments. Because his excess-commission policy would represent the "Independer difference," what he did in the end would be a major strategic decision. Finally, to keep pace with the company's aggressive plans for foreign expansion, Hilhorst knew he had to settle the issue quickly.

Conceiving the Company

Edmond Hilhorst had spent 12 years as a rapidly rising manager at ABN Amro, a Dutch bank that was one of Europe's largest. In Holland, he had succeeded in positions in marketing, sales, and consumer project management. But when he moved to a slot in New York City, he began to think about his career. "The place was so dynamic," he remembers, "that I started looking outward to new possibilities, to some kind of change. When I returned to Holland and got a prestigious promotion as a District manager, I felt unchallenged. It was too bureaucratic, too inflexible." Wondering what he should do next, he looked into the changes that were occurring in the financial services industries.

The Banking and Insurance Industries

The demand for financial services in the Netherlands has been above the European average for a number of years. As a percentage of GDP, the demand has been substantially higher in the Netherlands as compared to France and to the UK. In 1999, the Dutch market counted approximately 800 private insurance companies. The key players had a combined market share of approximately 60% in life insurances and 30% in non-life insurances. (An overview over the main insurance companies in Holland is given in Exhibit 2.) Brokers and intermediaries were responsible for the bulk of sales of insurance products (60%). According to the Dutch Statistical Office (CBS), the total gross premium for new life insurance for private individuals in 1999 was hfl12.1bn which equals €5.5bn (€1 = hfl 2.21).

In the banking sector, ABN-Amro, ING Group, and Rabobank dominated the retail market in terms of deposits or loans. SNS and Fortis were two medium-sized players. Together these five players accounted for about 80% of the market (Exhibit 3). Also, many banks had started to develop and sell their own insurance products.

The market used to be relatively stable, yielding high margins, but has been experiencing extraordinarily rapid change: not only were the two industries converging, but the Internet was opening exciting opportunities for new entrants as well as established firms. These movements promised to fundamentally alter the financial services industry. Among other things, that meant, however briefly, that there was room for entrepreneurs.

Channel Structure

Banks in the Netherlands distributed their products mainly through their network of branches but also through direct channels such as call centers. However, one could note differences in various product categories: mortgage distribution was dominated by intermediaries, traditional banking and saving products are to a large extent tied to the branch network, and the penetration of direct and telephone banking was generally low (>5%). The distribution of insurance products was dominated by brokers and intermediaries (60%), with banks and direct channels accounting for the remainder. The function of the traditional insurance broker extended well beyond policy writing. Most brokers covered the entire intermediary value chain (Exhibit 4). The bulk of the commission paid to the brokers (70%) covered customer acquisition and closing the sale.

Traditional intermediaries were aware that the increasing Internet usage and the convenience of this new channel could potentially weaken their position. However, to most of them it was not clear how profound this impact would be. Banks and insurances as well as brokers knew that the Internet could make consumer's search for financial services more efficient and that it could possibly increase pricing transparency. For example, the financial channel of AOL in the USA was already the most popular channel within the AOL site. Another concern of the existing providers was that they did not want to alienate their existing network of brokers. A marketing manager from a major insurance company said that:

> We only sell travel health insurances through the Web because we don't want to build up a channel that would undermine our sales rep network.

Starting in 1999, there were a growing number of niche players, who were presenting themselves as aggregators or intermediaries, i.e., they offered a comprehensive menu of sources of financial products at bargain prices (e.g., MoneyeXtra.com in the UK or Finanzscout24.de in Germany). Instead of attempting to provide everything to their customers, there were many signs that traditional bankers and insurers operated in different cultures and hence were poorly equipped to sell each others' products. These firms tended to specialize in one or at most a few areas, in which they excelled. Many, though not all, were also heavily invested in the Internet, typically in the form of "click-and-mortar" operations. Perhaps the best known of these firms was US-based Charles Schwab & Co., which provided stock brokerage services, with personalized advice, at lower prices; it had only recently entered the Internet.

During the 1990s, a series of mergers and acquisitions swept the banking industry. On the one hand, there were large new financial conglomerates, such as the merger between Citicorp and Travelers Group Inc. The logic behind these mega-mergers was to cross-sell each others' products through their existing distribution channels, in effect, increasing their reach along with the services they provided, all under a brand name. These were, they claimed, financial superstores, offering banking, brokerage, and insurance services at a single place. The advantages included economies of scale, greater breadth of product offerings, and seemingly unmatchable resources in bricks-and-mortar investment.[1] Regarding the competitive landscape, this meant that financial services were converging; while there was no legal separation of insurance and banking business in Holland, the restriction was recently removed in the USA (Glass-Steagall Act) and other countries were expected to follow.

Dutch Entrepreneurs

In December 1998, Hilhorst began to talk with Diederik de Groot van Embden, a friend and colleague at ABN Amro, who had worked in banking and insurance for the last 15 years. In particular, they discussed their customers in retail banking, where 60% of ABN Amro's profits were made. The customers, they observed, were dissatisfied with the service and advice they were getting and saw the Dutch banking industry as "arrogant, inward-looking, and concerned only with selling their own products." Furthermore, many customers were well aware of the fact that the so-called independent agents often sold the products that brought them the highest commissions. Hilhorst and Van Embden reasoned that traditional intermediaries couldn't fulfill key consumer demands (see also Exhibits 5 and 6):

- Lowest price

  Consumers want the best possible deal in the market. Traditional intermediaries generally offer only a limited range of products and brands. This means the best possible product is often not included in the offering.

- Independent advice

  Consumers are looking for objective decision support. However, traditional intermediaries are often commission-driven which means that their advice is biased.

- High convenience

  Financial products are more often than not low interest products. While consumers want to spend

as little time as possible, buying through intermediaries is generally time consuming and inefficient.

- Quality

  Consumers want to be sure of the quality of financial advice given to them. They are generally not able to judge the quality of the intermediary involved.

They thought that they could do better. The Internet, they thought, might provide the opportunity for them to do something about it. "We could," Hilhorst explained, "use the Internet as a means to bring independent advice on financial services products without an extensive distribution network. Consumers could just log in and compare the products themselves."

Hilhorst and Van Embden continued their discussions over the next few months, gradually realizing that they were serious about "doing something big." With the support of their families, they began to raise money and seek partners. It was a big risk for both of them: not only were entrepreneurs unusual in Holland and little admired, particularly when striking off on one's own meant abandoning their secure, "fast track" jobs, but they were burning their bridges with ABN Amro and would never be able to return to their old positions.

The Competition

After undertaking a quick survey of potential competitors, Hilhorst and Van Embden concluded that there was no one who was planning to do precisely what they wanted to do—at least in Holland. In other words, the banks and brokering firms on the Web offered the same mix of self-interested and restricted services that they did in their normal business, offering neither independent, unbiased advice, nor the full range of products that their company would. New startups were appearing on the horizon, however their content and functionality was far from Hilhorst and Van Embden's vision.

In Germany, there were several companies that started offering financial services comparisons, including Aspect-online.de, Compaer.de, and Finanzscout24.de. In the UK a company called MoneyeXtra.com was already operating. While these companies represented potential competition abroad, Hilhorst and Van Embden believed that they could do better with their company. In their analysis, these companies offered only superficial product comparisons, based almost exclusively on price, and with little analysis into the conditions (and restrictions)

---

[1] Peter Coy, "Great Big Company, Great Big Mistake?" *Business Week*, 20 April 1998, p. 40.

attached to the policies. To Hilhorst and Van Embden, that meant that there was room for an independent company that provided accurate and objective comparisons of price and policies in far greater detail, with the goal of imparting advice and facilitating and carrying out transactions. These were to be the precise point on which their company would add the most value.

Starting Ingredients

Hilhorst and Van Embden quickly agreed on a number of elements that their firm required. They decided that a "virtual structure"[2]—with the two of them leading a number of partners in a highly coordinated effort—was the quickest and most appropriate way to jumpstart their idea. Since they did not have the resources to jumpstart the company fast, engaging in a close partnership with well-known firms seemed the best approach. Their company would base itself on the following core propositions:

- The service would have to be consumer focused, providing independent and objective information with complete transparency. In addition to price comparisons, the site would translate product terms and conditions into language accessible to retail consumers. This was also a question of ethics: they would neither "cheat" their customers nor "sell" the customer information they collected for marketing purposes to other firms.

- Because existing distributors concentrated on a limited range of options to consumers—offering only their own products or those that paid them the highest commissions—a niche existed for a firm to offer comprehensive services in banking and insurance. "No existing firm was doing what we envisioned," Hilhorst said, "at least yet."

- In the age of global competition that the Internet was helping to bring about, consumer access was becoming a key to success. Explained Hilhorst: "Eventually, we want to enable a Frenchman to buy an Irish mortgage through a German intermediary."

- To establish a European brand, entry had to be made as quickly as possible. "We wanted to ensure that we had first-mover advantage," according to Hilhorst, "because other people were throwing the idea

around at the time. That meant choosing a timetable and sticking to it." Starting in Holland, they planned to expand into the major EU countries during 2000.

Though their company would be viewed as a dot.com startup, Hilhorst and Van Embden persisted in thinking that they were creating a new kind of financial services broker. It only used the Internet because it appeared to be the best available and most innovative technology at the time. They were also considering other means of accessing consumers, as in offering personal financial advice via telephone. But what would really distinguish their company from other dot.coms, they felt, was the revenue model they were developing. They would earn revenues not from advertising but directly from referrals and from transactions, which at a certain threshold, should turn profitable.

With these basic concepts in mind, Hilhorst and Van Embden turned to the tasks of raising money and building a network of devoted partners.

Virtual Partners

In April 1999, Hilhorst and Van Embden began to talk to potential partners. In addition to raising money from venture capitalists and other investors, they sought to bring together a web of expertise, not only in marketing and advertising, but in "startup incubation" as well (Exhibit 7). In other words, while guiding the effort as the core financial-service experts, they would outsource for their specialized needs to other professionals with expertise in both business and technology. Their formula was simple. At first, in exchange for stock in the company, the partners would supply their advice to Hilhorst and Van Embden; later, once investment funding had been secured, the partners would be paid for their participation, billing the company as much as they would their other clients.

One of the earliest partners was the Dutch office of DDB, a global advertising company (Omnicom Group) that specialized in loyalty programs and concept marketing. After overcoming DDB's initial reluctance to be paid only in stock during the early phases, DDB Managing Partner Herberth Jan Samson got deeply involved in discussions on how to develop the company. Given the mission of the company to offer unbiased advice in the interest of its customers, Samson explained, "we offered them insights on how to structure the company in a way that was convincing." Among other things, DDB helped

---

[2]Henry W. Chesbrough and David J. Teece, "When Is Virtual Virtuous? Organizing for Innovation," *Harvard Business Review*, Jan./Feb. 1996, pp. 65–69.

Hilhorst and Van Embden choose the name "Independer" for the company.

Another important partner was Bain & Co., which joined in December 1999. According to Geert van Engelen, a Bain manager working full time on Independer, "We provide advice to Internet entrepreneurs at many stages, from helping them write a business plan and implementing their rollout to pre-IPO consulting and the management of their concerns with on-going clients." "It was," he explained, "a hybrid of venture capitalism and consulting." Independer also allied itself of software companies, market research groups, and other specialists (Cap Gemini, Egon Zehnder, AC Nielsen).

So far, the virtual partnership worked. With all participants meeting once per week for updates and discussion, the relatively small group had gained credibility with, and confidence in the other members. Samson says, "We collaborated without elaborate, formal relations. Everyone just did as they promised, on time and according to plan." Nonetheless, Samson noted that the alliance was fragile: if one party failed to live up to its obligations, the whole structure could quickly fall.

The Revenue Model

Hilhorst and Van Embden strove to create a revenue model for Independer that they deemed innovative as well as realistic. While it would have to both support their ideals and advance the brand image they wished to carve out, the revenue model would also have to be viable and straightforward. They quickly agreed that Independer's revenues should be transactions based, i.e., directly connected to consumer decisions. However, no money should come from consumers.

After much discussion with their partners, Hilhorst and Van Embden settled on a two-pronged revenue model: leads and sales commission (Exhibits 8 and 9). Leads are generated when a consumer requests further information on a specific product via the Independer website, (the quality of the lead, Hilhorst emphasized, was more important than the number of leads). For example, in the case of a mortgage application, the consumers would:

1. Key their financial information into their website, thereby generating personalized comparisons on the conditions and prices available to them.

2. Ask them to pass their personal financial information to the bank that offered them the optimal deal.

3. The bank would pay Independer for the lead, regardless of whether a mortgage was finally offered or signed. Independer would hand over the request to the product provider who would handle all customer contact from there onwards.

It would operate in the same way for insurance companies and for other financial services. Of course the conversion rate of site users to actual referred customers was an important determinant of success. Conversion rates for similar US businesses are 28% for Insweb.com, 36% for Netquote.com, and 13% for Quotesmith.com. Independer would charge a fixed fee per customer request to the product providers, similar for all product providers. Naturally, this fixed fee would vary across product categories.

Sales commission would be generated when a customer actually purchased the product "online" via Independer. In the Netherlands, the lead-only model was quite new to the market, whereas the sales commission model was well known given the dominance of intermediaries as a distribution channel of almost all financial products. On average 70% of the commission value could be attributed to the activities covered by customer acquisition (obtaining the lead and closing the sale). For example, Independer estimated the value of a mortgage lead to be around €75 and that of a life insurance lead €15. The subsequent fulfillment aspect would have to be completed by either the provider or by other intermediaries.

Van Embden expected that, at least in the beginning, only a small percentage of the market would be comfortable purchasing generally high involvement financial products online. Likewise, it was expected that a much bigger percentage of the market would be willing to inform themselves on the offerings using the Internet. This latter group could be served by allowing them to compare online, after which they would be handed over to an offline closing channel. Estimates of percentage of consumers willing to close online varied between 2% and 5%. Percentages of people willing to inform themselves online varied between 20% and 40% (depending on study and product involved). This indicated that, at least in the short-term, the market for leads seemed to be a much bigger market than the online transaction market. Nevertheless, willingness to close online was expected to rise rapidly.

From a profitability point of view, the additional 30% sales commission on the fulfillment process would not show the same gross margins as leads. Fulfillment was a time-consuming process, the cost of which could sum to the first year sales commission. Only the recurring sales commission would make this process profitable (intermediaries receive recurring sales commission when a customer prolongs an insurance policy or maintains a credit/savings account after the first year).

For Independer, leads and sales commissions would exist in parallel. All visitors would start as potential leads, but only a subset of the leads would be converted to sales by Independer itself, via the Internet channel. In time, Independer could possibly develop other channels as well, to convert leads itself, e.g., through a call center. Initially, most of the leads would be converted by other parties through offline channels.

The typical customer would come from the "high social classes," i.e., the 10–15% of the population that was well educated, with upper bracket income, and "connected" to the Internet. They would also tend to be younger, "independent thinkers" rather than from the affluent, pre-computer generation. Less frequent customers—those that might consult the website and perhaps use it on occasion, would expand the pool to about 45% of the population. While they trusted these numbers, they were a "back of the envelope" calculation for now (Exhibit 10).

In keeping with its consumer-focused mission, the company would accept only a certain level of commissions, channeling the "excess" amounts into a consumer loyalty program. (While Hilhorst and Van Embden had originally envisioned returning the excess to suppliers, they were persuaded in discussions with their virtual partners, that it would be better to somehow return them to Independer customers.)

To preserve their independence and objectivity in the eyes of consumers, Independer would accept neither advertising on its website, nor sell information about its customers to other firms for marketing purposes.[3] "We will accept no banners [advertisements]," explained Van Embden. In addition, outside of the immediate purposes of the company to provide the best information available to consumers, he said, "We will respect their privacy completely. The value of independence for the company is far higher than the revenue we could generate from exploiting the data we will collect. It's short term versus

---

[3]Note: Dutch law was particularly stringent regarding the privacy of the financial information of individuals. Data on individual visits, for example, was prohibited by law from being given to third parties unless individuals had given their written permission (opt-in). However, data on aggregate groupings of consumers that avoided identifying individuals could in some circumstances be sold for marketing purposes. According to Marko Rijnsburger of AMI Database Marketing, which was an Independer virtual partner, legislation governing the Dutch Chamber of Privacy Registration was being strengthened in order to further protect consumer privacy.

long term." Independer has issued a privacy statement (Exhibit 11). The existence and the careful wording of its contents contribute to the willingness of persons to provide personal data. Finally this privacy statement shows that Independer complies with the obligations of the law and respects the rights of customers and site visitors.

Putting It All Together

With their virtual partners in place, Hilhorst and Van Embden were ready to tackle the issues of implementation. In July 1999, Hilhorst officially resigned from his position at ABN Amro and joined Van Embden in a makeshift office outside Amsterdam. Later on, Hein Swinkels, a former executive within Unilever's M&A department, joined them as Independer's chief financial officer. As their agenda turned from the conceptual to the practical, they faced a number of difficult choices, including: what range of products to cover, the level of detail they should go into for purposes of comparison, and a rollout timetable for Holland and then other EC countries. "We are allocating resources for the future now," explained Van Embden, "and we have to balance quality, speed, breadth, and depth. If we don't get it exactly right, Independer will die very quickly." To round out the virtual network, the company also secured a group of venture capital investors, who pumped over €10 million into the firm.

Broadening or Deepening

One of the first critical issues that Independer faced was the trade-off between category breadth and category functionality (depth). The financial services industry offered an extraordinary range of products, literally thousands of them, each with different conditions, costs, and regulations attached. Even if the data were accessible and compatible, it would cost too much in time and effort to cover them all in any useful way. Moreover, attempting to expand the range of coverage took precious resources away from more in-depth research, which was precisely the kind of information that consumers wanted from the site. Independer's choice in this matter would also affect the company's brand image.

Nonetheless, Independer had to cover a sufficiently broad range of products to attract the right mix of consumers. "We didn't want to be seen as a car- and home-insurance company," Van Embden explained, "so we knew that we had to include other products, such as mortgages and saving accounts." Moreover, greater breadth would surely increase the number of "hits" on the site, generating the higher traffic that was one measure of consumer interest to present to investors as evidence of consumer interest. However, as Independer employees quickly discovered, the availability of data on financial services varied starkly from country to country. In Holland, the company was able to exclusively allay itself early on with the one firm that had compiled such information—MoneyView Nederland. As no commercial database existed in France, they would have to build their own there; in Germany, several established firms were already selling the necessary data to potential competitors of Independer.

Regarding depth, Hilhorst and Van Embden felt that this area was crucial to generating customer loyalty and establishing the company brand. The option entailed to add transaction and advice capability to the existing categories. During launch time in Spring 2000, as there was no advice capability, Independer planned to add this functionality during the course of the year. The issue for Independer was to invest in technology development, and to create robust advice and transaction engines. The associated question was whether Independer had the necessary technology capabilities to implement this option. In essence, personalized advice capabilities lead directly to transactions that could be conducted through the website. Naturally, Independer was greatly interested in this capability, since it would immediately translate into higher revenues.

DDB argued that Independer should go into great depth in some product categories, such as mortgages, as a way to demonstrate what the firm could do. But once again, some compromise had to be found between resources and the immediate needs of the company. Moreover, there were questions about the depth of consumer demand for online financial services. There were only so many transactions that consumers would want to carry out at any given time. In addition, while there was a dedicated core of Internet users who enjoyed consulting the site, fear and suspicion limited the number of consumers willing to carry out the complex and highly personal exercises of a mortgage or life insurance application—they continued to prefer the personal contact of an office visit.

In the end, Independer settled on a pilot project of six products, which would be expanded gradually.[4] According to Van Embden, concerning mortgages, "To get a full overview, there are over 160 variables involved. For the site's inauguration, we settled on about 10 to 15 that

were needed for the comparison functionality. But for personalized advice, you need more, many more."

Approaching the Banks and Insurances

Independer's relations with its suppliers represented an extremely delicate issue. At issue was whether they would view the company as a threat or as an ally. On the one hand, the raison d'être for Independer was to challenge the traditional ways of doing business in the financial services industry. That meant changing the status quo. On the other hand, if the company went too far, it risked alienating or killing the source of its revenue—the suppliers. "We can't," explained Samson of DDB, "attack them in the heart." Moreover, it was not in Independer's interest to expose the disparities of banking and other commissions to the public, which in Van Embden's view could start a price war.

> We would not like to see our rates compared on the Internet if our services would not be explained. In case you can display the full service scope, Internet comparisons can be helpful.
>
> *Broker Support Manager of major mortgage bank*

> These days Internet financial service providers call me every day to sell their services. We are definitely interested in buying high quality leads and we would cooperate with good content providers. But we do not need just another set of unfocused addresses.
>
> *Internet Distribution Manager of direct bank*

After consulting a number of institutions, Van Embden was relieved to discover that they were interested in joining the effort. "Reactions were good," he said, "better than I expected. They saw us not as a competitor, but as a new and less expensive distribution channel." "In addition," he continued, "some banks viewed the company as a way for them to save money: a few of them even pushed for Independer to take over their customer relations responsibilities."

Once Independer had established itself as a reliable brand, Van Embden believed, it would become extremely difficult to dislodge. Indeed, the relationship between Independer and its suppliers had already begun to

---

[4]The initial products were mortgages, investment funds, health insurance, retail savings accounts, consumer loans, and disability insurance; in the coming months, Independer would expand into car insurance and life insurance.

deepen along a number of fronts. For example, Hilhorst received clear signs from a number of banks that they would quote Independer lower rates than their "official" rates, so that they would perform well in the comparisons (mortgage banks had used these "official" rates in the past to allow themselves room for discounts or negotiation, if the situation required such).

The Site

Though no one was sure what would work—what kind of site would inspire confidence—Independer and its virtual market research partner, Centrum Market Analysis, began to experiment with formats and the site's appearance in a series of consumer tests. Most important, of course, was that the site was easy to use: that customers could find what they want and, if they wished, interact with the system by supplying personal information. To illustrate a negative example, The Bank of Scotland (BoS) had offered mortgage services on a site in Holland which, observers said, was extremely difficult to understand and use. Although many visited the site to check the rates and ask for quotes, eventually, BoS wound up having to hire representatives to visit with potential customers.

Regarding the appearance of the site, Independer was entering virgin territory. According to Independer's marketing director, Ena Voute, "We chose a bland appearance for the site, not the bright orange or yellow of the earliest models. Bland is trustworthy, or that is our impression." (Exhibits 12 and 13)

Getting the Word Out

In the fall of 1999, Independer was just beginning to get the word out. The company had a Dutch-style consumer board in place, that is, some well-known people, who acted as "guardians" of Independer's values. This meant serving as an ombudsman that transmitted consumer views and complaints; quarterly discussions of the issues that faced the company; and the like. Among other things, this mechanism for self-regulation would help the company avoid litigation. So far, Independer had two members: Aad van den Heuvel, a journalist who frequently appeared on television to discuss consumer issues, and John Groen, the chairman of the Lawyer's Institute. Shortly, four other members were to join.

With the site launch scheduled for early Spring 2000, DDB and Independer were working on advertisements on the radio and television, in print, and on Internet banners. The campaign included:

- Radio. The company hired several well-known Dutch comedians to act in humorous sketches, of the "slice of life" variety, that complained of financial services in Holland and indicated that Independer offered a quick and easy solution.
- Television. Independer hired the winner of "Big Brother," the experimental (and controversial) television contest in which a group of strangers, placed in a house full of cameras, were voted out by viewers until only one was left. "His character fit the Independer image," Ena Voute explained. "He was seen as an independent thinker" and thus an ideal advocate for the company.
- Print media and Internet banners. These advertisements displayed a button that claimed that "objective advice" was just one click away.

So far, Independer was only offering comparisons of financial services and lead referrals in Holland. In the summer and fall of 2000, the company planned to expand these services to actual sales. In the company's view, it had achieved a "critical mass" there: a self-sustaining number of Internet-capable customers had become regular visitors to the site and were spreading the word. However, the newness of the Independer concept remained a challenge: as the first to market, the company had to build confidence that its new processes were trustworthy, particularly in the realm of lead referrals and later Internet purchases.

The Geographic Dimension

A further pull on Independer's resources were the founders' plans to expand their services to the major countries of Western Europe during the first year. While the site was getting a favorable reception in Holland, to be a major European player the company had to operate in France, Germany, and the UK. The other markets—the smaller but "highly wired" Scandinavian countries as well as the less developed (in terms of Internet adoption) markets of Italy and Spain—were viewed in the initial year as of secondary importance to the establishment of a European brand. Though a major financial center, Independer perceived the highly competitive UK as a higher risk and relatively more expensive. That left Germany and France as the most promising locations for the spring, though each of them presented unique challenges. According to Van Embden, "Once you get on this train, you have to go. You can't do it halfway. You just run and hope for the best."

In France, where the financial services database did not exist, Raymond Van Hulst and Michael Kosic, both INSEAD MBAs, had overseen the hiring of 10 analysts to collect the information. With the database almost complete, they were preparing to hire a country manager and 15 to 20 full-time managers to create a permanent organization and network.

The possession of the French database would be proprietary, establishing a competitive advantage that would last at least half a year.

The situation in Germany was somewhat different. With several databases easy to access and purchase, the Independer concept was not as new and the entry barriers were lower. Moreover, Deutsche Bank was initiating a big initiative to create its own comparison site, where it would sell its own products. "Germany will be the best test of our business model," Van Hulst argued. "We will not be able to leverage our access to a proprietary database and hence we have to compete there on our independence, on superior functionality, and on customer satisfaction. Our site will be more comprehensive and more objective. They won't be able to match our independence." The danger, he acknowledged, is that we will be unable to get that kind of differentiation into the minds of consumers.

The Decision

Hilhorst and Van Embden were convinced that the NASDAQ plunge would help their company more than hinder it. Investors were scrutinizing Internet operations much more closely and many pending IPOs had already been postponed. Nonetheless, they reasoned, because an Internet shakeout meant less "dot.com clutter," consumers and investors would see Independer as being on the "right side." After all, according to emerging commentaries, most dot.coms had had a remarkably poor business sense—presenting their technology-based companies as worthy ends in themselves rather than as a new means to cultivate customers and enter markets—and lacked realistic revenue models. These were precisely the areas in which Independer enjoyed the greatest strength. While it would become harder to raise money in the immediate future, Hilhorst acknowledged, "Investment banks were beginning to focus on real revenue and not 'hits' on the website. That means our business model will make sense to them." Moreover, their funding was assured by their current partners, at least for now, though, said Hilhorst, "it will take more time to widen our pool of partners."

Now Hilhorst returned to the options he was considering for the loyalty program that would govern excess commissions. Somehow, because the company was giving up the options of both using them for operating expenses and returning them to suppliers, they would have to be returned to consumers. In a way, consumers would get a double benefit. Not only would they get the lowest price, but they would stand to gain even more—at no additional cost—from the loyalty program. Because consumers would not learn what the actual commission was, they would have to be granted an average amount of excess-commission points according to the value and type of transaction. For example, the purchase of a life insurance policy might give 200 points, whereas a fifteen-year mortgage might award 1,000 points. Hilhorst's estimate was to generate €7m in excess commissions by 2001.

As he saw it, there were three ways to go:

1. An immediate cash rebate to the customer.

2. A membership in some form of consumer club, where Independer customers would "earn" credits to purchase various consumer items such as gift items, vacations, or services.

3. The issuance of certificates that, when Independer went public with an IPO, would turn into company stocks that could be sold or kept.

Hilhorst was leaning toward the third option. It was new and would demonstrate how innovative Independer was. Most importantly, he felt, it would entice consumers into a long-term and recurring relationship with the company, rather than function as a one-off cash rebate. This could build loyalty, which after all was the purpose of the fund. Of course, the downside of this option was also apparent. It was a complex scheme that consumers would need to understand; Independer would have to create a positive image of the program in the mind of consumers. Only one other company in Holland, which was also an Internet startup, had a similar scheme. In addition, consumers would implicitly be accepting part of the risk that shares in the company would become valuable in a year or whenever the company went through the IPO process.

The cash-back option had immediate and obvious benefits and would not take a lot of explaining. Bain and Company had long argued in favor of it as this "most aggressive course." Administratively, it was also the least complex: because no permanent structures would need to be created and monitored, there was very little overhead. However, it was likely to scare financial institutions, particularly if it revealed at the time of purchase what the commission rate really was. Finally, the consumer-club option appeared to be a kind of middle course: it would link Independer customers with the company on a longer-term basis and yet provide immediate, palpable benefits in whatever program they chose to create or join. The concept was employed by a number of firms and so would not require a long and costly advertising campaign to explain. However, the program might divert attention from the company, instead focusing consumers on the benefits rather than cementing their loyalty to the Independer concept.

Exhibit 1 Independer's Unique Commission Structure

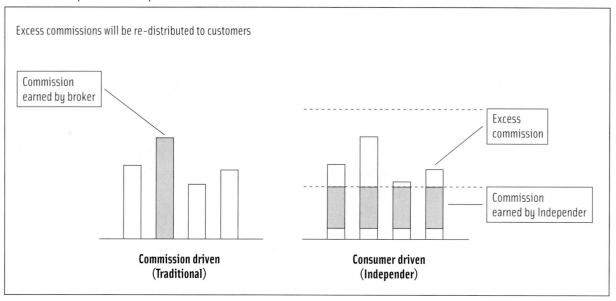

Exhibit 2 Main Insurance Companies and Premiums in the Dutch Market (in $m for 1995)

Insurance Company	Life Insurance	Non-Life Insurance
ING	3,725	1,720
Achmea Group	1,807	1,981
AEGON	1,986	499
Fortis	1,709	632
Interpolis	974	780
Stad Rotterdam	740	681

Source: International Business Strategies, Feb. '98

Exhibit 3 Degree of Banking Market Fragmentation: Different in Holland, France, and Germany: Market Share of Top 5 Banks

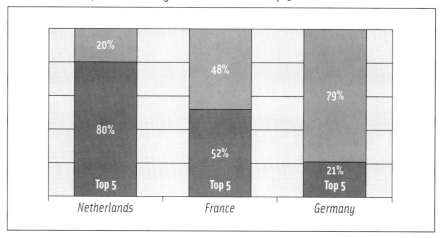

Exhibit 4 Insurance Broker Value Chain

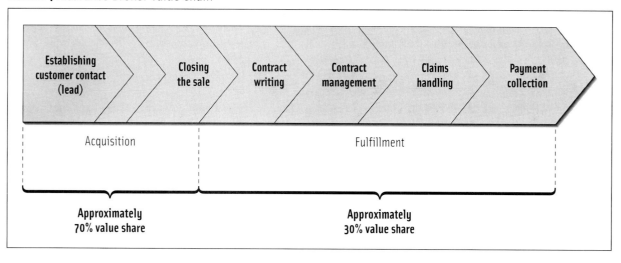

Exhibit 5 Comparing Financial Products Is Attractive for Consumers in The Netherlands, France, and Germany.

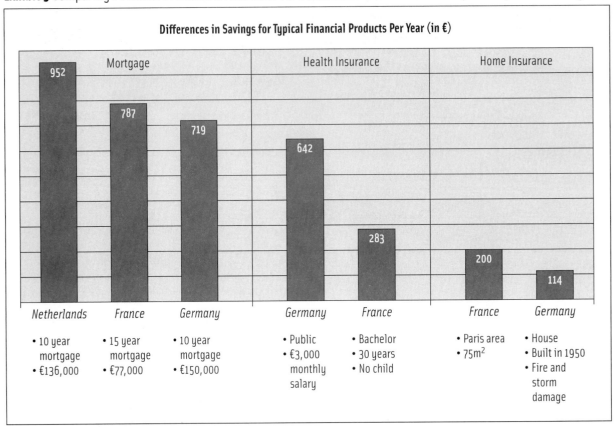

Differences in Savings for Typical Financial Products Per Year (in €)

Mortgage			Health Insurance		Home Insurance	
952	787	719	642	283	200	114
Netherlands	*France*	*Germany*	*Germany*	*France*	*France*	*Germany*
• 10 year mortgage • €136,000	• 15 year mortgage • €77,000	• 10 year mortgage • €150,000	• Public • €3,000 monthly salary	• Bachelor • 30 years • No child	• Paris area • 75m²	• House • Built in 1950 • Fire and storm damage

Exhibit 6 Marketing Research Results Regarding the Attitude Toward Purchasing Financial Services Using Traditional Channels

Study conducted by Independer partner Centrum Voor Marketing Analyses (CMA). Interviews conducted via CATI (computer aided telephone interview) for a representative sample of 500 individuals age 15–74. Target respondents were the financial decision makers in the households.

Whenever you require a mortgage, pension scheme or mutual fund, there are so many different options that it overwhelms and demotivates you as a consumer.

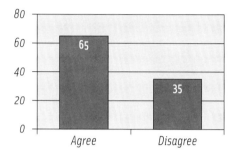

I am sure that an insurance intermediary (broker) only guards my interests (and not his own) when he advises me.

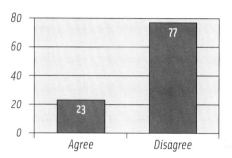

It takes a lot of time to develop a good overview of the offering with respect to financial products and possibilities from banks and other financial institutions.

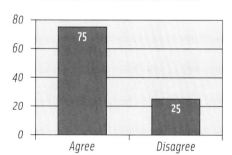

When I have made a choice for a certain financial product, for example mortgage, pension scheme or savings account, I am sure that that product is the best option for me.

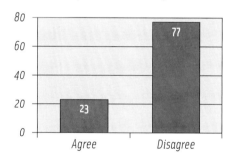

As a consumer you are an equal discussion partner for an insurance intermediary (broker) and you are not lectured about financial products. (Read: one is not grandfathered about financial products).

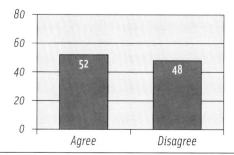

If I would have a better (read: more complete) overview of the existing mortgages, pension schemes and mutual funds, I would be able to find a cheaper solution.

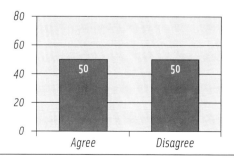

Exhibit 7 Independer's Networked Organization

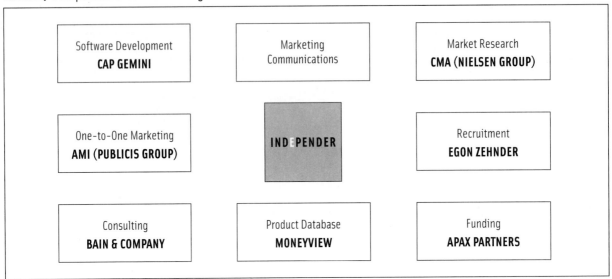

Exhibit 8 Independer's Revenue Model Rollout

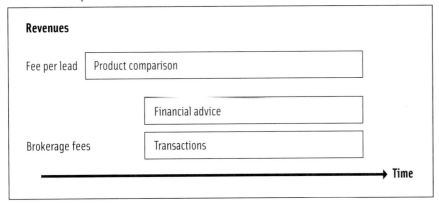

Exhibit 9 Independer's Business Model

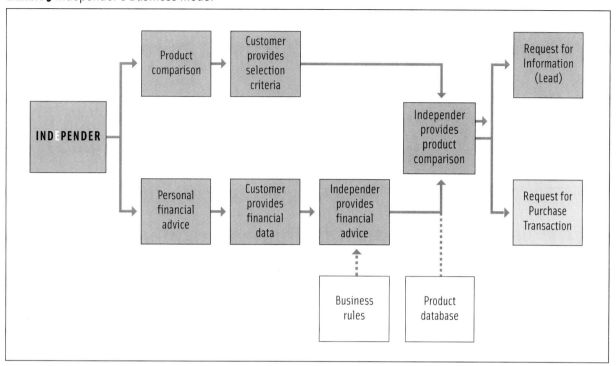

Exhibit 10 Technology Adoption Varies Across Europe in Millions of People over Age 16.

The Netherlands					UK				
Year	Population (mio)	Personal Computer (%)	Internet (%)	Digital Phone (%)	Year	Population (mio)	Personal Computer (%)	Internet (%)	Digital Phone (%)
1993	11.98	2.2	0.29	0	1993	45.11	9.6	0.79	0.02
1994	12.07	2.6	0.39	0.06	1994	45.26	9.9	1.01	0.75
1995	12.15	3.1	0.49	0.27	1995	45.36	11.8	3.82	1.77
1996	12.25	3.6	0.6	0.7	1996	45.61	12.7	5.11	4.14
1997	12.32	4.4	0.83	1.56	1997	45.81	14.3	6.2	7.42
1998	12.40	5.06	1.5	2.36	1998	45.99	15.73	8.11	11.04
1999	12.48	5.52	2.21	4.37	1999	46.24	16.8	10.25	14.8
2000	12.56	5.8	2.76	5.4	2000	46.43	17.7	12.51	18.11
2001	12.64	6.17	3.31	6.19	2001	46.62	18.9	14.32	21.91
2002	12.73	6.49	3.89	6.75	2002	46.87	20.4	15.81	24.37
2003	12.80	6.92	4.62	7.68	2003	47.06	21.7	17.43	26.82
Germany					**France**				
1993	65.64	10.2	1.12	0.98	1993	44.56	5.6	0.85	0.08
1994	65.80	12.5	1.73	1.76	1994	44.76	6.7	1.15	0.46
1995	66.03	15.6	2.97	3.13	1995	44.94	7.8	4.32	1
1996	66.26	19.1	4.32	4.97	1996	45.19	8.8	6.01	2.25
1997	66.43	21	5.53	7.7	1997	45.36	10.2	7.04	5.69
1998	66.57	23.31	7.29	11.32	1998	45.53	11.7	7.54	8.65
1999	66.81	24.82	10.39	14.03	1999	45.77	13.2	8.21	12.82
2000	66.96	26.31	12.68	18.75	2000	45.95	15	9.01	16.08
2001	67.12	27.59	14.21	24.16	2001	46.14	16.2	10.46	19.38
2002	67.36	29.4	15.61	29.64	2002	46.37	17.3	11.59	21.8
2003	67.51	31.45	18.91	34.43	2003	46.56	18.6	13.61	24.21

Source: Forrester Forecasts, November 1999

Exhibit 11 Privacy Statement

Independer acts as an online information broker, by selling and offering products and services specialised in financial care. For this concept to be successful, it is necessary that the visitors of the site are prepared to disclose personal information. Using this data, a match can be made with a selection of products and services. An essential condition herewith is that the visitors confide in the offered concept. To obtain the confidence of the user, emphasis on privacy aspects and related legal conditions is essential.

Legal framework

The most important legal framework at the moment is contained in the "Wet persoonsregistraties (WPR)" (Law on personal registration). Due to a European directive, this law will soon been replaced by the "Wet bescherming persoonsgegevens (WBP)" (Law on protection of personal data). Both laws have consequences for the organisation of data processing that will take place in the company activities of Independer.

In the WPR as well as in the WBP, three main elements can be distinguished:

- Obligations for the companies that collect personal data.
- Rights granted to persons whose personal data is being collected (customers including those rejected, and ex-customers, site-visitors).
- Independent supervision exercised by the "Registratiekamer".

At the moment of introduction of the WBP, the above-mentioned elements will be inflicted in a stricter way.

Although this new law is not effective yet, Independer has already taken into account its regulations. The notification of registrations and the use of personal data is performed according to the regulations of the current law (WPR). This is one of the obligations of this law. For the remaining obligations, the regulations of the newer law have been taken into account. On top of that, the rights granted to persons whose data have been collected are considered under the new law. This is because reviews of law compliance are often already done according to the new situation. Besides a late adaptation of the project could possibly have large consequences.

Rights and obligations

Overview of the most important obligations of the companies collecting personal data and of the rights granted to persons whose data has been collected.

Notification of the person registration

According to the current law, all person registrations must be reported at the "Registratiekamer". This independent institution controls the fulfilment of privacy laws. The notification describes, among other things, the controller (the company), the objective of person registration and the collected categories of personal data.

Description of the objective of person registration

The objective of the person registration, i.e., the purpose for which the data is processed, is of great importance. The new law prescribes that data only can be collected for purposes which are clearly described up front. Further processing is only allowed as long as it is not incompatible with the described purposes.

Obligation to inform

The controller of a person registration must inform the persons, whose data is being collected, of this registration. The purpose of collecting and processing this data must also be disclosed as well as the identity of the collector. Finally it is also necessary that the persons are aware that they have the right to object to the receipt of information of (other) products and services (opt-out). According to the new law, the above information should be given to the persons before the moment of the data collection.

The right of access data and the right of rectification

If an involved person so requests, a controller must inform them whether personal data has been collected and if so, which personal data. This is called the right of inspection. Besides this, the person has the right of rectification, erasure or blocking data, if the processing of this data does not comply with the provisions of the WPR/WBP, in particular due to the incomplete or inaccurate nature of the data.

The right to object

The WBP, introduces the right to object. This right offers the possibility to prevent data from being used in direct marketing activities. This right is of an absolute character and must be followed.

In addition to this, an obligation exists with every commercial communication to inform the involved person of his right to object. As stated before, the person should also be informed about this right when he is informed that his personal data is being collected.

Exhibit 12 Screenshot Main Page (April 2000)

Exhibit 13 Screenshot of Comparison Page–Savings Accounts (April 2000)

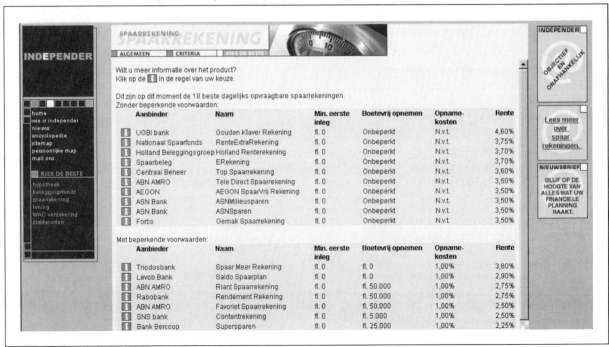

Customer Interface

4

CUSTOMER INTERFACE

In this chapter, we introduce the concept of a technology-mediated customer interface. This interface can be a desktop PC, subnotebook, personal digital assistant, cell phone, or other device. Furthermore, the interface may or may not be connected to the Internet. The key integrating mechanism is that the standard face-to-face interaction has been replaced by a technology-enabled interface. To illustrate this point, this chapter focuses on a wide variety of technology-enabled interfaces, including the personal computer (e.g., iVillage, Frontgate), television (e.g., QVC and its companion case in Chapter 5, iQVC; see pp. 416), telephone (e.g., Wildfire, first direct), and ATM (e.g., first direct). Simply put, the digital revolution is not specific to the Internet; it is about many different interfaces that frequently are used in combination.

Within a technology-mediated customer experience, the user's interaction with the company shifts from the face-to-face encounter in a traditional retail store to a screen-to-face interface. As this shift to screen-to-customer interface unfolds, it is important to consider the types of interface design considerations that confront the senior management team as they implement their business model. The seven design choices are content, context, community, communication, customization, connection, and commerce. Each of the 7Cs needs to fit and reinforce the others while at the same time satisfying the business model.

Context refers to the website's look-and-feel and can be conceptualized on two dimensions: form (or aesthetic) and function. Aesthetic designs focus on the artistic nature of the site. Function, on the other hand, involves the pragmatic usability of the site. Some argue that form and function are opposing design aspects with unavoidable tradeoffs, while others argue that advancing technologies lead to new techniques and new aesthetics. *Content* is defined as all digital subject matter on the site. This includes the form of the digital subject matter—text, video, audio, and graphics—as well as the domains of the digital subject matter, including product, service, and information offerings.

Community is defined as user-to-user communication and can be one-to-one or one-to-many. Websites can facilitate community-building through both interactive and non-interactive technologies. *Customization* allows users to personalize the site or, conversely, allows the site to tailor itself to users. The levers for personalization include log-in registration, personalized e-mail, content and layout configuration, storage, and agents.

Communication refers to dialogue that is initiated by the organization and may be undirectional or interactive. There are three forms of communication: broadcast, interactive, and a broadcast/interactive hybrid. *Connection* is the degree to which a given site is able to link to other sites. *Pathway-out* connections occur when links cause the user to exit from the website. *Pathway-in* connections retrieve material from the same or other sites without exiting the current website. *Commerce* is defined as the sale of goods, products, or services on the site.

Consistent with a tightly constructed business model, well-designed sites should simultaneously attract target segment customers and repel non-targeted customers. Compelling customer interfaces communicate the core value proposition of the company, and provide a compelling rationale for buying and/or visisting the site.

SYNOPSES OF CHAPTER CASES

iVILLAGE (2000)

Case Overview

This case examines the creation and challenges facing iVillage, a women-oriented content site that focuses on a variety of issues, ranging from motherhood to health to being in the workforce. Like most content providers, iVillage—one of the 50 most visited sites, according to Media Metrix—has attempted to scale up quickly but has lost millions in the process. As a result, its market capitalization has steadily declined after reaching a peak in late 1999. The iVillage site faces competition from Women.com, partially owned by Hearst Corporation, which publishes several leading women's magazines including *Cosmopolitan* and *Good Housekeeping*, and Oxygen.com, which includes input from television celebrity Oprah Winfrey.

Preparation Questions

1. Evaluate iVillage's business model. What can it do to become profitable?
2. What makes iVillage unique compared with Women.com and Oxygen.com?

first direct (A)

Case Overview

By 1996, first direct had become the largest "virtual" bank in the world, with over 630,000 current account customers and a growth rate of 12,000 new customers per month, with no physical branches. Moreover, first direct achieved the highest service quality ratings of any bank in the United Kingdom.

Kevin Newman, the bank's chief executive, stated the bank's commitment to reach one million customers by the year 2000. Implicit in this commitment was the idea that First Direct would continue to offer the highest quality service of any bank—physical or direct—in its national market. Newman believed service quality was first direct's competitive advantage, resulting from a company-wide commitment to six core values: individual contribution, openness, respect, responsiveness, getting it right the first time, and *kaizen* (continuous improvement). Maintaining that commitment, regardless of growth, was essential to preserving the firm's status as a premier service company in Great Britain's financial services sector.

Newman contended that the positive attitude and frame of mind of the "front line" service representatives distinguished first direct from its competitors. About two thirds of first direct's employees worked on the front line, dealing directly with customers on the telephone. One immediate need was expansion of the centralized telephone operations at first direct's sites in Leeds.

Preparation Questions

1. What is the customer interface for first direct?
2. How important is this interface?
3. What are the key components of its business model?
4. Was it important to concentrate phone center operations around headquarters?
5. Was it viable to draw all labor from a single city market?
6. Would changes in technology alter the bank's labor needs?
7. How could the front line expand to meet the demand without sacrificing the core values of customer service?

first direct (B)

Case Overview

first direct's unique banking model continued to appeal strongly to a new generation of consumers. Despite a leadership turnover, which resulted in the appointment of former IT Director Andrew Armishaw as CEO, by late 1997 first direct had increased its customer base to over 800,000 account holders and was adding 12,500 new customers per month. Word-of-mouth was working: 97% of the bank's customers reported that first direct delivered better services than other banks.

In order to accommodate a large and diverse customer base, first direct expanded its services into new channels. Steve Townend, Head of Lending, described these developments as a strategy to be "what, when, and where" the first direct customer wanted. In June 1997, first direct launched a PC-banking service, and announced plans to build a new call center on a 33-acre site near Glasgow, Scotland. first direct selected Glasgow based on extensive consumer research that revealed that customers responded not to regional accents so much as to the tone and warmth of representatives' voices. first direct therefore focused on identifying a location that had an abundance of well-educated, high-caliber, available workers. Glasgow emerged as a natural match.

Preparation Questions

1. Would first direct be able to create an infrastructure and customer interface that was scaleable to the emerging market of online banking consumers?
2. What other key services could it offer to compete with the traditional banking companies that were attempting to replicate first direct's business model?

QVC, INC.

Case Overview

QVC, the hugely successful, televised shopping channel, was founded in 1986 by Joseph Segel, founder of the multimillion-dollar mail-order company Franklin Mint. With $30 million in start-up capital and several seasoned television executives signed on, Segel began broadcasting the new QVC service with the following three customer-focused elements as the value proposition: Quality, Value, and Convenience (QVC). In its first full fiscal year,

QVC established a record in U.S. business history for revenues generated by a start-up company, with sales in excess of $112 million.

Several factors contributed to the unprecedented success of televised shopping. The number of dual-income families was growing as women continued to enter the workforce; plus, the number of teenagers, a group more inclined to embrace electronic shopping and interactive television, was becoming significant in the late 1990s. In 1996, approximately one half of all adults surveyed agreed that shopping in stores was an "unpleasant chore that they avoided doing whenever possible." QVC was the beneficiary of an increasing comfort with technology.

With this evolving backdrop for its business, QVC applied nontraditional marketing techniques to attract an incredibly diverse audience through the specific merchandise it featured. "We're so broad," Doug Rose, a director of marketing, observed, "that our audience is made up of countless niches—Clint Black fans, NASCAR fans, and Barbie fans."

In realizing the three principles of Quality, Value, and Convenience in day-to-day operations, employees focused on promoting high-quality and unique merchandise with a soft-sell approach and providing outstanding customer service, in which the company followed a philosophy of underpromising and overdelivering.

Preparation Questions

1. What business is QVC in?
2. What was the conventional channel of shopping? What is the new approach introduced by QVC?
3. What is QVC's value proposition? Is it sustainable? What are the key threats to its business model?
4. In 1996, after ten years of successful operations, how could QVC extend its consumer franchise? And how could it maintain its level of service, the key driver of its success, as it expanded to international markets and to new channels such as the Internet?

FRONTGATE CATALOG

Case Overview

Paul Tarvin and John O'Steen, President and CEO of the Frontgate catalog, had founded their business on making top-line, top-caliber products for the home. In six years, gross revenues of the Ohio-based catalog company had grown to nearly $100 million in 1997, from $300,000 in 1991. Tarvin and O'Steen knew that for Frontgate to continue to succeed, they needed to translate standards of quality into every aspect of operations, including a new potential sales channel, the Internet.

Plans for a Frontgate website were underway. Potentially, the site would take advantage of limitless webpages by providing extensive product information alongside product images. Site visitors would also be able to place orders online and submit e-mail inquiries. The catalog business already managed back-office functions, such as ordering, processing, and shipping, making entry into electronic commerce on the Web a natural next step. Additionally, the online customer profile seemed to coincide with that of Frontgate's catalog customer.

There was conflict within Frontgate, however, about how extensively to develop the website. While on one hand the Web offered an opportunity to take marketing to a higher level with customer profiling features, there was concern about the actual benefits and costs involved in maintaining a website. At that point in time, poor resolution and image quality on the Web were a primary concern in selling top-quality, high-end products.

In terms of costs, the moment online consumers picked up the phone to make an inquiry, all cost-savings benefits of the online order were eliminated. There was also the realization that once the company went online, customers would demand the same level of service to which they were accustomed over the phone. This would mean constantly updating the website and promptly answering untold numbers of e-mails, a potential financial drain.

What kind of human and financial resources should Frontgate allocate to the website? How should they extend the Frontgate brand image into the new media channel? Was Frontgate creating a site with limited or inadequate capabilities? Should the parent company, Cinmar, invest more into the site to provide additional features? How could Cinmar exploit the opportunities intrinsic to the online revolution without unnecessary investment of precious resources?

Preparation Questions

1. Why has Frontgate Catalog met with such success as a new catalog offering in an already crowded direct-mail market?

2. Who are the customers who buy from Frontgate Catalog? What aspects of its operations enhance its customers' levels of perceived value, satisfaction, and loyalty?

3. Given that customer lifetime value drives profitability of any direct marketing business, how should Frontgate managers maximize the value of the catalog's customer relationships?

4. Evaluate the existing Frontgate and related Cornerstone Group catalog sites on the Web. How well suited are these sites to building awareness, selling product, and providing customer service in the Web environment?

5. Is Frontgate's stated plan for its website implementation reasonable and sound? What changes in strategy or tactics would you recommend?

INTEGRATIVE QUESTIONS

As you consider the entire set of questions in the fourth chapter, you should also reflect on the following integrative questions:

1. Compare and contrast the community building features of iVillage and QVC. Many industry pundits believe that the Internet firms, such as iVillage, are better suited for community building as compared to other mediums such as TV, phone, and ATMs. However, QVC clearly has a distinctive community focus. What can iVillage learn from QVC? What can QVC learn from iVillage?

2. Face-to-face customer service is often thought to be superior to any technology-mediated interface. Yet first direct and QVC all seem to provide best-of-class customer service. How is this so?

3. Some pundits argue that a firm needs a single interface, while others (citing QVC, Frontgate, and others) argue that customers demand multiple interfaces. What are the arguments for and against multiple interfaces?

4. How are technology-mediated interfaces similar (or different) from face-to-face interactions? What implications does this have for customer service?

5. Is the 7Cs framework best suited for the Internet? Can it be extended to other technology-mediated interfaces such as television and telephones? Can it apply to nontechnology-based interfaces such as catalogs and face-to-face interactions?

SUMMARY

This chapter introduced the 7Cs of the customer interface. The interface—which is defined as a technology-mediated interface in e-commerce transactions—often can make or break the company. Building on the previous chapter, the interface logically follows from the business model. That is, a firm must first specify its complete business model prior to choice and construction of its customer interface. In the next chapter, we turn to a discussion of how best to implement the chosen strategy.

iVILLAGE.COM

*"I'm not that interested in cyberspace as a big deal; I'm
more interested in life as a big deal.[1]"*

Candice Carpenter
Cofounder and Chairwoman
iVillage.com

Candice Carpenter looked out her lower Manhattan office window and contemplated the future of iVillage. As co-founder and chairman, she was pleased with the company's success—iVillage.com was the 28th most frequented site on the web with approximately 8.3 million visitors per month[2] (see Exhibit 1)—but she also realized that iVillage was at a critical inflection point in its development. The presence of women online had grown significantly since 1996: women constituted one-half of the online population in 2000,[3] up from 40% just four years before.[4] This increased online presence was accompanied by increased competition among sites targeted specifically towards women. Although iVillage still remained the leading destination site for women in November 2000, a number of players sought to dislodge iVillage as the market leader.

The greatest competitive threats were posed by Women.com, the 29th most visited site on the Web[3], which was backed by the Hearst Corporation—a leading publisher of women's magazines, and Oxygen.com, whose investors included America Online and one of the most influential women talk show hosts of all time—Oprah Winfrey. Keeping iVillage ahead of the pack required that Carpenter not only leverage the company's key capabilities—an established brand and successful channel network—but also think of strategic ways to potentially work with competitors. These competitors ranged from online start-ups to established media players.

The second major challenge for iVillage was to achieve the profitability demanded by the market. Its market capitalization had declined sharply over the past year. Shares that had traded at $130 during the market high in April 1999 now traded at $1.50[6] (see Exhibit 2). Like many online operations, the bulk of iVillage's revenues came from advertising. However, unlike most of its counterparts, the company espoused an advertising model of online sponsorship packages rather than traditional banner advertising. A specialized sales force educated marketers on the value of creating such partnerships, but more marketers would need to embrace the iVillage model before the company could meet revenue targets. Despite iVillage's continued increase in quarterly traffic, registered members, and even revenue, the operating loss continued to widen. Revenues grew from $20 million in the first nine months of 1999 to $58 million during the same period in 2000, but operating losses also increased from $59 million to $161 million.[7] Excluding a one-time goodwill charge of $98 million related to the sale of iBaby.com to BabyGear.com in July 2000,[8] iVillage's operating loss during the first nine months of 2000 totaled $63 million.[9]

The iVillage sale of iBaby.com represented a larger strategic shift in the industry as content providers shied away from e-commerce. Women.com had shut down its e-commerce site, "She Gets Dressed," in March 2000,[10] while Oxygen did the same with its "Women's Hands," a site which sold craft items from female artists. iBaby.com was a site geared towards parents of children under three years old, offering a plethora of 14,000 products from nearly 500 manufacturers.[11] In March 1998, when iVillage acquired an interest in iBaby, the parent focused site seemed to be a strong complement to the women focused iVillage, with the added benefit of generating

*Madeline Choquette (MBA '99) and Dickson Louie prepared this case
using public sources, with the assistance of consultant Ellie J. Kyung,
under the supervision of Professor Jeffrey F. Rayport as the basis for class
discussion rather than to illustrate either effective or ineffective handling
of an administrative situation.*

[1]Denitto, Emily, "Entrepreneur, Candice Carpenter," *Crain's New York Business,* November 24, 1997.
[2]Media Metrix, "Top 50", October 2000.
[3]Pew Internet Research Study, May 9, 2000.
[4]Pew Internet Research Study, May 9, 2000.
[5]Media Metrix, "Top 50", October 2000.
[6]Couzin, Jennifer, "iVillage CEO says Farewell," *Industry Standard,* July 27, 2000.
[7]iVillage Investment Highlights, Third Quarter 2000.
[8]Couzin, Jennifer, "Women's Sites Shop for Profits," *Industry Standard,* July 24, 2000.
[9]iVillage Investment Highlights, Third Quarter 2000.
[10]Couzin, Jennifer, "Women's Sites Shop for Profits," *Industry Standard,* July 24, 2000.
[11]iVillage prospectus, March 18, 1999.

additional transactional revenue through e-commerce. It was a model iVillage had hoped to expand on in the future. While it had provided a key revenue source for iVillage, the transactional, fulfillment and customer service aspects of e-commerce proved challenging for a content oriented site, while further cutting into profits. iVillage made a strategic decision to focus on building content, and sold its stake in iBaby. The move away from e-commerce would force iVillage to find alternative sources of revenue to meet expectations.

Carpenter rose from her desk, considering three key strategic questions that faced iVillage and its new CEO, Douglas McCormick, who had replaced Carpenter in late July 2000.[12] First, what was the best way to target and attract women online, especially in light of the fact that the number of households—and thus women—online was expected to increase by 50% from 2000 to 2003?[13] Second, how would iVillage stay ahead of the pack and beat its competition? And finally, how could iVillage become a profitable operation without jeopardizing the growth of market share over the long run?

iVillage History

The Founders

iVillage was founded in June 1995 by Candice Carpenter, Nancy Evans and Robert Levitan. Each had experiences in different aspects of media, which they leveraged in the development of the company. Carpenter had been serving as a consultant to America Online when she left to start iVillage, and had previously served as an executive at American Express, Time-Life Video and Television, and Q2 (a sister channel of the QVC home shopping network.) Evans, who would eventually become the site's Editor-in-Chief, had a background in the publishing industry, having worked at *Family Life* magazine, Doubleday, and the Book-of-the-Month Club. Levitan was formerly the president and founder of Yearlook Enterprises, a video publishing company.

Carpenter reportedly conceived of the iVillage concept on a cocktail napkin in 1995 and discussed it with her colleagues.[14] The trio made the simple observation that, at the time, there was an absence of sites with relevance to everyday life in areas such as parenting, work, and careers.[15] They saw the Internet not only as a medium to create content around these issues, but as a platform to create virtual "communities" of individuals. Thus, the three set forth to create a company with the goal of "humanizing" cyberspace for both men and women alike.

Starting with "Parent Soup"

iVillage was fortunate in finding initial funding through America Online, TCI, the Tribune Company, and Kleiner Perkins Caufield & Byers. However, as a pioneer in its field, iVillage encountered numerous obstacles in its launch beyond securing funding. In 1995, there were no online technical or business models to learn from, and Carpenter and her colleagues were faced with the technicalities of designing and launching a customer friendly website themselves. The initial result was Parent Soup, launched in January 1996 as a site to provide expert advice and promote online discussions between parents on various family issues ranging from being a "Soccer Mom" to handling delicate child custody issues.[16]

By early 1997, Parent Soup had grown into an online community of 200,000 parents that each spent, on average, 10 minutes per session chatting with other parents.[17] Evans thought of Parent Soup as a "virtual 24-hour hotline and community center."[18] The regular congregation of these baby boomers online convinced Fortune 500 companies, such as Proctor & Gamble, Sony, and Fisher Price, to sign on as sponsors of the site.[19,20] Parent Soup proved to be a great success, and even in 2000, Parent Soup remained one of the strongest brands within the iVillage network of communities.

Expanding the Communities and Narrowing Focus

After the success of Parent Soup, iVillage invested in developing additional community channels.

[12]"iVillage CEO says fareware," *Industry Standard,* July 27, 2000.
[13]Baker, Lanny, Solomon Smith Barney Inc., "The Online Media Rule Book Volume 1", September 13, 1999.
[14]Candice Carpenter, Ernst & Young Entrepreneur of the Year Award profile.
[15]Kruger, Pamela and Mieszkowski, "Stop The Fight," *Fast Company,* September 1998.
[16]Eng, Paul N., "A Coffee Klatch for Moms and Dads," *Business Week,* May 5, 1997.
[17]Eng, Paul N., "A Coffee Klatch for Moms and Dads," *Business Week,* May 5, 1997.
[18]Eng, Paul N., "A Coffee Klatch for Moms and Dads," *Business Week,* May 5, 1997.
[19]Candice Carpenter, *Harvard Business School Bulletin,* April 1998.
[20]Eng, Paul N., "A Coffee Klatch for Moms and Dads," *Business Week,* May 5, 1997.

Supported by additional venture capital funding totaling $67 million, iVillage set out to create additional content sites, including About Work, Vices and Virtues[21], Better Health, and Armchair Millionaire.[22]

In late 1997, Carpenter and her team made an important discovery that shaped the face of iVillage: eighty-five percent of iVillage.com users were women. Further research determined that women tended to be more attracted to online communities than men and that they were less likely to browse randomly through the Web. Carpenter observed that "women . . . don't like to compartmentalize home, work, and family and use the Web to solve problems.[23]" Instead, they preferred to go to one reliable place online to source their information. Cognizant of the incredible marketing opportunity this implied, Carpenter and Evans decided to rework iVillage specifically into a destination site for women, using the existing online communities as content channels within the network.[24] In November 1997, the site became "iVillage.com, The Women's Network." By the end of that year, it had become the leading women's network online.

Growing the Company

By early 1999, iVillage had grown to include 14 channels, including Book Club, Money, Pets, Relationships, Shopping and Work from Home. In an extremely successful initial public offering led by the prominent investment banks Goldman Sachs, Credit Suisse First Boston, and Hambrecht & Quist, iVillage raised $81 million in capital.[25] While shares of the company sold at $24 per share on IPO day (March 18, 1999) the price quickly rose to $130 a share by April 1999. iVillage continued to expand its content through 1999, moving to acquire additional content sites, including the purchases of Astrology.Net and Family.Net.[26]

Early numbers indicated that iVillage was a success. As of December 1998, iVillage averaged 65 million page views per month from 2.7 million unique visitors.[27] Revenues had jumped dramatically during its years as a private company: $732,000 in 1996, $6 million in 1997, and $15 million in 1998. At the same time, operating losses also grew proportionately: $10 million in 1996, $21 mil-

lion in 1997, and $44 million in 1998.[28] At the time, however, Carpenter had not been overly concerned, noting that—as with any media company—iVillage "must delay profitability to build brand equity."[29]

Understanding iVillage and Its Cornerstones for Success

iVillage's success as the leading destination for women was based on two key factors: the structure of its online network and its unique business strategy.

Structure of the Network

The iVillage.com was the umbrella brand that connected individually branded channels. Its homepage (www.iVillage.com) served as a home base—a single point of entry into the family of iVillage sites (see Exhibit 3). The homepage was refreshed daily, promoting highlights of content, community, and featured channels. It was designed to be perceived as warm and inviting, but also useful and relevant. But more importantly, the homepage served as a platform for iVillage's networked structure.

The network structure was unlike that of portals, like Netscape, Yahoo! or Exite, which typically focused on Web search and dynamic chat. It was iVillage's key point of differentiation and provided a distinct advantage over the portal model: consistency and control over all aspects of the customer experience—particularly context, content, and community. In terms of context, iVillage ensured consistency of navigation and programming on its site, not only throughout each channel, also between channels to provide a uniform customer experience. With respect to content, each channel was specifically constructed by iVillage to provide a mix of expert advice, focused interaction, and interactive tools around a particular subject matter, unlike portals which served primarily to aggregate content. And finally through actively managed communities, versus the unmonitored chat rooms of portal sites, iVillage created a "safe, well-lit place" for members to interact under the watchful eye of assigned community "leaders" (detailed in the next section).

The network structure also allowed for the easy addition of value added features for its members, such as e-mail, personal homepages and instant messaging, as did the portal model.

---

[21]Napoli, Lisa, "Women and Venture Capital are a Fine Mix at iVillage," *The New York Times,* August 3, 1998.
[22]Candice Carpenter, *Harvard Business School Bulletin,* April 1998.
[23]Candice Carpenter, *Harvard Business School Bulletin,* April 1998.
[24]Candice Carpenter, *Harvard Business School Bulletin,* April 1998.
[25]iVillage Inc. Prospectus, March 18, 1999.
[26]iVillage Inc. Prospectus, March 18, 1999.
[27]iVillage.Inc. Prospectus, March 18, 1999.
[28]iVillage Inc. Prospectus, March 18, 1999.
[29]Candice Carpenter, *Harvard Business School Bulletin,* April 1998.

iVillage had developed fourteen channels by the time of its IPO in March 1999, which are detailed in Figure 1 below.[30]

More recent channel additions included "Election 2000," "lamaze.com", "Readers and Writers," and "Click! Computing." By November 2000, iVillage had nineteen separate content channels in its network.[31]

Business Strategy

The network system underscored the company's goal of becoming the leading online destination site for women, but it was supported by solid strategic vision. iVillage was built upon five key strategic principles:[32] (1) building strong brand awareness, (2) leveraging community to attract and establish a loyal user base, (3) using the network system to create diverse appeal, (4) pursuing strategic partnerships and alliances, and (5) creating revenue through sponsorship and advertising.

Building Strong Brand Awareness. iVillage used a combination of online and offline distribution agreements and localized public relations campaigns to establish itself as a brand among consumers, advertisers, and sponsors.

Figure 1 Description of iVillage Channels

Channel	Content Description
Astrology Net	Horoscopes, celebrity profiles, romance charts and monthly guidance
Book Club	Monthly Book Picks, Question of the Week, Reading Groups, book discussions and iVillage Bestsellers for readers interested in wide range of books
Career	Tools and resources for professional development / planning and career-related issues
Fitness and Beauty	Fitness and beauty information and interactive tools, including Body Calculators, Nutrition Experts and Community Challenges, to improve fitness level
Food	Information on meal planning, nutrition and recipes, including Food Experts and Cooking Basics
Health	Tools and information to assist users in becoming better health care decision makers, including approximately 200 bulletin boards and 150 weekly chats (some hosted through AOL)
Money	Keys to financial planning, including savings and investment strategies, steps to financial freedom, The Model Portfolio, and an investment center sponsored by Charles Schwab
Parent Soup	Parenting solutions, talk with experts, answers and support from fellow parents
ParentsPlace	Parenting community center site that included (through AOL and the Web) approximately 700 bulletin boards and 80 weekly chats in addition to information regarding childhood diseases
Pets	Information on selecting, adopting, purchasing, and caring for pets (designed in partnership with Ralston Purina Company) and a veterinarian finder tool sponsored by the American Humane Association and American Animal Hospital Association
Relationships	Information and conversation on love, marriage and family
Shopping	One-stop shopping destination with easy access to retail websites like Virtual Vineyards, Gymboree, Music Boulevard and Godiva
Travel	Vacation planning tools, travel related articles, reservation center, and currency converter
Work From Home	Home office tools and resources, such as Home Office Basics, a Tax Guide, and a Software Library

[30]Descriptions of each of these 14 content specific channels were adapted from iVillage Prospectus, March 18, 1999.
[31]iVillage home page, November 2000.

[32]iVillage, Prospectus, March 18, 1999.

The bulk of iVillage's online marketing efforts were through multi-million dollar distribution deals with portals and online media (banner) buys on sites with significant traffic. In December 1998, iVillage entered into a two year distribution agreement with AOL. In March 1999, it entered into a promotional agreement with NBC to purchase advertising on its Snap! portal site through 2001.[33] Other key distribution partners included Lycos, Infoseek, Hotmail and Excite.

Traditional offline media properties also offered strong distribution outlets, both for building brand awareness and creating revenue potential through brand extensions. As Editor-in-Chief, Evans often appeared as a guest on NBC's Today Show. Other such television and radio outlets were actively pursued by the public relations group. iVillage also had syndicated columns in over 500 daily newspapers and a Parent Soup book series.[34]

A critical—and unique—component of the iVillage marketing strategy was a series of locally centered public relations events. Local community members would be highlighted at targeted local events, such as PTA conferences or other conferences significantly attended by women, and promotional materials would be heavily distributed to advance the iVillage name.[35] Carpenter believed this strategy significantly contributed to iVillage's widespread brand recognition among women.

Leveraging Community to Attract and Establish a Loyal User Base.

iVillage's community aspect was the key to attracting and keeping users. Visitors needed to become registered members in order to participate in one of the 2,600 chats offered each month or post information on one of the 500 message boards with over 6,000 posts per day. Registered members were more likely to actively seek community and be familiar with the benefits of openly sharing their ideas and problems with other women. These community aspects brought stickiness to the website, resulting in increased visits with more page views per visit because users felt greater emotional involvement and trust in the site.

iVillage worked hard to foster this trust with its members, starting with the design of its community chats and message board systems. The Member Services area devised the original iVillage approach to community and membership. All community chats and message boards were monitored by "community leaders"— volunteers that committed to a complete training

program and one to thirty hours per week to monitor and take ownership for an aspect of the community. These one thousand volunteers not only saved iVillage the expense of 3,000 man hours per week, but also guaranteed the community was a positive place for women, monitored by its own users for the topics of the most relevance.

The results were evident in the number of iVillage registered users. The 3 million registered members in 1999 grew to 6 million the next year. iVillage members also tended to spend a great deal more time on the site than other websites, making it the 23rd most "sticky" site on the web in terms of minutes spent on the site per month. Eighty percent of these users were between the ages of 25 to 49, with an average user age of 33 years.[36] With this combination of women users and stickiness, marketers would pay a premium for access to iVillage.

Using the Network System to Create Diverse Appeal.

While "women" as a category of users was rather broad, iVillage was able to segment and service different women through its channel network. A key aspect of segmentation was through a woman's lifestage. This followed a woman through the various stages of her life: being single, getting married, becoming a parent, working from home, aging, etc. The network channels appealed to different women according to their lifestage, and users could self select into their areas of interest. For example, women who were parents could choose to enter Parent Soup to find information about raising children. From here, entering further user information could even segment users according to the ages of their children, offering information and community specifically relevant to them. iVillage worked to ensure that its channels were relevant to women across a diverse set of lifestages.

Pursuing Strategic Partnerships and Alliances.

iVillage pursued a diverse variety of strategic relationships to support the business. Media partners, such as Tribune, Cox, TCI, Intel, and Fast Company provided leverage to promote the iVillage name. Financial partners, which included Kleiner Perkins, Rho Management, CIBC Wood Gundy, Convergence, Boston Millennium, Cross-Technology Ventures and Moore Capital, provided equity investments in the business. Online partners like AOL, Microsoft, Excite, Lycos, Intuit and NBC drove traffic to the site.[37]

---

[33]iVillage, Prospectus, March 18, 1999.
[34]iVillage, Prospectus, March 18, 1999.
[35]iVillage, Prospectus, March 18, 1999.

[36]iVillage, Prospectus, March 18, 1999.
[37]iVillage prospectus, March 19, 1999.

iVillage also generated revenues from transactional partners, receiving a portion of sales from user purchases. These partners included Amazon.com (the exclusive book retailer and book club sponsor for iVillage.com), Charles Schwab (provider of the Investor Center), N2K (provider of Music Boulevard), and First USA (featuring iVillage branded credit cards).[38] iVillage.com even pursued relationships with key manufacturers interested in building new channels online while protecting their core distribution channels offline. All these partnerships were integral to iVillage business operations.

Creating Revenue through Sponsorship and Advertising.

The iVillage model for advertising focused on creating sponsorships rather than selling banner advertising. Evans explains the intent of the sponsorship model:

> When we started iVillage.com, we wanted our advertisers to be part of the village, the trusted shopkeepers who knew your name. That meant that they would deliver services and products relevant to women, that they would speak in our language.[39]

Sponsorship created value over traditional banner advertising not only for iVillage, but also for the marketer.

It allowed marketers to build far more powerful relationships with consumers that were already predisposed to focusing on relationships, women between the ages of 24 and 49 years old. As noted in *Advertising Age*:

> Women want a relationship. They'd rather buy a dishwashing liquid with less lemon from a company that sponsors after-school programs . . . Relationship innovation is just as important, if not more so, than product innovation.[40]

Through iVillage, marketers could reach a targeted group of consumers, and even target users of specifically relevant channels. Also, by virtue of being a partner of iVillage, it would benefit from some of the trust that users associated with the brand.

For iVillage, the sponsorship model optimized the economic value of the real estate within the iVillage.com network in a way banner advertising could not, especially when the sponsor targeted specific content channels. Sponsorship size and duration varied significantly, depending on its objectives, and accounted for 82% of revenue in 2000. By November 2000, there were 38 iVillage sponsors, including Career Builder, Kraft, Hertz, Huggies, and the Wedding Channel.com.[41] However, continuing to develop these sponsorships was proving challenging as these relationships were generally more expensive for the marketer. Continued revenue growth would require tapping into the brand, rather than solely interactive, budgets of corporations.

iVillage also had the advantage of being able to charge marketers more for even banner advertising. With its highly specialized and captive audience, iVillage was able to charge $45 cpm (cost per thousand page views), significantly higher than the industry average of $27 cpm.[42] With the shift away from e-commerce with the sale of iBaby.com, sponsorship would become an even more important source of revenue, as Carpenter noted that iVillage would "remain active in e-commerce through revenue-generating sponsorship agreements rather than carry the fulfillment side of the equation ourselves.[43]"

Marketing to the Community: Leveraging the Sponsorship Model

Sponsorship was a focal point in a relationship between iVillage, its members, and its sponsors. iVillage provided a free service to its members online and in the process aggregated a targeted audience. Marketers (the sponsors) sought access to this targeted audience while members wanted connections to the best brands. iVillage brought these members and marketers together to provide a value added service.

So how exactly did a sponsorship deal work? The answer is that each sponsorship deal with iVillage was unique. Often sponsors tested the waters by starting with a moderate investment in banners, email newsletters and polls. However, the far more effective models to leverage the iVillage.com real estate and its relationship with members usually involved community events and interactive tools.

For example, iVillage developed www.wrinklereport.com for Johnson & Johnson to promote Renova, an anti-wrinkle product. For two weeks, iVillage held a live conference with a wrinkle expert. The conference was heavily promoted and moderated, and Johnson & Johnson was able to interact with potential customers and

[38]iVillage prospectus, March 19, 1999.
[39]iVillage.com site, November 26, 2000.
[40]*Advertising Age*, November 10, 1997.

[41]iVillage.com site, November 26, 2000.
[42]Eng, Paul N. , "A Coffee Klatch for Moms and Dads," *Business Week*, May 5, 1997.
[43]Couzin, Jennifer, "Women's Sites Shop for Profits," *Industry Standard*, July 24, 2000.

promote their product in a relevant, meaningful context. Users could request free coupons, providing Johnson & Johnson with a measurable return on investment from those users that would actually try their product. After the conference, transcripts were posted so users could continue accessing the information on Renova.

Merck sponsored the development of a heart disease risk calculator to promote Zocor. Users entered personal information into the calculator and received a personalized health report. Depending on the results, the user could request to receive further health information through the mail. As an intermediary, iVillage emailed the users who requested information with a few questions. The response was incredibly favorable. Out of 1,500 users, 700 actually responded that they wanted to speak to their doctor. Approximately 77% of these people went to speak with their doctor about heart disease, and another 30% actually asked for Zocor by name. This in an example of how marketers can achieve measurable results that are not possible through traditional media campaigns.

Some of the most successful innovation to date had been a community challenge. The "Kick Butt" community challenge in Better Health helped members quit smoking while promoting Zyband. The "Never Say Diet" challenge in Better Health drew 20,000 users over 6 weeks. Armed with this customer data, iVillage sales teams were able to interest other diet related marketers, such as Jenny Craig, in sponsorships.

Health in general was an explosive advertising category for the web. The model for consumer products, such as laundry detergents, was not yet as compelling. Highly information intensive products seemed to leverage the interactive medium far better than physical products. An exception to this was the Polaroid sponsorship. iVillage.com designed a successful program for parents to boost their children's self-esteem using Polaroid film.

Financial Services were another information intensive field. Companies were also marketing heavily to women and even designing products specifically for them. iVillage.com created the Armchair Millionaire site for Quicken through multi-year sponsorship. The Schwab Investor Center on iVillage.com introduces women to mutual funds and basic investing advice. First USA offers a no fee, low interest credit card to iVillage.com users. Financial issues were highly relevant to women and the source of many questions, while financial services firms had money to invest.

iVillage constantly worked on other ways to further develop the sponsorship model, even considering ways to work with television advertising. With its critical role in generating revenue, constant innovation was key.

The Power of Women Online

The number of women online increased steadily through 2000, comprising nearly half the population of Internet users. By March 2000, there were approximately 28 million women online daily, six million of which had been introduced to the Internet only in the past six months.[44] This rapid growth was expected to continue with the proliferation of Internet access across the U.S.

The advent of the Internet had significantly changed the way women worked, purchased, played, and communicated. As the more time starved sex, often juggling work, children, and looking after the home, women were attracted to the Internet as a medium available to them at all hours of the day, providing information and services for every aspect of life, all from a PC.

Research done by the Pew Research Center in March 2000 showed that women used the Internet significantly differently from men, being more likely to use it to search for health information, religious guidance or play games, while men were more likely to make purchases, trade stocks, and seek political news.[45] E-mail also proved to be especially important to women as a way to "enrich their important relationships and to enlarge their networks,[46]" providing a convenient way to keep in touch with friends and family. Women also tended to spend less time using other mediums as they spent more time online: 55% spent less time watching television, 29% spent less time on the phone, 24% less time reading magazines, and 21% less time reading newspapers.

While women were not as comfortable making purchases online as men, they were making more online purchases each year. In 1997, only 37% of women using the Internet had made an online purchase, compared with 53% in 1998. This had significant implications as women wielded significant control over spending in the offline world. According to a November 1997 *Advertising Age* article, women controlled or had influence over nearly $3 trillion in consumer spending, including large

---

[44]Pew Research Center, "What Women Want," May 9, 2000.
[45]Jahnke, Art, "What Women Want," *Web Business Magazine,* May 30, 2000.
[46]Pew Research Center, "What Women Want," May 9, 2000.

ticket items like new cars (80% with influence over the purchase decision), home computers (60%), investment decisions (53%) and appliance choices (70%).[47]

Much of the increase in purchasing power of women is related to the increase in women's annual salaries and the greater number of dual-income families. Approximately 25% of women now earned more than their husbands. Women also constituted 62% of all new investors. They headed more households—nearly 42% of all households with incomes greater than $60K. In addition to simply earning more, an increasing number of women were self-employed and investing in their own businesses.

Not surprisingly, women have become the single largest target category of advertisers today. Roughly $35 billion is spent each year marketing specifically towards women, and a greater portion of these dollars was being spent online each year—an expected $17 billion (6% of total spending) by 2003.[48] (see Exhibit 4).

Competition

Given the amount of advertising dollars spent on women, there was no shortage of online and offline competitors for iVillage. These competitors ranged from women oriented websites, like women.com and Oxygen, to traditional print and cable television mediums geared towards women, like *Vogue*, *Cosmopolitain*, and the Lifetime Television network.

Online Competitors

Women-Oriented Sites. Any site targeted towards women was a competitor to iVillage, including everything from Women.com to Babycenter.com to Marthastewart.com (see Exhibit 5 for timeline of key competitors). Sites with offline partners were at a significant advantage. Women.com benefited from the strongly branded women's magazines and print publications of its partial owner, Hearst Corporation. Oxygen posed a particular threat with the backing of America Online, Oprah Winfrey, and other high profile corporations and individuals. A multi-media play across cable television, print media, and the Internet, Oxygen's model was significantly different from that of iVillage.com (see Exhibit 6). Gerry Laybourne, president of Oxygen, describes the potential for multiple revenue streams:

We have an economic model that includes subscriber fees, ad revenue, e-commerce and sponsorship. By Year Five, we think the television business and the Internet business will be valued about the same. That doesn't mean they're going to throw off the same amount of profits. Obviously, initially the cable business will be bigger. It's just the nature of cable television and the aggregation of eyeballs. We, like Wall Street, believe heavily in e-commerce and the Internet world, and we think there are lots of things we can do to help women run their lives. The promise we'd like to have is, Give us half an hour, and we'll give you back two hours[49].

The Oxygen cable network was launched in January 2000.

Despite the large market potential from reaching women online, Wall Street analysts were concerned about the fate of these women-oriented sites, believing that too many sites, which were already struggling for profits, would be competing for the same advertising dollars. Like iVillage.com, Women.com incurred heavy operating losses of $34 million in 1999 on revenues of $30 million (see Exhibit 7). Analysts were also skeptical that these sites were actually differentiated from each other in any way that could create significant value. Two media analysts at Salomon Smith Barney, Lanny Baker and Virginia Seitz, made the following observation of online competition in June 2000:

We believe investors are also concerned about stepping into the midst of fierce competition in the women's category, in which no clear leader has emerged. The two online leaders, Women.com and iVillage, are within half a point of each other in audience reach, a 5% difference in viewership, according to measurement from Media Metrix. Meanwhile, Oxygen Media, backed by Oprah, Gerry Laybourne, and Marci Casey, lurks in the wings as another potential force in the category. Furthermore, we believe that investors, as they consider the women's category, ask themselves the very question that underlines this report: Is there really room for several independent competitors to be successful in the women's category, and if so, are Women.com, iVillage, Oxygen, and the others really differentiated enough to have mutually thriving businesses in the long term? In our view, consolidation makes sense in this category as it does in the others we have already

---

[47]*Advertising Age*, November 10, 1997.
[48]Baker, Lanny, "The Online Media Rule Book, Volume 1," Salomon Smith Barney, September 13, 2000.

[49]Hamilton, Anita, "Geraldine Laybourne Brings Women A Breath of Fresh Air," Time Digital, March 8, 1999.

considered, and we believe that the women's category may ultimately be one of the larger opportunities in Online Media.[50]

On the road to profitability, iVillage faced significant challenges not only against other online competitors, but purely as an online entity.

Integrated Community Sites.

While integrated community sites were gender neutral, they competed with iVillage by appealing to the users interested in online community interaction. Geocities was one such competitor and was the first online community to go public, later acquired by Yahoo! While communities such as Geocities achieved strong traffic numbers, they did not have the stickiness of the iVillage communities (allowing users to jump from chat room to chat room) or the benefits of the volunteer community leader system that iVillage worked so hard to maintain.

Portal Sites.

In spite of all the benefits offered by content related sites such as iVillage, portals still had the largest reach among Internet users, with AOL, Yahoo! and Microsoft at the top. In addition to providing web searches, portals offered other free value added services, such as personal home pages, e-mail, instant messaging, message boards, and chat rooms. While in theory iVillage should offer a more meaningful online experience because it was tailored towards women, the reality was that many women users associated portals with a place to have their questions answered, and were simply not aware of iVillage. One of iVillage's key marketing challenges going forward was to have more women come to their site directly instead of a portal. Millions were spent annually on distribution deals to secure premier positioning within leading portals.

Offline Competitors

Because millions of women were not yet online, offline competition was also a considerable obstacle. There were a variety of resources women could go to offline to have their daily questions and concerns addressed.

Women's Magazines and Cable Television.

A plethora of traditional media competed for women's attention. Women's magazines, such as *Cosmopolitan* and *Redbook*, and women-oriented cable channels, such as Lifetime, captured hours of women's leisure time.

Women's publications also garnered significant advertising revenue, $2.3 billion in 1998, greater than that of business/money, auto and computer publications.[51] While these publications were supported by both subscription fees and advertising revenue, advertising comprised the bulk of revenue generated. Among the leading women's magazines in 1998 were *Better Homes and Gardens, Good Housekeeping* and *Woman's Day*. The top 32 women's titles had a total circulation of nearly 50 million readers, the publication category by far with the greatest number of subscribers[52] (see Exhibits 8, 9, and 10).

Offline Community Groups.

Physical community groups also provided competition for iVillage. These included local book clubs and special groups like Alcoholics Anonymous, Weight Watchers, and meditation and religious groups. iVillage had recently launched a book club channel in conjunction with its partner Amazon.com to compete with local book clubs, and promoted other channels in subject areas to attract people that were members of some of these groups. However, as the very nature of the interaction was significantly different in the physical v. online world, this proved to be a significant challenge.

Financial and Operating Results for 1999

iVillage continued to experience operating losses in 1999—an $87 million loss on revenues of $37 million. Although revenues had grown from $15 million the previous year, losses had also increased proportionately from $44 million. The 122% increase in spending for sales and marketing from the previous year, at $64 million, accounted for a significant portion of expenditures. Another $21 million was spent on production, product and technology while $13 million went towards general and administrative costs. A five fold increase in depreciation and amortization from the previous year, up to $26 million, was due to various acquisitions during the course of the year (see Exhibit 11).

---

[50]Baker, Lanny, "If you Can't Beat Em . . . ," Salomon Smith Barney, June 21, 2000.

[51]Baker, Lanny, "The Online Media Rule Book, Volume 1", Salomon Smith Barney, September 13, 1999.
[52]Baker, Lanny, "The Online Media Rule Book, Volume 1", Salomon Smith Barney, September 13, 1999.

Conclusion

iVillage was at a strategic inflection point in its development. While an increasing number of women flocked online, competition from other online competitors increased significantly, and the advent of the multimedia play—specifically Oxygen—posed an even greater challenge. With an advertising revenue model and significant competitors both online and offline, iVillage's goal of reaching profitability was further complicated.

Three strategic milestones lay ahead: capturing the attention of these new women as they moved online, winning in a space with increasing competition from a diverse set of competitors, and achieving profitability for a company that was focused around an advertising revenue model. How would iVillage go forward?

Exhibit 1 Top 50 Web sites—October 2000

	Top 50 Digital Media/Web Properties at Home & at Work Combined in the U.S. October 2000 Measurement Period (10/1/00 through 10/31/00)				
Rank		Unique visitors	Rank		Unique visitors
1	AOL Network- Proprietary & WWW	61,540	26	American Greetings	8,545
2	Yahoo!	56,535	27	News Corp. Online	8,477
3	Microsoft Sites	52,129	28	iVillage.com: The Women's Network	8,438
4	Lycos	30,967	29	Women.com Networks The	8,349
5	Excite Network	30,274	30	Weather Channel The	8,346
6	Go Network	22,953	31	FortuneCity Network	8,150
7	About The Human Internet	22,152	32	JUNO / JUNO.COM	8,092
8	AltaVista Network	19,311	33	GoTo	8,024
9	CNET Networks Digital	18,744	34	BIZRATE.COM	7,957
10	Infospace Impressions	18,029	35	Snowball	7,749
11	Amazon	17,335	36	PASSTHISON.COM	7,702
12	Time Warner Online	16,797	37	COOLSAVINGS.COM	7,553
13	NBC Internet Sites	16,489	38	CitySearch-TicketMaster Online	7,434
14	eBay	16,090	39	iWin Sites	7,401
15	LookSmart	13,696	40	Travelocity	6,927
16	Real.com Network	13,011	41	COLONIZE.COM	6,916
17	Ask Jeeves	12,903	42	Flipside Sites	6,864
18	eUniverse Network	12,372	43	ZMEDIA.COM	6,485
19	Viacom Online	12,274	44	eFront	6,470
20	Network Commerce Inc.	11,002	45	GOOGLE.COM	6,468
21	IWON.COM	9,951	46	NFL Internet Network	6,454
22	AT&T Web Sites	9,841	47	GRAB.COM	6,246
23	JOBSONLINE.COM	9,409	48	HOMESTEAD.COM	6,153
24	EarthLink	8,848	49	SPORTSLINE.COM SITES	6,108
25	MyPoints Sites	8,686	50	Barnes & Noble	6,107

Source: Media Metrix, October 2000

Exhibit 2 Stock Price of iVillage

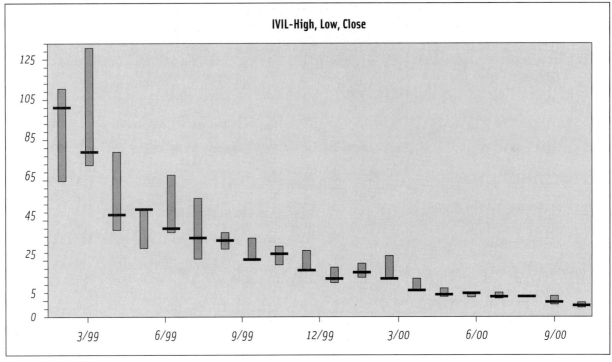

Source: America Online

Exhibit 3 *iVillage.com* Home Page

Exhibit 4 Computer Usage and Online Advertising Forecast

	(Millions) Total US Population	(Millions) Total US Households	(Millions) Households with PCs	(Millions) Households Online	Household Penetration		Online HHs Among PC HH	($Millions) Online Advertising	% of total US Advertising
					PCs	Online			
1993	258	96	30	3	31%	3%	10%		
1994	260	97	33	5	34%	5%	15%		
1995	263	99	35	11	35%	11%	31%	$55	0%
1996	265	100	39	13	39%	13%	33%	$300	0%
1997	268	101	44	18	44%	18%	41%	$600	0%
1998	270	102	48	24	47%	24%	50%	$2,100	1%
1999	272	103	52	28	50%	27%	54%	$2,800	1%
2000E	274	104	55	33	53%	32%	60%	$5,400	2%
2001E	276	105	56	39	53%	37%	70%	$8,700	4%
2002E	278	106	57	45	54%	42%	79%	$12,600	5%
2003E	280	107	59	50	55%	47%	85%	$17,200	6%

Table header: U.S. Online Computer Usage

Source: US Census Bureau, International Data Corporation, Smith Barney Inc./Salomon Brothers Inc. Research, Forrester Research

Exhibit 5 Online Women Sites: Timeline of Key Milestones

iVillage.com

1992	1993	1994	1995	1996	1997	1998	1999	2000

- 1995 Founded by Candace Carpenter
- 1999 Initial Public Offering

- Mar 99 Reports 1st Q Operating Loss of $16.2M on revenue of $4.8M. 1.6 million members and 7.7 million subscribers
- June 99 Reports 2nd Q Operating Loss of $15.0M on revenue of $6.4M. 2.0 million members and 8.5 million subscribers
- Sept 99 Reports 3rd Q Operating Loss of $24.9M on revenue of $8.6M. 2.7 million members and 11.6 million subscribers
- Dec 99 Reports 4th Q Operating Loss of $26.0M on revenue of $16.7M. Full year Operating Loss is $82.1M on revenue of $36.6M. 4.2 million members and 10.9 million subscribers

- Mar 00 Reports 1st Q Operating Loss of $22.0M on revenue of $18.1M. 4.9 million members and 11.9 million subscribers
- Mar 00 Chief Operating Officer resigns
- May 00 Sale of Baby.com announced
- June 00 Reports 2nd Q Operating Loss of $28.0M on revenue of $19.4M. 5.0 million members and 15.4 million subscribers. Has a reach of 10.2%
- July 00 Douglas McCormick named CEO. Carpenter becomes Chair.
- July 00 Women comprise 50% of all Internet users

Women.com

1992	1993	1994	1995	1996	1997	1998	1999	2000

- 1992 Company founded by Ellen Pack
- 1993 Dial-Up Service
- 1994 Marleen McDaniel named Chairman and CEO
- 1994 First round of venture capital
- 1995 Women.com launched
- 1996 First Online Sponsorship with Levi Strauss
- 1997 Partnership with Media OpenRoad Runner, Hallmark, Crayola, Rodal Press
- 1998 Distribution agreements with AOL and Yahoo!
- 1998 Reports Operating Loss of $27.2M on revenue of $11.6M
- 1998 Exclusive agreement with Bloomberg Financial
- Nov 98 Introduces personalized service with launch of myWoman.com

- 1999 Initial Public Offering
- Jan 99 Exclusive agreement with Hearst Corporation, MSN Women Central, Harlequin Books and Disney Investments
- Mar 99 Reports 1st Q Loss of $10.0M on revenue of $3.6M
- June 99 Reports 2nd Q Loss of $11.0M on revenue of $6.0M
- Sep 99 Reports 3rd Q Loss of $10.3M on revenue of $7.2M
- Dec 99 Reports 4th Q Operating Loss of $3.0M on revenue of $13.3M. Reports 1999 Operating Loss of $34.4M on revenue of $30.2M

- 2000 Acquired e2sharing. Three millionth member signed up
- Mar 00 Reports 1st Q Operating Loss of $7.6M on revenue of $14.4M
- May 00 Women.com expands wireless content offering
- June 00 Reports 2nd Q Operating Loss of $9.4M on revenue of $12.3M

Oxygen.com

1992	1993	1994	1995	1996	1997	1998	1999	2000

- 1998 Founded by Geraldine Layboumein partnership with Marcy Carsey, Tom Werner, Caryn Mandabaderd, Oprah Winfrey
- Feb 2000 Oxygen.com launches on February 2, 2000

Exhibit 6 iVillage and Online Competitors

SITE	URL	UNIQUE VISITORS PER MONTH (OCTOBER 2000)	BUSINESS MODEL	CHANNELS (NOVEMBER 2000)	INVESTORS	OTHER ASSETS
iVillage	www.ivillage.com	8,438,000	Supported mainly through advertising and sponsorships. Membership registration	19 content channels	TCI, Kleiner Perkins Tribune Company	Partnership with NBC and Snap!
Women.com	www.women.com	8,349,000	Supported mainly through advertising and sponsorships. Membership registration	17 content channels	Hearst Magazines	Hearst magazines: *Cosmopolitan, Good Housekeeping, Redbook*, etc.
Oxygen	www.oxygen.com	Not Available	Supported mainly through advertising and sponsorships. Some E-commerce	14 content channels	Oprah Winfrey, America Online	Oxygen cable channel

Sources: Individual sites, October 2000, Media Metrix, iVillage Prospectus

Exhibit 7 Income Statement for Women.com

	Women.com Income Statement 1997–1999 ($ 000)		
	1999	**1998**	**1997**
Revenues	$30,023	$7,247	$2,798
Operating Expenses:			
Production, product & technology	$22,364	$5,728	$2,922
Sales and marketing	35,368	12,042	3,907
General and administrative	7,015	1,374	1,101
Stock based compensation	2,987	1,170	0
Depreciation and amortization	20,482	517	0
Total Operating Expenses	$88,216	$20,831	$7,930
Loss from Operations	−$58,193	−$13,584	−$5,132
Interest (expense) Income, Net	$ (35)	$ (57)	$ (117)
Other Income, Net	1,455	596	154
Net Loss	−$56,773	−$13,045	−$5,095
Dividend Accretion on Mandatory Redeemable Convertible Preferred Stock	−$295	−$570	−$1,517
Net Loss Attributable to Common Stockholders	−$57,068	−$13,615	−$6,612

Source: Women.com 1999 10-K

Exhibit 8 Leading Magazine Categories by Circulation

Number of Titles and Total Circulation by Magazine Category		
Category	**# of titles**	**Circulation**
Women's	32	48.9 million
General News	10	33.1 million
Home	21	31.2 million
Sports	22	18.3 million
Business/Money	16	11.1 million
Health/Fitness	9	8.2 million
Men's	9	8.0 million
Computers	15	7.8 million
Auto	12	6.3 million
Music/Entertainment	8	5.0 million
Cooking/Cuisine	6	4.7 million
Kids'	4	4.7 million
Travel	4	3.1 million

Source: *Advertising Age* and Salomon Smith Barney

Exhibit 9 Estimated Revenue by Magazine Category

Category	Total ($)	Advertising ($)	Circulation
Women's	3,543 million	2,370 million	1,173 million
General/News	3,759 million	2,254 million	1,475 million
Home	2,078 million	1,366 million	712 million
Busines/Money	3,136 million	1,341 million	1,795 million
Sports/Outdoor	1,798 million	1,167 million	631 million
Computers	1,460 million	1,153 million	307 million
Music/Entertainment	630 million	434 million	196 million
Auto	599 million	427 million	172 million
Men's	569 million	310 million	259 million
Health/Fitness	420 million	227 million	193 million
Cooking/Cuisine	303 million	187 million	116 million
Kids'	174 million	69 million	105 million
Travel	136 million	63 million	73 million

Source: *Advertising Age* and Salomon Smith Barney

Exhibit 10 Top 25 Women's Magazines in the United States (1998)

	1998 Rank	Advertising Revenue ($Millions)	Average Paid Per Issue
Top 25 Women's Magazines in the United States by Advertising Revenue–1998			
Better Homes & Gardens	5	$410.10	7,614,682
Good Housekeeping	11	242.31	4,551,296
Woman's Day	13	229.23	4,156,126
Family Circle	15	218.81	5,004,998
Cosmopolitan	16	214.09	2,675,123
Ladies' Home Journal	17	213.31	4,548,983
Glamour	19	150.18	2,186,283
Vogue	20	149.99	1,168,678
Martha Stewart Living	23	133.59	2,295,004
Southern Living	25	128.84	2,494,467
McCall's	26	122.19	4,221,216
Redbook	27	121.14	2,861,200
Parents	30	107.92	1,742,226
Elle	31	105.88	958,295
In Style	34	90.64	1,207,777
Country Living	36	90.28	1,676,007
Seventeen	37	89.73	2,426,461
W	41	87.56	N/A
Bride's	42	83.52	N/A
Parenting	43	81.05	1,239,152
Modern Bride	44	80.90	N/A
Harper's Bazaar	45	78.25	N/A
Self	48	71.26	N/A
Sunset	49	68.92	N/A

Source: Magazine Publishers of America

Exhibit 11 iVillage.com Income Statement, 1995–1999 (in thousands)

	1999	1998	1997	1996	1995
iVillage.com **Income Statement** **1995–1999** **($ 000)**					
Revenues	$36,576	$15,012	$6,019	$732	$0
Operating Expenses:					
Production, product & technology	$20,652	$14,521	$7,606	$4,521	$629
Sales and marketing	63,526	28,523	8,771	2,709	329
General and administrative	13,165	10,612	7,841	3,104	656
Depreciation and amortization	25,720	5,683	2,886	109	17
Total Operating Expenses	$123,063	$59,339	$27,104	$10,443	$1,631
Loss from Operations	−$86,487	−$44,327	−$21,085	−$9,711	−$1,631
Interest (expense) Income, Net	$ 4,085	$ 591	$ (216)	$ 28	$ (7)
Loss on sale of Web Site	0	−504	0	0	0
Other Income	271	0	0	0	0
Minority Interest	0	586	0	0	0
Net Loss	−$82,130	−$43,654	−$21,301	−$9,683	−$1,638

Source: iVillage Prospectus and annual report

first direct (A)

What is first direct?
A higher form of banking
Where technology is a means to an end
Not an end in itself
Where time is conquered
24 hours a day
You're too busy working
To be busy banking
Life can be messy
Make it neater
Eliminating stress
By talking
Not lecturing
A gateway to freedom
Along the phone line
365 days a year
Even in the middle of the night
Helping you control your affairs
(and rule the world)
. . . without fail
And always at a fair price
So you can get on with your life
You can't touch us
You can't see us
But we're always here
Where kids play
While their parents work
Britain's hardest working bank
Feared by its competitors
Loved by its customers
Britain's hardest working bank
Invented for people not bankers.
—from "first direct—the movie"
produced for first direct by Chiat/Day

On the seventh anniversary of first direct's launch, Kevin Newman, the bank's 39-year-old chief executive, sat in the company cafeteria and reflected on his organization's progress to date and the challenges ahead. Newman had been a member of the original development team that established the business case for first direct within its parent organization, Midland Bank PLC,[1] and part of the first direct launch team, which in 1989 introduced 24-hour direct banking by telephone to the United Kingdom. By 1996, first direct was the largest "virtual" bank in the world, with over 630,000 current account[2] customers and a growth rate of 12,000 new customers per month, with no physical branches. Moreover, first direct achieved the highest service quality ratings of any bank in the United Kingdom.

Newman was pleased with the company's success to date. first direct had become profitable in 1994 and operated profitably since then. He expected operating income to exceed £10 million in 1996. But growth presented new challenges. During the previous two years, first direct had added roughly 120,000 customers a year—making it the fastest growing bank in the United Kingdom—which strained existing bank capacity. This put Newman under pressure to address issues related to how first direct would orchestrate its future growth. One immediate need was expansion of the centralized telephone operations at its sites in Leeds. Leeds had emerged in the early 1990s as the new center for financial services and high technology businesses in the United Kingdom; first direct had two phone centers there, one at Stourton and another at Arlington. Adding a third site in another part of the country seemed appealing by allowing the bank to tap other labor markets, but Newman wondered about the long-term impact on the company's service culture. Was it important to concentrate phone center operations around headquarters? Was it viable to draw all labor from a single city market? Would changes in technology alter the bank's labor needs?

first direct also had to consider the impact of increasing competition in direct banking as more and more competitors attempted to replicate its business model. Management also had to consider if organic growth from internal operations would be sufficient to meet

Research Associate Dickson L. Louie prepared this case under the supervision of Professor Jeffrey F. Rayport as the basis for class discussion rather than to illustrate either effective or ineffective handling of an administrative situation.

[1]Midland PLC was owned by the Hong Kong & Shanghai Banking Corporation.
[2]Current accounts were the equivalent of checking accounts in the United States.

demand, or if new channels or acquisitions would be appropriate.

These questions were critical, given Newman's stated goal. He had committed the organization to reaching one million customers by the year 2000. Implicit in this commitment was the idea that first direct would continue to offer the highest quality service of any bank—physical or direct—in its national market. Service quality was first direct's competitive advantage and resulted from a company-wide commitment to six core values—individual contribution, openness, respect, responsiveness, getting it right the first time, and kaizen[3]—and maintaining that commitment, regardless of growth, was essential to preserving the firm's status as a premier service company in Great Britain's financial services sector.

Project Raincloud

first direct was a subsidiary of Midland Bank, one of the four major—or "High Street"[4]—banks in the United Kingdom, along with Barclays Bank, Lloyds Bank, and National Westminster Bank (NatWest). In the late 1980s, the entire U.K. retail banking sector suffered poor reputations for service. Research from the U.K.'s Henley Center for Forecasting showed that retail banks scored lowest on service quality among all retail sectors in the United Kingdom. In addition to industry-wide concerns, Midland Bank had other problems. In 1988, Midland suffered significant losses (of £505 million), following write-offs related to the acquisition of Crocker National Bank in the United States and bad loans made to Third World countries. According to one executive, "The image of Midland was pretty bad in the late 1980s, and its reputation was way down there."

In June 1988, Midland chartered a task force to investigate options for re-positioning itself, including the possibility of new service channels. The project team, called "Project Raincloud," had a dual mandate: to find a viable alternative to branch banking and to devise a new approach to banking that put the customer first. After extensive research and analysis of consumer trends and preferences, the project team discovered that Midland

account holders were making decreasing use of the branch network. The research[5] showed that:

- 40% had not visited their branch in the last week (20% in the last month);
- 41% would rather visit their branch as little as possible;
- 48% had never met their branch manager; and
- 38% found it difficult to get to their bank during its business hours.

The most common bank transactions—withdrawing cash, making deposits, and paying bills—often did not require any type of personal interaction between account holders and staff. Transactions which required face-to-face interaction, such as obtaining foreign currency, arranging a loan or overdraft, or seeking financial advice, were relatively low in volume (see Exhibit 1 for bank usage by transaction type).

Even so, the research also revealed that account holders still put a premium on personal service and attention. Although many bank customers had never met their branch manager, almost 90% thought it was important to be able to see the manager when the need arose. And while 27% said they would like to do more business over the phone, 76% said they would prefer to speak with an individual instead of a computer or voice response unit when they called. The research also showed that consumers wanted to deal with friendly and knowledgeable staff, to have access to the bank during convenient opening hours, and to have the means to conclude transactions quickly and easily.

Finally, the research team asked if consumers would be interested in a person-to-person, 24-hour, 7-day-a-week telephone banking service, which was still an untested idea in the United Kingdom at the time. Fifty-six percent of respondents expressed some interest, of whom nearly half, or 25% of the sample, said they would be very interested The interest was greatest among certain customer groups: women; people who were heavy automated teller machine (ATM) users; and people who felt less organized regarding personal financial matters.

As David Hollely, director of mortgages at first direct and an early post-launch recruit, observed, "The concept for first direct was researched a lot. We found that you could have this service without a branch network. The

---

[3] "Kaizen" means "continuous improvement" in Japanese.
[4] Large commercial banks in the United Kingdom were known as "High Street" banks, because every town had a "High Street" where the branches of the banks were commonly located.

---

[5] Project Raincloud internal memo, summary of research findings, August 1989.

research showed that people no longer visited their branches nor saw their branch managers."

Using this research as a guide, Project Raincloud refined the concept of person-to-person banking services by telephone. Fifteen months after it started, Project Raincloud was prepared to become first direct.

Creating the Person-to-Person Banking Relationship at first direct

Please do not be alarmed. This is the first attempt to communicate across time. This experiment is being sponsored by first direct to celebrate our 21st anniversary; for us, it is the year 2010. To celebrate the 21st anniversary of first direct, we have returned to the date of our launch. We return you now to your programs with best wishes for your personal happiness in your own future.

—Television Commercial Spot
Launch of first direct
Midnight, October 1, 1989

At one minute past midnight on Sunday, October 1, 1989, first direct opened its phone lines to the public. At the same moment, a futuristic television commercial prepared by the advertising agency of Howell Henry Childecott Lury appeared across television screens throughout Britain, promoting first direct's new banking services. This attention-getting commercial was portrayed as a message from the year 2010, or 21 years after the launch of first direct, to report that the concept of telephone banking was widely accepted a generation later.

In its first 24 hours of operation, first direct took in over 1,000 phone calls at its Arlington site. By year-end 1990, the customer base had grown to 60,000; by year-end 1993, 360,000; and by year-end 1995, 580,000. (See Exhibit 2 for first direct's account growth history.) Kevin Newman, who had been the bank's director of information technology, became its CEO in October 1991. Under Newman's leadership, the bank continued to emphasize high quality service as its distinguishing feature. Newman recalled, "When we started out in 1989, we thought, how could we differentiate ourselves—would it be on product or would it be on technology? We convinced ourselves that the only point where we could differentiate ourselves would be on service."

Executives at the parent company, Midland Bank, had determined to brand first direct separately, partly to allay fears that any direct association with Midland might give the new entity an unfavorable image and partly to allow the first direct brand to develop as a corporate entity without any organizational "baggage." Midland, like the other High Street banks, had distinctly poor customer satisfaction levels associated with its retail banking operations. "You've got to credit Midland for deciding to build a separate brand image for first direct," observed one executive.

To be successful, Newman and other managers at first direct believed they needed to provide intense personalization of service at very low cost. They planned to achieve this high level of personalized service using new human resources strategies, sophisticated customer information systems, and widely accepted communications technologies. Observed Newman:

The scenario that we might measure ourselves against would be that of the personal banker. Let's say that if we went to college together or saw each other at the club, you would have confidence in me as your banker. If there was an investment opportunity, I would give you a call on what to do. That's the idea of a great financial services provider and it still works today in private banking—the only downside is that it is quite expensive to provide [to everyone].

When you pull back and look at the three key components of a personal banking relationship, there are data, communications, and trust. Those are the fundamental elements of an individual relationship that we are trying to provide, but in a different way. We provide data—financial data, propensity [preference] data, even attitudinal data—for an individual customer through information technology. As a service organization, this data management is an absolute must—the foundation of our success. The second component is communications. We don't use voice response units to answer our phones; we feel that a highly trained person at the end of the phone is the optimal form of communication. The third component is trust. How do you get trust? Not easily. Going the extra mile and looking at service from the customers' perspective. The customer may not always be right, but [he or she] always comes first and you have to do a lot to make it right . . . .

If we are able to do these three things and in many ways replicate the paradigm of individual banking relationships on a mass basis and at a fraction of the cost, we can pass on the savings to stockholders and to customers.

Newman believed that the key reason first direct was able to successfully replicate the personal banking relationship in a direct channel was its people, especially the "Banking Representatives" who handled all phone calls, and the "six core values" that defined the bank's working culture. (See Exhibit 3 for a list and definition of these values.) Added Matthew Higgins, Market Planning Manager:

> Something like 90% of customers tell us that we offer a more personalized service than their previous bank. And the interesting thing is that they're not seeing anybody and they're talking with a different person each time they call. We don't offer people personalized account managers, but, hopefully, every time they ring up, they get the same high level of service. All banking activity and detail is on the screen, so the banking representative knows what the customer asked the prior week and if the problem has already been resolved.

In fact, according to a National Opinion Polls (NOP) survey of current account holders in the United Kingdom, approximately 90% of the customers surveyed said they were extremely or very satisfied with first direct (see Table A below). Quarterly internal surveys also indicated a consistently high level of customer satisfaction: almost 90% of first direct customers said they would not transfer back to their previous bank, even if it offered a similar service to first direct's. Over 90% reported that they had recommended first direct to others—and, of those, over half had recommended first direct two or three times.

As Higgins observed, however, first direct's positive impact on customers derived as much from what the rest of the industry was *not* getting right as it did from first direct's apparently successful formula. Noted Higgins:

> In terms of the banking service industry, we're starting from a fairly low threshold. A lot of our customers [coming from other banks] are surprised and delighted at first that we generally get things right. When someone picks up the phone at first direct, they sound interested and warm. That makes a lot of difference to a lot of people. Our satisfaction levels are high; for a High Street bank, the satisfaction levels are still about 40%. People simply expect banks [in the United Kingdom] not to have very good service.

The first direct Customer

I'm going to have a place for my money I can call both night and day.
I'm going to speak to intelligent people there who will do anything I say.
They can give me instant decisions.
I get an overdraft automatically.

Table A Customer Satisfaction

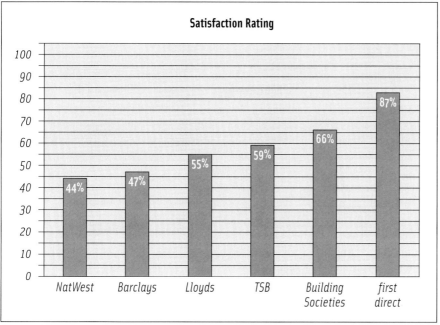

Source: NOP January 1996

first direct will be wonderful for you and me.
They don't have any branches.
They can spend more on their service you see.
first direct will be wonderful for you and me.
And it's free.
—Television Commercial, 1991
Optimistic View of first direct

Consumers interested in opening an account at first direct could dial a toll free number (0800-24-24-24) or mail a response form from a newspaper advertisement or direct mail piece to begin the process of submitting an account application. According to internal surveys (see Exhibit 4 for sources of new account acquisitions), since launch, 18% of first direct customers came through newspaper advertisements, 26% from direct mail solicitation, and 29% from customer recommendations. In the most recent 12-month period, direct mail accounted for almost 40% of acquisitions, and referrals accounted for 32%.

Direct mail pieces gave prospective customers an opportunity to open a checking account at first direct with a premium offer, such as a credit of £15, while newspaper advertisements (see Exhibits 5 and 6) emphasized the benefits of opening a first direct account in a pointed but humorous way ("Change your life/Change your bank"). In all of first direct's promotional material, the bank's colors of black and white were emphasized, reflecting the bank's underlying philosophy of "no small print" and "clear as black and white."

Not surprisingly, since launch, approximately two-thirds of first direct's customers came from the High Street banks—Midland, Barclays, NatWest, and Lloyds (see Exhibit 7). At first, many of the High Street banks were skeptical of the concept of telephone banking. Observed Higgins:

In the early days, the High Street banks said that the concept of first direct wasn't going to work as no one is going to be confident about doing business over the telephone. I hate to say, "I told you so," but that's the way it is with over 650,000 customers, almost exclusively from transfer banking—so our customers are not new to banking. There are two reasons for that. First, direct banking is still young and, second, it attracts a certain type of person—usually young professionals—who are comfortable about doing business over the telephone. first direct is now being copied by a new competitor virtually every week.

first direct's customers were both younger and more affluent than High Street bank customers (see Exhibit 8). Almost two-thirds of first direct's account holders were between the ages of 25 and 44. 86% owned their own homes and approximately one-third of account holders had household incomes in excess of £20,000 per year, compared with an average of less than a quarter of all banking customers with household incomes over this amount.

New applicants to first direct were screened and approximately 35% of all applicants were rejected, based on credit scoring. Applicants meeting first direct credit standards received 25 checks guaranteed up to £100 each, an automatic overdraft of £250, and an ATM card with which an individual could withdraw up to £500 per day. Guy Davis, Director of Credit, noted:

We screen out people because we have to. With our check guarantee card and checks you could write 25 checks at £100. That's like providing you with a loan of £2,500. The other reason for screening people is that if we are willing to loan people that much money, do we want to get into a relationship, where the answer to a future credit request is 'no'? It's better to terminate the relationship early on, rather than six to nine months later when you have a dissatisfied customer.

A first direct customer could deposit money into a checking account in three ways: by sending a check to first direct at a Leeds lockbox; by depositing money through ATMs; or by transferring money over the phone from one account to another. Cash could be withdrawn through either a phone transfer or through the ATMs operated by Midland, NatWest, and other major banks. When verifying a customer's identity over the phone, customers were required to tell the Banking Representative two letters of their chosen password and then answer one of five questions related to the customer's personal history.

New customers to first direct received a black welcome box (see Exhibit 9), specially designed to provide convenient storage for everything an account holder needed to manage his or her account, with the capacity to hold all bank-related information, including monthly bank statements. Approximately 95% of new accounts were opened as checking accounts; the other 5% were savings accounts. Checking accounts served as a gateway for cross-selling opportunities of other banking products such as VISA credit cards, savings accounts, and loans or mortgages offered by the bank's various business units. Noted Brian Carney, Director of Finance and Operations:

> The actual checking account is sort of a loss leader. It is the key point of acquisition. The principal products on which we get payback would be credit balances, the spread between savings and mortgages, and fees. Individual add-on products that we would cross-sell would be the secured loans, the savings accounts, and the competitive VISA card.

This portfolio of multiple banking products (see Exhibit 10) offered first direct an opportunity to increase the lifetime value of its customers. Over 95% of all first direct customers had been retained since launch. Internal surveys showed that a significant minority of first direct customers also held financial products at other banks or with a building society. The most common reasons for holding financial products with other financial institutions included categories of response, such as personal preference, too inconvenient to move, established institution, and credit history with the financial institution.

Upselling and service follow-through benefited first direct. One example was the increasing number in the amount of personal loans made by first direct to its customers—contributing to the Bank's profitability with increased interest revenue. Usually loan requests were generated either through direct mail pieces or from calls transferred from the Customer Service area to the Lending area. A typical loan usually took seven minutes to process. Noted Steven Townsend, Head of Lending:

> We sell only to our customers. We don't sell to anyone else, and there are several reasons why. One, the risk profile is good. Two, we've got a great deal of knowledge about the customer. Our processing costs and rejection rates are low.

One reasonably typical customer was Marcus J.J. Fedder, risk management director at an investment bank in London, who had been an account holder with first direct since its inception. Prior to first direct, Fedder had banked with NatWest and Midland. He commented:

> I was fed up with the slow service at the local bank branches. first direct's service is very good and always open—24 hours a day and 365 days a year. Their people are knowledgeable and friendly. Their rates are competitive and they have a good product range. I've referred about 10 of my friends to bank with first direct and some are now banking with them.[6]

---

[6]Interview with case writer, November 1996.

The Front Line

I've never actually seen the people at first direct. But I believe—I believe—they exist.
—Television commercial, 1992
first direct customer

"Our organization chart is upside down and our front line people are our most important assets," said Newman. "Their attitude and frame of mind distinguishes us from our competitors. That can only exist based on how the organization treats them. Customer service and company culture are two sides of the same coin." (See Exhibit 11.)

Almost 1,600 of first direct's 2,500 employees, or about two-thirds of its workforce, were front-line employees who dealt directly with customers on the telephone, either in the main call centers or in the specialized business units—mortgages, unsecured loans, and investments—offering specialized financial products. The frontline employees were trained to be attentive to the customer's needs and to listen for any cross-selling opportunities. Noted Guy Davis, who headed first direct's Customer Service area (see Exhibit 12):

> We may communicate in different ways to different customers. Some customers know what they want; others do not. The Banking Representatives are trained to pick up the pace and style of the customer they are dealing with as they are listening to the call. If you have five calls making a bill payment, each of those five calls will be slightly different based upon the interaction with the Banking Representative. A customer who is careful and cautious may check a balance and then want to ask about a series of transactions to see if it's in or not in that balance and then decide if and when they want to make an account transfer. Another customer may simply want to check if they've overdrawn their limit and that may only take 20 seconds. With five calls, each will be slightly different. That's how you get 1,600 people thinking and delivering the kind of service that first direct wants to deliver. You have to train people to listen—and use the information about customers our systems provide them. You can't do it by pronouncement by me or Kevin Newman.

Banking Representatives were trained to add relevant information, such as the purchase of a new house or the birth of a new baby, to a customer's profile in first direct's database (see Exhibit 13). In addition, customer profile modeling also supported the cross-selling of first direct's products. Added Davis:

> The screen in front of the Banking Representative is supported by models that predict what type of information the customer might be interested in—such as a traveler's check. What we know about the customer comes from modeling or from behavior—we would ask them in a conversation if they are interested in foreign currency, knowing that they were going on holiday, from their responses or from their profile. In modeling, we go beyond the typical demographics. We look at how risk-tolerant these customers are, how many products they buy, and what lifestage they are at now. We adopt different approaches and strategies to attract different customers.

A majority of Banking Representatives at first direct were women—many working mothers and housewives who were attracted by the bank's flexible hours, casual work environment, and child care centers located at both of first direct's sites. All Banking Representatives went through an initial training program, staying with the same team of 12 members and two trainers during a seven-week period. Prior banking experience was not required. Commented Davis:

> You do not need a banking background to be a Banking Representative. We get disaffected teachers. We get housewives and mothers who want to come back to work. We're looking for aptitude and personality—people who can communicate well, people who have a level of confidence and independence, and people who can make a decision to do it right the first time. We look for people who want to have a challenge. Say, the clock is ticking and the customer is angry and has to catch a train in two minutes. The Banking Representative needs to know how to respond.

After the initial training program was completed, the Banking Representatives assumed jobs in the call centers but they received additional training after a nine month period. first direct employees had a remuneration package which was in the top quartile of companies in the Leeds area; the package included a mortgage supplement and a bonus plan. In keeping with the core value of "openness," all employees at first direct were compensated with similar employee benefits. According to David Mead, director of personnel:

> Everyone is in the same pension, health, and life insurance plans, and bonuses are equal among the various units. We want to make sure that our status-

free concept is reflected in our rewards system. We're trying to create a sense of sharing as well as a sense of belonging. And unless you can create that sense of sharing in the profits of your business, then you don't deserve the high level of commitment and motivation of your people. The rewards policy that we adopt is a sense of sharing.

Front line employees in the call centers and business units were divided into teams—team names included "The King Pins," "The Top Kats," and "The Bank Robbers"—who often put their performance results on display on the "trading floor"—a large open area of terminals and desks—to provide other people in the company a sense of how their individual team was performing. Each team, except for several self-managed teams, had a team leader whose job was to inspire, motivate, and develop individual members. Team leaders, part-psychologist, part-resource manager, and part-preacher of the company's gospel on customer service, were often chosen by first direct's assessment center, which consisted of groups of first direct managers who evaluated personnel.

first direct's Infrastructure

> You've heard 'bout first direct.
> Won't work, I'm sure.
> They said they're a new kind of banking.
> No branches no more.
> But we've had branches for years.
> What they changin' it for?
> They say you can call their people 24 hours a day.
> They're far too new and different.
> They'll close down right away—Like tomorrow, honey.
> They're not an old institution.
> That's where my money stays.
> —Television Commercial, 1991
> Pessimistic View of first direct

While the front end of first direct's information system—the portion that provided the interface with the bank's customer—was new to U.K. banking, the financial systems infrastructure was outsourced to Midland Bank (see Exhibit 14). For example, first direct customers deposited and withdrew cash from Midland's ATMs and had their monthly bank statements processed and printed by Midland. Noted Andrew Arnishaw, director of information technology:

The biggest differentiation that we offer when you phone us is service—you don't get the traditional response typical of a U.K. bank. You are treated as a customer. Individually, we know if you've been on holiday, we know if you've purchased traveler's checks. We can create the mythical bank manager relationship that probably didn't exist for everyone anyway. The reverse side of this, which is sort of a halo effect that we have, is that the research shows that our customers rank the quality of "our" ATMs 15 to 20 points higher than Midland Bank customers yet physically it's the same machines.

Indeed, the cost structure of first direct differed from the cost structure of a typical High Street bank (see Exhibit 15). With less money allocated to overhead, a greater portion was devoted to marketing and brand-building. Using Midland Bank's infrastructure on a leased capacity basis, first direct avoided spending "megabucks" to develop its own account-management and data- and payment-processing systems. Instead, first direct's biggest investment was in "developing the brand," said Carney. "The second biggest investment would be building the front-end system, and the third largest building the skills sets and training" of the Banking Representatives.

Although specific financial results were not publicly available, Newman noted that first direct's "return on capital and equity is extremely attractive and the return on the substantial investment made in any year is geared to long-term rather than short-term profits."

Competition

"Tell me one good thing about your bank."
—first direct advertising campaign, 1995

The growth of first direct demonstrated that, with the use of technology, banking services could be distributed over electronic channels instead of physical bank locations. As a result of first direct's success, other banking concerns, financial services companies, and general merchandise retailers had joined the growing field of direct financial services providers.

Other Banking Concerns. Most banking concerns in the United Kingdom offered telephone banking services in three ways: human operators, touch-tone keypads, and voice response units. Product offerings and hours of service varied for each bank, ranging from full 24-hour service to limited weekday service, abbreviated to the

prime time hours from 8 a.m. to 8 p.m. (see Exhibit 16). The three most aggressive of first direct's competitors were the Royal Bank of Scotland's Direct Line (whose initial direct service was motor insurance; later it added direct banking services), Citibank Direct, and the Bank of Scotland's Banking Direct, all of which offered 24-hour, person-to-person banking and a full array of financial products.

Financial Services Companies. The largest provider of direct financial services in the United Kingdom was Direct Line, owned by the Royal Bank of Scotland. With a customer base between 2.5 and 3 million account holders of merchant and household insurance, Direct Line had acquired a banking license in 1995 which enabled it to expand its product portfolio to include mortgages and savings accounts. Direct Line had a strong brand image in the United Kingdom made famous by an icon of a red telephone on wheels featured in its advertisements, though Direct Line was often confused with first direct. Another potential competitor in the direct financial services market was Virgin Direct, led by Virgin entrepreneur Richard Branson, who had begun to offer life insurance and personal savings accounts for pensions beginning in July 1995. "People see Virgin as a little bit quirky and Branson as a champion of the underdog," said one first direct executive. "He wants to cut out the middleman. That's what people want. There are a lot of parallels with first direct."

Other Retailers. In addition to banks and financial services companies, retailers, such as the upscale Marks & Spencer department store, had also begun to offer banking services, such as loans and mortgages, through their telephone service operations and department store locations.

Future Opportunities

Looking to the future, senior management at first direct saw many opportunities for growth. Among these were increased cross-selling through improved data mining systems, offering banking by personal computer, or accepting a larger share of customer applications for accounts. Noted Stephen Robinson, head of sales and marketing:

Right now we're working on expanding the marketing database. We're doing overlays on the current database. By getting more data on customers, we're trying to reduce the cost of acquiring customers. We're also willing to spend more money on acquiring those customers with a higher lifetime value.

In addition, first direct's growth was fueled by the bank's entrance into retail finance markets. On January 1, 1997, first direct took over the loan portfolio business of Britain's Forward Trust Personal Finance Ltd., the consumer finance subsidiary of Forward Trust. The acquisition represented 420,000 new accounts for first direct. first direct renamed the service first direct Business to Business. This new unit offered secured lending to support first direct's product sales to consumers made by first direct's 20 newly designated business partners (the partners were retailers that bundled first direct financing packages with sales in sectors such as home improvement, home furnishings, and building societies). The new unit also offered loans marketed through employee benefit plans in U.K. companies. Noted Newman:

> We are entering the business-to-business market because we believe it will provide us opportunities to acquire customers through a new channel. When we launched in 1989, we set ourselves a clear goal of innovation in personal banking services; this is further evidence of this approach[7].

Senior management was also looking at ways to bring more customers, such as university students, into first direct at an earlier age. Observed one executive, "we're always looking at ways to expand our market base, and if getting these customers increases the lifetime value of our total customer population, we'll target them, even if the payoff is not as immediate."

---

[7]first direct press release, September 11, 1996.

Banking by personal computer presented another distribution channel for first direct, though only three million U.K. homes owned PCs. Two competitors had already launched PC banking. Said Higgins:

> We won't be the first, but we have the opportunity to be the first bank to do PC banking well and to get it right. Our first PC customers will be customers we already have and they will expect the same quality of service. It's important that we get it right. At the end of the day, it will just be another distribution channel, and it's the service behind it that will be important.

Lastly, Hong Kong & Shanghai Bank Corporation, parent of Midland Bank, was interested in the opportunities of replicating first direct's direct banking concept to other country markets around the globe.

Conclusion

As Newman walked down the sparse corridors of first direct's Stourton site, past the black and white posters from the bank's most recent advertising campaign, he was still pondering the key issues for the future. How might he best maintain first direct's preeminent customer service and still meet its goal of one million customers by the year 2000? In addition, he wondered what other ways, using the unique virtual channel to customers, first direct might augment the value it delivered to the market now and in the future.

Exhibit 1 Bank Usage by Transaction Type

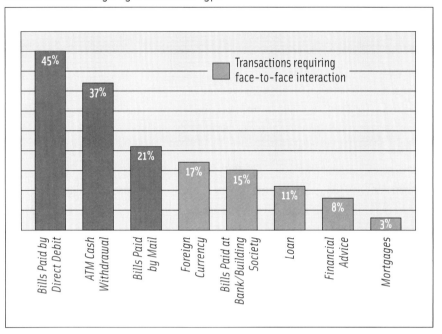

Exhibit 2 History of Bank Account Growth

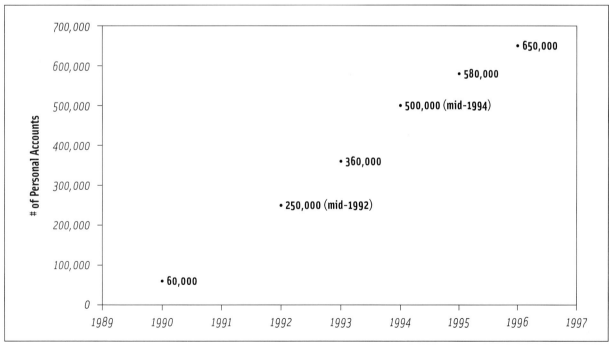

Source: first direct

Exhibit 3 Core Values

---

first direct's Core Values

In order to live the brand, we must practically define how this is to be achieved. We have identified six core cultural values of first direct, which shape and form the way we do things and why we do them. We all need to believe in and be committed to these values if we are to build the brand: which builds the business, which will become acknowledged as the best.

first direct's six core values are:

Responsive Responsive to our customers. Responsive to each individual. Responsive right now. Responsive as a company. Responsive to competitor weakness. Responsive to each other. Responsive in all we do.

Openness Always open. Open minded. Open plan. Open to new ideas. Open up. Open forum. Open to all. Open and honest.

Right first time Quality people. Quality research and design. Quality products. Quality systems. Quality control. Quality service. Quality loop.

Respect Respect yourself. Respect our customers. Respect each other.

Contribution Hard work. Commitment. Profit. Sharing. Mutual benefit.

Kaizen Continuous improvement.

Exhibit 4 Sources of Customer Acquisition

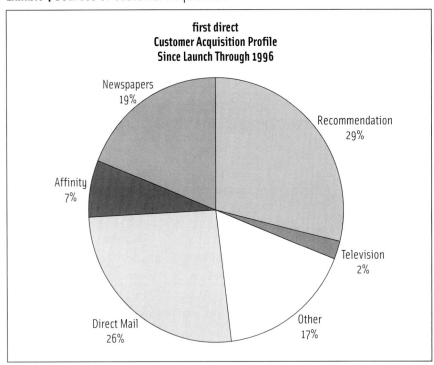

Source: first direct

Exhibit 5 Newspaper Advertisements

Exhibit 6 Newspaper Advertisements

Exhibit 7 Prior Financial Institutions of first direct Customers

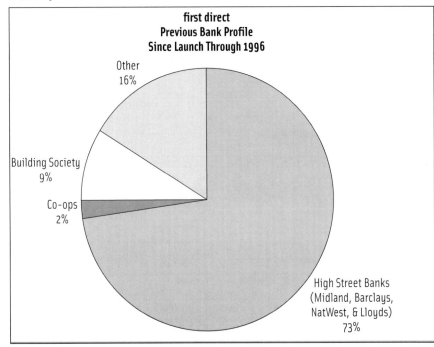

Source: first direct

Exhibit 8 Profile of first direct Account Holder

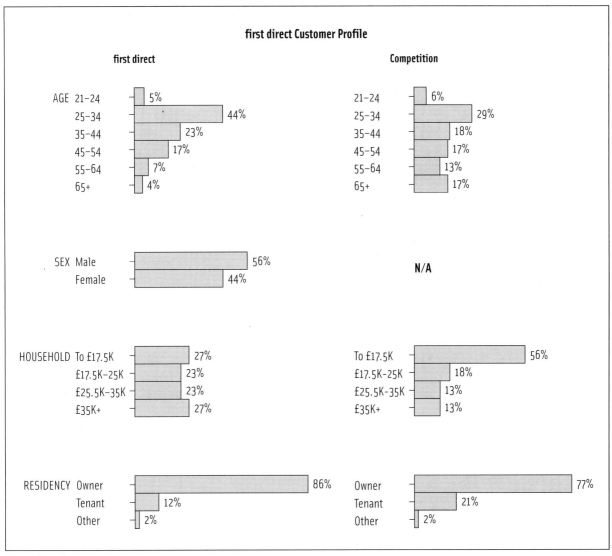

first direct Customer Profile

first direct	Competition

AGE
first direct		Competition	
21–24	5%	21–24	6%
25–34	44%	25–34	29%
35–44	23%	35–44	18%
45–54	17%	45–54	17%
55–64	7%	55–64	13%
65+	4%	65+	17%

SEX
first direct		Competition
Male	56%	N/A
Female	44%	

HOUSEHOLD
first direct		Competition	
To £17.5K	27%	To £17.5K	56%
£17.5K–25K	23%	£17.5K–25K	18%
£25.5K–35K	23%	£25.5K–35K	13%
£35K+	27%	£35K+	13%

RESIDENCY
first direct		Competition	
Owner	86%	Owner	77%
Tenant	12%	Tenant	21%
Other	2%	Other	2%

Source: first direct

Exhibit 9 Welcome Box Information

first direct in a box

black box

Produced as a result of our customers' suggestions, **black box** gives you the opportunity to organise all aspects of your financial affairs in a simple practical way by keeping everything in one place. It contains a section for each of our major service areas, as well as a place to file all your statements and credit and debit card receipts, and comes complete with several introductory brochures.

Each month, with your statements, we may send you further information about First Direct. We suggest that you use your black box as a library for this information.

statement and receipt holder

A clipboard is included to hold statements for all your accounts for up to two years. Please remember to keep them for a minimum of one full tax year. To help accurate checking of your statements there is a plastic pocket on the back of the holder for your credit/debit card receipts.

cheque book holder and card wallet

With our compliments.

calendar card

Use the calendar card to make a record of your key financial dates throughout the year. Never forget a policy renewal or review date again.

Cheque Account owner's manual

Tells you everything you need to know about your Cheque Account, including details of all the services and features it provides plus a look at the security measures you can take to safeguard your account.

service directory

An introduction to the wide range of services we can offer you, with the opportunity to obtain more detailed information about any service you happen to be interested in.

saving leaflet

Details our range of savings products, including the ideal Cheque Account partner - High Interest Savings Account.

Visa leaflet

All the facts about the First Direct Visa Card and how to apply for one, if you have not done so already.

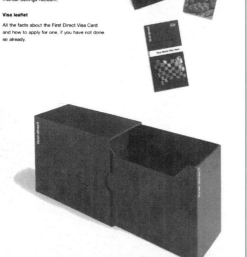

If you have any suggestions yourself regarding how we could improve black box in the future, we would be delighted to receive them. Call any time on **0345 100 100** or write to us at First Direct, FREEPOST, Leeds LS98 2RS.

Exhibit 10 Array of Bank Financial Products

Exhibit 11 Organizational Chart

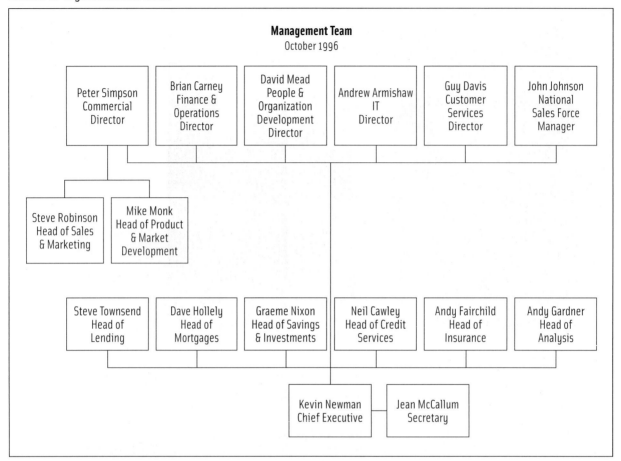

Management Team
October 1996

Peter Simpson
Commercial
Director

Brian Carney
Finance &
Operations
Director

David Mead
People &
Organization
Development
Director

Andrew Armishaw
IT
Director

Guy Davis
Customer
Services
Director

John Johnson
National
Sales Force
Manager

Steve Robinson
Head of Sales
& Marketing

Mike Monk
Head of Product
& Market
Development

Steve Townsend
Head of
Lending

Dave Hollely
Head of
Mortgages

Graeme Nixon
Head of Savings
& Investments

Neil Cawley
Head of Credit
Services

Andy Fairchild
Head of
Insurance

Andy Gardner
Head of
Analysis

Kevin Newman
Chief Executive

Jean McCallum
Secretary

Exhibit 12 Call Center, Stourton Site

Exhibit 13 On-Screen Customer Service Menu

EDGE-FRONT OFFICE MENU

LIVE	INTRODUCTION SCREEN	MAIN

SELECT: SERVICE REQUIRED

CUS01

VADAFLIV

SERVICES AVAILABLE FOR EXISTING ACCOUNTS

1 OPEN NEW ACCTS	11 A/C ENQUIRIES	21 AUTO TRANS	33 SALES STATUS
3 REQ FOR LIT	12 TRANSFERS	22 TRAVEL	34 ACTION REQUEST
4 VIEW AC TFR LET	13 A/C CHANGES	23 CUSTOMER DETAILS	36 ADD PRODUCTS
5 TAKE SEC DET	14 PAPS	24 PRODUCTS	
6 ORDER PINS	15 BILL PAYMENTS	25 ACTIONS	
7 PEPS	16 STOPS	26 NOTICE A/C WDL	
	17 CARDS	27 ACCOUNT DETAILS	
9 VIEW REF BOOK NOTES	18 STATEMENTS	29 EMERGENCY ENC	
10 OTHER SERVICES	19 CHQ/CR BOOKS	30 SPECIAL PRES	
	20 3RD PARTY TRANS		

ENTER

F1 CONTINUE	F5 REAL TIME MI
F2 SWITCH TO PROSPECT MENU	F6 OPERATIONS UTILITIES MENU
F3 LOAN QUOTATIONS	F7 CALL INTERRUPTED
F4 SYSTEMS UTILITIES	F8 QUE LIMITS

4   AV03   CAPS   S8 DEFS LOADED   70

F1		F3		F4		F9		SUBSET 0		F5		F6		F7		F8
F9		F10		F11		F12		SUBSET A		PAS/PAPS		ENQ		AUTOCCN		MAIN MENU

Exhibit 14 Interface/Midland Bank Infrastructure

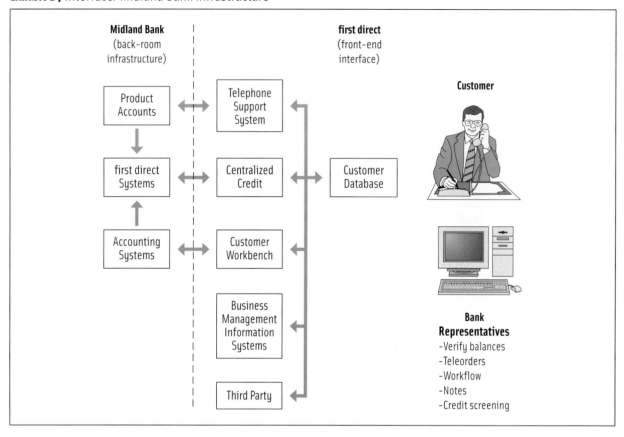

Exhibit 15 Revenue and Cost Structure

Revenue:	
Net Interest Income	54%
Commission/Fee Income	46%
Total Revenue	100%
Expenditures:	
Marketing (mainly brand-building and acquisition)	15%
Staff costs	45%
Midland Bank cross-charges (IT/Operations)	13%
Depreciation	4%
Other Operational Expenses	15%
Bad Debt Charge	8%
Total Expenditures	100%

Source: first direct

Exhibit 16 Product Offerings by Competitors

	first direct	Bank of Scotland Phoneline	Barclays Barclay Call	Citibank Citibank Direct	Direct Line Instant Access Savings
Service Proposition	Optional Servic Dedicated Telephone Bank	Optional Service Customer Subscribes	Optional Service Customer Subscribes	Optional Service Customer Subscribes	Part of Dedicated Telephone Operation
Method of Operation	Human Operator	Human Operator	Human Operator	Voice/Response then Human Operator	Human Operator
Hours of Operation	24 hours	6 a.m. to 1 a.m. weekdays 6 a.m. to mid. weekends	7 a.m. to 11 p.m. weekdays 9 a.m. to 4 p.m. Saturdays	24 hours	8 a.m. to 8 p.m. weekdays 8 a.m. to 5 p.m. Saturdays
Location	Leeds	Edinburgh	Coventry	Heminensmith	Glasgow
Balances	Yes	Yes	Yes	Yes	Yes
Stop Cheques	Yes	Yes	Yes	Yes	No
Transfers	Yes	Yes	Yes	No	No
Order Statements	Yes	Yes	Yes	Yes	No
Order Chequebooks	Yes	Yes	Yes	Yes	No
Bill Payment	Yes	Yes	Yes	No	No
Overdrafts	Yes	No	No	No	No
Loans	Yes	No	No	No	No
Credit Card Balances	Yes	No	Yes	Yes	No
Standing Orders	Yes	Yes	Yes	No	No
Direct Debits	Yes	Yes	Yes	No	No
Foreign Currency	Yes	No	Yes	No	No
Mortgages	Yes	No	No	No	No

	Lloyd's Lloydirect	Midland Bank CSC	NatWest Actionline	Royal Bank of Scotland Direct Banking	Scotland Bank Phonebank
Service Proposition	Optional Service Customer Subscribes	All Customers	Optional Service Customer Subscribes	Optional Service Customer Subscribes	Optional Service Customer Subscribes
Method of Operation	Human Operator	Human Operator	Automated Services	Human Operator	Human Operator
Hours of Operation	6 a.m. to 10 p.m. weekdays	8 a.m. to 8 p.m. weekdays 8 a.m. to 1 p.m. Saturday	24 hours	24 hours	24 hours
Location	Southend	Leeds/Swansea/Hemell	Bradford/Berkshire	Regiona Cermes	Newpost/Glasgow
Balances	Yes	Yes	Yes	Yes	Yes
Stop Cheques	Yes	Yes	No	Yes	No
Transfers	Yes	Yes	Yes	Yes	Yes
Order Statements	Yes	Yes	Yes	Yes	Yes
Order Chequebooks	Yes	Yes	Yes	Yes	Yes
Bill Payment	Yes	No	No	Yes	Yes
Overdrafts	No	No	No	No	Yes
Loans	No	No	No	No	Yes
Credit Card Balances	No	No	Yes	No	Yes
Standing Orders	Yes	Yes	No	Yes	Yes
Direct Debits	Yes	Yes	No	Yes	Set up/Cancel
Foreign Currency	Yes	Yes	No	No	Cancel
Mortgages	No	No	No	No	No

first direct (B)

first direct's unique banking model continued to appeal strongly to a new generation of consumers. Unexpectedly, Kevin Newman, first direct's CEO, left the bank in April 1997 to join Citicorp in New York as Global Delivery Director, where he became responsible for managing Citicorp's portfolio of electronic banking products throughout world markets. In November 1997, first direct named Andrew Armishaw, former IT Director, as Newman's successor.

Despite the leadership turnover, first direct by late 1997 had increased its customer base to over 800,000 account holders; the bank was adding 12,500 new customers a month; and it had captured 2% of the British retail banking market. first direct employed 4,000 people, fielding an average of 38,000 calls each weekday and 22,000 calls each day on the weekends. first direct attributed this steady growth, in part, to customer referrals: In December 1997, 87% of its customers reported that they had recommended the bank to a friend, and 29% of new customers joined the bank on a friend's recommendation.[1] Indeed, 97% of the bank's customers believed that first direct delivered better services than other banks.[2]

In order to accommodate a large and diverse customer base, first direct expanded its services into new channels. Steven Townsend, Head of Lending, described these developments as a strategy to be "what, when, and where" the first direct customer wanted.[3]

In June 1997, first direct launched a PC-banking service. To access the service, first direct customers dialed into the bank's Intranet, which was a secure, private network. first direct expected more than 50,000 customers to sign up for the service by year-end 1998. Site functionality included balance updates, direct debit bill payment, money transfers, e-mail inquiries, new account openings, loan and mortgage applications, travel insurance, and card replacement.

first direct also announced plans to build a new call center on a 33-acre site near Glasgow, Scotland, to accommodate the increased demand for its services. first direct selected Glasgow after conducting extensive consumer research. Originally, the bank's management believed that customers might react positively or negatively to various regional accents. As a result, it tested responses to banking representative accents associated with various potential call center locations in the United Kingdom and Ireland. Researchers concluded that customers responded not to regional accents so much as to the tone and warmth of representatives' voices. Having come to this conclusion, first direct focused on identifying a location that was abundant with well-educated, high-caliber, and available workers. Glasgow emerged as a natural match; it was an industrial city in which many industries had shut down, leaving it with a surfeit of unemployed, yet skilled and experienced, workers. According to Keith Whitson, Midland's CEO, the new call center would create 5,000 jobs over seven years, "expanding business well into the next century."[4]

first direct would complete the five-building Glasgow campus in stages, with an opening for the first structure in spring 1998.

Research Associate Carrie L. Ardito prepared this case under the supervision of Professor Jeffrey F. Rayport as the basis for class discussion rather than to illustrate either effective or ineffective handling of an administrative situation.

[1]Company Press Release, August 1997.
[2]Company Documents, December 1997.
[3]Casewriter interview with Steven Townsend, Head of Lending, first direct, January 21, 1998.
[4]Company Press Release, May 1997.

QVC, INC.

I don't think there's anyone at QVC who doesn't love this business and doesn't believe that we will change the way the world shops.

—Fred Siegel, Senior Vice President- Marketing

The last items of the 1996 Olympics merchandise appeared for sale on the QVC television screen. The show's host was broadcasting live at a remote site in Atlanta from the company's mobile television studio (dubbed "The QVC Local"). He spoke over the air to another show host, located at the main studios in West Chester, Pennsylvania, just outside of Philadelphia. With the order number for each item appearing at the top of the television screen, the price on the left side, and a toll free telephone number to call at the bottom, the show's host spoke to the viewing audience about the benefits of owning a replica of the warm-up, Champion-designed jacket worn by the U.S. Olympic team. Then he described the thrill of buying a special Dream Team Olympics T-shirt and purchasing a unique collector's Olympics pin set.

Having just celebrated its tenth anniversary in June 1996, executives at QVC were looking ahead to the electronic retailer's future. Over the preceding four years, the $1.6 billion franchise, available to 56.1 million cable and satellite TV households in the United States, had extended its lead over long-time rival, Home Shopping Network (HSN), in the highly competitive $4 billion TV home shopping market. At year-end 1992, both QVC and HSN were nearly equal in size on the basis of net revenue—defined as gross revenue after returns. But while HSN's net revenue had dropped from $1.1 billion to $1 billion between 1992 and 1995, QVC's net revenue grew at an average annual rate of 14% during the same period. Indeed, QVC had just celebrated its first $20 million day in January 1996 and shipped its 200 millionth package in March 1996.

Research Associate Dickson L. Louie prepared this case under the supervision of Professor Jeffrey F. Rayport as the basis for class discussion rather than to illustrate either effective or ineffective handling of an administrative situation.

History[1]

QVC was founded in 1986 by Joseph Segel, founder of the Franklin Mint, a multi-million dollar mail order company that sold commemorative coins, collectors' editions of fine books, and vintage model cars. Earlier that year, Segel had tuned into HSN, a pioneer of the televised shopping concept, and was unimpressed. The programming was crude, the products were down-market, and the proliferation of inexpensive jewelry turned him off. But Segel saw an opportunity to promote more upscale merchandise through higher quality programming using a distinctly different approach from that of HSN.

In November 1986, with $30 million in start-up capital and several seasoned television executives who had signed on, Segel began broadcasting the new QVC service from its headquarters in West Chester, Pennsylvania, and aimed to guide the company according to three customer-focused elements that constituted a new kind of value proposition: these were Quality, Value, and Convenience, comprising the initials of QVC. In its first full fiscal year, QVC established a record in American business history for revenues generated by a start-up public company, with sales in excess of $112 million.

The concept of televised shopping had originated in July 1977 in St. Petersburg, Florida, when Roy Speer, a radio operator, accepted a box of can openers as payment in kind from one of his advertisers who was unable to settle advertising bills in cash. To liquidate the can openers, Speer tried an experiment, asking a local disk jockey to offer them for sale on a radio talk show. The can openers sold out in minutes and Speer had spotted an opportunity.

Over the next two years, Speer and his partner, Lowell "Bud" Paxson, worked to transfer the shop-at-home concept from radio to television. In late 1982, HSN, a television network dedicated exclusively to home shopping programming, began transmitting from Tampa, Florida. In 1985, HSN expanded to cable-TV systems and satellite dish receivers across the United States, and this offering was called HSN1. HSN2, a separate programming signal,

---

[1]This section is based upon an earlier case, "The TV-Home Shopping Wars: QVC and Its Competitors," HBS case No. 395-014.

was introduced in 1987, carried part-time by both cable systems and broadcast-TV stations during channel downtimes, when regular programming was not scheduled. Sales growth for HSN paralleled its increase in household penetration. From 1988 to 1993, HSN's revenues increased from $13 million to over $1 billion. In fulfilling customer orders, HSN was able to compile a database of over five million households that had made purchases from the service.

In the meantime, under Segel's direction, QVC had grown rapidly, largely through acquisition, purchasing two of its largest competitors in 1990, the Cable Value Network (CVN) and J.C. Penney's TV home shopping network. In 1992, Barry Diller, the former chairman of Paramount Pictures and Fox Inc., saw the potential of TV home shopping as a gateway to interactive media and invested $25 million of his own personal wealth in the QVC network. In January 1993, Diller became chairman of QVC, replacing Segel, who retired.

During Diller's tenure, with Douglas Briggs as president, the company overtook its long-time rival HSN. While both companies reached nearly $1.1 billion in net revenue in 1992, QVC's net revenues rose to $1.2 billion in 1993 and $1.4 billion in 1994, while HSN's net revenues remained flat at $1.1 billion. Under Diller's and Brigg's leadership, QVC pursued several ventures to expand the company's marketing efforts and viewership. They launched a joint venture with Rupert Murdoch's British Sky Broadcasting in the United Kingdom in October 1993, resulting in a British version of the QVC shopping channel. Diller and Briggs also launched Q2, a sister retail channel aimed at more upscale audiences, in April 1994, which involved separate production operations in new studios established in Long Island City, New York. And Briggs masterminded "The Quest for America's Best—QVC's 50 in 50 Tour," a year-long search to discover a thousand of the best new products from American entrepreneurs; the "quest" took shape in September 1994 with a mobile TV studio—the "QVC Local"—that would tour America, running local product competitions and then national shows featuring the winning products. These events and shows were slated to take place in 50 states in 50 weeks.

In February 1995, two of the nation's largest cable-TV operators, Comcast Corporation and Telecommunications, Inc., acquired QVC, with Comcast assuming the majority position. Diller had attempted to use QVC as his base to acquire two major media properties, the CBS television network, and Paramount, the movie studio. Both bids failed; CBS was ultimately sold to Westing

house and Paramount to Viacom. Diller left subsequently and assumed the helm of rival HSN in November 1995. Briggs, a long-time QVC veteran, replaced Diller as head of the electronic retailer.

By late 1995—almost ten years after QVC's founding and almost 20 years after the concept of televised shopping began—net sales for the televised shopping market in the United States had risen to $4 billion. The key competitors in the marketplace were QVC, which had $1.6 billion in revenues and 40% market share, and HSN, which had $1 billion in revenues and 25% market share (see Exhibit 1 for a comparison of the two retail channels' net revenues). With net sales of $1.6 billion in 1995, QVC had already exceeded several well-known retailers in its scale of operations, including Bloomingdale's and Saks Fifth Avenue.

The Changing Shopping Environment[2]

By 1996, 20 years of lifestyle and demographic changes were reflected in evolving shopping formats. The most widely heralded change was the growing number of women entering the workforce, and thus the large number of dual-income families. Also, the number of teenagers and young adults, a group more inclined to embrace electronic shopping and interactive television, was expected to become significant in the late 1990's.

Department store sales increased from nearly $127 billion in 1985 to $218 billion in 1994, yet they lost market share to discount stores, warehouse clubs, manufacturers' outlet stores, and specialty retail stores. Many department stores were downsized, restructured, and remerchandised to emphasize fashion apparel. As department stores declined and consolidated, specialty apparel and accessory stores posted increased sales from $70 billion in 1985 to $110 billion in 1994. Specialty retailers, such as computer stores, home improvement outlets, and book retailers, grew even more dramatically from $184 billion in 1985 to $337 billion in 1994.[3]

Consumers were expected to spend roughly $80 billion on catalog sales in 1995, compared to $51.5 billion in 1992. In 1994, more than 10,000 mail-order companies sent out 12.8 billion catalogs and about 61% of the adult population purchased consumer goods through the mail. The growth of catalog retailing could be explained by an increase in dissatisfaction with

[2]Ibid.
[3]United States Department of Commerce, *Statistical Abstract of the United States*, 1995.

traditional shopping environments. Consumers cited many reasons for their displeasure, including lack of adequate parking, poor service, long lines, and growing crime rates. Approximately one half of all adults surveyed in 1996 agreed that shopping in stores was an "unpleasant chore that they avoided doing whenever possible."[4]

The appeal of televised shopping, like catalog shopping, was the opportunity to avoid many of these ills. At the same time, quality, price, and convenience were emphasized by consumers as reasons specifically for televised shopping, although many potential customers often viewed the medium as a channel that offered lower quality merchandise. Some attributed the rise in popularity of televised shopping to consumers' increasing comfort with technology. In 1995, approximately 11% of all U.S. adults had purchased on one of the televised shopping channels, and 8% from an infomercial (see purchase rates by marketing channel in Exhibit 2). Many consumers, particularly those with computers and VCRs, perceived that new technology could become a personal tool. Estimates for retail revenues occurring over the Internet—an electronic retail channel—ranged from $200 million to $2.5 billion during 1995, either of which was less than one percent of all retail sales for the same year.[5] Though small in number—8% of consumers had made a purchase through the Internet in 1995—the purchase rate was twice that for the segment of the population that was 18 to 35 years of age. Estimates projected that retail sales on the Internet would grow to $165 billion[6] by the year 2000.

QVC vs. HSN

Although the audience reach for both HSN and QVC was more than half of U.S. households, there were several key differences between QVC's and HSN's customer profiles. For example, the average annual dollar purchase of a QVC customer was 50% greater than that of an HSN customer; 10% more QVC customers made repeat purchases within 12 months than HSN customers; and the merchandise mix for QVC was less dependent on jewelry sales than was HSN's. Jewelry sales made up one-third of QVC's merchandising, whereas it comprised almost 40% of HSN's (see Table A for a comparison of QVC and

HSN buyers).[7] Products offered on QVC included well-known brand names in consumer electronics such as Krups, Sunbeam, Cuisinart, JVC, Panasonic, Sony, Nintendo, and Kodak, and in apparel brands such as Liz Claiborne, Nike, Coach, Maidenform, Kenneth Cole, Esprit, and Susan Graver.

QVC's merchandising mix and service approach also generated higher gross margins and operating margins (see Exhibit 3 for financial comparisons). Between 1991 and 1994, when jewelry sales made up almost one-half of HSN's sales,[8] QVC gross margins were approximately 40% or 5% to 8% higher than those of HSN. During the same period, QVC operating margins increased from 9% to 11%, while HSN's operating margins fluctuated between 2% and 8%, including an operating loss in 1993. "People believe all televised shopping is the same thing," observed Fred Siegel, senior vice president of marketing. "But the Home Shopping Network and QVC are two different animals. The merchandise selection is different and the pricing strategy is different."[9]

The average income and educational levels of the QVC customer were higher than the national average (see Exhibit 4 for income profiles of the QVC customer), with median household income in 1995 of $46,000, nearly 40% higher than the national average. In other regards, however, QVC's customer base defied straightforward demographic characterization. Instead, it represented a broad cross-section of U.S. cable households. QVC's viewership was not predetermined in terms of size or demographic make-up. Instead, it was constantly changing, and much of the change was driven by merchandising. Depending on what product QVC put on the air, the composition of viewers might change dramatically. In that sense, QVC could not, and did not, rely on conventional TV industry measures such as viewership data generated by A.C. Nielsen or consumer studies on "HUT" levels (Households Using Television). As Doug Rose, a director in marketing, observed, "We're so broad that our audience is made up of countless niches—Clint Black fans, NASCAR fans, and Barbie fans."

Data from two research firms, Nielsen and Claritas, confirmed the diversity of QVC's audience: the age and gender profile of a QVC cookware hour differed radically from that of a QVC baseball hour (see Exhibit 5). In fact, a recent Nielsen survey showed that during a video game hour on QVC, more male teenage viewers were watching QVC than MTV. As a result, while television

---

[4]Deloitte & Touche Consulting Group, *The Dawning of the Age of Electronic Consumerism*, June 1996.
[5]Ibid.
[6]Ibid.

[7]Direct Marketing Association, 1996 *Statistical Fact Book*, page 173.
[8]Ibid, page 171.
[9]Jane L. Levere, Advertising, *The New York Times*, August 15, 1996.

Table A Comparison of QVC and HSN Customers

	QVC Inc.	Home Shopping Network
Annual Net Sales (Fiscal Year '95)	$1,600,000	$1,018,625
Number of Homes Reached via cable and satellite	56 million	48 million
Reached via broadcast	–	21 million
Number of Active Customers	4.8 million	5 million
Percentage of active customers who shop more than once in last 12 months	60%	50%
Number of Calls per Day	190,000	177,000
Mean dollar spent (1995 NIMA survey)	$282	$192
Average Number of Packages Shipped per Day	110,000	62,000
Merchandise Mix	Jewelry 35%	Jewelry 39%
	Home/Lifestyle 35%	Home/Lifestyle 37%
	Apparel, etc. 20%	Apparel, etc. 14%
	Other 10%	Cosmetics 10%

Sources: QVC; NIMA Fact Book, Spring 1996; Home Shopping Network, Inc. 1995 Annual Report

executives programmed based on anticipated audience demographics determined by "day part"—specific blocs of programming time throughout the day[10]—QVC executives had not achieved success using day part-based logic. Instead, they attracted unique audiences at all times of the day or night based on specific merchandise featured.

This iconoclastic approach to programming reflected an equally divergent philosophy of retailing. Just as QVC defied the logic of day parts, so it defied the retailing rationale of focus. As Darlene Daggett, executive vice president of merchandising/sales and product planning, explained, "Everyone in traditional retailing is niche focused, while our strength is our diversity." She went on to observe:

We probably have a more diverse mix than any conventional retailer. We can change our storefront every hour instead of on a weekly or quarterly basis. No one else has that flexibility, and we use that to our advantage. We stay away from demographics and psychographics. If you do demographics on a national basis, you always get vanilla. Demographics shift with our product. You get different demographics for

promoting Windows 95 and Aptiva computers, selling 160,000 cookbooks, or doing a live remote broadcast from Michael Jordan's restaurant in Chicago.

Siegel echoed Daggett's point of view. In spite of his previous positions as a creative executive with major advertising agencies, he was convinced that the logic of QVC defied everything he had ever learned about marketing and promotion:

QVC does not fit any existing marketing theory. When I came here, people said we would never sell heavy rock and roll stuff. We put Pink Floyd on and sold $400,000 worth of merchandise in an hour. People said that QVC is into jewelry and your customer should be the single woman. So how do you explain the millions of dollars of NFL merchandise that QVC sells? It doesn't fit the conventional model, because people watch for many different reasons. It's like watching news for different reasons. It turns the whole concept of marketing upside down.

As a result, one significant difference in what Siegel called "upside down" marketing was the absence at QVC of traditional marketing research. The reason was simple. When QVC executives wondered about the appeal of a particular product, they had one easy, low-risk way to address the question. As Daggett observed, "We don't labor a lot over what we should test; we put the product

[10]Examples of major day parts were daytime, early fringe, prime access, prime time, and late night. Though networks might define the specific time blocs differently season by season, the basic logic of this structure had persisted in the industry for decades.

on the air and find out. The traditional retail and catalog folks are laboring over those decisions for weeks and months. In the meantime, we figure out what all the selling points are, and we are off into the next thing, and they haven't even taken the product to market yet." However, Daggett was not cavalier about on-air experimentation. "Airtime is very precious," she pointed out. "Besides our people, it's our second greatest asset." Nonetheless, QVC's live, 24-hour, direct connection to its customers changed the dynamics of marketing, sales, and service.

The QVC Difference

Employees at QVC attributed much of the company's continued success to the three basic principles that founder Joseph Segel had established: Quality, Value, and Convenience. In realizing the principles in day-to-day operations, employees focused on promoting high quality and unique merchandise, offering such merchandise with a soft-sell approach, and providing outstanding customer service, in which the company followed a philosophy of underpromising and overdelivering. The company's values were defined in "The QVC Difference" given out to each employee (see Exhibit 6). Daggett commented on the significance of these values to the organization:

> The QVC Difference really speaks to our culture, which is what makes us distinctive for the people who work here. It's not only the things we believe in but things that we take action on everyday. There are the eight key values that we really focus on. They're significant. There is a strong customer focus, which

means exceeding the customer's expectations in every possible way from the initial customer interface, to the quality of the product, to how it's delivered, to how it gets handled in terms of product information The first ten years we primarily focused on the external customer. Now we take a closer look at how we can interface with one another so we provide the external customer with better service. That's becoming a critical piece of what we do.

Siegel's views reflected a similar emphasis on the "internal customer." To him, it was intrinsic to trust within the organization, which allowed the company to respond quickly to changes in the market. For instance, Siegel contrasted the QVC approach to new ideas with that of more traditional firms. "I've been in situations where people have an idea and someone goes into a deep dive into all the numbers and says, 'Here's the plan.' Then you start working off the plan. It doesn't work like that here. It's, 'Let's do it!' And everyone's on the same page. We are a company that has a culture of picking out a goal and then figuring out a way to do it."

Key Drivers to Customer Adoption

In considering how TV viewers became QVC customers, executives at QVC had identified certain key drivers of consumer adoption for the service. They believed that such drivers (see Figure A below) included quality and value, presentation and information, customer service, and ease of doing business. An internal survey showed that over 70% of QVC customers discovered the network through channel surfing. Approximately 24% of QVC

Figure A Key Drivers

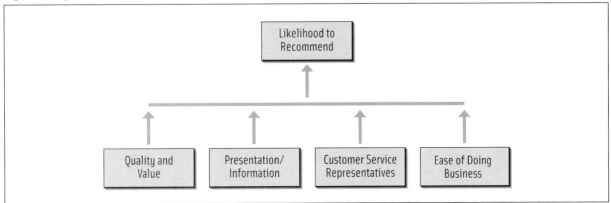

customers located the service based on a recommendation by a relative or a friend. As a result, management believed that an integrated approach to improve key drivers of adoption and orchestrate positive word-of-mouth were essential to QVC's success. Working at QVC, said Robb Cadigan, senior vice president of programming and broadcasting, was like "a relay race. The buyer in merchandising brings the product in. Merchandising hands the baton off to programming, which hands it off to broadcasting, which hands it off to customer service." If the "relay race" was executed perfectly, success developed a momentum of its own. Indeed, QVC implemented this process with an error rate in mid-1996—reflected in customer complaints and fulfillment errors tracked by QVC—of 0.5%.

Quality and Value

Approximately 15%, or 250 of the 1,600 products featured on the air each week, were new products. These were selected by QVC's buying staff of over 104 career merchants, most of whom had come to the retail shopping channel after successful careers in conventional retailing environments. Each buyer specialized in what QVC called a merchandise "department"—sporting goods, kitchenware, books, music, computers, and so forth—and looked for products that offered features and benefits that were demonstrable on air, often involving the latest technologies. According to Daggett:

> Different people champion different products at QVC. At QVC, we start with differentiation—items not readily available elsewhere or those that have something unique to offer. The way I look at it is that we are a virtual mall. Expect the unexpected, expect the first, expect the launch, and expect the highest quality and value. We can't claim to offer the lowest price, because category killers will always do better on price. But then, if you compete on price alone, you'll be out of business no matter what you do.

Many manufacturers and designers viewed televised shopping as a tremendous selling opportunity. It represented an additional channel of distribution. In addition, promoting products through QVC was often less expensive than dealing with traditional retailers, because suppliers could reduce many costs incurred in traditional retail environments (such as co-operative advertising, slotting allowances, point-of-sale promotion, and other channel and consumer incentives). In that way, some designers or entrepreneurs with limited funds for promotion found televised shopping to be their only economically feasible channel of distribution. At the same time, some well-established retailers, such as Home Depot and Sears, viewed QVC as a low-cost extension of their physical retail stores.

Along these lines, QVC had proven itself an effective platform for product launches in a wide variety of categories. These included the premiere of Microsoft Windows 95 on July 15, 1995. In a single two-hour show, QVC recorded over 12,200 orders for the new operating system at a price of $89.99; total sales of Windows 95 exceeded $1.5 million for the day. Likewise, Saban Entertainment's "Mighty Morphin Power Rangers"-licensed products logged $1.9 million in sales in two hours on November 6, 1994. Well-established QVC brands could also record robust sales results. Designers Susan Graver and Joan Rivers sold exclusive fashion or jewelry lines on QVC, with Graver selling over $50 million of sportswear merchandise on QVC over a three-year period. Within minutes after the 1995 Super Bowl, QVC sold over 16,000 Super Bowl Champ T-shirts of the Dallas Cowboys.

As Daggett observed, this kind of retailing required flexible buyers who were willing to take non-traditional approaches to merchandising:

> The people you find here buying for QVC are so different from those in traditional retail. The whole issue of matrix buying[11] is absolutely the worst strategy in the world. It may be great for the consolidation of stores and it may make sense from a balance sheet perspective. But the customer is unhappy. The assortments are ultimately the same from department to department and store to store. There is no personality. Unless you look up when you walk through the store's front door, you don't know where you are. Customers want things that are unique and different and that's not happening in traditional retailing. Creativity and passion are the differences between QVC and traditional retail.

Once a product was selected for sale through QVC, it was cleared by Quality Assurance. The 130-member department performed a random sampling test of each product's quality and validated manufacturers' claims. In 1995, the Quality Assurance Department rejected three million units, preventing specific product lines from

---

[11]Matrix buying usually involved merchandisers reporting to two or more chains of command, often by product line to headquarters and department by store or territory.

being sold on-air or certain batches from being accepted by the warehouse. Sometimes, a product's quality became questionable after Quality Assurance approval. In these instances, QVC's commitment to quality stood out. Daggett commented:

We are often asked to do the impossible. For instance, at one point we ended up with a product on the air—one of our high profile products—a gold bracelet. It had a laser weld on it. In a close-up shot, the show's host pulled on it and it snapped. This was the first time it had ever happened in ten years of on-air selling. The line-producer was very quick; we switched the shot and the show's host never missed a beat—she didn't get unnerved. What went on behind the scene was extraordinary. Literally everyone stopped what they were doing and did quality assurance on the entire batch. We had the vendor on the telephone and we wanted to understand the weld. The bottom line is that we were able to segregate a very small percentage—120 items—that had the defect, and we were able to ship 10,000 items of the product that otherwise met our quality standards. We are a 24-hour business but, ultimately, we have to take care of the customer. And we will do anything it takes to make sure that it happens so fast so that we never miss the customer's expectations. We simply will never knowingly ship them a bad product.

QVC believed that the costs associated with maintaining this high level of quality was essential to the business. In an internal survey, QVC customers ranked QVC higher on trust than regional department stores and national department stores. "If you look at the economics of promoting quality one item at a time, you'll never do it," said Daggett. "You have to look at the big picture. You have to look at exceeding customer expectations. The biggest reason why people shop at QVC is trust. Once you have violated that trust, you've opened the door just a crack for them to say, 'Why should I buy that product from QVC?'"

Pricing of each product was determined by competitive benchmarking, category by category, and then selecting the middle of the price band. On QVC's television screen, two economic benchmarks usually appeared on the air—the suggested retail value and the QVC price (see Exhibit 7). Each day, one product was selected by buyers for intermittent promotion throughout the day; it was referred to as Today's Special Value or, simply, "the TSV." With both regular merchandise and TSVs, QVC engaged in no price cutting, progressive discounting, or

price promotion. "The focus here is on building long-term customer retention," said Rose. "Approximately 60% of the customers who have made a purchase once, do so again. We can do a lot of tricks to build up a lot of volume in the short run, but we simply don't—and won't."

Information and Presentation

Entertainment and education for viewers were important elements of QVC's presentation or merchandise on air. "Television is a very personal medium," said Siegel. "It's probably more personal than most other selling environments. You go into a Home Depot store, and those people with aprons are very important to your experience. If you go into a store and no one knows what's going on, that can be very frustrating. But that's what most retailers are like these days, because their margins have been squeezed and they've cut back on sales help. How do you get personal interaction in a world like that?" Added Daggett:

To me, the value of QVC is information. This is an information age and people want to make intelligent decisions about the products that they buy. If you can bring a product to life with a demonstration on the air, then you can add value for the consumer that they can't get elsewhere. We take this to a new level at QVC. For example, on products that may intimidate customers—these range from fine jewelry to exercise equipment to computers—the common denominator is that they're all hard to shop for. Think about the vast majority of Americans who have ten or more pounds to lose. Would you like to buy that motorized treadmill in person from a twenty-something salesperson who is leading a totally different lifestyle? Also, computers are one of those things that you want a lot of information on and you get wild extremes in traditional stores, from the techno-geek who you can't understand to the five-dollar-an-hour clerk who's trying to figure out where the power switch is. That's a big gap in between. QVC makes it easy for customers to get information just by asking them to tune in.

Once Daggett approved product selections by her merchandisers, she handed off the products to the Programming Department for "packaging" on the air. Approximately 110 themed programs appeared on the QVC channel each week, ranging from "NFL Team Shop" to "The Fashion Outlet" to "The Computer Clinic with Steve Bryant" (see Exhibit 8 for an example of QVC's weekly shows). Each show usually lasted one hour and presented six to 10 products—with each product's inventory usually limited by QVC to avoid overstocking and to reduce related inventory costs. Cadigan, who got many of his programming ideas from visiting shopping malls across America, compared great programming to "great theater."

Programming for QVC could be classified into three categories: *basic programs*, such as "In the Kitchen with Bob" or "QVC Morning Show"; *special shows*, such as "Star Wars Collectibles" or the "Joan Rivers Classics Collection"; and *opportunity events*, such as shows appearing immediately after the Super Bowl or in conjunction with the Atlanta 1996 Summer Olympics. New shows were always being added to attract new viewers and ultimately convert them into customers of QVC. One senior executive estimated that it took six months of viewing for a person to make their first purchase with QVC. Upon making that purchase, customers became "members" of QVC, receiving a "Q-number" and a membership card. Every month, QVC members received a program guide (see Exhibit 9), outlining the upcoming programming schedule. According to internal research, many QVC viewers scheduled "shopping appointments" with specific shows on the network.

Cadigan occasionally reviewed market research numbers for specific shows, but spent little time analyzing such data. "We have the best rating system in the world," added Cadigan. "If the phone rings often enough, we know we have a hit. We don't look at the Nielsens. We're not up against *Seinfeld*.[12] It doesn't matter how many eyeballs we get. What matters is how many sales we make."

On-air program hosts for QVC were often selected through open casting calls in major cities. As a result, hosts reflected a cross section of the U.S. population, and they were evaluated based on their ability to relate to a television audience while engaging in a "soft sell" of a product, rather than promoting directly either the product or themselves. "The program host must be credible, sincere, and talking to you," said Jack Comstock, vice president of TV sales and a former Air Force fighter pilot. "We have no pressure." He was adamant that QVC hosts would never behave like hawkers of product in infomercials, where the atmosphere was driven by a "get 'em now! Call us now! Call us now!" approach.

"A lot of viewers find us entertaining," continued Comstock. "They build a relationship with the host. Consequently, when I look for hosts—on-air salespeople—I look for people who are real, people who are credible, people who are talking to you about why you may want to buy a product—not pressuring you to buy. They're educating, entertaining, presenting to you the benefits or a product in a conversational, not pushy, way."

An example of QVC's on-air approach was *The Morning Show* host Lisa Robertson. While selling a sterling silver bracelet, she made the following comments:

> This is a bracelet which is also available from Beverly Hills Silver. The Beverly Hills Silver is one of our most popular sellers at QVC. Because when you take the sparkle of Beverly Hills—and they're known for the illusion cutting and the diamond cutting—and you put it with silver, which is the most highly reflective metal, you get a great look for $38.50. This one is about seven inches long and just about a quarter of an inch wide, and has a lobster-claw clasp so it will stay on exactly where you want it to be—on your wrist—and not end up falling off. And it will give you an illusion of a diamond or diamonique phase, because it has that sparkle that goes all around. It will be something that will be extremely affordable, but it will give you a lot of look and a lot of shine. I think this has sold out the last five or six times it was on the air. Once again, if you're doing sterling silver, one of the things that I am amazed with is QVC's quality, value, and selection when it comes to sterling silver. When I shop for sterling silver, I get a few pieces, they're real expensive. QVC gives you a lot of options, and if you want something real sparkly and pretty, this is going to be in style 20 years from now as it is now. You can put it on by itself or you can wear it with something else. It's a great gift idea if you want to put something away for Christmas or for college.[13]

Previous job experiences of QVC program hosts have included positions such as school teacher, television news reporter, and radio announcer. Program hosts underwent rigorous training before appearing on the air, involving both coaching by Comstock and mentoring by senior program hosts. When new hosts appeared for the first time on-air, they often began in the early morning hours when QVC's viewing audience was small. Eventually, they graduated toward the more popular daytime or weekend hours. All hosts were hired as generalists, with an expectation that they could prepare themselves to

---

[12]*Seinfeld* was one of the top three most watched shows in the U.S. for the 1995–96 television season. The show appeared on NBC Television Network on Thursday nights.

[13]*The Morning Show*, QVC, August 30, 1996.

handle all products in all categories that QVC sold. Some did, over time, develop areas of specialization. For example, QVC's most popular host, Kathy Levine, was legendary for the success of her jewelry shows. Nonetheless, Levine had appeared recently selling personal computers, a category she knew little about prior to her preparation for the show. As Comstock observed:

> There is the need for the host to have a relaxed, easy, friendly persona in front of the camera, which are broadcasting skills. But a host can't have the talent mentality, saying, 'I'm the reason the show is here' or 'I am the star.' The product is the star, and the host is playing the supporting role. To get people who understand the sales side, understand the camera, and understand that the product is the star—those people are hard to find.

To prepare for a show, the program hosts could use the company's computerized inventory system, which provided key facts on products slated to appear on air. The program hosts transcribed notes onto blue cue cards to remind them of product benefits when speaking to the television audience. Support staff for individual shows checked each product in advance, cleaned or polished product samples, and laid them out in the order they would appear on the air.

Hosts were supplied more than information and products; they were supported on-air by line-producers who communicated with them continuously through an intercom worn as an ear-piece. "The on-air sales team includes the producer," said Comstock. "The producer is in the host's ear saying if the product is doing well, if the product is not doing well, or if we can wrap this and go on to the next product. The producer manages the host. Using an Air Force analogy, the pilot up front is the host and the backseater is the producer, who like a navigator, says, 'Go this way or go that way.'" The producer also determined the sequence of products presented throughout the hour.

Guests with knowledge of a particular product, such as Marie Osmond promoting her hand-made porcelain dolls or Joy Mangano promoting her miracle mops, appeared on-air to chat with hosts and viewers. Their presence often accelerated product sales. (For example, Osmond appeared in August 1996 on a single show and drew such a large audience that her entire inventory of 20,000 dolls, priced at $191 each, sold out in a one-hour show.) Often, many viewers would tune into QVC just to obtain more information on a particular product. Daggett remarked:

Guests are a critical part of the sell. For people who have significant personal brand equity that they want to protect and enhance, this is the ultimate medium. It's wonderful to have the person who was key for the product's development or a champion of it in-house to interface with the consumer. Usually, the host is a very competent generalist. The guest provides information. The host sells.

Most of the shows were broadcast from the first floor studio of QVC's headquarters in West Chester. A rotating, circular platform with four sets—each quadrant contained one set, including one with a built-in, fully functional kitchen—was used to change the set almost instantaneously at the top of the hour for each show (see Exhibit 10 for a photo of the QVC set). The line-producer was often seated in front of the set to direct the show's host. From the control room located on the second floor, the executive producer decided what camera shots and graphics should appear on the air. From the host's point of view, however, the three robotic video cameras, with lights indicating which camera was on-air, remained the focus of attention. At the base of the set, large TV monitors indicated show time remaining, products in queue, call volume, and unit sales.

Occasionally, viewers were invited to give testimonials (or T-calls) about the products shown on air through phone calls. "In many ways, T-calls are as good for the viewing customer as they are for QVC," Daggett observed. "They're third party endorsements. If a customer calls in and says that I bought this product last week for friends at Christmas and got wonderful feedback, that's fabulous," she added.

Finally, QVC had invested heavily from the beginning in establishing the quality of its signal. Segel's goal had been to deliver picture and sound quality that exceeded network television in its quality. According to John Link, executive vice president of information technology and chief information officer, QVC had maintained that advantage throughout its first decade by investing in state-of-the-art studio equipment and lights, digital video editing systems, and satellite uplinks.

Customer Service Representatives

Television viewers interested in buying merchandise from QVC or seeking more information about a particular product could dial a toll-free number (1-800-345-1515) and speak to a customer order-entry or service representative over one of 5,300 phone lines operated by the network. QVC always answered its phones in less than two rings; many calls were answered before the first ring. If a caller wanted to order a product, the representative asked for the product number, the customer's name and billing address, and his or her phone number; if customers had ordered from QVC before, they simply provided their Q-number. When new customers were assigned a Q-number, their information was also entered into a profiling and transactions database. On average, QVC's 4,000 customer representatives each received more than 30 hours of training before they took their first phone call. For situations where customers had problems or concerns, the customer representatives were trained to assume the customer was always right. Inbound calls were randomly monitored to assure quality of service. When taking phone orders, customer representatives never promoted other items for sale and they seldom engaged in idle chat. The average phone call took less than two minutes. (See Exhibit 11 for a sample phone conversation.)

QVC received 70 million phone calls in 1995—the equivalent of 190,000 phone calls per day and 8,000 per hour. The network operated customer phone centers in three locations: West Chester, Pennsylvania; Chesapeake, Virginia; and San Antonio, Texas. To monitor customers' perception of quality, tracking information on all telephone calls were input automatically into an integrated database, classified by category, and summarized into a report called the "Daily Activity Report." On this report, negative calls that numbered more than one in a hundred for a specific category were identified for further analysis. For example, if specific problem patterns were identified for certain types of products or vendors, corrective action was taken immediately.

Ease of Doing Business

Orders paid by credit card were shipped from the company's four warehouses in Lancaster, Centerville, West Chester, Pennsylvania, and Suffolk, Virginia. Orders paid by check were not shipped until the checks cleared. Over 80 percent of orders were filled within 24 hours of receipt. Because QVC sold no products on air that were not in its warehouse (the only exceptions were large items such as exercise equipment, which were sometimes drop-shipped), the network delivered virtually 100% of merchandise within the time period promised by the order entry representative. All orders were delivered using the United Parcel Service and the United States Postal Service in boxes with the QVC logo on it (see

Exhibit 12). The packing strip reminded the customer of QVC's services through a series of verbal communications. One said:

QVC: \kyu\ve\se a: QUALITY. VALUE. CONVENIENCE. b: a better way to shop that resides in your television. c: of or pertaining to shopping, entertainment, information, interactivity, value. d: 24 hours a day, seven days a week, 364 days a year. e: where to find the highest quality merchandise at terrific prices. f: the origin from which Q2 is derived. g: window to the future with unique possibilities —see ELECTRONIC RETAILING.

Siegel explained the distinctive appearance of QVC boxes and packaging. "In all our communications — advertising, public relations, or programming—we try to bring a little smile to the face of the customer. If you look at the outbound box, the tape on it is fun. Whoever thought that a shipping box could make you smile? But that's part of what QVC-ness is all about. What we do is to confirm for the customer that the customer did the right thing by ordering from us."

Included in the box was a packing slip which provided the customer with a summary of the transaction, including the item ordered, customer service numbers, and total cost. All merchandise purchased through QVC was covered by a 30-day, money-back guarantee; the packing slip provided information on how to return the merchandise. There were no special charges, such as a "restocking fee" or a "handling fee," for returned merchandise. In 1995, QVC shipped over 40 million packages—an average of 1.2 packages every second.

While QVC operations appeared seamless, the success of the process was dependent on the coordination of countless interlocking parts. The "relay race" to which managers referred was not only complex, but it was also continuous. As Comstock observed, "The pace here never stops. Some call it pressure. I think of it as a heartbeat, and it's a pulse that runs throughout the building. It's a live show that goes on 24 hours a day, seven days a week. It's 12 o'clock and it's already the next show. It's a lot of fun."

The Customer's Experience

QVC customers ranked the network highest on attributes related "to the ease of doing business" and "to price competitiveness," when compared with other retail competitors such as catalog companies, regional department stores, and national department stores (see Exhibit 13).

Table B Ratings of QVC on Key Customer Attributes

	Active Customers	One-Time Only Customers	Inactive Customers
Excellent value	51%	51%	41%
Excellent quality	60%	57%	50%
Excellent ease of doing business	86%	74%	74%
Definitely can trust	83%	60%	72%
Definitely would recommend	80%	60%	58%
Definitely would reorder	87%	53%	54%

Source: 1995 QVC Quantitative Tracking Program

As indicated in Table B, active customers—those who had ordered from QVC at least twice in the previous 12 months—rated QVC highest on attributes related to the ease of doing business and trust. Eighty percent of active subscribers said they would recommend QVC to others and 87% said they would order again. One-time customers and inactive customers showed similarly favorable—albeit lower—ratings on these dimensions.

One example of the opinions underlying this data came from Rick Rickers, a Philadelphia-based van driver who had been a QVC customer for over four years. He articulated this satisfaction:

> My wife and I have been customers of theirs for over four years. I've only had to return one item—a canvas chair that ripped up—and they refunded me the money right away. No third-degree treatment. I keep an eye on the monthly program guide that QVC sends out. If I missed a show that I would have wanted to have seen, I simply look at the program and circle the next showing on my calendar. When I buy something on TV, I'm informed about it before I buy it. The host and hostesses are very important to me, my wife, and anyone who shops at QVC. You can tell if someone is a phony and I don't like phonies. The host and hostesses got to be like the audience and have a sense a humor; they can't be stern. I get teed off by rude people. When I'm bored with regular TV—especially with re-runs and when I feel like buying something—I just channel surf to QVC. But two things would turn me off from ever buying from QVC again—if their service representatives were ever rude and if my package didn't arrive within the six or seven days they promised.[14]

Another customer who had purchased a Diamonique ring, wrote in a letter addressed to the network, "the ring is everything you said and more. The information that you give your customers is more than I have received from anyone before. The deciding factor though for me in purchasing this ring was the fact that I had a 30-day money back guarantee. You do not have to worry about me returning this ring, though. I love it and so does my husband."

Current QVC Marketing Efforts

Sponsorships

By the mid-1990's, QVC increasingly turned to innovative event marketing, corporate sponsorships, and marketing alliances as ways to broaden the retail shopping channel's awareness. For example, in 1994, the company launched the QVC Local (see Exhibit 14 for photo), a bus with a state-of-the-art broadcast studio on the interior and the world's largest road map of the United States painted on the exterior. The Local was used to promote weekly segments on "The Quest for America's Best: QVC's 50 in 50 Tour." The show hosts visited each state of the nation to discover the best new products from American entrepreneurs and meet with local QVC viewers. Other efforts included QVC's sponsorship of the Geoff Bodine Racing team in the NASCAR Winston Cup racing series (and the introduction of the QVC race car, as shown in Exhibit 15); promotional alliances with the Metropolitan Museum of Art in New York, the Smithsonian Institution in Washington, and the Philadelphia Museum of Art; and the sponsorship of the Fashion

---

[14]Interview with case writer, August 8, 1996.

Footwear Association of New York "Shoes on Sale," which raised more than $1 million for breast cancer research.

Q-Checks

The network also launched an awareness-building marketing campaign on network and cable television, with a series of what it called "Q-checks." These were 30-second advertising spots that appeared first in March 1996, inviting viewers to channel surf to QVC during commercial breaks on regular television. Q-checks used well-known celebrities, such as soap opera star Susan Lucci, pop star Paula Abdul, composer Isaac Hayes, comedian Louie Anderson, and television game show host Chuck Woolery, as advocates of QVC:

> Announcer: When do you Q-check?
>
> Susan Lucci: During the Emmys.
>
> Isaac Hayes: During shampoo commercials.
>
> Chuck Woolery: When I don't make a connection.
>
> Announcer: Got a minute? Do a Q-check. You might find something that you're looking for.

QVC International, Q2, and iQVC

Finally, additional retail shopping channels—abroad, domestic, and in cyberspace—provided other ways for QVC to expand its audience and customer base.

In 1993, QVC, Inc. expanded overseas and entered the United Kingdom with "QVC: The Shopping Channel," a joint venture with BSkyB. With a separate organization and its own indigenous product mix and programming, this London-based service reached five million subscriber households throughout the United Kingdom and had over 400,000 active customers. In late summer 1996, the company announced plans to extend QVC into Germany and Canada; this move would add an additional 30 million households to QVC's worldwide viewership.

Q2, QVC's sister cable channel, launched originally in April 1994, was available in approximately 10 million U.S. subscriber homes by the end of 1995. The channel was initially launched by Diller as a separate retail shopping channel that would appeal to more upscale audiences. Six months following launch, Q2's programming was reformatted as a headline-style service, much like CNN's Headline News, presenting the best products and show segments from the previous 48 hours on QVC. With a live anchor providing continuous updates, Q2 offered a fast-paced mix of taped and edited demonstrations.

In 1996, QVC launched a new Internet-based shopping service on the World Wide Web at www.qvc.com after first appearing on-line on the Microsoft Network in December 1995.[15] The new interactive service, called iQVC offered the same standards of customer service, order delivery, and hassle-free shopping that the network had established on air (see Exhibit 16 for screen print of iQVC's home page). With the ability to compare various products within a single category, customers could navigate through electronic aisles with the click of a mouse, exploring products that included those promoted on the air and also a range of others exclusive to iQVC. Management viewed iQVC, though still in a start-up phase, as a significant attempt to extend the company's electronic retailing franchise.

Conclusion

It was clear to QVC executives that the original philosophy espoused by founder Joseph Segel—a commitment to Quality, Value and Convenience—had provided the company and its employees with a mission that had resulted in a successful first ten years of operations. Now, the challenge that stood before them was how to continue to grow the company, how to extend its consumer franchise, and how to maintain its level of service.

---

[15]Also see case, "iQVC," HBS case No. 897-123.

Exhibit 1 Comparison of QVC's and HSN's Net Revenue (1990 to 1995)

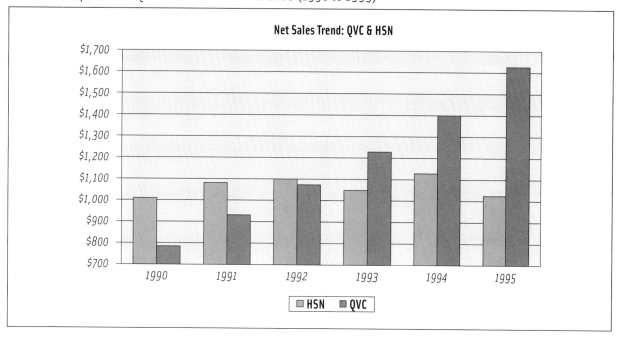

Net Sales Trend: QVC & HSN

Exhibit 2 Purchase Rate by Marketing Channel

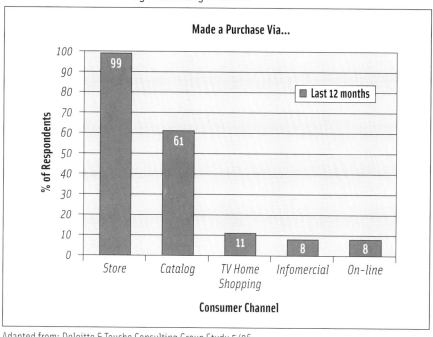

Made a Purchase Via...

Adapted from: Deloitte & Touche Consulting Group Study 5/96

Exhibit 3 Selected Financial Data from HSN and QVC

QVC–Income Statement 1991–94 (in $Millions)				
	1991	**1992**	**1993**	**1994**
Net Revenue	$921.9	$1,070.6	$1,222.1	$1,390.1
Gross Profit	387.2	448.8	499.0	541.6
Operating Income	84.4	118.2	152.2	158.6
Gross Margin	42.0%	41.9%	40.8%	39.0%
Operating Margin	9.2%	11.0%	12.5%	11.4%

HSN–Income Statement 1991–94 (in $Millions)				
	1991	**1992**	**1993**	**1994**
New Revenue	$1,078.6	$1,097.8	$1,046.6	$1,126.5
Gross Profit	389.4	406.2	342.5	396.0
Operating Income (exc. restructuring costs)	64.5	82.3	−6.9	26.9
Gross Margin	36.1%	37.0%	32.7%	35.2%
Operating Margin	6.0%	7.5%	−0.7%	2.4%

Sources: QVC and HSN annual reports (1991–94)

Note: QVC became a subsidiary of Comcast Corporation in 1995. Separate financial results for QVC are not available for fiscal year 1995, except for reported net revenue of $1.6 billion. HSN reported a net operating loss of $61.9 million, excluding restructuring charges of $18.4 million, on net revenue of $1.0 billion in fiscal year 1995.

Exhibit 4 Distribution of Household Income Among QVC Customers

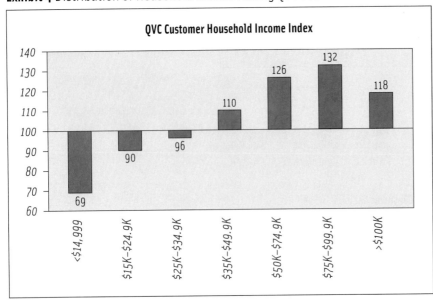

Exhibit 5 Claritas Profile of QVC Customers

Accordingly, the QVC customer base is not one homogeneous group, but instead represents a broad cross-section of the U.S. cable household population. PRIZM data reveals a variety of geo-demographic clusters represented within the customer mix.

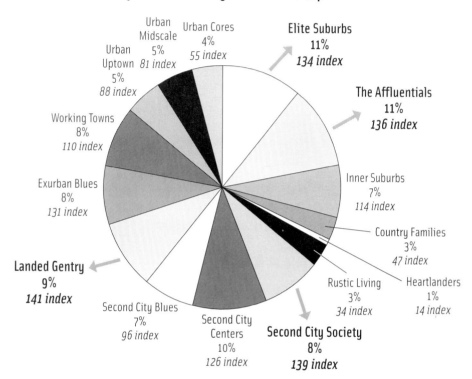

QVC Customer Mix by PRIZM Social Group

In broad terms, QVC's customer base skews toward metro suburban and affluent "second city" segments and away from heavily urban and rural social groups. Note that the four largest PRIZM social groups—both in terms of absolute percentage as well as index versus the adult population—are "elite suburbs™", "the affluentials™", "second city society™", and "landed gentry™".

Again, the above pie chart reflects QVC's *total* active customer base of nearly five million adults. It's important to remember that QVC's audience profile is constantly "morphing" from one hour to the next, as each new product attracts its own interest groups.

Source: Claritas/PRIZM 1994

Exhibit 6 The QVC Difference

THE QVC DIFFERENCE

We are dedicated to these values:

Customer Focus–Exceeding the expectations of every customer.

Teamwork–Working together to succeed.

Pioneering Spirit–Initiating and embracing new ideas with enthusiasm.

Commitment To Excellence–Acting to make a differencce, being responsible for our actions and continually striving to improve.

Respect And Concern For Each Other–Accepting and supporting each other personally and professionally.

Ethics And Integrity–Keeping our word and doing the right thing.

Openness And Trust–Relying on each other and communicating with honesty and acceptance.

Fun Along The Way–Recognizing contributions, maintaining perspective and celebrating successes.

Exhibit 7 QVC Television Screen

Exhibit 8 QVC Weekly Schedule

week of 1/22-1/28

The NFL™ Team Shop has your ticket to the Super Bowl. Join us the night before the big game live from "The NFL Experience" in Phoenix when you can make your picks. Choose from apparel featuring the Super Bowl XXX logo, plus officially licensed jerseys and jackets of all your favorite teams. Get ready for the action with QVC – the official electronic retailer of the NFL.

The NFL™ Team Shop
Live from The NFL Experience
Sat., Jan. 27th, 5-8pm ET

EASTERN	PACIFIC	MONDAY JANUARY 22	TUESDAY JANUARY 23	WEDNESDAY JANUARY 24	THURSDAY JANUARY 25	FRIDAY JANUARY 26	SATURDAY JANUARY 27	SUNDAY JANUARY 28
12m	9pm	Casual Connection	Necessities	It's a secret that can't be kept...	Vermont Teddy Bears/The Master Bedroom	Jewelry Essentials - Joan Rivers	Gold Sampler	Quick & Easy Cooking
1am	10pm	Around the House	Fun & Leisure	It's a secret that can't be kept...	Make Life Easier	Western Jewelry	Gold Sampler	Fun & Leisure
2am	11pm	The Jewelry Showcase	Diamonique® Jewelry	that can't be kept...	Now You're Cooking	Valentine's Day Gifts	Make Life Easier	The Jewelry Showcase
3am	12m	Valentine's Day Gifts	The Linen Closet	There's gold in this here show!	The Linen Outlet	Around the House	Valentine's Day Gifts	Now You're Cooking
4am	1am	Fun & Leisure	Valentine's Day Gifts	There's gold in this here show!	Fun & Leisure	The Jewelry Showcase	The Jewelry Showcase	Around the House
5am	2am	The Jewelry Showcase	Now You're Cooking	California Gold Rush	The Ring Showcase	Make Life Easier	Fun & Leisure	The Jewelry Showcase
6am	3am	The Jewelry Showcase	Watch Gallery	California Gold Rush	Collectible Dolls	Heart Jewelry Collection	Around the House	All Plugged In
7am	4am	The QVC Morning Show Style Edition	The QVC Morning Show - Valentine's Day Gifts	California Gold Rush	The QVC Morning Show	The QVC Morning Show Weekend Preview - Get to Know Us	The Bracelet Showcase	Make Life Easier
8am	5am	The QVC Morning Show Style Edition	The QVC Morning Show - Valentine's Day Gifts	California Gold Rush	The QVC Morning Show	The QVC Morning Show Weekend Preview - Get to Know Us	AM Style	The Home Sampler
9am	6am	Happily Ever After - Wedding Gifts	Jewelry Gift Ideas	California Gold Rush	Graver Studio with Susan Graver	Health & Fitness	AM Style	Silver Jewelry
10am	7am	Happily Ever After - Wedding Gifts	The Bed & Breakfast Inn	California Gold Rush	The Linen Closet	Fine Jewelry Collection	Fine Jewelry Collection	Smart Cooking
11am	8am	The Fashion Outlet	Collectible Dolls	24 hours' worth of 14k gold...	The Linen Closet	Joan Rivers Classics Collection - Joan Rivers	Get to Know Us	Shape Up for '96
12n	9am	Beauty by Tova with Tova Borgnine	The QVC Clearance Sale	24 hours' worth of 14k gold...	The Jewelry Showcase	Joan Rivers Classics Collection - Joan Rivers	Get to Know Us	In the Kitchen with Bob
1pm	10am	Weekend Spirit	The QVC Clearance Sale	all brand-new...	The QVC Sampler	Valentine's Day Gifts - Joan Rivers	Joan Rivers Classics Collection - Joan Rivers	The Jewelry Showcase
2pm	11am	Valentine's Day Gifts	The QVC Clearance Sale	all brand-new...	Now You're Cooking	Quick Takes	Joan Rivers Classics Collection - Joan Rivers	Bette Ball Dolls - 5th Anniversary
3pm	12n	Now You're Cooking	The Jewelry Showcase	all at special prices	Warm & Cozy Linens	The Jewelry Showcase - Joan Rivers	Valentine's Day Gifts	Now You're Cooking
4pm	1pm	Marcasite Jewelry	The Home Sampler	all at special prices	Fashion Formulas®	The Toy Box	The Jewelry Showcase	Joan Rivers Classics Collection - Joan Rivers
5pm	2pm	Fashions Under $50	Heart Jewelry Collection	good for one day only... this day...	Fashion Formulas®	The Jewelry Outlet - Joan Rivers	The NFL™ Team Shop - Live from the NFL Experience via the QVC Local	Joan Rivers Classics Collection - Joan Rivers
6pm	3pm	The Jewelry Showcase	Cooking with T-Fal	good for one day only... this day...	The Jewelry Showcase	Around the House	The NFL™ Team Shop - Live from the NFL Experience via the QVC Local	Kitchen Ideas
7pm	4pm	The QVC Sampler	Cooking with T-Fal	good for one day only... this day...	Make Life Easier	Gourmet Holiday	Get to Know Us	Get to Know Us
8pm	5pm	The NFL™ Team Shop	Things You Hate to Carry Home Anniversary	The California Gold Rush is on!	Decorating on a Budget Anniversary	Joan Rivers Classics Collection - Joan Rivers	Get to Know Us	Get to Know Us
9pm	6pm	Valentine's Day Gifts	Warner Bros. Studio Store	The California Gold Rush is on!	Silver Jewelry	Joan Rivers Classics Collection - Joan Rivers	The Elegance of 18K Gold Valentine Special	Diamonique® Jewelry
10pm	7pm	Idaho Garnet	Warner Bros. Studio Store	The California Gold Rush is on!	Valentine's Day Gifts	Carlos Falchi® Workshop	The Elegance of 18K Gold Valentine Special	The NFL™ Team Shop - Super Bowl Wrap-Up
11pm	8pm	Idaho Garnet	Problem Solvers	The California Gold Rush is on!	Around the House	Carlos Falchi® Workshop	The Elegance of 18K Gold Valentine Special	The NFL™ Team Shop - Super Bowl Wrap-Up

In the Mountain Time Zone, program times are 1 hour later than Pacific Time. In the Central Time Zone, program times are 1 hour earlier than Eastern Time. Program times may change without notice. Shop with us any time. Some items you see may not be in stock. But our Customer Representatives will be happy to check product availability.

Exhibit 9 QVC Program Guide and Membership Card

Exhibit 10 QVC Set

Exhibit 11 Sample Telephone Conversation Between Customer and QVC
           Representative

A transaction with QVC usually went this way over the phone:

Customer Representative: What is the number of the item you would like to order?

Customer: C27484

Customer Representative: The Geoff Bodine QVC Race Car?

Customer: Yes.

Customer Representative: That's $21. How many would you like to order?

Customer: Just one.

Customer Representative: OK. At this time can I have your Q membership number?

Customer: That's 8765-4321

Customer Representative: And your first and last name?

Customer: John Doe

Customer Representative: Would you like us to ship it to your home address on Veteran Avenue in Los Angeles?

Customer: Yes.

Customer Representative: And what credit card would you like to use Mr. Doe?

Customer provides/confirms credit card information

Customer Representative: The grand total for your Geoff Bodine QVC Race Car is $26.48, including shipping and handling. The estimated delivery date is six days. Is there anything else I can do for you today?

Customer: No, that's it.

Customer Representative: Thanks for shopping with QVC. Do have a great day.

Exhibit 12 QVC Shipping Box

Exhibit 13 Attributes of Shopping Through QVC

Attribute	QVC	Catalog/ Mail Order	Regional Department Stores	National Department Stores	Discount Stores
Comparison of Ease of Doing Business	78%	74%	57%	56%	62%
Comparison of Price Competitiveness	37%	35%	27%	29%	59%
Comparison of Trust	72%	81%	69%	65%	70%

Sources: 1995 QVC Quantitative Assessment

Exhibit 14 Photo of QVC Local

Source: QVC, Inc.

Exhibit 15 Photo of QVC NASCAR Race Car

1996 QVC Racing Ford Thunderbird

Driver: Geoff Bodine

Source: QVC, Inc.

Exhibit 16 QVC Home

iQVC SHOP

FEATURES:

iQVC's Gourmet Gallery
Gem Day Favorite

Search

DEPARTMENTS:

Arts & Leisure	Furniture and Accessories	Personal Care
Beauty	Hardware, Lawn & Garden	Photo and Optical
Collectibles	Home Office	Sports & Fitness
Computers and Software	Intimate Apparel and Hosiery	Tabletop
Domestics	Jewelry	Women's Accessories
Electronics	Kitchen	Women's Apparel

WHAT'S NEW	**CORPORATE HQ**	**BACKSTAGE**	**ASSISTANCE**
Special Events	Tour	Backstage Tour	Feedback Desk
Press Releases	Business Overview	In the Spotlight	Return Info.
Online Kitchen	Press Releases	The Host Lounge	Service FAQ's
Program Guide	Employment		Phone Numbers
	Corporate Facts		

FRONTGATE CATALOG

There will be a fair amount happening on the Internet from a competitive standpoint. It's going to be harder to distinguish yourself on the Internet than in traditional catalog retailing. That's why we need to be at the front end rather than the back end.
—Paul Tarvin, President, Cinmar, L.P.

Even if the Frontgate customer isn't on the Internet today, we need to have it figured out to some degree three years from now when big bandwidth starts getting into the house and our customer starts getting on-line.
—Greg Berglund, Director, Business Development, Cinmar, L.P.

Leaning back in his sumptuous black leather chair, Paul Tarvin gazed with pride at several Frontgate catalogs laid out on his office coffee table. Tarvin, the company's president, and John O'Steen, the company's CEO, founded the Frontgate catalog in 1991 and emphasized from the start the operation's commitment to quality. Making top-line, top-caliber products available to the public had been the foundation of Frontgate's success. In six years, gross revenues of the Ohio-based catalog company had grown to nearly $100 million in 1997, from $300,000 in 1991. Tarvin and O'Steen knew that for Frontgate's continued success, they needed to translate standards of quality into every aspect of operations, including a new potential sales channel, the Internet.

Plans for a Frontgate Web site (*www.frontgate.com*) were underway. Tarvin and O'Steen hired Greg Berglund, who had previously founded a catalog-based wine business in California, to the position of Director of Business Development. Berglund's responsibilities included the development and implementation of the Frontgate Web site. By late 1997, Berglund had planned a first version of

the site. The site would take advantage of the limitless pages accessible using the Internet by providing extensive product information alongside product images. Site visitors would also be able to place orders on-line and submit e-mail inquiries.

Tarvin couldn't help but wonder what challenges lay ahead for Frontgate and the new sales channel. Compared to other direct retailers, for instance L.L.Bean (*www.llbean.com*), Sharper Image (*www.sharperimage.com*), and others, Frontgate was entering the on-line scene late. However, Tarvin knew Frontgate would face common challenges of Web site development: How extensively to develop the Web site, what kind of human and financial resources to allocate to the site, and how to extend the Frontgate brand image into a new media channel.

Catalog Marketing in the United States

History—Catalogs in the 1700s. Benjamin Franklin, one of the United States' founding fathers, produced the first catalog distributed in America in 1744, which offered scientific and academic volumes to its customers by mail. Franklin also wrote the first catalog customer service pledge, which read, "Those persons who live remote, by sending their orders to said B. Franklin, may depend on the same justice as if present."[1] Over 250 years later, Franklin had proven himself a pioneer in more than just democracy and electricity: He introduced to the United States a popular, distance-based home shopping experience.

The Montgomery Ward catalog, established in 1873, offered customers a wider range of goods, such as hoop skirts and harnesses, and more affordable prices than were available locally. Similarly, the Sears and Roebuck catalog, first printed in 1881, offered its customers an enormous variety of products from watches to washing machines. The advent of the teletype machine, telephone, and the completion of railway lines enabled widespread diffusion of catalogs, making them staples of

Research Associate Carrie L. Ardito prepared this case, with the assistance of Holly S. Camercon (CPA, M.Div.), under the supervision of Professor Jeffrey F. Rayport as the basis for class discussion rather than to illustrate either effective or ineffective handling of an administrative situation. This case is based, in part, on a research report prepared by Greg Berglund (MBA '97) and Luc Sirois (MBA '97). Some numbers in this case have been disguised at the company's request.

[1]The Direct Marketing Association. *Direct Marketing: An American Success Story.*

American life in the early 1900s. The Direct Marketing Association observed, "A century ago, the only books in many American homes were the Sears Roebuck and Montgomery Ward catalogs, and the Holy Bible."

With the exception of the Montgomery Ward and Sears and Roebuck books, retail catalogs were not abundant in consumer homes until the early 1980s. At that time, "category killers," catalogs and retail stores that focused on particular retail categories such as outdoor clothing, lingerie, books, and computers, experienced rapid growth. Examples of "category killers" in the retail world included Home Depot for do-it-yourself home repairs, Barnes & Noble for books, and Crate & Barrel for kitchen wares; catalog "category killers" included L.L.Bean for outdoor apparel, Victoria's Secret for lingerie, and Williams-Sonoma for kitchen wares.[2] Although "conventional wisdom" 20 years ago suggested that only certain narrow categories of products could be sold through catalogs, by 1997, catalogs offered almost everything—from clothing, computers, videos, and household products, to food, flowers, and personalized pet collars. (See Exhibit 1 for catalog sales by product categories.)

The newfound success of catalog marketing was often attributed to U.S. lifestyle and demographic changes. The most widely heralded change was the growing number of women entering the work force, and the resulting larger number of dual-income families. This change also led to a decrease in consumers' available time for traditional shopping. With less time but more discretionary income, many consumers turned to the convenience and availability of catalog shopping.

The L.L.Bean (founded in 1912) and Lands' End (founded in 1963) catalogs experienced rapid growth in the late 1970s through the 1980s. Their success in casual outdoor apparel and equipment paved the way for many clothing and sporting goods catalogs to enter the catalog market. L.L.Bean and Lands' End pioneered an unprecedented commitment to customer service—including unconditional satisfaction guarantees—that set standards for service in the catalog industry. Gary Comer, founder of Lands' End, wrote in the Lands' End fall 1997 catalog:

> Quality in the apparel business, we learned early in our life, is an ephemeral thing. Making clothing remains essentially an art form. Things do occasionally get out to you that shouldn't, which is why we back everything with one unqualified guarantee: Guaranteed. Period. A guarantee that makes everyone try harder to get it right the first time, then attend to

the problem (not the terms of the guarantee) if something goes wrong.[3]

In 1997, Lands' End and L.L.Bean rated in the top ten direct merchandisers for customer service, and ranked nine and 12, respectively, for catalog sales in the United States. Computer catalogs Dell, Gateway 2000, Digital,[4] and Micro Warehouse dominated the top five in catalog sales,[5] reflecting the increase in the number of American households purchasing personal computers and peripherals and the higher prices of such items. (See Exhibit 2 for top 20 catalogs by revenues.)

The Direct Mail and Catalog Business.

Catalog marketing was a sector of the direct mail business. Direct mail, a marketing device, was usually letter-format mail sent directly to consumer homes and businesses, while catalogs provided extensive retail selections of products for consumer or business purchases. Direct mailers sent information to targeted households by renting mailing lists of prospects determined by consumer demographics and buying history, and by utilizing lists of consumers' names that had purchased in the past from their catalogs (these customers were referred to as belonging to "house lists"). Response rates—the number of people accepting an offer or ordering a product as a percentage of the number of pieces of mail sent—determined a direct mail campaign's profitability. Catalog response rates for "house lists" were higher than for rental lists. Direct mailers such as credit card, music club, and book club companies tended to measure success in terms of customer lifetime value: The net value of a new customer increased the "lifetime" of the customer/vendor relationship, offsetting acquisition costs of the direct mail campaign.

With lower overhead expenses as compared with physical retailing—rent for retail space and budgets for associated personnel and equipment—catalogs could experience strong profitability. Profit margins for the catalog industry were significantly higher than for the retail industry as a whole: In 1997, catalog industry profit margins averaged between seven and ten percent, while the retail industry averaged one to three percent.[6] (See

---

[2]Crate & Barrel also offered a catalog under the same brand name; Victoria's Secret and Williams-Sonoma also operated retail stores under the same brand names.
[3]Introduction to Lands' End catalog, October, 1997.
[4]This catalog company was not related to Digital Equipment Corporation.
[5]*Catalog Age/DIRECT Source Book*, 1997.
[6]*Catalog Age/DIRECT Source Book*, 1997.

Table A Catalog Industry Sales Growth[8]

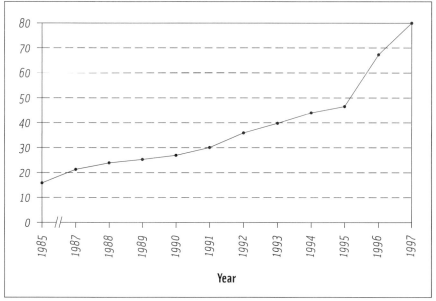

Source: U.S. Department of Commerce, *Statistical Abstract of the United States*, 1985-1996.

Exhibit 3 for a typical catalog business profit and loss statement; see Exhibit 4 for a comparison of catalog and retail businesses.)

The Catalog Industry in the 1990s.

By the 1990s, catalogs still represented viable businesses, despite rising postal rates and postal reclassifications, increased paper prices, heightened consumer concern over privacy, and growing competition from alternative media, such as televised home shopping and infomercials. In 1997, 87% of the U.S. population received catalogs. Of those 87%, over half had purchased from a catalog within the previous year. Consumers were expected to spend $80 billion on catalog sales in 1997, a 125.4% increase from 1992 sales of $35.5 billion and a 286.5% increase from 1987 sales of $20.7 billion.[7] (See Table A for historical catalog sales growth.)

The average catalog buyer of non-computer-related products was female, professional, married, and between the ages of 45 to 64. Additionally, this buyer had children ages 4 to 18 living at home, earned a bachelor's degree or higher, was a home owner, and had an annual household income of $40,000.[9]

There were a variety of new factors that contributed to the continuing success of catalog marketers. In addition to changing lifestyles, industry experts attributed catalog industry growth in part to express delivery by Federal Express (FedEx) and the United Parcel Service (UPS). *The Journal of Commerce* noted, "FedEx and UPS have stormed into the direct marketing industry this decade, signing contracts with major catalogers. There's no question what it has done. It has made [catalogers] competitive with retailers." For example, express delivery eliminated the need to rush to a mall during the week before Christmas. With the availability of express delivery, consumers could delay purchases until the last week of December, with confidence that UPS or FedEx could still deliver packages from catalogs in time for the holidays.[10]

The ultimate success of catalog shopping was also attributed to rising standards of convenience and ease. Catalog customers felt that the level of service provided by catalog operators was far superior to that of retail stores.[11] Todd Simon, Vice President and General Manager of Omaha Steaks, a direct marketer of steaks and other gourmet foods, commented on the importance of customer service:

---

[7]*Catalog Age/DIRECT Source Book*, 1997.
[8]The Department of Commerce did not incorporate the retail category "Catalogs" into their data until 1985. Data prior to that included mail-order sales only.
[9]"Maybe they're cutting back on snacks." *Direct*, July 1997.
[10]*Journal of Commerce*, December 6, 1996.
[11]*Catalog Age/DIRECT Source Book*, 1997.

Table B Top Five Reasons to Shop By Catalog

Reason	Percent Citing This as a Major Reason to Shop By Catalog
It saves a lot of time compared to shopping in stores	55%
Items bought in catalogs are usually not conveniently available in stores	47
It's nicer to shop at home than go through the hassle of shopping at a mall or individual store	46
You don't have to deal with sales clerks or other people trying to sell you things	32
Merchandise in catalogs tends to cost less than equivalent merchandise in stores	28

Source: *Catalog Age/DIRECT* Source Book, 1997.

We owe our success to our customers. The feedback we get from them, in the form of orders, calls, and correspondence, allows us to tailor our merchandise, marketing, and service to meet their needs. We listen to our customers and then respond with high quality products and service. None of this comes as a surprise to anyone, but the key is relentless application of the idea every day, every minute of every day.[12]

Indeed, the nature of the catalog purchasing experience, taking place primarily in a one-to-one interaction on the telephone between a customer and a customer service representative, allowed greater customization and opportunity for market feedback. Customers purchasing merchandise over the telephone generally felt comfortable calling a company back to offer negative or positive feedback. Retail store consumers were less likely to return to stores to find the appropriate person to register a complaint.[13] (See Table B for consumer reasons to shop by catalog.)

Challenges, however, lay ahead for the catalog industry. The most serious was the threat of margin erosion resulting from large numbers of new entrants. For example, it was clear that over-stuffing of consumer mailboxes with catalogs led to declining response rates. *Catalog Age* reported: "A good 58% of polled consumers in DIRECT's consumer issues survey said that they do not even look at their direct mail before they toss or recycle it."[14] The enormous numbers of catalogs mailed to consumers, and the consumer outrage that it sometimes incurred, was even the subject of a late October 1997 "Seinfeld" episode on NBC.[15]

Smaller catalog players were experiencing financial difficulties due to rising competition. As a result, industry consolidation was a growing trend—in just two months of 1997, twenty-one mergers and acquisitions took place. Larger consolidations included U.S. Office Products' acquisition of Childcraft Education Corporation from Disney Enterprises, and Genesis Direct's addition of toy catalog GlobalFriends to its catalog collection[16] (see Exhibit 5).

Frontgate History: Paul Tarvin and John O'Steen

As a high school student in 1974, Paul Tarvin, following advice his father gave him ("Never say no to an opportunity"), accepted an offer to work in the warehouse of Sportsman's Market, an aviation supply catalog. Many years later, as Vice President of Marketing, Tarvin initiated creative marketing decisions and promotions, including the introduction of a plane giveaway sweepstakes and a line of leather jackets endorsed by pioneering test pilot Chuck Yeager. During Tarvin's tenure, annual catalog

---

[12]"Catalogers Report Increased Profits and Response Rates for 1997 Spring Season." Direct Marketing Association, On-line Headline News.

[13]*Catalog Age/DIRECT Source Book*, 1997.

[14]Negus, Beth. *Catalog Age/DIRECT Source Book*, 1997.

[15]"Seinfeld," an NBC sitcom, was one of the America's most popular television programs in 1997.

[16]Section adapted from Greg Berglund's and Luc Sirois' paper, *Front gate On-line?*

sales rose 5000% to $50 million in 1991 from $1 million in 1974.

John O'Steen, a former Proctor & Gamble manufacturing manager and professional race car driver, also had experience in the catalog-based direct marketing industry. From 1984 to 1990, O'Steen was the president and CEO of Cincinnati Microwave, a direct marketer and manufacturer of police radar warning receivers and other electronic products and services.

While working at Sportsman's Market, Tarvin recognized an opportunity in what he viewed as a neglected market:

> What I felt was that there were a lot of people serving the mid-market, companies like Brookstone and The Sharper Image. I saw an opportunity to go after the very high-end category with functional products. Not really decorative, but products that added beauty and function to the home. That was really the core of the merchandising concept for Frontgate. The name "Frontgate" symbolized the entire home environment inside and out.

In March 1991, O'Steen and Tarvin founded Cinmar L.P., a Delaware limited partnership, in Lebanon, Ohio—just outside of Cincinnati—to pursue their objectives. That September, they mailed the first Frontgate catalog to 300,000 homes. From the outset, the venture proved financially successful; each quarter the company surpassed its revenue and profit projections. Reflecting this rapid growth, in 1997 Cinmar employed 350 people up from 140 in 1996, circulated 28 million catalogs, and had projected revenues of $95 million.

The Frontgate Catalog and Value Proposition

Mission. Cinmar's success was attributed to the clear vision of its founders, with quality as the foundation of the business. O'Steen and Tarvin remarked on this in the Cinmar, L.P. Statement of Purpose:

> Cinmar will circulate more than 30 million catalogs in 1998. But size alone is rarely a measure of success

nor its guarantee. Rather, it's the ongoing adherence to the guiding principles of our mission statement:

> *The mission of Cinmar is to be a leader in supplying high quality goods of lasting value to discriminating homeowners via direct marketing. Cinmar will be customer focused, building recognition for its brands by providing unmatched service and products which exceed our customers' expectations. Cinmar will maintain a reputation for professionalism and integrity among suppliers and associates throughout the industry. Cinmar will provide its employees with an environment which fosters personal and professional growth and satisfaction. We will accomplish these objectives in a way that will provide an excellent return for our investors.[17]*

Catalog. Frontgate mailed its catalog, proportioned generously at a newsweekly magazine trim size (slightly larger than 8 1/2" by 11"), 12 times a year. Five to six of these catalogs represented were completely new seasonal publications.[18] The remaining five to six catalogs contained previously offered products under new covers, a common catalog industry practice to deliver "fresh" editions without repurposing all of the inside pages.

Each catalog included between 270 and 300 products, with three to four products per page. Photography for the cover shot cost Frontgate from $1,000 to $3,000, while standard product shots inside cost $500. Cinmar printed the catalog on premium grade paper, chosen for its ability to render superior color purity and sharpness of images. Stuart Kennedy, Cinmar's production manager, added:

> We spend a ton of time making sure photos are color-accurate. We make sure that the image truly matches the product. Before we actually go to the printing press we get a proof, which represents what the press conditions will be, and put it next to the product. If the greens don't match, we'll go back and manipulate that electronic image again, get a new proof, and make sure that they match. Once the proof is right, I actually sit down there at the printing plant while the press is running with my proof and line them up. (See Exhibit 6 for the Frontgate catalog cover.)

Products

Every product in this catalog has one thing in common: long-lasting value. We look for well-thought-out design and timeless styling, not trends. Strong, sturdy

---

[17]Cinmar, L.P., company documents.
[18]Total number of catalogs mailed in a year has been disguised. Historically, the catalog was printed in four cycles. This grew to six in order to accommodate large shifts in merchandise mix between spring and summer and late August and autumn.

materials and honest workmanship, not flimsy dispos-
ables. Because many Frontgate products are the best in
their category, they invite real pride of ownership. They
also invite imitation, so while you may find knock-offs
elsewhere, we guarantee you won't find better value
anywhere.

—John O'Steen and Paul Tarvin, from the
Welcome to the 1997 Holiday Catalog

Frontgate offered products from various premium-branded vendors, including Sony Electronics, Motorola, Viking Grills, Saeco, and imported Italian ceramic art from Deruta and Montelupo.[19] Frontgate's product managers specifically sought items that were not commonly available elsewhere and that customers did not previously know existed but would feel compelled to purchase. Examples of these products included The Jiffy Garment cleaner, a personal clothes steamer that produced results similar to those of a professional dry-cleaner, and a massive outdoor Viking grill with a griddle and infrared roaster (see Exhibit 7). Tarvin commented on the selection process for Frontgate products:

> I think flexibility is the key. We try not to put things in that don't fit into who we are and that we don't believe in. There is a subtle definition of a Frontgate product. One thing we try not to waver on is the quality side. If we're selling a towel, it needs to be bigger and thicker and better quality then what you're going to find in a department store. The idea is that if you're selling a bath shelf or a grill, the quality and the positioning should be consistent from one product category to the next.

Rigorous testing of products took place prior to inclusion in the Frontgate catalog. Before granting final approval for any product, Frontgate asked product vendors to submit guarantees that the product was adequately packaged for reshipment. On the quality of Frontgate products, Rob Guiher, the company's Chief Information Officer, commented on the reality of the high quality in Frontgate products:

> I guarantee it. In fact I own a Frontgate mailbox and about two years ago somebody ran it over. They ran it over, snapped off my six-by-six inch redwood post,

the mailbox skidded about forty feet down the asphalt, and all that happened was it was scratched up a little bit where it had skidded. Not a single dent in it. I had to put a new post in, unfortunately, but the mailbox itself was great.

Pricing. Just as Frontgate defied traditional catalog practices of offering products at varying quality levels, so it defied standard retail pricing models. The catalog did not seek to appeal to the average price-sensitive, bargain-shopping customer. Frontgate customers were 61% female, between the ages of 35 to 54; 74% were married; their median home value was $300,000 and annual household income was over $100,000.[20] (U.S. average annual household income was $35,492 in 1997.)[21] Tarvin remarked, "We're not competing with the masses out there. There's a lot more competition in the $799 price point for a table and chairs than there is for a $2,000 price point—$10 and $15 grill utensils do not sell well in our catalog."

Frontgate had tested low price items in the catalog, and they fared poorly. Pricing, therefore, remained stable; consumers did not find red-slashed items for sale in the Frontgate catalog. If a product did go on sale, Frontgate lowered the price in the next catalog without drawing attention to the new price. Due to the high-end character of the catalog's products, Frontgate's profit margins were higher than industry averages.

Customer Acquisition. To acquire new customers, Frontgate mailed its catalog to approximately 20 million prospective households each year, 12 times a year, at a cost of $.50 per piece. These addresses were obtained through the purchase of targeted mailing lists at approximately $.10 per name. Of these prospective households, approximately 1.4 percent, or 280,000 new customers, ordered a product through the Frontgate catalog, with an average order of $115.[22]

Customer Retention. Repeat customers were divided into three categories: Those who made another purchase within the last 12 months; those customers who had not made a repeat purchase for the last 12 to 24 months; and those customers who had not made a repeat purchase in more than 24 months. Customers who fell in the first category—approximately 317,000 households—received the Frontgate catalog 10 times a year and had a response rate of roughly four percent per catalog mailed. Customers who fell in the second category—approximately 183,000 households—received the Frontgate catalog six times a year and had a response rate of approxi-

---

[19]The villages of Deruta and Montelupo were considered centers of the Italian pottery renaissance.
[20]Cinmar, L.P., Company Profile, 1996 and interview with Greg Berglund.
[21]United States Census Bureau, 1997.
[22]All numbers have been disguised.

mately three percent. Customers who fell in the third category—approximately 262,000 households—received the Frontgate catalog only four times a year and had a response rate of approximately two percent. The average order for repeat customers was $135. The gradual reduction in catalogs sent to non-purchasing households reflected the company's effort to reduce marketing costs by targeting customers more aggressively who were more likely to make a repeat purchase.[23]

Spin-Off Catalogs.

Cinmar also introduced three spin-off catalogs: The Search for the Perfect Gift—"the Frontgate gift collection," The Ultimate Grill—a "catalog of outdoor cooking," and Splash—a swimming pool accessory supply catalog (see Exhibits 8, 9, and 10 for catalog covers). Frontgate mailed each spin-off catalog twice a year. Berglund remarked:

> What these three spin-off catalogs allow us to do is to prospect for new customers more effectively. We could send Frontgate catalogs to all of those prospects, but we found if we target the merchandising mix more closely to the customer segment we're mailing to, we can really take marketing to another level, by increasing our response rates and lowering our acquisition costs.

Each spin-off had varying percentages of overlapping products with the anchor Frontgate catalog. Noted Berglund:

> We really need to be careful with brand positioning. There are some powerful arguments saying that you should put your best selling products in multiple book titles—grills go on patios, pools have patios. We could sell grills and grill accessories in Splash. But if you go overboard with this, your previously distinctive brands or titles start merging together. [See Exhibit 11 for brand positioning statement.]

Consolidation.

In 1995, Cinmar was acquired by holding company International Cornerstone Group. Cornerstone acquired TravelSmith, a leisure and travel catalog, in 1995; in 1996, it added other high-end catalogs including Garnet Hill, The Territory Ahead, and Ballard Designs. Tarvin noted that the merger's opportunities for pooled resources among the catalogs would provide operational advantages in Cinmar's back office. These included negotiating credit card contracts, freight con-

tracts, phone contracts, UPS contracts, and consolidating order processing, warehousing, material handling, technology, tracing orders, and paper and printing costs. Consolidation would also enable sharing of customer records across catalog databases. Tarvin pointed out that Cornerstone had the opportunity to build its own inhouse database that could focus on a consumer pool more pertinent to Frontgate.

The Customer Experience

Ordering.

The Frontgate call center, open for business 24 hours a day and seven days a week, consisted of 50 workstations. These supported 30 phone service representatives, 10 product specialists, and 10 customer service representatives. In addition, seven "roamers," senior Frontgate employees, patrolled the call center in order to ensure quality of customer service. Upon dialing the Frontgate toll-free phone number (1-800-626-6488), 92% of customers reached a phone service representative within 20 seconds. A digital light display capable of running headlines on each wall of the call center identified the number of operators talking to customers, available operators, and customers waiting to speak with a representative. Warning bells sounded when all of the representatives were occupied with customers, and new calls were holding in line to be answered. Every employee, including Tarvin and O'Steen, was trained to jump in to handle calls if necessary.

Phone service representatives entered order and billing information into a catalog management system called Mail Order and Cataloging System (MACS).[24] MACS served as the operational backbone of the company by integrating order entry, customer service, credit card processing, shipment receiving, and warehousing data. For example, using the MACS system, phone service representatives could tell a customer immediately if a product was in-stock.

MACS' limitations, however, made it less useful for retrieval of extensive product information. MACS was able to store and display two or three screens or windows of product information. Frontgate held the remaining product information in 15 filing cabinets co-located with the product specialists. MACS' other limitation was its service customization and personalization features, which were minimal. When viewing customer information screens, phone service representatives found it difficult to access customer purchasing or return histories. Without that information, it was challenging for

---

[23]All numbers have been disguised.
[24]MACS was made by Smith Gardner. Smith Gardner had already integrated Web sites with the program.

Frontgate phone service representatives to offer special attention, such as cross-selling additional products pertinent to specific customers.[25]

Product Specialists. Frontgate phone service representatives connected customers to product specialists for detailed product information and inquiries such as product comparisons and usability. Product specialists generally began as phone service representatives and received an additional six to eight weeks of training to gain expertise on every product in the four Frontgate catalogs. Pete McAdams, Product Specialists Manager, remarked:

> They know the products backwards and forwards. They have used the products and tested them themselves. We try to have the specialists positioned so they are like an in-house representative of the manufacturer. I would put any of our people up against any one of our product supplier's customer service representatives. I don't think the manufacturer has specific individuals that know their product as well as we know their product.

A product specialist fielded a customer inquiry:

Product Specialist: Thank you for calling Frontgate, this is Gary. How may I help you?

Customer: I just received the Frontgate catalog for the first time and am intrigued by these expensive Viking and DCS (Dynamic Cooking Systems) grills. I was wondering if you could provide some more information about their features.

Product Specialist: Well, we've been offering the DCS grills for about five years and have had very favorable responses from customers. We've only been offering the Viking grills for about four months, so we have less testimonials for those products. I can answer specific questions for both grills.

Customer: Are they weather resistant?

Product Specialist: They both come with a heavy duty vinyl case. And the hardware is also stainless steel, so if you left it out it would not rust anyway. The stainless steel has a lifetime guarantee and the burners have a five-year guarantee. [Burners] may rust but all you have to do is take a wire brush and scrape the rust off.

Customer: Can you talk about the differences between the Viking and DCS grills?

Product Specialist: I personally feel that because the DCS grills have a more rounded look, they are more aesthetically pleasing. But the Viking grill has some better features like larger side trays and a warming tray for breads and things. Viking grills also have flavor generators. There is a grid under the meat, above the burners, that catch drippings from the meat. Heat dissipates drippings into steam and comes back up at the meat to re-flavor it.

I can mail you our grill catalog to provide you with even more information on the grills, if you would like.

Inventory. Frontgate filled orders for the Frontgate catalog, as well as for the TravelSmith catalog, from a 120,000-square-foot, on-site warehouse and a 40,000-square-foot, off-site warehouse for large grills and furniture, both located in Lebanon, Ohio. When Tarvin and O'Steen started filling orders three years earlier, the on-site warehouse was one-quarter of its current size.

Phone service representatives immediately informed customers of items not in stock and when they expected the items to arrive. Frontgate aimed for a mid-90% fill rate of all orders (clothing catalogs and manufacturers usually aimed in the 85% range, due to the complexity of managing size and color specifications for apparel).[26] Guiher remarked on the company's inventory planning methodology:

> If [a product] was carried before, you've got history to go on. Preferably, it was carried last year at the same time, in a similar presentation, in a similar book, in which case the results are usually fairly comparable. There are obvious caveats to this. The difficult job is when you don't have past history, or carried the product in a different season. In this case, you can use existing similar products to judge customer interest. Where you really get into trouble is where you have an item, especially given the uniqueness of our items, that you've never carried before. Then you look at factors like positioning in the catalog, the amount of space it's been given—all of the things that relate to how motivating the presentation is to the purchaser.

---

[25]These types of features had almost become standard on many Web sites due to applications capable of extensive user customization. In late 1997, for example, Amazon.com was able to offer new and old customers book recommendations based on their buying histories.
[26]Interview with Greg Berglund, Director, Business Development, Cinmar, L.P.

Shipping. Frontgate's central geographic location just north of Cincinnati had advantages for shipping; it was able to reach half the nation in just two days via UPS ground service. In fact, *Catalog Age* ranked Ohio as the best state in the country for outbound shipping.[27] Frontgate offered a pledge for same-day shipping on in-stock orders received before 7:00 p.m. Eastern Time, and it packed merchandise in heavier grade paper than standard packing in order to insure safe shipping. (See Exhibit 12 for a Frontgate packing slip.)

Returns. Returns, in line with catalog industry standards, were hassle-free. Customers could call customer service representatives to check order status and to discuss return information. Frontgate catalog return rates were less than industry averages of 10% to 14% returns on hard items and 20% to 25% returns on soft items (apparel). Frontgate extended the typical industry 30-day product guarantee by a full year, to 395 days, and created an alternative returns process. Rather than utilizing a code system, in which customers matched a pre-allocated problem to their own, the Frontgate form had blank lines for customer comments (see Exhibit 13). Product specialists found that these comments were often specific and accurate, enabling the catalog to serve their customers better in the future. McAdams added:

> Any time a customer returns a product, they'll tell us why. Its one of those advantages we have as a retailer, that we can capture exactly why people are returning goods. Every time we get a return we put it in a category and process it by the primary factor for returning it. What we did was eliminate the codes that the customer would put in and, instead, invite the customer to put comments down. It's much more effective. I can look at a frequently returned product and actually look at the comments on the returned packing slips. We are doing [the customer] a service: If [customers] tell us why, then we are better able to adjust what we do here internally or through our product selection to offer a better service.

While sometimes the catalog had agreements to return unwanted or damaged products to suppliers, Frontgate generally liquidated returned merchandise with warehouse sales. The catalog had never used a liquidator for these purposes.

The On-Line Catalog Industry

Estimates of the Internet user population were between 13 and 48 million in 1997.[28] Forrester Research projected that by 2000, 51% of all Americans would live in households connected to the Internet, compared with 15.8% in 1997.[29] On-line retail sales were also expected to grow: Forrester predicted sales on the Internet to approach $7 billion by 2000, from $518 million in 1996.[30] (See Exhibit 14 for on-line commerce projections by product category.) The average on-line user was male and college-educated, with an average household income of approximately $59,000 a year (see Exhibit 15).[31]

Because most catalogs already managed back-office functions, such as ordering, processing, and shipping, many industry analysts considered catalogs obvious candidates for entry into electronic commerce on the Web. An analyst at International Data Corporation, a research firm in Framingham, Massachusetts, echoed this sentiment: "Given the similarity of managing databases and page production for the Web to the applications used by the catalog business, it's not a huge leap of faith to think it's not difficult for them to move pages to the Web. They already have the infrastructure to sell on-line."[32] Ray Sparks, an MIS manager at Frontgate, agreed, stating, "We already have the things in place to make [a functioning Web site] happen. The players are all there." Additionally, the on-line customer profile seemed to coincide, in some respects, with that of a catalog customer. In a survey of on-line customers conducted by the Direct Marketing Association, half of respondents made purchases from a catalog during the same period that they made purchases on-line.[33]

In 1995, 11% of catalogs surveyed reported that they offered catalog services on-line. In 1997, 60% of catalogs offered an on-line catalog; 60% of those offered on-line ordering and a complete catalog. Most of the on-line consumer catalogs cited improving consumer brand awareness as the primary goal of their on-line catalog.[34]

[27] *Catalog Age/DIRECT Source Book*, 1997.
[28] Veronis, Suhler & Associates, *Communications Industry Forecast*, July, 1997; CommerceNet/Nielsen, *Electronic Commerce Overview*, Spring 1997.
[29] Adapted from Greg Berglund's and Luc Sirois' paper *Frontgate On-line?*
[30] *Forbes Magazine*, February 10, 1997.
[31] CommerceNet/Nielsen, *Electronic Commerce Overview*, Spring 1997, and Yahoo Internet Life, August 1997.
[32] Ricadela, Aaron. "Mail Order Finds Friend in On-line Sales - Catalog Operations Complemented By Web Efforts." *Computer Retail Week*, June 2, 1997.
[33] "How Consumers are Shopping Using Interactive Media." Direct Marketing Association, On-line Headline News.
[34] Chiger, Sherry. "The Future of On-line Commerce is Now." *Catalog Age*, September 1, 1997.

(See Exhibit 16 for Web site costs related to functionality.) In late 1997, Frontgate's direct and indirect competitors—1-800-Flowers, Campmor, Eddie Bauer, J. Crew, J. Peterman, Lands' End, L.L.Bean, Omaha Steaks, Orvis, Sharper Image, and Sundance—offered on-line companions to their print catalog, with varying degrees of functionality.

Frontgate On-Line

In light of the on-line ventures of his competitors, Tarvin was sure that Frontgate needed to move forward with the development of a Web site. Hiring Greg Berglund was the first step toward that goal. But Tarvin was aware of contrasting views among key decision-makers in the company.

Some Cinmar employees questioned the value of a Frontgate Web site. Central to this argument was the poor resolution and image quality of data accessed through home modems and viewed on PCs with consumer (as opposed to professional) monitors. Guiher expressed the sentiments of many of his colleagues, "Grainy thumbnails, in our minds, do not sell $4,000 products [such as high-end grills]. It is not going to be easy on the Web to convince someone to buy something that costs twice what they might spend at Wal-Mart, even if the product is twice or three times the quality."

Patrick Butler, Cinmar Vice President and Controller, expressed similar concerns with respect to modems' speeds, "Our customer is very high income with a tight schedule. If the process on the Web slows them down, our service image may become damaged."

Butler also remained unconvinced that costs involved in the maintenance of a Web site were as minimal as often quoted. A two-minute phone call was far more expensive than an order via e-mail. However, Butler pointed out that the moment on-line consumers picked up the phone to make an additional inquiry, all cost-saving benefits of the on-line order were eliminated. Additionally, the Web's potential use as a source of information for product specialists required a commitment throughout the company to adopt the Web as a way of life. The file cabinets were easy to expand, but Web page maintenance required employees to enter new product information into the system. If the customer service center received e-mails on a consistent basis, Frontgate customers would demand the same level of service to which they were accustomed over the phone. Those e-mails would need to be fielded promptly, which represented yet another potential financial drain.

Tarvin believed that inferior graphics were a necessary trade-off given the Web's convenience and ease-of-use. Berglund shared this opinion, stating that a transactional Web site would appeal to the segment of younger Frontgate customers who were accustomed to the Web and on-line shopping: "People who are just coming into some disposable income, look at the Frontgate catalog and say, 'I really want my home to look like that.' Those people are Internet-savvy today—because many have made their money using technology."

Tarvin and Berglund also saw value in the Web as a potential testing ground for products. "When you print 10 million catalogs, with half a page of space, you're going to spend $25,000 to $50,000 promoting an individual product," Tarvin remarked. "The Internet can really provide a testing vehicle for that product. In just an afternoon, we could gauge consumer interest in a new product."

Berglund felt the Web offered the opportunity for Frontgate to take marketing to a higher level. Frontgate could make anecdotal stories available on-line about products from customers and employees. Berglund also envisioned a customer profile feature, in which the Frontgate database used individual preferences to respond to individuals' wants and desires by offering products in their preferred categories.

Web Site Options

Frontgate's competitors had developed sites along six levels of investments. These levels, outlined in Exhibit 16, ranged from a site with minimal functionality—one or two pages of content and a posted phone number for catalog requests—to a fully developed site with capabilities such as transactions, sound and video, and chat. Tarvin found it useful to consider development of the Frontgate Web site in light of these investment levels:

- **Option A: Limited Web Site (Levels 1–4)** This site would consist of limited pages of product and contact information for users to order catalogs. It appealed to people within the Frontgate organization who questioned whether the Internet was an appropriate medium for delivery of Frontgate products at all.

- **Option B: Content-Based Web Site (Level 5)** The middle option for the on-line catalog would include product images, detailed information, and ordering functionality, with e-mail inquiries sent to customer service. Product specialists could also access the information digitally, rather than sorting through physical file cabinets. Berglund envisioned this site complementing the catalog by providing additional information that could not be justified in print. This model used the Internet to close the sale, rather than generate new sales; marketing techniques in the catalog would generate an inquiry, and the transaction would take place on the Web.

- **Option C: Full-Scale Web Site (Level 6)** These Web sites would not only provide ordering functionality and product information, but also value-added content that built a sense of community to boost the catalog's brand equity in the eyes of existing and prospective customers. An extensively developed Web site with customization features offered businesses the power of one-to-one marketing. Catalogs could target individuals rather than marketing to entire population segments. This fully developed site, with a great deal of money invested in it, would involve a "push" approach for Frontgate, potentially attracting and acquiring new customers on-line. This would include advertising on other sites and possible inclusion in on-line "malls"—conglomerates of on-line shopping sites.

Conclusion

Tarvin was pleased with the progress of the Frontgate Web site. He believed that the site would provide yet another valuable service for Frontgate's customers. At the same time, though, he worried that Frontgate was once again a step behind in the Internet race. Was Frontgate creating a site with limited or inadequate capabilities? Should Cinmar invest more in the site to provide additional features? He knew that the answer was not simple. Most importantly, Tarvin did not want to find Cinmar and Frontgate missing the opportunities intrinsic to the on-line revolution, but he also resisted increased investment just because everyone else was pouring resources into the Web.

Exhibit 1 Catalog Sales by Product

Product Category	Percent of Catalog Shoppers Ordering This Merchandise 1997	Percent of Catalog Shoppers Ordering This Merchandise 1996
Books, music, video	62%	61%
Gifts for others	60	63
Women's apparel	54	56
Men's apparel	38	34
Kitchen/household products	33	34
Gardening items	32	33

Source: *Catalog Age/DIRECT Source Book*, 1997 and 1996.

Exhibit 2 Top 20 Catalogs in the United States, 1995 and 1996

Company	1996 Sales ($ millions)	1995 Sales ($ millions)	Market Segment
1. Dell Computer	$7,554	$5,296	Computer hardware
2. Gateway 2000	5,035	3,676	Computer hardware
3. J.C. Penney	3,772	3,738	General merchandise
4. Digital	3,300	3,000	Computer hardware
5. Micro Warehouse	1,916	1,308	Computer supplies
6. Spiegel	1,681	1,751	General merchandise
7. Fingerhut	1,638	1,826	General merchandise
8. Viking Office Products	1,182	920.7	Office supplies
9. Lands' End	1,112	1,030	Apparel
10. Computer Discount Warehouse	927.9	634.5	Computer supplies
11. Global Direct Mail Corp.	911.9	634.6	Computer, office, and industrial supplies
12. L.L.Bean	908	945	Apparel
13. IBM Direct	900	1,070	Computer hardware
14. Harry Schein Inc.	829	616.2	Medical and dental supplies
15. Brylane	736	601.1	Apparel
16. Hanover Direct	700.3	749.8	General merchandise
17. Victoria's Secret	684	661	Apparel
18. J. Crew Group	650	640	Apparel
19. Deluxe Direct	603.5	678.5	Business supplies
20. Newark Electronics	550	600	Industrial electronics

Source: *Catalog Age/DIRECT Source Book*, 1997.

Exhibit 3 Typical Catalog Profit and Loss Statement: As Percentage of Net Sales

Gross product sales	110%
Returns	10
Net sales	**100**
Cost of Goods sold	50
Gross margin	**50**
Fulfillment (order receiving, data entry, warehousing)	10
Net postage	(2)
Marketing and catalog costs	30
General and administrative	5
Total expenses	**43**
Operating income	**7**
List rental income	1
Interest expense	(.5)
Net income	**6.5**
Depreciation	1
Pre-tax net income	**5.5**

Source: Estimates from J. Schmid & Associates and Greg Berglund.

Exhibit 4 Profit Margin Examples–Catalog, Category Retail, and General Merchandise Retail for Fiscal Year 1996

	Catalog: Lands' End % of Total Sales	Category Retail Store: Pier 1 Imports % of Total Sales	Retail Store: Saks & Company % of Total Sales
Total Sales	**100%**	**100%**	**100%**
Costs of goods sold	53	59	69.3
SG&A expense	39.4	29	25
Other operating	NA	NA	.1
Depreciation	NA	2.1	NA
Unusual income/expense	.1	NA	0.0
Total Expenses	**92.6**	**90.1**	**94.4**
Interest expense, non-operating, other–net	(.1)	(.1)	(3.7)
Pre-Tax Income	**7.6**	**8.9**	**1.9**

Source: Company Documents, 1997.

Exhibit 5 Catalog Industry Merger and Acquisition Activity, 1995–1997

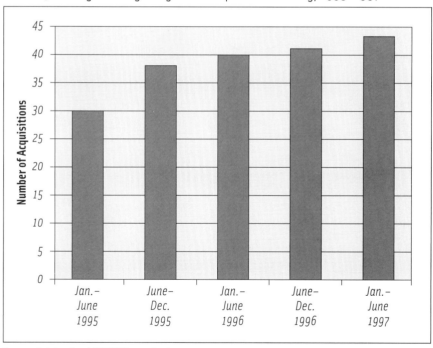

Source: *Catalog Age/ DIRECT Source Book*, 1995–1997.

Exhibit 6 Frontgate Catalog Cover, Holiday 1997

Exhibit 7 Sample Frontgate Products

Professional clothing care at home

The Jiffy Garment Steamer is used world-wide by clothing stores and cleaners because it yields fast, professional results. Your formal wear, business suits, and even casual clothing will appear fresh and wrinkle-free. Steaming is more convenient and gentler to your wardrobe than ironing, and you'll never again pay for unnecessary dry cleaning just to remove wrinkles. Steam is generated within a minute of filling the one gallon reservoir with tap water. Safety features include an automatic shutoff if the water runs low and a nozzle that stays cool to the touch. Effective on all fabrics as well as upholstery, draperies, and tablecloths. Aluminum housing is sturdier than plastic steamers and rolls easily on four casters. Hose and rod remove for storage. We recommend periodic use of the cleaning solution to remove mineral deposits from the Steamer's internal parts. 110V. 13½"W x 7½"D x 66½"H. 16 lbs. USA.
2653 Jiffy Garment Steamer $215.00
2655 Solution for Cleaning Steamer $8.50

36 FRONTGATE

Built-in rangetop burners open up new possibilities for cooking outdoors

Outdoor cooking isn't just about grilling anymore. Now you can prepare your secret Bar-B-Q sauce, sauté mushrooms to smother the steaks, or sizzle bacon for burgers without leaving the grill (or your guests) thanks to this grill's twin 15,000 BTU rangetop burners. They're outfitted with porcelainized cast iron grates and a protective stainless steel cover that doubles as a work surface. Place our optional griddle plate on top to prepare open-air weekend brunches, or add the wok grate to stir fry entrées and side dishes in your wok. The main event is individually-ignited 20,000 BTU cast iron burners at the heart of the grilling area. Both the two-burner 41" long grill and the three-burner 53" grill are equipped with a built-in smoker system, and either grill can be outfitted with an infrared rotisserie for spit-roasting meats to succulent perfection. Stainless steel carts have two 16" x 24" fold-down side shelves, a slide-out tray for easy access to the LP tank, and in-board 10" rubber wheels and locking casters for maneuverability. Double-walled doors open onto two storage shelves (41" has a single door, 53" has two doors). Includes heavy cloth-backed vinyl cover. Offered in natural gas or propane (20 pound tank provided). Grills are 31½" deep, 52½" high. USA.
4520 Professional 41" Grill with Integrated Dual Rangetop Burner $3200.00
4524 Professional 41" Grill with Integrated Dual Rangetop Burner and Infrared Rotisserie $3650.00
5320 Professional 53" Grill with Integrated Dual Rangetop Burner $3650.00
5324 Professional 53" Grill with Integrated Dual Rangetop Burner and Infrared Rotisserie $4100.00
4161 Griddle Plate (23½" x 11½", 10½ lbs.) $145.00
4168 Wok Grate (12" diameter. 3¼ lbs.) $50.00
Please specify propane or natural gas
Prices given for all-stainless grills.
For stainless with brass, add $150.00.
For forest green with brass, add $300.00.
For blue with stainless, add $150.00. *

Exhibit 8 The Search for the Perfect Gift Cover

Exhibit 9 The Ultimate Grill Cover

Exhibit 10 Splash Cover

Exhibit 11 Positioning Illustration for Frontgate Catalog Sub-Brands

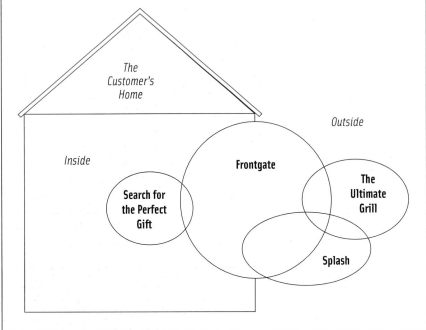

Source: Greg Berglund, Cinmar, L.P.

Exhibit 12 Frontgate Packing Slip

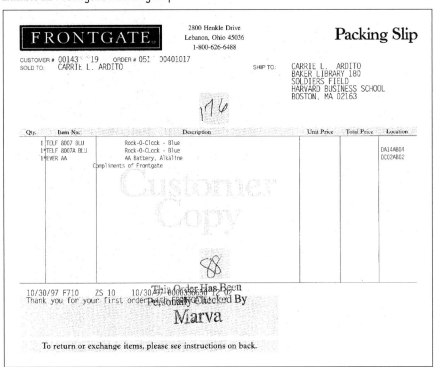

Exhibit 13 Frontgate Return Form

Return Information

For a quick solution to any of the following problems,
please speak with a Product Specialist by calling 1-800-537-8484.
Many concerns can be resolved by phone.

- Difficulty with assembly or operation
- Need for replacement parts
- Dissatisfaction with your selection
- Questions about price protection

**Frontgate's
395 Day Signature Guarantee**
We've extended the typical
30 day guarantee by a full year. If any
product fails to meet your expectations
within 13 months of purchase, we will
promptly refund your payment or replace
the item, whichever you prefer.

Price Protection
If you purchase from Frontgate and see
the same item for less (including shipping
and taxes) in another catalog within 90 days,
we will gladly refund the difference.

Printed on Recycled Paper ♻

If you find it necessary to make a return, please complete the information below.
Let us know whether you prefer an exchange, a gift certificate for later use, or a refund.
Be sure to tell us the reason for your return, too.

1. Merchandise you're returning

Item No.	Description	Qty.	Total Price	Indicate Exchange, Gift Certificate, or Refund

2. Did you receive the item(s) as a gift?   Yes _____   No _____

3. Reason for return. Be as specific as possible. _____

4. Merchandise you're ordering in exchange

Item No.	Description	Qty.	Total Price

Net Payment/Refund _____

Method of Payment   ☐ Visa   ☐ MasterCard
☐ Discover   ☐ American Express   ☐ Check or Money Order

Credit Card # _____

Exp. Date _____

Signature _____

Daytime Phone # (_____) _____

5. Enclose this form in the package with your merchandise, affix the preprinted shipping label provided below, and return to us via **UPS** or insured parcel post.

6. We welcome your comments and suggestions. _____

Exhibit 14 Projections of On-Line Commerce, 1996–2000 ($ millions)

Segment	1996	1997	1998	1999	2000
Computer products	$140	$323	$701	$1,228	$2,105
Travel	126	276	572	961	1,579
Entertainment	85	194	420	733	1,250
Apparel	46	89	163	234	322
Gifts/flowers	45	103	222	386	658
Food/drink	39	78	149	227	336
Other	37	75	144	221	329
Total	$518	$1,138	$2,371	$3,990	$6,579

Source: Forrester Research, 1996.

Exhibit 15 Profiles of Catalog Shoppers, Frontgate Customers, On-Line Users, and On-Line Shoppers

	Catalog	Frontgate	On-Line User	On-Line Shopper
% Female	61	61	42	45
% Male	39	39	58	55
Average age range	45–64	35–54	25–49	25–49
Average household income ($)	40,000	100,000	59,000	60,000
% Married	73	74	NA	NA
% With college degree	56	74	35	45

Source: "Maybe They're Cutting Back on Snacks." *Direct*, July 1997, Cinmar L.P., Company Profile, Yahoo Internet Life, August 1997, and CommerceNet/Nielsen, *Electronic Commerce Overview*, Spring 1997.

Exhibit 16 Cost Comparison of Putting Up a Web Site, by Six Degrees of Functionality[35]

Levels of Functionality	High Cost-of-Living City	Low Cost-of-Living City
1. Vanity site: One or two pages raising awareness of the company with a posted phone number and mailing address	$1,000 per page	$1,000 per page
2. Advanced vanity site: Two to three pages and e-mail capability to the company to request materials without company response	$4,000	$4,000
3. Advanced vanity site with e-mail responses from the company	$5,000	$5,000
4. Basic/small-sized Web site: 20 pages, e-mail accounts, product pictures and information, ability to update documents, Internet service for five people	$85,000	$18,900
5. Medium-sized Web site: 100 pages, e-mail accounts, user registration, password protected directories, search engine, database services, transactional capabilities, Internet service for 25 people, custom programming	$185,000-$500,000	$89,150-$404,150
6. Large Web site: Large searchable database, chat features, digitization and integration of sound and video, transactional capability, advertising banners to place on other sites	$425,000-$3,000,000	$175,000-$1,000,000

Source: "How Much Does it Cost to Put Up a Web Site?" *Advertising Age,* September, 1997, Industry Expert Estimates, and Casewriter's Estimates.

[35]Estimates do not include on-going maintenance costs such as periodic updates and monthly charges of hosting and servers. *Advertising Age* estimates those costs at $200 to $1,000 per month. Estimates also do not include personnel resources: 84% of Webmasters in 1997 made $45,000 and above; 10% earned $95,000 and above. (Gardner, E. "Backlash Against the Title Webmaster." *WebWeek,* September 15, 1997.)

Market Communications and Branding

5

MARKET COMMUNICATIONS AND BRANDING

One of the fascinating developments of the Internet has been the importance of branding. According to the American Marketing Association, a brand is a "name, term, sign, symbol, or design, or a combination of them intended to identify the goods and services of one seller or group of sellers and to differentiate them from those of competition." Market communications refer to all the points of contact that the firm has with its customers. This includes the obvious offline communications, such as television advertising, promotions, and sales calls, as well as the emergent advertising approaches on the Internet. Any discussion of market communications in the New Economy must include a blended discussion of both offline and online approaches.

One useful way to categorize market communications is to consider a simple two-by-two matrix that crosses audience focus (individualized target versus broad audience) or communication media (offline versus online). Given these two dimensions, we can distinguish between four categories of marketing communications: (1) personalized online, (2) broad online approaches, (3) traditional mass media, and (4) face-to-face communications.

A good online brand provides positive customer responses (e.g., positive brand awareness and brand associations) and benefits to both the company (e.g., reduced marketing costs, increased margins) and to the customer (e.g., confidence, satisfaction). Good brands begin with a strong value proposition that is deeply based on providing a unique customer experience. The value proposition, in turn, is executed with integrity, is consistent over time, and requires patient investment.

One difficult question that arises is whether to leverage an offline company's brand into the online environment. Proponents of the "keep the same brand" school argue that, first, it takes an enormous amount of time and money to build strong brands. Second, customers who decide to purchase online can be assured that services will occur offline. Third, it is difficult to uncover interesting new brand names. Fourth, the online and offline brand can have a synergistic effect—one that is greater than either brand operating alone. Finally, target customers will not be confused by brand offerings that appear on new sites (e.g., K-mart brands appearing on Bluelight.com).

Opponents argue that using an existing brand limits the growth of the user base. That is, it is easier for customers to believe that Travelocity or Expedia is the most comprehensive travel site as compared to their majority stockholders (i.e., American Airlines and Microsoft, respectively). Second, existing offline brands "don't get the net." Hence, their user interfaces are likely to be less useable, hip, and interesting as compared to true dot-com brands. Third, it is possible to sign up more partners—potential competitors, collaborators, and others—when a third party name is used (e.g., General Motors, Ford, and Chrysler).

Good brands, whether they leverage an offline brand or are strictly online, provide a clear message to the market about the nature of the offering. Strong brands provide not only a clear message about the functional offering but are simultaneously differentiated by their emotional, symbolic, and experiential benefits for both employees and target customers.

SYNOPSES OF CHAPTER CASES

MONSTER.COM

Case Overview

Founded in April 1994, the Monster Board was rapidly changing the way many people looked for jobs. From the beginning, the Monster Board positioned itself as a full-service resource and one-stop shop for job seekers. For corporate clients, the Monster Board provided a means to improve their quality of recruiting while lowering overall hiring costs. In 1995, TMP Worldwide acquired the Monster Board, by then one of the most recognized brands on the Web, and the site became the flagship site of TMP's Interactive division. With the full support and resources of TMP Worldwide, including dozens of offices around the world, millions of dollars in clients' advertising billings, and sites already averaging nearly a million hits per day, it seemed that the only scarce resource for the Monster Board was management's time and its ability to predict the future.

Jeff Taylor, Founder of the Monster Board and Executive Vice President of TMP Worldwide (overseer of the firm's interactive division, TMP Interactive), was once again considering critical strategic issues facing the company. He knew that the Monster Board was well-positioned for continued growth and category dominance, if it could resolve pressing issues pertaining to branding, strategic alliances, and consumer needs. In many ways, the Monster Board was already a monster success.

By the end of 1997, Monster had more than 50,000 job listings and 1.3 million visitors a month, achieving Jeff Taylor's goal of turning the Monster Board into a megabrand. TMP had forged 20 strategic alliances with Web content providers that promised to drive visitors to the Monster site, including AOL, Excite, and Yahoo! New features aimed at providing a higher quality career center for users and alliance members included "Monster Entry Level," expansion to international markets, and an alliance with Rent.net for apartment searches.

In July 1999, the company entered into the free agent market by launching an auction site, Monster Talent Market, whereby prospective employers could place bids for the services of independent professionals. Five months later, in December 1999, Monster.com entered into a four-year, $100 million deal with America Online to be the online service provider's exclusive career information provider. Monster.com also continued to build its brand internationally with Monster sites in 8 countries outside the United States by the end of 1999 and planned to enter 11 other countries in 2000.

In the wake of these initiatives, Jeff Taylor considered future challenges, including an increase in the number of niche job placement sites, such as casino.com for gaming industry employees and MBAfreeagent.com for MBA professionals; the importance of building community and personalization into Monster.com to encourage repeat visits by users; and maintaining the company's innovative culture as it expanded across geographic boundaries.

What would the next five years be like for Monster.com? What would be the next monster idea? How could Monster.com continue to be innovative and retain its dominant position as the world's leading online career brand while continuing to expand into new markets?

Preparation Questions

1. What are the Monster Board's strengths and weaknesses with respect to its competition? What factors account for its business success to date?

2. How might Monster Board strengthen its franchise, given Jeff Taylor's options—building its brand, launching vertical sites as brand extensions or increasing geographic expansion?

3. How might Monster Board gain maximum leverage as a subsidiary of TMP Worldwide?

4. Are there new economic models, new sources of user value, or pricing policies that Monster Board could adopt to enhance revenues and profitability?

E-LOAN, INC.

Case Overview

This case examines the Service Profit Chain in an online brokerage environment and the uses of electronic interfaces to help customers achieve value-added efficiencies when searching for a home mortgage. Through the Internet, E-LOAN attempts to replace the traditional, brick-and-mortar mortgage broker by offering its customers access to a larger number and wider range of mortgages from which to choose. While the mortgage brokerage industry is highly fragmented, one of the challenges facing E-LOAN is whether its brand can scale up quickly to be a national player and thereby become profitable. Its key competitors include Countrywide, Quicken, and MoneyTree.com.

Preparation Questions

1. How does E-LOAN's philosophy simultaneously benefit customers, employees, and shareholders?

2. How do E-LOAN's customers benefit from the company's value proposition over that of traditional mortgage brokers?

3. How does E-LOAN's interface support its value proposition?

INTEGRATIVE QUESTIONS

As you consider the entire set of questions in the fifth chapter, you should also reflect on the following integrative questions.

1. Is branding different in the New Economy? Is branding more or less difficult in the online environment?

2. If Jeff Taylor was hired as a consultant to advise E-LOAN on branding and market communications, what advice might he provide? Would you agree with this advice for E-LOAN?

3. How should marketing communications effectiveness be measured in the online environment? What are the challenges in measuring the impact of the combination of online and offline effectiveness?

SUMMARY

This chapter focused on market communications and branding. Market communications should be broadly conceived to include both online and offline communications. One key feature of the online environment is the shift from broadcast-based communications to custom, interactive communications. To measure the overall impact of communications, both mediums should be examined. Branding is one of the central outputs of an effective market communications campaign. The brand should symbolize the value proposition of the firm functionally, emotionally, and experientially. A brand should be managed over time. Key metrics for successful brands include relevance to the target audience, memorableness of the brand, strength of positive associations with the brand, and consistency.

MONSTER.COM

"When I grow up, I want to be forced into early retirement."
—Monster.com television advertisement 1999

*Two roads diverged in a yellow wood
And sorry I could not travel both
And be one traveler, long I stood
And looked down one as far as I could . . .*

*. . . And both that morning equally lay
In leaves no steps had trodden black . . .*

*. . . Two roads diverged in a wood, and I—
I took the road less traveled by,
And that had made all the difference.*
—Monster.com television advertisement 2000, adapted from the poem by Robert Frost

Most companies are evolutionary. But to be successful in the new economy, you have to be revolutionary.
—Jeff Taylor, founder and CEO, Monster.com

As Jeff Taylor (Harvard Business School OPM '99), the 39-year-old founder and CEO of Monster.com, looked out of the window from his fifth-floor office at the company's headquarters in Maynard, Massachusetts, on a clear and crisp day in February 2000, he could not help but reflect on how far the company had come since its founding almost seven years earlier. By all accounts, Monster.com was now the clear leader among the estimated 25,000 active job sites on the Web, with 50% share of the online recruitment advertising market.[1] Over the past four years, Monster.com's revenue had increased almost twenty-fold from $6.9 million in 1996 to $133.5 million in 1999,[2] and had contributed significantly to its parent company TMP Worldwide's market capitalization of over $6 billion. The site's traffic—averaging 3.6 million unique visitors in January 2000 and reaching over 5% of all U.S. Internet users, ranking Monster.com as the 82nd[3] most visited site on the Web—was substantially greater than that of three of its nearest competitors, CareerMosiac.com, HotJobs.com, and Careerpath.com[4] (see Exhibit 1).

For the second year in a row, Monster.com had taken an aggressive approach to building its brand by purchasing two 30-second television advertising spots during Super Bowl XXXIV in January 2000. A year earlier, Monster.com had launched its first-ever television spot—it was one of only two Internet-based companies to do so during Super Bowl XXXIII—showing fresh-faced, elementary school-aged children aspiring to achieve dead-end jobs as a way of emphasizing the importance of finding a satisfying career online (see Exhibit 2). The response to this advertising campaign, entitled "When I Grow Up," was tremendous. Within a 24-hour period after the spot's airing, searches on Monster.com increased by 450%. Over the next 12 months, Monster.com continued to run the television spot, which almost quadrupled its reach among all Internet users in the U.S. from 1.4% in December 1998 to 5.3% in January 2000; its paid job listings on Monster.com grew by almost 75%, from 186,000 to 315,248;[5] and its resume database tripled from 1 million to 3 million (see Exhibit 3). The Monster.com television spot which aired during Super Bowl XXXIV (see Exhibit 4) centered around the Robert Frost poem, "The Road Not Taken." This ad showed similarly strong results, with 4.4 million job searches within a 24-hour period—double the number of job searches that Monster.com had received the day after Super Bowl XXXIII.

Despite the high brand awareness of Monster.com among human resource professionals and job seekers, Taylor knew that both he and his executive team could not afford to rest on the company's past success. In order to maintain Monster.com's dominant position in an

---

[1]Media Metrix, January 2000. Fifty percent market share refers to percentage of eyeball minutes among career sites.
[2]Media Metrix, January 2000.
[3]As of December 1999. Brean Murray Institutional Research Report, December 2, 1999.
[4]Careerpath.com was a joint venture of several major newspapers, including *The New York Times, Washington Post,* and *Los Angeles Times,* to place their print help-wanted ads online.
[5]December 1999 figure from William B. Drewry, Newspapers.com report, Donaldson, Lufkin & Jenrette, February 15, 2000.

industry that was expected to grow from $265 million in 1999 to $1.74 billion dollars in 2003, Taylor knew that he had to move aggressively. In July 1999, the company entered into the free agent marketspace by launching an auction site, Monster Talent Market (*www.talentmarket.monster.com*), whereby prospective employers could place bids for the services of independent professionals. Five months later, in December 1999, Monster.com entered into a four-year, $100 million deal with America Online to be the online service provider's exclusive career information provider. Monster.com also continued to build its brand internationally with Monster sites in eight countries outside of the United States (see Exhibit 5) by the end of 1999 and planned to enter 11 other countries in 2000.

In the wake of these initiatives, Taylor considered the future challenges for Monster.com. These challenges included an increase in the number of niche job placement sites, such as casino.com for gaming industry employees and MBAfreeagent.com for MBA professionals; the importance of building community and personalization into Monster.com to encourage repeat visits by users; and how to maintain the company's innovative culture as it expanded across geographic boundaries and entered new marketspaces.

With over 340 employees located in its Maynard headquarters—out of 580 employees worldwide—Taylor sought to maintain the distinctive culture of an Internet start-up. Monster.com's new offices were designed with this in mind: an employee lounge was overseen by a giant mural of the company's mascot, the monster Trump (See Exhibit 6); a breakfast bar offered free refreshments and snacks; and an employee gym. As he walked out of his office and down the hall toward the breakfast bar, Jeff Taylor wondered what the next five years would be like for Monster.com and what the next monster idea would be.

The Recruitment Advertising Market[6]

Recruitment advertising traditionally involved companies creating and placing "help wanted ads" for specific positions in the classified sections of newspapers. While recruitment advertisements historically had been a cyclical business, during the period from 1990 through 1997, the U.S. market grew at a compound annual growth rate of approximately 12%. Classified readership by job seekers had remained constant over the previous ten years and in 1996, 85% of companies used newspapers to attract potential employees. While the market was robust, industry experts estimated that only 20% to 30% of job openings were advertised using traditional print media; most positions were filled by internal placement, employee referral, employment agencies, and job fairs. The full range of services provided by recruitment advertising agencies could be complex, including the design and placement of classified advertising and creation of comprehensive image campaigns seeking to brand a client as a preferred employer. For 1998, total spending in the United States in recruitment classified advertising in newspapers was approximately $12 billion.[7] Agencies earned commissions [that were] equal to 15% of gross billings, which amounted to agency revenues of nearly $1.8 billion.

Recruitment classified advertising had long represented the "bread and butter" business of local newspapers, providing 85% to 95% profit margins as a category, and making the difference between profit and loss for many newspapers (see Exhibit 7 for advertising revenues for U.S. newspapers and Exhibit 8 for help wanted recruitment advertising rates in *The Boston Globe*).

While the number of people in the United States having access to the Internet expected to rise from 80 million in 1998 to 120 million in 2000,[8] the percentage of *Fortune* 500 companies actively recruiting online was expected to show an even more impressive increase over the same time period, from an estimated 17% in 1998 to a projected 70% by end of 2000.[9] As a result of this change, over the next five years recruitment advertisers were expected to shift more of their advertising budgets to the Internet and away from traditional media as spending for online recruitment advertising was projected to increase from $265 million in 1998 to $1.74 billion in 2003 (see Exhibit 9). There were several reasons for this shift. Ad spending was following job seekers online: industry analysts estimated that by 1999, nearly 20% of job seekers used the Internet as part of their search, up from essentially 0% in 1995. Also, online advertising was more cost-effective and faster for companies, a crucial advantage in the tight labor market of the late 1990s. Companies such as Cisco, the manufacturer of computer networks, had used the Internet to recruit employees and had demonstrated its effectiveness: two-thirds of Cisco's

[6]Portions of this section were adapted from an earlier case on Monster Board written by Michelle Toth (HBS #N9-897-148).
[7]Nancy Moyer and Jesse Pichel, C.E. Unterberg, Towbin, "What Is TMP Worldwide?" analyst report, November 1, 1999.
[8]Jupiter Communications, *Wall Street Journal*, December 6, 1999.
[9]Daniel Eisenberg, "We're for Hire, Just Click," *Time Magazine*, August 16, 1999.

new hires originated from the Internet and the company had shaved its time to fill an open position to 45 days from 113 days three years earlier.[10] In 1998, several major newspapers, including the *San Jose Mercury News*, and the *Dallas Morning News*, showed year-over-year declines in recruitment classified advertising of 9.2% and 3.6%, respectively,[11] despite a robust U.S. economy.

Monster.com generated most of its revenue from prospective employers, who paid about $275 per job listing for an eight-week period, with discounted rates for larger subscriptions or multiple recruiter access.[12] Advertising sales were generated through four channels: field, telesales, ad agencies, and posted job features on Monster's home page. Approximately 30% of Monster.com's sales came from the field channel, where the ultimate customer was usually the corporate human resource department of companies with 500 or more employees. The average order size for the field sales channel, staffed by 80 sales representatives, was $100,000. The telesales channel was used to reach [companies ranging in size from] start-ups to mid-sized . . . and accounted for 60% of Monster.com's revenue. The average order size in telesales was $3,000 and this channel was staffed by 163 telesales representatives.

Job seekers could search Monster.com for employment opportunities at no cost. Monster Search allowed the job seeker to access the full Monster.com database according to job location, discipline, and keyword search, allowing a user to enter specific keywords to match skills, job titles, or other requirements. Finally, through My Monster.com, job seekers could now personalize their career start page on the site (see Exhibit 10). Using My Monster.com, job seekers could store up to five different resumes, track their online applications, and allow the Monster search agent to notify them by e-mail if any job listings matched their keywords. By January 2000, more than 6 million job seekers had registered for My Monster.[13] Taylor observed:

> My Monster is a customized desktop, stored by user name and password, which allows an individual to

manage all aspects of their career on the Monster.com site. In other words, "your career operating system." Not unlike using Quicken to manage personal finances, job seekers are now using My Monster to manage their careers.

The Job Placement Industry[14]

Segments of the job placement industry ranged from temporary staffing companies that placed individuals on a short-term basis to high-end executive search firms that worked on retainer and collected a fee from the hiring company equivalent to one-third of the annual salary for the position filled. Industry-wide, permanent placement firms generated revenues of $11 billion, while the temporary help industry generated over $40 billion in revenues in 1996 (Exhibit 11 shows industry size by segment).

Temporary Help Firms

Temporary help firms filled positions in the categories of office/clerical, industrial, medical, technical/computer, and professional and specialty positions. When individuals were employed by temporary help firms on an ongoing basis, the positions included benefits such as training and healthcare. Clients were generally charged an hourly rate (usually with a four-hour minimum) which included estimated average markups of 20% to 50% of the wages paid individuals; the markup covered the temp agency's expenses and profits. Many temporary firms offered "temp-to-perm" placement, which was designed to move individuals from temporary posts into permanent positions within client companies. Some temporary firms also had permanent staffing divisions which focused on helping firms and individuals make permanent placements. Among the largest temporary staffing firms in the world were Manpower, Inc. (with revenues of $8.5 billion in 1999), Kelly Services ($4.4 billion in 1999), Adia SA ($3 billion worldwide in 1999),[15] and Robert Half ($1.8 billion in 1999).

Permanent Placement Firms

The permanent placement segment included employment agencies and placement agencies. These firms focused on placing individuals in permanent positions for clerical, administrative, and entry-level through

---

[10]Jerry Useem, "For Sale Online: You," *Fortune*, July 5, 1999.

[11]Felicity Barringer, "Newspapers Seek Cyberpartners to Fight On-line Ads," *The New York Times*, August 30, 1999.

[12]Nancy Moyer and Jesse Pichel, C.E. Unterberg, Towbin, "What Is TMP Worldwide?" analyst report, November 1, 1999.

[13]TMP Worldwide 1998 Annual Report.

[14]Portions of this section were adapted from an earlier case on Monster Board written by Research Associate Michelle Toth, under the supervision of Professor Jeffrey F. Rayport (HBS #897-148).

[15]Revenue figures from Hoover's Online (Manpower and Kelly) and OneSource (Adia SA).

middle-management positions. Such firms generally operated on a contingency basis, meaning that they were compensated only when they successfully placed a candidate. TMP estimated that these agencies earned the equivalent of 15% to 30% of the first-year annual salary of individuals placed. While the general range of salaries placed was in the range of $20,000 to $120,000, most contingency work focused on positions with salaries in the range of $20,000 to $49,000. Such companies were viewed by the market as an alternative to "help wanted" newspaper classified advertising.

Retainer Firms

Companies filled approximately 15% of all executive and managerial appointments using recruiting firms paid on a retainer basis. Retainer firms received part of their total fee at the start of a search and generally billed on an installment basis during succeeding months. Retainer firms usually placed individuals at a salary level of $70,000 and up, with fees equal to approximately one-third of each individual's starting salary. The largest retainer firms in the world were Korn/Ferry International, Heidrick & Struggles, and Spencer Stuart.

Internet job services were putting pressure on head-hunters to achieve results faster and at lower cost. Michael Boxberger, president of Korn/Ferry International, noted in 1996: "Such services are hurting recruitment firms that specialize in finding candidates for middle management jobs on a contingency-fee basis. That's because some companies are discovering that the Internet job services had not succeeded in taking business from Korn/Ferry or other high-end firms." Another industry expert, Tom Rodenhauser, managing editor of *Executive Recruiter News,* agreed, stating that "computers can't replace a recruiter's skill in judging who will fit into which corporate culture."

The History of Monster.com[16]

In the early 1980s, Jeff Taylor was a distracted student at the University of Massachusetts, Amherst, who found little motivation for classes but a natural affinity for managing people and running businesses. Unsure about college after his freshman year, Taylor took off his sophomore year and drove a truck for a retail company.

As he recalled, "That experience helped me to know what I *didn't* want to do with the rest of my life." Newly motivated to improve his long-term prospects, Taylor returned to the Amherst campus and became president of a 60-member fraternity, advertising manager of the *Daily Collegian,* the college newspaper, and coordinator of an 18-student team that gave campus tours. With some fraternity brothers, Taylor started a business offering "Freshmen Survival Kits," which marketed products to anxious freshmen parents.

Just short of earning his undergraduate degree, Taylor left the University of Massachusetts and worked as a disc jockey in several large Boston nightclubs. He tapped into a network of people in the staffing/recruitment field. Convinced by a friend to interview at some local firms, Taylor applied to three and got three offers. "Only after I started work did I realize that with most recruiting companies, as long as you were breathing, you were hired," Taylor recalled.

Taylor spent two years working as a recruiter focused on filling technical positions for high-tech companies on a contingency basis, getting most of his leads out of the help-wanted classified advertising section of *The Boston Globe* and other local newspapers. When their help-wanted ads did not work, Taylor pitched his consultative services to listed companies as an alternative. In the process, Taylor often found himself making suggestions to improve the effectiveness of his clients' ads and soon realized his talents and preferences were more aligned with the creative demands of the advertising side of the business. Shortly thereafter, Taylor left recruiting and joined JWG Associates, an agency that created and placed help-wanted ads for company recruiters.

After three years at JWG Associates, Taylor began thinking about branching out on his own. In May 1989, with six investors, he started ADION, a niche advertising agency that concentrated on designing and placing recruitment advertisements in traditional media for high-tech clients in and around Boston. Such clients were more open to exploring new approaches to recruiting. By summer 1993, Taylor had built the firm to 30 people and $6 million in billings. In the post-recession economy of the mid-1990s, high-tech firms had begun to aggressively increase their hiring. As a result, Taylor was soon feeling pressure from his clients to offer innovative solutions to their staffing problems. He remembered:

> For weeks, we'd been trying to come up with something big and different to offer our clients, who were really pushing us for new ideas. But everything we came up with were print-based solutions. One day, I

---

[16]This section was adapted from an earlier case on Monster Board written by Research Associate Michelle Toth, under the supervision of Professor Jeffrey F. Rayport (HBS #897-148).

woke up at four in the morning with this "monster" idea.

I'd been hearing about the Internet. I went over to the offices of BBN [a Boston-based engineering firm where much of the design work for the earliest versions of the Internet had been completed during the early 1970s] and hung around for an entire day. At the time, engineers were the only ones who knew anything about the Internet. After I'd been there for five or six hours and asked many questions, management politely asked me to leave. But I convinced them to help me and they sent me to see Net Daemons (NDA), a consulting company nearby. This is how my education on the Internet began.

So, having a little bit of knowledge about the Internet and a dream-induced brainstorm, I began to sketch out this completely new platform for matching job seekers with employers, and The Monster Board was born. The monster theme was important, because we were talking about something really big, with attitude, that would stand out—like a monster.

In autumn 1993, Taylor formed a separate subchapter S corporation called ADION Information Services (Monster) and, by January 1994, he was spending 60% of his time on the Internet idea. Taylor explained his staff's reaction to this: "Consensus was that I had lost focus; in their eyes I was doing 'computer crap.' The proof of this, in their minds, came when I borrowed one of our lead designers and had him draw monsters for three weeks."

The Monster Board had, in Taylor's words, "a noisy, awkward arrival on the Internet." The Internet at the time, despite the rapid development of the Web, was still primarily non-commercial. Into that world, The Monster Board—the 454th Web site in the world—brought one of the first examples of graphics combined with deep content on the Web, in a site that changed constantly with new information. The Monster Board also worked hard to build awareness of the Web itself. "We were the first company to advertise on the radio with a URL. After that, we received e-mail from some MIT students saying 'Welcome!' and one e-mail from an engineering student saying, 'NO! Stop this commercialization of the Web!' as a response to our radio advertising." Taylor elaborated:

It was challenging to actually launch The Monster Board, because we had to have both job seekers and employers. We convinced 30 of our best [Monster] clients to let us "use" their jobs for free, and then we spent $50,000 on radio advertising to jumpstart the applicant flow. And we got no response. As a result, we gave away our services to about 50 companies. It was precarious in the beginning.

By fall of 1994 we had about 400 jobs on the board and about 100 visitors a day. We hit a tense moment when the employers wanted to take their jobs down, and the newspapers wouldn't run advertising for our site. But we made sure we had good jobs, we kept doing radio, and we kept emphasizing our brand. Eventually, we turned the corner. We're still turning, actually. It's just that the corner—the opportunity—has turned out to be huge.

Through 1995, Monster struggled to become a national, and ultimately global, operation. Taylor's vision for The Monster Board as a brand had always been global, because the Internet could provide the company with global reach. The team considered hiring local salespeople to develop a client base in major cities other than Boston, where the company's presence was well-established, when TMP Worldwide proposed an acquisition. With its vast global network of offices and client relationships, TMP had local presence in most major cities in the United States and around the world. Two months after their first meeting, Taylor signed a letter of intent to sell ADION and Monster to TMP Worldwide. Monster began marketing The Monster Board to TMP clients even before the acquisition was closed in November 1995.

TMP Worldwide

TMP Worldwide was founded in 1967 by Andy McKelvey, chairman and CEO, who built the firm into a global player in the Yellow Pages and recruitment advertising business and took it public in December 1996. In 1999, TMP Worldwide generated total gross billings of $1.8 billion and commissions and fees totaling $765.8 million. Breaking down the commissions and fees, $178.1 million came from recruitment advertising; $101.3 million from Yellow Pages advertising; $295.6 million from search and selection services; $133.5 million from Internet advertising; and $57.1 from temporary contracting services (see Exhibit 12 for income statement). During the Fourth Quarter 1999, TMP's Internet Operations earned an operating profit of $7.7 million.[17]

---

[17]TMP Worldwide Press Release, March 7, 2000.

TMP's Recruitment Advertising Business. TMP entered the recruitment advertising business in 1993 with the acquisition of Bentley, Barnes & Lynn, Inc., and grew both organically and through acquisitions thereafter. In 1996 alone, TMP acquired 28 agencies. In addition to its 45 domestic offices, the company had 25 locations outside the United States and maintained affiliate relationships with 24 other agencies throughout the world. As a full-service shop, TMP offered clients comprehensive recruitment advertising services, including creation and placement of classified advertising, development of employer and corporate image campaigns, creation of collateral materials (such as recruiting brochures), and implementation of alternative recruitment programs (such as job fairs, employee referral programs, and campus recruiting). TMP received commissions generally equal to 15% of recruitment advertising gross billings, but it also earned fees from value-added services such as design, research, and other creative and administrative services.

TMP's Yellow Pages Business. With approximately 2,100 clients, or 30% of all national accounts in the U.S. Yellow Pages advertising market,[18] TMP was the largest Yellow Pages advertising agency in the world and three times larger than its nearest competitor.

TMP's Search and Selection Business. In addition to recruitment advertising and Yellow Pages, TMP also participated in the search and selection business. The company worked on retainer to help clients search for executives and on a retainer and contingency basis to help place mid-level executives earning between $50,000 and $150,000.

TMP's Temporary Contract Business. With the January 1999 acquisition of Morgan & Banks, Limited, in Sydney, Australia, the company also provided temporary contract employees in Australia and Asia, ranging from executives to clerical workers.

Clients. Overall, TMP Worldwide had more than 17,000 clients, including 90 *Fortune* 100 companies and 450 of all *Fortune* 500 companies. No account represented more than 5% of TMP's recruitment advertising commissions and fees. Table A shows some of TMP's larger recruitment advertising clients by category.

Table A Selected Recruitment Advertising Clients of TMP

Technology	Finance	Retail
Cisco Systems	Bank America Corporation	Good Guys
Compaq Computer Company	Morgan Stanley Dean Witter	Kohl's Corporation
Gateway 2000		Federated Department Store
IBM		Nike
Motorola		Office Max
Sun Microsystems		Target Stores
Pharmaceuticals	**Restaurants**	**Transportation**
Abbot Laboratories	Darden Restaurants	J.B. Hunt Transport Services
Genentech	Pizza Hut	
Consulting	**Healthcare**	
Price Waterhouse, LLP	Cigna Corporation	
System Software Associates	Kaiser Permanente/Kaiser Foundation Health Plan	
	Nova Care	

---

[18]TMP Worldwide 1998 Annual Report.

James J. Treacy, TMP's chief operating officer, explained the synergies between Monster.com and the parent company:

A lot of the jobs come from TMP. A lot of the content comes from TMP. When they're hosting a chat or message board about some really sophisticated employment issue and there's a specialist that works in the TMP network on that issue, they'll ask that person to come over to host the chat or message board.

Building the Monster.com Brand

Following the acquisition of the Monster Board, TMP Worldwide set up a new division, TMP Interactive, which also included the Online Career Center (OCC), another online career site that was acquired by TMP Worldwide in December 1995. Both sites were merged in January 1999 to form Monster.com.

In January 1999, Monster.com aired its first television advertisement. Taylor explained the rationale for launching the national television campaign and spending 15% of Monster.com's estimated 1999 advertising budget of $32 million[19] on a single 30-second Super Bowl spot:

In February 1998, about a third of our traffic came through 90 strategic alliances and partnerships [with vertically-focused websites such as Cahner's Manufacturing Marketplace and The Gartner Group] with many of the Internet's most popular Web sites. By August 1998, traffic generated from the alliances had fallen below 15% (under 10% today). But traffic to Monster.com was going through the roof. With these facts in hand, I decided to change our focus from the three-year strategy of using strategic alliances to build our traffic to going directly to the consumer.

In launching the television campaign, we thought that we could go from being the "leader" in our category to becoming the "dominator." It worked: we ended up almost quadrupling our reach. One of our goals was to get America Online's attention so we could become the exclusive career search site for them. In order to get their attention we had to be "best in our class" in terms of market share. AOL had 20 million members who spent 80% of their time within the confines of AOL. By offering a partnership with them [in December 1999], we could go directly to the

consumer and greatly expand our reach. The AOL relationship confirmed our leadership, promised massive increases in traffic, and our $100 million investment could be accretive as AOL revenue kicked in.

Anne Hollows, Monster.com's vice president for branding, explained the urgency to build the Monster.com brand quickly: "You don't have 20 years. By any measure, since [the Super Bowl in] January 1999, Monster.com has created a pre-emptive lead against our competitors and an effective barrier to entry." Over the next 12 months, the "When I Grow Up" commercial would continue to air on television—along with the introduction of the Monster.com blimp (which provided Monster.com with the image of "being big but not scary") on national sporting events, such as ABC-TV's *Monday Night Football* (see Exhibit 13)—and help boost traffic to the Monster.com site.

Under the AOL deal—completed after nearly five years of on-again and off-again negotiations—Monster.com agreed to pay America Online $100 million over four years to be the exclusive search site across all of the AOL properties—AOL, AOL Canada, AOL.com, Compuserve, ICQ, Netscape Netcenter, and Digital Cities. James J. Janesky, an analyst with Bank of America Securities, noted that the Monster.com/America Online deal would allow Monster.com to "customize its job boards to fit each local job market, which will benefit both employers and job seekers."

In addition to building the Monster.com brand in the United States—where one survey reported that it had a 92% name recognition among its customers, mainly human resource executives[20]—Taylor and his executive management team were moving quickly to make Monster.com a global career brand as well. At the end of 1999, Monster.com had sites in eight countries: the United Kingdom, Australia, Canada, the Netherlands, France, Singapore, New Zealand, and Belgium. The company planned to enter 11 more countries by the end of 2000. Andrew Wilkinson, Monster.com managing director of Europe, observed that while most of Europe was behind the United States in Internet usage, the goal was to apply the lessons learned from Monster.com to the development of its sister sites overseas. He described the competition there:

Our competitors usually fall into three groups: traditional, which is equivalent to careerpath.com or newspapers putting their classifieds online; local sites

---

[19]Nancy Moyer and Jesse Pichel, C.E. Unterberg, Towbin, "What Is TMP Worldwide?" analyst report, November 1, 1999.

[20]Nancy Moyer and Jesse Pichel, C.E. Unterberg, Towbin, "What Is TMP Worldwide?" analyst report, November 1, 1999.

Figure A Monster.com Newsletter

THE MONSTER.COM NEWSLETTER

Monster.com is your online career network, whether you want to find a
hot new job or heat things up at your current one. What's up at Monster.com this week?

IN THIS ISSUE: Week of February 28, 2000

-- Handling the Salary History Question When You Want to Make More
-- So You Want to Work in Politics . . . on the Web?
-- THE MONSTER.COM POLL: Workers Wanted: What to Do?
-- HEARD ON THE BOARDS: I Don't Know My Own Skills!
-- AND FINALLY...JOBS, JOBS, JOBS!

Handling the Salary History Question When You Want to Make More

Question: "In an interview, how do I respond to questions about salary history when I am currently grossly underpaid and I am trying to correct that?"

Keep the interviewer focused on what would be an appropriate amount for you to make now, given your experience, skills and credentials. How can you direct the discussion in this direction? First, do your homework. Knowing what others make for this position gives you leverage. Second, be prepared to explain WHY you are seeking a jump in your salary. Third, click here for more help: http://midcareer.monster.com/articles/negotiationtips/salaryhistory/

So You Want to Work in Politics...on the Web?

The proliferation of political Web sites has opened a whole new field of work for techno/political types. If you love politics, this might be your next great job. So what skills do you need? Doug Bailey, co-founder of FreedomChannel.com, says a political background is more important than a technical one. Click here to learn more: http://dotcom.monster.com/articles/pluginandvotep2/

THE MONSTER.COM POLL: Workers Wanted: What to Do?

Last week, we asked: "Should your company pay for employees'substance abuse programs?"

You said:

-- This should be covered in the health program, but not be paid directly by the company: 52%

-- No, it's not the company's responsibility to take care of employees' personal problems: 29%

-- Yes, it shows the company cares about its workers: 17%

Total votes: 30830

This week's poll: What should our country do to satisfy the demand for workers?

What do you think? Tell us here:

http://www.monster.com

HEARD ON THE BOARDS: I Don't Know My Own Skills!

Monster.com Member Catiope writes: "I've been teaching elementary and secondary school for about four years. Now I find I want to do something else -- a 9-to-5 job where I would not have to work nights and weekends. But what can I do? It's hard to find something when you don't know what else you can do! Any suggestions?"

The Nonprofit Career Expert answers: "It sounds as if you need a little direction, but don't worry...the Web has great resources that can help you!

Try looking into some of the following online career tests:

http://www.ncsu.edu/careerkey/careerkey.html

http://www.temperament.net or http://10steps.careerpathsonline.com

After you figure out what career path you might follow, investigate the specific occupations at sites like:

http://www.jobprofiles.com and http://stats.bls.gov/ocohome.htm

Source: Monster.com

in the local countries, which are usually "two guys in a garage"; and three or four other sites in Europe which are trying to build a European network.

Building Communities Online

Taylor also saw an opportunity to incorporate community into Monster.com as an obvious step toward enhancing the site. Taylor explained:

> We see the creation of community around the Monster.com site as a natural progression. We look at our operation as a large resource where we want to be more than just the place you go when you are looking for your next job. To be relevant to people who are happy with their current positions, we have to offer career specific networking opportunities, career development support, salary survey information, and virtual career fairs. We think of community as a way to build a "lifetime learning" model into users' experience of Monster.com.

On the Monster.com site, job seekers could obtain resume writing tips, compensation information, and networking advice as well as an opportunity to participate in a daily online poll or one of 20 chat rooms. Under the direction of Doug Handy, the site's editor-in-chief and vice president of content, Monster.com e-mailed 20 different newsletters each week (see Exhibit 14) to 410,000 subscribers in targeted audiences—ranging from dot.com careers to health care careers—to encourage visitors to think about career planning and regular use of Monster.com's career center.

Creation of the Talent Market Site

Beginning on Independence Day, July 4, 1999, contractors, independent professionals, consultants, and freelancers could auction off their skills and talents to the highest bidder through Monster.com's Talent Market site. By filling out a profile that outlined their ideal assignment, desired pay rate, skills and education, and product scope, an independent contractor could field bids from employers seeking to fill project needs. At the beginning of March 2000, Monster.com had roughly 12,000 registered employers and 161,000 registered independent contractors. The number of auctions averaged around 40,000 per day and Monster.com received a commission of up to $1,000 for each match made. The creation of the Talent Market site reflected Monster.com's move into the $86 billion staffing market and an effort to reach an estimated 8.5 million free agents in the United States. Other online competitors trying to reach this market included freeagent.com, guru.com, and e-lance.com (see Exhibit 15).

Oversight for the talent market site came under the direction of Linda Nathansohn, Monster.com's senior vice president of ventures. The ventures group was created in 1999 to serve as an incubator for new projects and to review potential acquisitions. Nathansohn explained:

> One of the overriding missions for Monster.com is to innovate. . . . If there is one thing about competing in the Internet world it is the speed to develop, the speed to market, the speed to close the deal. Sometimes if you come across a delay, the competition woos a company away from you. The learning company moves faster and smarter. We'll be a 1,000-person company by year-end 2000, but we want to continue to think like a 10-person company.

Conclusion

As Taylor returned to his office from the breakfast bar, he began to scribble some thoughts he had for Monster.com on a large whiteboard. Taylor believed that the only scare resources for Monster.com would be management's time and its ability to predict the future. He knew that Monster.com was well-positioned for continued growth and category dominance, especially with the full support and resources of TMP Worldwide, which had dozens of offices worldwide and millions of dollars in clients' advertising billings. With these advantages, Taylor pondered how Monster.com could continue to be innovative and thereby retain its dominant position as the world's leading online career brand, and to continue to expand into new markets and marketspaces. A Post-it note taped to his whiteboard stated "Only the innovative thrive . . . versus only the paranoid survive."

Exhibit 1 Top Ranked Career Sites on the Web—January 2000

Major Online Career Sites January 2000			
	Unique Visitors (000)	Reach	Page Views	Power Ranking
Monster.com	3,595	5.3%	29.8	157.9
Careermosaic.com	1,508	2.2%	6.1	13.4
Hotjobs.com	1,253	1.8%	14.3	25.7
Careerpath.com	1,087	1.6%	8.9	14.2
Headhunter.net	893	1.3%	27.7	36.0
Careerbuilder	717	1.0%	6.1	6.1
Dice.com	395	0.6%	17.7	10.6
Kforce.com	304	0.4%	4.6	1.8

Power Ranking = Reach Multiplied by Page View
Source: Media Metrix

Exhibit 2 Print Version of Monster.com Super Bowl XXXIII
Advertisement—January 1999

Source: Monster.com

Exhibit 3 Monster.com—Key Metrics

	December 1998	March 1999	June 1999	September 1999	January 2000
Monster.com Key Metrics—December 1998 to January 2000					
U.S. Internet users visiting Monster.com	1.4%	3.4%	4.2%	4.1%	5.3%
Direct traffic (non-alliance)	81.0%	90.0%	94.0%	95.0%	NA
Page views	48 million	82 million	122 million	146 million	158 million
Paid job listings	186,000	204,000	252,000	255,000	315,000*
Resume database	1.0 million	1.3 million	1.6 million	2.0 million	3.0 million
Registered members	NA	2.5 million	3.6 million	4.2 million	6 million

* As of December 1999
Source: Bean Murray Institutional Research, Monster.com, Media Metrix

Exhibit 4 Print Ad Based on Monster.com Super Bowl XXXIV Advertisement—January 2000

Source: Monster.com

Exhibit 5 Monster.com International Sites—December 1999

United Kingdom	The Netherlands	New Zealand
Australia	France	Belgium
Canada	Singapore	

Source: Bank of America Securities, TMP Worldwide, analyst report, January 28, 2000

Exhibit 6 Monster.com's Maynard, Massachusetts, Headquarters

Photos: Dickson Louie

Exhibit 7 Newspaper Advertising Breakout

		U.S. Daily Newspaper Advertising Expenditures ($ millions) 1965–1998		
Year	National Advertising	Retail Advertising	Classified Advertising	Total Newspaper Advertising
1965	$783	$2,429	$1,214	$719
1970	891	3,292	1,521	1,036
1975	1,109	4,966	2,159	1,631
1980	1,963	8,609	4,222	2,754
1985	3,352	13,443	8,375	4,181
1990	4,122	16,652	11,506	5,743
1995	4,251	18,099	13,742	7,254
1996	4,667	18,344	15,065	7,636
1997	5,315	19,242	16,773	8,111
1998	5,721	20,331	17,873	8,511

Source: Newspaper Association of America

Exhibit 8 Boston Globe Classified Recruitment Advertising Rates (March 2000)

Boston Globe Help-Wanted Classified Advertising Rates	
Daily and Sunday Basic Rates	
Daily rate per line	$16.25
Sunday rate per line	$20.00
Repeat Rates within a 7-day Period	
1st day	$5.55 per agate line
2nd day to 6th day	$3.75 per agate line/day
2nd Sunday repeat	$10.00 per line
Add-On Charges	
4-color premium	15% of cost
Minimum 4-color premium	$800
Spot color	10% of cost
Minimum spot-color premium	$600
Commissions	
Rates are commissionable to recognized advertising agencies.	
Paid Circulation	
Daily	462,850
Sunday	730,348

Note: All classified advertisements are listed online at Careerpath.com at no additional cost.
Source: Boston Globe (March 2000) and September 1999 FAS-FAX report, Audit Bureau of Circulations

Exhibit 9 Online Recruitment Advertising (1997 to 2003)

Online Job Classified Market 1997 through 2003 (in Millions)	
1997A	$48
1998A	$105
1999E	$265
2000E	$525
2001E	$895
2002E	$1,340
2003E	$1,740

Source: Forrester Research, Inc.

Exhibit 10 My Monster.com

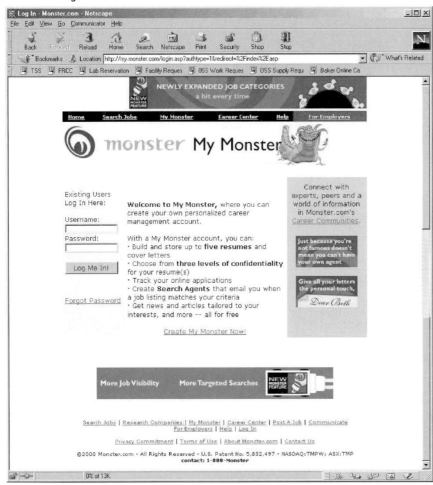

Source: Monster.com

Exhibit 11 Job Placement Industry

Industry Size by Segment—1996 ($ in billions)	
Industry Segment	**1996 (F)**
Temporary help	$45.1
Medical	4.0
Professional/specialty	4.8
Technical/computer	11.4
Office clerical	13.7
Industrial	11.2
Placement and search	$9.0
Contingency	4.5
Permanent placement	1.8
Recruiting	2.8
Temp-to-perm	1.9
Retained search	2.5
Staff leasing	$17.6
Outplacement	$0.9
Total staffing industry	$72.6(a)

(a) Does not include outsourcing
Source: 1996 by Staffing Industry Analysts, Inc.

Exhibit 12 TMP Income Statement, 1996–1999

<table>
<tr><td colspan="5">TMP Worldwide Income Statement
For Years Ended December 31, 1996 to 1998
(in $Millions)</td></tr>
<tr><td rowspan="2">Gross Billings:</td><td>(Unaudited)
1999</td><td>1998</td><td>1997</td><td>1996</td></tr>
<tr><td></td><td></td><td></td><td></td></tr>
<tr><td>Internet</td><td>$151.6</td><td>$54.2</td><td>$19.6</td><td>$6.7</td></tr>
<tr><td>Recruitment</td><td>811.8</td><td>794.2</td><td>604.4</td><td>342.4</td></tr>
<tr><td>Search and Selection</td><td>298.9</td><td>92.6</td><td>76.5</td><td>53.3</td></tr>
<tr><td>Temporary</td><td>57.1</td><td>-</td><td>-</td><td>-</td></tr>
<tr><td>Yellow Pages</td><td>532.3</td><td>485.2</td><td>469.3</td><td>443.6</td></tr>
<tr><td>Total</td><td>$1,851.7</td><td>$1,426.2</td><td>$1,169.8</td><td>$846.0</td></tr>
<tr><td colspan="5">Commissions and Fees:</td></tr>
<tr><td>Internet</td><td>$133.5</td><td>$48.5</td><td>$18.6</td><td>$6.7</td></tr>
<tr><td>Recruitment</td><td>178.1</td><td>167.2</td><td>127.2</td><td>71.7</td></tr>
<tr><td>Search and Selection</td><td>295.7</td><td>91.6</td><td>75.7</td><td>53.3</td></tr>
<tr><td>Temporary</td><td>57.2</td><td>-</td><td>-</td><td>-</td></tr>
<tr><td>Yellow Pages</td><td>101.3</td><td>99.4</td><td>98.0</td><td>95.9</td></tr>
<tr><td>Total</td><td>$765.8</td><td>$406.7</td><td>$319.5</td><td>$227.6</td></tr>
<tr><td>Salaries and related costs</td><td>$436.3</td><td>$223.7</td><td>$179.3</td><td>$126.5</td></tr>
<tr><td>Office and general</td><td>179.6</td><td>126.8</td><td>102.5</td><td>75.1</td></tr>
<tr><td>Marketing costs (1)</td><td>64.1</td><td>-</td><td>-</td><td>-</td></tr>
<tr><td>Merger costs</td><td>63.1</td><td>21.5</td><td>0.0</td><td>0.0</td></tr>
<tr><td>Restructuring costs</td><td>2.8</td><td>-</td><td>-</td><td>-</td></tr>
<tr><td>Amortization</td><td>11.4</td><td>8.9</td><td>6.3</td><td>4.4</td></tr>
<tr><td>Special compensation and CEO bonus</td><td>0</td><td>1.3</td><td>1.5</td><td>52.0</td></tr>
<tr><td>Total</td><td>$757.9</td><td>$382.2</td><td>$289.6</td><td>$258.0</td></tr>
<tr><td>Operating Income</td><td>$7.8</td><td>$24.4</td><td>$29.8</td><td>−$30.3</td></tr>
</table>

(1) Marketing expenses broken out separately for 1999 unaudited income statement
Source: TMP Worldwide annual reports, March 7, 2000, TMP Worldwide press release

Exhibit 13 Monster.com Blimp

Source: Monster.com

Exhibit 14 List of Monster.com e-Newsletters—February 2000

Monster.com newsletter	Bulletin d'information Monster.ca
Technology newsletter	Lettre d'infos Monster.fr
HR newsletter	Monster.com.au newsletter
Monster Talent Market newsletter	Monster.ca HR newsletter
Healthcare newsletter	Bulletin d'information RH Monster.ca
International newsletter	Monsterboard nl HR Nieuwsbrieven
Campus newsletter	Monster.be Nieuwsbrieven
Monster.co.uk newsletter	Monster.be—Nieuwsbrieven
Monster.ca. newsletter	Monster.be—La lettre d'info
Dot.com Careers newsletter	Monster.be—Newsletter
Monsterboard.nl Nieuwsbrieven	

Source: Monster.com

Exhibit 15 Free Agent Sites on the Internet (February 2000)

Some Major Web Sites for e-Lancers		
Company and Web site	**Service**	**Headquarters**
Ants.com	Helps companies find freelance help as quickly as possible	Santa Barbara
Aquent Partners (www.aquent.com)	Combination traditional staffing business and online job matching service	Boston
ELance.com	e-lancers bid auction-style for short-term company projects	Sunnyvale
Ework Exchange (www.ework.com)	Employers, staffing agencies, and project seekers decide what they want to pay eWork Exchange to obtain successful matches for short-term, off-site projects	San Francisco
FreeAgent.com	Matches independents with projects; sells insurance and administrative support packages	New York
FreeAgentNation.com	Provides advice, articles for e-lancers	Washington D.C.
FreetimeJobs.com	Helps small businesses find temporary help for short-term, part-time projects	New York
Guru.com	Matches independents with projects; offers extensive content and services	San Francisco
IcPlanet.com	Hooks up professional and management-level contractors with hirers	San Rafael
iNiku.com	Matches IY and management professionals with projects; offers business support services through partners	Redwood City
Skills Village	Matches information technology contractors with companies or staffing agencies	Santa Clara

Source: *San Francisco Chronicle*, February 25, 2000

E-LOAN

A Better Way to Get a Loan
E-LOAN promotional tagline, 2000

At the close of a workday in late March 2000, a crowd of approximately 200 employees streamed into a large auditorium-sized room. The auditorium was part of E-LOAN's office compound, located in Dublin, California, about 35 miles east of San Francisco (see Exhibit 1). Its bare, cement walls bore messages spray-painted by employees during the excitement of the company's IPO the previous summer. One message reflected the company's intent to become the nation's dominant provider of mortgage loans. It simply read: "E-LOAN—A better way to get a home loan." Another message summarized the collegial spirit among the start-up's employees. It read: "Your E-LOAN tag team." And finally, a third message summarized the essence of E-LOAN, becoming an often-used quote by Frank Siskowski, the company's CFO, during the E-LOAN pre-IPO roadshows. It read: "We are a consumer driven model which brings real value to the consumer in the most important single financing transaction of their lifetime."

As a reflection of E-LOAN's customer driven focus, the employees were gathered on this particular day to honor individual colleagues for outstanding customer service—the company's key differentiating feature from its competitors, both online and offline. Each month, members of the company's management team selected the two employees they believed to have demonstrated the most outstanding service to E-LOAN customers. These awards—titled the E-Service Awards—were presented in a company-wide ceremony which bestowed the recipient with a black-and-white leather varsity jacket embossed with a large gold "E." Excitement would build during the ceremony as a member of the senior management team would read testimonials of the outstanding service provided by the employee, without actually iden-tifying them. Then, in a moment of crowning glory, the winning employee would be identified and fitted with their jacket in front of all E-LOAN employees (see Exhibit 2). On this day, two employees would win the company's coveted E-Service Award—a customer loan consultant and a technician who had provided much behind-the-scenes systems support.

As the E-Service Awards were being presented, the company's two co-founders, Chris Larsen and Janina Pawlowski, and president, Joe Kennedy, stood nearby and reflected upon the challenges ahead. Just prior to the Awards presentation, 38-year-old Larsen announced plans for expansion into the European market. This was a major milestone for a company which had spent the past nine months since its IPO building itself as an operation and laying the foundation for making E-LOAN a U.S. household name. However, Larsen, Pawlowski, and Kennedy knew several key challenges lay ahead for E-LOAN which faced most Internet-based companies: scaling operations rapidly, building outstanding customer service for an online organization, gaining brand recognition, and of course, achieving profitability.

Like most Internet-based companies, E-LOAN had seen its market capitalization decline over the past year. On IPO day, June 29, 1999, E-LOAN's share price soared from $14 to $43 per share, raising $50 million in capital.[1] In the week following the IPO, the stock price peaked at $64 per share with a company valuation of $2.4 billion. By the next year, in March 2000, the company's share price had declined to $10 a share. Although part of the decline could be attributed to the steady increase in mortgage interest rates which had dampened the demand for home refinancing nationwide (see Exhibit 3), it was largely a reflection of the market's demand to see profitability.

In spite of this setback, E-LOAN still seemed to be well on its way towards reaching its goals. The company continued to grow at a rapid pace with revenues tripling from $7 million in 1998 to $22 million in 1999. Over 90% of customers rated its service as being very good or excellent. Over $3 billion in loan originations had been

[1]Hof, Robert D., "Inside an Internet IPO," *Business Week*, September 6, 1999.

recorded across four different product categories—home mortgages, auto financing, credit cards, and small business loans.[2]

However, three key questions remained as E-LOAN poised to reposition itself from simply an online mortgage provider to a leading online loan center. How quickly could the company scale to dominate the consumer loan market, especially in the home mortgage and auto loan categories? How could E-LOAN become profitable sooner than any of its competitors? And finally, to what degree would customer service and branding—E-LOAN's key assets—be key differentiators in a highly fragmented and competitive industry?

U.S. Mortgage Industry Overview
History of the Mortgage Industry

Fueled by the lowest mortgage rates in over three decades, a strong national economy, and continued low unemployment,[3] the home mortgage market in the U.S. totaled $1.2 trillion in loan originations with over $20 billion in origination fees in 1999.[4] (This included mortgages of both new home purchases and refinancing of existing mortgages.)

Despite its large size, the mortgage loan market was highly fragmented, comprised of approximately 20,000 small local brokers and single-source lenders, with no nationally branded multi-lender or agent having market share greater than seven percent.[5] Until the late 1970s, retail banks and savings and loan institutions handled all aspects of the mortgage process internally, from originating, underwriting, and closing the loans using their own customer deposits to actually servicing the loans.[6] In the 1980s this vertical production chain was broken by two major developments: the emergence of pure mortgage banks (which could purchase mortgages from mortgage brokers and sell to government-sponsored mortgage investors, such as Fanny Mae and Freddie Mac) and the evolution of a large, secondary funding and trading market for mortgage debt.[7] This led to the separation of the front-end activities of loan origination

and mortgage funding from the back-end activity of loan servicing.[8] Among the largest retail leaders in the mortgage industry were Norwest (with $34 billion in loan originations in 1999), Bank of America ($28 billion), Countrywide ($20 billion), Washington Mutual (WAMU) ($17 billion), and Chase ($16 billion).

On the whole, retail mortgage originators were slow to migrate online. The mortgage origination and funding process was very complex, expensive, and manually driven, often resulting in reams of paperwork and untimely responses. Developing a process to automate these activities was slow-going, and by the end of 1999, only eight of the top fifteen retail mortgage originators had online functions (see Exhibit 4).[9]

In the meantime, a number of online mortgage companies sprang up to serve the market. In addition to E-LOAN, key online mortgage companies by the end of 1999 included QuickenLoan.com, Mortgage.com, and Lending Tree (see Exhibit 5 for competitor profiles and Exhibit 6 for home pages). According to Forrester Research, the share of mortgages migrating online was expected to grow rapidly, from $18.7 billion (1.6%) in volume in 1999 to $91.2 billion (9.6%) by 2003 (see Exhibit 7). This implied over $1 billion available in online origination fees. The top online lenders, including E-LOAN and Lending Tree, accounted for approximately 50% of total online mortgage volume in 1999, while traditional leading mortgage banks, including Countrywide and Bank of America, accounted for only $3 to $4 million of this volume.[10]

Obtaining a Home Loan in the U.S.

Although virtually the same percentage of Americans owned their homes in 1998 vs. 1980 (66% and 64% respectively),[11] housing prices and the average age of the first-time homeowner rose significantly. During the 1980s, a rapid increase in home prices and interest rates prevented many people from buying homes, causing homeownership rates to remain flat. In 1980, the median purchase price for a new home was $68,714 while the average monthly mortgage payment was $599 per month (roughly 32.4% of total household income.)[12] In 1998,

---

[2]E-LOAN 1999 Annual Report and 10K Statement.
[3]"Housing", *New York Times 2000 Almanac.*
[4]Marks, Jim, "The Great Wall Street Roller Coaster Ride," Credit Suisse First Boston, 2000.
[5]Kiggin, Jamie, "E-Loan," Donaldson, Lufkin & Jenrette, August 12, 1999.
[6]E-LOAN, Prospectus, June 28, 2000.
[7]E-LOAN, Prospectus, June 28, 2000.

[8]E-Loan, Prospectus, June 28, 2000.
[9]Marks, Jim, "The Great Wall Street Roller Coaster Ride," Credit Suisse First Boston, 2000.
[10]Marks, Jim, "The Great Wall Street Roller Coaster Ride," Credit Suisse First Boston, 2000.
[11]"Housing", *New York Times 2000 Almanac.*
[12]"Housing," *New York Times 2000 Almanac.*

the median purchase price of a home in the U.S. was $167,000 while the average monthly mortgage payment was $1,212 per month (roughly 32.3% of total household income.)[13]

The increase in home prices was also reflected in the average age of the first-time homeowner, up to 32 years old in 1998 from 28 years old in 1980. The average age of the repeat home buyer also increased from 36 years old in 1980 to 41 years old in 1998. Even the average percentage down payment for first-time buyers reflected the burden of higher home prices, decreasing from 21% of sale price in 1980 to 13% in 1998.[14]

For the prospective U.S. homeowner, these rising home prices were complicated by the confusing and frustrating mortgage qualification process which involved credit bureaus, inspectors, settlement attorneys, title insurers, surveyors, and often a host of other individuals.[15] Securing a loan to purchase or refinance a house required qualification for a home mortgage based on the individual's income and debt levels. As a rule of thumb, monthly mortgage payments should be no greater than 30% of a homeowner's monthly gross income. These monthly payments varied according to the amount of debt taken to purchase a home and the mortgage interest rates. For example, an individual earning $60,000 per year could borrow up to $139,000 at 11% interest but up to $261,000 at 5% interest (see Exhibit 8 for further variation according to interest rates.)[16] Homeowners could choose from a number of loan programs to try and reduce the dollar amount of these monthly mortgage payments.

Mortgage Types

The most common types of loan programs are fixed rate mortgages and adjustable rate mortgages (ARMs). Other less common loan programs include, but are not limited to, 5/25 mortgages, COFI (cost of funds index) adjustable rate mortgages,[17] 40-year terms, 3% down payment, and no down payment mortgages.

Because of the recent decline in interest rates, the number of buyers selecting fixed rate mortgages increased from 55% in 1995 to 80% in 1998 while the number of buyers selecting variable rate mortgages (ARMs) decreased from 36% to 14% during the same period.[18] With a fixed rate mortgage, the customer locks into the same monthly payment for the entire life of the loan—usually 15 or 30 years.[19] In contrast, monthly payments for ARMs vary according to the changes in the national interest rate. ARMs typically have lower interest rates for the first several years of the loan term and higher rates in the later years. Prospective homeowners normally choose ARMs over a fixed rate mortgage if they were unable to qualify for loans at the current fixed rate.[20] For most ARMs, interest rates are capped at 2% per year and not more than 6% over the life of the loan.[21]

The remainder of the market is served by a number of other loan types. In a 5/25 mortgage—a 30-year mortgage—the mortgage interest rate remains fixed during the first five years of the loan, but can be reset to current fixed rates during the 25 years afterwards. Unlike an ARM, there is no cap on the increase in interest rates.[22] In a cost of funds index adjustable rate mortgages (COFI ARM), rates are based upon the average that Western banks pay their depositors in the Federal Home Loan Bank's 11th district. Interest rates for a COFI ARM are typically lower than traditional ARMs, but fluctuate from month to month during the term of the loan.[23]

Prospective homeowners could also pay "points" upfront in order to obtain a lower mortgage interest rate, where one point is equivalent to one percent of an outstanding loan. For example, if the current fixed interest rate is 8%, a homeowner who is willing to pay for one point can obtain a mortgage with a lower 7% rate over the life of the loan. The price of these points is determined with the settlement costs for a loan, which also include title insurance, escrow fees, loan processing fees, and transfer and recordation taxes.

Use of Mortgage Brokers

While many prospective homeowners work with real estate agents to find the ideal home, many also enlist the

[13]Chicago Title and Trust Company, "Who's Buying Homes in America."
[14]Chicago Title and Trust Company, "Who's Buying Homes in America."
[15]Edelman, Ric, *The Truth About Money,* Harper Collins Publishers, Inc.
[16]This paragraph draws from Edelman, Ric, *The Truth About Money,* Harper Collins Publishers, Inc.
[17]Edelman, Ric, *The Truth About Money,* Harper Collins Publishers, Inc.
[18]"Housing," *New York Times 2000 Almanac.*
[19]"Housing," *New York Times 2000 Almanac.*

[20]Edelman, Ric, *The Truth About Money,* Harper Collins Publishers, Inc.
[21]Edelman, Ric, *The Truth About Money,* Harper Collins Publishers, Inc.
[22]Edelman, Ric, *The Truth About Money,* Harper Collins Publishers, Inc.
[23]Edelman, Ric, *The Truth About Money,* Harper Collins Publishers, Inc.

services of a mortgage broker to secure the ideal loan for their needs. A mortgage broker will work to pre-qualify the homeowner for a loan and determine what financing options are available through the variety of loan programs. Their commission is typically 1.25% to 1.5% of the loan amount.[24] This commission also constitutes the bulk of the mortgage broker's income, causing obvious conflicts on interest for the customer.[25] Mortgage brokers are often middlemen that represent banks and other lending agencies, such as Norwest, Countrywide, and Bank of America.

From this tight, fragmented market, Larsen and Pawlowski had a vision for what would become E-LOAN.

The History of E-LOAN

The Early Years

Prior to co-founding E-LOAN, Larsen and Pawlowski started a brick-and-mortar mortgage brokerage company called the Palo Alto Funding Group, in October 1992. Larson, a Stanford MBA and the son of a United Airlines mechanic, had previously worked in the area of financial systems design at both the Chevron Corporation and NASA/Ames Research. Pawlowski, a Cornell University undergrad and Rochester University MBA, had previously worked as an analyst with Xerox before becoming an independent real estate agent and loan officer. The American-born daughter of Polish immigrants who had opened a credit union in Rochester, New York, to assist other post-World War II immigrants in buying their first home, Pawlowski was no stranger to the mortgage industry.[26]

As the Internet became increasingly widespread, Larsen and Pawlowski saw potential to empower the consumer in the mortgage lending process. Pawlowski explains the evolution of the E-LOAN concept beyond their brick-and-mortar company:

We had a traditional brokerage with loan agents. We started that in 1992. What we were trying to do was to give people a better way to pick products and to compare mortgages. Because I was a loan agent for a long period of time, I knew that a lot of people didn't like the "face-to-face" contact which could be very embarrassing and the most difficult part of taking the loan application. The Internet presented itself in 1995. And when we saw what the Internet could do as a tool, we started to come up with ways to eliminate the agent.[27]

With the Internet, Larsen and Pawlowski could streamline an otherwise cumbersome loan transaction process to offer better services than a traditional loan officer with a greater number of choices among lenders and better rates. By removing the often distasteful face-to-face interaction, the process could be what Larsen referred to as a "customer-focused" rather than "sales-focused."[28] On this principle, E-LOAN was founded in August 1996.

The initial $450,000 of funding for E-LOAN came from the co-founders' friends and family, and the company developed at a rapid pace. The first office opened on University Avenue in downtown Palo Alto, California, and in June 1997, just ten months after being incorporated, the E-LOAN website (*www.eloan.com*) was launched—one of the first sites to offer home mortgages online. For the remainder of 1997, E-LOAN incurred a net loss of $1.4 million, on revenues of $1.0 million in origination fees and operating expenses of $2.4 million (see Exhibit 9). At the end of 1997, E-LOAN secured its first round of institutional financing with an infusion of $5.5 million from Benchmark Capital and Technology Partners, and growth began in earnest.[29]

Taking It to the Next Level: The Softbank/Yahoo! Investment

In 1998, interest rates fell to a 30-year low (7.0% for a conventional 30-year fixed loan) and the dollar value of mortgage originations exploded by 70% to $1.5 trillion. Market conditions, as well as a rapid rise in Internet usage, resulted in dramatic growth at E-LOAN: 447 loans were closed in 1Q 1998 while 1,635 loans were closed 3Q 1998. What is more, the dollar amount of these loans increased from $105 million to $219 million during the same period.

This increased loan activity quickly dried up E-LOAN's cash supply. With a burn rate of $250,000 per month, 150 employees on payroll and additional funds needed for an advertising campaign, Larsen and Pawlowski began to search for alternative financing options in

---

[24]E-LOAN Prospectus, June 28, 2000.
[25]Edelman, Ric, *The Truth About Money*, Harper Collins Publishers, Inc.
[26]Wooley, Scott, "Should She Keep the Baby," *Forbes*, April 19, 1999.

[27]E-LOAN Promotion Video, 1999.
[28]E-LOAN Promotion Video, 1999.
[29]Wooley, Scott, "Should She Keep the Baby," *Forbes*, April 19, 1999.

August 1998, either through an outright sale or an outside infusion of cash.[30]

Two options became available.[31] One was to sell the company to Intuit for $130 million and fold E-LOAN into the operations of Quicken Mortgage (now Quicken Loan). Larsen and Pawlowski, who then owned a combined 40% stake in the company, would each receive $26 million from the offer—$10 million in cash and $16 million in Intuit stock. The second option was to sell a 23% equity stake in the company to Softbank, a major investor in Yahoo!, for $25 million.

While the Softbank/Yahoo! offer would keep E-LOAN independent, its valuation of $110 million was less than Intuit's offer and would turn Intuit into a rival rather than an investor. Larsen and Pawlowski were divided over the two options. Larsen recalled several Internet start-ups—such as PointCast and BigBook—that had spurned such offers from larger corporations, only to end up being sold at bargain basement prices. Pawlowski sought to keep E-LOAN independent, even at the prospect of a lower valuation. Pawlowski recalled:

> During our negotiations with both Intuit and Yahoo!, I had a weird dream. I'm on the tram at Disneyland when a toddler falls off. I reach out to pick the baby up and it has been decapitated. From this I realize that I shouldn't sacrifice the company that I had brought into the world. With a deal with Yahoo! I realized that the E-LOAN brand could live on, although the company would be valued less.[32]

Thus driven, she eventually persuaded Larsen to pursue the offer with Softbank/Yahoo!.

Building the Business Through 1998

With the additional funding from Softbank/Yahoo!, Pawlowski and Larsen focused E-LOAN activities on establishing a national brand and building the business from that of a mortgage broker into that of a mortgage bank. The advertising agency of Saatchi & Saatchi was brought on board to help launch the company's first advertising campaign. Expanding beyond the in-house print and radio ads that were written by Pawlowski in the past, the campaign in late summer 1998 promoted E-LOAN in Los Angeles, Seattle, and San Francisco through outdoor, radio, print, and television advertising. Sharon Ruwart, then vice president of marketing, recalls the hopes for the new endeavor:

> Our strategy is to build a national brand. Our strategy is not to focus on just California . . . there has never been a national multi-lender company, and that's the opportunity. Mortgage brokers have traditionally been local, with many being mom-and-pop operations.

E-LOAN sought to become the first nationally recognized brand in its field.

During its early branding effort, E-LOAN also sought to become a mortgage bank, in addition to a mortgage broker, in all 50 states in the U.S. This effort was led by Steve Majerus, vice president of secondary markets, who had previously owned his own mortgage lending company. Most online competitors, such as Quicken Mortgage and Lending Tree, employed a referral business model, serving essentially as marketplaces where quotes from lending partners were delivered to customers, and firms paid a fee upon obtaining new customers. In contrast, E-LOAN employed a processor firm business model, actually processing and underwriting all of its loans. In-house loan representatives handled the paperwork and correspondence needed to complete each loan.

This critical difference gave E-LOAN full control over the entire customer experience from the loan application to the completion of funding. Revenues were higher on a per fee basis because E-LOAN sold nearly all its loans to secondary markets at lower wholesale rates. Majerus observed:

> What we did when we started growing the mortgage bank unit internally was to sign up as many secondary market investors as possible, so that even within our lending organization we were still providing maximum choice to our consumers. We were still playing all of the secondary markets investors against each other, in just the same way we played the wholesale lenders off each other as a mortgage broker.

By the end of 1999, E-LOAN had licenses as a mortgage bank in 46 states and the District of Columbia.

In 4Q 1998, E-LOAN closed 1,635 mortgage loans totaling $339 million. During all of 1998, E-LOAN had closed 3,865 mortgage loans totaling $835 million.[33] Operating revenue in 1998 grew seven-fold from $1.0 million in 1997 to $6.8 million (see Exhibit 9), while operating losses grew nearly eight-fold from $1.4 million

---

[30]Wooley, Scott, "Should She Keep the Baby," *Forbes*, April 19, 1999.
[31]This paragraph is adapted from Wooley, Scott, "Should She Keep the Baby," *Forbes*, April 19, 1999.
[32]Wooley, Scott, "Should She Keep the Baby," *Forbes*, April 19, 1999.
[33]E-LOAN Prospectus, June 28, 1999.

in 1997 to $11.3 million. The increased loss was due primarily to increase in operations and sales and marketing expenditures. However, in spite of its successful growth, E-LOAN had not achieved national brand status—approximately 83% of the loans closed in 1998 were made in California.

The E-LOAN Value Proposition[34]

Challenged with establishing this national brand, Larsen and Pawlowski thought seriously about the E-LOAN value proposition as an online provider of consumer debt. Fundamentally, they believed E-LOAN could offer customers the ability to obtain a suitable loan product—whether it be a mortgage, home equity loan, auto loan, credit card, or small business loan—from a wide variety of lenders at a reduced cost. Larsen notes:

> What we want to achieve for E-LOAN is what online brokerage and mutual fund companies had done for the left [asset] side of the balance sheet in helping consumers manage their assets. What we want to do is to focus on the right side of the balance sheet and help consumers manage their debt. We want to show consumers that a home mortgage and an auto loan are not necessarily mutually exclusive. For example, it might make sense for someone to use a home equity loan to finance a car purchase and E-LOAN can provide that need to the consumer.

Through E-LOAN's website (see Exhibit 10), mortgage applicants could efficiently compare multiple products from multiple lenders tailored to their financial profile and complete their transactions online. E-LOAN provided value to the customers during the process through several key attributes: (1) inherently better product offering with increased selection and savings, (2) sophisticated and customized online tools, (3) superior customer service, and (4) a streamlined financing process.

Increased Selection and Savings

E-LOAN offered mortgages from over 70 leading sources, including nationally recognized institutions. Each customer inquiry triggered a proprietary rate search algorithm that sorted through 50,000 products in the E-LOAN database, which was updated in real time.

The results were delivered in seconds and represented the set of the most competitively priced loans available that best matched the individual customer's criteria (see Exhibit 11). Matt Roberts, director of finance, makes the following observation of the process:

> We're not a mortgage broker that provides loan options from only five people who happen to be my buddies or because I want to get a higher spread on the loan. It's something that you can't do unless you have the technology to do it.

The large selection of lenders and loans available in a single destination saved borrowers time and effort from having to search for the most suitable mortgage through individual mom-and-pop operations.

At the same time, E-LOAN offered significant savings to its customers by eliminating unnecessary commissioned intermediaries, such as loan agents. Savings of over 50% of origination costs could be achieved over traditional brokers or single source lenders: the typical loan agent received a commission of 1.25% to 1.50% of the loan amount; E-LOAN charged a commission of 0.65%.[35] On a loan balance of $200,000, customer savings could range from $1,000 to $1,200.

Sophisticated and Customized Online Tools

In addition to its exceptional product offering, E-LOAN's website was technically designed to offer prospective borrowers easy access to rate quotes, information about loan fulfillment, and tools and services to aid in making financing decisions. Loan recommendations were formulated through powerful comparative and analytical tools designed to assist the borrower in determining the most suitable product available through E-LOAN and was based entirely on borrower-provided information and criteria. This approach differed substantially from traditional mortgage brokers who often recommended and promoted products based on associated commissions, which can vary by lender.

Once customers had made financing decisions, E-LOAN also provided ongoing mortgage monitoring. Customers could obtain information to make refinancing decisions by continuously comparing their existing loan to new products available through E-LOAN. E-LOAN would alert customers to opportunities to save money over the life of their loan, significantly increasing its capability to promote long-term relationships with its customers.

---

[34]Parts of this section adapted from E-LOAN 1999 Annual Report and 10K Statement.
[35]E-LOAN Prospectus, June 28, 1999.

Superior Customer Service

E-LOAN offered superior service, staying attuned to customer needs both through the website itself and through actual human contact. Improvements were made to the website on a continuous basis. Bill Crane, vice president of engineering, comments on E-LOAN's philosophy of making incremental improvements to its website daily:

> We get feedback from our customers on a regular basis. First, making a change one or two days after receiving it makes our customers feel good that they are being heard. Second, there is less engineering risk, when you make changes gradually.
>
> A customer can comment on our site at any time. When a customer says "this is hard, I don't understand Question 6, or what do you mean by a reverse mortgage," we analyze the problem and then decide if we should add a FAQ [Frequently Asked Question], hyperlink or rework the sentence. We analyze all of the customer comments.
>
> As soon as we hear the feedback, we focus on it, improve it, push it out and then we're done with it. If you add the feedback to a big pile, it becomes a big project and never gets done because you don't have the time to complete it. We don't have projects that take more than a month. We usually have the idea on Monday, work on it Tuesday and take it live by Friday.

E-LOAN practiced its customer-centric philosophy on a consistent basis through its daily site evolution.

On a person-to-person level, E-LOAN offered customized service by assigning each customer a personal loan consultant once an application for a mortgage loan was completed. This consultant would serve as a simple point of contact and support through the entire transaction process, available by phone, e-mail, or fax until a loan was closed. Karen Steele, a loan consultant, describes her typical day:

> Consumers can reach me in a variety of ways—by phone, by fax, or by e-mail. Each morning, I would check my e-mail and voice-mails and address those messages which have the most time-pressing issues first. During the day, documents, such as third party appraisals, which need to be set up in order to get a loan closed comes to me for processing. Before I leave each day, I contact the people that need to be contacted. I usually close about 18 loans per month, which include both refinances and purchases.

During those hours when their representative might not be available, customers could check on the status of their loan with the E-Track loan application tracker, a password-protected window which updated the status of loans in real time (see Exhibit 12). A 24-hours-a-day, 7-days-a-week online service, Pawlowski referred to E-Track as a "FedEx tracking process that lets you check on the status of your loan."

Satisfaction with this service was tracked through a survey customers were asked to complete upon the closing of a loan. One such customer compliments E-LOAN for its "high-touch, high-tech" service:

> My transaction was not real typical since I was selling a manufactured home to fund the conventional home. There are many little oddities in the manufactured home process of which E-LOAN (and my real estate agent for that matter) were not aware. Overall, my home purchase, using E-LOAN, went much more smoothly than my home sale, which went through a different company. Using an out-of-town, online broker was not a problem at all. The accessibility and knowledge of my representative far exceeded my expectations and provided more convenience than if the broker had been located across the street. A big "thank you" to Alison Joy and E-LOAN!

Overall, 90% of E-LOAN customers professed to finding the service "very good" or "excellent."

Streamlined Financing Process

All of these services helped E-LOAN streamline the traditional mortgage process, simplifying the paper-based manual process, providing early approval to lock in interest rates, and improving customer relationships. Figure 1 [page 398] details the key differences in the mortgage process for typical providers vs. E-LOAN.

Expanding the Franchise

E-LOAN sought to put its customer-centric philosophy to work in franchises beyond mortgages, adding car loans, credit cards, home equity loans, and small business loans to its product mix by the end of 1999.

E-LOAN's expansion into the $400 million car loan market (the second largest consumer debt market after mortgages) was made possible through its acquisition of Bank of America's CarFinance.com in the summer of 1999. The online application process was similar to that

Figure 1

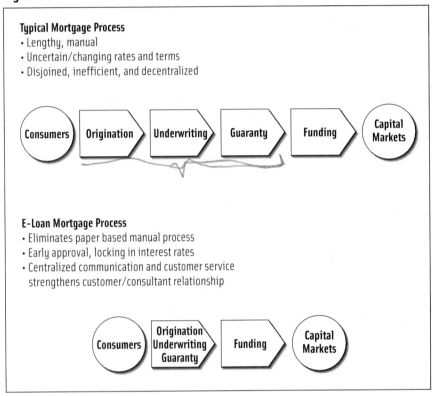

Typical Mortgage Process
- Lengthy, manual
- Uncertain/changing rates and terms
- Disjoined, inefficient, and decentralized

Consumers → Origination → Underwriting → Guaranty → Funding → Capital Markets

E-Loan Mortgage Process
- Eliminates paper based manual process
- Early approval, locking in interest rates
- Centralized communication and customer service strengthens customer/consultant relationship

Consumers → Origination Underwriting Guaranty → Funding → Capital Markets

Source: Kiggin, Jamie, E-LOAN, Donaldson, Lufkin & Jeanrette, August 12, 1999

of mortgages: customers applied for and obtained auto loans through the E-LOAN website, receiving immediate credit decisions. Once approved, E-LOAN provided next-day check drafts, eliminating the often distasteful need to negotiate auto financing at the dealership, and again separating the purchasing decision from the financing transactions. E-LOAN effectively removed dealer control over financing terms and often offered customers a lower loan rate than the dealers themselves could provide. As with mortgage loans, a loan consultant was assigned to each auto loan customer.

Customers could also obtain instant online approval for credit cards with valued added services such as online balance transfers to the new card or in some cases obtaining a 0% introductory APR. For small business loans, online applications could be processed with approval within five minutes for loans of up to $50,000 from a number of lending sources.

Expansion into car loans, credit cards, and small business loans were all part of E-LOAN's strategy to become the complete online loan center.

Key Strategic Milestones[36]

Joe Kennedy, E-LOAN's president, believed the time was ripe for the type of company E-LOAN hoped to become:

One advantage is that the debt side is significant. There are weak standalone mortgage companies—such as Countrywide—and there are the big bank brands, such as Citicorp. But there has never been a category winner. The customer acquisition model for bricks-and-mortar mortgage companies is not built on brand building. The sales agent relationship model that mortgage bankers use is very expensive. Same with car loans. Car loans are usually made through car dealers. Lender brands for home mortgages and car loans are weak. Bank brands are powerful but no one assumes a benefit on the consumer side. This is branding a new territory—there is no such thing as a multi-lender debt player in the offline world.

[36]Parts of this section adapted from E-LOAN 1999 Annual Report and 10K Statement.

No one in the bank world would help you understand what the best [loan] product is. For example, if you want to finance a car, your best option might be a home equity loan with a lower after-tax cut. Most of the time, however, debt products are like chimney products. You want a car loan, you get a car loan. Brands represent an opportunity for multiple lenders rather than individual debt products.

On the road to becoming the leading Internet-based provider of debt management services for customers, E-LOAN was tackling four key strategic challenges: (1) leveraging technology to further bring efficiencies to the industry, (2) expanding the choice and selection of its offering to meet customer needs, (3) building a strong brand, and (4) expanding internationally.

Leveraging Technology to Create Industry Efficiencies.
The ultimate goal of using technology in this industry was to eliminate inefficiencies in the existing mortgage system and bring borrowers closer to the capital markets with the funds they needed. However, this required the correct balance of promoting ease of navigation on a site through simplicity while providing sufficient information to the customer. Providing real-time information was also extremely important in the customer experience, but providing secure, private connections for this information was also a challenge. E-LOAN continued to make changes to its site based on feedback from engineers, staff, focus groups, and consumers.

Expanding Choice and Selection of the Offering.
E-LOAN sought to expand its choice and selection for consumers through further building its base of multi-source lenders, expanding the multi-lender model across every major category of consumer debt, and actually helping consumers manage their debt. By further building upon its existing base of multi-source lenders, E-LOAN could offer customers more choice and selection, often at lower cost. By expanding the multi-lender model across every major category of consumer debt, E-LOAN could become a category winner in the debt offering market, which was currently fragmented without a market leader. By helping consumers manage their debt, E-LOAN could fulfill a perceived customer need while further developing deeper customer relationships.

Building a Strong Brand.
Building brand awareness and strong customer loyalty was critical in the highly fragmented mortgage industry and to E-LOAN's goal of building a nationally scalable business. Kennedy reflected on the challenges of building the E-LOAN brand:

> Consistency and continuity are how you get a brand built. The Super Bowl helps build the message and presence of a brand, but not consistency and continuity. What does the E-LOAN brand mean? At the highest level, the brand contrasts the old way to get debt and the new way to get debt. E-LOAN represents the new way to get debt. We talk about more lenders, lower rates and better service. Multi-brand. EZ Loan provider. Lower rates. Efficiency and better service. We don't work banker hours, we work 24 x 7. Also very important is the straightforwardness of our approach. Better service, underwriting, credit decisions are much faster. Overall, the big idea is comparing the old way with the new way.

In addition to building a consistent brand image, E-LOAN worked to increase its brand awareness both online and offline. A series of nearly 50 online partnerships, developed under the direction of Doug Galen, vice president of business development, involved a variety of sites from Yahoo! to E-Trade with the aim of building traffic to the E-LOAN site. E-LOAN was also the exclusive provider to REMAX, an offline national real estate company whose agents encouraged customers to use the E-LOAN site. In 1999, approximately 22% of all loans closed by E-LOAN came through these partnership agreements.[37]

Expanding Internationally.
E-LOAN looked not only to building a strong brand in the United States, but in other parts of the world where there was a need for its type of services. Through a series of joint ventures with strong local partners, exchanging technology and expertise for equity stakes, E-LOAN exported its online loan solution abroad. These joint ventures launched online operations for various types of consumer loans in the United Kingdom, Australia, Japan, France, and Germany.

Additional Strategic Challenges.
To Larsen and Pawlowski, one of the greatest strategic challenges would be to maintain the E-LOAN company culture they had worked so carefully to establish while trying to achieve these broader goals. Larsen details the characteristics he hoped the organization would maintain:

---

[37]E-LOAN 1999 Annual Report and 10K Statement.

What we're trying to do here is to build a lasting company that will last for several generations. The values that we cherish are risk-taking, innovation, customer-focus and learning from our mistakes. If we do all of those, we will succeed.

Pawlowski further reflected these sentiments when thinking about the typical E-LOAN hire:

Our values are reflected in the type of people that we hire. Our new hires do not necessarily have to come from the mortgage industry, but they must be radically pro-consumer. We want people to come from other industries where we can learn from as well. We want to create a functional, self-improving organization.

In the E-LOAN spirit of always considering the needs of others, the company donated 75,000 shares of its stock to establish the E-LOAN Foundation. The Foundation was established to support charitable causes in the San Francisco Bay Area, with the Davis Street Community Center being the first recipient in September 1999, and was just one of many manifestations of E-LOAN's commitment to promote and preserve its corporate culture.

1999 Operating Results

The company continued to grow rapidly after it went public in June 1999. In 1999, a total of 24,000 mortgage loans were closed, a six-fold increase from 1998. Operating revenue also grew three-fold from $6.8 million to $22.1 million during the same period. ($2.9 million of 1999 revenue was from auto loans.) However, due to continued increased expenditures from operations and sales and marketing, E-LOAN's operating loss grew further from $11.3 million to $76.1 million. (Of these expenditures, $23 million came from amortization of unearned stock-based compensation and another $11.6 million came from amortization of goodwill—see Exhibit 9).

Additionally, increased mortgage interest rates in 1999 caused the number of refinancing mortgage loans to decline. The mix of mortgage loans shifted from 5% purchase and 95% refinance in 1998 to 63% purchase and 37% refinance during the fourth quarter of 1999.[38]

Kennedy believed that in light of these issues, quickly building the E-LOAN brand was critical to long-term success:

Brands are not built in a day or even in two years. Brands are being built faster, but consistency and continuity remain the keys. E-commerce is accelerating the building of brands. Here, many start-up companies are attempting to become big players in big categories. Channel conflicts prevent big traditional players from significant online opportunities and provide a window for startups while there is a vacuum—a vacuum of the established brands. However, I don't believe this will last for 10 years.

Online stock trading provides an analogous—though not perfect—comparison. Ameritrade, Datek, E-Trade, all tried to become the brand leader while Merrill Lynch was not involved. They had maybe 5 years to do so. That brand vacuum is now getting more air in it. Through aggressive marketing, E-Trade has built a substantial position during the vacuum brand period. Lesser players could get in then. Ameritrade achieved secondary status. Now, new players don't have the brand vacuum to work with. The vacuum only allows 1 or 2 new brands.

Despite its losses, the company believed that it was still on the path to achieving profitability by pursuing market growth and the advantages of its market "vacuum." By the end of 1999, E-LOAN remained the leading online mortgage company, ahead of Mortgage.com, Lending Tree.com, and Countrywide.com based upon the number of loans closed. In early March 2000, two key competitors—Mortgage.com and FiNet.com—withdrew from the business-to-consumer markets to focus entirely on a business-to-business strategy. In 1999, Mortgage.com had experienced losses of $46.9 million on revenues of $61.3 million. Citing that it was too expensive to brand directly to customer to acquire business, Mortgage.com pursued partnerships with real estate agents and homebuilders who would send customers to Mortgage.com.[39]

Meanwhile, E-LOAN continued its plan of building a national, customer-recognized brand. With the help of its nationwide brand-building campaign in radio, television, and print in selected key markets (see Exhibit 13), E-LOAN was able to reduce the percentage of its mortgage loans sourced solely through California in 1999. In 2000, E-LOAN expected revenues to exceed operating costs for the first time, with the exception of marketing costs.

---

[38]E-LOAN 1999 Annual Report and 10K Statement.
[39]"Mortgage.com Quits Marketing to Customers, Targets Firms," American Banker Online, March 2, 2000.

Conclusion

As Larsen, Pawlowski, and Kennedy turned to leave the E-Service Awards, they were convinced that E-LOAN offered customers a unique value proposition, but the overarching strategic questions remained. How could E-LOAN position itself so the customer would recognize them more broadly as an online loan center, rather than just an online mortgage provider? Could it continue to differentiate itself through customer service? And most importantly, could it leverage the national brand recognition it strove to develop into scaling its customer base and achieving profitability?

Exhibit 1 E-LOAN Headquarters (Dublin, California)

Photo: Dickson Louie

Exhibit 2 E-Service Awards Ceremony

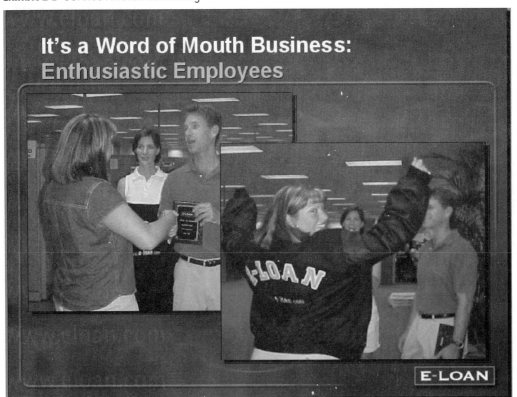

Source: E-LOAN

Exhibit 3 U.S. Mortgage Interest Rates

	1970	1980	1985	1990	1997	1998
Conventional new home	8.52%	13.95%	12.28%	10.08%	7.76%	7.00%
Conventional existing home	8.56%	13.95%	12.29%	10.08%	7.76%	7.01%

Source: Board of Governors of Federal Reserve System

Exhibit 4 Top Retail Mortgage Originators in the United States

Online Status of Leading Retail Mortgage Banks		
Retail Originators	**Retail Origins[1]**	**Online Applications[2]**
1. Norwest	$34.0	No
2. Bank of America	$28.0	No
3. Countrywide	$20.0	Yes
4. Washington Mutual	$17.0	Yes
5. Chase	$16.0	Yes
6. Cedant	$15.0	Yes
7. GMAC	$11.0	Yes
8. FT Mortgage	$8.0	Yes
9. National City	$8.0	No
10. Golden West	$8.0	Yes
11. CTX	$7.0	No
12. Dime	$7.0	No
13. SunTrust	$6.0	Yes
14. PNC Mortgage	$6.0	No
15. Prism	$6.0	No

[1] In billions of dollars, annually
[2] Online applications as of December 31, 1999
Source: Credit Suisse/First Boston

Exhibit 5 Key Online Mortgage Originator Competitors

	E-LOAN				
	Profile of Key Online Competitors				
Site	**URL**	**Loan Volume(1)**	**Business Model**	**Corporate Parent**	**Other Info**
Quicken	www.quickenloans.com	N/A	Refers customers to lenders online	Intuit	Formerly QuickenMortgage.com
Countrywide	www.countrywide.com	$860	Handles entire loan transaction; direct lender	Countrywide Home Loans, Inc.	Largest Direct Online Lender. 550 branches
Lending Tree	www.lendingtree.com	$501	Refers customers to lenders online	LendingTree.com	—
iOwn	www.iown.com	$291	Handles entire loan transaction; direct lender	iOwn.com	Formerly LoanShark.com
Get Smart	www.getsmart.com	N/A	Refers customers to lenders online	Providian	—
Home Advisor	www.homeadvisor.com	N/A	Refers customers to lenders online	Microsoft	—
Washington Mutual	www.wamu.com	N/A	Handles entire loan transaction; direct lender	Washington Mutual	—
People First	www.peoplefirst.com	N/A	Lends to customers directly	PeopleFirst.com	One of largest online auto lenders. Founded in 1995.

Note: (1) Loan volume in millions of dollars, first three quarters of 1999, Credit Suisse/First Boston
(2) Other sources: Individual online sites

Exhibit 6 Web Addresses of Home Pages of Competitor Sites

Countrywide: *www:countrywide.com*

GetSmart.com: *www:getsmart.com*

HomeAdvisor.com: *www:homeadvisor.com*

iOwn.com: *www:iown.com*

LendingTree.com: *www:lendingtree.com*

QuickenLoans.com: *http://quickenloans.quicken.com*

Washington Mutual Bank: *www:wamu.com*

PeopleFirst.com: *www:peoplefirst.com*

Exhibit 7 Forecast of Mortgages Originated Online

Source: Forrester Research

Exhibit 8 Effect of Interest Rates on Lending Limits

How Lending Limit Affects a Person Earning $60,000			
If the Rate Is	**You Can Borrow**	**If the Rate Is**	**You Can Borrow**
5.00%	$260,794	8.50%	$182,075
5.25%	$253,530	8.75%	$177,958
5.50%	$246,570	9.00%	$173,995
5.75%	$239,901	9.25%	$170,176
6.00%	$233,508	9.50%	$166,497
6.25%	$227,377	9.75%	$162,951
6.50%	$221,495	10.00%	$159,531
6.75%	$215,850	10.25%	$156,232
7.00%	$210,431	10.50%	$153,049
7.25%	$205,226	10.75%	$149,976
7.50%	$200,225	11.00%	$147,009
7.75%	$195,418	11.25%	$144,142
8.00%	$190,797	11.50%	$141,373
8.25%	$186,352	12.00%	$138,695

Source: Ric Edelman, *The Truth About Money,* Harper Collins Publishers, Inc.

Exhibit 9 E-LOAN Financial Statement ($000) (1997–1999)

	1999	1998	1997
Revenues	$22,097	$6,832	$1,043
Operating expenses			
Operations	22,779	8,257	1,319
Sales and marketing	30,286	5,704	470
Technology	3,595	1,346	102
General and administrative	6,859	1,619	524
Amortization of unearned stock-based compensation	23,116	1,251	—
Amortization of goodwill	11,589	—	—
Total operating expenses	98,224	18,177	2,415
Loss from operations	($76,127)	($11,345)	($1,372)
Other Income, net	3,152	173	(2)
Net loss	($72,975)	($11,172)	($1,374)

Source: E-LOAN 1999 Annual Report

Exhibit 10 E-LOAN Home Page

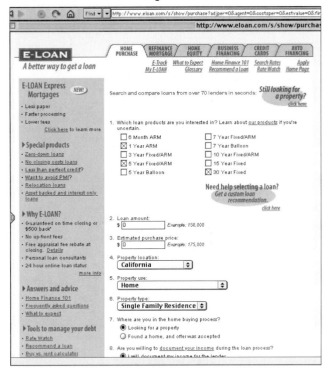

Exhibit 11 E-LOAN Rate Comparison

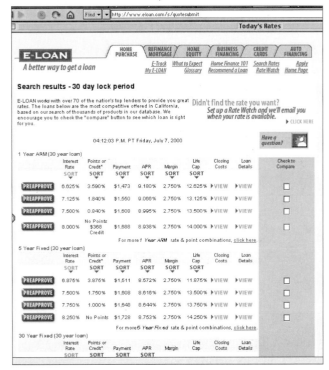

Source: E-LOAN

Exhibit 12 E-LOAN: Changing the Mortgage Process

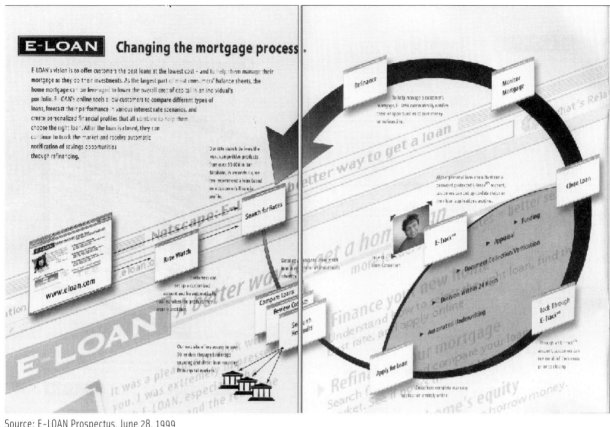

Source: E-LOAN Prospectus, June 28, 1999

Exhibit 13 E-LOAN Newspaper Advertisements as Run in *The Wall Street Journal* (1999)

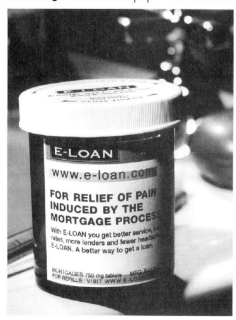

Source: E-LOAN

6

Implementation

IMPLEMENTATION

The purpose of this chapter is to introduce the firm-specific infrastructure that must be created and configured to go to market. In particular, we discuss two broad categories of infrastructure—the delivery system and the innovation process.

In the first phase of the online implementation process, the firm is concerned with the delivery of the offering to target customers. This delivery system is comprised of five key components: people, systems, assets, processes, and supply chains. A company's delivery system is the most detailed and concrete expression of that company's value proposition. Once the strategy has been defined and necessary capabilities identified, it becomes a matter of defining the structures, processes, reward systems, and human resource practices that will produce the needed competencies and capabilities.

In the second phase of implementation, the firm is concerned with the extent to which the offerings and infrastructures can be modified to fit the evolution of the market. In the offline world, a firm will typically cast a wide net to capture as many innovative ideas as possible, then progressively narrow down to a small set of ideas that are actively developed and brought to market. The purpose of this funnel process is to make internal choices about innovations that have the highest chance of succeeding.

The erosion of traditional constraints on innovation enables a faster, cheaper, and more adaptive innovation process but also intensifies uncertainty, in turn fueling the demand to innovate. Two fundamentally different process models attempt to accommodate this additional uncertainty: (1) the "flexible development process," in which concept development and implementation are tightly integrated and overlap, and (2) the "distributed innovation model," whereby the company tracks the evolution of each source of uncertainty, constantly adjusting the current online offering to the latest innovations.

Increased speed and intensity of competition in the online environment means online implementation mistakes are likely to be punished much more severely and quickly. Six implementation challenges for online companies are the following: higher visibility to errors, lower switching costs, more dynamic competitive environment, more fluid organizational boundaries, more dynamic market environment, and more complex linkages within and outside the organization.

SYNOPSES OF CHAPTER CASES

iQVC (A)

Case Overview

The iQVC website was launched the day after Labor Day in 1996. While the volume of sales generated through iQVC had rapidly increased since the launch, Stuart Spiegel, its Vice President and General Manager, wondered what might represent the best ways for iQVC to compete in the long-term, as a general merchandising store in a virtual world against specialized Internet retailers (virtual "category killers"). These category killers included new entrants, such as Amazon.com (booksellers), CDNow (compact discs), and Virtual Vineyards (wines), as well as other established retailers seeking to create a presence on the Web, such as Barnes & Noble, Tower Records, and Land's End. Even as iQVC developed more niche businesses, its management team sought to balance the site's promotion of its general merchandise character with the focused environments of its niche businesses. The challenge was to define iQVC as a single brand while providing adequate flexibility and resources for subbrands to flourish on the site.

This balance was not simple. Spiegel knew that he and his management team were by no means alone in their retailing ambitions on the Web. The online extension of the QVC television shopping franchise faced a variety of horizontal (general merchandise) competitors, along with even more vertical (niche-oriented) players. With all of them chasing the same limited consumer demand that QVC hoped to serve through iQVC, growing the iQVC business rapidly remained the key challenge.

To successfully replicate the QVC franchise online, Spiegel believed there were two important elements: the on-screen interface for electronic sales and the behind-the-scenes infrastructure for order fulfillment and customer service. Site designer, award-winning Web architect Clement Mok, aimed to make ordering as easy as it was on the QVC toll-free phone lines. In terms of fulfillment infrastructure, iQVC used a nationwide distribution network of vendors who shipped directly to consumers. This strategy allowed iQVC to expand merchandise selection over the cable-TV franchise, reduce inventory carrying costs, and provide opportunities for comparison shopping on the site.

How could iQVC keep its customer base growing through acquisition and retention strategies to render it a viable marketing channel for the scale of an organization such as QVC? At the same time, how could iQVC provide site users with increased levels of personalization, and of the recognized benefits of Internet shopping?

Preparation Questions

Please note: Students should take time to explore the iQVC website. Those who are wired for cable TV may also wish to watch the QVC and Q2 channels to better understand the core business. Shopping is encouraged!

1. Compare QVC's cable-TV service with the iQVC website. What are the key success factors for each business? How do they differ between the cable-TV and web platforms?

2. What are the key implementation challenges for both QVC and iQVC?

3. What aspects of QVC's core franchise contribute most to the business potential of iQVC? To what extent are the QVC brand and existing operations a liability for the Web-based business?

4. What are the strengths and weaknesses of the iQVC site? How effective is the screen interface as a virtual storefront?

5. What role might virtual communities play in achieving higher levels of user satisfaction and retention on the site?

6. What key sources of differentiation must iQVC develop to meet the intensifying competition from other vertically and horizontally focused Web-based retailers?

7. How does iQVC innovate?

iQVC (B)

Case Overview

In September 1997, Stuart Spiegel and Clement Mok collaborated to expand and redesign the iQVC site in anticipation of increased holiday traffic. Mok and iQVC changed the block design of the iQVC homepage to a living room scene, with site options placed in picture frames around a mantel. New software on the site's back-end was integrated with additional Web servers to enable the service to handle up to five times the average iQVC volume. Included in the new site were a number of interactive personalization features that provided information and product offerings driven by individual customer preferences.

Without advertising or marketing beyond QVC's cable-TV networks, revenues on the site were reaching impressive numbers—over $5 million in sales in December 1997. In January 1998, in response to customer demand, iQVC launched an entirely new website, *GemsandJewels.com.*, which linked to the iQVC home page, and vice versa. By January 1998, the iQVC website was receiving 20 million hits a week and nine million page views a day.

Preparation Questions

1. With the redesign of the main site and the new jewelry site, would iQVC continue to prosper as one of the Internet's most successful electronic retailers?

2. How could iQVC continue to benefit from exposure on the company's cable-TV networks?

MARSHALL INDUSTRIES

Case Overview

As 1998 drew to a close, Robert Rodin, CEO of Marshall Industries, had every reason to celebrate. Marshall, the fourth largest global distributor of industrial electronic components, had logged annual revenues of $1.4 billion, having successfully reinvented itself as what Rodin called a "virtual distributor." Not only was Marshall one of the first companies to conduct electronic commerce on the Internet, but it had created one of the most robust and widely used business-to-business websites.

In 1992, in a radical move viewed by the industry with great skepticism, Rodin had scrapped the company's entire internal system. He eliminated commissions, contests, forecasts, budgets, the organizational chart, and most dramatically, individual performance-based bonuses. Rodin argued that these changes were crucial for preparing the company to go virtual by eliminating internal distractions and allowing his managers to focus on designing customized solutions for customers. In effect, he shifted the company's culture from a sales-based to a service-based organization.

In 1994, the company launched "Marshall on the Internet," which replaced the bulky product catalogs, and MarshallNet, an intranet system that enabled customers to check order status. By 1998, the transformation was complete. Rodin described the company as a "high-speed junction box" that connected suppliers with customers. Many observers predicted that the Internet would render obsolete distributors and other so-called middlemen. Electronics distributors, including Marshall, had so far survived the disintermediation threat by stepping up their offering of value-added services. Marshall boasted not only the most comprehensive feature set of any distributor's website but also a transparent, uncluttered, and easy-to-use interface.

Yet despite Marshall's successes, Robert Rodin eyed the future with trepidation. Customers were squeezing distributors harder than ever, resulting in declining margins. Meanwhile, many nontraditional competitors were emerging, threatening to make the struggle for market share even more intense. How could Rodin continue to develop innovative new businesses and services fast enough to generate earnings and maintain its edge as the leading innovator in distribution? How could the company continue to distinguish itself as the best virtual distributor in the face of newly formed "vortex site," or pure Internet, distributors and even freight forwarders like FedEx and UPS?

Preparation Questions

1. What roles do distributors play in the electronic components industry? Why and how are those roles evolving?

2. What is Marshall's position in the industry? How have changes in the industry affected the viability of this position?

3. Can Marshall secure a sustainable competitive advantage from its website?

4. Was Rodin's decision to scrap sales commissions a wise one?

5. If you were a pure Internet distributor like Netbuy or Fast Parts, how would you attack a traditional distributor like Marshall?

INTEGRATIVE QUESTIONS

As you consider the entire set of questions for the sixth chapter, you should also reflect on the following integrative questions:

1. How important are supply-chain issues for online businesses? What are the lessons learned from iQVC and Marshall?

2. How are the order-fulfillment and supply-chain issues similar and dissimilar for QVC/iQVC and Marshall?

3. Some have argued that online companies have unique implementation challenges, while others have argued that the same basic issues confront brick-and-mortar companies. State your opinion.

4. Comment on the following quote: "Increased speed and intensity of competition in the online environment means implementation mistakes online are likely to be punished much more severely and quickly." Do you agree or disagree?

SUMMARY

Implementation entails all of the firm-level activities that are necessary to bring the firm's value proposition to market. This includes structures, processes, people, activities, and resource allocation. Many of the implementation challenges that confront traditional brick-and-mortar companies also appear to affect online companies. The implementation challenge is also compounded by the constant need to innovate. Traditional innovation approaches that required time-intensive, sequential decisions must be replaced by innovation approaches that involve less time, more interwoven decisions, and quick modification of the firm's offerings.

iQVC (A)

www.qvc.com

As the number of shopping days before Christmas 1996 began to dwindle, the staff at iQVC, the interactive shopping arm of QVC, Inc., was considering new ways to stimulate sales through its Web site (*www.qvc.com*). The most obvious driver was the regularly scheduled cross-promotion of the iQVC site on the company's two cable television network channels, QVC and Q2, as a surge in the number of "hits"[1] coincided with each time the Web site was mentioned on-air. Less obvious drivers included alteration of the iQVC home page on the Web—similar to a merchant's storefront window—to highlight top-selling items, making it easier for users to navigate through the site's 21 product categories, and making detailed product information available on each item sold to consumers (such as how to care for teddy bears).

While the volume of sales generated through iQVC had rapidly increased since the site was officially launched the day after Labor Day 1996, Stuart Spiegel, its vice president and general manager, wondered what might represent the best ways for iQVC to compete, long-term, as a general merchandising store in a virtual world against specialized retailers, or vertical "category killers," on the Internet. These category killers included new entrants, such as Amazon.com (booksellers), CDNow! (compact discs), and Virtual Vineyards (wines), as well as other established retailers seeking to create a presence on the Web, such as Barnes & Noble, Tower Records, and Land's End. Another question that Spiegel wrestled with was how to keep growing iQVC's customer base through acquisition and retention strategies to render it a viable marketing channel for the scale of an organization such as QVC.

The Changing Shopping Environment[2]

By 1996, 20 years of lifestyle and demographic changes were reflected in evolving shopping formats. The most widely heralded change was the growing number of women entering the work force, and thus the large number of dual-income families. Also, the number of teenagers and young adults, a group more inclined to embrace electronic shopping and interactive television, was expected to become more significant in the late 1990s.

Department store sales increased to $218 billion in 1994 from nearly $127 billion in 1985, yet lost market shares to discount stores, warehouse clubs, manufacturers' outlet stores, and specialty retail stores. Many department stores were downsized, restructured, and re-merchandised to emphasize fashion-forward apparel. As department stores went bankrupt and were subsequently consolidated during the 1980s, specialty apparel and accessory stores posted increased sales to $110 billion in 1994 from $70 billion in 1985. Specialty retailers, such as computer stores, home improvement outlets, and book retailers, grew even more dramatically—rising to $337 billion in 1994 from $184 billion in 1985.

Consumers were expected to spend roughly $80 billion on catalog sales in 1995, compared with $51.5 billion in 1992. In 1994, more than 10,000 mail-order companies sent out 12.8 billion catalogs and about 61% of the adult population purchased consumer goods through the mail. The growth of catalog retailing could be explained by an increase in dissatisfaction with traditional shopping environments. Consumers cited many reasons for their displeasure, including lack of adequate parking, poor service, long lines, and growing crime rates. Approximately one-half of all adults surveyed in 1996 agreed that shopping in stores was an "unpleasant chore that they avoided doing whenever possible."[3]

Research Associate Dickson L. Louie prepared this case, with the assistance of Research Associate Michelle Toth, MBA '95, under the supervision of Professor Jeffrey F. Rayport as the basis for class discussion rather than to illustrate either effective or ineffective handling of an administrative situation.

[1]A "hit" is defined as "every file request made to a Web server." A typical Web page generated several hits each time it was served.
[2]This section adapted from two earlier cases, "The TV-Home Shopping Wars: QVC and Its Competitors," HBS case No. 395-014, and "QVC, Inc.," HBS case No. 897-050.
[3]The WEFA Group, News & Information, Direct Marketing Association, "Meet the New Competition: Emerging Home Shopping Alternatives," p. s18.

The appeal of televised shopping, like catalog shopping, was the opportunity to avoid many of these ills. At the same time, quality, price, and convenience were emphasized by consumers as reasons specifically for using televised shopping, although many potential customers often viewed the medium as a channel that offered lower quality merchandise. Some attributed the rise in popularity of televised shopping to consumers' increasing comfort with technology. In 1995, approximately 11% of all U.S. adults had purchased something from one of the televised shopping channels and 8% from an infomercial[4] (see Exhibit 1).

Estimates for retail revenues occurring over the Internet—an alternate electronic retail channel—was estimated by Jupiter Communications to be about $200 million in 1995, which was less than one percent of all retail sales for the same year. Though small in number—8% of consumers had made a purchase over the Internet in 1995—the purchase rate was double that for the segment of the population that was 18 to 35 years old.[5] Internet commerce was projected to increase to nearly $7 billion by the year 2000 (see Exhibit 2) as the number of Web users worldwide increased by an estimated seven-fold to 152 million in 2000 from 23 million in 1996 (see Exhibit 3). Corresponding to increases in Web users was the increasing percentage of personal computer users with access to the Web, which was expected to grow to 67% in 2000 from 15% in 1996.

Emergence of Electronic Commerce on the Internet

According to Forrester Research, an Internet research company based in Cambridge, Massachusetts, computer products, travel, and entertainment were dominant retail categories in on-line commerce (see Exhibit 4).

By year end 1996, several start-up companies had established a foothold in on-line retailing. Advantages to consumers making purchases on-line included 24-hour access to information and services, large inventory selections, and an abundance of product information on demand. Increased security for credit card transactions over the Internet, built into new releases of Netscape and

Microsoft Web browsers, eased consumer concerns about on-line purchases. Among the most prominent retailers on-line at the end of 1996 were:

Amazon.com (*www.amazon.com*). Billed as "the Earth's largest bookstore," Amazon.com provided visitors to its site with a selection of over one million titles. The Seattle-based company offered books at a 10% to 30% discount from regular retail prices; visitors could read book reviews posted by authors and readers. Visitors could search through Amazon.com's inventory by using keywords for subject, title, or author. Sign-on to a personalized notification system called "Eyes" or "Editor" provided visitors with e-mail alerts of forthcoming books in selected categories such as favorite authors or subject areas.[6]

CD Now! (*www.cdnow.com*). CD Now! enabled visitors to browse through a large collection of CDs, ranging from Broadway musicals to punk rock. Accessible 24 hours a day, CD Now! gave potential customers a chance to sample music on-line and read the latest reviews on its Web pages.

Internet Shopping Network (*www.isn.com*). An on-line computer retailer purchased in 1994 by Home Shopping Network—QVC's long-time competitor in the televised home shopping arena—Internet Shopping Network (ISN), based in Palo Alto, California, competed with over 200 other computer retailers on the Web. Visitors to the site could search for computers and peripherals by category (drives, memories, and multimedia hardware), read product reviews from the trade weekly, *InfoWorld*, or download the latest versions of Microsoft's Word, Excel, and PowerPoint software, among others.

Travelocity (*www.travelocity.com*). Owned by AMR, the parent company of American Airlines, Travelocity provided busy travelers with the capability to book their own tickets, read about travel destinations, and check the weather forecasts in various cities.

Virtual Vineyards (*www.virtualvin.com*). One of the oldest Web-based retailers, Virtual Vineyards provided visitors with an inventory of California wines with reviews and transactional capabilities for secure purchases over the Internet. If visitors were unsure of the type of wine that they needed for a special occasion, an e-mail message to the "Cork Dork" yielded a personalized response.[7]

---

[4]Deloitte & Touche Consulting Group, *The Dawning of the Age of Electronic Consumerism*, June 1996.
[5]Ibid.
[6]Also see case, "Amazon.com," HBS case No. 897-128.
[7]Also see case, "Virtual Vineyards," HBS case No. 396-264.

Other on-line retailers included AOL Marketplace, operated by America Online, which provided links to merchants, such as Land's End, JCPenney, Starbucks Coffee, Godiva, and the Nature Company, for over 150,000 members daily as well as The Internet Mall (*www.internetmall.com*) which had links to over 20,000 stores, including Macy's and the Disney Store Online. In addition, in 1996, Wal-Mart, the large discount retailer, and Microsoft, the software giant, announced plans for a joint on-line venture. By year end 1996, industry experts estimated that 14% of all U.S. retailers had Web sites or planned to build sites within a year, compared with only 4% a year earlier.[8]

Security was a major concern for on-line consumers, whose perception was that Internet transactions were fraught with risk—though most experts believed that on-line transactions were, in fact, much safer (by an order of magnitude in terms of incidence of credit card fraud as a percent of sales) than using a credit card in a physical retail environment. The perception was beginning to change as companies started to take advantage of available technology to build secure systems using Netscape's Secure Sockets Layer (SSL) technology and other secured server technologies. The Secured Electronic Transactions (SET) specification—the security standard for credit card transactions proposed by MasterCard and Visa and others—was widely expected to become operational in late 1997, which would presumably further increase consumer comfort with on-line transactions.

The History of QVC[9]

QVC was founded in 1986 by Joseph Segel, founder of the Franklin Mint, a multi-million-dollar mail order company that sold commemorative coins, collectors' editions of fine books, and vintage model cars. Earlier that year, Segel had tuned into the Home Shopping Network (HSN) on his cable-TV system, a pioneer of the televised shopping concept that had originated in 1977, and was unimpressed. The programming was crude, the products were downmarket, and the proliferation of inexpensive jewelry items turned him off. But Segel saw an opportunity to promote more upscale merchandise

through higher quality programming using a distinctly different approach from that of HSN.

In November 1986, with $30 million in start-up capital and several seasoned television executives who had signed on, Segel began broadcasting the new QVC service from its headquarters in West Chester, Pennsylvania, and aimed to guide the company according to three customer-focused elements that constituted a new kind of value proposition in televised home shopping: these were Quality, Value, and Convenience, comprising the initials QVC. In its first full year, QVC established a sales record in American business history for a start-up public company, with revenues in excess of $112 million.

Over the next seven years, under Segel's direction, QVC grew rapidly, largely through acquisition of its largest competitors, the Cable Value Network (CVN) and JCPenney's TV home shopping network, in 1990. In 1992, Barry Diller, the former chairman of Paramount Pictures and Fox Inc., believed televised home shopping would become a gateway to interactive commerce and invested $25 million of his personal wealth in the QVC network. In January 1993, Diller became chairman of QVC, replacing Segel, who retired.

During Diller's tenure, with Douglas Briggs as president, the company overtook in sales its long-time rival HSN. While both companies had reached nearly $1.1 billion in net revenue in 1992, QVC's net revenue rose to $1.2 billion in 1993, and $1.4 billion in 1994, while HSN's net revenue remained flat at $1.1 billion in both those years. Under Diller's and Briggs' leadership, QVC pursued several ventures to expand the company's marketing efforts and viewer base. They launched a joint venture with Rupert Murdoch's British Sky Broadcasting in the United Kingdom in 1983, resulting in a British version of the QVC shopping channel. Diller and Briggs also launched Q2, a sister retail channel aimed at more upscale audiences, in April 1994, for which QVC established separate production operations in studios located in Long Island City, New York. Briggs also masterminded "The Quest for America's Best—QVC's '50 in 50 Tour,'" a year-long search to discover a thousand of the best new products from American entrepreneurs across all 50 states.

In February 1995, two of the largest multiple-system cable operators in the United States, Comcast Corporation and Telecommunications, Inc. (TCI), acquired QVC, with Comcast assuming the majority position. Diller left subsequently and became CEO of rival HSN in November 1995. Briggs, a long-time QVC veteran continued to build the QVC brand as president of QVC. In December 1995, QVC's first interactive on-line site was launched on

[8]Angwin, Julia, "Attention Internet Shoppers," *San Francisco Chronicle*, December 25, 1996.
[9]This section adapted from two earlier cases, "The TV-Home Shopping Wars: QVC and Its Competitors," HBS case No. 395-014, and "QVC, Inc.," HBS case No. 897-050.

the Microsoft Network. QVC established a separate, stand-alone Web site on the Internet several months later. In September 1996, the company announced plans to establish QVC channels in Germany, adding to the retailer's worldwide viewer base.

By the end of 1995—almost 10 years after QVC's founding and 20 years after the concept of televised shopping appeared—sales for the televised shopping market in the United States had risen to $4 billion. The key competitors in the market were QVC, which had $1.6 billion in revenues and 40% market share, and HSN, which had $1 billion in revenues and 25% market share. With sales of $1.6 million in 1995, QVC had already exceeded several well-known traditional retailers in its scale of operations, including Bloomingdale's and Saks Fifth Avenue.

Development of QVC's Web Site

By 1995, accessing the Internet through a personal computer had emerged for electronic commerce as the clear alternative to interactive television. Although the Internet had been in use for over a generation—it was created during the 1960s by the U.S. Department of Defense as a means of accessing vital information in the event of a nuclear exchange that crippled the Bell System—its primary use had been to serve as a communications tool for educational and government institutions to transmit and share research information across computer networks. The introduction of the first Web Browser— Mosaic, which was superseded by Netscape Navigator— in the mid-1990s helped spur the growth in commercial Internet use.

Spiegel, a marketing and retailing executive living in California who had worked with Macy's, NY, Ralph Lauren, Liz Claiborne, and Sony Signatures, was hired by QVC's executive vice president of information technology and chief information officer, John Link, in May 1995, to become the vice president and general manager of the company's new retailing venture in cyberspace. Recalled Spiegel:

> When QVC called, I took the interview because I was interested in what QVC was doing. I didn't know anything about the on-line world. I went into a magazine store and bought everything that had the words "Internet" or "Net" in it, read voraciously, and went to the interview. Fortunately, QVC was looking for a merchant and business person—not a techie. And here I am.

Once aboard at QVC, Spiegel and his executive team concluded that the mission of their venture was to expand QVC's existing franchise on a different platform, not to create a completely separate business as the early on-line business models and prototypes had previously assumed. Link and Spiegel also decided to move cautiously into cyberspace—choosing to go with the Microsoft Network (MSN), which was being launched in December 1995, instead of partnering with a much larger and established partner, such as America Online. The overriding priority was for the company to learn from early on-line efforts before launching a Web site of its own. Recalled Spiegel:

> We went with MSN because it had a controlled audience structure, and we wanted the ability to develop our on-line presence very carefully. Our goal was to build processes and infrastructure methodically before plunging onto the World Wide Web. We believe the lessons learned from an audience of 400,000 would translate effectively to an audience of 40 million.
>
> If we went with America Online, it would be America Online's identity because it's on their template. Every "store" looked like America Online; the "stores" didn't present their own identities. Also, the Internet wasn't really ready in summer 1995 and people were just beginning to talk about it. So Microsoft afforded us the freedom technically to say, "What do I want to look like?" So our first mission was: "What do we want to look like and how do we want to market our brand?"

With colleague Steve Hamlin, iQVC vice president of operations, focusing on the project's back-end and logistics (these tasks included procedures for delivering packages to customers and finding the best ways for QVC's information systems to interface with its vendors), Spiegel and Clement Mok, the founder and information architect of San Francisco-based Studio Archetype, Inc., focused on developing the project's front-end—iQVC's screen interface with its customers. Mok had previously served as director of communications for Apple Computer's Macintosh during the mid-1980s before establishing his own brand-identity consulting firm in 1989.

Regarding iQVC, Mok recalled that there were three critical challenges in putting iQVC on-line. The first challenge was how to extend QVC's brand and customer base using on-line platforms, such as MSN, the Internet, and Intercast.[10] The second challenge was how to design an interface that appeared consistent on different on-line platforms and sustained QVC's visual appeal. The final challenge was how to make on-line business transactions easy and intuitive for customers.[11] Noted Mok:

> When Stuart came on board, timing was such that interactive television was on its way out and on-line was in. The Internet was just becoming credible, but this was happening fairly rapidly. Stuart and his team had looked at the Microsoft Network as vehicles for their first forays into the on-line world, but they knew that the Internet would probably be a thing to be reckoned with in the near future.
>
> So we worked with them in trying to figure out how you can have incremental learning curves and all your fingers in all different pieces of the pie and still move forward in a commercially meaningful way. With Stuart and his team, we put together a functional master plan for which we could look at ways to stage the various steps as the site was deployed on different platforms. That's what we were engaged in first, assisting with the master planning. The second piece was the actual execution for on-line delivery. And the third piece was the deployment and adaptation of the full Internet platform itself. That was staged over a nine-month period.

By November 1995, QVC's site on MSN was ready for launch. Spiegel and Link believed that the key to becoming a retail success in a digital world was to avoid becoming enamored by any specific technology. They determined it best to continue focus on the customer and the retail fundamentals of merchandising. Observed Spiegel:

> Today's obsession with technology in a virtual world is virtually beside the point. If this were 100 years ago—and we were obsessing over creating something new and different, such as a department store—would we be focusing on the bricks, their size or shape, or the mortar? Or the shelves and whether they

are made of wood or glass or even metal? Of course not. We'd be talking about the merchandise, the assortments, the signage, and the displays. We would be talking about in-store service and training. We would be talking about the stuff retailers are really made of. Obviously, the technology is critical. But it's only the platform, a detail to how we conduct business. Let's forget about the technical "how" and discuss for "whom" and "what" we are marketing. The growth of digital commerce will be driven the old-fashioned way, through content. The reality is that we cannot afford to think of ourselves as digital retailers, but simply as retailers.[12]

QVC's senior management believed that the company's existing infrastructure for providing services to customers—centered around the principles of quality, value, and convenience—would also benefit iQVC. Added Spiegel:

> At QVC, we concentrate on things like: Who is the customer? How do you plan to deliver your products? How do you assure quality? What does your product assortment look like? How do your customers return merchandise? How is the merchandise packed? How quickly do you process an order? Who does the customer call for complaints? At QVC, we have concentrated on the basics and have emphasized our ability to execute. We expect iQVC to execute business as smoothly as QVC does—the standards of excellence are the same across platforms.[13]

iQVC was launched on MSN on December 9, 1995, to coincide with QVC's offering of a Packard Bell Pentium personal computer as "Today's Special Value,"[14] a regular feature on QVC. The promotion generated approximately $10 million in sales for QVC that day alone, demonstrating the potential of the combined marketing channels.

After launching iQVC on MSN, Spiegel and his team turned their attention to building a Web site. By early summer 1996, iQVC's Web site was up and running—though not yet widely publicized on-air—and allowed users to "browse" through and order nearly all the merchandise offered by QVC on the air. "We didn't tell a soul," recalled Spiegel, "until after Labor Day, because we wanted to make sure that everything was running right before going public with the site."

The initial users of iQVC's Web site were its existing customers. With regularly scheduled on-air cross-promotion from its two sibling cable-television networks, which appeared in three-minute formats two to

---

[10]Intercast was a media platform which allowed a television viewer to see, simultaneously, a broadcast or cable-TV channel and its corresponding Web site on a TV screen. In early 1997, however, there were only a few information providers doing business on Intercast. In addition to QVC, NBC and CNN also provided Intercast services.

[11]Mok, Clement, *Designing Business*, Adobe Press, 1996.

[12]Stuart Spiegel, speech to "Digital Shopping and Electronic Commerce Conference," September 22, 1995.

[13]Ibid.

[14]"Today's Special Value," or TSV, referred to the product QVC buyers selected for special promotion at an attractive price throughout each 24-hour programming period.

three times a day, Spiegel noted that whenever iQVC was mentioned on the air, "the server spiked, highlighting the willingness of QVC network viewers to try the site out right away." He added:

> We've got over 5 million customers. We assume that a third of them have computers and, of those, another third are connected to the Internet. We'll target those potential customers—our network customers—first; they are already established QVC users and therefore represent, we believe, a good place to begin. We have pursued this strategy despite the popular, and clearly incorrect, belief that QVC customers are not "sophisticated" or technology-savvy enough to surf the Web or know how to connect to the Internet.

> We are introducing iQVC to these customers by demonstrating the added value of the medium. In three minutes, our regular QVC hosts can show them how iQVC's database expands our offerings beyond the nine or ten items available each hour on the core cable-TV service. We plant the seed of an idea with our viewers that our on-line world is bringing more to choose from, anytime they want to visit.

> The strategy is causing our business to just rocket. I'm seeing between a 5% and 10% increase in business every week. And our traffic is steadily increasing to over a million hits a day.

Creating Quality, Value, and Convenience on the Web

In establishing iQVC's Web site, Briggs and Link commissioned Spiegel and his team to build a new marketing channel to reflect QVC's core customer values—Quality, Value, and Convenience. The Web site, they believed, should serve as an extension of the electronic retailer's storefront, which originated on cable-TV but now reached onto the Internet; in this sense, iQVC would augment QVC's brand equity much as the addition of Q2, a separate network with similar merchandise and different presentation, had done. To successfully replicate the QVC franchise on-line, Spiegel believed there were two important elements: the on-screen interface for electronic sales and the behind-the-scenes infrastructure for order fulfillment and customer service.

---

[15]"QVC, Inc.," HBS case No. 897-050.

The Interface

iQVC's home page on the Web (see Exhibit 5) provided visitors with a "peek" at what merchandise was available in the general merchandise "store." The home page changed with the seasons (see Exhibit 6 for the site's original storefront and Exhibit 7 for its Christmas season storefront). As Frankie Babin, iQVC's on-line editor, observed:

> We're trying to be a general merchandiser first, before adding specialty shops. The design has to be easy to download. I want it to be attractive and exciting. The important thing is to just get you into our store.

One of the key elements attributed to the success of QVC's two television channels was the product information that its on-air hosts provided to the viewing audience. Noted Jack Comstock, vice president of television sales at QVC, regarding his selection of the television hosts:

> A lot of viewers find us entertaining. They build a relationship with the host. Consequently, when I look for hosts—on-air salespeople—I look for people who are real, people who are credible, people who are talking about why you may want to buy a product—not pressuring you to buy. They're educating, entertaining, and presenting to you the benefits of a product in a conversational, non-pushy way.[15]

But there was a difference between cable-TV viewing and Web surfing. Customers shopping on one of QVC's cable-TV channels tended, Spiegel believed, to have a more passive approach; they enjoyed being entertained and leaned back during their viewing. Shoppers on the Internet, by contrast, were usually aggressive by nature and habit; they frequently knew what they were looking for and leaned forward as they interacted with keyboard and screen. He added:

> Consumers are passive when watching TV and QVC creates spontaneous "calls to action." On iQVC, we have the opportunity to facilitate both browsing and considered purchasing. iQVC's consumers, we believe, are in a more pro-active mode—so they often are looking for something. Our job is to make it easy and fun and fast for them to find what they want.

Approximately 40% of iQVC's Web customers used its search engine to find products, while the remaining users simply explored the site. The majority of purchase activity took place on weekends—despite lower overall traffic on the site—while the majority of browsing took place during weekdays, presumably from a mix of home and office users. When designing the site, Mok had aimed to make ordering through the iQVC site as easy as ordering a product through QVC's toll-free lines—if not more so. Recalled Mok:

> An important interface design consideration was the transaction process. QVC is known for the speed, quality, and efficiency of its ordering system, so we paralleled QVC's established procedure in iQVC's ordering process. There are no time constraints in the computer environment, and for iQVC shoppers the service's main benefit is its customized, instantaneous responses. This meant that iQVC's service had to be as good as, if not better than, QVC's toll-free phone service. QVC customers are used to instant purchase gratification—"I want that product, I'm going to order it now." As a result, getting that same kind of confirmation in a digital environment couldn't take any longer than a few mouse clicks. The design challenge was not so much in creating the interface's look-and-feel; the real challenge lay in assuring its performance from a transactions perspective.[16]

In his work with iQVC, Mok had followed what he called the "two-click rule." As he recalled, "We wanted the customer to be able to find anything that they needed in two clicks or less. If the customer has to make more than two clicks, then we believed they were likely to get frustrated and might not purchase the item they were looking for even if they found it."

Along similar lines, Mok had made user convenience a priority. A visit to the iQVC home page highlighted several QVC promotions simultaneously—"Today's Special Value," the "Current On-Air Item," and Search—and emphasized the multi-functional aspects of selling several products on the Internet simultaneously. As Mok observed, there was a key difference between selling on television and selling on the Internet:

> The cable broadcast, being linear, could be used to promote only one "hot item" at a time. Information on the Web is multi-functional. The Web window could show links to all the current promotions at once, giving customers access to more iQVC promotions in less time.[17]

This meant that, in building iQVC's Web site, two of QVC's key sales features in its core service—in particular,

the "Current On-Air Item" and "Today's Special Value"—had to be fully integrated with the site to retain the familiar context of the service. Remarked Spiegel:

> The "Current On-Air Item" and "Today's Special Value" are very solid parts of our site. We probably do 15% of our business in these two areas. Our thought in planning the site was to demonstrate that both iQVC and QVC are fully integrated electronic merchants. Where else in the world can you click on the Web and get exactly what's on television right now? Sometimes CNN or MSNBC, but only in the case of selected programming. We're fully integrated 24 hours a day.

On iQVC's home page, images of cubbyholes and drawers—each with a specific promotion or product category—were used to make popular high-traffic areas easier for users to find, in a manner similar to product placement at eye level in a supermarket aisle. This was crucial in designing the overall structure of the Web site. As Mok observed:

> Just as an architect uses a master plan to lay out spaces and orchestrate traffic patterns in a building, we used a bubble diagram [see Exhibit 8] to plan and develop the cluster of shopping and information-seeking activities [Products, Corporate Information, Chats/ Events, etc.] that defined iQVC.

To provide the kind of product information supplied by QVC's television hosts on-air, iQVC provided on-line visitors with product information for every selection, including a color digitized image, along with feature pieces provided either by manufacturers, by the company's staff of research librarians (see Exhibit 9), or by the electronic retailer's editorial staff, often drawing on the knowledge of the on-air hosts (see Exhibit 10). Spiegel believed that having this content was essential to meeting the needs of his on-line customers in order to pre-empt iQVC from becoming simply another Web-based electronic catalogue. He noted:

> iQVC can tap into the infrastructure of QVC's core business. This allows us to achieve both a digital and a physical advantage over our competition. iQVC uses the organization's core logistics system to ship products that are also sold on-air; in addition, it draws upon the company's expertise in packing, packaging, and shipping for all its fulfillment through the "virtual" infrastructure. Despite those advantages, it's access to QVC's Information Services division that is really our secret weapon. Not many retailers have the ability

---

[16]Mok, Clement, *Designing Business*, Adobe Press, 1996.
[17]Ibid.

to tap into the skill sets offered by highly trained staff librarians to build a database of product and feature descriptions. Ultimately, our customers will be able to research virtually any level of detail that interests them about the product they are considering for purchase. Additionally, we have another asset unavailable to our competition—our hosts. For example, Bob Bowersox is a true professional in the kitchen. He shares his expertise with our Web users by writing a monthly column for the site and "publishing" his recipes weekly in digital form. This adds both information and entertainment to what we're all about.

The Infrastructure

Most of the products purchased on-line from iQVC were drop-shipped directly by the manufacturer to the consumer once an order was placed (see order page on Exhibit 11). First-time customers were issued a Q-Member number, provided credit card or other payment information, and chose a unique personal identification number (PIN); those who had already received a Q-Member number as users of the core service simply provided a credit card number and selected a PIN to make use of the site. Once an order was placed, iQVC displayed an order number for the customer's record and estimated delivery dates. iQVC transmitted the order information, along with the Q-Member number and appropriate shipping instructions, electronically to vendors. Vendors usually acknowledged receipt of data within 24 hours and shipped within 48 hours. Throughout the order cycle, users could call any of QVC's 4,000 customer service representatives to get information about order status, since the Q-Member number allowed the core franchise to track individual shipments throughout network and Web-based operations.

Using a nationwide distribution network of vendors who shipped directly to consumers allowed iQVC to expand merchandise selection over the cable-TV franchise, reduce inventory carrying costs, and provide opportunities for comparison shopping on the site. iQVC vendors were subject to the same vigorous product testing and screening process as vendors on QVC's core network, in which two of every three products were rejected or returned for modification. The rationale for maintaining such rigorous selection standards was the preservation of QVC's core brand equity and the high level of customer trust. Because of the large and varied inventory on iQVC, however, quality assurance for iQVC products was based on initial screening, spot checks, and monitoring of returns, rather than periodic testing in QVC's Quality Assurance department. In addition, vendors doing business with iQVC were required to adhere to iQVC's "drop-ship" procedures. Added Spiegel:

We have "virtual" warehouses all over the country, in the sense that, unlike QVC, we don't own or control most of our distribution infrastructure. As a result, iQVC's operations team is charged with ensuring that customer order fulfillment is delivered at the same level of quality as from our own warehouses. Our distribution network follows stringent guidelines and our vendors ship using our own packing slips. Our customers can return any product directly to QVC's central returns facility simply by peeling or cutting off part of the label. This service is available to our customers regardless of which warehouse the product is shipped from. QVC is all about exceeding customer's expectations; it is no different if you happen to purchase from us over the Internet.

In addition, QVC's management information systems provided Spiegel with real-time information on product sales, allowing him to decide which items to promote online more aggressively and which should be dropped from the site. Explained Spiegel, "If I noticed that blood pressure monitors were selling well, I would ask myself, 'Should we enhance that product? How can I bring sales up to the next level? And how many units should we have in inventory for each SKU?' In the physical world, you could walk the floor at Macy's and try to figure out what was moving. In the Internet environment, I can sit in my office and click through real data."

To date, the data QVC had for shoppers on its Internet site was surprising—or, at least, counter-intuitive—according to widely noted demographics for Internet usage.[18] Spiegel explained:

Approximately 75% of the shopping done on iQVC is done by women. Interestingly, there is a higher proportion of women shopping on-line than in our cable-TV network counterpart. On QVC, the mix is 65% women and 35% men. On iQVC, it is 75% women and 25% men. Today, however, the mix for new customers—those that have never shopped with QVC—is split evenly between men and women.

---

[18]In 1996 an estimated two-thirds of Internet users were men. "The Internet," *The Wall Street Journal*, December 9, 1996.

During the Christmas season, in November and December 1996, iQVC shipped goods worth $2 million in sales. While Spiegel could not release specific financial figures for iQVC performance, he observed that the site was exceeding its financial projections and had, in addition, begun to make money.

Creating Niche Businesses within the General Merchandising Store

iQVC's management team believed the strategy of using Web technology to create niche businesses while realizing substantial leverage from QVC's centralized operations infrastructure had great potential. For example, Spiegel pointed to the compelling logic of highlighting even a minor merchandise category, such as teddy bears, on its home page during the Christmas season:

> We consistently change our storefront on television, so changing our Web page with the seasons is just as important. One of the opportunities that we have is our ability to create niche businesses alongside our general merchandise environment. During the Christmas holiday season, we wanted to test a boutique concept. We decided to highlight teddy bear collectibles in order to represent the site in a strong visual manner, while also intensifying a particular merchandise category. I'm happy to report the results: it worked.

The capability to create niche retailing categories essentially on demand was significant in Spiegel's mind. When combined with existing QVC infrastructures for customer service and order fulfillment, innovative merchandising (beyond the network's on-air items) could flourish through presentation in appropriate niche-focused environments. As Spiegel noted:

> With the teddy bears, we created a specialty niche out of a general merchandise category. We believe we can leverage the company's product strengths into several niche merchandise boutiques. By first going after our core competencies—jewelry, collectibles, and home goods—we could build strong stand-alone environments to rival any specialty operation. For example, I am certain that we could have the world's largest jewelry store on-line. In fact, the most likely outcome is that the store would eventually have its own Web

address while remaining accessible from the general store called iQVC.

> Merchandising a general specialty store in conjunction with several stand-alone specialty stores affords us the ability, among other benefits, to capture consumer demand for seasonal products. If our whole store was a specialty store offering ski equipment, we would have a limited sales window in which to conduct business. But with ski equipment included in our general merchandise store, we could highlight it when appropriate in a niche format without concern to seasonality, because we can always move other products into other niche stores when a category of seasonal items has passed.

> The challenge is clear. Even when you're juggling several balls at once, they're not all up in the air at the same time. My job is to figure out which balls to raise and when, making them available to all consumers at any time.

Teddy bears were not the only niche iQVC had created. For example, just before Christmas 1996, iQVC launched an on-line bookstore. Consistent with its other niche businesses, iQVC placed an icon for the bookstore on the home page, allowing easy access for users. As Spiegel observed, while traditional retailers in the United States had lost market share to category killers and specialty retailers in the past decade, he believed the evolution of digital retailing might follow a different pattern. As a model, he cited the pattern of traditional department store retailing in Japan. Specifically, he expected that large general retailers in the on-line world, as on the Ginza in Tokyo, might succeed in operating general merchandise environments that comprised successful niche boutiques for branded and private label goods alike, while also selling a wide variety of less differentiated branded and non-branded goods. Observed Spiegel:

> What I see happening is like the evolution of the Japanese department store—a Mitsukoshi, for example, a Takeshimaya, or a Seibu. Seibu has Ralph Lauren. Isetan has Calvin Klein. These are both private label brands for them. Although manufacturers control the use of these brands by their Japanese licensees, these are really branded departments under one roof belonging to a general merchandiser. That is likely the direction we will all be going on the Web, as we are driven by the imperative to achieve scale in fulfillment operations and back-end customer service.

Future Developments

A major issue for iQVC's future was the challenge of providing site users with increased levels of personalization. "Right now," noted Spiegel, "we're in the first phase of the development of electronic commerce. We are functional, efficient, and reliable, and we hope to exceed our customers' expectations on those performance dimensions." In the near future, however, he expected that he would need to provide customization of the site and order fulfillment on an individual customer basis. One initial approach to such one-to-one service was an e-mail alert to customers regarding orders placed or items just in, to encourage repeat sales through iQVC and to attract iQVC customers who were not regular viewers of QVC or Q2 and therefore not subject to hosts' reminders regarding products and services available on the Web. Commented Spiegel:

> On the docket in the next iteration of iQVC, which we release in Summer 1997, is essentially the first major upgrade of the site since launch. New features such as "My iQVC" are intended to give customers a way to communicate their needs directly to us. For example, a doll collector might ask iQVC to advise them by e-mail when a major doll program was appearing on one of the networks or when a particular doll was currently in stock. This type of personalization will enable our on-line operation to become a highly efficient and productive sales vehicle. What it does is allow us to offer the same kind of personalization that best practice retailers, such as Nordstrom, furnish to their best customers. For instance, my Nordstrom salesperson will routinely notify me when a particular brand of dress shirt comes in. They are hard to get, and I asked her to call me. These kinds of robust value-adding experiences are what will build our site, and others on the Web, into a sales medium unlike any other.

Additionally, Spiegel believed there were ways to make the experience of shopping on iQVC more "personal," in ways analogous to what the networks' television hosts did on QVC and Q2. Spiegel commented:

> On air, the hosts speak extemporaneously from QVC research and from their personal experiences. They personalize the products and their features, and that enables them to communicate in a manner that feels one-to-one for the viewer. The cable-TV selling environment is information rich and highly personal. On-line retailing can differentiate itself from its "landlocked" competitors by giving pertinent, valuable information to the customer in similar ways, with a distinct point of view and editorial tone in some cases or simply in-depth information in others. If you go into a department store, the clerks may not know where a particular piece of merchandise came from or who its vendor is. Electronic retailing is all about the information moving fluidly to the customer, and the more personal we can make that information the better. That's what we're all about.

The use of live chat rooms and bulletin boards was also a capability in which iQVC had invested to build repeat visits on the site. From the beginning, iQVC had planned to establish an electronic community for its visitors, beginning with an electronic bulletin board service (BBS). The BBS allowed postings and threaded discussion among interested site visitors; indeed, it had often proved overwhelmingly popular. (By March 1997, iQVC had shut down its BBS several times due to extreme spikes in volume of posted messages which threatened to "melt down" the site's servers.) BBS Forums included "Dear iQVC Buyer" (questions about products and requests for additional products), Kitchen, Electronics, Jewelry, Home Office, Water Cooler, Collectibles, Computers & Software, Sports & Fitness, and Women's Apparel. Spiegel and his staff planned to replace the BBS with live chat in March 1997; the live chat areas would be located in the Conversation department on the iQVC site. On-line chat would become a 24-hour "gathering hall" for the site's visitors, with live on-line events, moderated by celebrity guests and QVC hosts, along with network support for activities of on-going virtual communities centered around QVC's and iQVC's products and "programming."

While the chat area was expected to bring no additional revenues to iQVC, Spiegel believed that iQVC could use chat to increase user satisfaction and retention, while providing another way to build consumer excitement about on-line and televised shopping. In fact, the area would allow users to gather product information and evaluations from one another (in the "Shop Talk" forum) as well as from iQVC specialists (in "The QVC Scoop" forum). Through these areas, iQVC shoppers could also share experiences related to specific product categories requiring user sophistication or background knowledge, such as home office equipment, collectibles, or fashion. The chat area would also serve to provide iQVC management with unique access to, and perspective on, its on-line customers, enabling the site to customize and personalize product presentation more effectively both in general and on a "segment of one" basis.

One new feature that the combination of QVC and iQVC infrastructure made possible was the introduction of QVC's "Personal Shopper," which was launched in March 1997. Personal Shopper was a customized personal service available to all QVC customers. Through the service, customers could call QVC, without first visiting the Web site or viewing the cable-TV channel, for assistance in searching for, learning about, and then purchasing products in specific categories. To support this service, special QVC customer service representatives, trained as Personal Shoppers, would provide customers with descriptions of product attributes such as manufacturer's brand, price range, features and functions, and other details within a product category. If a customer wanted a specific product and brand from QVC, Personal Shoppers could access detailed information for the product or, if it was not available, suggest potential substitutions from a menu of comparable items that would appear on merchandise database screens at each call center workstation. For example, if a QVC member was looking for a Toastmaster toaster, within a price range of $15 to $30, operators could enter these parameters and then read from a list of toasters that qualified. The Personal Shopper feature was available either by phone, with 800-number access to one of the network's four call centers, or on-line, in product category listings on the iQVC Web site.

To date, iQVC had used only the QVC and Q2 networks to promote its services and URL. By late 1997, Spiegel noted, the approach would change. iQVC, he predicted, "will start looking at other media to market and build its brand. Right now, we're still consistently increasing our traffic and getting a new user rate of 10% to 15% daily."

Conclusion

Even as iQVC developed more niche businesses, its management team sought to balance the site's promotion of its general merchandise character and the focused environments of its niche businesses. Indeed, the challenge was to define iQVC as a single brand, while providing adequate flexibility and resources for sub-brands to flourish on the site. As Spiegel noted, achieving this balance was not simple:

> iQVC is a hybrid between general merchant and mega-niche retailer. We have an opportunity on the Web to serve many different segments of consumers. If a customer wants to learn more on the history of the teddy bear, for example, she will probably step into our site's Bear Store and browse the information there. If she wants to get a Gund bear in a hurry for her niece, she may go to the department in the general store and order it straight away. It's her choice. Our challenge is to communicate the options available to our customers effectively across all the possible options for accessing our site. After that, the challenge is simply to serve them as well as QVC would serve them—and better than anyone else on the Web.

Spiegel knew that he and his management team were by no means alone in their retailing ambitions on the Web. The on-line extension of the QVC franchise faced a variety of horizontal (general merchandise) competitors, along with even more vertical (niche-oriented) players. With all of them chasing the same limited consumer demand that QVC hoped to serve through iQVC, growing the iQVC business rapidly remained the key challenge.

Exhibit 1 Percentage Purchase Rates by Physical and Electronic Retail Channels

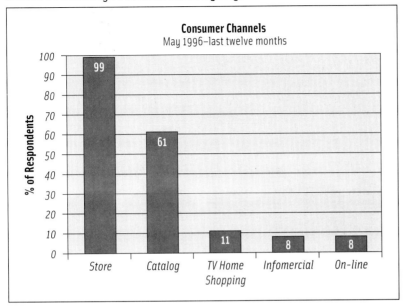

Consumer Channels
May 1996–last twelve months

Adapted from Deloitte & Touche Consulting Group Study, May 1996

Exhibit 2 Various Estimates of Present and Future Consumer Internet Commerce (in millions)

Source	1996	2000
Forrester Research	$ 530	$ 7,170
Yankee Group	730	1,000
International Data Corp.	140	32,000
Jupiter Communications	1,200	7,300
Cowles/SIMBA Information	733	4,300
Estimated U.S. Gross Domestic Product		9,000,000

Adapted from *Inter@ctive Week*, "Online Shoppers: Their Numbers Are Growing," February 10, 1997

Exhibit 3a Projected PC and Web Users Worldwide, 1995–2000 (in millions)

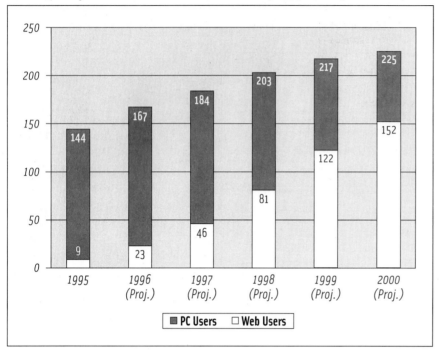

Source: The Internet Report, 1996, Morgan Stanley (NY), SIMBA Information Inc.

Exhibit 3b Projected Growth of Users for Electronic Channels Worldwide, 1995–2000 (in millions)

	1995	1996	1997	1998	1999	2000
Users of PCs	144	167	184	203	217	225
E-mail	35	60	80	130	180	200
Net/web	9	23	46	81	122	152
Online/hybrid	8	13	18	23	27	30

Source: Morgan Stanley, February 1996

Exhibit 4 Electronic Commerce Forecasts by Market Segment, 1996–2000
(in millions)

Segment	1996	1997	1998	1999	2000
Computer products	$140	$ 323	$ 701	$1,228	$2,105
Travel	126	276	572	961	1,579
Entertainment	85	194	420	733	1,250
Apparel	46	89	163	234	322
Gifts/flowers	45	103	222	386	658
Food/drink	39	78	149	227	336
Other	37	75	144	221	329
Total ($M)	$518	$1,138	$2,371	$3,990	$6,579

Source: Forrester Research, Inc., May 1996

Exhibit 5 iQVC Home Page (March 1997)

Source: *www.qvc.com*

Exhibit 6 iQVC Home Page—Initial Launch (September 1996)

Source: *www.qvc.com*

Exhibit 7 iQVC Home Page—Christmas Season (Fall 1996)

iQVC SHOP

FEATURES:

Dynamic and Durable Toys
Electronic Gifts for the Gals
M & I Seafood
Great Gifts

Search

DEPARTMENTS:

Arts & Leisure
Beauty
Books
Christmas Shoppe
Collectibles
Computers & Software
Domestics

Electronics
Furniture and Accessories
Hardware, Lawn & Garden
Home Office
Intimate Apparel and Hosiery
Jewelry
Kitchen

Personal Care
Photo and Optical
Sports & Fitness
Tabletop
Teddy Bears
Women's Accessories
Women's Apparel

WHAT'S NEW

Special Events
Press Releases
Online Kitchen
Program Guide

CORPORATE HQ

Tour
Business Overview
Press Releases
Employment
Corporate Facts

BACKSTAGE

Backstage Tour
In the Spotlight
The Host Lounge

ASSISTANCE

Feedback Desk
Return Info.
Service FAQ's
Phone Numbers

Source: *www.qvc.com*

Exhibit 8 iQVC Bubble Diagram of Possible Service Functions

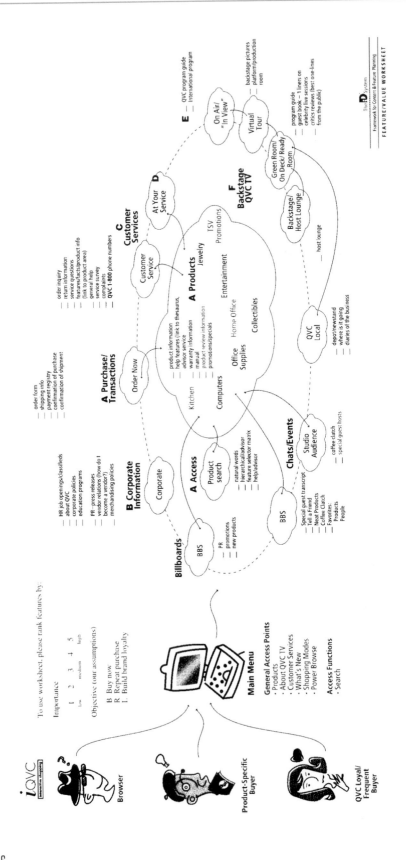

This bubble diagram is our assessment of the features and contents of QVC's service. We used it to determine iQVC's possible functions, which we then asked QVC to prioritize. We also used the diagram as a worksheet in two ways: to facilitate group discussion with QVC and the programmer, and to set internal priorities before the service's release.

Exhibit 9 Online Product Information from Research—Care & Feeding of Bears

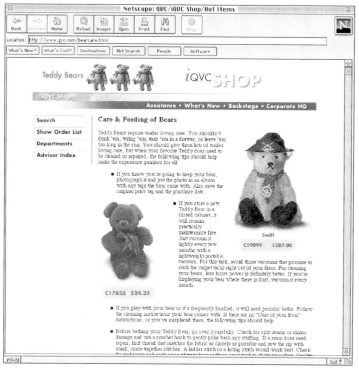

Source: *www.qvc.com*

Exhibit 10 Online Product Information from Hosts—Column by Bob Bowersox

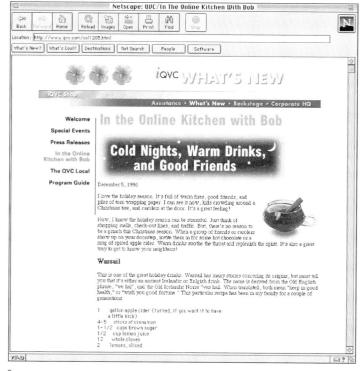

Source: *www.qvc.com*

Exhibit 11 iQVC Order Page

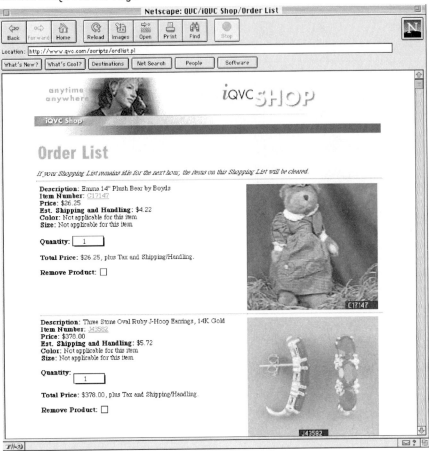

Source: *www.qvc.com*

iQVC (B)

By January 1998, the iQVC Web site was receiving 20 million hits a week and nine million page views a day. Without advertising or marketing beyond QVC's cable-TV networks, revenues on the site were reaching impressive numbers. In December 1997, iQVC surpassed $5 million in sales. PC Meter estimated that iQVC saw 2.9% of all Internet traffic worldwide, and it ranked iQVC the top General Merchant on the Web. With a pending launch of a new jewelry site, Stuart Spiegel, iQVC's general manager, felt confident of continued growth.

On September 5, 1997, iQVC expanded and redesigned the iQVC site in anticipation of increased holiday traffic. Spiegel's team created the new site in collaboration with Clement Mok, an award-winning and celebrated Web architect who had designed the original iQVC site. Mok and iQVC changed the block design of the iQVC home page to a living room scene, with site options placed in picture frames around a mantel. The iQVC redesign incorporated "frames" software technology that enabled the display of multiple windows of information on each Web page, while improving site navigation and search functions. New software on the site's back-end was integrated with additional Web servers to enable the service to handle up to 5 times average iQVC volume.

Included in the new site were a number of interactive personalization features. "My iQVC"—incorporating the features "My Style Advisor" and "My Mailing List"—provided information and product offerings that addressed individual customer preferences. "My Style Advisor" was a personal fashion profiling service, created by fashion expert Doris Pooser, that helped users develop a personal style of dress. Users filled out an on-line questionnaire with questions pertaining to skin type, eye color, and body type, and received a personal profile rec-

ommending selected clothing and cosmetics. "My Mailing List" enabled iQVC customers to receive e-mails "pushed" on a regular basis on selected QVC topics, such as information on specific programs and listings. Additionally, "Feature Finder" presented merchandise keyed to individual customers' specific tastes and needs. A "Quick Compare" feature allowed users to array several product images on one dynamically published Web page for easy comparison.

In January 1998, iQVC launched an entirely new Web site, "Gems and Jewels.com" (*www.gemsandjewels.com*). iQVC created the site in response to consumer demand, given that 30% of iQVC's new customers in 1997 made their first purchases from the QVC jewelry department.[1] While "Gems and Jewels.com" had its own URL, users could access the site from the iQVC home page through a hotlink, and conversely the "Gems and Jewels.com" home page hyperlinked back to the iQVC home page. "Gems and Jewels.com" sold QVC's lines of jewelry exclusively—including silver, gold, gems, and Diamonique—and it furnished additional editorial content and fashion slide shows, which highlighted product trends and insights on the jewelry industry. "My Viewing Pad," a virtual "velvet pad" or viewing option, could display images of up to nine selected products on one page. "My Style Advisor" provided a personalized fashion profiling service with customized jewelry advice and specific jewelry recommendations tailored to each user's tastes.

Spiegel was confident that iQVC, with a redesigned main site and the new jewelry site, would continue to prosper as one of the Internet's most successful electronic retailers, while continuing to benefit from exposure on the company's cable-TV networks at a rate of four demonstrations each day.

Research Associate Carrie L. Ardito prepared this case under the supervision of Professor Jeffrey F. Rayport as the basis for class discussion rather than to illustrate either effective or ineffective handling of any administrative situation.

[1]iQVC Press Release, January 19, 1998.

MARSHALL INDUSTRIES

*In the end, business all comes down
to supply chain vs. supply chain.*
—Robert Rodin, CEO, Marshall Industries

As 1998 drew to a close, Robert Rodin, CEO of Marshall Industries, had every reason to celebrate. Marshall, the fourth largest global distributor of industrial electronic components, had logged annual revenues of $1.4 billion, the sixth consecutive year the company had reported record net sales. But more important, Rodin believed, the company had, in the same six-year period, successfully reinvented itself as what he called a "virtual distributor." Not only was Marshall one of the first companies to conduct electronic commerce on the Internet, but it had also created one of the most robust and widely used business-to-business Web sites. The industry had taken notice. Marshall had been named best business-to-business Web site two years in a row by *Advertising Age.* In 1997 and 1998, *Business Marketing* named Marshall the top business-to-business marketing Web site.

The 52-year-old company, based in El Monte California, distributed industrial electronic components such as semiconductors, connectors, and computer peripherals. It worked with more than 150 suppliers, including Advanced Micro Devices (AMD) and Toshiba, and served more than 60,000 customers, including IBM and computer contract manufacturer Solectron. One of its largest customers was Web TV, which made set-top boxes that enabled television sets to provide Internet access. In addition to selling and delivering hundreds of thousands of electronic parts, Marshall offered customers value-added services like component testing and programming, just in time (JIT) inventory management, and kitting.

Marshall almost single-handedly had disproved the notion that the Internet would kill the distribution business. Yet despite its successes, Rodin eyed the future with trepidation. True, he was a self-described worrier, but his concerns were not just a figment of his imagination. The industry had always felt chronic margin pressures, and customers were squeezing distributors harder than ever, resulting in declining margins across the industry. Then there was the competition. Though midsize Marshall had successfully differentiated itself as the pre-eminent virtual distributor, there was no denying that size still mattered. The industry had long been dominated by two 800-pound gorillas, Arrow and Avnet, which together controlled more than 40% of the electronics distribution market. Meanwhile, many nontraditional competitors were emerging, threatening to make the struggle for market share ever more intense.

Finally, Rodin continued to worry about the Byzantine politics of the industry. For years, major U.S. semiconductor makers like Motorola had followed an unwritten policy of preventing their major distributors from carrying Japanese parts. The ban had effectively prevented Marshall, which had franchises with several leading Japanese suppliers, from carrying any major U.S. chipmaker lines. Quite unexpectedly, in 1998, the "us or them" policy was modified to "us and one of them," as Motorola and other large U.S. chipmakers each agreed to share distributor shelf-space with one Japanese semiconductor supplier. The top industry players had already begun scrambling to find a Japanese partner; after the dust settled, Rodin wondered, what would the industry look like—and how would Marshall be affected?

Amid these distractions, Rodin believed the company had to focus on the major forces that had and would continue to reshape the industry: increasing bandwidth, globalization, demographic population shifts, super-compressed product life cycles, and customized services. Marshall's ability to ride these trends and take advantage of emerging opportunities lay in what Rodin described as the company's four core "intellectual property" assets: supply chain management services, engineering design services, a deep understanding of the .com space, and expertise in what Rodin characterized as the "plumbing" of distribution, i.e., transporting goods.

Marshall Industries Background

Marshall Industries was founded by Gordon Marshall in 1946. Marshall, who had been a ham radio operator in

Research Associate Cathy Olofson prepared this case under the supervision of Professor Jeffrey F. Rayport as the basis for class discussion rather than to illustrate either effective or ineffective handling of an administrative situation.

his youth and a decorated B-24 pilot in World War II, started the company when he was unable to get a job in manufacturing after graduating from college. In its early years, the company was a general distributor, selling anything from poker chips to army surplus goods. But in the early 1950s, as television sets, portable radios, and other mass-produced consumer electronics were beginning to enjoy widespread demand, the company made the decision to specialize in electronics components. The company went public in 1959.

Marshall, who built the company on a foundation of aggressive selling and exceptional customer service, earned a reputation as an innovative leader. The company was one of the first distributors to carry semiconductors, a move that helped lift Marshall to $100 million in revenues by the late 1970s. Marshall was also the first to make Japanese parts widely available to American customers.

In 1992, Robert Rodin, who had joined the company nearly a decade before as a sales manager, succeeded Gordon Marshall as CEO. Rodin soon began to distinguish himself as an innovator and risk-taker in his own right, upending the traditional sales force compensation and structure and building a Web presence as early as 1994, well before the rest of the industry.

In 1997, Marshall acquired $360-million Sterling Electronics Corporation. Sterling's expertise lay in serving smaller customers who bought in limited lot sizes. Marshall also had stakes in electronics overseas distributors, including Sonepar Electronique International (SEI), which distributed primarily in European markets, and Serial Systems, which was based in Asia. In 1998, Marshall employed approximately 2,300 people and offered coverage and support in 36 countries from 164 locations.

A Cultural and Technological Revolution

By 1992, when Robert Rodin succeeded Gordon Marshall as CEO, Marshall's sales had topped $600 million. The company had a good track record of growth; customer base and volume were both growing steadily. Its motto, "Satisfaction Through Service," and mission of "Number One in the Marketplace" were enthusiastically embraced by employees.

Like most distributors, the company was a sales-driven organization, with a complicated compensation system on a complex system of management by objectives (MBOs). People were reviewed and rated on individual performance: division managers were evaluated on their division's profits and losses; salespeople on gross profit dollars; and product marketers on sales versus forecast and inventory budgets. Internal sales contests and supplier-sponsored promotions—sometimes 20 at a time—ratcheted up the internal rivalry, encouraging employees to aggressively outsell each other with the promise of cruises, TVs, VCRs, and other prizes.

On the surface, the system bred a spirit of high-energy fun and camaraderie among employees, particularly salespeople. Programs like "March into March," a month-long series of rallies and prizes, did increase sales and generate excitement. But Rodin worried about the downside: the system bred fierce internal competition and gamesmanship—often at the expense of customers. Marshall kept running into the same vexing, though not dire, problems. Among them:

- The company was consistently shipping 20% of total sales in the last three days of each month, resulting in a desperate scramble to get product—any product—out the door.

- Salespeople would ship ahead of schedule to make a number or win a prize in a contest, even though customers measured delivery in a window of one day early to zero days late.

- Divisions would hide inventory from one another to make sure their own customers got parts that were in short supply; managers would often ship the product out of state so they could honestly tell other divisions they were out of stock.

- Divisions also argued about cost-allocation, often delaying important capital investments and improvement. While everybody could agree that a new computer system or new training programs were critical, no one wanted these costs allocated to their P&L.

Though the compensation system had been part of the company for years, Rodin believed it bred short-term thinking: it rewarded people for closing sales, not for creating solutions. There was no brand development or long-term relationship building; instead of penetrating the marketplace, the sales staff was simply going after the easiest orders to book. What's more, Rodin believed, the current system was ill-equipped to deliver on increasing customer requests for just-in-time delivery and rising expectations of quality and service. Inspired by a Deming quality seminar he attended, Rodin decided to scrap the system—and to reinvent the organization. Rodin explained:

> Marshall had become a web of conflicts; a company of 40 different fiefdoms. Every time a supplier or customer asked us for something more, we'd try to jump, hoping that luck and skill would hold it all together and keep us from falling flat. Our only chance for the future was to present a common front, a unified identity that made doing business with Marshall different from doing business with anybody else.[1]

Rodin concluded that the only way to pull off such a major cultural transformation was to go to the heart of what motivated people: namely, money. And so Rodin and his management team targeted a major overhaul of compensation and performance-evaluation systems. To start with, they eliminated contests, and prizes, commissions, and most radically, individual performance-based bonuses. Under the new system, everyone at Marshall would be paid the same way and share in a companywide bonus pool. Eventually, Rodin eliminated commissions, as well.

Out too went performance evaluations based on P&Ls, forecasts, budgets, and monthly numbers. Employees would be evaluated, instead, on a matrix of fundamental business skills: business skills, communication skill, product knowledge, system knowledge, personal development, and knowledge of the company.

At first, Marshall employees greeted the changes with mixed feelings. On the one hand, there was no denying that some salespeople would see their pay decline, their salary no longer padded by big bonuses and commissions. On the other hand, the new system would not penalize the sales force for "missing" targets or even losing customers. After the initial shock, most employees were receptive to the new system, though eventually, a few top salespeople left the company.

Outside of Marshall, the reaction ranged from bewilderment to derision. Industry insiders and competitors regarded the changes with skepticism; one critic even labeled the system "communistic." Suppliers were uncomfortable with the no-promotions policy, since they had long regarded promotions as an important incentive for encouraging distributors to push their products over a competitors'.

But Rodin thought differently. The system overhaul was not some radical political experiment; it was a strategic decision that would give Marshall a competitive edge in an era of increasing customer demands. Rodin was simply designing the right incentives that would eliminate counterproductive competition and create a culture based on teamwork and a common mission—serving the customer. Most important, the new system would allow the company to transform itself from a sales-based to a service-based organization. Salespeople would no longer be motivated to simply make sales and ship product, in short, to chase numbers. Instead, they would be encouraged to invest as much time as necessary to develop and nurture new business relationships, to provide solutions to customers, to form long-term partnerships. In the company's new mission statement, written to reflect the emerging organization, the word "distribution" was conspicuously absent: "Marshall Industries serves our business partners by adding value with a commitment to continuous improvement, innovation, and mutual satisfaction."

Organizationally, the new system effectively broke down barriers between Marshall and the customer, dismantled the bureaucracy, and created an awareness of internal mutual independence. (See the company's new organization chart, Exhibit 1.) Looking back, Rodin argued that the new organization also gave the company a distinct advantage as the industry increasingly went virtual:

> We have a structure that can deliver on the promise of virtual supply chain management. I'm not saying a competitor can't do what we do, but they may be doing it with horsepower instead of with systems. Maybe the customer doesn't care, because they don't peel back the onion, but I believe you can't manage that kind of complexity with old systems.

In 1994, only 90 days after Rodin first saw a demo of the Web browser Mosaic, Marshall had a digital strategy. In short order, the company launched "Marshall on the Internet," which replaced the company's bulky product catalogs, and MarshallNet, an intranet system that enabled customers to check order status. Marshall installed Lotus Notes across the company and gave laptops to the entire sales force—at that time almost as radical a notion as abolishing bonuses and commissions. Marshall also began designing software to do time-phased order planning, supply management, and demand modeling for its customers.

As changing expectations of quality and service had pushed Marshall to rethink its relationship with the customer, so did the Internet push the company to reconsider how it viewed the customer. If the Internet ethos was free-flowing information, available anytime and any-

---

[1]From *Free, Perfect, and Now*, by Robert Rodin with Curtis Hartman (Simon & Schuster, 1999).

where, then the Marshall Web site would embrace, not resist, this ideal. The company made most of its Web features free and accessible to anyone, no registration required. As Rodin explained:

> The Internet hasn't changed what customers want; it's just given them more freedom to find it. Marshall's definition of a customer changed as soon as we went online. We weren't doing business with this division of IBM or that department at HP anymore. Instead, we were dealing with individuals, often engineers, sitting before a screen, exploring for ideas. . . . Now Jack in purchasing needed inventory details, Sonya at the plant needed order status, and David, a hobbyist from Nevada, was looking for tips on sale parts. Our home-page had to make them all feel welcome and give them what they came for.[2]

By 1998, Rodin described the company as a "high-speed junction box" that connected suppliers with customers. The company was not simply connecting people to the goods they wanted; it was connecting people to information. It was no longer just selling parts; it was selling solutions. Marshall's network of branch locations served more than 60,000 customers and delivered sales and technical support 24 hours a day, 7 days a week. Sales per person had more than doubled since 1991, from $360,000 to $740,000.

Industry Trends

The electronic components distribution industry developed in the 1940s and 1950s when the consumer electronics industry emerged. Early on distributors traded in capacitors, resistors, and vacuum tubes, and later connectors and semiconductors. With the rise of the computer industry, distributors also began carrying computer peripherals and components.

While many suppliers sold directly to their high-volume customers, they relied on distributors to reach myriad small and midsize customers. Distributors, for most of their history, provided a straightforward service: they bought in volume and acted as an extension of their suppliers' sales forces, which alone could not reach a broad market as cost-effectively. In return, suppliers often provided technical support and sales referrals, allowed a certain percentage of returns, and some price protection.

---

[2]Ibid.

In the 1950s and 1960s, suppliers and distributors began formalizing their relationships. Companies like Texas Instruments offered price and inventory protection as well as buying privileges to their distributors. Throughout the 1980s and 1990s, as competition increased, companies sought to expand nationally; they also began to more fully automate their operations and services.

Shelf-Sharing Restrictions

From the early days of the industry, large electronics companies had often imposed some form of shelf-sharing restrictions on distributors. The 1990s were no different. U.S. chipmakers Motorola, Intel, and National refused to make their products available through distributors that carried competing Japanese semiconductor lines. While most of the leading distributors complied with the ban and distributed no Japanese chips, Marshall went in the other direction, providing a wide array of products from Japanese, European, and domestic suppliers. Though the company was restricted from carrying the three major U.S. chipmakers, in 1995, Advanced Micro Devices unilaterally abandoned the shelf-sharing ban and franchised Marshall as a distributor.

The restrictions had other consequences. In 1997, Marshall was on the verge of entering into a joint venture with competitor Wyle Electronics. But major chipmakers objected to the deal and exerted pressure on the companies to comply with the ban: either Marshall would have to give up its Japanese lines, or Wyle its U.S. chip line. The deal was abandoned.

By early 1999, soon after relaxation of the shelf-sharing ban, major distributors had begun aligning themselves with Japanese partners. Arrow announced that it had signed a deal for exclusive distribution of Toshiba's high-power semiconductor products in North America beginning in April 1999. Avnet's Hamilton-Hallmark Electronics unit struck a deal to carry Hitachi products. Distributors Pioneer-Standard and Future were expected to follow suit.

The Digital Revolution and the Changing Face of the "Middle Man"

In the 1980s and 1990s, several accelerating forces converged to reshape the electronics and distribution industry. Product design and manufacturing grew in complexity; products went from containing hundreds to thousands of parts. Parts proliferation increased, too, as more low-cost competitors entered the market, and the result was an often bewildering selection of components with the same functionality. At the same time, product cycles were shortening as companies scrambled to get products to market faster. As a result, companies began outsourcing parts of their value chain in an effort to capture efficiencies, save costs, and stay focused on core competencies.

Managing the supply chain was never so crucial—or difficult. As middlemen, distributors were perfectly positioned to help their customers coordinate supply chain activities and reduce manufacturing costs. They had expertise in inventory management; they had vast product knowledge and availability; they had deep relationships up and down the supply channels. And so by the mid-1990s, most distributors had begun offering an array of services: inventory control, assembly services such as kitting, logistics planning, design solutions, and materials management. Value-added services as a percent of sales for the industry were about 25% in 1994, up from 15% in 1989. The figure was expected to reach 40% in 1999.[3]

Many observers predicted that the Internet would render obsolete distributors and other so-called middlemen. The Web would enable suppliers of services and products to skip the intermediaries—from retail stores to distributors—and go directly to the customer. In reality, there had been few casualties. Electronics distributors had so far survived the disintermediation threat by stepping up their offering of value-added services and, most important, leveraging the Internet to offer new, as well as enhance existing, value-added services. Distributors' Internet-based services typically fell into one of four categories: (1) logistics, including auto-replenishment capabilities through electronic data interchange (EDI) systems; (2) information, including downloadable supplier data sheets and other design support; (3) service, including easy access to customer support and order tracking; and (4) e-commerce, including parts ordering and payment.

Suppliers and Customers

Distributors supplied services and components to a variety of markets, including auto manufacturers, consumer product companies, medical device makers, and net-working and telecommunications companies. Estimates suggested that Fortune 1000 customers accounted for about $8 billion, or about 30% to 35%, of distribution sales. Midsize companies, with sales around a few hundred million dollars, as well as smaller companies, with sales under $100 million, each accounted for $6 to $8 billion of distribution sales.[4]

Experiencing cost and cycle-time pressures, large OEMs (such as Hewlett Packard, IBM, Cisco, and Ericsson) were increasingly looking to outside sources to perform non-core activities as a way to better utilize their own asset bases. Just as OEMs handed off manufacturing to contract manufacturers, they had also begun to rely on distributors to manage supply chain logistics and procurement.

Suppliers, from semiconductor makers like Intel and Motorola to industrial manufacturers like 3M, were also focusing on core competencies. Most typically didn't have the resources to offer design expertise and support, except for their major customers to whom they sold direct. But because products and components were more complex than ever, being able to provide design expertise and support was essential to making a sale. Complicated products also raised legacy issues. Once designers and engineers learned about and felt comfortable with a part, they were likely to want to use it for as long as possible—reducing the possibility of replacement sales. Thus it was particularly important for suppliers to get their parts *designed* into original products. (Exhibit 2 shows at what stage in the design process engineers typically used distributor Web sites and which services they favored.)

Industry Consolidation and Growth

Over the previous two decades, the industry had been consolidating to an unprecedented extent. The top 25 distributors had increased their market share to more than 85% in 1998.[5] Part of this was a response to globalization. As supply chains spread across the globe, distributors sought to extend their reach. Most companies made investments in or acquired at least one European and Asian distribution partner. Consolidation was also a response to new competitive anxieties, as distributors sought to round out their line cards and service offerings by acquiring specialty distribution partners. Acquisitions had also helped distributors reduce operating costs and spread SG&A costs over a larger revenue base.

Distributors were also profoundly affected by the cyclical nature of the electronics industry. In 1998, the Asian economic crisis and an oversupply of semicon-

---

[3]Merrill Lynch report, "Electronics Distribution," February 1999.
[4]Merrill Lynch report.
[5]Ibid.

ductors put pressure on low average selling prices and already declining gross profit margins. For example, average gross margins of the top five distributors declined from 24% in 1990 to 15% in 1998.[6] (See Exhibit 3 for margins of leading distributors, as well as other industry benchmarks.) Despite the squeeze on profits, analysts noted that component suppliers increasingly turned more business over to distributors, while OEM customers relied on distributors for products and other value-added work. Analysts expected that these factors would help average dollar sales growth increase slightly for 1998, to just under 1% industrywide. In 1985, approximately 25% of electronic components sold in North America were sold through distributors. In 1995, about 31% were sold through distributors.

Marshall Industries Service and Operations

Marshall differentiated itself through exceptional customer service, an innovative and aggressive approach to e-commerce, and a semiconductor line card that offered more Japanese semiconductor products than any other North American distributor. In fiscal 1998, semiconductors accounted for 64% of Marshall's sales. (See Exhibit 4 for Marshall's income statement.) Marshall was the only distributor that provided manned 24 by 7 customer support, via call centers as well as online chat sessions.

Sales and Marketing

> "No one ever asks for a salesperson: they ask for someone to help them."
> —Rob Rodin

Rodin believed that Marshall's unorthodox compensation structure and heavy investments in information technology systems allowed the company to move from a sales focus to a service focus. Information technologies simplified and speeded routine activities such as order tracking and billing, freeing up salespeople to spend more time with customers, learning about technologies, and crafting custom solutions. IT advancements also made possible new value-added services, such as auto replenishment.

Where once the sales mandate was to close sales, the new sales mandate was more complicated: provide cus-

tomized solutions. Salespeople, no longer driven by bonus competition or commission to pursue only sure-thing deals (known as SWAT, or "sell what's available today"), had the freedom to commit themselves to long-term customer relationship management. Rodin recalled:

> There was a firm in Palo Alto, called Artemus Research. It was a 30-person operation, doing no business when we first visited the company. We put a salesperson on the account for two years, during which time Artemus didn't book a single order. Then the company became Web TV, was bought by Microsoft, and now it's our biggest customer. We couldn't have been that patient if we hadn't eliminated commissions.

The company formalized this service philosophy through its Marshall Process, a training program designed to help salespeople develop stronger business relationships with customers. (See Exhibit 5.) The Process guides employees toward an understanding of each customer's needs, teaching the key questions to ask: Who are the target customers? Do they have supply-chain problems? How does the customer define quality? The goal was to enable each salesperson to create custom solutions that address long-term and short-term needs, in short, to form partnerships with customers. The program emphasized equally each step of the business process—market research, marketing, prospecting, qualifying, presenting, commitment (which replaced "closing"), and following up—and captured strategic customer data in a database. Salespeople were awarded and promoted according to how well they executed the Process.

Internet and intranet technologies, in combination with database management systems, also enabled companywide access to key corporate knowledge management tools: a Marshall dictionary and performance matrix. Both tools were repositories for accumulated company knowledge and best practices, and the information was available to all employees. The dictionary provided definitions, how-to information, and guidance for a variety of business tasks and functions; for example, it showed how to use sales reports to analyze sales to budget. The matrix provided detailed information on customers, suppliers, products, and market activity. Users wanting to learn more about a customer's chip market, for example, could find information about competition, suppliers, trends, demand projections, even daily product activity, down to the last fax sent.

---

[6]Ibid.

About 46% of Marshall's work force was in sales. Despite its unusual compensation structure, Marshall's sales structure did not break the mold: VP, branch manager, sales managers, area managers, salespeople. The sales force included field applications engineers, who had design and engineering expertise and were crucial to technical sales to customers.

Value-Added Services

Marshall offered a range of supply-chain management services in manufacturing, materials and logistics management, and design and engineering. The company estimated that 35% of its revenues were derived from its value-added services. Marshall performed the majority of these services in-house.

Manufacturing programs helped customers reduce inventory and accelerate manufacturing cycles. Kitting services aggregated multiple sub-components, destined for the same final product, into a pre-sorted parts kit. Marshall's turnkey programs offered comprehensive supply chain management, from part procurement, assembly, and project management, to relationship management.

Component services comprised semiconductor device programming, systems integration, and PC system solutions, and cable and connector assembly. Marshall's three in-house semiconductor facilities programmed and tested memory and logic chips, as well as performed bundling activities such as "tape and reel." In 1998, Marshall signed an exclusive agreement with Comit Systems, an engineering firm, which strengthened Marshall's custom design capabilities.

Logistics and materials management services helped companies manage their just-in-time manufacturing activities. Marshall offered handling, procurement, and pipelining services, as well as component stores based on forecasts. Through an electronic data interchange (EDI) system, Marshall offered auto-replenishment systems, which allowed customers to send its stock status directly to Marshall. The system would order automatically as supplies neared depletion. The EDI connected customers' computers directly to Marshall's and allowed for seamless data transmission. Marshall also developed proprietary software packages that generated forecasts and helped minimize part shortages and oversupplies.

Finally, Marshall offered design and engineering services, many of them through the Web. While most value-added services targeted customers like OEMs and contract manufacturers, services that supported suppliers' products—including assembly, design expertise, programming, and testing—also generated demand for them.

Virtual Services

For two years, Marshall had been named by *Business Marketing* as the top Web site; no other leading dis-tributors made the list of 200 sites. (See Exhibit 6 for Marshall's home page.) Its Web site boasted not only the most comprehensive feature set of any distributor's site but also a transparent, uncluttered, and easy-to-use interface. Its open architecture gave it unsurpassed connectivity.

Marshall was exceptional in its ability to integrate its value-added supply chain services with its information systems. Its intranets/extranets connected suppliers, customers, and its own distribution operation, allowing it to offer a wide range of electronic customer services. These included parts searching, ordering, tracking; round-the-clock customer support; auto-replenishment; and training and education. The system processed over 750,000 daily transactions. Descriptions of Marshall's key Internet-based services follow:

Macro.Link. An ambitious virtual supply chain management tool, Macro allowed supply chain partners to streamline communication, automate decision-making, and remove administrative inefficiencies from the system. In some cases, decisions that used to take weeks could be made and executed in a day. Using Internet technology and data-warehousing techniques, Macro connected computers up and down the supply chain—from supplier to manufacturer to value-added reseller. The system was programmed according to rules established by a steering committee of the supply chain partners; the rules set certain specifications any design change had to meet, for example, and also dictated the kind of orders that could be processed automatically.

A product engineer considering replacing one part with another, for example, could initiate an engineering change order (ECO) and get immediate information from partners on the replacement part availability, functionality, revised sales, and delivery forecasts, and estimated costs. If all the information met design specifications, the order would be executed automatically. (See Exhibits 7 and 8 for diagrams of supply chain management via Macro.Link.)

Order Center. With a purchase order account or credit card, customers could order and track parts at any time of the day. Marshall's "order agent" tool resided on suppliers' Web sites and allowed them to hand off customers with smaller orders directly to Marshall. The agent transparently took users to the Marshall site where Marshall would fulfill the order through its own system. In 1998, about 10 suppliers used the order agent. A single click direct-linked users to UPS's package-tracking feature.

Electronic Design Center.
The EDC featured parts-number and manufacturer searching, as well as parametric searching, which allowed users to plug in parameters like voltage and dimensions. (Parts searching was also available from Marshall's home page.) Users could then view side-by-side comparisons of similar parts from different manufacturers. (See Exhibit 9.) Through XML connections with suppliers, users could review supplier product information, such as data sheets, without appearing to leave the Marshall site. (See Exhibit 10 for a sample data sheet.) The EDC also contained links to technical resources as well as industry news.

Marshall Connection.
This login/ID extranet maintained customer accounts and profiles. Customers could access as backlog and order status, inventory status, and contract pricing information. The Connection also featured an automated quote process, as well as the ability to cross-reference and track multiple part numbers.

@Once.
A Marshall subsidiary, this sales lead-management and follow-up service supported demand-creation efforts for suppliers. It also provided marketing services.

Help@Once.
This chat service offered online support, 24 hours a day. Visitors could log on and chat in real time with a Marshall engineer, who provided assistance with product availability, pricing, order status, and using the Marshall Web site.

Education News & Entertainment Network.
ENEN, a subsidiary of Marshall, was a leading provider of Internet broadcasting services for the electronics industry. ENEN's Web site incorporated real-time video, audio, and interactive chat to deliver live, interactive training sessions, product announcements, and other events via the Internet. ENEN offered three core services. Net-Seminars were live broadcasts over the Internet that featured audio and chat interactivity among participants. NetPresentations were streamlined versions of NetSeminar that delivered on-demand presentations, available to audience members any time of the day. NetInterviews used audio feeds and digital photography to broadcast live reports from trade shows or other events.

ENEN also offered related event management and marketing services, including audience development, real-time transcription, and multilingual capabilities, fulfillment and real-time audience reporting. Marshall marketed the service to its own suppliers, as well as competitors' suppliers, who paid a fee to use the technology and to provide technical support and training for their products. The service was free to customers.

Quotecart.
This virtual service streamlined quoting. Customers uploaded or pasted in a bill of materials or parts list in spreadsheet form, reviewed quotes, and could then directly order parts.

Suppliers and Customers

Marshall served approximately 60,000 customers, the majority of which were small and midsize computer companies, capital and office equipment companies, and systems integrators. One of the company's largest customers was Web TV; no single customer exceeded 4% of total sales. Marshall also worked with contract manufacturers, which built and shipped computers and other electronic products for OEMs. Rodin believed that as contract manufacturers took on more manufacturing and purchasing functions for their customers, and as their role in the supply chain became more complex, they would comprise a growing market for Marshall's customized forecasting and materials management software solutions.

The company's line card represented about 200,000 products, and its average product selling price was $5.00 The distribution of electronic components accounted for approximately 95% of total fiscal 1998 sales.

Marshall's key suppliers included AMD, Toshiba, AMP, and Lucent. Its ten largest suppliers accounted for approximately 51% of the company's total sales in fiscal 1998. (See Exhibit 11 for a list of Marshall suppliers.) The standard supplier distribution agreement was a non-exclusive agreement with a 30-day cancellation clause. As a result, Marshall competed with other distributors that sold the same or similar products, as well as with its suppliers, which tended to sell directly to their larger customers.

Physical Operations

Marshall had 77 sales and distribution facilities and six corporate support and distribution centers. Its main distribution center was 258,000 square feet, and it owned and leased several hundred thousand more square feet for warehousing.

Competition

The electronics distribution industry comprised hundreds of competitors, but a handful dominated the field. (See Exhibit 12 for the top ten distributors by revenue.) In 1997, total industry sales reached nearly $27 billion.

By the late 1990s, electronics distribution companies had transformed themselves into service organizations that provided a package of services to help customers reduce the time it took to bring a product to market. As the industry consolidated and the distributor profile became more complex, a once-undifferentiated industry had begun to look slightly more heterogeneous. Competitors sought to differentiate themselves according to a number of factors: size and reach of its distribution coverage, selection of components, combination of services, ease and quality of customer service, and their Internet and information technology offerings.

All of the large distributors, including Arrow, Pioneer-Standard, Marshall, and Avnet, had extensive Web sites. Though few offered parts ordering and other e-commerce options, most featured a standard set of features: company information, line card details, technical information, and parts availability and pricing information.

Arrow Electronics

Arrow was the world's largest distributor of electronic components and computer products, with 1997 sales of $7.8 billion and average inventory of over $1 billion. The company, based in Melville, New York, worked with more than 600 suppliers and 160,000 original equipment manufacturers and commercial customers. It had a massive global presence, with distribution centers in 32 countries. Throughout the late 1990s, Arrow had been on a buying spree, which allowed it to supplant rival Avnet as the leading global distributor. In 1998, Arrow acquired two competitors, Bell Industries, one of the ten largest distributors in North America, and Richey Electronics, a specialty distributor of interconnect devices.

Arrow was the largest distributor for most of the world's semiconductor suppliers. Semiconductors accounted for more than 60% of sales in 1998, while computer products accounted for an additional 25% of sales. Intel topped the supplier list, accounting for 16% of products purchased.

Arrow was increasingly offering sales, service, and technical support, as well as value-added services such as materials management, which helped customers reduce their time to market and cost of ownership; automated inventory management; and business-needs analysis. To improve service, the company in 1997 realigned its North American components operations by customer segment. The seven new business groups included Arrow's Supplier Services Group and the Semiconductor Group.

The company had not completely found its footing on the Internet. Customers could search for part availability, though the search could only be done by part number and/or manufacturer. Other Internet features included package tracking and industry news alerts. While the Gates/Arrow division, which distributed computer systems and software to value-added resellers, featured a more fully featured parts search and order tracking system, as of early 1999 it was not available from Arrow's main Web site.

Avnet

The number two distributor, founded in the 1950s, had 1998 sales of $5.9 billion, up from just over $2 billion in 1993. The Phoenix-based company distributed parts from 250 manufacturers to more than 100,000 customers, including Eastman Kodak, AT&T, and Hewlett-Packard. About half of the company's 1997 sales came from its Hamilton Hallmark unit, which distributed semiconductors for top chip makers such as AMD, Intel, and Motorola. In 1998, 54% of its sales came from semiconductors, 27% from computer products, and 19% from connectors and other items.

In the 1990s, Avnet had pursued acquisitions aggressively. The company outbid Wyle Laboratories for Hall-Mark Electronics in 1993, and it acquired Penstock, the top U.S. distributor of microwave radio-frequency products, the next year. Between 1992 and 1998, the company purchased a total of 20 firms, most of them based outside the United States.

The company's feature-rich Web site was the closest rival to Marshall's. It offered parts searches (again by number and/or manufacturer only), order tracking, downloadable catalogs and data sheets, and technical resources. In 1998, both Avnet and Marshall were among the top ten in *Information Week*'s ranking of the most innovative users of information technology. As of early 1998, however, customers could not order parts from the site.

Other Traditional Distributors

Though other competitors, including Future and Pioneer-Standard, lacked the depth and breadth of Avent and Arrow, they too offered a range of value-added services, many increasingly through the Internet. Pioneer-Standard's Web site provided technical data, product availability, and pricing information; the site also allowed buyers to purchase parts with a credit card or by setting up a line of credit. For large, established customers, Pioneer Standard set contract pricing on the system.

Pure Internet Distributors

Newly formed "vortex site" Internet companies—including Digital.market, Netbuy, and Fast Parts—aggregated inventory from multiple electronics distributors and made it available through the Web. At Netbuy, for example, online buyers could search for and order components, which Netbuy typically would then acquire from one of its 29 distributor partners, who actually held the inventory. (When Netbuy sold a part, it did not disclose the name of the distributor.) By early 1999, Netbuy had more than $1.4 billion in virtual inventory. QuestLink, the second leading e-distributor, had more than $1 billion in inventory available online and partnerships with leading distributors and semi-conductor vendors. These sites targeted professional electronics buyers.

Emerging Competitors

Contract manufacturers and freight forwarders were slowly grabbing pieces of the supply chain management territory. Freight forwarders like FedEx and UPS, with extensive transportation fleets and logistics expertise, were poised to compete with distributors in services like logistics management and aggregation of bills and materials. Contract manufacturers had massive manufacturing infrastructures and could supply low-cost component purchasing and other manufacturing services.

Conclusion

Marshall had prospered in the first stage of industry dis-intermediation and emerged at the beginning of 1999 with a reputation for exceptional customer service and technology innovation. Looking ahead to 2000 and beyond, Rob Rodin suspected the industry would continue to feel the same constraints it had in the last several years: margin pressures, ever-more demanding customers who wanted everything "free, perfect, and now," and fickle supplier policies. Rodin believed that Marshall would be successful only to the degree that it addressed these "time bombs"—and that the best strategy for doing this lay in what he described as "dynamic alignment": the process of bringing the company's products, services, strategies, and partnerships in line with the market's constantly changing needs and capabilities. He summarized: "The Marshall mandate is to find new ways to connect products to the marketplace, people to people, people to technology, products to market, answers to questions, solutions to problems, and order to chaos."

Exhibit 1 Marshall Organization

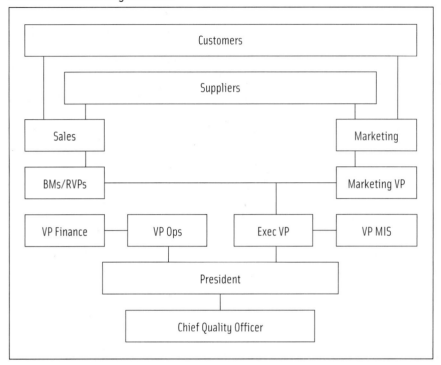

Exhibit 2 Engineers' Uses of the Internet During the Design Process

	North America	Europe	Asia
Evaluating products	70%	69%	71%
Developing concept	44	47	52
Seeking design tips	43	47	43
Establishing specs	50	45	30
Selecting a supplier	36	42	45
Locating a brand	44	24	16
Purchasing a product	23	21	48
Other	3	4	2

Most Common Web Site Services Used by Engineers

	North America	Europe	Asia
Technical information on parts	66%	76%	73%
Pricing information	68	60	45
Technical service information	53	62	65
Accessing the vendor data book/materials	53	53	58
Company information	38	33	51
Contact names, e-mails, and/or phone numbers	37	40	46
Transactions (e.g., ordering parts, paying for parts)	28	12	31
Other	7	1	3

Source: Adaptation of data from *Cahners 1998 Electronics Industry Yearbook*

Exhibit 3 Key Distributor (Pioneer-Standard, Avnet, Arrow, Marshall Industries) Benchmarks

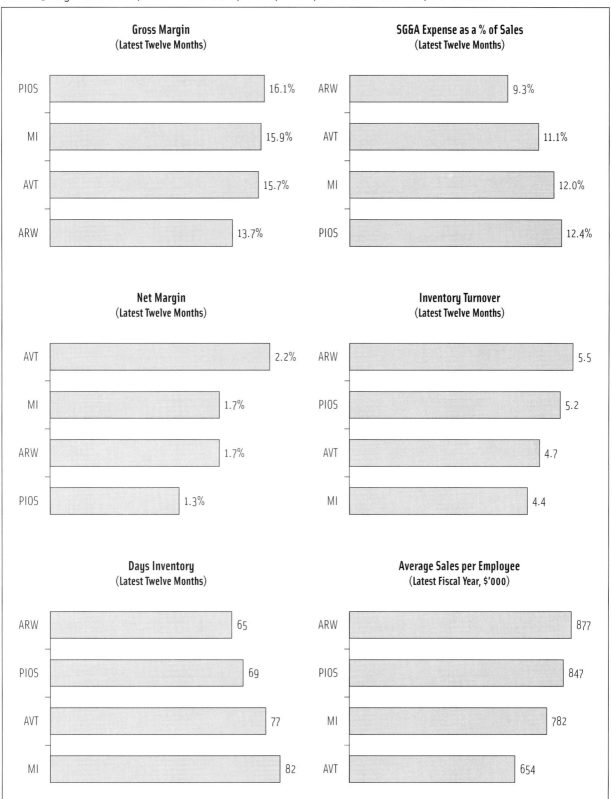

Source: Adaptation of data from Merrill Lynch "Electronic Distribution Report," February 1999

Exhibit 4 Marshall Income Statement and Consolidated Operations

Consolidated Statement of Income			
	Years Ended May 31		
	1996	1997	1998
		(in thousands except for per share data)	
Net sales	$1,164,812	$1,184,604	$1,461,363
Cost of sales	955,331	988,371	1,232,026
Gross profit	209,481	196,233	229,337
Selling, general and administrative expenses	123,188	128,927	163,556
Income from operations	86,293	67,306	65,781
Interest expense (income) and other–net	989	(1,197)	7,480
Income before income taxes and extraordinary gain	85,304	68,503	58,301
Provision for income taxes	35,250	28,850	24,958
Income before extraordinary gain	50,054	39,653	33,343
Extraordinary gain from termination of joint venture (Net of income taxes of $10,535)	–	–	14,615
Net income	$ 50,054	$ 39,653	$ 47,958
Earnings per share (basic):			
Income per share before extraordinary gain	$ 2.90	$ 2.35	$ 2.01
Extraordinary gain per share	–	–	0.88
Net income per share	$ 2.90	$ 2.35	$ 2.89

Consolidated Results of Operations			
	Years Ended May 31		
	1996	1997	1998
Net sales	100.0%	100.0%	100.0%
Cost of sales	82.0	83.4	84.3
Gross profit	18.0	16.6	15.7
Selling, general and administrative expenses	10.6	10.9	11.2
Income from operations	7.4	5.7	4.5
Interest expense (income) and other–net	.1	(.1)	.5
Income before provision for income taxes and extraordinary gain	7.3	5.8	4.0
Provision for income taxes	3.0	2.4	1.7
Income before extraordinary gain	4.3	3.4	2.3
Extraordinary gain (net of income taxes)	–	–	1.0
Net income	4.3%	3.4%	3.3%

Exhibit 5 Marshall Process

Exhibit 6 Marshall Industries Home Page

Source: *www.marshall.com*

Exhibit 7 Supply Chain

Exhibit 8 Macro.link Flow Chart

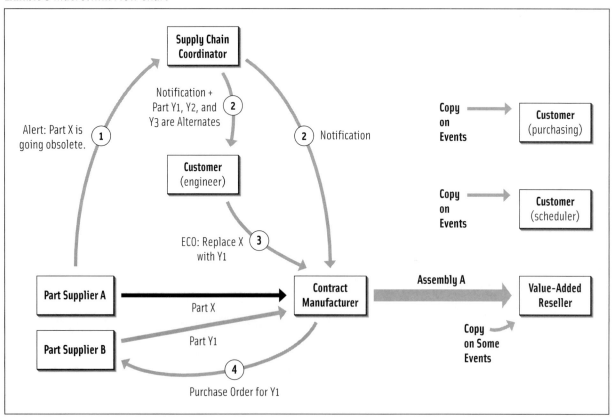

Exhibit 9 Marshall Industries Product Comparison Feature

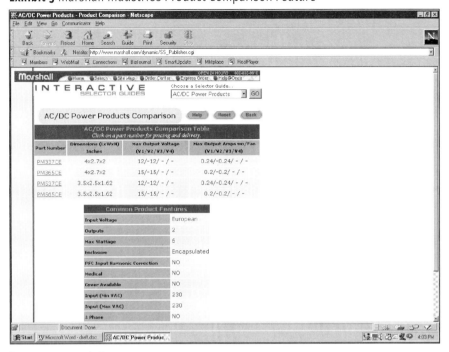

Source: *www.marshall.com*

Exhibit 10 Sample Data Sheet from Marshall Industries Site

Accu-P®

0402 Typical Electrical Tables

/A\VX

Capacitance & tolerance* @ 1 MHz (pF)	Self resonance frequency (GHz) typical	3/4 lambda				5/4 lambda				7/4 lambda				9/4 lambda				11/4 lambda			
		ref freq (MHz)	typ. C(eff) (pF)	typ. Q	typ. ESR (ohm)	ref freq (MHz)	typ. C(eff) (pF)	typ. Q	typ. ESR (ohm)	ref freq (MHz)	typ. C(eff) (pF)	typ. Q	typ. ESR (ohm)	ref freq (MHz)	typ. C(eff) (pF)	typ. Q	typ. ESR (ohm)	ref freq (MHz)	typ. C(eff) (pF)	typ. Q	typ. ESR (ohm)
1.00±0.05	7.7	247	1.16	1635	0.34	494	1.15	1283	0.22	742	1.13	870	0.23	991	1.12	620	0.25	1240	1.14	474	0.26
1.20±0.05	7.2	245	1.34	1564	0.31	491	1.33	1153	0.21	738	1.31	727	0.23	986	1.30	503	0.25	1234	1.33	372	0.25
1.50±0.05	6.5	242	1.63	1454	0.28	486	1.63	1002	0.20	731	1.61	638	0.21	978	1.60	438	0.23	1226	1.65	316	0.25
1.80±0.05	6	240	1.93	1343	0.26	481	1.93	897	0.19	726	1.91	583	0.20	972	1.91	401	0.21	1219	1.97	294	0.22
2.20±0.05	5.1	237	2.28	1302	0.22	476	2.27	893	0.16	718	2.26	581	0.17	964	2.27	396	0.19	1212	2.35	289	0.19
2.70±0.05	4.5	233	2.84	1290	0.15	469	2.83	778	0.15	711	2.82	464	0.16	956	2.86	313	0.19	1203	3.00	224	0.19
3.90±0.05	3.9	224	4.01	1210	0.13	457	4.01	649	0.13	697	4.02	384	0.15	943	4.11	251	0.16	1191	4.37	172	0.18
4.70±0.05	3.5	220	4.75	1170	0.11	450	4.74	632	0.11	690	4.74	378	0.12	937	4.86	244	0.14	1186	5.18	159	0.16
5.60±0.05	3.3	214	5.74	1127	0.11	443	5.75	591	0.11	684	5.81	340	0.12	932	6.01	205	0.14	1182	6.62	127	0.15
6.8±0.1	2.8	208	6.92	1105	0.09	436	6.94	578	0.09	678	7.04	334	0.10	926	7.39	198	0.11	1177	8.22	119	0.13
8.2±0.1	2.6	202	8.35	1042	0.09	430	8.36	542	0.08	673	8.48	306	0.09	922	8.93	186	0.10	1174	10.04	109	0.12
10.0±1%	2.4	196	10.14	936	0.08	424	10.24	385	0.08	668	10.55	202	0.09	919	11.49	118	0.10	1171	13.75	70	0.12
12.0±1%	2.2	189	12.16	889	0.08	418	12.30	348	0.08	664	12.77	173	0.08	915	14.16	95	0.09	1168	17.63	52	0.11

Capacitance & tolerance* @ 1 MHz (pF)	Self resonance frequency (GHz) typical	13/4 lambda				15/4 lambda				17/4 lambda				19/4 lambda				21/4 lambda			
		ref freq (MHz)	typ. C(eff) (pF)	typ. Q	typ. ESR (ohm)	ref freq (MHz)	typ. C(eff) (pF)	typ. Q	typ. ESR (ohm)	ref freq (MHz)	typ. C(eff) (pF)	typ. Q	typ. ESR (ohm)	ref freq (MHz)	typ. C(eff) (pF)	typ. Q	typ. ESR (ohm)	ref freq (MHz)	typ. C(eff) (pF)	typ. Q	typ. ESR (ohm)
1.00±0.05	7.7	1489	1.18	380	0.26	1739	1.25	314	0.26	1988	1.32	265	0.26	2240	1.38	229	0.27	2493	1.41	200	0.28
1.20±0.05	7.2	1483	1.37	307	0.25	1732	1.45	251	0.25	1982	1.54	208	0.25	2234	1.59	173	0.26	2488	1.62	149	0.27
1.50±0.05	6.5	1474	1.72	252	0.25	1724	1.82	203	0.25	1974	1.94	169	0.25	2227	2.01	143	0.25	2481	2.03	135	0.26
1.80±0.05	6	1468	2.06	239	0.22	1717	2.19	197	0.21	1968	2.33	165	0.21	2222	2.41	140	0.21	2476	2.42	123	0.21
2.20±0.05	5.1	1461	2.47	228	0.21	1711	2.65	183	0.19	1964	2.83	149	0.19	2217	2.91	126	0.19	2473	2.91	108	0.20
2.70±0.05	4.5	1453	3.18	164	0.20	1703	3.47	122	0.19	1956	3.75	94	0.19	2211	3.89	78	0.19	2466	3.89	66	0.20
3.90±0.05	3.9	1442	4.72	121	0.19	1695	5.26	87	0.18	1948	5.77	76	0.18	2204	5.94	62	0.18	2461	5.82	59	0.19
4.70±0.05	3.5	1437	5.60	118	0.17	1690	6.23	82	0.17	1944	6.72	70	0.17	2200	6.71	59	0.18	2457	6.35	54	0.19
5.60±0.05	3.3	1434	7.43	92	0.16	1687	8.75	65	0.16	1942	10.03	48	0.18	2199	10.42	39	0.18	2456	10.07	48	0.20
6.8±0.1	2.8	1430	9.41	88	0.13	1684	11.43	61	0.13	1940	13.36	45	0.14	2196	13.72	37	0.14	2454	12.85	36	0.14
8.2±0.1	2.6	1428	11.64	79	0.12	1682	14.43	52	0.13	1938	16.85	38	0.13	2195	16.65	32	0.14	2453	15.32	31	0.14
10.0±1%	2.4	1425	17.60	41	0.11	1680	26.51	21	0.12	1936	40.16	11	0.11	2194	45.46	8	0.13	2452	39.54	8	0.13
12.0±1%	2.2	1423	24.14	29	0.11	1678	43.51	13	0.12	1934	92.97	5	0.11	2192	123.19	3	0.13	2450	82.44	4	0.13

* Other tolerances are available, contact AVX

Exhibit 11 Marshall's Major Suppliers

Selected Products and Suppliers: Semiconductor Products
AMD
Atmel
Cypress Semiconductor
Fujitsu
Hitachi
Lattice Semiconductor
Linear Technology
Mitel Semiconductors
NEC
Philips
Siemens
Sony
Texas Instruments
Toshiba America
Computer Systems and Peripherals
Fujitsu
IBM
NEC
Quantum
Sony
Toshiba America
Passive Components, Connectors, and Interconnect Products
AMP
AVX
Molex
T&B/Ansley
Industrial Production Supplies
Cooper Industries
Fluke
Litton Industries
Loctite
3M
Tektronix

Exhibit 12 Top 10 Distributors by North American Revenues, 1998 (US $)

Rank	Company (Headquarters)	1998 North American Revenue ($ millions)	1998 Total Revenue ($ millions)
1	Arrow Electronics Inc. (Melville, NY)	$5,341	$8,345
2	Avnet EMG (Great Neck, NY)	4,871	6,165
3	Veba Electronics (San Jose, CA)	2,150	4,300
4	Pioneer-Standard Electronics, Inc. (Cleveland, OH)	2,133	2,133
5	Future Electronics (Pointe Claire, Quebec, Canada)	1,870	2,200
6	Marshall Industries (El Monte, CA)	1,700	1,700
7	Premier Farnell PLC (West Yorkshire, England)	780	1,200
8	Bell Microproducts (San Jose, CA)	661	661
9	Kent Electronics (Sugar Lane, TX)	622	622
10	Savoir Technology Group (Campbell, CA)	593	593

Source: Adaptation of data from *Electronic Business* and *Electronic News*

Valuation

VALUATION

This chapter is about valuing companies that are new and have high growth but no earnings. In the late 1990s and now in the early years of the new millennium, we are confronted with company valuations with wide fluctuations—from unreasonably high in spring 2000 to unreasonably low in winter 2001—that appear to be unreasonably high multiples for companies that did not exist even a few years ago. The purpose of this chapter is to demonstrate that many, but of course not all, of the multiples that are being paid in the market do have a rational basis if one applies sound analysis. However, it is important to choose the right analysis for the situation at hand.

The earliest phase in the life cycle of most companies is "embryonic." These companies have no track record, have a small but rapidly growing sales base, and expect no profit for several years. Yet embryonic companies sometimes sell for over a hundred times their sales revenue. If a company survives its start-up phase without being acquired, or more likely going bankrupt, it makes the transition to an "emerging growth" company that is really a small portfolio of projects with high optionality (growth options that require the use of real option analysis to understand their multiples). Finally, there is the "robust growth" company, like AOL or Amazon.com, which is large but still growing rapidly and which is selling for 15 to 25 times sales.

The valuation of Internet companies at any of these three phases can be achieved by applying the appropriate methodology. The standard discounted cash flow (DCF) valuation works well for large companies with robust growth. Using analyst forecasts, coupled with some careful thought about a logical industry structure a decade from now, it is possible to build a company's valuations that are easily within the trading ranges. The estimated values are sensitive to relatively small changes in the assumptions.

Emerging growth companies are companies at an inflection point. Either they will break into robust growth, resulting in the valuable option to expand, or they will fail and should be abandoned. The real option approach (ROA) applies best to those situations where the company value depends on the success or failure of a few projects that have wide variability in their possible outcomes. Finally, valuations of embryonic companies that may justify high multiples should be based on how they might affect the discounted cash flows of the large, high-growth companies that would acquire them.

In all three cases, the valuation can be tied to logical roots and therefore be understood. Acquirers can estimate a range of prices that is justified and can keep from overpaying. Of course, not all prices that are paid are necessarily justifiable: In many situations, emotion and the magic of "smoke and mirrors" win the day. Remember that the guiding principle of valuation is the value of an asset in its best use. The value of a target company should be based not on its stand-alone value but rather on its value impact on the companies that acquired them. The appropriate valuation is the discounted value of the change in cash flows of the acquiring companies. For the target company to get the maximum price, there should be several potential buyers; otherwise the bargaining power of the much larger acquirer may result in a lower transaction price.

SYNOPSES OF CHAPTER CASE

TOM.COM

Case Overview

Early in 2000, the Internet investment craze was starting to catch on in Hong Kong. Tom.com Limited, a Hong Kong–based Internet start-up company, was planning an initial public offering on the Hong Kong Stock Exchange. Tom.com (Tom) was striving to be a major multilingual portal with a focus on Chinese-related content. Three core markets were the non–Chinese-speaking audience interested in the "China Experience"; the PRC market, which was interested in the "Lifestyle for Chinese" content; and overseas Chinese-speaking audiences. The potential Chinese market was huge, but a number of competitors had already jumped into the market. One of Tom's unique advantages was its connection with Hong Kong's major tycoon Li Kai-Shing.

Tom had just released a prospectus for its planned $HK 640 million IPO for 15% of the total post-IPO shares of the firm. A portfolio manager for EuroGlobal Funds was to provide his professional opinion on the value of this investment and its appropriateness for different investors. He was aware of the difficulties in valuing Internet companies and the debate over the choice of valuation methods. Among these, one approach was to analyze the implied hypergrowth rate in revenues that Internet companies had to achieve in the next five years in order to justify their current valuations. His challenge was to determine the worth of Tom's shares, and decide on the best investment strategy for EuroGlobal Funds.

Preparation Questions

1. Assess Tom's overall business model, revenue and growth potential, risks, and major shareholders.

2. What are the some of the valuation challenges with a firm like Tom as compared to the valuation of well-established "blue-chip" firms?

3. Apply the implied average annual growth rate approach to Tom (as suggested by Perkins and Perkins), as well as any other valuation approaches. Clearly state any assumptions you are making. What do you think is the worth of Tom's shares compared to the suggested IPO price range?

4. What would you recommend to Andy Lau and EuroGlobal regarding the purchase of Tom shares?

INTEGRATIVE STUDY QUESTIONS

As you consider the entire set of questions in the seventh chapter, you should reflect on the following integrative questions:

1. Does the valuation of Internet companies make sense?

2. What is the valuation approach to Tom.com?

3. What are the advantages and disadvantages of discounted cash flow approaches to valuation? What are the advantages and disadvantages of the real options approach?

4. What are the advantages and disadvantages of an IPO vs. being acquired?

SUMMARY

One of the biggest changes confronting New Economy businesses is valuation. Using conventional approaches that are based on discounted cash flow can result in significantly undervaluing a company. More recent approaches—such as real options theory—offer an alternative point of view that addresses the limitations of DCF analysis. The critical point is that the value of the company—particularly the embryonic company—is the value of the asset in use. For example, if a large company was to acquire a new formed company with no revenues, the value of the new company should be based on the incremental valuation for the acquiring company.

TOM.COM

valuation of an asian internet company[1]

Tom.com seemed to embody everything the Internet frenzy is about. The start-up aims to be a multi-lingual mega-portal focusing on delivering China-related content worldwide ... as the Internet wave piqued the interest of local Chinese investors and international investors. A number of competitors already have jumped into the Chinese markets hoping to tap the potential of one billion consumers, most of whom have never used a computer. Tom.com is distinguished from its competition much in part due to its connection with Hong Kong's most high-profile tycoon Li Kai-Shing.[2]

On Feb. 19, 2000, the day after Tom.com Limited (Tom), a Hong Kong based Internet portal, released its prospectus for the planned $640 million[3] initial public offering (IPO), Andy Lau, a portfolio manager for EuroGlobal Funds, was immersed in digesting the 200-page information package. EuroGlobal was one of Europe's leading families of mutual funds. Its Asia Growth Fund had more than US$800 million of funds under management and had been in the top quartile of Asian based funds ranked by total return performance for all five of the years the fund had been in existence.

Tom had been a focus of attention by the financial community since the announcement of its IPO. Headline after headline had been reporting the grand scale of the mega-

portal for China-related content, its affiliation with the Li family and, most of all, its potential market price. Emerging out of the two-year-long Asian financial crisis, the "get rich fast" Hong Kong spirit would not likely see such an event pass without plenty of buzz. However, Lau knew his job was to make professional opinions on the value of such an investment and its appropriateness for different investors. Valuation of "dot-com" companies had been one of the most controversial subjects in the investment realm ever since the technology stock-dominated NASDAQ index shot up almost 84 percent in 1999,[4] powered mostly by Internet related companies (and biotechnology companies). Various new valuation techniques had been suggested to replace the more traditional Discounted Cash Flow (DCF) and Price Earnings Multiples (P/E) approaches. With only four days left until the closing of applications, Lau decided to use a variety of valuation methods he knew and "try to unveil" the true value of Tom.

Tom.com Limited[5]

Creation of Tom

In 1996, Metro, an information, entertainment, and radio programming business owned 50 percent by the Cheung Kong Group and 50 percent by the Hutchison Whampoa Group,[6] launched its first Web site, *metroradio.com.hk* to provide online details of Metro Radio's

IVEY *Peter Yuan prepared this case under the supervision of Professors Larry Wynant and Steve Foerster solely to provide material for class discussion. The authors do not intend to illustrate either effective or ineffective handling of a managerial situation. The authors may have disguised certain names and other identifying information to protect confidentiality.*

[1]This case has been written on the basis of published sources only. Consequently, the interpretation and perspectives presented in this case are not necessarily those of Tom.com or any of its employees.
[2]Gabriella Faerber, "Tom.com: Just an Illusion," *Worldlyinvestor.com*, April 2000.
[3]Unless otherwise stated, all currencies in the case refer to Hong Kong dollar. US$1 = HK$7.75
[4]NASDAQ closed at 2208.05 on Jan. 4, 1999, and 4069.31 on Dec. 31, 1999.
[5]Much of the information in this section is drawn from the prospectus of Tom.com Limited.
[6]Both the Cheung Kong Group and the Hutchison Whampoa Group were listed companies on the Hong Kong Stock Exchange. The Cheung Kong Group was the majority shareholder of Hutchison Whampoa Group. Mr. Li Ka-Shing and his immediate family members had effective control over Cheung Kong Group through their shareholdings.

programming. In 1998, a second Web site, *104fm-select.com*, was launched to provide information and live streaming of radio programming. In July 1999, a third Web site called *sochannel.com* was launched to provide up-to-date information on local and international music and the entertainment scene.

As penetration of the Internet accelerated in Hong Kong, Hutchison Whampoa and Cheung Kong realized that the target market should be expanded beyond the limited potential of the existing Metro Web sites. They saw that there was the potential of a portal which offered a total China experience, particularly to mainland and overseas Chinese communities. In order to provide a new and refreshing brand for the range of content being developed, "Tom" was created as the single brand under which to launch and promote the broader portal concept. Subsequently, through reorganization, all of the Web sites and event production expertise of Metro were acquired by Tom for a cash consideration of $310 million. On Oct. 5, 1999, Tom.com Limited was registered in the Cayman Islands.[7]

The Business Plan

Tom intended to leverage its core strengths in technology, media foundation, content acquisition and presentation, as well as shareholder support to achieve its goal of becoming the leading multi-lingual China-related mega-portal.[8] The mega-portal would provide "Lifestyle for Chinese" content and e-commerce to the worldwide Chinese population both in the Greater China region and overseas Chinese-speaking communities and broad "China Experience" content and e-commerce to the rest of the world.

Believing that Hong Kong had always acted as a natural bridge between China and the rest of the world for popular culture and entertainment exchange, Tom would focus on three core markets:

1. The non-Chinese-speaking audience, which would be interested in "China Experience" style content;

2. The PRC audience, which would be more interested in "Lifestyle for Chinese" content; and

3. Overseas Chinese-speaking audiences, which would be interested in both.

The "China Experience" content would provide a comprehensive guide to China covering classical and contemporary topics including news and business, travel information and services, classical arts and literature, modern arts and literature, wisdom and popular culture. On the other hand, the "Lifestyle for Chinese" content would cover day-to-day interests for Chinese people, such as food and wine, sports and leisure, entertainment and music, fashion and beauty, popular technology and fun and self improvement.

To propel Tom into a leading China-related portal, Tom built and launched a new and unique Chinese language information and entertainment content platform branded Tomcast. It provided a personalized real-time information channel and Internet navigation tool. Subscribers to *www.tom.com* were asked to sign up and download a small piece of software onto their hard drives.

Some analysts had expressed concern over a potential user's acceptance of such hurdles to accessing the Web site. They had also questioned whether there was a lack of focus by targeting such a broad range of audiences with a relatively wide range of contents. Besides, marketing to the worldwide Chinese audience would be extremely expensive.[9]

Revenue Model

Exhibit 1 provides the audited financial statements of Tom for the two years ending Dec. 31, 1999.

Directors of Tom stated that the company would target four revenue streams over time. Advertising revenue had been the major source of income for Internet portals. Like traditional media companies, Tom would sell advertising space on its Web sites to advertisers. Advertising revenue was linked to the number of page views that Tom expected to generate. The quality of content was a key factor in increasing page views. As Tom increased its online e-commerce capability, it would also receive revenue from transactions and subscriptions from products and services offered through tom.com. Commission revenue was generated through commission agreements with companies who had banner advertisements or hyperlinks placed on the tom.com Web sites. With an extensive content provision network in

---

[7]Many public companies in Hong Kong were registered in Cayman Islands for tax and political reasons. The bulk of their operation was still centered in Asia.

[8]Portals, such as Yahoo!, were Web sites that attract visitors by offering free information or free services on a daily basis. The portal site would be used as a basis to explore the Web. A portal was an entry point and gateway for surfing the Internet that provided useful Web-related services and links.

[9]Gabriella Faerber, "Tom.com: Just an Illusion?," *Worldlyinvestor.com*, April 2000.

place, Tom also expected to sell syndicated content to both cyber and other media.

Current Businesses

By January 2000, Tom had 143 staff and had established five operating units: Super Channel, Super Web, itravel, EClink Shenzhen, and OneAsia (see Exhibit 2).

Super Channel. Super Channel was a wholly owned subsidiary created to operate the Web sites and manage strategic investments. Tom used cutting edge software and hardware components, both developed in-house and procured from third party vendors, to build a common backend infrastructure that provided a reliable and scalable platform. The company also planned to deliver its products via local or mirror servers located in the vicinity of the target markets. The overall architectural design of Tom's infrastructure would follow the principles of distributed Web architecture to enable maximum information availability and provision efficiency to end-users.

Super Channel also supervised the Web content management team. To date, Tom had entered into 10 content provision and license contracts with external content providers regarding travel, culture, science, learning, arts, fashion, games, news, sports, and "infotainment." The content would be repackaged and edited, while at the same time, Tom would also develop its own content. These content providers included PRC organizations, Metro and OneAsia. Due to the short history of Tom, most of [the] license agreements were still subject to finalization. (Several content provision agreements and joint venture agreements with PRC companies were subject to PRC government approval.)

Super Web. Super Web was established in November 1999 to hold the Web sites acquired from Metro for a total cash consideration of $310 million in December 1999. According to the company's internal data, the Metro Web sites comprising metroradio.com.hk, metro997.com, metro104.com, and sochannel.com, had reached 100,000 daily pageviews and 7,000 registered members within two months from the re-launch in July 1999. These Web sites focused on updated on-line local and international news in Hong Kong.

itravel. A joint venture between Tom and CTN Holdings, itravel, would sub-brand its Web sites with tom.com to offer travel related products and services both in B2C (business to consumer) and B2B (business to business) markets. Tom had invested $16.7 million for 55 percent of itravel, while CTN Holdings owned by China International Travel Service Head Office (CITSHO), the largest PRC state-run travel agency, would bring expertise in servicing inbound tourists. itravel planned to launch its Web site in the first quarter of 2000, and would enter into a commercial agreement with Tom to share transaction revenue generated by users entering itravel through Tom's portal.

EClink Shenzhen. EClink Shenzhen, a wholly owned subsidiary of Tom, had been involved in the development of Electronic Data Interchange (EDI) customs declaration software to provide a secure electronic transaction platform. It would bring Tom capability in software development, electronic network systems, and other computer network systems in PRC.

OneAsia. OneAsia.com was a Web site that sold Chinese produced music and video products to Chinese communities in the Greater China region and Chinese communities living overseas. At the time, it was one of the few companies that had payment handling and fulfillment capabilities. Tom indirectly held 15 percent of OneAsia and had the option to increase its shareholding to 50 percent. OneAsia would sub-brand with tom.com. The two companies were also in discussion to amalgamate their customer databases.

Tom had also entered into a number of content provision and license contracts with providers for cultural events, sports, culinary arts, and games.

Future Businesses' Plans

Tom would initially focus on the "China Experience" themed content, targeting a worldwide audience, as the company believed that the more advanced distribution infrastructure and established e-commerce models outside of China provided a more ready market. Tom would establish mirror sites in major cities in the world with local editorial teams to develop local content.

Significant Shareholders

After the reorganization, Tom had six major shareholders: Easterhouse, Romefield, Cheung Kong, Schumann, Handel, and Pacific Century CyberWorks Limited (PCCW).

The Li Family

Through their subsidiaries, Mr. Li Kai-Shing and his family members held 62 percent of Tom immediately before the IPO through three related entities. Easterhouse, a wholly owned subsidiary of Hutchison, held 38 percent of Tom. Romefield, a wholly owned subsidiary of Cheung Kong, held 19 percent and PCCW held five percent.

Cheung Kong, the flagship investment holding group controlled by the Li family, owned 49.9 percent of Hutchison. Both companies were listed on the Hong Kong Stock Exchange with a broad business scope ranging from property development and investment, ports operation, telecommunications, retailing, and manufacturing. Including its majority shareholdings in two other listed companies, Cheung Kong Infrastructure (Holdings) Group and Hong Kong Electric Group, Cheung Kong had $59 billion of consolidated profits attributable to its shareholders in 1999.

Richard Li, one of the sons of Mr. Li Ka Shing, served as chairman and chief executive officer of PCCW, a joint venture that Intel had a 13 percent stake in. A leading technology company, PCCW was developing an innovative satellite to cable distribution system to deliver broadband Internet service in Asia. It was also actively involved in the investment and development of the Cyberport, an information infrastructure project initiated by the Hong Kong government to create a strategic cluster of information technology and Internet service companies and a critical mass of professional talent in Hong Kong.

Being one of the first companies to invest in Mainland China, Cheung Kong was also the most successful. Its PRC portfolio included properties, infrastructure, ports, and retail projects. Through their philanthropic activities and extensive business dealings, the Li family was generally recognized to enjoy good "*Guanxi*" (the Chinese term for personal network) with different levels of the PRC government.

Hutchison and Cheung Kong recently announced the establishment of two other Internet-related projects focused on the development of the groups' overall e-commerce ability. One was an alliance between Hutchison and priceline.com. The other one was iBusinessCorporation.com, a joint venture between Cheung Kong, Hutchison, Hong Kong and Shanghai Banking Corporation (HSBC), and Hang Seng Bank.[10]

---

[10]Total assets of HSBC in 1999 were US$559.2 billion. Hang Seng Bank is a member of the HSBC Group with total assets of HK$442 billion.

Schuman and Handel

Schuman and Handel were engaged in the provision of management consulting services and [were] owned and managed by a group of consultants with extensive experience in the planning and development of projects in China, such as the Beijing Oriental Plaza, a US$2 billion investment by Cheung Kong. The consultants helped Tom to secure the content provision and license agreements with various PRC partners. Schuman held 23.75 percent of Tom while Handel had a 14.25 percent stake.

The Share Offering

The planned share offering would float 15 percent of Tom, a total of 428 million shares excluding the over-allotment option[11] on the recently established Growth Enterprise Market (GEM)[12] of the Hong Kong Stock Exchange (see Exhibit 3). The offer price of the common shares would be between $1.48 and $1.78 for total net proceeds of about $640 million (see Exhibit 3). The final offer price would be set by the underwriters at the end of the application period and would depend on the strength of the interest shown for the Tom issue. The proceeds would be used for capital expenditures, promotion and marketing activities, development of the e-commerce business, strategic investments, and general working capital (see Exhibit 4).

Placing

Ninety percent of the 428 million offered shares, or 385.2 million shares, would be placed with professional institutional investors, qualifying subscribers and certain employees and executive directors of Tom at the offer price. Professional investors included brokers, dealers, fund managers in Hong Kong, Europe, and other jurisdictions outside the United States. Allocation would be based on several factors, including the level of demand and whether or not investors would likely buy further shares, or hold or sell their shares after the listing.

---

[11]Over-allotment up to an aggregate of 64,200,000 additional shares could be exercised at the discretion of the underwriters.
[12]GEM was established by the Stock Exchange of Hong Kong in 1999 to accommodate companies with high investment risks and were targeted at professional and informed investors. Companies listed on GEM were not required to have a track record of profitability or forecast of future profitability. By the end of 1999, seven companies were listed on GEM which raised an aggregate of $1.6 billion. In January 2000, daily trading volume averaged $83 million. Total market capitalization of the GEM stocks reached $11 billion by the end of January.

Ten thousand seven hundred Hong Kong residents, registered as subscribers of Tom's Internet services and selected by Tom, would be qualifying subscribers, each entitled to subscribe to 2,000 shares at the offer price. Qualifying subscribers were generally individuals who had visited Tom's Web site and joined on-line as a Tom member.

Up to one percent of the offer shares would be offered by Tom to certain employees and executive directors of Tom at the offer price.

Public Offering

Forty two million eight hundred thousand shares representing 10 percent of the shares being offered would be for public subscription. Applicants would be required to pay, on application, the maximum offer price of $1.78 per share, in addition to a brokerage and stock exchange transaction levy. Allocation of public offer shares would be based on the level of application. Shares would be allocated on a pro-rata basis and could involve balloting if the shares were heavily over-subscribed, a norm in Hong Kong for such high-profile IPOs. Already, there was speculation that Tom could break the 1,200 times over-subscription record held by Beijing Enterprise Holdings that had its IPO on the Hong Kong Stock Exchange in 1997 (see Exhibit 5). Funds accompanying an application would be held for about a week until the application was deemed successful. If an application was not successful, payment for the shares would be refunded without interest to the unsuccessful applicant. In addition, if the issue was priced at less than the specified maximum, the difference between the final offer price and maximum offer price would also be refunded to successful applicants.

Waivers

The GEM Listing Rules required the initial management shareholders of a new issuer not to dispose of their interests for a period of two years from the listing date, which was referred to as the moratorium period. A moratorium period was implemented to ensure commitment by the initial management and significant shareholders to the growth of the company. However, as a result of an application made on behalf of Tom, the Hong Kong Stock Exchange had granted an adjustment in the moratorium period applicable to Easterhouse and Romefield, which together held 48.4 percent of the issued share capital of Tom after the IPO, to be reduced to six months.

Tom had also applied for and was granted a waiver regarding the number of shares that it could issue to its employees in a Stock Option Scheme. Tom was allowed to increase the Stock Option Scheme limit from the regular 10 percent up to 50 percent of authorized shares.

The Internet in Greater China

Emerging economies in Asia had always been among the most aggressive in investing in new technologies. According to International Data Corporation (IDC), a global leader in information technology analysis, the number of Internet users worldwide would grow from approximately 155.6 million at the end of 1998 to 526 million by the end of 2003, while the user base in Asia (including Japan) would increase from 24 million to 155 million over the same period, a compound annual growth rate of 45.4 percent. The Internet explosion was supported by a progressive penetration of computers and peripherals. The PC penetration rate in Asia was 1.3 percent in 1998 and expected to reach 5.3 percent in 2003.

Tom believed that the substantial growth in the number of Internet users and Web sites was fuelling the expansion of two key Internet business areas: on-line advertising and e-commerce. IDC estimated that worldwide e-commerce revenues would grow from US$48.4 billion as of the end of 1998 to US$1.3 trillion by 2003, representing 93.3 percent cumulative annual growth rate (CAGR). Over the same period, Asian on-line spending would grow at 104 percent CAGR, reaching US$118.4 billion in 2003.

A lot of attention had been focused on the adoption of the Internet in the PRC, but little verified industry data was available. China Internet Network International Center, an institution under the PRC Ministry of Information, estimated that at the end of 1999, Internet penetration in the PRC was about 0.74 percent.[13] Some of the most popular PRC portals, Sina.com, 163.com, and Sohu.com, reported page views[14] per month ranging from 210 million to 399 million. According to IDC, e-commerce spending would grow from US$43 million in 1999 to US$6.5 billion by 2003. However, according to

---

[13]Based upon a population of 1.2 billion.
[14]Page views were a commonly used statistic for measuring Web site activity. One page view was recorded each time a single page on a Web site is viewed. Another statistic used was called a "hit." One hit was counted each time a user accesses a different file on a Web site. Each page viewed on a Web site might contain many such files, so a single page view could account for multiple hits.

The New York Times, China's online advertising industry only generated US$12 million in 1999, while according to AC Nielsen, a leading market research firm, advertising expenditures on traditional media was US$4.1 billion.

Besides the infancy of the Internet in [the] PRC, it was also not clear what policies the PRC government would adopt to develop the Internet. It had from time to time halted the distribution of information over the Internet that it believed to be socially destabilizing by blocking Web sites maintained outside of China. Currently, the Internet sector was off-limits to foreign investment, even though it was expected to gradually open up. Foreign investors,[15] such as Tom, had been trying to participate through content provision agreements. In addition, within the PRC, access to the international gateway was controlled by the government's backbone. Tom also relied on this backbone and China Telecom, the state-owned monopoly in the PRC, to provide data communications capacity and depended upon the PRC government to establish and maintain a reliable Internet infrastructure.

The Valuation Challenge

Valuing these high-growth, high-uncertainty, high-currently-unprofitable Internet firms had been a challenge, to say the least. Some practitioners had even described it as a hopeless one.[16] To be more precise, the real challenge had been to justify the incredibly high values that the market had awarded these dot-coms when many of them were simply producing interesting concepts instead of earnings. For example, in 1999, Amazon had a loss of US$720 million with revenues exceeding US$1.6 billion.

Calculating the Implied Average Revenue Growth Rates

After identifying and studying 133 publicly traded Internet companies with market capitalization over US$100 million, Anthony Perkins and Michael Perkins summarized their findings in a book called *The Internet Bubble.* Based on their assumptions of how the Internet industry would turn out to be in the future, they found that the current share prices implied extremely aggressive revenue growth rates in the next five years for most Internet companies.

Assumptions[17]. The Perkins' approach assumed the Internet companies would experience a period of hyper-growth for a limited time period, such as the next five years, during which time revenue growth could be phenomenal. After that time, growth would diminish to more normal levels, profits would be achieved, and the stock would be valued in more traditional ways. The Perkins assumed that by the end of the hyper-growth period, the average P/E ratio would be in the range of 20 to 40 times and the net profit margin would be in the normal range experienced by traditional businesses, between 5 and 15 percent (see Exhibit 10).

The Perkins further assumed that investors in Internet companies would expect a return on capital of 15 to 25 percent. This assumption was based on examining the betas of more traditional technology companies. By applying the forward-looking discount rate, the future market capitalization of Internet companies in five years could be derived. For example, the market capitalization of Amazon in the second quarter of 1999 was US$17.1 billion. If a 20 percent required rate of return was assumed, Amazon would need to grow to a market capitalization of US$42.6 billion in June 2004 in order to generate the return required by investors.

Because most Internet companies used stock options in employee remuneration, the Perkins further assumed a dilution in the equity base of five percent. In the case of Amazon, the market capitalization would need to grow to US$44.7 billion.

Using a P/E ratio of 40 times and a net profit margin of five percent, earnings and revenue of Amazon would need to reach US$1.1 billion and US$22.3 billion respectively in five years. By comparing the future revenue to Amazon's past 12-month revenue of US$816.3 million, revenue growth in the next five years would have to achieve a cumulative annual growth of 94 percent.

The Perkins categorized 133 Internet companies into commerce, content, enabling services, enabling software, and enabling telecom services. Based on stock data and revenue data as of second quarter 1999, they calculated the average Internet company in the set would need to generate revenue growth of approximately 80 percent every year for the next five years (see Exhibit 6 for selected companies from the Perkins analysis).

---

[15]The PRC government classified and treated investments from Hong Kong, Taiwan, and Macau as foreign investments.
[16]Driek Desmet et al, "Valuing Dot-coms," *McKinsey Quarterly,* Number 1, 2000.

---

[17]Source: *www.redherring.com/internetbubble/*

Other Valuation Approaches

Lau realized that investment professionals used a variety of other valuation approaches for Internet companies. The most popular valuation method, the discounted cash flow analysis, required an estimation of future earnings, growth in those earnings, the capital and working capital expenditures required to fuel growth and the company's cost of capital. Analysts often estimated earnings over the next five years and then applied a constant growth rate beyond that period. However, Tom would more than likely experience negative free cash flows in the foreseeable future because of high marketing expenses and high development spending. To deal with these issues, elaborate projections over an extended period of time would have to be made.

A related approach was based on scenario analysis. While it was particularly difficult to determine the one "best guess" of projected cash flows for these types of firms, a variety of free cash flows were projected based on "most likely," "pessimistic," "optimistic," and other possible scenarios. After discounted cash flows were estimated for each of the scenarios, a probability was attached to each in order to estimate a weighted-average current value. Scenario analysis allowed for incorporating a small probability of a large potential value with more realistic (and more probable) possibilities.

Relative valuation was widely used on Internet companies, as most investors who invest in these firms did not do so because of their judgments on intrinsic value, but more on their judgment of relative value, the value of a firm relative to how similar firms were valued by the market at the moment. Multiples such as price-earnings, price-book value, price-sales were some of the most popular. However, because most Internet companies had negative earnings, and their book values did not reflect their earnings power, price to sales (P/S) was most widely used with Internet companies. Exhibit 7 provides information of several U.S. based Internet companies.

Besides the P/S ratio, various new multiples for valuing Internet companies were being introduced. Among them, Price to Monthly Page Views[18] and Price to Unique Users[19] were often used for portals. Monthly Page Views measured the number of pages of a particular Web site accessed by the market, and Unique Users measured the number of users that the Web site possess. As portals derived most of their income from advertising, and advertisers pay for the size, quality, and frequency of the audience their message reached, the value of portal companies was driven principally, it was argued, by the number of viewers they attracted, much like the traditional media companies.

The Decision

Andy decided to start with the cumulative average growth rate approach to examine the revenue growth implied in Tom's current IPO price. Exhibits 8 and 9 provide information on risk free rate and equity risk premium in Hong Kong and the United States. He agreed that one advantage of this approach was that it was based upon past revenue data, which was readily available. Besides, it avoided the almost impossible task of forecasting future cash flows since Tom, like most Internet companies, had very short histories and immature business models. This approach produced one yardstick, cumulative average revenue growth in the next five years, to assess what an Internet company had to achieve during the hyper-growth stage.

Lau realized that even with the revenue growth data, he still didn't have enough information to decide whether such growth would be attainable. However, by comparing the revenue growth data of Tom with those of other Internet companies, Lau believed that he at least had some indication whether Tom was a relatively good Internet stock to buy at this moment.

The EuroGlobal Fund family had always looked to long term value in choosing its investments. Therefore, Lau knew his decision would be based on Tom's value and its prospects of becoming an industry leader in the budding Internet sector in Asia. However, the temptation to view any IPO as a quick-in and quick-out opportunity was particularly high for Tom. Even if Tom's long term prospects could not justify its offering price, Lau wondered whether the Asian Growth Fund should buy into Tom and benefit from a short term boost in prices while the frenzy for Internet based stocks continued.

---

[18]NetRatings Inc., a subsidiary of AC Nielson, provided page view information of major Web sites.
[19]Media Metrix Inc. provided unique user information of major Web sites.

The Richard Ivey School of Business gratefully acknowledges the generous support of The Richard and Jean Ivey Fund in the development of this case as part of the RICHARD AND JEAN IVEY FUND ASIAN CASE SERIES.

Exhibit 1

HK$'000	Income Statement (For years ending December 31)	
	1998	**1999**
Turnover	39,717	51,695
Cost of sales	(31,051)	(43,492)
Gross profit	8,666	8,203
Other revenue	1,160	410
Website/portal development costs	(906)	(29,945)
Software development costs	(1,090)	(1,113)
Advertising and promotion costs	-	(7,364)
Distribution costs	(2,837)	(2,861)
Administration expenses	(22,017)	(31,726)
Amortization of goodwill	(16,022)	(16,022)
Operating loss	(33,046)	(80,418)
Finance costs	(61)	(711)
Loss for the year	(33,107)	(81,129)
Minority interests	279	
Loss attributable to shareholders	**(32,828)**	**(81,129)**

Balance Sheet	
	As at December 31, 1999 HK$'000
Intangible assets	288,404
Fixed assets	25,129
Current assets	
Receivables and prepayment	8,843
Cash and bank balance	22,369
	31,212
Current liabilities	
Amounts due to related companies	8,039
Other payables and accrued charges	29,588
	37,627
Net current liabilities	(6,415)
Net assets	307,118
Deduct:	
Loans from shareholders	362,877
Net liabilities	**(55,759)**

Source: Prospectus of Tom.com Limited

Exhibit 2

Headcount of tom.com Limited		
	Headcount	
	December 1999	**February 2000**
Management	11	19
Information technology/Web development	16	47
Finance & administration	11	16
Sales & marketing	1	7
Business development	2	3
Operation/other support staff	8	51
	49	**143**

Source: Prospectus of Tom.com Limited

Exhibit 3

Share Offering Plan		
	Number of Shares	**Percentage**
Shares to be issued under the share offer	428,000,000	15.0%
Placing shares	385,200,000	13.5%
Public offer shares	42,800,000	1.5%
Shares in issue	2,421,000,000	85.0%
Easterhouse	920,000,000	32.3%
Romefield	460,000,000	16.1%
Schumann	575,000,000	20.2%
Handel	345,000,000	12.1%
PCCW	121,000,000	4.2%
Total Outstanding Shares	**2,849,000,000**	**100.0%**
Midpoint of the offering price per share ($)	1.63	
Market capitalization ($)	4,643,870,000	
Total offering proceeds ($)	697,640,000	
Total issuing cost ($)	58,000,000	
Net Offering Proceeds ($)	**639,640,000**	
Over-allotment	104,646,000	

Source: Prospectus of Tom.com Limited

Exhibit 4

Use of Proceeds (US$ millions)		
Capital expenditure in relation to technology development and content development for the year ending Dec. 31, 2000	$	240
Promotion and marketing activities for the year ending Dec. 31, 2000		150
Development of e-commerce business for the year ending Dec. 31, 2000		10
Strategic investments and additional general working capital		240
Total	$	640

Source: Prospectus of Tom.com Limited

Exhibit 5

	Over-Subscription Ratio of Selected Companies Listed on the GEM Market of Hong Kong Stock Exchange	
Listing Date	Company	Subscription Ratio (times)
1999/11/25	China Agrotech Holdings Ltd.	58.7
1999/11/26	Pine Technology Holdings Ltd.	66.0
1999/12/02	SIIC Medical Science and Technology (Group) Ltd.	495.2
1999/12/02	T S Telecom Technologies Ltd.	200.3
1999/12/16	Asian Information Resources (Holdings) Ltd.	394.0
1999/12/17	Qianlong Technology International Holdings Ltd.	312.0
Average		254.4

Source: The Official Web site of the Hong Kong Stock Exchange, *http://www.sehk.com.hk/*

Exhibit 6

Implied Revenue Growth Rate of Selected Internet Companies Based on the Perkins Methodology (Data as of second quarter 1999) ($ millions)				
Name	**Market cap**	**Revenue**	**Future Revenue**	**Implied CAGR**
Commerce				
Amazon.com	17,100.0	816.3	22,338.9	94%
eBay	20,800.0	75.4	10,869.0	170%
Priceline.com	13,600.0	84.6	7,106.0	143%
Content				
America Online	107,700.0	4,190.0	70,348.0	76%
Lycos	3,660.0	109.4	3,187.5	96%
Yahoo!	27,600.0	258.7	24,037.2	148%
Enabling Software				
Broadvision	1,500.0	59.3	653.2	62%
Inktomi	4,460.0	39.9	1,942.1	118%
Enabling Telecom Service				
Earthlink	1,400.0	214.4	914.5	34%
Global Crossing	22,100.0	602.1	14,435.4	89%
MindSpring	1,980.0	154.9	1,293.3	53%

Source: *www.redherring.com/internetbubble/*

Exhibit 7

Selected Information for U.S. Based Internet Companies (As of Dec. 31, 1999)				
	Yahoo!	**Ebay**	**Amazon.com**	**AOL**
Revenue 1999 (US$ Million)	588.6	224.7	1639.8	4777
Revenue 1998 (US$ Million)	245.1	86.1	609.8	3091
	343.5	138.6	1030	1686
Cumulative revenue *Growth in the past 4 years*	355.9%	745.4%	652.7%	110.5%
Current assets 1999 (US$ million)	945.9	459.8	1012.2	1979
Current debt 1999 (US$ million)	192.3	88.8	738.9	1725
	753.6	371	273.3	254
Current assets 1998 (US$ million)	617.7	97.6	424.3	1263
Current debt 1998 (US$ million)	95.9	24.7	161.6	1155
	521.8	72.9	262.7	108
	231.8	298.1	10.6	146
Beta	2.64	2.39	1.63	1.54
Price to book	33.9	19.1	450.8	19.2
Price to sales	74.7	60.8	5.8	19.1

Source: Bloomberg. Cumulative revenue growth rate of Ebay is for the past three years.

Exhibit 8

Yields (as of Feb. 19, 2000)	Government Debt Yield (%)	
	Hong Kong	U.S.
3 month	5.86	5.75
6 month	5.98	6.03
1 year	6.33	6.23
2 year	6.70	6.63
3 year	6.91	n.a.
5 year	7.19	6.70
7 year	7.37	n.a.
10 year	7.65	6.49
30 year	n.a.	6.19

Source: Bloomberg

Exhibit 9

Return and P/E of S&P 500 Index, NASDAQ Index and Hang Seng Index (1995–1999)			
	S&P 500	NASDAQ	Hang Seng Index
Total Return (%)			
1999	20.9	86.0	72.7
1998	28.3	40.0	(3.0)
1997	33.1	22.1	(17.0)
1996	22.7	23.0	36.9
1995	37.1	40.8	26.8
P/E (1995–1999)			
Hi	34.7	n.a.	28.5
Low	16.0	n.a.	8.1
Average	23.5	n.a.	15.7

Source: Bloomberg

Exhibit 10

Net Income of Selected U.S. Companies for FY1999 (US$ million)			
Company	Revenue	Net Income	Net Profit Margin
Computer-Services			
Microsoft Corp.	19,747.0	7,785.0	39.4%
Oracle Corp.	8,827.3	1,289.8	14.6%
Adobe Systems Inc.	1,015.4	237.8	23.4%
Novell, Inc.	1,272.8	190.8	15.0%
Citrix Systems, Inc.	403.3	116.9	29.0%
Publishing			
Time Warner, Inc.	14,582.0	168.0	1.2%
McGraw-Hill Cos., Inc.	3,729.1	341.9	9.2%
Dow Jones & Co., Inc.	2,158.1	8.8	0.4%
Washington Post Co.	2,110.4	417.3	19.8%
Retail			
Wal-Mart Stores, Inc.	139,208.0	4,430.0	3.2%
K Mart Corp.	33,674.0	518.0	1.5%
Venator Group Inc.	4,555.0	3.0	0.1%
Advertising			
Interpublic Group of Cos. Inc	3,968.7	309.9	7.8%
Omnicom Group, Inc.	4,092.0	285.1	7.0%
Grey Advertising, Inc.	935.2	25.9	2.8%

Source: *Mergent Industry Review,* Vol. 19, No.3, Jan. 21, 2000

Network Infrastructure

8

NETWORK INFRASTRUCTURE

Mostly linked by telephone lines, the Internet is an expansive network of individual computer networks that allows for the exchange of news, information, entertainment, and other forms of communications in digital form. The World Wide Web is the most used portion of the Internet. Created by researcher Tim Berners-Lee in 1989, the World Wide Web allows for the transmission of multimedia documents (videos, audio, etc.) across the Internet.

Customers and businesses usually transfer information over the Internet by using a personal computer, an Internet browser, an analog modem, and standard telephone lines. A customer uses the personal computer and modem to dial up an Internet service provider (ISP) to access a business's website. Once the business's site recognizes the customer through his or her screen name and encrypted password, the customer can then interface with the business services to search for products, order merchandise, or request services, such as making airline or hotel reservations.

The Internet browser, which is the software that allows a user to visit the World Wide Web, usually stores the user's screen name, password, and other information to a particular site (through "cookies") so that the user does not have to retype his or her password every time or reinput his or her credit card number to purchase merchandise when revisiting the site. All commercial data is usually encrypted, through the browser software and by firewalls, to prevent hackers from stealing an individual's information online.

Analog technology uses continuously varying signals as electronic waves to transmit information and is limited in its ability to carry multiple types of information. Digital technology, on the other hand, treats incoming and outgoing information as a string of zeros and ones—the binary language of computer code—which allows for more complex uses, such as interactive television and video-conferencing.

The convergence of digital technology is of great interest to both telephone companies and cable operators because it offers the opportunity to provide the "last mile" of broadband services into the house. DSL (digital subscriber line), cable modem, and satellite transmissions will be some of the faster ways to access the Internet. As broadband connections—those greater than 128 kilobytes per second—become more available over the next five years, demand is expected to grow rapidly for new services, such as video-on-demand, software sale, online, and other services.

Companies with PC-based information systems can better manage their business processes, such as customer service, supply-chain management, and procurement, by creating an intranet—an internal network on the Web—whereby individual managers can obtain information in real time from a centralized database to analyze customer opportunities or to order supplies.

Laws governing privacy, taxation, access, patents, free speech, and network economies and monopolies in the United States are currently under review as a result of increased usage of the Internet. While many of these issues still need to be resolved, they are being addressed at all levels of government—local, state, and federal.

SYNOPSES OF CHAPTER CASES

NORTEL NETWORKS: INTERNET POINT OF PRESENCE

Case Overview

Consequent to its merger with Bay Networks, Nortel Networks became a key player in the Internet infrastructure space. Deregulation, first in the United States in the early 1980s and then in Europe, created a window of opportunity for Nortel and other vendors to build competitive telecommunications networks. In many countries, this meant that vendors moved from having one customer to having many customers. Led by Manager Eme Dean-Lewis, Nortel launched the iPoP (Internet Point of Presence) product for Northern European Internet Service Providers (ISPs) in 1999.

The emergence of ISPs is a critical trend. The iPoP solution, in essence a signal "switcher" housed in a box that facilitates access to the Internet, is targeted primarily to ISPs but also to voice resellers. The iPoP solution integrates data and voice capabilities and comes with a package of professional services and financing options, with total prices ranging from $100,000 to $1,000,000,000. When an ISP purchases iPoP, it simplifies the data transmission, eliminating the need for additional connectivity providers and in so doing simplifies the revenue flow. The benefit to the ISP is that as traffic increases, the ISP may collect "call termination" revenues previously not accessible. Since greater use actually increases revenues, many ISPs with iPoP offer free dial-up access. If the business case is favorable, the call termination revenues will, at minimum, cover the lease payments for iPoP.

For each country, this revenue is dependent on a number of factors. These include: (1) interconnection call termination rate per minute for each tariff band (however defined for the particular country); (2) expected rate of growth or decline in interconnect tariffs; (3) average minutes per month per subscriber in each tariff band and the growth trend; and (4) growth rate of subscribers for a particular ISP (depends on Internet penetration rate and market share for a particular ISP). It is important to note that the incumbent operator is not *losing* interconnect revenue to the ISP. Rather, the increased Internet usage is generating new call minutes on the operator's network. In effect, the operator is *gaining* a share of new call revenue.

As Eme Dean-Lewis reviewed the iPoP innovation, she wondered what Nortel Network's position would be in the Netherlands and other European markets.

Preparation Questions

1. What competitive response should Nortel Networks expect, and what should be their countermove?

2. How should iPoP change in the future? How would developments in the regulatory environment, the evolution of the market, and the target customers influence those changes?

3. Are there other markets that can be tapped with the iPoP product? If so, how?

MINDSPRING

Case Overview

Founded in 1994 by CEO Charles Brewer, MindSpring was a leading ISP based in Atlanta, Georgia. In a business that many analysts had called increasingly commodity-like, MindSpring's strategy was focused on superior customer service. Brewer's philosophy was based on a set of core values and beliefs described in a letter to stockholders, outlining his plan to base the company on integrity and respect for employees and customers alike.

MindSpring's strategic service vision consisted of identifying a target market segment, developing an operating strategy to support the service concept, and designing an efficient service-delivery system to support the operating strategy. About 83% of MindSpring customers defected from another ISP, usually because they experienced service problems such as busy signals, failed connections, poor technical support, or slow transmission. MindSpring's value proposition—Internet access that was easy to install, easy to use, and easy to fix— aimed to meet the needs of this market more effectively than its competitors.

By all accounts, Brewer's strategy had paid off. 1997 had been a record year, and in the fourth quarter, MindSpring became the first national ISP to record a quarterly profit. Its revenue had risen 190% since 1996, and its subscriber base had grown from 13,000 in 1995 to 341,000 in the first quarter 1998, an increase primarily accomplished through customer referrals and word-of-mouth. MindSpring had graduated from regional to national ISP status, offering local dial-up service in some 320 U.S. locations.

The issue of growth—how to achieve it, and with what trade-offs—raised a number of strategic and tactical questions. Was the company's customer-service model scalable to 500,000, 1 million, or even 2 million subscribers? Would traditional ISPs be left out in the cold when cable and DSL took off? Should MindSpring pursue acquisitions more aggressively? Should it seek a partnership similar to the recent Sprint/Earthlink deal or remain independent?

Preparation Questions

1. Describe MindSpring's target customer. Assess how well the company has tailored its strategy to profitably serve this target group.

2. Determine whether MindSpring should accelerate its growth. If it does so, explore whether MindSpring should acquire established ISPs or intensify its marketing efforts within its existing units. Also consider whether it would benefit MindSpring to pursue a merger or alliance with a long-distance phone company.

3. The addendum to the case provides data to calculate MindSpring's market value per customer. Assess whether the company's cash flow per customer and its growth prospects warrant its current valuation levels. Determine what this situation implies for strategy.

INTEGRATIVE QUESTIONS

As you consider the entire set of questions in the ninth chapter, you should also reflect on the following integrative questions:

1. What are the characteristics of a "killer app"? How does a firm (or set of firms) establish a killer app? Are killer apps largely driven by consumer needs, or are they driven by supply-side needs?

2. Who will win the fight for the last mile—DSL, cable modems, satellite, or wireless?

3. How is the wireless revolution impacting the non-wireless side of the infrastructure?

4. How is the management of technology-based firms similar or dissimilar to the traditional retail store?

SUMMARY

The network infrastructure can be conceived as the "plumbing" of the Internet. The network is comprised of hardware, software, and associated business applications. Two key themes emerge in any infrastructure discussion. The first is the emergence of standards and the associated lock-in around the standard. The second theme is one of convergence. Convergence in this context refers to the converging of multiple industries—telecommunications, cable, satellite, and wireless—to provide the so-called last mile into the consumers' homes.

NORTEL NETWORKS

Internet Point of Presence[1]

Introduction

Consequent to its merger with Bay Networks, Nortel Networks had become a key player in the Internet infrastructure space. With dot coms, ISPs and established firms, all moving to do business online, innovation was taking place at a rapid pace. In Europe, one of the products that Nortel had launched was the iPOP product for ISPs in 1999 and was now reviewing the way forward. Eme Dean-Lewis was the manager responsible for moving the iPOP product in the Northern European market.

As she reviewed the genesis and launch of IPOP she was faced with many challenges. What should be Nortel Networks' position for iPoP in the Netherlands and other European markets? What competitive response should Nortel Networks expect in the Dutch and other European markets ? What should their counter move be? What should be the future changes, if any, in the iPOP product? How should those changes be affected by developments in the regulatory environment, evolution of the market and the target customers? Are there other markets that can be tapped with the iPOP product? If so, how?

Background

Telecommunications is an industry that has developed over more than a century evolving a national monopoly structure of operators providing telephony service to business and residential customers. Vendors to the industry were domestic monopolists (such as Alcatel in France, Siemens in Germany); oligopolists (such as STC and GEC in the UK) or were vertically integrated (such as AT&T in the US). Deregulation first in the US in the early 1980s and then in Europe introduced competition using various models. For Nortel Networks and the other vendors, this created a window of opportunity as licenses were awarded to new players and new networks built. In many countries, it meant that vendors moved from having one customer to having many customers. This wave of change was not yet complete in Europe although the richer economies have progressed the furthest.

During the 1990s the growth of the Internet has been rapid and its effect on the telecommunications industry, dramatic. It changes again the landscape of the industry. Convergence of circuit switched voice networks and packet switched data networks creates a market discontinuity in which most of the "old rules" no longer apply. The speed of change is captured by the following comment: "Telecom 99[2] was held in 1999. I find it remarkable that at the last Telecom—Telecom 95—no one mentioned the Internet, in 1999, no one talked about anything but the Internet."[3] This remark captures the essence of the magnitude and speed of recent changes in the telecommunications industry.

The emergence of Internet Service Providers (ISPs) is a critical trend. The ISPs are developing a relationship with consumers to whom vast quantities of information are easily accessible. The iPoP solution is targeted at voice resellers and ISPs. Initial focus is on the ISPs. The solution includes data and voice capabilities and comes with a package of professional services and financing options. David Perry, who is responsible for iPoP productisation, says "iPoP is not a technical innovation."[4]

The lead market for iPoP is the UK. Market testing was conducted in the first half of 1999 in several other European countries including France, Germany, Spain and Italy as well as the Netherlands. For Nortel Networks iPoP addresses some important needs of the changing operator marketplace. Firstly, it is targeted at the ISPs: a new customer base focused on services to consumers. Secondly, the ISPs are typically smaller customers which means that they rely on their vendors for expertise in many areas (e.g., technology, network planning, implementation, operations and maintenance). Again, this is a

---

[1]Eme Dean-Lewis of Nortel Networks prepared this case with Assistant Professor of Marketing Arvind Sahay to be used as a basis for class discussion rather than to illustrate either effective or ineffective handling of an administrative situation. Confidential data have been disguised.

---

[2]Telecom 99 is the major telecommunications industry exhibition. It is held every 4 years.
[3]John Roth, CEO Nortel Networks
[4]Interview held October 1999

trend which began with the emergence of Alternative Operators (AOs)—entrants into monopoly market structures. Before deregulation, the incumbent PTT (Public Telephone and Telegraph) companies were typically funded by their governments to develop in-house expertise. Thirdly, given attractive markets and an appropriate "whole product"[5] package, the sales cycle for iPoP is short: weeks rather than months or years. Generating orders quickly contributes to achievement of analyst expectations.

Nortel Networks

Nortel Networks Globally

Nortel Networks is a global company of 75,000 people roughly a quarter of whom are working in research and development. It operates in 150 countries with research laboratories in over 40 countries. In 1998, it reported revenues of US$18 billion. This revenue was balanced across its main "lines of business"—Public Carrier Networks, Broadband, Wireless and Enterprise. It was split geographically between Canada 8%, US 56%, Europe 21% and Other 15%.

The company began life in Canada as Northern Electric in the 1890s. Nortel is "the father of" digital switching which was introduced to the market in the 1970s. Nortel still leads this segment in installed base and current market share. In the 1980s, Nortel launched Fibre-World—high speed network backbone architecture. This underlies recent success in very high capacity networks—for example, seven out of eight pan-European networks built in 1998 used Nortel Networks equipment. Nortel leads the bandwidth race: it has built terabit backbones in 1999.

Nortel Networks concentrates on building "Unified Networks."[6] This means the company is focused on meeting the challenge of convergence of everything to IP: voice and data; fixed and mobile; carrier and enterprise. A feature of the internal cultural shift associated with the Unified Networks story is the concentration on reducing time to market: working in "Web Time."

In 1998, Nortel (undoubtedly a leader in voice switching) acquired Bay Networks—a successful data company competing with Cisco Systems in the router segment—paying US$9 billion. The new company is called Nortel

Networks. Bay Networks brings credibility and skills in the data market space. The acquisition was completed in only 60 days and has been followed by rapid integration of personnel. However, the possible collision between the voice and data world is present. Even Dave House, the chairman of Bay who became president of Nortel Networks, has said, "One thing I've learned joining Nortel is that I underestimated the phone system and all its requirements."[7]

In early 1999, Nortel Networks had a Lines of Business (LoBs) organisation structure which identified profit responsibility by product family. Some solutions—such as iPoP—incorporate products or services from several LoBs.

Nortel Networks in Europe

Nortel Networks has been working in European markets since the early 1980s. There are now 20,000 employees in Europe (the majority in the UK) working in all areas of the business—sales, marketing, research and development, installation, maintenance, training and manufacturing. Revenue for 1998 was US$3.8 billion.

In 1991, Nortel acquired STC (Standard Telephones and Cables) and so became an incumbent supplier to BT in the UK. There are also several Joint Ventures in Europe such as Nortel Matra (with Matra Communications) in France and Nortel Dasa (with Daimler-Benz) in Germany.

The Telecommunications Market

Review of Global Trends

The growth of the Internet is a key factor driving bandwidth demand as more people want access to more services more quickly. Significant network build to satisfy this demand has been undertaken. Companies such as Qwest in the US have built their business on providing very high capacity networks to other carriers. The rapid increase in bandwidth demand is accompanied by dramatic decreases in prices. John Roth, CEO of Nortel Networks, has written, "Moore's Law is driving down prices at an average rate of one percent per week."[8]

---

[5]See Geoffrey Moore—Crossing the Chasm
[6]Unified Networks is a trademark.

[7]Terry Sweeney and Tim Wilson—The state of internet working—users resist one-stop shopping
[8]John Roth—The importance of time.

Liberalisation is another key trend. It makes market entry possible for new operators. Entry is still controlled by licenses but increased deregulation makes these licenses more accessible. Monopolistic incumbent PTTs are facing competition for the first time. The US has led liberalisation with the splitting of AT&T into a long distance carrier (AT&T) and several local carriers (the "Baby Bells"). The UK is ahead of much of Europe although a different liberalisation model has been used. BT remains vertically integrated and faces competition from other national carriers (such as MCL in the first phase of duopoly) and local access offerings from cable television companies.

For vendors in the industry, deregulation creates enormous opportunity as new networks are built. However, as the number and type of customers increase sharply, there is a challenge for organisational culture to respond to satisfying a range of customer needs. In particular, it means that the vendors need to consider the new customers. John Borland has written, "the big local phone companies have been famously unsuccessful at building thriving ISP services over the last few years, while Net companies like AOL [America On Line] have captured millions of dial-up subscribers."[9] Regulation is a defining feature of the voice market—but not of the Internet. Stagg Newman, chief technologist at the FCC (Federal Communications Committee) has said, "We don't regulate the Internet, per se, . . . we don't police packets."[10]

Globalisation is a further characteristic of the industry. Major carriers are consolidating. An example is the battle in 1998 for the US carrier MCI which was won by Worldcom. In addition, US operators are moving into Europe—investing in joint ventures with domestic operators (for example, the joint venture between Qwest and the Dutch PTT, KPN—called KPNQwest) or in entrants (such as SBC's stake in diAx—a venture with Swiss utilities). Finally, "data is growing much faster than voice, and voice will be a data application," as per Rick Roscitt, CEO AT&T Solutions.[11]

However, this convergence has elements of collision. On the one hand, there is an implication for speed of working: the data world is characterised by fast market response. "[The telecommunications equipment vendors] are used to product cycles of around seven years, not just six months like in the Internet world," wrote Pim

Bilderbeek, International Data Corp.[12] Conversely, the voice segment is used to "five nines" reliability (99.999%). The reliability, scalability, and availability assumed in the voice world are unknown in the data world. As Rick Roscitt, CEO AT&T Solutions, has said "even compressed voice would require you to stack routers from the floor to the ceiling to handle a reasonable amount of voice traffic."[13] Mobility is another important trend for the industry. Penetration of mobile phones is rapid. As voice and data networks converge, and third generation technology becomes a reality, the challenge of delivering mobile data faces the industry.

Review of European Trends

Liberalisation creates a window of opportunity. The European Directive mandating the deregulation of telecoms is effective from January 1998 although some member states have opted for some extra time. According to *Forbes* magazine, "in our assessment, the most promising market in Europe is the UK, an exciting place these days with a strong technology infrastructure and a healthy appetite for innovation. Scandinavia's technology infrastructure beats the UK's but the Nordic countries are too small to offer economies of scale."[14] As already mentioned, deregulation has created an opportunity for US expansion into Europe—for example, AT&T's involvement in Unisource (in partnership with the Nordic PTTs).

Internet penetration varies across Europe although in general it is increasing. Some Scandinavian countries have higher penetration than the US (but much smaller populations). This leading indicator means that some European markets are more attractive than others for investment. It should be noted that tariff structures create significant differences between European and US markets: "Europe's expected boom in home-based Internet use will also complicate the telephony landscape in countries where local calling is expensive, because those local call revenues subsidize long-distance rates."[15]

For Europe—as is the global trend—Internet Protocol (IP) will eventually dominate the network but this

[9]John Borland—Bells stumble over broadband AOL
[10]Intelligent Network News, Packet service over cable—a regulatory no-man's land
[11]Cassimir Medford, Roscitt converses about convergence—the president and CEO of AT&T Solutions gives IP a thumbs-up

[12]William Boston, For Europe's telecom titans, it's now or never on the Net
[13]Cassimir Medford, Roscitt converses about convergence—the president and CEO of AT&T Solutions gives IP a thumbs-up
[14]Forbes Digital Tool, How does Europe stack up on the Internet? A country by country ranking
[15]David J. Wallace, Changes in phone service are mixing up Net issues in Europe

is not yet understood in all countries—some are still struggling with the introduction of competition. According to Neil Barton, Technology Analyst at Merrill Lynch, "We think carriers will have to . . . implement IP in their backbone networks. Many in the U.S. have decided that the case has been made, but it's a different story in Europe. BT . . . KPN . . . . Telia have been convinced, but the majority have not."[16]

Attractiveness of the Dutch Telecommunications Market

Macroeconomic data provide an overview of the Dutch economy.[17] There are fifteen and a half million people in the Netherlands. GDP at US$400bn is sixth in Europe. Dutch GDP per head at US$25K is higher than the UK although eleventh in Europe. Trade with the EU accounts for 80% of exports and 64% of imports. The Netherlands' main trading partner is Germany. The other BeNeLux countries—Belgium and Luxembourg—are next in importance.

Key data for the Netherlands by comparison with the UK and US are given in Figure 1.

Outgoing telephony traffic statistics unsurprisingly show a correlation with the main trading partners—23% (350 million minutes) in 1997 to Germany, 17% to Belgium followed by the UK and France. However, the national traffic balance (total incoming international minutes minus total outgoing international minutes) has moved from a deficit of 55 million minutes in 1994 to a surplus of 177 million minutes in 1997.[19] This means the Dutch are now receiving more calls than they are making. With the general growth in Internet traffic, this may be related to the large number of Internet hosts in the Netherlands (Figure 2). It may also be driven by the growth in call centres (which generate a lot of inbound traffic)—"about 40 percent of the pan-European call centres—where four or more languages are spoken—are in the Netherlands."

The state of the technology infrastructure is relevant to market attractiveness for iPoP since the solution relies on interconnecting with an existing network. In this regard, the Netherlands is attractive. According to the

Figure 1 Comparative Key Data for the Netherlands (extract)[18]

Country	GDP ($ billions)	Population (millions)	Main Lines (thousands)	Lines per 100	Cellular users (thousands)	PCs (thousands)	Internet users (thousands)
Netherlands	360.5	15.6	8,860	56.6	1,717	4,400	900
UK	1,288.2	57.6	30,292	51.8	14,993	11,200	6,000
US	8,079.9	268.0	170,568	64.0	80,312	109,000	70,000

Source: Telegeography

Figure 2 Internet Hosts by Economy 1993–1997 (extract)[20]

Country / Region	Number of Internet Hosts 1997	CAGR 1993–1997
The World	29,700,605	90.00 %
The Americas	19,394,554	90.70 %
Of which: US	17,247,802	90.00 %
Europe	7,213,888	85.10 %
Of which: UK	1,347,322	80.40 %
Netherlands	503,225	79.20 %

Source: Telegeography

---

[16]William Boston—For Europe's telecom titans, it's now or never on the Net
[17]EIU Country Profile—Netherlands
[18]Telegeography Inc 1999—Indicators

[19]Telegeography Inc 1996, 1997, 1998 Largest Telecommunications Routes
[20]Telegeography Inc 1998—Internet hosts by economy 1993–1997

Economist Intelligence Unit, "the telecommunications network is of a high standard, being fully digitised and consisting of fibre-optic cabling only, apart from the local loop."[21] In a study by *Forbes* magazine,[22] the Netherlands was rated B+ in terms of market attractiveness to investors. The study included Western European countries with populations over one million and reviewed a wide variety of key data in three main categories: technology penetration, the state of the economy and the business environment. The UK (with A−) was ranked the most attractive market. Holland was graded B+ along with Scandinavia.

Figure 3 shows some leading indicators for market attractiveness in the new world of the Internet. Personal Computer (PC) penetration affects market size for Internet penetration until other access mechanisms—such as television monitors—are available to the mass market. Debit and credit card usage may impact the rate of growth of eCommerce. For the Dutch market, Internet penetration is above the European median. The Netherlands is promoting itself as a continental Internet hub, along with London and Stockholm.

In Spring 1999, the Dutch market for providing Internet service was dominated by a few players who each had several hundred thousand subscribers. World On Line (owned by the Sandoz Foundation and of the Nina Brink fame) had the largest market share followed by companies owned by the incumbent PTT, KPN: World Access/Planet Internet and Xs4all. Apart from these large players, the market was highly fragmented: there were hundreds of ISPs.

On deregulation, "full liberalisation of the telecoms sector occurred on July 1, 1997, only six months ahead of an EU directive."[24] This means that the Netherlands was behind some other European markets such as the UK which began the path to deregulation in the 1980s.

However, the regulator, OPTA (Onafhankelijke Post en Telecommunicatie Autoriteit) has created a liberal regime aimed at encouraging entry. OPTA is following the lead of OFTEL (Office For Telecommunications) in the UK and requiring only one Point of Presence (PoP) to obtain an operator's license.[25] In addition, the new national telecommunications law determines that interconnected ISPs are entitled to keep the interconnect revenue. These factors are important for the iPoP business case. For example, in some European countries, multiple PoPs are required in order to apply for interconnection with the incumbent PTT. The more PoPs stipulated, the higher the barrier to entry for a new operator: greater financial and operational resources are necessary.

KPN Telecom offers interconnection at the transit level only. The Netherlands is divided into 20 transit interconnection areas. In each interconnection area, there is one single Point of Interconnection (PoI). At each PoI, KPN Telecom offers national access and regional access for both call termination and call origination. KPN Telecom was planning interconnection at the local level (interconnection at local exchanges) but this was excluded from the Regional Interconnection Offering in Spring 1999.[26]

Each PoI covers several area codes for telephone numbers. For example, area codes 020, 0294, 0297, 0299, 075 can be accessed from the Amsterdam PoI. Note that in any code area, all adjacent code areas are treated as local calls. This means that by carefully selecting the code areas for siting PoPs (correlating telephone codes with population figures), an entrant can access a large proportion of the Netherlands' population with a handful of PoPs—much less than the twenty (i.e., one PoP at each PoI) theoretically required for national coverage. For example, code area 079 (Zoetemeer) is

Figure 3 Key Indicators for Market Attractiveness[23]

Country	Percent of People Online	PCs per 1000	Cost to Get Online ($)	Annual Disposable Income ($)	Credit/Debit Cards per 1000
Netherlands	9%	450	40.23	14,062	21
UK	9.5%	441	46.17	15,996	100
Europe Median	6%	405	46.15	14,976	26
US	16%	580	34.87	21,928	148

[21]EIU Country Profile—Netherlands
[22]Marius Meland, Europe: The next frontier
[23]Marius Meland, Europe: The next frontier (table constructed from country data in the report)
[24]EIU Country Profile—Netherlands
[25]OPTA website, March 1999
[26]KPN website, April 1999

particularly attractive because callers from Rotterdam and Den Haag (two large population centres) are tariffed at the local rate. There are many ISPs in Zoetemeer.

Nortel Networks in the Netherlands[27]

Nortel Networks established a sales and marketing presence in the Netherlands in the late 1980s selling its Meridian PBX (Private Branch Exchange) systems to Enterprise customers. The first Carrier business was won in the early 1990s. The initial win has supported business growth—notably with new operators. Several hundred employees now work in offices near Amsterdam. The functions supported in Holland include sales, marketing, installation, maintenance and training.

All About iPoP

The iPoP Proposition

Lucia Kelley[28] who is responsible for iPoP Market Development, describes iPoP as follows: "There are four parts to the proposition: data, voice, finance and services—build and install, two years technical support, maintenance and warranty. There is an option for help with interconnect. . . . The message is: let us concentrate on the technology, you concentrate on your business."

The iPoP solution includes the CVX1800 Remote Access Server (a data product which can pass traffic to the Internet) and as Lucia Kelley says, a "feature rich voice switch." This is either the Multi-Media Carrier Switch (MMCS) or, for higher capacity, a Digital Multiplexing Switch (DMS). Several financing structures are offered—for example a 24-month lease purchase arrangement. Professional services are provided from in-country offices where possible and supplemented from one of the European hubs. Some core product information is included in Exhibit 1.

iPoP presents an opportunity for ISPs to move into lucrative voice services or for voice resellers to move into data services. Details of the services offered by iPoP, extracted from a Nortel Networks white paper are included in Exhibit 2. Note that for established telecommunications operators, voice revenues far exceed data

revenues—even though data traffic overtakes voice traffic. This is because voice revenues are now driven by high value advanced services such as voicemail.

History of iPoP

The iPoP programme evolved from another programme —"Telco in a Box"—an MMCS–only proposition targeted at new, small alternative operators (mainly switchless voice resellers). The opportunity to combine the MMCS with the data functionality of CVX1800 arose in 1998 when the Remote Access Server (RAS) entered the portfolio. According to Lucia Kelley, it was then that the revenue-generating possibility for an ISP from the regulatory structure was spotted.

Call termination revenue is normally a settlement mechanism between operators who carry calls for each other and rates are usually set by the national regulatory authority (NRA)—at least for the dominant players. Thus operators generally both pay and receive call termination revenue. The unusual feature about ISPs is that they generate a large number of call minutes but all those call minutes are destined for the Internet and will not go back into another operator's network. Thus they can receive call termination revenue but have no corresponding payment.

Lucia Kelley describes the importance of the ISPs as follows: "The ISPs are the operators of the future . . . [they] will be bought by the big guys or they'll become the big guys or they'll be content providers." On developing the iPoP solution to include services, she explains that "the ISPs don't have a voice competency"—hence they need to draw on Nortel's expertise.

In early 1999, Telinco became the lead customer in the UK for the iPoP solution. Telinco is a "leading UK-based facilities management service provider for ISPs."[29] It is operating as an ISP wholesaler to smaller ISPs and is seen as a "pioneer in the field of outsourced Internet services."[30]

The Importance of Call Termination Revenue

Call termination revenue can be important in the short term. The inclusion of a voice switch in the iPoP package means that an ISP (after a successful operator license application) can apply to interconnect to an incumbent operator—for example, BT in the UK. Nortel has already

---

[27]From discussions with the Dutch sales and business development teams—Spring 1999
[28]From interview notes—October 1999

[29]Nortel Networks—Carrier Solutions Business Case—iPoP
[30]Nortel Networks—Carrier Solutions Business Case—iPoP

conducted successful interconnect testing for all the voice switches incorporated in the iPoP solution in many countries in Europe. This brings two key benefits. Firstly, Nortel staff have experience which is valuable to the new operator in planning and conducting these complex tests between the new operator's switch and the incumbent's network. Secondly, the tests required are typically scaled down or conducted more quickly because the incumbent has interconnected with equipment of the same type on previous occasions.

Once interconnection is achieved, a new operator can receive calls to its switch because it can issue telephone numbers for end users to call. (Operators normally purchase telephone numbers in blocks from the national regulator.) The incumbent may still be billing the end user. However, the new operator is entitled to a share of the call charge billed to the end user for calls made to telephone numbers residing on the new operator's switch. This share of the call charge is known as call termination revenue or interconnect revenue. It is important for iPoP because it increases with traffic growth: the more call minutes, the more call termination revenue. In the case of traffic destined for the Internet, the number of call minutes is rising rapidly. This is not only because there are more users (Internet penetration is increasing) but also because the length of calls from each user is rising (there are more websites to explore and more online applications to use).

If the business case is favourable, the call termination revenue will at least cover the lease payments for iPoP. For each country, this revenue is dependent on a number of factors. These include:

- interconnection call termination rate per minute for each tariff band (however defined for the particular country)
- expected rate of growth or decline in interconnect tariffs (dependent on the NRA [national regulatory authority])
- average minutes per month per subscriber in each tariff band and the growth trend (dependent on national pattern and—maybe—number of free ISPs [subscribers may sign up to more than one])
- growth rate of subscribers for a particular ISP (in turn depends on Internet penetration rate and market share for a particular ISP)

It is important to note that the business case for buying a voice switch and RAS in the medium term can be made if appropriate high value services are offered. An important point about the call termination revenue is

that it allows the ISP to take a low risk step into the voice world and enjoy that revenue (given that the regulatory structure allows it).

In addition, if the interconnect revenue does indeed cover the lease payments—giving a favourable cash position for the ISP, then offering free Internet access will improve the situation further. Internet usage faces a downward sloping demand curve—i.e., if access is free (only call charges to pay) more people will use it more of the time. This means that the interconnect revenue will be even higher. From this point of view, if the case for free access can be made on the base figures, free access generates upside potential as usage increases. It is probable that this "interconnect arbitrage" will evaporate over time as incumbents and regulators amend the rules. However, the call termination revenue de-risks the move to voice services for an ISP.

It is important to note that the incumbent operator is not "losing" interconnect revenue to the ISP. Rather, the increased Internet usage is generating new call minutes on the operator's network. So the operator is "gaining" a share of new call revenue. Further, note that most voice traffic on an incumbent's network occurs during the business day (peaking mid-morning and mid-afternoon). However, residential Internet traffic typically peaks late in the evening. Thus, many of the new call minutes generated by free Internet access constitute traffic on the network when it has redundancy. New call minutes at "quiet times" on the network are very high margin minutes for the incumbent. Thus, an ISP by encouraging its subscribers to use the Internet is generating new call minutes for the backbone network, i.e., the consumer is making calls which would not otherwise have been made.

Market Testing: The Seminar Programme

In the first half of 1999, the iPoP marketing team introduced market-testing seminars in several European countries—working with the in-country teams. One purpose of these was to identify a lead customer in each country being considered for the solution. The seminar programme includes database building, telemarketing and targeted mailshots with supporting collateral as well as running the seminar event. This lead generation process is targeted primarily at non-customers of Nortel Networks. In the Netherlands an iPoP seminar was conducted in May 1999. Of the hundreds of small Dutch ISP businesses, several dozen attended the seminar. Feedback was positive. Some interesting leads were identified.

Productisation

In developing the iPoP programme, Lucia also insisted that the package be productised. She wanted the solution to be easy to buy and easy to sell. David Perry[31]—responsible for productisation—describes it as "definition of specific packages." He comments, "Nortel is used to dealing with a relatively small number of relatively large customers." Often it is appropriate to have a "bespoke way of dealing with carrier class customers" where each solution is tailor-made. However, in approaching the iPoP solution, he notes, "simplification was the goal . . . to find an optimum way of [offering the services]." It was "difficult to size the switches because there was no impedance [from the customer] . . . the customer didn't know [what traffic was expected]." David decided, "[we had to] put [ourselves] in the mind of the customer and think . . . [at first] we thought it was just a matter of answering questions but when it came to it, we weren't sure what some of the questions were . . . [The iPoP productisation] raised a lot of issues we needed to address anyway."

Productisation has included central support for the lead generation and the market testing seminars including production of collateral and regulatory monitoring. For follow up there is the provision of a portable, PC based business modelling tool and management of a lead tracking database. On the data and voice side, modular multi-line of business configurations were adopted by David Perry which enabled simple pricing structures and faster order management. To these were added a standard set of services and specific financing packages.

Competitors

"Nortel Networks principal competitors are large telecommunications equipment suppliers, such as Lucent Technologies Inc. (Lucent), Siemens AG and LM Ericsson, and data networking companies such as Cisco Systems, Inc and 3Com Corporation."[32] Key competitors for iPoP are drawn from these groups. In particular, in the Internet space Nortel Networks is one of "internetworking's new Big Three"[33] along with Cisco and Lucent.

Competitor analysis can be conducted for each element of the iPoP solution. Several competitors have data and voice products which provide the functionality required. They do not all have so comprehensive interconnection experience in Europe. However, in terms of the whole solution, iPoP is targeted at a new market. On this point, Eme Dean-Lewis estimates, "we are six months ahead of the game" relative to the other big players.

Business Case for Dutch ISP Customers

The business case for Dutch ISP customers is reviewed by considering the revenue flows before and after the deployment of iPoP (see Figures 4 and 5). Note that the iPoP revenue flows shown here apply to European markets. In the US, where local calls have traditionally been free, the economics are quite different. In the "before" case, note that the ISP's primary source of revenue is subscription and advertising revenue. Receiving calls from subscribers is a source of cost for the ISP through PRI rental. Call revenue is collected by the operator (and may be shared with an alternative operator). In the "after" case, the ISP benefits from calls made by subscribers—they are a source of revenue, not cost. Since the revenue is usage based, the ISP can consider dispensing with monthly subscriptions altogether and offering "free" Internet access; i.e., the user only pays usage based call charges.

Consider the case of Dixons, a high street consumer electronics retailer in the UK with a well-known brand. When it launched its Freeserve offering, Dixons became the largest ISP in the UK in a few weeks. It attracted hundreds of thousands of subscribers. Within a few months it had nearly a million subscribers. Many of those subscribers were new to the Internet. The Dixons' Freeserve operation generates call termination revenue which is shared between the ISP and the backbone network provider. Free dial access is a killer application for an ISP: it can change the Internet penetration rate.

The same may be true for Holland. In Spring 1999, some free access offerings existed, e.g., from CasTel in Northern Holland or "HetNet" (a Dutch Intranet service) from KPN, but their market share was small.

The question remains whether the interconnect tariffs in the Netherlands support the Business Case for iPoP. Using information from OPTA and KPN and conservatively estimated usage (500 minutes per month), Nortel Networks' business model indicates that iPoP has a payback period of one to two years for an initial subscriber base of a few tens of thousands.

---

[31]From interview notes—October 1999
[32]Nortel Networks Annual Report 1998 page 27
[33]Terry Sweeney and Tim Wilson—The state of internetworking—users resist one-stop shops

Figure 4 Typical ISP Dial Access Revenue Flows (without iPoP)[34]

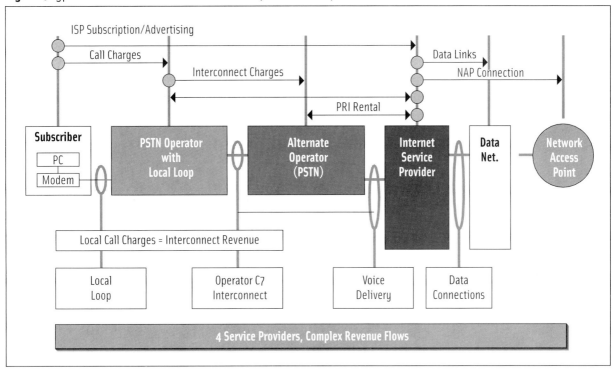

Figure 5 Primary Revenue Flows for Dial-in Access (with iPoP)[35]

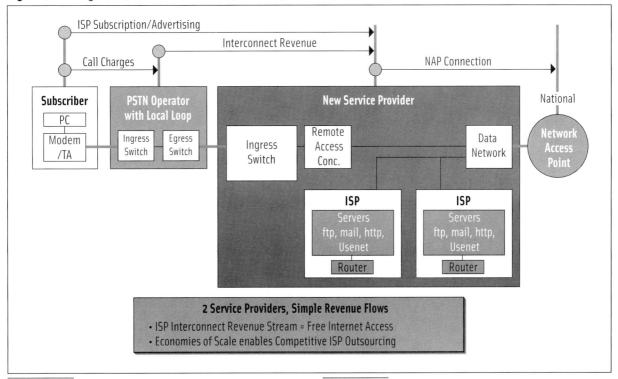

[34]Nortel Networks—White Paper—iPoP   [35]Nortel Networks—White Paper—iPoP

The typical Dutch Internet user is online 3 days per week, spending an average of 56 minutes online.[36] Also, the growth in eCommerce is an additional source of revenue not included in the base case model. A parameter exists to include the upside potential flow of a commission charge per transaction made. Importantly, eCommerce is predicted to increase in the Netherlands. "An estimated 170,000 people reported having bought . . . something online [during the two-week survey] . . . up from 82,000 . . . five months previously."[37]

Thirdly, the model takes no account of the positive effect of Freeserve on demand. So the fact that the market will grow more quickly as a result of launching Freeserve is understated.

Fourthly, while OPTA may move to change the interconnect tariffs eventually, they have no plans to do so at the moment. Regulators do not usually change their approach in weeks or months. Thus, any closing of the window of opportunity for iPoP would be signalled by NRAs well in advance.

In short, the business case to invest in iPoP for an ISP with only a few tens of thousand subscribers is supported in the Netherlands. For larger ISPs the initial investment may be greater but the payback period is in the same range.

Conclusion

As Eme Dean-Lewis reviewed the iPOP innovation, she thought about the future road map for the product. What should be Nortel Networks' position for iPoP in the Netherlands and other European markets? What competitive response should Nortel Networks expect in the Dutch and other European markets? What should their counter move be? What should be the future changes, if any, in the iPOP product? How should those changes be affected by developments in the regulatory environment, evolution of the market and the target customers? Are there other markets that can be tapped with the iPOP product? If so, how?

---

[36]Pro Active—2.3 Million Dutch Users Online in March 1999
[37]Pro Active—2.3 Million Dutch Users Online in March 1999

Exhibit 1 Core Data and Voice Product Information

The CVX 1800 Remote Access Switch

The CVX 1800 (Figure [1]) is a Carrier Grade Access Switch. In a comparative Remote Access Server (RAS) test[38] between the competing products, the CVX 1800 had the best availability—"the only RAS to approach 99 percent uptime." It was also the "most reliable" server—completing 98.8% of calls. In addition, the CVX 1800 was best for "connect speed consistency" ("a high number of calls completed at 49.3kBit/s"). Connect Speed is the factor which most affects users' perception of an ISP. As the ISP market segment becomes more competitive, quality of service provided will increasingly become a differentiator.

Figure [1]: Nortel Networks CVX 1800 Access Switch[39]

Starting at around a hundred thousand dollars (for 96 ports) the CVX 1800 is scaleable up to 1152 ports and so ties investment to successful business growth.

---

[38]David Newman—Monster RASs: Growing pains
[39]CVX1800 Access Switch—Nortel Networks Data Sheet, 1999

The MMCS (Multi-Media Carrier Switch)

The MMCS (Figure [2]) has been developed from Nortel Networks' PBX (Private Branch Exchange) family (Meridian) as an entry-level product with multiple features. It has the reliability of Nortel Networks' carrier switches designed in and has many voice services supplied "as standard." A key benefit of the MMCS is its price point. Starting at a few hundred thousand dollars, it lowers the capital investment barrier to entry normally enjoyed by incumbent operators. Its lowest price is comparable with the most expensive PC based "soft switch" solutions. This makes it an attractive option for experienced voice resellers who want to grow their business.

In Europe, the MMCS was packaged for start-up operators as 'Telco in a Box'. It is a single box entry product for a new operator. For a larger operator, the DMS-100 Small Exchange is better suited.

Figure [2]: The Nortel Networks Multi Media Carrier Switch[40]

The DMS (Digital Multiplexing Switch) Family[41]

The DMS family is deployed by major network operators worldwide. The DMS-100 Small Exchange is a specially developed small version of the DMS-100 platform. It comes in three package sizes—SX32, SX64 and SX96. For operators planning for higher traffic levels, the DMS-100 Small Exchange offers a route into high traffic switching. It is upgradeable to larger DMS configurations. Thus investment is protected. Starting at around a million dollars, the DMS-100 Small Exchange is the most cost efficient way to invest capital as traffic grows.

[40]MMCS Point of Presence—Nortel Networks Data Sheet 1999
[41]DMS Family—Nortel Networks Data Sheets 1997, 1999

Exhibit 2 Extract from Nortel Networks White Paper, iPoP: Free Internet Access Solutions with
Unified Networks, 1999[42]

New Service Provider Services

Today iPOP delivers the following services:

- **SS7 & Interconnect**: Essential to the revenue sharing proposition and key to the incumbent PTT [acceptance] is the use of proven and tested platforms from reliable equipment manufacturers like Nortel Networks.

- **Modem Wholesaling**: Allows the sale of virtual ports. These are no longer physically allocated to a customer. Allocations are made on a call by call basis with decisions based on sophisticated rules in a central database.

- **Virtual PoPs & Virtual Routers**: Virtual iPoP allows operators to partition the iPoP system into a series of mutually independent iPoP servers, each of which has its own authentication method, database, billing system, and management interface. This is ideal for wholesaling Internet access and outsourcing corporate remote access.

- **Voice Services**: Indirect Access, CLI [Calling Line Identification] Screening, [Authorisation] Code, VPN [Virtual Private Networks], Calling Card, Number Translation (Premium/Freephone), Least Cost Routing.

- **Unified Voice & Data Billing**: One stop shopping for users.

- **VoIP**: iPoP can perform direct and indirect telephony over IP, effectively acting as an integrated gateway and gatekeeper to perform VoIP toll bypass.

---

[42]Nortel Networks—White Paper—iPoP

References

Borland, J; Bells stumble over broadband AOL, 11 March 1999, CNET News.com (from *www.mews.com*)

Boston, W; For Europe's telecom titans, it's now or never on the Net, 15 March 1999—*Wall Street Journal Europe* (Bonn)

Economist Intelligence Unit, Netherlands Country Profile 1997–98

Forbes Digital Tool; How does Europe stack up on the Internet? A country by country ranking. 29 March 1999 (from *www.forbes.com*)

Harriet, J, and Scopel, C; All Providers Sector Opportunity Pack—Customer Value Research 05 March 1999—Nortel Networks Internal Document

Intelligent Network News; Packet service over cable—a regulatory no-mans land, 12 May 1999

Medford C; Roscitt converses about convergence—the president and CEO of AT&T Solutions gives IP a thumbs-up, 10 May 1999, *VARBusiness*

Meland, M; Europe: The next frontier, Forbes Digital Tool 29 March 1999 (from *www.forbes.com*)

Moore, G A; *Crossing the Chasm*, 1998, Harper Collins

Newman, D; Monster RASs: Growing pains, 21 April 1999, DataCommmunications (from *www.data.com*)

Nortel Networks; Annual Report 1998

Nortel Networks; CVX 1800 Access Switch—Nortel Networks Data Sheet, 1999

Nortel Networks; DMS Family—Nortel Networks Data Sheets, 1997, 1999

Nortel Networks; Carrier Solutions Business Case—iPoP transforming Telinco's business, 1999

Nortel Networks; White Paper—iPoP: Free Internet Access Solutions with Unified Networks, 1999

Nortel Networks; MMCS Point of Presence—Nortel Networks Data Sheet, 1999

OPTA website—*www.opta.nl*

Pro Active—2.3 Million Dutch Users Online in March 1999 (from *www.proactive.nl*)

Roth, J; The importance of time—Internal Employee Bulletin, May 1999

Roth, J; Internal Memorandum, Spring 1998

Sweeney T and Wilson T; The state of internetworking —users resist one stop shops, 10 May 1999, *InternetWeek*

Telegeography Inc 1996,1997,1998 Largest Telecommunications Routes (from *www.telegeography.com*)

Telegeography Inc 1998—Internet hosts by economy 1993–1997 (from *www.telegeography.com*)

Telegeography Inc 1999—Indicators (from *www.telegeography.com*)

Wallace, D J, Changes in phone service are mixing up Net issues in Europe, 09 April 1999, *New York Times*

The argument for the importance of developing an ISP customer base was strong in each European country. However, some countries, such as Ireland and Austria, had an unfavourable regulatory environment and were therefore excluded from the testing programme.

MINDSPRING

We want to build a truly great company. Our vision of what the company should be like is expressed by the MindSpring Core Values and Beliefs. We want to change the way the world does business by demonstrating that a company based on integrity and respect for the individual can do an outstanding job of serving its customers, providing meaningful work for its employees, delivering a favorable return to its owners, and being a force for good in its community.
—Letter to Stockholders,
MindSpring 1997 Annual Report

As the mild winter day in Atlanta, Georgia, neared a close in December 1999, Charles Brewer, MindSpring's 40-year-old CEO and founder, sat back in his office chair and reflected upon his company's achievements since its founding in Spring of 1994 and thought about the challenges which laid ahead, especially with its proposed merger with EarthLink Network, Inc., the nation's fifth largest Internet Service Provider (ISP), that was announced just three months earlier and which was scheduled to be completed by early 2000. While his dog, Louis, who often accompanied Brewer to work, slept untroubled on a plastic lawn chair nearby, Brewer took satisfaction in knowing that the five-year-old Mind-Spring by itself, was now the sixth largest ISP—with over one million subscribers—and was just recognized by the firm of J.D. Powers & Associates as being the leading ISP in the area of customer satisfaction. While the jury was still out on whether MindSpring had changed the way the world did business, Brewer felt confident the company had changed the way the world viewed ISPs.

In a business that many Wall Street analysts had called increasingly commodity-like—especially with the emergence of several ISPs during 1999 which offered free subscriptions—MindSpring's strategy was to build its paid subscriber base by focusing on providing outstanding customer service. MindSpring provided easy-to-use start-up software to its customers, built and maintained its own network of local modems and routers (points-of-presence, or POPs), and made customer retention a priority. As of December 1999, the company offered local Internet access in some 800 locations nationwide. Through its dial-up service, subscribers could browse the World Wide Web, send electronic mail, participate in online chats, use MindSpring's servers to host their own home pages, and access over 20,000 newsgroups. Mind-Spring also provided Web design and hosting for small businesses. At the same time, the company aggressively sought to control costs. In many ways, MindSpring's strategy mirrored its culture, which stressed values like frugality and fun.

By all accounts, MindSpring's strategy had paid off. In the fourth quarter 1997, MindSpring became the first national ISP to record a quarterly profit (see Exhibit 1 for company financial data. Its annual revenue had risen 632% from 1996 to 1998, and its subscriber base had grown from 13,000 in 1995 to over 1 million by the third quarter of 1999, an increase primarily accomplished through customer referrals, word-of-mouth and acquisitions. MindSpring had graduated from regional to national ISP status, as it now offered service throughout the United States. And the company had won numerous accolades for outstanding service. In addition to being recognized by J.D. Powers, MindSpring had also received *PC World* magazine's prestigious "World Class Award" in July 1998 as the best ISP in the United States.

Brewer knew that it was important to maintain momentum. The number of Internet users in the U.S. was projected to grow from 20% to 25% annually over the succeeding five years,[1] and it was important for the new EarthLink/MindSpring company to capture as many of those newcomers as possible. The industry, though fragmented, was dominated by America Online (AOL)—which had 17.9 million subscribers at the end of the third quarter of 1999—and many analysts were predicting a shakeout. With the completion of the proposed merger of EarthLink and MindSpring, the new Earth-Link/MindSpring company would have almost 3 million subscribers—leapfrogging ahead of Compuserve, the

Joe Keough, MBA '98 and Research Associate Cathy Olofson prepared this case under the supervision of Professor Jeffrey F. Rayport as the basis for class discussion rather than to illustrate either effective or ineffective handling of an administrative situation.

---

[1]Forrester Research, Inc.

Microsoft Network (MSN), and AT&T as the second largest ISP.

The issue of growth—how to achieve it, and with what trade-offs—and how to merge the cultures of the two companies had raised a number of strategic and tactical questions. Should the new EarthLink/MindSpring company make significant marketing investments to acquire new customers and build its brand—even at the risk of reduced or negative profitability? Internal brand awareness surveys at both EarthLink and Mindspring had showed that prior to the proposed merger, neither company had better than 10% brand awareness whereas AOL had 80% brand awareness.[2] Should the company modify its pricing structure, especially with the inroads made by ISPs that were now offering free subscriptions? One such ISP, NetZero, had gained over 1.5 million subscribers in less than a year by adopting this pricing strategy. And was the company's customer-service model scalable to 3 million, 5 million, or even 10 million subscribers? As a public company, the new EarthLink/MindSpring company would continue to face earnings-per-share pressures on a quarterly basis, and continued revenue growth was important. Should it provide more ancillary services like Web hosting and telephony as a way to augment revenues? Meanwhile, the cable-TV companies and regional Bell operating companies (RBOCs) were making substantial investments in high-speed access technologies like broadband using cable modems and digital subscriber lines (DSL), respectively. Would traditional ISPs be left out in the cold when these technologies took off?

A Brief History of MindSpring

After receiving his MBA from Stanford in 1987, Charles Brewer moved to Atlanta looking for a company that he could buy or start. He worked for a short time as a venture capitalist at Sanders & Company. In 1989, he joined AudioFax, a fax technology company, where he was the CFO and later CEO. He resigned in 1993, dissatisfied with the company culture. Instead of taking another job, he began thinking about starting his own company. He wasn't sure what the business would do or what industry it would be in; but he did know how the business would be run. He formalized his company vision by writing "Core Values and Beliefs," a manifesto that espoused respect, fun, and integrity in the workplace

(see Exhibit 2). When he read the statement to Mike McQuary, his friend and later MindSpring's COO, Mike asked, "Sounds good, but what does this company do?" "Don't bother me with details," Brewer responded, "I'm on a roll."

In early 1994, Brewer found his opportunity. Following an unpleasant first-time experience on the Internet—after spending several days trying to get connected due to limited customer start-up documentation and unresponsive technical support—Brewer immediately realized the need for a user-friendly ISP that could be built on four key customer service elements: a software package that installed easily and configured itself; a graphical front-end that made the software easy to use; a technical support staff that was accessible, friendly, and competent; and a reliable connection. Working out of his Atlanta apartment, Brewer enlisted the services of a software developer to design the graphical interface that he wanted for MindSpring. For the first five months, the enterprise was virtually a one-man show. Brewer was working 18-hour days and decided it was time to get some support. In June 1994, employee number two, Robert Sanders, a 20-year-old Georgia Tech dropout, was hired to provide the technical support and to build the network. (Sanders would later become chief technology officer—see Exhibit 3 for profiles of key MindSpring executives). Initial users loved the service and provided ideas for improving the interface. Word quickly spread about MindSpring's focus on service and support. By the end of summer 1994, MindSpring had a few hundred paying customers.

In November 1994, ITC Holding Company, Inc., was brought on board as a major investor. ITC had helped finance several telecommunications companies, including Powertel, which provided cellular phone services in the Southeast. With ITC's significant investment, MindSpring was able to build local POPs in areas around the southeastern United States. ITC recently held a 20% interest in MindSpring and had two of its officers on the MindSpring board.

In March 1996, MindSpring (NASDAQ: MSPG) became a public company. Since its IPO, which raised $32 million, the company had used the public equity markets to fund growth, including secondary offerings in 1998 that raised an additional $170 million. But the company was wary of relying too heavily on the capital markets. Michael McQuary, MindSpring's COO, believed that real earnings growth, through increased revenues from subscribers, was the key to the company's long-term health and sustainability. By the spring of 1999, MindSpring's stock price had risen dramatically to an all-time high of

[2]Elinor Abreu and Jason K. Krause, "David's Team Up to Take on Goliath," *Industry Standard*, October 4, 1999.

$66.50 per share, adjusted for splits. As of December 1999, MindSpring had over 1.1 million customers and 1,790 employees.[3]

The Merger with EarthLink

Founded in July 1994 by Sky Dayton, EarthLink was a pure Internet service provider (ISP) with approximately 1.5 million subscribers at the end of September 1999. Like MindSpring, EarthLink claimed to offer simple, efficient, and effective access to the Internet, offering easy-to-install software and 24-hour toll-free customer service. It had received several industry awards, including *PC Magazine*'s Editors' Choice for best ISP in 1997, and its customer satisfaction ratings in a 1999 J.D. Powers & Associates survey were second only to those of MindSpring (See Exhibit 4 for customer satisfaction survey results).

EarthLink had historically spent more on marketing than MindSpring both on an absolute dollar basis and as a percentage of sales. (See Exhibit 5 for EarthLink financial data.) Its marketing campaign included affinity marketing programs with companies like Sony, aggressive radio and newspaper advertising, and a referral program, which offered one free month of service to current customers for each customer referral. Approximately 40% of gross subscriber additions came from affinity programs, 35% from advertising, and 25% from customer referrals.[4]

EarthLink started as a regional provider, offering service in California through its own network of POPs. As the company expanded nationally, it began leasing POPs from third-party providers like UUNET Technologies, Inc., a subsidiary of WorldCom Inc., and PSINet Inc. EarthLink's leasing strategy decapitalized the intense infrastructure requirements and mitigated associated capital expenditures of ownership; the cost of operating, maintaining, and upgrading the network fell to the third-party provider. EarthLink also believed that the risk of technological obsolescence associated with owning an extensive network of POPs was too high, given the potential of cable modems and DSL.

In February 1998, EarthLink and Sprint announced an agreement to create a single, unified Internet service called EarthLink Sprint. The deal provided EarthLink with $24 million in cash, a $100 million credit line, approximately 130,000 new members (those previously signed up on Sprint's Internet service), as well as

commitments from Sprint to deliver a minimum of 750,000 new members to EarthLink over the next five years. Sprint acquired a 28% minority interest in Earth-Link and two seats on its board.

Upon completion of the EarthLink and MindSpring merger in early 2000, the new company's headquarters would be based in Atlanta and the company would take the EarthLink name. MindSpring founder Brewer would be the chairman of the new company, while EarthLink CEO and chief executive Charles Betty would be its chief executive. McQuary, MindSpring's president, would be the new company's president.[5]

Analysts saw the new combined company, with its focus on service, as a viable alternative to America Online. The new EarthLink company, noted Joan Barter Kline, director of research in the telecommunication services sector at J.D. Powers & Associates, "will be a strong player to counter America Online."[6]

The Consumer Online Industry

The consumer online industry included a variety of local, regional, and national companies serving the mass market of individuals who used modem-equipped personal computers to connect to the Internet. Within the consumer online industry, there were predominately two types of companies—online service providers (OSPs) and Internet service providers (ISPs). (This distinction was fading, though, as features were slowly converging.) OSPs like AOL sold bundled services of software, content, and local access lines. Their subscribers could access the Internet but were required first to go to the company's proprietary start page, which supplied a variety of exclusive content. Most ISPs, on the other hand, offered direct access to the Internet. Subscribers could select any Web site as their home or start page when they connected to the Internet. Some ISPs, including MindSpring, provided links to search engines such as GoTo.com, Yahoo!, Excite, and Go Network on their home pages, but few offered exclusive or original content.

Online providers generated revenue by charging access fees to customers. Typically, they offered different levels of service at different price points. For example, MindSpring offered service ranging from the Light plan, which included five hours of service for $6.95 per month, to the Unlimited plan, which offered unlimited

[3]MindSpring press release, December 1999.
[4]Everen Securities' estimates.

[5]Elinor Abreu and Jason K. Krause, "David's Team up to Take Goliath," *Industry Standard*, October 4, 1999.
[6]Elinor Abreu and Jason K. Krause, "David's Team up to Take Goliath," *Industry Standard*, October 4, 1999.

access for $19.95 per month. Standard services included Web server space for home pages, e-mail, a Web browser, online chat groups, and newsgroups.

Increasingly, ISPs and OSPs were looking to generate additional sources of revenue from e-commerce, advertising, and Web hosting. Web-hosting services encompassed Web site development and monitoring services for businesses. Typically, an online provider would design the Web site, drive traffic to the site through its home page, and evaluate the site by providing detailed reports regarding the numbers of hits, sources of hits, and so on. Web hosting was considered by many to be a high-margin, high-growth business, because it leveraged the existing dial-up infrastructure. Increasingly, ISPs sought to differentiate themselves by offering more features than competitors—multiple e-mail accounts, more server space for home pages—and by providing higher quality customer service.

Customer service had long been the ISPs' weakest link. Long wait times, busy signals, and network down time were common complaints, though throughout 1998 customer surveys across the industry indicated that satisfaction was improving. ISPs typically allocated 20% to 30% of their costs to customer service. Unlike Mind-Spring, which kept its support and service operations in-house, most national ISPs outsourced their customer service activities. Local ISPs provided in-house support but usually limited calls to day-time hours. (See Exhibit 6 for a summary of ISP service offerings and rates.)

Network Connectivity: The Back Office Operations of an Online Provider

Dial-up ISPs used a common set of networking technologies and processes to enable subscribers to connect to the Internet. Subscribers typically dialed into a point-of-presence (POP), a collection of modems, digital lines, and routers operated locally. Most ISPs had POPs in each geographical market, allowing subscribers to use a local (and therefore toll-free) number to connect. The POP routed traffic from the local modems to the ISPs' servers, high-end computers that stored user e-mail, news, and proprietary content. For connections to the broader Internet, routers directed data packets to "national backbone" providers, which operated huge networks capable of hosting thousands of Web sites and sending massive amounts of data quickly.

ISPs and OSPs could either lease POP network capacity from third parties or build and own their network of POPs. Building and owning POPs included the following steps:[7]

1. Purchasing or leasing a rack of modems and a router from a supplier (3COM or Cisco, for example).

2. Rented a location for the modems, typically in a facility of a long-distance phone company or a competitive local-exchange carrier.

3. Installing local phone, or ports, enabling users to connect to the service via a local phone number. The number of phone lines required was a function of the number of users in a particular area.

4. Leasing a dedicated line, typically a T1, from a long-distance company. The T1 was a high-speed line that transmitted data from the local POP to the company's servers.

5. Selecting a national backbone provider for wider access to the Internet. Backbone providers included WorldCom, IBM, GTE, and Intermedia Communications.

If an ISP opted to lease POP network service, third-party providers, including PSINet, WorldCom, or GTE, would perform steps one through five.

Connection Technologies

In 1997, 22.9 million online accounts used dial-up technologies. About 100,000 accounts used cable modems, and about the same number used ISDN lines or wireless connections. Most dial-up providers were upgrading from 28.8 to 56 kilobytes-per-second (Kbps) modems. By year-end 1997, approximately 92% of local ISPs and 70% of national ISPs had upgraded their POPs to 56 Kbps.[8]

Still, many analysts argued that if the Internet were to achieve widespread acceptance, faster access would have to become available to the mass market at a fair price. From 1997 through 1999, the largest cable companies were making billion dollar investments to rebuild their systems to handle digital traffic so they would be able to provide telephone service and Internet access. Cable's broadband infrastructure would eventually allow high-speed Internet access up to 100 times faster than a 28.8 Kbps dial-up modem.

[7]Everen Securities.
[8]Forrester Research, Inc.

Telephone companies were experimenting with digital subscriber line (DSL) technology, a new modem technology that converted existing telephone lines into access paths for multimedia and high-speed data communications. DSL was expected to accelerate the rate at which data could travel across "twisted pair" copper phone lines. With DSL, data could be delivered to a user at home at 1.5 megabits per second (Mbps), 30 times faster than a 56 Kbps modem. DSL would also enable users to receive voice and data simultaneously, allowing home offices and small businesses to leave computers plugged into the Net without interrupting phone connections. Despite the obvious attractions of DSL, the service was still considered expensive to deliver—carriers had to send out technicians in trucks to install equipment; moreover, many experts considered the technology unproven.

Despite the cable companies' slow start on broadband, and the uncertain feasibility of DSL for the RBOCs, many analysts predicted that total broadband access, including cable modems and DSL, would take off in the next few years, commanding as much as 26% of the online market by 2002.[9]

Brewer worried that MindSpring would have trouble getting access to this new technology. Cable companies were not common carriers and thus did not face regulatory pressure to allow competitive access to their network. In theory, incumbent local-exchange carriers had to allow access to their distribution infrastructure. However, many had been hesitant to make large, widespread investments in DSL, given questions regarding its viability. In addition, the Baby Bells were lobbying Congress to free high-speed pipes from regulation and hence shut off access to competitors.

Competition

By 1999, approximately 54 million individuals in the United States were online.[10] Given the expanding market, many big and small competitors were rushing to enter the business. All of the local and long-distance telephone companies were establishing a presence in the online industry, and Microsoft had aggressively entered the market with its MSN service. (See Exhibit 7 for the major online access providers' market share.)

America Online. AOL was the world's leading online service, with 17.9 million subscribers as of October 1999. In 1997, AOL had acquired a competitor, CompuServe, and added approximately 2.5 million subscribers. AOL's business model was focused on leveraging subscriber relationships by selling a variety of products and services. A significant source of revenue came from advertising. As its scale continued to grow, AOL was attempting to develop content to attract a mass audience so that it could compete with TV networks for advertising revenue. In 1997, AOL had on average 400,000 simultaneous "prime-time" users. This audience size was competitive with quarterly-hour TV audiences for MTV and CNN.[11] AOL was also forging e-commerce relationships with a growing number of companies as a way to generate additional revenue. Companies like Amazon.com, Intuit, Monster.com, and 1-800 Flowers paid fees for promotion on AOL's service and sites and for purchases made by AOL subscribers.

In 1998, AOL acquired NetChannel, a struggling Web-based television company. NetChannel, which had 10,000 subscribers at the time of the purchase, provided Internet access via cable to television viewers through TV "set-top" boxes. AOL was expected to use NetChannel's technology and programming experience to develop and deliver branded interactive content, which many analysts forecasted would be increasingly in demand as broadband technology became available to the mass market. In early 1998, AOL announced that it would undertake, with GTE Internetworking, commercial trials of DSL technology. The service was to be offered in five markets: Washington, D.C.; San Francisco, CA; Richmond, VA; Phoenix, AZ; and Birmingham, AL.

MSN. Microsoft's MSN service was the number two ISP in the nation. It had the ability to leverage its relationships with millions of Windows users. Like AOL, the company's value proposition was ease-of-use and ease-of-access, along with exclusive branded content. Microsoft was also positioned to leverage its technology assets: it had its own browser, had investments in cable, and owned Web TV, a service which allowed consumers to access the Internet using television sets. As 1998 progressed, MSN was shedding some of its proprietary content and moving toward streamlined ISP features. The company had in its early days received poor marks for customer service, but its service in recent months had improved dramatically.

[9]Forrester Research, Inc.
[10]U.S. Department of Commerce and e-stats; *The New York Times Almanac*, 2000.
[11]Sourced from AOL's 1997 Annual Report.

NetZero. Calling themselves the "Defenders of the Free World," NetZero was launched in October 1998. The company provided consumers with free and easy access to the Internet while offering advertisers a highly effective way to target those users. Subscribers to NetZero provide basic demographic and geographic information with data on their hobbies and interests. This information enabled NetZero to build a personal profile that was unique to the user and to customize the information that users saw in their advertising window throughout the entire time they were online.[12]

Other Competitors. There were a number of other large, cash-rich players in the online industry. They included the RBOCs, as well as long-distance carriers AT&T, Sprint, and MCI/WorldCom. In addition, there were more than 3,000 small local ISPs offering service, many of which were profitable.

The RBOCs and the long-distance carriers were able to bundle communications services (a combination of local, long-distance, cellular, and Internet access), which simplified access and billing for customers. Though slow to establish Internet service, the RBOCs had the advantage of strong brand awareness among its telephone service customers. As of mid-1998, the phone companies had experienced only moderate success in signing up ISP customers.

Cable companies had recently spent considerable sums upgrading their infrastructure and were poised to enter the Internet access market aggressively. Companies like Media One and @Home Network, a consortium of cable companies, promised not only faster access but the potential for richer content. @Home offered high-speed Internet access and content services; it claimed connection speeds up to 100 times faster than a 28.8 dial-up modem. As of September 1999, @Home had 840,000 subscribers. Through agreements with various cable companies, @Home had exclusive access to 67 million American households through the year 2002. However, only 6 million of those households were wired for @Home access.

In addition, other companies providing free Internet access were emerging. @bigger.net, K-mart's BlueLight.-com, and other free ISP providers sought to draw revenues exclusively from advertising. This model had not yet proven itself, and many free ISP providers had already closed their doors. McQuary observed, "Once a year somebody offers a free service, and then they go bankrupt just in time for the next guy to try it."[13]

The MindSpring Model

MindSpring's strategic service vision consisted of identifying a target market segment, developing an operating strategy to support the service concept, and designing an efficient service delivery system to support the operating strategy.[14]

Target Market and Service Concept

MindSpring defined its target market as predominantly male (60%), ranging in age from 18 to 49, already using another online provider, and with a median income ranging from $25,000 to $75,000. About 83% of MindSpring customers defected from another ISP, usually because they experienced service problems like busy signals, failed connections, poor technical support, or slow transmission.[15] MindSpring's value proposition—Internet access that was easy to install, easy to use, and easy to fix—aimed to meet the needs of this market more effectively than its competitors.

Operating Strategy

MindSpring's operating strategy allowed for the maximization of "the difference between the value of the service to customers (service concept) and the cost (operating strategy and service delivery system) of providing it."[16] The maximization of this difference was positive cash flow (EBITDA) and bottom-line profitability. Elements of the operating strategy included the company's Core Values and Beliefs, a highly reliable network infrastructure, and a simple, low-cost marketing strategy.

Core Values and Beliefs

MindSpring's Core Value and Beliefs statement was the company's Constitution. Employees often referred to the

---

[13]Elinor Abreu and Jason K. Krause, "David's Team up to Take Goliath," *Industry Standard*, October 4, 1999.
[14]The strategic service vision was developed by Harvard Business School Professor James L. Heskett in "Lessons in the Service Sector," *Harvard Business Review*, No. 87206.
[15]This information was sourced from MindSpring customer surveys.
[16]Heskett, "Lessons in the Service Sector," op. cit.

---

[12]NetZero press release, 1999.

statement when they were debating company policies or strategic direction. As John Bushfield, vice president of human resources, put it:

> Our Core Values and Beliefs are the driving force of the company. People like to know that they are working for a company with good intentions and character. The values are embedded in our culture, in everything that we do. We believe that the result of having this strong culture is superior performance from our employees.

Owning and Operating POPs

As MindSpring expanded beyond the Southeast and became a national player in the United States, it relied on third-party providers for its infrastructure. After problems with respect to quality and control, MindSpring decided to build, own, and operate its own network of POPs. By May 1998, approximately 77% of MindSpring subscribers were calling into company-owned POPs. (See Exhibit 8 for an economic analysis of owning and operating a POP.)

In areas where it was economically feasible to own a POP (that is, where the cost per user to own was less than the cost per user to lease), MindSpring believed it was able to offer better service at a lower cost. Third-party providers charged MindSpring approximately $9 to $11 per month per subscriber to use their POP networks. In areas with a significant subscriber base, the cost was as low as $6 per subscriber per month on company-owned POPs. Since the investment was modular, modems could be added and subtracted as needed, and the latest technology and fastest modems could be installed as they became available. When there was a problem with the network, company employees repaired the problem. As former CFO Michael Misikoff reasoned, "If you own something as opposed to renting it, there is a better chance that you will take care of it."

Marketing Strategy and Customer Acquisitions

MindSpring's customer acquisition costs were among the lowest in the industry. On average, MindSpring spent $36 in marketing costs per customer addition, compared to the industry average of $100 and EarthLink's average of $44.[17] MindSpring relied heavily on inexpensive mar-

keting methods like word-of-mouth and direct referrals, though the company also increasingly used advertising as well as bundling or original equipment manufacturer (OEM) agreements.

In 1997, approximately 45% of new MindSpring customers were acquired through word-of-mouth and referral programs; advertising accounted for another 45% of gross additions. All national marketing was handled by a PR firm that marketed MindSpring in industry trade magazines. Regionally, MindSpring advertised in local newspapers and on the radio. To support the advertising campaigns, MindSpring hired a territory manager in each key city, who performed a number of grass-roots marketing activities, including negotiating media trades, visiting radio stations, making presentations in the community, and so on. The remaining 10% of customer acquisitions in 1997 came from software bundling and OEM deals. MindSpring's partners in these programs included US Robotics, Sierra Online, Cybermedia, and Blizzard Software.

In the Fall of 1999, MindSpring launched its first nationwide television in 12 markets to build its brand. The television ads campaign, designed by the advertising agency of Fallon McElligot in New York City, featured "The MindSpring Guy"—sort of a Forrest Gump-like character—who expresses his feeling about using the ISP service to a passerby in a park. Lance Weatherby, executive vice president of sales and marketing, explained the rationale:

> This advertising campaign and accelerated marketing plans is designed to grow our subscriber base quickly and efficiently over the next four quarters and build brand-awareness. MindSpring's new TV spots present our brand attributes in an engaging and entertaining way that appeals to both first-time Internet users and those already online.[18]

Since its inception, MindSpring had also used acquisitions to grow its subscription base. In February 1999, the company completed a $245 million acquisition of Net Com, a major ISP, with over 371,000 individual Internet access accounts, 22,000 Web hosting accounts, and 3,000 Internet access accounts, for both cash and stock. Two years earlier, in 1997, MindSpring had gained more than 7,500 customers by acquiring several small, local ISPs such as Terra-Link, in New York, and Spyderbyte, in Greensboro and Winston-Salem, North Carolina.

---

[17]MindSpring estimates.

[18]MindSpring press release, September 6, 1999.

Service Delivery System

Customer and technical support is often the Achilles' heel of online providers. We believe it is a source of competitive advantage.
—Greg Stromberg, executive vice president of MindSpring Biz and former executive vice president, Call Centers

MindSpring's service delivery system was consistent with its operating strategy. The delivery system included an easy-to-use software and interface program; internal technical and customer support; and a state-of-art internal customer service database system.

MindSpring Software and Start Page

After signing up for MindSpring service, a customer received a floppy disk or CD-ROM software package in the mail. The start-up package listed the user's temporary password and included a comprehensive instruction manual for getting started. Installation was straightforward; on-screen cues walked the new customer through the process. Once installed, the MindSpring screen interface was simple and intuitive; clearly marked windows made it easy to find and run a Web browser, check e-mail, search the Web, find answers to technical questions, and so on.

MindSpring's Web site (*www.MindSpring.com* or *www.MindSpring.net*) was positioned as a good starting point for subscribers. (See Exhibits 9 and 10 for screen shots of the MindSpring Web site.) It featured information on the company's various subscription packages, technical advice and updates, and real-time customer service information, like current wait times to talk to call center representatives. The start page also featured news headlines and organized links to third-party online content providers like the *New York Times*, ESPN, the Weather Channel, and Nickelodeon. Users could read short news summaries and site descriptions, and, if interested, click on a link to go to the content provider's Web site. MindSpring had several revenue-sharing agreements with its content partners and advertisers, whereby it received a small fee for each user who linked to a partner's site and viewed a banner ad. This was not a significant source of revenue, though; in 1998 it accounted for just less than 1% of total MindSpring revenues.

---

[19]*Industry Standard* (*www. Thestandard.com*), "EarthLink Moves Up to Number Two," October 1999.
[20]E-mail correspondence with casewriter.

Call Centers and Technical Support

The customer and technical support functions of online providers were notoriously difficult to manage. Most employees found answering phone calls for 8 to 10 hours a day tedious, and few stayed in support positions for long. MindSpring, however, had generally experienced low employee turnover and, in its opinion, high-quality results. Wait times in the fourth quarter of 1997 averaged only three minutes. In general, customers had been extremely satisfied with MindSpring's customer service and technical support. *PC World* magazine agreed, naming MindSpring the ISP with the best customer support in 1997. Front-end support, to reduce the number of connect time problems—according to industry surveys, 81% of users switch ISPs for this single reason[19]—was managed by Technical Support. Frederique Delius P. de Reuss, a network management engineer who supervised MindSpring's technical support area in Atlanta, commented:

> My job is to monitor and maintain the MindSpring Network. That includes all machine rooms that we currently run nationwide. I want to insure that users all over the country can log on, receive e-mail, and browse the Web 24 hrs, 7 days a week. We isolate and in most cases repair the problems. If we are not able to repair problems from our desk, such as hardware swaps, we handle the dispatch of contractors to the sites.[20]

MindSpring had struggled with customer support in its early days. When Stromberg became vice president of technical support in October 1995, MindSpring's then-7,000 customers were being supported by 10 full-time sales-desk employees and 20 full-time technical- and customer-support employees. (Of these 30 employees, 12 had started just the week before Stromberg arrived). An inadequate phone system failed to produce call reports, the call-tracking system was rudimentary at best, and there was no training program for new employees. Call wait times were high (typically more than 20 minutes), customers were angry, and employees felt overwhelmed. Stromberg was spending over 50% of his time dealing with customer complaints.

In 1996, Stromberg consolidated MindSpring's call center operations—located in a former West Peachtree Street office building (see Exhibit 11) where IBM once housed a giant mainframe system but abandoned 15 years earlier—and created three departments: sales desk, customer service, and technical support. All three departments handled customer phone calls and e-mails. The sales desk handled in-bound sales inquiries and signed up new customers. Customer service handled non-technical questions, including billing questions, account changes, and general interest questions about MindSpring. Technical support handled questions related to software installation, network connectivity, and software applications.

Another department, Electronic Services, provided the call centers with up-to-the-minute internal technical information. Electronic Services also created the help and support documentation designed for customers. By providing as much comprehensive and clear information directly to customers, thus allowing them to troubleshoot or prevent problems, MindSpring was able to reduce the number of calls.

While most of the service operations were centralized in Atlanta, MindSpring had call centers in five other locations: Harrisburg, PA; Phoenix, AZ; Seattle, WA; San Jose, CA; and Dallas, TX. When customers called the toll-free support number, they were routed to the first available representative at any one of these sites. The company did not outsource its call center services because they were considered, according to McQuary, "a strategic advantage." McQuary explained:

There are three ways for ISPs to differentiate themselves through customer service. The first way is the software that you provide in allowing the customer to easily hook up to the Internet. The second way is being able to provide high speed connections with no busy signals. Both of these ways are becoming harder to differentiate. The third way is to provide outstanding technical support to the customer user. If the modem doesn't work, the end user might think that the Internet is broken. Not too many people are aware of all the possible technical problems that may exist.

By 1998, MindSpring had also begun to take training very seriously. The technical support staff went through two weeks of classroom training before starting at the call centers. Each service representative was matched with a mentor and was evaluated 90 days after starting. Emphasis for evaluating individual service representatives was not placed upon the volume of calls taken—as some customer calls could last up to 90 minutes—but on customer satisfaction levels attained, as measured by the online quality surveys returned to MindSpring.

When employees did leave the call center they often moved to other departments within the company. Greg Stromberg, executive vice president of MindSpring Biz who had overseen the company's call centers from 1995 to 1998, believed that this was a benefit. "Starting at the call centers gives employees a keen understanding of the needs of the customer, which improves their ability to handle other jobs, whether they be in accounting, marketing, product development, or human resources."

Database Tracking System

MindSpring also used a homegrown, proprietary call-tracking database (which replaced an earlier, off-the-shelf, turnkey data tracking system). The system, called Hercules, integrated billing, e-mail, and phone records. All company departments had access to Hercules, and anyone could post to Hercules major issues or developments affecting customer service on a day-to-day basis. In addition, customer issues that needed the attention of specific departments could be forwarded to the appropriate department. Each customer account had a detailed chronology of past calls, e-mails, and service or technical issues. The database tracked common problems and had reporting capability, so problems affecting a large number of customers could be identified quickly. The Hercules system also allowed the customer and technical support departments to automatically send quality surveys (see Exhibit 12) to customers who had contacted MindSpring with a problem. MindSpring typically experienced a 35% response rate, which could be tracked to individual representatives. Approximately 90% of the calls coming into MindSpring's call centers came from individuals who were customers 45 days or less with MindSpring.

Operating Results

MindSpring's service concept and operating strategy had created impressive results. Cost of call-center operations as a percentage of sales had decreased from 25% in 1995 to 12% in 1998, prior to the acquisition of NetCom. At the same time, value offered to customers had increased significantly as customer complaints had all but disappeared and feedback from customer surveys steadily improved. As Stromberg observed in 1998, "I used to spend the better part of each day trying to console irate customers. Now I may have to deal with one or two customer complaints per month."

Moreover, MindSpring's strategy of retaining customers through superior service was clearly paying off. In 1998, prior to its acquisition of NetCom, its monthly "churn rate" (the rate at which customers cancelled service) was 3.4%, compared with AOL's 13.2%. (See Exhibit 13 for comparative industry churn rates.) Operating margins continued to improve as the POP network was built out, and more and more subscribers were dialing into company-owned POPs.

The Future of EarthLink/MindSpring

Such results were actually old news for Brewer as he was now thinking about the future of the new combined EarthLink/MindSpring company. Issues like broadband access, opportunities for alternative sources of revenue, brand-building, and scalability competed for his attention. Also important was how to determine how the merged company could continue to use customer service as a way to differentiate its product from other ISPs. As he thought about the issues confronting EarthLink/MindSpring, he decided it was time to take his dog Louis for a walk to ponder these strategic issues further.

Exhibit 1 MindSpring Enterprises—Income Statement (000s)

	Quarter Ending 9/30/99	Quarter Ending 6/30/99	Year Ending 12/31/98
Revenues			
Access	$ 72,631	$71,620	$95,852
Subscriber Start-up Fees	0	0	4,086
Business Services	15,548	14,044	14,735
Total Revenues	88,179	85,664	114,673
Cost and Expenses			
Cost of Revenue	28,367	29,120	34,336
Gross Margin	59,812	56,544	80,337
General and Administrative	28,363	26,460	38,446
Selling	22,366	14,366	18,881
EBITDA	9,083	15,718	23,013
Depreciation and Amortization	5,517	4,692	8,179
Acquired Customer Base Amortization	23,302	23,720	7,048
Operating Income	(19,736)	(12,694)	7,786
Interest (expense) income, net	1,977	1,183	1,214
Income (loss) before taxes	(17,759)	(11,511)	9,000
Provision for Income Taxes	6,925	4,430	1,544
Net Income (loss)	$(10,834)	$ (7,081)	$ 10,544

MindSpring Enterprises—Balance Sheet (000s)

	9/30/99	12/31/98
Assets		
Cash and Equivalents	$386,833	$ 167,743
Current Assets, Other Than Cash	16,852	7,457
Property Plant and Equipment, Net	78,561	35,841
Intangible and Other Assets	237,297	36,558
Total Assets	719,543	247,599
Liabilities		
Current Liabilities	$59,110	$38,094
Long-term Liabilities	180,502	2,424
Total Liabilities	$239,612	$40,518
Total Shareholders' Equity	479,931	207,081
Total Liabilities and Shareholders' Equity	$719,543	$247,599

Source: MindSpring financial statements and prospectus

Exhibit 2 Core Values and Beliefs

- We respect the individual, and believe that individuals who are treated with respect and given responsibility respond by giving their best.

- We require complete honesty and integrity in everything we do.

- We make commitments with care, and then live up to them. In all things, we do what we say we are going to do.

- Work is an important part of life, and it should be fun. Being a good businessperson does not mean being stuffy and boring.

- We are frugal. We guard and conserve the company's resources with at least the same vigilance that we would use to guard and conserve our own personal resources.

- We insist on giving our best effort in everything we undertake. Furthermore, we see a huge difference between "good mistakes" (best effort, bad result) and "bad mistakes" (sloppiness or lack of effort).

- Clarity in understanding our mission, our goals, and what we expect from each other as critical to our success.

- We are believers in the Golden Rule. In all our dealings we will strive to be friendly and courteous, as well as fair and compassionate.

- We feel a sense of urgency on any matters related to our customers. We own problems and we are always responsive. We are customer driven.

Exhibit 3 Resumes of Key Personnel

Charles M. Brewer
Chairman, Chief Executive Officer

Charles Brewer, the 40-year-old founder of MindSpring, was born in Louisville, Kentucky. Before he founded MindSpring, Brewer had worked at Wertheim & Company, an investment banking firm; he also served as vice president of Sanders & Company, a venture capital firm. From 1989 to 1993, Brewer was CFO and then CEO of AudioFAX, a fax technology company. Brewer, an outdoor enthusiast, was a Phi Beta Kappa graduate of Amherst College, where he received a BA in economics. He received his MBA from Stanford University.

Michael S. McQuary
President, Chief Operating Officer

Mike McQuary, age 39, was MindSpring's president since April 1996 and its chief operating officer since September 1995. Prior to joining MindSpring, McQuary served for twelve years in a variety of management positions with Mobil Chemical Company, a division of Mobil Corporation, including regional sales manager from April 1991 to February 1994 and manager of operations (reengineering) from February 1994 to June 1995. In addition to serving on the MindSpring board of directors, he also served on the Georgia Center for Advanced Telecommunications Technology. McQuary received a BA in psychology from the University of Virginia and an MBA from Pepperdine University.

Juliet M. Reising
Executive Vice President, Chief Financial Officer

Juliet Reising, age 48, has served as vice president and chief financial officer of MindSpring since February 1999. Reising has a strong background as a financial executive having served as CFO for Atlanta-based companies including most recently AvData Systems, Inc., InterServ Services Corp., and Coin, Inc. Prior to this she was vice president, finance, for Norrell Corp. and controller for Cox Communications. She started her career with Ernst & Young where she received her CPA. Reising graduated summa cum laude with a BBA in accounting from the University of Georgia.

Robert D. Sanders
Vice President, Chief Technical Officer

Robert Sanders has been MindSpring's vice president since September 1996 and chief technical officer since January 1995. Robert served as MindSpring's vice president of network engineering from December 1995 to December 1996 and MindSpring's senior engineer from June 1994 to January 1995. Prior to joining MindSpring, Robert worked as a software engineer and system administrator of Harry's Farmer Market, Inc. from March 1994 to May 1994. Sanders attended the Georgia Institute of Technology.

Samuel R. DeSimone, Jr.
Executive Vice President and General Counsel

Sam DeSimone, age 39, joined MindSpring in November 1998. DeSimone's most recent position was vice president of corporate development with Metrix Corporation of Forest Grove, Oregon. He was previously a partner with Lane Powell Spears Lubersky of Portland and an associate attorney with Testa Hurwitz & Thibeault of Boston, Massachusetts. He is also a co-founder of the Oregon Young Entrepreneurs Association and a former director of the Oregon Entrepreneurs Forum. DeSimone earned his JD from New York University School of Law in 1984 and was a Phi Beta Kappa graduate of Amherst College in 1981.

Gregory J. Stromberg
Executive Vice President, MindSpring Biz

Greg Stromberg, age 46, has served as an executive vice president since March of 1999. He is currently responsible for MindSpring Biz organization, the MindSpring Y2K Compliance Program and the integration of Netcom's customers and services into MindSpring. Greg joined MindSpring as vice president of technical support in October 1995, served as executive vice president of call centers beginning in August 1998. From June 1993 to September 1994, he served as a regional manager for Digital Financial Services, a computer leasing company, after which he traveled until he joined MindSpring. Greg worked for Digital Equipment Corporation between 1983 and 1993 in a variety of sales and operations positions. In addition, Greg served as a sales representative and product manager for Burroughs Corp., a computer hardware company, from June 1978 to June 1983. Greg was an avid runner, having won the St. George Marathon Master's Division in 1994, along with a number of other road races. Greg received a BS in business management and an MBA from the University of Utah.

Lance Weatherby
Executive Vice President, Sales and Marketing

Lance Weatherby, age 37, was executive vice president of sales and marketing since April 1998. Previously, he was MindSpring's vice president of business development and acting vice president of business development. Weatherby joined MindSpring as market development manager in September 1995. Prior to that, he held a variety of sales, sales management, and marketing positions with Mobil Chemical Co., a petrochemical company, from 1990 to 1995, including district sales manager from 1992 to 1995. From April 1990 to October 1990, Weatherby served as an account executive with United Parcel Service, Inc., a shipping company. Weatherby received a BBA in marketing from Eastern Kentucky University and an MBA from Indiana University.

Source: MindSpring Press Release

Exhibit 4 Customer Satisfaction Survey with ISPs

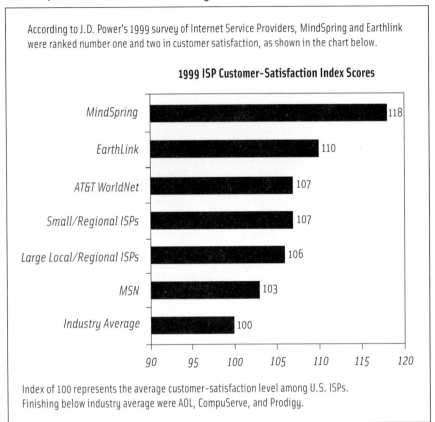

According to J.D. Power's 1999 survey of Internet Service Providers, MindSpring and Earthlink were ranked number one and two in customer satisfaction, as shown in the chart below.

1999 ISP Customer-Satisfaction Index Scores

ISP	Score
MindSpring	118
EarthLink	110
AT&T WorldNet	107
Small/Regional ISPs	107
Large Local/Regional ISPs	106
MSN	103
Industry Average	100

Index of 100 represents the average customer-satisfaction level among U.S. ISPs. Finishing below industry average were AOL, CompuServe, and Prodigy.

Source: Adaptation of data from J.D. Power & Associates, "1999 National ISP Online Residential Customer Satisfaction Survey."

Exhibit 5 EarthLink Network Inc.—Income Statement (000s)

	Year Ended		
	31-Dec-97	**31-Dec-98**	**31-Dec-99**
STATEMENT OF OPERATIONS DATA:			
Revenues			
Narrowband access	$ 74,228	$ 161,009	$ 310,868
Web hosting	5,202	7,537	11,554
Broadband access	1,143	3,285	6,756
Content, commerce and advertising	315	4,110	13,110
Total revenues	80,888	175,941	342,288
Operating costs and expenses			
Cost of revenues	38,065	77,223	132,679
Operations and member support	30,607	53,765	104,842
Sales and marketing	25,971	42,837	125,992
General and administrative	14,699	21,720	38,010
Acquisition-related costs	–	42,635	65,072
Total operating costs and expenses	109,342	238,180	466,595
Loss from operations	(28,454)	(62,239)	(124,307)
Net interest income, (expense)	(1,462)	2,457	16,059
Net loss	(29,916)	(59,782)	(108,248)
	31-Dec-97	**31-Dec-98**	**31-Dec-99**
BALANCE SHEET DATA			
Cash and cash equivalents	$ 16,450	$ 140,864	$ 308,579
Total assets	46,887	266,341	423,475
Long-term debt	8,218	7,701	8,259
Total liabilities	40,812	68,997	96,937
Accumulated deficit	(66,072)	(133,454)	(255,809)
Stockholders' equity (deficit)	6,075	197,344	326,538

Source: Adaptation of data from Earthlink Network, Inc. FORM 10-K filed March 30, 2000.

Exhibit 6 Comparison of Leading ISPs' Services, Rates, and Features (1998)

	Startup Fee?	Basic Monthly Unlimited Access Plan	Connection Speed	Technical Service (telephone)	Proprietary Content?	Successful Connection Rate[a]
MindSpring	$25 (occasionally waived)	$19.95	• 56K in most areas • ISDN support	800 number Available 24/7	No	88–89.9%
EarthLink	$25 (occasionally waived)	$19.95	• 56K in most areas • ISDN support	800 number Available 24/7	No	90–92%
MSN	No	$19.95	• 56K in most areas • ISDN support	Toll call Available 24/7	Yes	Above 95%
AOL	*$25 (occasionally waived)	$21.95	• 56K in most areas • No ISDN	800 number Available 24/7	Yes	Below 88%
Prodigy	No	$19.95	• 56K in most areas • No ISDN	800 number Limited hours	Yes	93–95%
ATT WorldNet	No	$19.95/month for 150 hours; 99 cents per additional hour	• 56K for approx. 40% of its POPs • No ISDN	800 number Available 24/7	No	93–95%
NetCom	$25 (occasionally waived)	$19.95	• 56K in most areas • ISDN	800 number Available 24/7	No	90–92%
MediaOne Express	$99–$175 installation fee	$29.95–49.95 (depending on leased or owned modem)	1,500K to computer/ 300K from computer	800 number Available 24/7	No	Connection always on
@home	$99 installation fee	$29.95–49.95, depending on locations	1,500K to 3,000K	800 number Limited hours	No	Connection always on

Source: Adaptation of data from Inverse Network. Testing performed July 1997.

Exhibit 7 Leading ISP Subscriber Levels (September 1999)

The merger of MindSpring and EarthLink would make it the second largest Internet Service Provider (ISP) in the United States. Prior to the proposed merger in September 1999, EarthLink and MindSpring were the fifth and sixth largest ISPs, respectively.

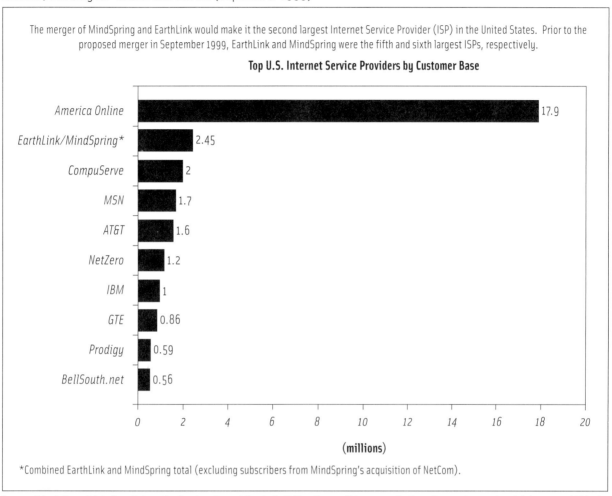

Top U.S. Internet Service Providers by Customer Base

*Combined EarthLink and MindSpring total (excluding subscribers from MindSpring's acquisition of NetCom).

Source: Adaptation of data from Interactive Services Report Quarterly Online Census, Telecommunications Reports International, July 1999 published in *The Industry Standard,* October 1999.

Exhibit 8 Estimated Cost of Building and Operating a Point-of-Presence (POP), March 31, 1998

Start-up Equipment Costs	
Equipment: Rack of 23 modems and a router	$30,000
Cost per additional modem rack	20,000
Equipment costs for 184 subscribers (1 modem rack)	30,000
Equipment costs for 1,000 subscribers (5 modem racks)	110,000
Equipment costs for 10,000 subscribers (48 modem racks)	970,000
Equipment costs for 25,000 subscribers (100 modem racks)	2,010,000
Monthly Costs—84 subscribers, 8-to-1 subscriber-to-modem ratio	
Monthly rent—local facility	$1,000
Average monthly phone line charge per line	34
Total phone line charge with 23 modems	782
Monthly lease cost T-1 dedicated line	1,000
Total monthly POP costs	$2,782
Monthly cost per subscriber	**$15.12**
Monthly Costs—1,000 subscribers, 8.5-to-1 subscriber-to-modem ratio	
Monthly rent—local facility	$1,000
Average monthly phone line charge per line	34
Total phone line charge with 118 modems	4,012
Monthly lease cost T-1 dedicated line	1,000
Total monthly POP costs	$6,012
Monthly cost per subscriber	**$6.01**
Monthly Costs—10,000 subscribers, 9-to-1 subscriber-to-modem ratio	
Monthly rent—local facility	$2,000
Average monthly phone line charge per line	34
Total phone line charge with 1,111 modems	37,774
Monthly lease cost T-1 dedicated line (one T-1 per 250 modems)	5,000
Total monthly POP costs	$44,774
Monthly cost per subscriber	**$4.48**
Monthly Costs—25,000 subscribers, 11-to-1 subscriber-to-modem ratio	
Monthly rent—local facility	$3,000
Average monthly phone line charge per line	34
Total phone line charge with 2,273 modems	77,282
Monthly lease cost T-3 dedicated line	20,000
Total monthly POP costs	$100,282
Monthly cost per subscriber	**$4.01**
Approximate Cost Per Subscriber to Lease POP Service via Third Party Provider	**$9–$11**

Source: Adaptation of data from Everen Securities

Exhibit 9 MindSpring Home Page

Source: MindSpring

Exhibit 10 MindSpring Call Center Snapshot Page

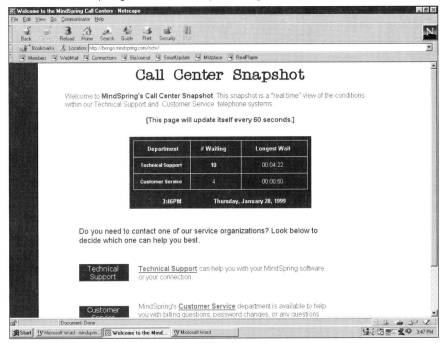

Source: MindSpring

Exhibit 11 MindSpring Office Building

Photo: Dickson Louie, July 1999

Exhibit 12 Online Customer Survey

Dear [insert customer name here]:

Thank you for contacting MindSpring Technical Support. We truly want to exceed your expectations. Please help us better serve you by completing the following questionnaire:

To begin filling out the survey use the "REPLY" feature on your email program and place an X in the line next to the appropriate statement. Then "SEND" the message.

1. How do you feel about your OVERALL experience with MindSpring as your Internet Service Provider?

   1____   Excellent

   2____   Good

   3____   Sufficient

   4____   Poor

   5____   Very Poorly

2. How do you rate your MindSpring connection [Including reliability, speed, busies, etc.]?

   1____   Excellent

   2____   Very Good

   3____   Adequate

   4____   Poor

   5____   Very Poor

3. How would you rate the MindSpring software for ease of installation and use?

   1____   Excellent

   2____   Very Good

   3____   Adequate

   4____   Poor

   5____   Very Poor

4. Approximately how long were you on hold before being helped by our representative?

   1____   Less than a minute

   2____   1-5 minutes

   3____   5-10 minutes

   4____   10-20 minutes

   5____   Do Not Remember

Our records indicate that you spoke with David S., a MindSpring technical support representative and you were issued case number 990723-5816726. Please answer the following questions regarding the service you received from David S.

Exhibit 12 Online Customer Survey (continued)

5. How would you rate David S.'s friendliness?

    1___   Extremely Friendly

    2___   Very Friendly

    3___   Friendly (Typical for MindSpring)

    4___   Neither Friendly nor Unfriendly

    5___   Unfriendly

6. How would you rate David S.'s degree of professionalism?

    1___   Extremely Professional

    2___   Very Professional

    3___   Professional (Typical for MindSpring)

    4___   Neither Professional nor Unprofessional

    5___   Unprofessional

7. To what extent would you say that David S. was interested in solving your problem?

    1___   Extremely Interested

    2___   Very Interested

    3___   Interested (Typical for MindSpring)

    4___   Neither Interested nor Disinterested

    5___   Disinterested

8. When solving your problem, how would you rate the information David S. provided? Would you say the information was:

    1___   Extremely well presented and understandable

    2___   Well presented and understandable

    3___   Sufficient to solve the problem (Meets your minimum expectation)

    4___   Difficult to understand

    5___   Extremely difficult to understand

9. Which of the following statements best describes your initial contact with David S.?

    1___   David S. understood my problem immediately

    2___   David S. understood my problem quickly

    3___   David S. understood my problem with some effort (Meets your minimum expectations)

    4___   David S. had some difficulty in understanding my problem

    5___   David S. had an extremely difficult time understanding my problem

Exhibit 12 Online Customer Survey (continued)

10. Was your problem solved on this call?

      Yes   _____

      No   _____

      Don't Remember   _____

10a. If your answer to Question #10 was No, why

      1___   The problem was caused by a piece of software other than MindSpring Software.

      2___   The problem was due to a network or server outage

      3___   The problem was with my system or phone lines

      4___   I got frustrated and decided it was not worth fixing my problem.

      5___   David S. lacked the knowledge to resolve my problem correctly.

11. If you needed to contact MindSpring's technical support again, would you like to speak with David S. again?

      Yes   _____

      No   _____ [If No, Please Explain]

      Undecided   _____

      If No, why Not?

12. Comparing MindSpring's technical support to other companies' technical support, would you say that, overall

      1___   MindSpring's technical support is much better than other companies' technical support

      2___   MindSpring's technical support is better than other companies' technical support

      3___   MindSpring's technical support is about the same quality as other companies' technical support

      4___   MindSpring's technical support is worse than other companies' technical support

      5___   MindSpring's technical support is much worse than other companies' technical support

      6___   I have never contacted another company for technical support

13. Please share any additional comments or suggestions you may have:

    Thank you for helping us improve our service. If you require further assistance, please send a separate e-mail to support@mind-spring.com. This will ensure a timely response. We can also be reached at 1-800-719-4660 24 hours a day, 7 days a week.

Source: MindSpring email survey sent to casewriter.

Exhibit 13 Customer Churn Rates (March 1998)

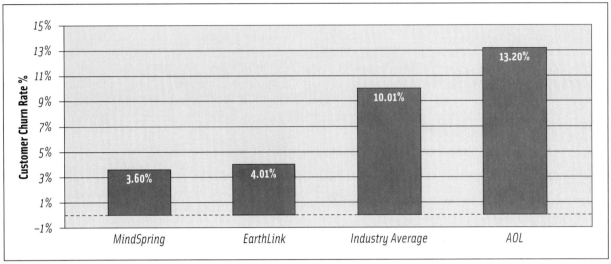

Source: Adaptation of data from The Strategis Group

Media
Convergence

MEDIA CONVERGENCE

The purpose of this brief overview is to provide an understanding of media convergence. Broadly defined, **media convergence** is the evolution of different types of media content (news, information, and entertainment) that were traditionally found on different types of media platforms (print, audio, and video) into a single digital media base available on the Internet platform.

Digital technology provides the common platform for placing all types of media content into binary form. Once audio, video, or graphics are broken down into digital form, they can easily be transmitted across the Internet and reassembled onto a receiving platform, such as a personal computer, television set, or any other type of Internet device. With the emergence of broadband access, not only will traditional graphics, streaming video, and streaming audio become available on one platform but so will video-on-demand, software distribution, books-on-demand, and multi-player games.

The use of digital technology represents both a blessing and a curse for moviemakers and the recording industry. On the plus side, digital technology enables the possibility of media convergence and allows for both movies and music to be transmitted across a variety of platforms. On the negative side, digital technology can allow for increased piracy once the digital codes are broken and raises the issue of how artists, recording companies, and studios can protect their copyrights.

The Telecommunications Act of 1996 overhauled the federal communications laws for the first time since 1934. This bill deregulated the telecommunications industry and, for the first time, allowed telephone, cable, and utility companies to compete directly against one another. With the passage of this law, competition between telephone and cable companies has intensified, especially over the issue of broadband delivery of Internet services to the household.

Some of the recent mega-media mergers that have resulted from deregulation include the marriage of Disney and ABC/Capital Cities, Viacom and CBS, Tribune Company and Times Mirror, America Online and Time Warner, and Time Warner and Turner Broadcasting. These new media companies can achieve synergy by sharing content on different platforms. For example, in the case of Disney, through its acquisition of Infoseek and the ABC Network and subsequent creation of the GO Network, the company can use content from ABC News's television and radio broadcasts for placement on ABCNews.com. The use of content on multiple platforms helps create synergy and *theoretically* helps improve the revenue line. As with all mergers, however, the merging of company cultures can also *limit* potential synergies.

Some of the legal issues confronting the increased concentration of media ownership include fewer editorial voices and potential conflicts of interest. Proponents of media mergers believe that laws limiting cross-ownership of other media companies—newspapers and television stations—are outdated and should be eliminated. These proponents believe that with the growth of new media, more sources of news and information are now readily available and create a highly fragmented usage of media by the public. The concept of media convergence and its associated "synergistic benefits"—fueled by advances in digital technology and the expected increase in household use of broadband access—has been the key driver behind the mega-mergers of media companies.

SYNOPSES OF CHAPTER CASES

THE NEW YORK TIMES ELECTRONIC MEDIA COMPANY (A)

Case Overview

With an editorial staff of over 1,200 employees collecting, interpreting, and disseminating information around the world, the senior management of *The New York Times* believed that the use of electronic channels—television, Internet, or video—offered new and exciting ways to extend the information franchise both nationally and globally. As a result, in 1995, *The New York Times* publisher Arthur Sulzberger established *The New York Times* Electronic Media Company. While the new team, led by President Martin Nisenholtz, was deciding how much to invest, where to invest, and how to measure the return on these new electronic ventures, two key strategic issues emerged on expanding *The New York Times* brand.

First, would *The Times* be better served by a horizontal extension online—with all of the newspaper's content available at a single locale? Or should it become a vertical extension online—where key sections of the newspaper, such as *Book Review*, *Travel*, and *Business Day*, would be branded separately like magazines to compete with subject-specific sites, such as Amazon.com, Travelocity, and Motley Fool, to create online communities of interest?

Second, what financial model should *The Times* pursue on the Internet? Should it be entirely advertising based, like the *Wall Street Journal* Interactive Edition; or should it be a subscription-based or pay-per-view model? Were these models mutually exclusive, or could a website with branded content attract both advertising and electronic commerce revenue in a hybrid model, such as ESPNET SportZone?

Preparation Questions

1. What are the strengths and weaknesses of *The New York Times* Company's current positioning in its print media markets?

2. How much equity does *The New York Times* brand have in print markets? What aspects of the brand are best suited to applications in digital-information markets? What aspects of the brand, if any, represent liabilities in electronic markets?

3. Evaluate the Electronic Media Company's website (*www.nytimes.com*). What attributes have made it a top news site on the Web?

4. Evaluate the economic model presented for *The Times*'s Web-based business in the case. How would you predict the model will evolve, in light of a variety of possible revenue streams, such as subscriptions, advertising, lead generation, retail transactions, and fee-based services?

5. Given your assumptions regarding future economic model(s) for the site, who are *The Times*'s present and future competitors on the Web? Are they news sites, retail sites, entertainment sites, community sites, or others?

THE NEW YORK TIMES ELECTRONIC MEDIA COMPANY (B)

Case Overview

By year-end 1997, the nytimes.com site was averaging nearly 900,000 page-views a day and had registered over 3 million users, with an average user visit of approximately 26 minutes. Martin Niseholtz, president of *The New York Times* Electronic Media Company, had come to believe that the site's initial marketing strategy requiring registration before use had been premature. He had hoped that data generated through user registration would enable the site to deliver highly specific target market segments of site users to advertisers. Nisenholtz commented: "I still feel that the Internet is a great medium for using database marketing for targeting and accountability. But, as it turns out, most of the advertisers at this time are just not prepared to use the Web for database marketing."

As a result, Nisenholtz pursued an industry-standard strategy to increase page-views through increased traffic and frequency. From his perspective, a model something akin to broadcast TV was emerging as the dominant approach for content businesses aiming to generate revenues on the Web. As a result, sites that could generate large quantities of raw mass-market traffic such as Yahoo!, which averaged 300 million page views a day at year-end 1997, garnered the largest online advertising revenues.

The nytimes.com site had become a commercial success, ranking 24th among all websites in advertising revenue for the first half of 1997. As Nisenholtz pondered the site's future, he was also planning the launch of a flanker site called New York Today, an online guide that the Electronic Media Company would debut in spring 1998. This site was specifically designed for people living in, visiting, or doing business in New York. While Nisenholtz was optimistic about the commercial possibilities of New York Today, its primary goal was defensive: to protect local newspaper advertising dollars, especially those from classified ads, from predation by online entrants.

Preparation Questions

1. Would the locally focused site strategy help *The New York Times* reach meaningful scale and become a business akin to the Yellow Pages as Nisenholtz envisioned?

2. Were there other media to exploit and integrate into *The New York Times* brand?

CBS EVENING NEWS

Case Overview

In January 1998 Andrew Heyward, president of the CBS News Division, considered future directions of the *CBS Evening News with Dan Rather.* In 1997, the *Evening News* had climbed back into second place, behind NBC's *Nightly News* program and ahead of third-place ABC's *World News Tonight.* Since 1980, however, total viewership of all three network evening newscasts had eroded from a historical high in the 1970s. News observers attributed the decline to a combination of factors including the following: the availability of 24-hour cable television, the expansion of local news programs, the increase in prime-time news magazines, the shift in airtimes to 6:30 P.M. from 7:00 P.M., and the proliferation of viewers' channel options with the rising acceptance of cable-TV and direct-broadcast satellite services.

Despite the fragmentation of news audiences, total viewership in 1998 remained large, with 25 million households—34 million Americans—watching a network evening news program each night. The evening news represented a valuable franchise that went beyond the creation of a mass audience. Celebrity news anchors helped build networks' brand equity, highly rated network newscasts provided a strong lead-in for affiliates' local prime-time programming, and network evening newscasts had the potential to influence, if not determine, the national news agenda.

Preparation Questions

1. Were the network's evening news franchises irrevocably declining? If so, should some of the network's resources be used to develop other programming produced by the News Division? Or, with increased fragmentation, did the audience size of the *Evening News* represent an important base from which to build audiences for other News Division programming?

2. Should Heyward aim to attract a larger share of the existing evening news audience with renewed emphasis on serious and foreign news coverage?

3. What about other media? How could Heyward increase CBS's marketshare and advertising revenues by exploiting the Internet for disseminating the news? How would these news channels work together?

CBS MARKETWATCH

Case Overview

In June 2000, CBS.MarketWatch.com's site had become the 40th most visited site on the Web. It had passed other leading financial news and information sites such as Bloomberg.com, CNBC.com, CNNfn.com, and Intuit. Despite becoming one of the leading financial news content sites, Larry Kramer, CEO of MarketWatch.com, knew there were a number of basic challenges ahead. One obvious concern was competition. For example, CNBC.com was planning to revamp its website with rumors of a more tight integration with CNBC—the leading financial news channel. TheStreet.com, in cooperation with *The New York Times,* also aired a weekly news program on Fox, and CNNfn was part of the recently announced merger of AOL-TimeWarner. In short, media convergence was accelerating with multiple points of contact with key target customers.

As Kramer reflected on what he and his senior management team should do next, he considered three key questions. First, what should the MarketWatch.com franchise do to become profitable and meet Wall Street expectations? Second, how could MarketWatch.com become even more dominant in domestic markets? Third, how could he expand MarketWatch.com globally—in areas where the CBS brand name had little or no meaning?

Preparation Questions

1. Evaluate MarketWatch.com's business model. How can it become profitable?

2. How does MarketWatch.com leverage off the brand name of CBS?

3. How does MarketWatch.com leverage off the operations of CBS?

4. How can MarketWatch.com expand globally by replicating the CBS.MarketWatch.com model in Europe and Asia?

RCA RECORDS: THE DIGITAL REVOLUTION

Case Overview

Bob Jamieson, president of RCA Records, considered the recording industry in 1999 to be a frightening chaos that needed to be managed. Jamieson, since joining RCA in 1995, and Executive Vice President and General Manager Jack Rovner had turned the company around by pursuing a "less is more" strategy. The management team wondered, however, whether it could continue to be successful in the face of retail and radio consolidation, "market clutter," and increasing marketing costs that were reducing net profit margins generated by physical product. Digital distribution, whereby musicians marketed and sold music directly to consumers via the Internet, posed another threat.

Between 1995 and 1997, the number of U.S. music retail outlets had dropped 20%. Consolidation among radio stations resulted in less risk-taking with newer artists, with shortened playlists dominated by "sure-fire hits," translating into higher costs for marketing. In addition, the market share of the independent labels (or "indies") had increased from 10 to 20% since 1990.

Enter MP3 and its competitors, Liquid Audio and AT&T's a2b music. The Internet was creating new, efficient, cost-effective retail and distribution opportunities for artists and labels alike. Piracy also posed a significant and unresolved threat.

Preparation Questions

1. How could companies such as RCA manage the chaos and turn this new sales and distribution channel into revenues, thereby turning the digital threat into an opportunity?

2. How would the new technology alter traditional rights and contract agreements between labels and artists?

3. How could labels respond to the changing market in which the need to "own" music was itself called into question?

4. How would recording companies that were part of an international conglomerate exploit the global reach of the Internet while maintaining discrete value propositions and profit centers?

INTEGRATIVE QUESTIONS

As you consider the entire set of questions in the tenth chapter, you should also reflect on the following integrative questions:

1. How has media convergence transformed the business model of both old media (e.g., CBS News) and new media (e.g., cbsmarketwatch.com) companies?

2. Why is industry consolidation occurring? Who will ultimately win in this space? What attributes would you look for in "winning" media companies?

3. Most of the cases in this chapter have great content, yet their revenue models are often questionable. What advice would you give to companies that are looking for advertising-based revenue models?

4. Some media companies have purchased infrastructure companies, while the reverse is also true; infrastructure companies have purchased media companies. What is the argument in favor of this type of integration?

SUMMARY

This chapter focused on the media convergence evolution of different types of media content—news, information, and entertainment—that were traditionally found on different types of media platforms—print, audio, and video—into a single digital media base available on the Internet platform. This convergence intensifies the level of competition in heretofore noncompeting firms (e.g., *TV Guide* now competing with E! Online) but simultaneously provides enormous opportunity for the firm that is able to see the future of market evolution. Stakes in the media convergence game are high, but the payoff can be quite substantial.

THE NEW YORK TIMES ELECTRONIC MEDIA COMPANY (A)

Ours is a business of value-added information. It's a business of original material, carefully collected, edited, packaged, and distributed to our customers in a way that pleases them, informs them, makes their lives easier to manage, and even entertains them. . . . The plain truth is that I don't give a tinker's damn how we distribute our information. For as long as our customers want it on newsprint I'll do all I can to give it to them on newsprint. . . . But if they want it on CD-ROM, I'll try to meet that need. . . . Quite frankly, if someone would be kind enough to invent the technology, I'll be pleased to beam The New York Times *directly into your cortex. . . . We'll have the Metro Edition, the National Edition, and the Mind Meld Edition."*[1]

—Arthur O. Sulzberger, Jr., Publisher

As dawn broke across the Manhattan skyline on a crisp October morning, newsstand vendors were busy unbundling the morning editions of various newspapers and getting their newsstands ready for another day of business. The City's three major newspapers, *The New York Times*, *The New York Daily News*, and *The New York Post*, had stories on the major news events of the previous 24 hours: the upcoming presidential debates; the hometown New York Yankees preparing for the American League playoffs; and the recent surgery performed on Pope John Paul II.

On West 43rd Street, near Times Square, Arthur Sulzberger, Jr., the newspaper's 44-year-old publisher, was already in his office on the eleventh floor of *The New York Times* building. For the past 10 months, *The Times* had been celebrating the centennial anniversary of its purchase in 1896 by Adolph Ochs, Sulzberger's great-grandfather. As the publisher read through his morning edition of *The Times*, he wondered what the next century would be like for the newspaper. With a daily and Sunday circulation of almost 1.1 million and 1.7 million,[2] respectively, and net revenue of $1.2 billion, *The Times*

was considered by many Americans to be the most influential newspaper in the nation. Beginning in 1997, and for the next 18 months, the print version of *The Times* would be launching several editorial enhancements for its readers—a Late City Edition with later sport articles and scores: a new Northeast Edition to be printed, via satellite, in Boston and Washington, D.C., and additional sections of the daily newspaper, some to be printed in color for the first time.

Yet, Sulzberger thought *The Times* could be more than just a newspaper. With an editorial staff of over 1,200 employees collecting, interpreting, and disseminating information around the world, Sulzberger and his senior management team believed that the use of electronic channels—television, Internet, or video—offered new and exciting ways to extend the information franchise of *The New York Times*, both nationally and globally. As a result, *The New York Times* Electronic Media Company, a subsidiary of the newspaper, was established in 1995 to examine these new growth opportunities. While Sulzberger, Joseph Lelyveld, *The Times*' executive editor, Janet Robinson, *The Times*' president and general manager, and Martin Nisenholtz, president of *The New York Times* Electronic Media Company, were deciding how much to invest, where to invest, and how to measure the return on these new electronic ventures, two key strategic issues emerged on expanding *The Times* brand. First, would *The Times* be better served by a horizontal extension on-line—with all of the newspaper's content available at a single locale—or by a vertical extension on-line—where key sections of the newspaper, such as *Book Review*, *Travel*, and *Business Day*, would be branded separately like magazines to compete with subject-specific sites, such as Amazon.com, Travelocity, and Motley Fool, to create on-line communities of interest?[3] Second, what business model should *The Times* pursue on the Internet? Should it be entirely advertising-based, as many content providers, such as CNN Interactive and c/net, were; subscription-based, like the *Wall Street Journal* Interactive Edition; or a hybrid, pay-per-view model,

[1]Speech by Arthur O. Sulzberger, Jr., "Jefferson or Barnum: The Values of Our Information Age." Tufts University, April 9, 1996.
[2]Audit Bureau of Circulations, FAS-FAX report, September 30, 1996.
[3]Arthur Armstrong and John Hagel, "The Real Value of On-line Communities," *Harvard Business Review*, May–June 1996 (Reprint 96301).

like Starwave's ESPNET SportsZone, which charged Web users a fee for its premium services?

The History of *The New York Times*

The first issue of *The New-York Daily Times*—a four-page newspaper—was published on September 18, 1851. The newspapers' principal owners, Henry J. Raymond, a working newspaperman, and George Jones, a businessman, were among the seven men who put up $100,000 to publish the newspaper.[4] Previously, both Raymond and Jones had worked at *The New York Tribune*, owned by Horace Greeley, and believed that a newspaper venture of their own would also be profitable. Active first in Whig, and later in Republican, politics during the Civil War, Raymond served as the newspaper's first editor and publisher. As editor he emphasized the coverage of the city, the courts, and the literary world. Unlike the other newspapers of the "penny press"[5] era, Raymond promised his readers that *The Daily Times* would be an objective publication, and noted that "there are very few things in this world worth while to get angry about." Following the death of Raymond in 1869, Jones became the newspaper's publisher. Under Jones' leadership in the early 1870s *The Daily Times*, together with *Harper's Weekly* magazine, became famous for leading an investigation of William Marcy Tweed, the political boss of Tammany Hall. Jones reportedly turned down a $5 million bribe to quash the stories and Tweed was eventually convicted for fleecing New York City of millions of dollars in public works contracts.

Following Jones' death in 1891, and due to the lack of financial support from readers and advertisers following the newspaper's endorsement of Democrat Grover Cleveland in 1884, the newspaper was sold in August 1896 to Adolph S. Ochs, publisher of the *Chattanooga Times* in Tennessee. Promising to make the newspaper the best in New York City, Ochs quickly added sections—the *Book Review* and the *Sunday Magazine*—and additional staff, enabling the publication to expand its readership base. During Ochs' first year of ownership, the slogan, "All the News That's Fit to Print," first appeared on the front page of *The Times*. Looking for a phrase to summarize the newspaper's editorial policy of being fair and objective, Ochs himself came up with the slogan. But he challenged his readers to come up with a better one, offering $100 as prize money. Although another slogan won the contest, "All the World News, but Not a School for Scandal," Ochs kept the original slogan on the front page where it has appeared every day since February 10, 1897.

With Ochs' passing in 1935, control of the newspaper went to his son-in-law, Arthur Hayes Sulzberger. During Sulzberger's 26-year tenure as publisher, which spanned the Great Depression, World War II, and the Korean War, *The Times* became one of the most influential newspapers in the world. "Beyond simply reporting news of the day, writers for *The Times* tried to better interpret and analyze events—to tell readers not just what happened, but how it happened and why it is important."[6] Specialized reporting was added, as well as features such as the daily and Sunday crossword puzzles, the weather map, and the *Book Review*'s bestseller list.

Following Arthur Hayes Sulzberger's retirement as publisher in 1961 and the death of his successor and son-in-law, Orvil E. Dryfoos, in 1963, Sulzberger's son, Arthur Ochs Sulzberger, Sr., became head of *The Times*. During the younger Sulzberger's 29-year tenure as publisher, which saw the Civil Rights Movement, Vietnam, the Pentagon Papers, Watergate, and Reaganomics, *The Times* would greatly expand its breadth of coverage with new editorial features and reach across the country with a National Edition. Pulitzer Prize writers such as James Reston, Max Frankel, and Tom Wicker dominated the news pages, while other writers such as Craig Claiborne, George Vescey, and Philip Dougherty covered stories, respectively, for the food, sports, and business sections. In April 1976, *The Times* began its expansion from a two-section into a four-section newspaper—adding a different section, such as *Weekend, Home, Sports Monday, Science Times*, and *Living*, on different days of the week—to attract both readers and advertisers.[7] To further increase its circulation base outside the Northeastern region, a National Edition was launched in Chicago in 1980, eventually expanding to six print sites and growing to a daily circulation base of 280,000 by 1996. During Sulzberger's tenure as publisher, the total daily circulation of *The Times* would grow by almost 50%, from over 800,000[8] in 1964 to just under 1.2 million in 1992.

By 1992, Arthur Ochs Sulzberger, Jr., succeeded his father as publisher, following a 16-year apprenticeship through various posts at *The Times*. The junior Sulzberger's previous positions included assistant metropolitan

---

[4]Richard F. Shepard, "The Paper's Papers: A Reporter's Journey Through *The New York Times*," Times Books, 1996, page 15.
[5]Called "penny press" because newspapers during the mid-19th century sold for one or two cents.

[6]"Facts About *The New York Times*," page 35.
[7]Virginia Cahill and Donald Morrison, "Coping with the New *New York Times*," *Time Magazine*, August 15, 1977.
[8]Gay Talese, "The Kingdom and the Power," World Publishing, 1969, page 337.

editor, financial planning analyst, and deputy publisher. Since 1992, the newspaper had maintained the largest daily and Sunday circulation of any metropolitan newspaper in the United States (see Exhibit 1) and had won more Pulitzer Prizes than any other U.S. newspaper for its editorial coverage (see Exhibit 2). In addition to the *New York Times*, The New York Times Company, the corporate parent, also owned *The Boston Globe* (acquired in June 1993), 21 regional newspapers, 10 magazines, 6 television stations, 2 radio stations, and part interest in the *International Herald Tribune* (see Exhibit 3). In 1995, on net revenue of $2.4 billion, The New York Times Company earned $228.6 million in operating profit (see Exhibit 4).

Newspaper Economics

The revenue mix of the typical metropolitan newspaper was comprised of two key sources: advertising and circulation. Advertising revenue made up most of a newspaper's revenue base and came from the purchase of newspaper space by advertisers (roughly 55% to 60% of a newspaper was devoted to advertising, the rest to news or the "newshole") such as retail outlets, financial institutions, and other businesses and individuals seeking to promote the sales of goods and services to the newspaper's readership. Circulation revenue usually made up one-quarter to one-third of the total revenue base and came from sales of home delivery subscriptions or copies purchased through a newsstand or a vending machine (also called single copy sales).

Advertising was broken up into two main categories: display and classified. Retail display advertising was usually made up of local accounts, such as department stores, supermarkets, and other retailers, and national accounts, such as airlines, media companies, and financial institutions. Classified advertising was made up largely of help wanted, automotive, and real estate advertising. Because of the mergers of many companies and increased competition from other forms of advertising, such as direct mail and cable television, the amount of advertising revenue taken in by newspapers in real dollars had fallen between 1987 and 1995 (see Exhibit 5). For most newspapers, this shift in advertising dollars placed more pressure on managers to grow circulation revenue to shore up financial results.

With the downsizing and mergers of several companies in the New York City market during the late 1980s and early 1990s, advertising lineage for *The New York Times* reflected the nationwide drop in retail and classified advertising (see Exhibit 6). Although national display advertising remained strong, largely due to the upscale demographics of the newspaper's nationwide audience and the importance that many advertisers placed on image advertising in *The Times*, increases in subscription and single-copy prices of the newspaper (see Exhibit 7) helped offset some of the losses in advertising revenue. *The Times'* business strategy to generate increased profits was two-fold. First, *The Times* provided quality journalism to upscale readers willing to pay a premium subscription price. Second, it delivered this upscale readership audience to upscale advertisers who would pay a premium to reach them (see Exhibit 8). Previously, *The Times* had pursued a strategy of increasing profits by charging premium rates to only its upscale advertisers, not readers.

In its newsroom, unlike many metropolitan and suburban newspapers, *The New York Times* provided virtually all of its own local, national, and international reporting—employing a staff of over 1,200 editorial staff, including correspondents stationed at 19 domestic and 32 foreign bureaus—without having to rely on wire or other news services, except for background. In fact, some of the newsroom expense was offset by the sale of *Times* editorial content through its News Service to 650 newspapers around the world.

While the cost of the newsroom and other staffing was fixed, newsprint costs—which could account for as much as 20% of the cost structure—could fluctuate greatly. For example, between 1987 and 1995 the average annual growth rate in the cost of newsprint was roughly 2.4% per year. However, between 1994 and 1995 the cost of newsprint rose over 40%, from $466 to $658 per metric ton (see Exhibit 9), reflecting a worldwide shortage of newsprint and making it harder for newspaper publishers to predict their newsprint costs with certainty.

The Creation of *The New York Times* Electronic Media Company

With the uncertainty in advertising revenue and newsprint prices, many newspaper publishers began to look at alternate ways of generating new revenue and profits. While the average profit margin of newspapers dropped from 20% in the mid-1980s to 12% in the mid-1990s,[9] many newspaper executives feared that profit margins could erode further, especially if classified advertising shifted from print to on-line media through such ventures as America Online's Digital Cities or

[9]The Morton Research Report.

Microsoft's Sidewalk (formerly Cityscape). Both were examples of on-line sites devoted to provide local content—local news, weather, sports, events, and traffic reports—to on-line users in select U.S. cities.

By year-end 1996, over 400 newspapers in the United States were expected to have World Wide Web sites on the Internet, digital agreements with on-line companies, or electronic bulletin boards.[10] While many newspaper publishers considered these experiments in new media defensive moves to prevent further shifts in advertising dollars, the investments in electronic media represented a renewed interest by newspapers in extending their franchises outside of the print medium.

In the mid-1980s, Times Mirror, the parent company of the *Los Angeles Times* and *Newsday*, and Knight-Ridder, the corporate owner of the *Philadelphia Inquirer*, *Miami Herald*, and *San Jose Mercury News*, had attempted to venture into electronic media. Times Mirror, with its investment in VideoText, had tried to introduce on-line news services, at-home banking, and other electronic activities through interactive television. Knight-Ridder, through its ViewTron project headed by Roger Fidler,[11] had tried to do the same using television and personal computers. Both ventures, well ahead of consumer demand and infrastructure diffusion, failed. As a result, many newspapers retreated from electronic to print media, allowing third party on-line services such as America Online (though partially owned by The Tribune Company, owners of the *Chicago Tribune*), Prodigy, and Compuserve to emerge in the late 1980s in an uncontested market. By the early 1990s, these on-line services offered many newspapers an electronic platform for distributing editorial content and several partnerships were created: the *Los Angeles Times* established Times Link, on Prodigy; the *San Jose Mercury News* created Mercury Center, on America Online; and the *Washington Post* launched Digital Ink, on AT&T Interchange.[12] Using these platforms, newspapers were able to extend their franchises electronically while providing the on-line services with branded content. They had, however, ceded control of the electronic channel to a variety of new entrants.

The New York Times Company followed a similar path in developing electronic products. In the mid-1980s, the company had launched New York Pulse, an on-line guide to entertainment and news services in New York City. The project was shut down after a year. Although *The Times* had made content available to businesses—recognizing the strong archival value of its articles—since the late 1980s through its agreement with Mead Data Central's Nexis service, it only began to make its editorial content available directly to consumers through its @times service with America Online in June 1994, through its corporate New Media and New Products' subsidiary.

Initially, content appearing from *The New York Times* on @times was limited to the day of publication. On-line visitors could not electronically retrieve past articles. This was largely due to an agreement that The New York Times Company had entered in January 1983 with Lexis-Nexis, when it had sold the electronic rights to *The New York Times* editorial content, realizing the large archival value of its articles in business-to-business applications. Only after the Dayton, Ohio-based company was sold in fall 1994 to Reed Elsevier PLC, did The New York Times Company untangle itself from its original contract and regain the rights to make its content directly available to consumers through its on-line services.

In late 1994 a report by the management consulting firm of McKinsey & Co. recommended that new electronic products targeted for consumers be created at the operating unit level, or within the newspapers of The New York Times Company (such as *The New York Times* and the *Boston Globe*), instead of through the corporate staff. Sulzberger believed that many information-based products could be launched by *The Times* on several electronic distribution channels, in addition to the Internet. He remarked:

> The truth of the matter is that we have a lot to fight with—and we're a global organization. It's really more than just the Internet. Electronic distribution is also television; it is also radio. If you think of it as broadly as you can, it's anything where you don't have to use a printing press to put out *The Times*.

The publisher thought that the quality of information—and what made it unique—generated by the newspaper's editorial staff was what consumers valued most in *The Times*, regardless of distribution method:

> In a world defined merely by the quality of information, what should *The New York Times* be scared of?

---

[10]Newspaper Association of America, Facts About Newspapers, 1996.
[11]Fidler would also head up Knight-Ridder's Information Design Laboratory in the mid-1990s. This venture, to create the underlying software for reading newspapers of the future on an electronic tablet, ended in March, 1996. Knight-Ridder's New Media Center took on responsibilities for creating Web sites for that company's 31 newspapers.
[12]Also see Harvard Business School case 396-273, "Digital Ink (A)," by Bill McIntosh under the supervision of Professor Jeffrey Rayport.

We have the best information in the world, with our commitment to quality journalism, our commitment to honest reporting, and our commitment to provide reporting that people read to make their lives successful. In an era defined as the information age, that has to have some value. Our business is information—quality value-added information. What defines us—and what is to me the core of newspapering—is taking the information and making it valuable . . . putting it in context . . . making it accessible to your audience. If you accept that, then everything else is just a means of distribution.

As a result, in early 1995, *The New York Times* created a separate unit of the newspaper, *The New York Times* Electronic Media Company, to build a portfolio of new information-based products, aimed at the consumer market, on electronic platforms. Martin Nisenholtz, a former senior vice president with the advertising agency of Ogilvy & Mather and director of content strategy at Ameritech, a regional telephone company, was appointed president of the new unit in June 1995, after a nationwide search. Nisenholtz had long been interested in the applications of interactive media. As an assistant professor at New York University he helped create the Interactive Telecommunications Program, and at Ogilvy & Mather he established the first creative development group devoted to interactive communications within a major advertising agency. He echoed Sulzberger's thinking about using different electronic means to distribute the editorial content of *The Times* and to expand the brand globally:

> Bytes are bytes. You can't separate the output of an Atex Sytem [the computerized news editing system used by the newsroom at *The Times*] from the output of a video-camera. We must understand how our brand translates into things that move and speak before the world goes broadband in four or five years.

Establishing an Internet Presence at *The New York Times*

Initially, *The New York Times* Electronic Media Company was concerned with immediate defensive moves to protect its classified advertising base—approximately $300 million in 1996—against potential upstarts like America Online and Microsoft and to establish a presence on the Internet. In October 1995, *The New York Times* entered into a partnership with six other newspapers—*The Atlanta Constitution Journal, Boston Globe, Chicago Tribune, Los Angeles Times, San Jose Mercury News,* and the *Washington Post*—to create CareerPath.com, a site on the Internet, allowing Web viewers to search the database of the help-wanted classified advertisements of all seven newspapers. A similar partnership was entered into earlier in September 1995, by *The New York Times* and eight other newspaper companies—many of the same newspapers involved with CareerPath.com—to create the New Century Network, an Internet site *(www. newcentury.net)* which allowed visitors to read top news articles written by member newspapers and which served a hub linking viewers to individual newspaper sites.

On January 19, 1996, after a year of planning and the dramatic increase in the number of Web sites worldwide—largely due to the commercial launch of the Netscape Navigator Web browser in 1994—*The New York Times* launched its own site, *www.nytimes.com* (see Exhibit 10). Prior to Nisenholtz' arrival, Sulzberger had appointed a team of four *Times* managers—Daniel Donaghy and Steve Luciani from the business side, and Kevin McKenna and Bill Stockton from the editorial side—in January 1995, to write a business plan for the newspaper's Web site, noting that the *Raleigh News and Observer* had already launched one of the first Web sites within the newspaper industry. Said Nisenholtz about *The New York Times*' Web site launch:

> Why does this matter to *The New York Times*? There are essentially two reasons: First, millions of people use the Internet and the World Wide Web. Some of these people have begun to use the Web to gain access to information about job openings, homes for sale, and other categories that fall into our marketplace. We need to build an on-line presence so that advertisers who use *The Times* to sell effectively today extend their "reach" to the people who are looking for jobs, homes, or other products and services on the Net.
>
> Second, the Web has created a new digital publishing platform to deliver news and information to a worldwide audience. When we went live on the Web, we instantly became available to Internet users in over 100 countries. While the Web is still in its nascent stage, most news organizations, including existing and emerging competitors, have begun to learn about this new medium. To the extent that readers choose to use the Internet to get their news, we need to become the choice—to be the greatest "newspaper" in the

cyberspace world and to attract new forms of "interactive" advertising.[13]

The worldwide number of personal computer users with access to the Web was expected to increase over sixfold between 1996 and 2000, from 23 million to 152 million.[14]

Web Content. Approximately 95% of the content—from the page one stories to the crossword puzzles—found in the pages of *The New York Times* print version was also available on the Web site (see Exhibit 11). Notable exclusions were the Sunday *Book Review* section, the *Sunday Magazine* and the daily chess column. Each night, the production staff of 22 professionals, under the direction of former *Times* foreign editor and diplomatic correspondent Bernie Gwertzman, would produce the Web pages in parallel production with that of the newspaper. The editorials and the Letters to the Editor were usually among the first pages produced electronically each night. Before midnight, page one and the Sports sections were the last pages to be produced. After midnight, once the pages had been reviewed by the news editor and his assistants for accuracy and style, they were then downloaded to three Web servers for general access by the public. Even after the pages had been transmitted, the staff would continue to enhance pages, edit copy, and add new material up until 3:00 a.m. when the last edition of the Late Final went to press. Added Gwertzman:

> The news editor, the director of editorial operations, and I would often provide the staff with some journalistic balance. Because the staff is so young, we try to instill in them some of the journalistic values of *The New York Times*, often reminding them to follow the stylebook and to balance the news coverage—to get pictures from both sides instead of just one.

To attract users, *The New York Times* Web site also contained some additional content not found in the newspaper: Cyber Times, a daily feature devoted to news on new media (see Exhibit 12); special sections on the presidential elections, Bosnia, and the downsizing of America (see Exhibit 13); discussion areas, inviting debate on key political issues; and interactive features, including a sensitivity analysis that allowed Web visitors to calculate the impact of Senator Dole's proposed 15% tax cut during the 1996 presidential campaign on their

individual household income (see Exhibit 14); and a forecast of the transmission of the HIV virus throughout American society using Web-based simulations.[15] Commented Nisenholtz:

> *The Times* on the Web is much more than a recycling of our newspaper content through an electronic channel. It is the beginning of our exploration in a world where digital text, graphics, photography, audio, and video collide to create new forms of journalism and advertising.[16]

Web Economics. Although there were no subscription fees—except for international accounts—to visit *The Times* on the Web, all users were required to register. This information allowed *The Times* to provide advertisers on the Web with detailed information on the demographics and preference profiles of the site's users. By March 1997, approximately 1.0 million individuals had registered for the site. On a regular day, excluding the days of major news events, approximately 60,000 unique users[17] visited the site. Approximately 170,000 unique users visited the site each week with an average site time visit of 12 minutes. Many of the Web readers were prompted to visit the site through cross promotions in the newspaper (see Exhibit 15). Approximately 80% of the site users were male, had an average household income of $80,500 (more than twice the national average), and averaged 44 years of age. Approximately 45% of users were not regular subscribers or buyers of *The New York Times* newspaper and 58% also subscribed to a local newspaper.

To generate advertising revenue for the Web site—which *Times* senior management hoped would eventually cover most of its costs—*The New York Times* offered advertisers exclusive partnerships within specific advertising categories, whereby an advertiser received exclusive marketing information (page impressions, click-views, etc.) on the site's users in exchange for a 12-month sponsorship fee of $150,000. Among the eight initial sponsors were AT&T, Chemical Bank, IBM, Maxwell House, and Toyota. Banner advertising was also available to nonsponsors at fees ranging from $30,000 (for 857,000 page views or a cost per thousand [CPM] of $35) to $120,000 (for six million page views or a CPM of

---

[13]*Times Talk*, "Martin Nisenholtz Leads the Team That Put *The Times* on the World Wide Web," January/ February 1996.
[14]"The Internet Report," Morgan Stanley, 1996.

[15]The reading note, "A Day in the Life of on the Web" HBS case No. 897-125, provides additional information on the daily production of *The New York Times* Web site.
[16]*Times Talk*, January/February 1996.
[17]Unique user is defined as a single person using the service at least once a day.

$20). By late 1996, *The Times* Web site was averaging over 550,000 to 625,000 page views[18] per day, reaching a peak of 771,000 page views the day following election night.

Redefining the Competition

In a physical world, newspapers had often considered other newspapers as their direct competitors for both advertising dollars and readers. While many editors looked at *The Wall Street Journal*, the *Washington Post*, and the *Los Angeles Times* as their primary competitors on national and international stories, business managers considered national newspapers, such as the *Journal* and *USA Today*, as competitors for both national advertisers and readers, and local newspapers, such as the *New York Daily News*, *New York Post*, and the *Bergen Record*, as competitors for local advertisers and readers.

Because of the Internet, some at the *New York Times* Electronic Media Company were beginning to think of the television news organizations, such as CNN and MSNBC, as direct competitors. Noted Pete Young, news editor of *The New York Times* on the Web:

> Right now, we're in the early days of the Internet, much like the early days of radio. Many of the people now on-line are "early adopters"—people who aren't intimidated by the machines and don't mind reaching under the hoods and jiggling the wires. The real numbers will start coming when bandwidth opens up and access get simpler and more reliable. Over time, with the convergence of the media and with increased usage, more newspapers will see other news organizations, such as CNN and NBC, as key competitors. As a result, many newspapers will probably need to rethink about when news stories are filed, doing it more often than just once a day before the paper's traditional evening deadline.

Nisenholtz believed that the context of *The New York Times* presented a special challenge in expanding the newspaper's Web presence. Unlike CNN Interactive and *USA Today* Online—the two most popular news sites on the Internet—whose punchy and up-to-the-minute stories made both news organizations tailor-made for the Web, *The New York Times*' strength was its long, in-depth articles best suited for the print medium. Noted Nisenholtz:

Having long, well-written, in-depth articles is what distinguishes *The New York Times* as a Pulitzer Prize-winning newspaper. But how can we turn that strength into an advantage for *The New York Times* on the Web? Both CNN Interactive's and *USA Today*'s style of using short stories and constant updates fits the Web medium perfectly. CNN is averaging between two and three million page views a day[19] and we're only averaging 700,000 page views. Obviously people are tuning into CNN more than just once a day.

As the *New York Times* Electronic Media Company began to think of its news competitors differently from its print counterparts, Nisenholtz also believed that the Internet redefined *The New York Times*' competitors for new advertising dollars and consumers. The new competitors—usually content providers—could also be defined on the basis of specific or "vertical" interest areas—unlike a newspaper of general or "horizontal" interests—and would include on-line sites such as c/net for technology news, amazon.com for book publishing news, and Motley Fool for investment and financial news (see Table A).

In addition to its traditional "hard news" coverage, Nisenholtz believed that *The New York Times* had the foundation to compete with these emerging vertical areas of interest on the Internet—although he felt more resources would be needed in the future to compete in a different medium. For example, while the editorial content of *The New York Times* was traditionally focused around its coverage of national and international news, its "back of the book" sections[20] on the coverage of Business, Travel, Home, Science, Books, and the Arts, provided additional opportunities for creating on-line areas of interest in an electronic age, similar to that of magazines, but under the umbrella brand name of *The New York Times*. Given the ability of electronic distribution to go beyond geographic boundaries and to segment markets by areas of interest instead of just by demographics or by household penetration, Nisenholtz believed that developing these vertical editorial products of *The Times* offered new opportunities for the franchise's consumers and advertisers.

The genesis for many of these "verticals" had begun in the mid-1970s with the expansion of *The New York Times* into a four-section newspaper. Recalled Louis

---

[18] Also know as "impressions." Each time an end user retrieves an HTML document counts as a page view. This differs from "hits," where a single hit can be one graphic file or one text file. A typical Web page generates several hits each time it is served.

[19] CNN Interactive updated its home page while a viewer was on-line. In January 1997, *The New York Times* on the Web added a page feed service from Associated Press that provided updated news and page views.
[20] Called "back of the book" because these sections were often behind the Main News (A section) and Metropolitan News (B section).

Table A Horizontal and Vertical Competitors on the Internet

HORIZONTAL SITES:

Site	URL	Description	Page Views/wk	Demographics
CNN Interactive	*cnn.com*	News from CNN/Wires	12 million	86% male/14% female
Pathfinder	*pathfinder.com*	News from Time Inc.	10 million	83% male/17% female
USA Today Online	*usatoday.com*	News from USA Today	13 million	82% male/18% female

VERTICAL SITES:

Site	URL	Description	Page Views/wk	Demographics
C/net	*cnet.com*	Technology News	2.6 million	87% male/13% female
E! Network	*eonline.com*	Entertainment News	Not available	45% male/55% female
ESPNET Sportszone	*espnet.com*	Sports News	19 million	94% male/6% female
Family Planet	*family.starwave.com*	Family Activities News	225,000	39% male/61% female
NBA.com	*nba.com*	NBA Basketball News	3 million	92% male/8% female
Wall Street Journal	*wsj.com*	Financial News	Subscriber-based	90% male/10% female

SEARCH ENGINES:

Site	URL	Description	Page Views/wk	Demographics
Yahoo!	*yahoo.com*	Search Engine	140 million	83% male/17% female

Source: Advertising/Media kits of individual Web sites; press releases; interviews

Silverstein, former assistant managing editor of *The New York Times*, who oversaw redesign of the newspaper during that period:

> The idea of producing a different third section, the C section, on a different subject each weekday was born on the Brooklyn-bound 7th Avenue subway . . . . On this subway ride, John Profret [then assistant general manager of *The Times*] brought up the "What should the third section be?" question. Entertainment, fashion, lifestyle, sports, and food were strong candidates. I said, "Why not all of them, a different one each day? We would be giving the reader in effect a different magazine with each day's paper."[21]

The addition of these new sections attracted new readers and advertisers to *The New York Times*—an estimated increase of 35,000 copies were sold on the days the new sections appeared.[22]

During the 1980s and the 1990s, *The New York Times* positioned the print version of itself as the "marketplace" for news and information, asking readers to "Read What You Like." Max Frankel, then-executive editor of *The Times*, believed that the newspaper offered its readers a wide menu of articles to read. From analysis on the president's domestic policy decision-making to the impact of the fall of the Berlin Wall to the latest theater review on Broadway, readers could read as much or as little as they wanted (see Figure 1).

However, segmenting *The Times*' editorial content on the Internet by interest area, would pose some interesting editorial challenges. Newspapers, some argued, gave communities a common agenda to work from. Noted Sulzberger:

> Should I care if the Travel section of *The New York Times* is on the same Web site as the *Book Review*? No, because you're back into distribution. We should care about producing the best section we possibly can. But what shouldn't be lost in this debate at all is the role of the newspaper in a democracy to give a nation a common understanding of what is going on in the world and how we as a nation should be doing.

Choosing the Business Model

Nisenholtz believed that the key to choosing how much *The New York Times* Electronic Media Company should

---

[21]Louis Silverstein, "Newspaper Design for *The Times*," van Nostrand Reinhold, 1990, page 104.
[22]Virginia Cahill and Donald Morrison, "Coping with the New *New York Times*," *Time*, August 15, 1977.

Figure 1 *The New York Times* and Its Vertical Editorial Products

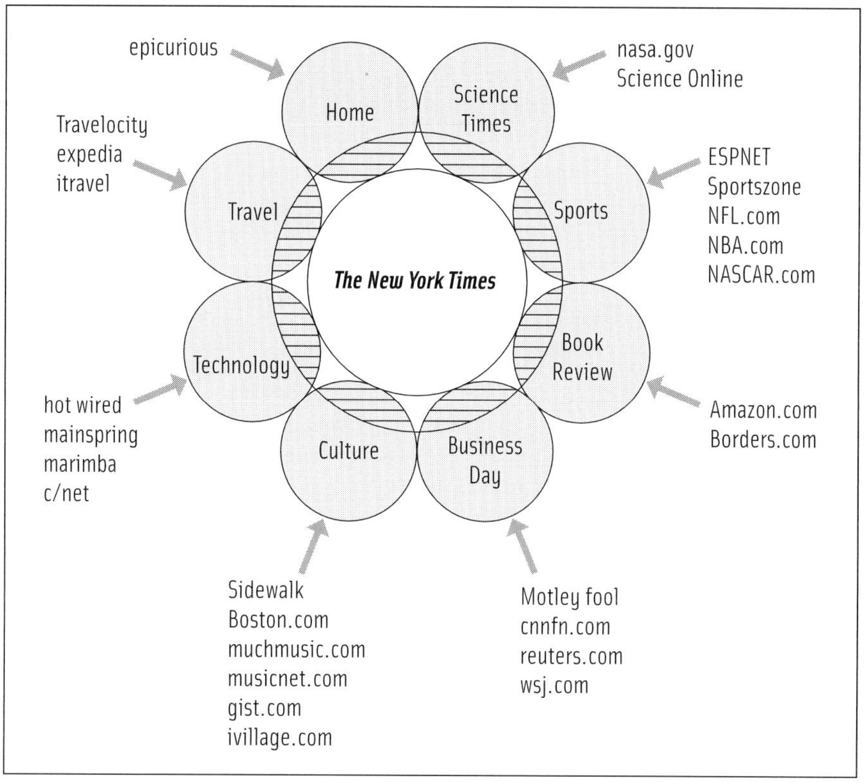

Source: The New York Times Company

invest in developing electronic vertical sites depended largely on what business model would become dominant on the Internet. Nisenholtz foresaw the development of three possible business models on the Internet.[23]

The first model was a search engine-based model where "advertisers seek a mass reach through search engines of random browsing." In this scenario, the search engines—and not individual Web sites with branded content—benefited from creating a marketplace for advertisers by attracting a traffic flow of Internet users through their individual Web sites. Search engines included Yahoo!, Excite, WebCrawler, Lycos, AltaVista, HotBot, and InfoSeek. According to PC Meter, the top search engine, Yahoo!, reported an average of 140 million page views per week at the end of 1996.[24]

The second model was a Web site based upon branded content—the direct opposite of the search engine-based model—where viewers went directly to a Web site network with branded content, similar to that of Disney.com, Pathfinder.com, or c/net. Like the search engine model, almost all of this model's revenue was generated through advertising. In this business model, however, Nisenholtz believed that "consumers would ultimately spend more time with individual megabrands" as these Web sites would be "providing highly personalized entertainment and information value." Over time, these Web sites would create a highly-targeted marketplace whereby advertisers could reach customers "based on discretely segmented interest areas and purchase behavior histories."

The third model was centered on electronic commerce. In this model, "the dominant customer use is commerce augmented by practical work-at-home applications." In this scenario, consumers could use the Internet for such activities as downloading a prospectus from a mutual fund provider to obtain targeted newsletters.

[23]Martin Nisenholtz, speech to On-line Advertising '97, December 4, 1996.
[24]"Yahoo! Reports Fourth Quarter Profit, Yahoo!" January 14, 1997. In fourth quarter 1996, Yahoo! reported a net profit of $96,000 on revenues of $8.6 million. For fiscal year 1996, Yahoo! reported a loss of $2.3 million on revenues of $19.1 million. Advertising base increased to 550 accounts.

Supporting each business model were the strong revenue projections for on-line businesses. Advertising revenue on the Internet was expected to increase from $343 million in 1996 to $5 billion[25] in 2000, while electronic commerce revenue was expected to grow from $518 million to $6.6 billion over the same time period (see Table B). Subscription fees,[26] making up a smaller portion of the revenue base due to the amount of "free" information on the Web, were expected to grow from $120 million in 1996 to $966 million in 2000.[27]

In Nisenholtz' opinion, none of the three models were mutually exclusive. For example, a Web site with branded content could attract both advertising and electronic commerce revenue. One project that was being considered by *The New York Times* Electronic Media Company was to segment its *Book Review* section as a separate—or vertical—Web site, using the *Book Review*'s 100 years of book reviews to compete with amazon.com in book retailing over the Internet.

Another aspect of the business model was if information provided on the Internet should be of a "pull" or "push" nature. The former referred to the behavior of Web viewers having to proactively pull up bookmarked Web sites for viewing; the latter referred to having information from a site delivered automatically to a viewer's computer terminal. Having an automatic and customized delivery system such as Pointcast, which began to deliver *The New York Times* on the Web to its subscribers in September 1996, helped build the retention of regular Web viewers. Noted Young:

The choice between having a reader's news "pulled" or "pushed" is of great interest to us. If you had to call up the circulation department of the paper every day and say "I'd like *The Times* delivered, please," pretty soon you'd get tired of it, you'd forget, and other things would get in the way. That's why we have subscriptions, so you call once and the paper's on your

Table B Projections for Electronic Commerce and Advertising on the Internet

Electronic Commerce ($ million)					
Categories	1996	1997	1998	1999	2000
Computer products	$140	$323	$701	$1,228	$2,105
Travel	126	276	572	961	1,579
Entertainment	85	194	420	733	1,250
Apparel	46	89	163	234	322
Gifts/flowers	45	103	222	386	658
Food/drink	39	78	149	227	336
Other	37	75	144	221	329
TOTAL	$518	$1,138	$2,371	$3,990	$6,579
Advertising Revenue ($ million)					
	1996	1997	1998	1999	2000
Advertising revenue	$80	$200	$1,000	$2,700	$4,800

Source: Forrester Research

[25]By comparison, in 1995, local newspapers recorded $13.3 billion in advertising revenue; network TV, $12.4 billion, and cable TV networks, $3.4 billion. *Advertising Age*, October 14, 1996.
[26]*The Wall Street Journal* charged a subscription fee for its Web site (*www.wsj.com*). The annual cost was $29 year for its newspaper subscribers; $49, for non-newspaper subscribers.
[27]Jupiter Communications, *Business Week*, September 23, 1996.

doorstep every morning. It's the same way with the Web; right now, you have to reach into the computer and drag the site to your screen, you have to go in and get it. What we want is to deliver it right to your screen, so that it's there first thing when you sit down at your computer.

Other Electronic Platforms

Nisenholtz believed that the electronic distribution—the Internet, television, and video—and the convergence of the media around content, provided the offensive means to augment and gain leverage from *The New York Times* brand in the future. Nisenholtz observed:

I see an unprecedented opportunity on the electronic side, not so much as a defense against erosion of classified advertising, but as an offense against an increasingly fragmented television marketplace and an increasingly costly direct response marketplace.[28]

The diagram below (see Figure 2) summarized senior management's thinking on how multiple media platforms—both electronic and print—built around *The*

New York Times editorial content would generate new growth for the franchise through increased distribution.

Entering new electronic platforms would require *The Times* to think in new ways for a different media in the future. Added Sulzberger:

You can't do what you do with newsprint on another vehicle and say it's a success. You have to find the elements that make it a successful electronic transaction—Internet, television and so on—and then adapt the information to those vehicles. We will need to understand new ways of thinking and to adopt to accept the fact that what you're going to do in print is not the same as in electronic media. Can we do to our information as what *National Geographic* magazine has done with theirs in print, television, and video?

Nisenholtz believed that television—although often overlooked with the general public's excitement over the Internet—offered an easier way to distribute content online in the immediate future and with a quicker payoff. While only 10% of all households in the United States had access to the Internet (see Exhibit 16), virtually all households had access to a television set and almost 70% of those homes had access to cable television. Said Nisenholtz:

Figure 2 *The New York Times* and Multiple-Media Channels

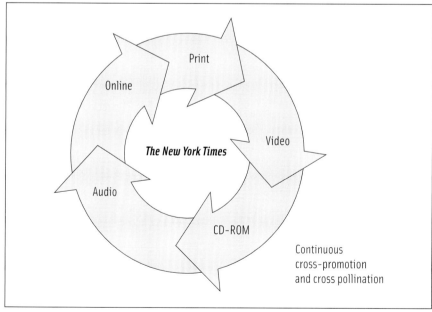

[28]American Press Institute, Curtis Memorial Seminar, "The Future for Newspaper Advertising", September 1996.

When I got here, everyone thought that the Internet was the answer for growth. I thought otherwise.   In my mind, the potential of the Internet was not yet fully recognized and I thought that the short-term opportunity for growth would be in television.

The first of these new electronic ventures included the launch of *Science Times* with the Video News International—another of The New York Times Company's subsidiaries—on the Learning Channel, and a Saturday night program designed to preview the Sunday *New York Times* on the cable news channel, MSNBC.

Measuring the Success of the New Ventures

Another key question that faced Nisenholtz was how to measure the success of these new electronic ventures— from both a financial and nonfinancial perspective. *The Times'* investment in new media was modest, being described by one senior corporate executive as being no "blackhole.com" financially. However, all classified advertising that appeared in the newspaper also appeared on the Web site, providing classified advertisers with an additional benefit for advertising in the core franchise. While the financial payoff was not immediate, Nisenholtz also believed that the other benefits from these ventures would be equally important:

As an organization, we need to look at the traditional industry benchmarks—such as the market share, revenue, etc.—in addition to softer measures—skill development, creating partnerships and organizational learning—that mean just as much at the end of the day.

Russell Lewis, the president of The New York Times Company, who, as general manager and president of the newspaper, had hired Nisenholtz to develop the electronic media company, compared its venture to an investment in research and development: "This is a skunkworks-type operation. It lets us try to see what works and what doesn't. We're here to learn from this experience."

Conclusion

Sulzberger knew that the products of *The New York Times* Electronic Media Company would take time to perfect. Said the publisher:

If Adolph Ochs—or even the man who started *The New York Times* in 1851, Henry Raymond—had to wait until the paper he created was *The New York Times* of today, a four-part newspaper of 1.2 million circulation and a Sunday newspaper weighing in at six pounds, *The New York Times* would never be created. It started out as an eight-page newspaper with very limited distribution among many competitors and it grew and adapted. Why can't we think when we create a new vision for *The New York Times* that we can't take the same opportunities to grow and adapt to make it better?

Nevertheless, while Sulzberger knew that the future direction of *The New York Times* franchise was pointed to electronic distribution, he knew that he and his management team needed to decide where to invest and how.

Exhibit 1 Top 15 Daily and Sunday Newspaper Circulation in the United States

Top 15 Dailies		Top 15 Sunday	
The Wall Street Journal	1,783,532	The New York Times	1,652,800
USA Today	1,675,091	Los Angeles Times	1,349,889
The New York Times	1,071,120	Washington Post	1,122,276
Los Angeles Times	1,029,073	Chicago Tribune	1,046,777
Washington Post	789,198	New York Daily News	888,759
New York Daily News	734,277	Philadelphia Inquirer	876,669
Chicago Tribune	609,151	Detroit News and Free Press	789,666
Long Island Newsday	564,754	Dallas Morning News	785,934
Houston Chronicle	545,348	Boston Globe	763,135
Dallas Morning News	502,894	Houston Chronicle	748,082
Chicago Sun-Times	496,030	Atlanta Journal-Constitution	687,397
San Francisco Chronicle	486,977	Long Island Newsday	656,895
The Boston Globe	471,024	San Francisco Chronicle and Examiner	633,513
New York Post	429,642	Newark Star-Ledger	605,627
Philadelphia Inquirer	427,175	Phoenix Republic	553,192

Source: Audit Bureau of Circulations, FAS/FAX Report, September 1996.
Note: Both *The Wall Street Journal* and *USA Today* are considered to be national, not metropolitan, newspapers. This classification makes *The New York Times* the largest daily metropolitan newspaper.

Exhibit 2 Pulitzer Prizes Won by *The New York Times* Staff

Year	Recipient	Citation
1918	*The New York Times*	For most disinterested and meritorious public service–coverage of World War I
1923	Alva Johnston	For distinguished reporting of scientific news
1926	Edward M. Kingsbury	For most distinguished editorial–Hundred Neediest Cases
1930	Russell Owen	For graphic news dispatched from Byrd Antarctic Expedition
1932	Walter Duranty	For reporting from Russia
1934	Frederick T. Birchall	For unbiased reporting from Germany
1935	Arthur Krock	For distinguished correspondence, impartial and analytical Washington coverage
1936	Lauren D. Lyman	For distinguished reporting–Lindbergh's departure for England
1937	Anne O'Hare McCormick	For distinguished foreign correspondence
1937	William L. Laurence	For distinguished reporting of Harvard's Tercentenary Celebration
1938	Arthur Krock	For distinguished Washington correspondence
1940	Otto D. Tolischus	For articles on economic and ideological background of war-enraged Germany
1941	*The New York Times*	Special citation for "public education value of its foreign news reports"
1942	Louis Stark	For distinguished reporting of important labor stories
1943	Hanson W. Baldwin	For series of articles on tour of Pacific battle areas
1944	*The New York Times*	For most disinterested and meritorious public service–survey of teaching American History
1945	James B. Reston	For news dispatches on Dumbarton Oaks Security Conference
1946	Arnaldo Cortesi	For distinguished correspondence from Buenos Aires
1946	William L. Laurence	For eyewitness account on bombing of Nagasaki and atomic bomb articles
1947	Brooks Atkinson	For distinguished series of articles on Russia
1949	C.P. Trussell	For "consistent excellent coverage in covering the national scene from Washington"
1950	Meyer Berger	For distinguished local reporting–Killing of 13 people by berserk gunman
1951	Arthur Krock	Outstanding instance of national reporting–Exclusive interview with President Truman
1951	Cyrus L. Sulzberger	Special citation for interview with Archbishop Stepinac of Yugoslavia
1952	Anthony H. Leviero	For distinguished national reporting
1953	*The New York Times*	For its "Week in Review" section
1955	Harrison E. Salisbury	For a series based on six years in Russia
1955	Arthur Krock	Special citation for distinguished correspondence from Russia
1956	Arthur Daley	For his sports column, "The Sports of *The Times*"
1957	James B. Reston	For distinguished reporting from Washington
1958	*The New York Times*	For distinguished coverage of foreign news
1960	A.M. Rosenthal	For perceptive and authoritative reporting from Poland
1963	Anthony Lewis	For distinguished reporting on the proceedings of the U.S. Supreme Court
1964	David Halberstam	For distinguished reporting from South Vietnam
1968	J. Anthony Lukas	For distinguished local reporting–An article on a murdered 18-year-old girl and her two lives
1970	Ada Louise Huxtable	For distinguished architecture criticism
1971	Harold C. Schonberg	For distinguished criticism, music
1972	*The New York Times*	For distinguished example of meritorious public service–Publication of the Pentagon Papers
1973	Max Frankel	For distinguished international reporting–President Nixon's trip to China
1974	Hedrick Smith	For distinguished foreign affairs reporting–Coverage of Soviet Union
1976	Sydney H. Schanberg	For distinguished foreign affairs reporting–Fall of Cambodia
1976	Walter W. (Red) Smith	For distinguished criticism–"Sports of *The Times*" column
1978	Henry Kamm	For articles on plight of Indochinese refugees
1978	Walter Kerr	For distinguished criticism–Drama
1978	William Safire	For distinguished commentary–The Bert Lance Affair
1979	Russell Baker	For distinguished commentary–Observer column
1981	Dave Anderson	For distinguished commentary–"Sports of *The Times*" column
1981	John M. Crewdson	For distinguished national reporting–Illegal aliens and immigration
1982	John Darnton	For distinguished international reporting
1982	Jack Rosenthal	For distinguished editorial page writing
1983	Thomas Friedman	For distinguished international reporting–War in Lebanon
1983	Nan Robertson	For distinguished example of feature writing–Toxic shock syndrome
1984	Paul Goldberger	For architecture criticism
1984	James Noble Wilford	For national reporting
1986	Donal Henahan	For distinguished criticism–music
1986	*The New York Times*	For explanatory journalism–articles on the Strategic Defense Initiative
1987	Alex S. Jones	For distinguished specialized reporting–Fall of a Louisville newspaper dynasty
1987	*The New York Times*	For national reporting on the *Challenger* spaceshuttle disaster
1988	Thomas Friedman	For distinguished international affairs reporting–Coverage of Israel
1989	Bill Keller	For distinguished international affairs reporting–Coverage of Soviet Union
1990	Nicholas D. Kristof & Sheryl WuDunn	For distinguished international affairs reporting–Coverage of China
1991	Natalie Angier	For distinguished beat reporting–Coverage of molecular biology and animal behavior
1991	Serge Schmemann	For distinguished international affairs reporting–Reunification of Germany
1992	Anna Quindlen	For "Public & Private" column
1992	Howell Raines	For feature writing–"Grady's Gift"
1993	John F. Burns	For distinguished international affairs reporting–Bosnia
1994	*The New York Times*	For local reporting–World Trade Center bombing
1994	Isabel Wilkerson	For distinguished feature writing–"Children of the Shadows"
1994	*The New York Times*	For photo by Kevin Carter of starving child in the Sudan
1995	Margo Jefferson	For distinguished criticism
1996	Rick Bragg	For distinguished feature writing
1996	Robert D. McFadden	For spot news
1996	Robert B. Semple, Jr.	For distinguished editorial writing

Exhibit 3 Subsidiaries of *The New York Times* Company

Newspapers:	
The New York Times	New York, New York
The Boston Globe	Boston, Massachusetts
Regional Daily Newspapers:	
Times Daily	Florence, Alabama
The Gadsden Times	Gadsden, Alabama
The Gainesville Sun	Gainesville, Florida
Times-News	Henderson, North Carolina
The Courier	Houma, Louisiana
Lake City Reporter	Lake City, Florida
The Ledger	Lakeland, Florida
The Dispatch	Lexington, North Carolina
Ocala Star-Banner	Ocala, Florida
Daily World	Opelousas, Louisiana
Palatka Daily News	Palatka, Florida
Santa Barbara News-Press	Santa Barbara, California
The Press-Democrat	Santa Rosa, California
Sarasota Herald-Tribune	Sarasota, California
Spartanburg Herald-Journal	Spartanburg, South Carolina
Daily Comet	Taibodaux, Louisiana
The Tuscaloosa News	Tuscaloosa, Alabama
Wilmington Morning Star	Wilmington, North Carolina
Regional Non-Daily Newspapers:	
News-Leader	Fernandina Beach, Florida
Marco Island Eagle	Marco Island, Florida
The News-Sun	Sebring/Avon Park, Florida
Part-Ownership:	
International Herald Tribune	Neuilly-sur-Seine, France
Magazines:	
Cruising World	Newport, Rhode Island
Golf Digest	Trumbull, Connecticut
Golf Shop Operations	Trumbull, Connecticut
Golf World	Trumbull, Connecticut
Sailing Business	Newport, Rhode Island
Sailing World	Newport, Rhode Island
Snow Country	Trumbull, Connecticut
Snow Country Business	Trumbull, Connecticut
Tennis	Trumbull, Connecticut
Tennis Buyer's Guide	Trumbull, Connecticut
Broadcast:	
KFSM-TV	Fort Smith, Arkansas
WHNT-TV	Huntsville, Alabama
WNEP-TV	Scranton, Pennsylvania
WQAD-TV	Moline, Illinois
WREG-TV	Memphis, Tennessee
WTKR-TV	Norfolk, Virginia
WQXR (FM)/WQEW (AM)	New York, New York
NYT Video Productions	Scranton, Pennsylvania
NYT Video News International	Philadelphia, Pennsylvania
Information Services:	
The New York Times Syndicate	New York, New York
The New York Times Syndication Sales Corp	New York, New York
The New York Times News Service	New York, New York
NYT Custom Publishing	New York, New York
NYT Business Information Services	New York, New York
The New York Times Index	New York, New York
Times On-Line Services	Morris Plains, New Jersey
Forest Products:	
Donohue Malbaie, Inc.	Quebec, Canada
Madison Paper Industries	Madison, Maine
NYT Shared Services Center, Inc.	Norfolk, Virginia

Exhibit 4 The New York Times Company—Income Statement ($ thousands)

Revenues	1995	1994	1993
Newspapers	$2,161,356	$2,006,184	$1,563,281
Magazines	162,941	280,061	394,463
Broadcasting	85,106	71,318	61,910
Total	$2,409,403	$2,357,563	$2,019,654
Operating Profit (Loss)			
Newspapers	$208,465	$207,489	$125,597
Magazines	28,741	19,204	12,330
Broadcasting	18,941	13,626	8,138
Unallocated corporate expenses	(27,569)	(29,077)	(19,484)
Total	$228,578	$211,242	$126,581
Interest Expense, Net of Interest Income	25,230	28,162	25,375
Net Gain on Dispositions	11,293	200,873	0
Income before Income Taxes and Equity in Operations of Forest Products Group	$214,641	$383,953	$101,206
Income Taxes	92,832	173,868	43,231
Income before Equity in Operations of Forest Products Group			
Products Group	$121,809	$210,085	$57,975
Equity in Operations of Forest Products Group	14,051	3,264	(51,852)
Net Income	$135,860	$213,349	$6,123

Source: The New York Times Company, 1995 annual report.

Exhibit 5 Advertising Dollars—Spending Index

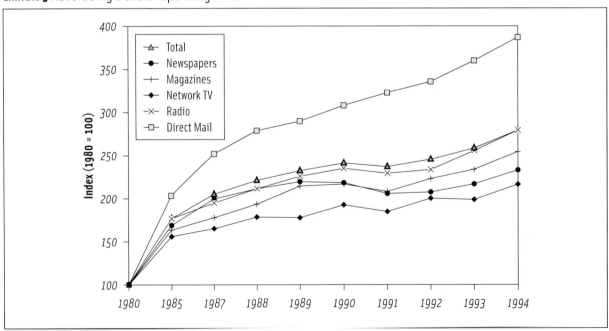

Source: Data from "Red Sky at Morning: The Newspaper Industry," by Tod A. Jacobs, Bernstein Research.

Exhibit 6 *The New York Times* Advertising Revenue

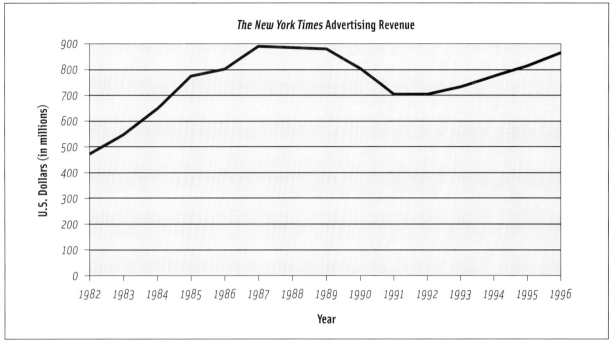

Source: The New York Times Company, Presentation to Financial Analysts, April 27, 1955, and the New York Times Company, 10-K reports, 1995 and 1996.

Exhibit 7 *The New York Times* Revenue Mix, 1996 vs. 1993

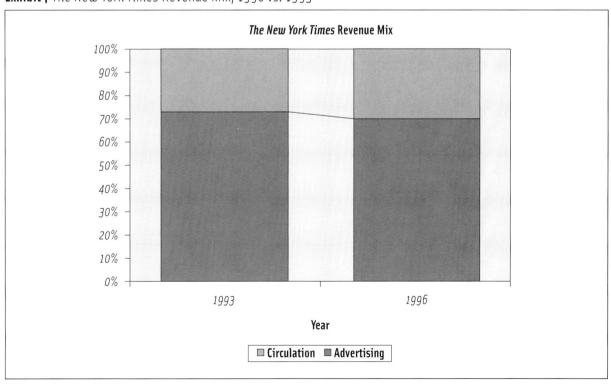

Note: In 1996, circulation made up 30% of total revenue; in 1994, circulation made up 27% of total revenue.
Source: The New York Times Company, 10-K reports, 1993 and 1996.

Exhibit 8 *The New York Times* Business Strategy

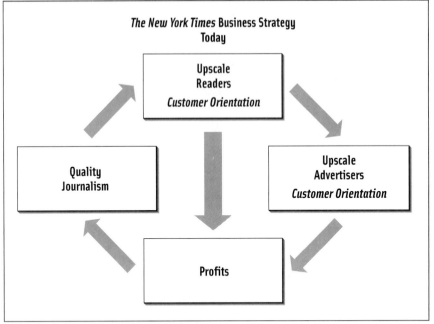

Source: The New York Times Company, Presentation to Financial Analysts, April 27, 1995.

Exhibit 9 Newsprint Prices

Year	Price (per metric ton)	Year	Price (per metric ton)
1970	$176	1983	$465
1971	$184	1984	$496
1972	$191	1985	$500
1973	$200	1986	$490
1974	$248	1987	$548
1975	$301	1988	$601
1976	$304	1989	$564
1977	$331	1990	$553
1978	$348	1991	$530
1979	$384	1992	$440
1980	$430	1993	$453
1981	$472	1994	$466
1982	$485	1995	$658

Source: Adapted from *Facts about Newspapers 1996,* Newspaper Association of America.

Exhibit 10 Home Page of *The New York Times* on the Web

Source: *www.nytimes.com*

Exhibit 11 Content Page of *The New York Times* on the Web

The New York Times

Contents

Home	Sections	Contents	Search	Forums	Help

Today's Front Page
- Front Page: Headlines: With Links to Articles
- Front Page: Quick Read: A Summary, With Links to Articles
- Front Page: Image: A 130KB Image of the Printed Page

- Late News Update available weekdays, after 1 P.M.

Sections
- Editorials
  - Letters
- Op-Ed

- CyberTimes
  - CyberTimes Index
  - Navigator: A Selective Guide to the Internet

- Business
  - Outlook '97
  - Current Market Quotes: Stocks & Indexes
  - Banking Center
  - Business Connections: A Guide to Internet Resources
- Politics
  - Political Points: A Guide to Political Sites on the Web

- Arts & Leisure
- Travel
- Real Estate
- Job Market

News by Category
- International
- National
- Metro
- Politics/Washington
- Science
- Financial
- Sports
- Style
- Arts
- Obituaries

Web Specials
- Netrospective: The Year in Review **NEW**
- Gallery in the Round : 360-Degree Photography

Politics/Issues
- The Congress Quiz **NEW**
- Issues '96: From The Times on the Web and National Public Radio
- Barely Four Walls: Housing's Hidden Crisis
- Convention '96: The Democrats
- Convention '96: The Republicans
- The Downsizing of America
- An American Place: The Election Year From Canton, Ohio

Sports
- Knicks/Celtics: One on One
- The 1996 World Series
- 1996 NFL Preview
- Atlanta 1996: The Olympic Games

From The Times Magazine
- Heroine Worship: The Age of the Female Icon
- The Magazine at 100: Looking Forward, Looking Back
- The Magazine at 100: Memorable Articles
- The Magazine at 100: Memorable Photos

Services
- Times File From DocuMagix **NEW**
- The New York Times Direct: News Delivered Daily via Netscape 3.0 Mail
- The New York Times on PointCast™
- The World Wide Web Directory: An Advertising Marketplace
- The New York Times Systems and Information Technology Job Fair: Job Listings From Participating Companies
- ETV Host: Your Personalized Electronic Television Guide
- Case Shiller Weiss: Automated Home Valuations

Diversions
- Crossword Puzzle
- Trivia Quiz

Classifieds
- Help Wanted
- Residential Real Estate
- Commercial Real Estate
- Automotive **NEW**
- Auto Dealer Directory **NEW**
- Place an Ad

Source: *www.nytimes.com*

Exhibit 12 CyberTimes Page Front

Source: *www.nytimes.com*

Exhibit 13 Special Sections of *The New York Times* on the Web

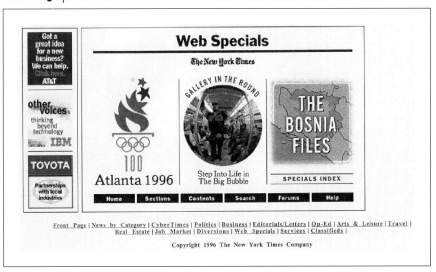

Source: *www.nytimes.com*

Exhibit 14 Example of New Media Tools for *The New York Times* on the Web

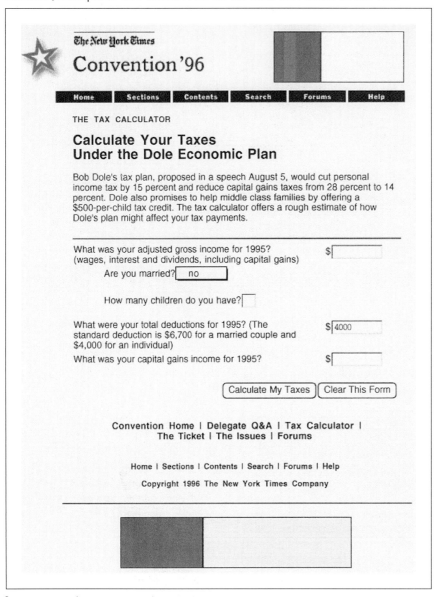

The New York Times

Convention '96

Home | Sections | Contents | Search | Forums | Help

THE TAX CALCULATOR

Calculate Your Taxes
Under the Dole Economic Plan

Bob Dole's tax plan, proposed in a speech August 5, would cut personal
income tax by 15 percent and reduce capital gains taxes from 28 percent to 14
percent. Dole also promises to help middle class families by offering a
$500-per-child tax credit. The tax calculator offers a rough estimate of how
Dole's plan might affect your tax payments.

What was your adjusted gross income for 1995? $ [   ]
(wages, interest and dividends, including capital gains)

Are you married? [no]

How many children do you have? [ ]

What were your total deductions for 1995? (The $ [4000]
standard deduction is $6,700 for a married couple and
$4,000 for an individual)

What was your capital gains income for 1995? $ [   ]

[Calculate My Taxes] [Clear This Form]

Convention Home | Delegate Q&A | Tax Calculator |
The Ticket | The Issues | Forums

Home | Sections | Contents | Search | Forums | Help

Copyright 1996 The New York Times Company

Source: *www.nytimes.com*

Exhibit 15 Cross Promotion of *The New York Times* on the Web in *The New York Times* Newspaper

If the Web is a community, think of this as its town square.

CYBERTimes

The New York Times

www.nytimes.com

It's part newspaper, part gathering place ────────────

Available only on-line, this is CyberTimes, a cornerstone of The New York Times on the Web. CyberTimes serves as the daily chronicle of the on-line world. It's like a town square for the globally connected to share information, and for anyone else interested in discovering intelligent life on-line.

Created by a special staff of New York Times editors, reporters and writers, CyberTimes goes far beyond being just news. It is a compendium of news, columns, on-line forums, in-depth features and guideposts for anyone trying to fully grasp this constantly shifting medium. CyberTimes examines the impact of cyberspace from all perspectives, then presents it in workable, fascinating pieces.

Columns include Monday's Digital Metropolis, which explores the people and technologies driving New York's Silicon Alley. Hyperwocky takes you each weekend to hidden corners of the World Wide Web, where everyday people turn into publishers and put their passions on display for the world. Wednesday's Surf &Turf explores the impact of computer technology, from games to artificial intelligence to new-media publications. arts@large, which appears on Thursdays, takes on the evolving relationship between the arts and new media. On Fridays, Internet Q&A solves problems for puzzled readers.

All this combines with the day's Internet news stories, reader forums, a glossary of Internet terms and "Navigator," the New York Times newsroom's own reference database, which provides useful links to nearly any kind of general information.

In a world as complex as the Web, it's reassuring to know there is, in fact, a town square.

Source: The New York Times Company

Exhibit 16 Household Usage of Electronic Appliances in American Households

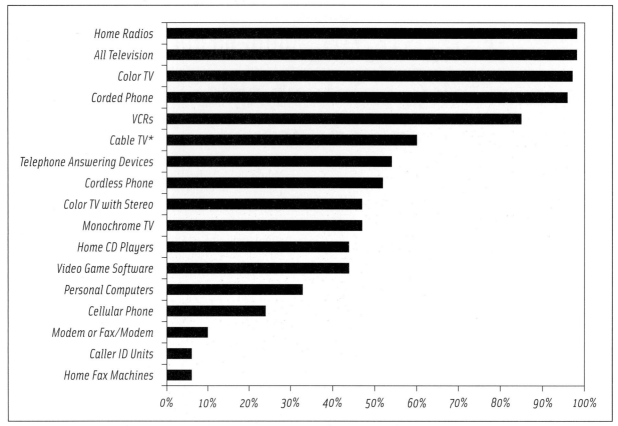

Source: Electronic Industries Association Consumer Electronics Group, 1995. *Morgan Stanley Research Estimate.

THE NEW YORK TIMES ELECTRONIC MEDIA COMPANY (B)

In January 1998, Martin Nisenholtz, president of *The New York Times* Electronic Media Company, reflected upon his unit's activities during the previous year. By year-end 1997, the *www.nytimes.com* site was averaging nearly 900,000 page-views a day, and it had registered over 3 million users. The average length of a user visit was approximately 26 minutes.[1] By comparison, in March 1997, the site averaged between 550,000 to 625,000 page-views a day, it had roughly one million registered users, and the average visit was approximately 12 minutes.[2]

Nisenholtz wondered if the site's initial marketing strategy requiring registration before use had been premature. He had hoped that data generated through user registration would enable the site to deliver highly specific target market segments of site users to advertisers. Nisenholtz commented:

> I still feel that the Internet is a great medium for using database marketing for targeting and accountability. But, as it turns out, most of the advertisers at this time are just not prepared to use the Web for database marketing. So if you are out there alone with this strategy of using the Web and no one else is pursuing it, then you are not following the standards. Some of our sophisticated advertisers have taken advantage of the database, but it's an evangelistic job for us. It's a tough sell. As a result, we had to pursue a strategy where we would conform to the existing standards and increase our page-views through increased traffic and frequency.[3]

It was apparent to Nisenholtz that something akin to a broadcast-TV model was emerging as the dominant approach for content businesses aiming to generate revenues on the Web. The alternative—a target-marketing model used by niche magazines and direct response marketers—had not gained widespread acceptance. As a result, sites that could generate large quantities of raw mass-market traffic such as Yahoo!, which averaged nearly 300 million page views a day at year-end 1997, garnered the largest on-line advertising revenues. Nisenholtz explained:

> From a traditional media perspective, advertising on Yahoo! is like advertising on the Super Bowl. If you're interested in reaching all of the fly-fishermen in the United States on the Web, it might be easier to advertise on Yahoo! than on *The New York Times* site. Never mind that the advertiser may have wasted 80% or 90% of advertising dollars in pitching its message to the vast majority of Yahoo! users who are not fly-fishermen. It may be cheaper to advertise on Yahoo! and find all the fly-fishermen in the United States than to advertise on *The New York Times* Web site and reach only the 50,000 fly-fishermen that we can identify in our database [of registered users].[4]

Despite such frustrations, the nytimes.com site had nonetheless become a commercial success. While CNN Interactive was winning the electronic news wars as the Web's most popular news site (it averaged 8 million page views a day in December 1997[5]), nytimes.com ranked 24th among all Web sites in advertising revenue[6] for the first half of 1997.

As Nisenholtz pondered the site's future, he was also planning the launch of a flanker site called *New York Today (www.nytoday.com)*, an on-line city guide that the Electronic Media Company would debut in spring 1998. Unlike the *Times* site, which targeted a national audience, *New York Today* was designed "specifically for people living in, visiting, or doing business in New York."[7] Business support for *New York Today* would come not only from on-line advertising (both retail and electronic classified), but also from the design and hosting of Web pages in the site for local advertisers. Nisenholtz expect-

---

[1] *The New York Times* on the Web, Media Kit, February 1998.
[2] See *The New York Times* Electronic Media Company (A), HBS Case No. 897-051.
[3] Interview with casewriter, December 11, 1997.
[4] Interview with casewriter, December 11, 1997.
[5] Interview with CNN Interactive Marketing Department, February 1998.
[6] Jupiter Communications, *Webtrack*, Advertising Survey, January–June 1997.
[7] Press Release, *New York Today*, October 20, 1997.

ed that *New York Today*'s key on-line competitors would be America Online's *Digital Cities New York*, Microsoft's *NewYork.Sidewalk*, and *Yahoo! New York City*.

While Nisenholtz was optimistic about the commercial possibilities of *New York Today*, its primary goal was defensive—to protect local newspaper advertising dollars, especially classified, from predation by on-line entrants. "You don't need to reach critical mass nationally to have an on-line business potentially," observed Nisenholtz. "You might be able to do it by concentrating locally and then tapping into local advertising dollars. The question then becomes this: Can you reach meaningful scale locally and become a business akin to the *Yellow Pages*, with the kind of terrific economics that go with it?"

CBS EVENING NEWS

At 6:20 p.m. on Monday, January 4, 1999, Dan Rather, the anchor and managing editor of *CBS Evening News with Dan Rather*, was ready to record the program's headlines for the day's top news stories:

> Cat and mouse with missiles: we take you aboard an aircraft carrier as Saddam Hussein tries to lure U.S. pilots into danger into the no-fly zone. . . . The huge winter storm that turned part of the United States into a no-fly zone now transforms much of the country into an Arctic misery zone. . . . And *Eye on America* investigates so-called reality TV programs that turn personal tragedy into prime time entertainment.

As Rather settled into his chair (see Exhibit 1), Andrew Heyward, the 48-year-old President of the CBS News Division, sat in his office at the CBS Broadcast Center in mid-town Manhattan and considered future directions for the *Evening News*.

Since 1980, total viewership of the three network evening newscasts had eroded from a historical high in the 1970s, when an average of 40% of U.S. households tuned in to at least one newscast each weekday night, to 1998 levels when that proportion had fallen to 25% of households (see Exhibit 2). News observers attributed the decline in viewership to a combination of factors; these included the availability of 24-hour cable television news; the expansion of local news programs; the increase in prime-time news magazines; the shift in airtimes to 6:30 p.m. (or earlier in Central and Western time zones) from 7:00 p.m.; and the proliferation of viewers' channel options with the rising acceptance of cable-TV and direct-broadcast satellite services.

Despite the fragmentation of news audiences, total viewerships nonetheless remained large, with close to 25 million households—or 32 million Americans—watching a network evening news program each night in 1998.

By comparison, the daily circulation of *USA Today* and *The New York Times*, both distributed nationally in the United States, were 1.6 and 1.1 million, respectively;[1] the weekly circulation of *Time* and *Newsweek*, two major newsweeklies, were less than 4 million each; and the average prime-time audience of the Cable News Network (CNN) was less than 700,000 households.[2] The networks' evening news programs represented a valuable franchise that went beyond the creation of a mass audience. For example, celebrity news anchors helped build networks' brand equity; highly-rated network newscasts provided a strong lead-in for affiliates' local prime-time programming; and network evening newscasts had the potential to influence, if they did not actually determine, the national news agenda.

The fragmentation of the market for news and the dwindling but still substantial evening news audiences presented Heyward with a paradox. Were the networks' evening news franchises declining? If so, should some of its resources be used to develop other programming produced by the News Division? Or, with increased fragmentation, did the audience size and brand of the *Evening News* represent an important base from which to build audiences for other News Division on-air programming or on-line programming?

As Heyward looked at the weekly ratings report on his desk, he was encouraged that the *Evening News*—the flagship show of the News Division, which also produced *60 Minutes*, *60 Minutes II*, *48 Hours*, and *Face the Nation*, among other shows—was in a tight race with ABC's *World News Tonight with Peter Jennings* and NBC's *Night News with Tom Brokaw*. In fact, on a season-to-date basis, the *Evening News* had achieved a 7.7 rating[3]—with each rating point representing 1% of the 99.4 million U.S. television households.[4] The *CBS Evening News* trailed first-place NBC by a 0.6 rating point and second-place ABC by a 0.5 rating point.

Heyward felt he had three immediate options—none of them mutually exclusive—to pursue if he wanted to

Research Associate Dickson L. Louie prepared this case, with the assistance of Holly S. Cameron, CPA, M.Div., and Research Associate Michelle Toth, MBA '95, under the supervision of Professor Jeffrey F. Rayport, as the basis for class discussion rather than to illustrate either effective or inffective handling of an administrative situation. Some of the data in this case has been disguised.

[1]Audit Bureau of Circulations, *Fas-Fax*, September 30, 1997.
[2]"Rick Kaplan to Shake Things Up at CNN," *USA Today*, January 15, 1998.
[3]Nielsen Ratings, weeks ending September 21, 1998, to February 19, 1999.
[4]CBS Research.

grow the *Evening News* franchise. (1) The show could aim to attract a larger share of the existing evening news audience, with an emphasis on serious and foreign news coverage. (2) The show could try to attract an audience of non-traditional viewers to its network evening news. Or the show could seek to increase the frequency of viewing among current viewers of the news program. Heyward was intrigued by a report sent over to his office by CBS Research showing that, of the approximately 8 million households tuning into the *Evening News* on any given night, 3.8 million households, or approximately 50% of the audience, watched the *Evening News* only once a week. If CBS could succeed in shifting once-a-week viewers to twice-a-week, the Research Department estimated that the show's ratings would increase by 0.8 points—the equivalent of 800,000 additional households—and become the number one newscast.

Network Television Broadcasting Economics

Unlike most businesses, which produced or sold tangible products and services, TV broadcasting at the network level was "essentially a programming service."[5] The three major networks in the United States, each with approximately 200 local television affiliates, generated revenues by creating and delivering audiences to advertisers. On average, each network aired 90 hours of programming a week. The amount of money that a network or station could charge advertisers for commercial spots (or avails) within a show depended on the size and composition of program audiences. The larger the audience for a particular show, the higher the advertising rates, because advertising was sold on a cost per thousand or CPM basis. At the same time, CPM rates varied considerably, based on particular audience demographics. In contrast with other media, such as newspapers, magazines, cable television, and Web sites, broadcast television was fully supported by advertising revenues rather than user fees.

The size and demographics of a television show's audience were measured each week through a sampling of viewers conducted by the A.C. Nielsen Company. Audiences were measured on the basis of "ratings" and "share." Ratings referred to the percent of total U.S. television households tuned in during an average minute within a specific program. Share referred to the percent

of households using television (or HUTs) tuned into an average minute of a specific program.[6] For example, during the week ended February 21, 1999, *60 Minutes* was the top-rated show on CBS with a 14.9 rating and a share of 25. This meant that an estimated 14.9% of all TV households in the United States watched the show, and this was equivalent in the time period to 25% of TV households actually using television.

The viewing audience was also broken down by Nielsen into several demographic categories: children, teens, and adults; men and women; and age cohorts. Adult age groups were categorized initially in two key segments—18 to 49 and 25 to 54. Additionally a new group was emerging in demographic breakdowns: baby-boomers 35 to 54. Advertisers often paid premiums for placement within programs with large concentrations of viewers between the ages of 18 and 49, based on a long-held belief among marketers that younger audiences were more susceptible to influence with respect to brand preferences.

"The actual [advertising] rates for each television program are proprietary information of the networks. It is a rate card that changes by the hour," noted David Freeman, a research manager with the Television Advertising Bureau. "All television advertising is inventory. It's sold on the basis of supply and demand. The networks will charge the highest price they can get. Like unfilled airplane seats, any unsold spots represent lost income."[7]

Affiliates played an important role in determining a program's distribution and therefore its audience size. Between 1948 and 1985, to prevent concentration of media ownership, the U.S. Federal Communications Commission limited the number of local television stations owned by a single entity to five VHF[8] and two UHF[9] stations.[10] Under this constraint, the three major television networks focused direct ownership of stations in five of the largest U.S. metropolitan markets (the network-owned stations were known as "owned and operated" or O&O stations). To ensure additional distribution,

---

[5] David Poltrack, *Television Marketing: Network, Local, and Cable*, McGraw-Hill, 1984.

[6] CBS Television Network Sales/Marketing Services.

[7] Interview with casewriter, February 9, 1998.

[8] VHF referred to Very High Frequency channel and corresponded to channels 2 to 13.

[9] UHF referred to Ultra High Frequency channel and corresponded to channels 16 to 63.

[10] The federal communications law which restricted television ownership to five VHF and two UHF stations was changed in 1985. The new federal communications law allowed for ownership by a single entity of up to 12 television stations as long as total ownership did not exceed coverage of more than 25% of the national audience in the United States. This law was revised in 1996 to allow ownership of an unlimited number of television stations and coverage up to 35% of the national market.

networks contracted with independently owned stations in the next 200 largest markets for signal carriage or "clearance" of their programs. Network programming was categorized according to "dayparts," among them: Morning (7 a.m. to 9 a.m.); Daytime (10 a.m. to 4 p.m.); Evening News (6:30 p.m. to 7 p.m.), Prime Time (8 p.m. to 11 p.m.), Late Night (11:35 p.m. to 2 a.m.), and Late Late Night (2 a.m. to 6 a.m.). Less important network dayparts included Saturday Morning Children's Programming, Sunday Morning Information Programs, Specials, and Sporting Events.[11]

To carry network programming in local markets, affiliates were paid a "clearance" fee by the network. On rare occasions, affiliates might choose to preempt network feed in favor of a local program (for example, to provide coverage of local sporting events or weather disaster conditions). When an affiliate preempted the network, it would forfeit its clearance fee for the bumped program. In network programming, affiliates were granted limited commercial opportunities with respect to advertising; generally, each 30-minute program from the network left several 30-second avails for affiliates to sell. The only network programming which had no local avails was evening news.

Time periods outside of network dayparts belonged to affiliates, and they retained all revenues generated by avails in local dayparts. Local dayparts included Morning (9 a.m. to 10 a.m.), Early Fringe (4 p.m. to 6:30 p.m.), Prime Access (7 p.m. to 8 p.m.), and Local News (11 p.m. to 11:35 p.m.). During these times, stations sourced their own programming content, which included local news and syndicated programs (these were shows purchased from production companies after network contracts for original broadcast had been fulfilled). Typical programs in multiple cycles of syndication were talk shows such as *The Oprah Winfrey Show* and game shows such as *Wheel of Fortune*. (The only exception was Daytime, which often represented a combination of national network and local affiliate programming.)

The History of CBS Corporation

In 1928, William S. Paley, the 27-year-old son of a Russian-Jewish immigrant cigar maker, borrowed $400,000 from his father and purchased controlling interest in the one-year-old Columbia Broadcasting System (CBS) radio network. Paley led the fledgling radio system

[11]David Poltrack, *Television Marketing: Network, Local, and Cable*, McGraw-Hill, 1984.

through rapid expansion, differentiating CBS from its entertainment-oriented rival National Broadcasting Company (NBC) by focusing on news and public affairs throughout the 1930s and 1940s. With the outbreak of World War II, prominent CBS correspondent Edward R. Murrow and his team of journalists, known as "The Murrow Boys," ranked among America's most respected and popular newscasters.

After the war, Paley transformed CBS into a television network while retaining its presence in radio. He assailed NBC's stronghold in entertainment programming by signing top NBC talent like Jack Benny and successfully promoting new talent like Lucille Ball and Jackie Gleason. Over the next three decades, CBS's commitment to quality and family-oriented programming was reflected in its lineup of the most-watched entertainment shows in the United States, including *The Honeymooners, I Love Lucy, Gunsmoke*, and *The Mary Tyler Moore Show*, and it became known among American consumers as the "Tiffany" network.

Following years of top-rated prime-time shows and expansion into records and book publishing, CBS ended the 1980s under siege. Prime-time ratings fell during the mid-1980s as the network became the target of several hostile take-over attempts. Ted Turner, founder of CNN, tried to acquire CBS and failed. Laurence Tisch, the New York investor who ran Loew's Corporation, succeeded in 1986. Under Tisch's management CBS cut staff, sold the network's music and publishing divisions, and reduced its investments in other media, such as cable television. Jim McKenna, Vice President of Finance and Administration for the CBS News Division and a 25-year veteran of the company, recalled how CBS retrenched under Tisch:

> Tisch was very successful at buying and selling. Unfortunately, I think the company, and the people who were running it at the time, didn't realize, recognize, or understand that this was his strategy. And it is unfortunate because at the same time that Tisch acquired CBS, Capital Cities acquired ABC. Both companies were purchased for nearly the same amount of money—roughly $5 billion—at around the same time in the mid-1980s. When you leap forward about ten years to 1995, both companies were sold again. CBS was sold to Westinghouse for about $5 billion. Capital Cities/ABC sold out to Disney for about $19 billion. At the end of the day, what did Tisch's strategy of buying and selling do for the company? It didn't do anything for the company; it actually hurt the company. But it was great for Tisch. And when you look at ABC, they were left with a company

that was prosperous, diverse, multimedia, and international. And the value its shareholders got was equally significant.

With the emergence of three new networks—Fox (owned by Rupert Murdoch's News Corporation), UPN (United Paramount Network, controlled by Viacom), and WB (Warner Brothers, controlled by Time Warner)—during the early 1990s, the value of local TV stations doubled as affiliates with a VHF signal found themselves in demand. (Because VHF stations tended to have stronger signals and lower channel numbers on broadcast dials, they were deemed superior as distribution vehicles in local markets by networks.)

In 1994, CBS felt the pinch of this additional competition, when it attempted to extend the network's TV rights for National Football League games. The negotiation became a bidding war with Fox over the NFL franchise, and Fox won, paying $1.58 billion for rights for a period of four years. CBS's failure to re-sign the NFL also hurt the network's affiliates, given that the loss of football meant, in part, lower ratings in local markets. As a result, certain CBS affiliates defected from the network—in key markets such as Atlanta, Cleveland, Dallas, Detroit, Milwaukee, Phoenix, Seattle, and Tampa—and switched their affiliation to Fox. Many industry observers viewed the shift in NFL rights as a signal moment in the history of broadcast television in the United States—the three-way network oligopoly was broken. With NFL, Fox became a contender for major network status, elevated from its position as a second-tier player fighting for leftover programming and advertising dollars with UPN and WB.

From McKenna's perspective, the NFL loss genuinely crippled CBS. The affiliate losses had an obvious and materially negative impact on the News Division. "The other interesting dynamic," McKenna observed, "was the impact on the *Evening News*." As he recalled, "We went back and did the research and measured the impact [on the *News*] of these affiliate changes. It was about a six-tenths of a ratings point [net] difference. CBS lost five-tenths and NBC gained one-tenth. If you know the evening news ratings, six-tenths of a ratings point is major. We went from a position of being second to ABC to being third and last."

In 1995, Westinghouse Electric Corporation acquired CBS for $5.4 billion.[12] The merger of CBS with Westinghouse's Group W broadcasting properties resulted in a combined O&O network of 14 television and 39 radio stations.[13] With the acquisition in 1997 of Mel Karmazin's Infinity Broadcasting—a radio chain that included talk-radio personalities Don Imus and Howard Stern—the number of CBS-owned radio stations increased to 175 nationwide. In 1996, the Westinghouse/CBS Group had sales of $4.1 billion in media, including $2.6 billion from the TV network.

At year-end 1997, 10 of the network's 14 O&Os operated in top-20 markets, and 64 of its 77 radio stations were concentrated in top-ten markets (see Exhibit 3 for a map of CBS properties). In addition to its O&Os, CBS had 192 affiliates serving 214 markets in the United States (see Exhibit 4 for a map of CBS TV affiliates). According to Peter Schruth, CBS's President of Affiliate Relations, the network's goal was to defend its stronger affiliates and upgrade its weaker ones from UHF to VHF stations whenever opportunities arose:

> One challenge of a fragmented, more active marketplace is to hold on to strong [VHF signal] affiliates that are under attack from other networks. Everyone wants to take our VHF stations away. Whoever has a UHF station tries to take over a VHF station. We were under attack in St. Louis, where we have one of the strongest CBS affiliates in the country. ABC was on Channel 36. ABC came after us. Because of the affiliate's fear of the unknown, we were able to hold on to the station.

On December 1, 1997, Westinghouse renamed itself CBS Corporation to reflect its transformation from an industrial to a media-based business.[14] For fiscal-year 1997, CBS Corporation had revenues of $5.4 billion. Of those revenues, the CBS Network accounted for $2.8 billion and the O&Os generated an additional $836 million. (See Exhibit 5.)

A month later, in January 1998, CBS entered a bidding war with NBC for NFL rights—this time for the American Football Conference games—and won with an offer of $4 billion for eight years. The NFL's National Football Conference games remained with Fox. CBS affiliates shared in the cost of acquiring the NFL through a mix of cash and inventory. Don Hewitt, executive producer of *60 Minutes*, whose show was one of those hit hardest from the NFL loss, added "I think it's like restoring part of the CBS logo."[15]

---

[12]"Turner Board Looking at Options," *Advertising Age*, August 19, 1995.

[13]Westinghouse Electric Company Annual Report, 1996.
[14]*ValueLine*, CBS Corporation, December 1997.
[15]Gary Paul Gates, *Air Time: The Inside Story of CBS News*, Harper & Row, 1978.

Leslie Moonves is President and Chief Executive Officer of CBS Television, the corporate entity that oversees all programming activities at CBS, including CBS News, CBS Sports, and CBS Entertainment. Moonves, too, views the return of the NFL as an important building block in the corporation's comeback story, but in no way more important than the re-establishment of CBS News as a key determinant of the CBS corporate image and character. "The return of NFL football helped the public once again view us as an industry leader and a media force to be taken seriously," he observed.

CBS News benefited from that increase in viewing audience, promotional power and all-around credibility. But the same benefits that our entire company saw from the return of football were also conferred by the return of CBS News to a position of unparalleled leadership in its field. CBS News is an integral part of the service we provide to the public, and a crucial part of our image and our public standing. As with football, we are simply not the CBS people know and respect without a healthy, growing CBS News. And the *CBS Evening News* is central to that overall role in the company—and in society.

In late 1997, in addition to the *Evening News*, the CBS News Division managed a diverse portfolio of news programs (see Exhibit 6). Its first significant program each weekday was *CBS Morning News* a half-hour news program (any time between 5 a.m. and 7 a.m.), followed by *CBS This Morning* (7 a.m.–9 a.m., Monday–Friday), a breakfast-time news show that competed with NBC's *Today Show* (7 p.m.–9 a.m., Monday–Friday) and ABC's *Good Morning America* (7 a.m.–9 a.m., Monday–Friday). CBS had also pioneered the newsmagazine format with its long-standing franchise *60 Minutes* (7 p.m.–8 p.m., Sundays), which was widely imitated both within the CBS News Division and across other networks. For example, in January 1999 CBS debuted *60 Minutes II* (9 p.m.–10 p.m., Wednesdays). CBS also broadcast the long-successful *48 Hours* (10 p.m.–11 p.m., Thursdays). These newsmagazines had viewing profiles similar to the *Evening News,* with median ages ranging from 55.3 to 57.9 years. Meanwhile, ABC ran newsmagazines *20/20* (8 p.m.–9 p.m., Mondays, 10 p.m.–11 p.m., Wednesdays, and 9 p.m.–10 p.m. Fridays and Sundays). NBC countered with *Dateline* (10 p.m.–11 p.m. Mondays and Tuesdays, and 8 p.m.–9 p.m. Wednesdays and Sundays). ABC also ran a program that stood alone in its time-slot, *Nightline* (11:35 p.m.–12:05 a.m., Monday–Friday).

The increase in the number of network newsmagazines was driven by audience interest and broadcast production economics. Five of the 20 most-watched Prime-Time shows during the 1997–98 season were newsmagazines. CBS's *60 Minutes* ranked seventh with a rating of 13.9. ABC's *20/20* was sixteenth with a 10.9 rating, ABC's *Prime-Time Live* was nineteenth with a 10.5 rating, and NBC's *Dateline-Tuesday* was thirteenth with an 11.5 rating. *Dateline-Monday* was fourteenth with an 11.4 rating. The average cost to produce a newsmagazine was estimated at $400,000 to $600,000 an hour, roughly half the cost of an average Prime-Time non-news program.[16]

The CBS Evening News with Dan Rather

The first regular evening newscast on CBS aired in Spring 1948 with Douglas Edwards as anchor. Originally known as *CBS TV News*, the show was initially broadcast to four markets before expanding nationwide in 1951. In 1962, Walter Cronkite replaced Edwards as the show's anchor and began a 19-year reign. CBS was the news leader for 15 of Cronkite's 19 years at the helm. Between 15% and 17% of all U.S. households tuned into the *Evening News with Walter Cronkite*. On that program, CBS News covered the Civil Rights Movement, Vietnam, Space Exploration, and Watergate during the 1960s and 1970s.

In March 1981, Dan Rather, who had joined CBS News as its Dallas bureau chief in 1962, succeeded Cronkite as the *Evening News* anchor and managing editor. Rather had served as CBS White House Correspondent during the Johnson and Nixon Administrations and as a correspondent for CBS's *60 Minutes* (see Exhibit 7 for a biography of Rather). He was known as a tough, no-nonsense reporter. In November 1963, Rather was in Dallas, and broke the news of President John F. Kennedy's assassination. During the early 1970s, officials in the Nixon Administration tried to have Rather removed from the White House beat because of his aggressive demeanor. As an anchor, he still went on reporting assignments and enjoyed the challenge of covering major news stories himself. In 1997, Rather still believed in his responsibility to maintain the network's commitment to quality journalism:

---

[16]Jane Hall, "Magazines Spread Across TV's Table," *Los Angeles Times*, September 30, 1997.

I'm primarily a story hunter, a story writer, and a storyteller. My job here is to see that the quality of CBS News is maintained. CBS News has been an important part of the brand image of CBS—I believe that the quality reporting we do here is a key intangible asset for the entire network. When people tune into CBS, they expect to see first-rate reporting and nothing less.[17]

The *Evening News* maintained its first-place standing in the ratings among the network newscasts during the first eight seasons of Rather's 16-year tenure. By the end of the 1989–1990 season, however, the *Evening News* dropped into second place behind ABC's *World News Tonight*. ABC, once known as the network that invested least in news, began investing aggressively to upgrade its News Division. Under the direction of Roone Arledge, who also headed ABC Sports beginning in 1978, ABC News added both star TV journalists and new prime-time news programs. Arledge hired David Brinkley from NBC and Diane Sawyer from CBS and developed *Nightline*, *20/20*, and *Prime-Time Live*.[18] Such programming helped ABC achieve a seven-year reign atop the ratings of the evening news programs. By the 1990–1991 season, CBS was suffering again: the *Evening News* had fallen to third place behind *NBC Nightly News*.

When the *Evening News* regained second place among the network news shows in the 1992–1993 season, News Division management attempted to build on a winning trend by installing Connie Chung, anchor of CBS's *Eye to Eye* newsmagazine, as co-anchor with Rather. The logic was that Chung would help the *Evening News* attract new viewers.[19] Despite the show's increasing emphasis on news features, the formula did not succeed. The *Evening News* fell to third place once more, and Chung departed as co-anchor in May 1995. From that point, Rather was sole anchor of the *Evening News* and achieved a 7.3 rating in the 1996–1997 season.

Under Westinghouse's ownership in early 1996, a new management team was brought in to lead the News Division. Heyward, the *Evening News'* executive producer, was promoted to CBS News president and Jeff Fager, a former *60 Minutes* senior producer, was appointed as Heyward's replacement for the *Evening News*. Both were long-time CBS News veterans. Under Heyward and Fager, the *Evening News* set a new course to climb out of the ratings basement. Rather remembered how the change in direction came about:

We set ourselves on a course about two years ago. We stopped, thought, assessed, and asked ourselves what we can do better. And what we said to ourselves was: "You know, we think we're the best hard news broadcast of the network Big Three, but we'd like to be a bit harder. And we would like to increase the broadcast's reputation of being the broadcast of record and a broadcast of quality." So we rededicated ourselves to that.[20]

Fager recalled that the change in ownership from Tisch to Westinghouse had a positive impact on the surviving News Division personnel, who had weathered nearly a decade of turbulence under ownership apparently insensitive to the quality of network news. Even Fager seemed surprised that the spirit of Edwards, Murrow, and Cronkite—the passion to produce outstanding news programming—still flickered. "After Tisch left," Fager commented, "everyone in the News Division looked around, stood up, and realized that we were still alive, after all. We had made it through one of the toughest periods in our history."

Declining Viewership of Evening News Shows

Observers cited several reasons for the decline in viewership of evening news shows. These included TV channel proliferation, the emergence of CNN, expansion of local news programming, and shifts in the start time of network news programs.

Channel Proliferation. With the erosion of broadcast-television audiences for network programming beginning in the 1980s, almost all of the losses went to cable television (see Exhibit 8). The decline in network viewership was not just restricted to news, but was reflected in prime-time and sports programming. For example, CBS's *Dallas* was the top-rated show during the 1980–1981 season with a 31.2 rating. In contrast, NBC's *Seinfeld* was the top-rated show during the 1997–1998 season with 22.0 rating—a 29% drop. In sports, NFL viewership dropped from a 15 rating in 1980–1981 to a 10.3 rating in 1998—a 31% decline.[21]

[17]Interview with casewriter, December 16, 1997.
[18]Marc Gunther, *The House That Roone Built: The Inside Story of ABC News*, Little Brown, 1994.
[19]Jane Hall, "Rather's Reality Check Keeps Him Anchored," *Los Angeles Times*, March 9, 1996.

[20]Steve McCleallan, "Dan's Back!," *Broadcasting and Cable*, January 5, 1998.
[21]CBS Research.

Emergence of CNN. Founded by Ted Turner in June 1980, Atlanta-based Cable News Network became the first channel to offer 24-hour news programming on television. By 1997, CNN had access to approximately 75 million cable-TV households in the United States.[22] CNN reached its peak viewership during the Gulf War when approximately 100 million people in the United States tuned in for live coverage (on cable and via CNN's broadcast affiliates) of the Baghdad bombing on January 17, 1991.[23]

In 1996, two additional all-news cable channels entered the market. NBC News and Microsoft Corporation launched MSNBC in July 1996 and News America Corporation launched the Fox News Channel in October 1996. In the MSNBC joint venture, Microsoft committed to invest hundreds of millions of dollars to develop the channel, while NBC News provided editorial and production resources. Besides CNN, MSNBC, and the Fox News Channel, several all-news cable channels emerged in regional markets. These channels included BayTV in the San Francisco Bay Area, Chicagoland TV in northern Illinois, and New England Cable News serving the northeastern United States.

Expansion of Local News Programming. In the 1980s, affiliates expanded local television news to compete in Early Fringe and Prime Access. Many affiliates found local news more cost-effective to produce than to buy shows in syndication. As affiliates expanded local news coverage, they drew on news feeds from CNN for video images of national and international news, which they could not get from the networks. To counter the use of CNN footage, network news divisions buckled under pressure and made available their own packaged news feeds to affiliates.[24] CBS called this service NewsPath. The shift was controversial, because it ran the risk of having affiliates in a position to "break" network news stories. David Poltrack, CBS Executive Vice President of Research and Planning, observed that services such as NewsPath did have a significant impact on network news audiences:

> Previously, NewsPath took all of the news that the network did not use and fed it out for use by the local affiliates. When the affiliates began to include national and international news in their newscasts, CNN started to provide a competing news service to these stations. To keep CNN out of the affiliates, the network had to add their main stories to NewsPath. The network didn't include the main stories before, because it didn't want to cannibalize its evening newscasts. However, if you wanted to compete with CNN, you now had to put your major stories on NewsPath.

Shifts in Start Time of Network News Programs. During the 1980s, many affiliates shifted the network news from a 7:00 p.m. to a 6:30 p.m. start (or earlier in the Central and Western time zones). Their goal was to capture the more valuable audiences in Prime Access with local programming rather than cede it to the networks (see Exhibit 9). The airtime decision was driven by local economics. Advertising revenues in Prime Access, if programming was local, were retained by affiliates. When affiliates ran syndicated programs such as *Entertainment Tonight, Wheel of Fortune,* or *Jeopardy,* they could sell most or all of the avails in their metro markets—and those avails were worth more if they ran later in the day. The same logic worked against the networks. When evening news ran earlier, it attracted smaller audiences with older viewers, rendering the avails—sold exclusively by the network on a national level—less valuable to advertisers. In short, the time shift for network news enabled the affiliates to maximize revenues at the expense of the networks.

The *CBS Evening News* Audience

Demographics. Over half of *Evening News* viewers were female and 60% were aged 55 years or older (see Exhibit 10). *NBC Nightly News* and ABC's *World News Tonight* viewers were somewhat, though not substantially, younger. This was consistent with CBS' position as the network with the highest median age among the Big Three in the 1998–1999 season (see Exhibit 11). Poltrack offered some research-based insight into another factor, other than timing, that drove these demographics. As viewers aged, he observed, they typically watched more television news:

> In the 1960s, we took a look at television behavioral patterns in a study sponsored by CBS. We repeated the same study in the 1970s and again in the 1980s. We looked at cohorts and we found that as each group went from their 20s into their 30s, they increased their

---

[22]"Top Ten Cable Networks, 1996," *New York Times Almanac*, 1998.
[23]*CNN Milestones*, CNN Public Relations Department, January 1998.
[24]By early 1998, CNN had over 350 broadcast-TV affiliates in the United States; many of these were also network affiliates. To remain competitive, such stations held the option to take both CNN and network newsfeeds. Phone interview with Steve Haworth, CNN, February 10, 1998.

news and information viewing and reduced their sitcom viewing. It is clear that increased television news viewership at a later age is a life-stage phenomenon. This trend has been seen in every generation of the postwar era.

Customer Acquisition and Retention.

George F. Schweitzer, CBS's Executive Vice President of Marketing and Communications, believed that the network's "reach of millions of people every night" provided CBS with a huge base to "promote" the *Evening News*. He noted that current CBS strategy to boost ratings was to "regain and retain viewers." Schweitzer commented:

> Your best customer is the customer you have now. If we can retain those viewers one more night a week, we'll be in first place. The next best customers are those who are familiar with us, but are not watching. We would like to get them back. You then build out from the bull's eye, with the outer-most ring being people who won't watch no matter what you do. If the bull's eye represents your current customers, then the inner-most ring represents your formerly-current customers. You can get those recent defectors back with a program of enhanced editorial interest.

CBS Research found that approximately 75% of evening news viewers were brand loyal. These loyal viewers were divided evenly among the three networks, with CBS, ABC, and NBC each claiming roughly 25% of viewers among their loyals. The remaining 25% were brand switchers (see Exhibit 12). Another CBS research report showed that, on any one night, approximately 50% of its network news audience consisted of once-a-week *Evening News* viewers, as compared with five-times-a-week viewers who constituted just 9% (see Exhibit 13). Schweitzer commented:

> There's also a pool of news viewers who just hunt around every night. There's not a whole lot of new people who are coming in to watch. It's a pre-set pie. We looked at different strategies. The strategy of "regain and retain" is what we're working on now.

In addition to cross-promoting the *Evening News* on affiliates' local news shows, anchors on *48 Hours*, *60 Minutes*, and *60 Minutes II* also highlighted upcoming shows. Duplicate viewership for the newsmagazines and the *Evening News* was significant. Robert Schlaepfer, CBS's Director of News Research, commented on the cross-promotion strategy:

> *60 Minutes* is the best example of a show where we use our cross-promotion. Before we decide where to cross-promote, we look at the duplication of audiences with *Evening News* viewers across all our news programs—in Prime Time, Morning and Saturday/Sunday Weekends, Daytime, and Late Night. On shows where duplication is high, we often choose to cross-promote. We cross-promote because we believe that viewers of these shows, if they are not already doing so, would be the most likely to watch the *Evening News*. *60 Minutes* has the largest duplication with the *Evening News,* but we have other CBS news programs where there is also strong duplication. When we cross-promote to these audiences, it's like "preaching to the choir."

Impact of Affiliate Lead-ins on Viewership.

When compared to NBC, Poltrack noted that the *Evening News* did better in second-tier markets—such as Minneapolis, Green Bay, and Baltimore—than in major metropolitan markets, such as New York, Los Angeles, or Philadelphia, where local newscasts by O&Os were weaker than the competition. The strength of O&Os in news had a direct impact on the ratings for the *Evening News*. As Poltrack observed:

> We are significantly disadvantaged in our major urban markets. There are a couple of reasons for this. First, the ratings of the CBS O&Os are not as strong as those of NBC or ABC in the largest markets. Second, the viewership of the lead-in programs for the evening newscast aired by our O&Os are not as strong as ABC's. Lead-ins are a major contributor to viewership of local news shows. Over the past several years, *The Oprah Winfrey Show* has been the dominant force in pre-news in the 4:00 p.m. to 6:00 p.m. time period. Viewers of *Oprah* are news viewers. They watch the news program that follows *Oprah*. *Oprah* airs on many of the ABC affiliates and not on many CBS affiliates. In fact, when *World News Tonight with Peter Jennings* went number one in 1989–1990, we could show you a statistical analysis that attributed its entire leadership position to *Oprah*. So CBS is at a disadvantage in major markets, though the *Evening News* is stronger in smaller markets where our affiliates have a strong news presence.

In addition, Rather believed that the weak UHF signals of the five new CBS affiliates, which replaced the old CBS VHF stations that joined the Fox Network in 1994–1995, meant that CBS had compounded the problem with inadequate distribution:

We've been operating with a handicap since we lost several of our affiliates to the Fox network. The stations who replaced them had weak signals, and our new management team is now working on improving our distribution. That will be a tremendous help. When we lost our affiliates, we went to hell in a handbasket. You can have the best milk in the world, but if you do not have the distribution to deliver it, it does not matter.[25]

Advertising Sponsors. In every *Evening News* 30-minute broadcast, seven minutes were allocated to 14 to 15 advertising spots. Key advertisers for the *Evening News* included Johnson & Johnson, General Motors, American Home Products, Bayer, Pfizer, and Charles Schwab. Joseph D. Abruzzese, President of Sales for the CBS Television Network, explained how advertising for the *Evening News* was sold:

> Selling the *Evening News* to advertisers was easier four years ago prior to the increase in the number of Prime-Time newsmagazines. The older audiences for the *Evening News* sometimes make it a tough sell—advertisers are not interested in paying a premium on audiences over 55 years of age. Although *60 Minutes* has an older audience, too, it also has the largest percentage of viewers making more than $100,000 a household than any other television show. That story makes it easier for us to sell *60 Minutes*.
>
> We're always trying to find a good story on why advertisers should buy time in the *Evening News*. Too often, our advertisers tell us that they would rather spend their money instead on a newsmagazine program. With a newsmagazine, advertisers can not only reach older viewers already watching the *Evening News* but also younger viewers not watching the newscast.
>
> It's a challenge. Unlike some of our competitors, we do not sell the *Evening News* as a package with other news programs but as a stand-alone program.

The *Evening News* Broadcast

The 30-minute *Evening News* broadcast was divided into five segments with four interstitial periods for commercials. Network research indicated that key attributes that

attracted news viewers were anchor appeal, news content, reporting and writing, and end-of-show feature pieces:

Anchor Appeal. Poltrack noted that Rather's appeal—he was on-air for approximately eight minutes of every 30-minute newscast—cut across various age groups. He ranked high on dimensions of "trustworthiness" and "experience," which Poltrack found were top motivators for people who tuned in. Gil Schwartz, CBS's Senior Vice President of Communications, added:

> People do want to get a feeling of trust from the *Evening News*. The viewers want a newscast that is truthful, honest, and "there" [on the scene of the news]. CBS is the same place that brought you Edward R. Murrow and Walter Cronkite.

A 1988 study commissioned by the Times Mirror Company and conducted by The Gallup Organization also confirmed Rather's trustworthiness with the American public. Rather's believability rating was 81%, higher than the 75% average for all three network anchors and greater than that of then-President Reagan's rating of 67%.[26] Some past controversy did, however, surround Rather. For example, the network went off the air for an unprecedented six minutes prior to an *Evening News* broadcast in September 1987, when Rather reportedly stormed off the set after having the newscast delayed by CBS Sports' coverage of the U.S. Open.[27] He was also criticized for appearing pointedly aggressive in a 1988 interview with Vice President George Bush, in which Bush accused Rather of "ambushing" him. Nonetheless, Rather remained popular. John Nichols, a security administrator for the state of California and a long-time *Evening News* viewer, observed:

> My wife and I have watched the *Evening News* for over 25 years. We like Dan. He's a real reporter. We know that when he's telling us something, he's telling us the truth as he knows it. Trustworthiness is the key. We've tried watching ABC and NBC, but we always come back to CBS. The people behind Dan are good, too.

---

[25]Interview with casewriter, December 16, 1997.

[26]Survey results, "The People, The Press, and Politics," *Times Mirror*, 1988.

[27]The September 11, 1987, blackout was later attributed to a communications problem between CBS News and CBS Sports, when Rather was in Miami for the coverage of Pope John Paul II's visit. Instead of doing a planned post-game show after a U.S. Open Tennis match, CBS Sports returned the network signal back to CBS News, which was caught unaware. Also see *The Camera Never Blinks Twice* by Dan Rather, Simon & Schuster, 1994.

While CNN may be best on breaking news, we watch CBS for its in-depth reporting.[28]

News Content. Andrew Tyndall, editor of the TV industry newsletter eponymously named the *Tyndall Report*, noted that CBS' *Evening News* coverage in 1997 emphasized more serious news than ABC and NBC. "CBS has the most traditional, hard-news broadcast among the three programs," said Tyndall. "NBC is the most feature-oriented. And ABC has been alternating between the two approaches."[29]

Tyndall's analysis of network news shows during 1998 showed that CBS had carried 3,067 minutes of hard or serious news, compared with 2,600 minutes for ABC and 2,432 for NBC. CBS also increased its coverage of international news, surpassing ABC's, which had long been identified with foreign coverage. NBC de-emphasized foreign coverage, carrying only 1,130 minutes (see Table A), while putting more emphasis on news features, such as reports on health, sex, and the family. The investigation by special prosecutor Kenneth Starr into President Bill Clinton and Monica Lewinsky and the resulting impeachment dominated the network nightly news in 1998. In total, all three networks spent three times as many minutes on this subject than the second-most covered story: the confrontation with Iraq (Exhibit 14).

In 1998, NBC continued to lag behind the other two networks in foreign news coverage. Tyndall believed that NBC News executives made the decision "to cut way back on foreign news and to concentrate on the everyday lives of people and lifestyle issues,"[30] following ratings increases during coverage of the Simpson trial in 1996.

CBS has the opposite view. Rather said that he would like to see CBS differentiate itself from the other two networks by increasing the *Evening News'* coverage of Washington and overseas stories. "I would make our newscast even 'harder,'" Rather commented.[31]

Rather believed that pursuing soft news to attract an entirely new audience of non-news viewers would be "suicide" for the *Evening News*. Rather noted:

I would certainly like to believe that our staying the course—being steady, consistent, and constant—in such things as international reporting has something to do with whatever good news we had in the ratings. And I do believe it. I fully understand that there is little, if any, empirical evidence of that. But my experience and intuition tell me that these have been factors.[32]

Many at CBS felt that ABC News, under Arledge, benefited from the constant format changes of the *Evening News* during the early 1990s. With CBS in turbulence, ABC had seized CBS' long-held position as the source for hard, serious news. Poltrack commented on the re-positioned ABC News:

When ABC was the dominant newscast, from 1989–1990 to 1995–1996, they were considered to be the authoritative news source. They got that position primarily with *Nightline*. So when they had a major event, they could double-team it by covering it on their evening news program and on *Nightline*. Viewers who watched *Nightline* on the first night would

Table A Minutes by News Topic on Network Evening News Programs, 1998 *Tyndall Report* Survey

	ABC	CBS	NBC
Hard news	2,600	3,067	2,432
Features, interviews, commentary	2,260	1,972	2,459
Total	**4,860**	**5,039**	**4,891**
Foreign (international and foreign policy combined)	1,392	1,424	1,130
Inside the beltway	1,252	1,351	1,375
Domestic (nongovernment, national, regional and local)	2,236	2,264	2,386
Total	**4,860**	**5,039**	**4,891**

Source: *Tyndall Report*, February 3, 1998

---

[28]Interview with casewriter, February 2, 1998.
[29]Jane Hall, "CBS Evening News' Climbs to Second Place in Ratings," *Los Angeles Times*, December 5, 1997.
[30]Peter Johnson, "CBS Nudges ABC Aside in Evening News Ratings," *USA Today*, November 19, 1997.

[31]Interview with casewriter, December 16, 1997.
[32]Steve McClellan, "Dan's Back!," *Broadcasting and Cable*, January 5, 1998.

then follow it on their evening news program the next night. Peter Jennings added to ABC's positioning with his cosmopolitan reputation. ABC's *World News Tonight* was well-positioned to become the serious news viewer's program—and they took that position away from us.

Once ABC was no longer leading the news ratings, it found itself stuck between NBC and CBS. Tyndall observed that, "ABC wrote off CBS [as a competitor in 1997] and [began to develop] more features like NBC." However, ABC "had failed to attract any of NBC's audience." Meanwhile, "[ABC's] core hard-news audience went back to CBS. ABC doesn't know what to do—be a hard newscast or do lifestyle news? It has lost the identity of its audience."[33] In fact, from November 1997 to January 1998, the *Evening News* had posted an 8.4 rating as compared with NBC's *Nightly News* which had an 8.7 rating. Third-place ABC delivered an 8.2 rating. At that time, the race between the three evening news broadcasts had tightened considerably.

Reporting and Writing.
CBS Network executives believed the key to quality at CBS News was its correspondents' ability to develop sources, find stories, and write well.

Jonathan C. Klein, former executive vice president of CBS News, characterized CBS correspondents:

Take a guy like Jim Stewart, who's based in Washington and covers the FBI and the Justice Department. He's nothing of what a local news consultant will tell you to hire as a television reporter, yet he has the ability to develop sources and find great stories as a correspondent. The same is true of David Martin, who's our Pentagon correspondent. But he's a guy who can make great stories. Those guys get on the air and break the stereotypes. Their exclusives are the driving force behind them. There's no substitute for it. I don't want to say that we don't work cosmetic factors, but cosmetic factors have got to take a backseat to great reporting.

While CBS News was criticized for responding slowly to the death of Princess Diana on August 31, 1997, CBS News correspondents had broken numerous stories in succeeding months on the *Evening News*. These stories included a report in December 1997 that Defense Secretary William Cohen would recommend curtailing integration of the sexes in military training,[34] and the revela-

tion that the U.S. military had previously identified, and then withheld the name of, the Unknown Soldier from the Vietnam War.[35]

Feature Pieces.
Near the end of every news broadcast, an *Eye on America* segment usually aired. This segment provided viewers with a special in-depth report—usually three to four minutes in length. In addition to the January 4 segment on reality TV, some of the other *Eye on America* pieces in the 1998–1999 season focused on the new face of organized crime, a big-time bank's unpopular impact on a small town, and unqualified exterminators who end up poisoning humans instead of pests. Schweitzer commented:

There's a commodity status to the evening news on any network. They're all going to tell you what's happening in the world. But there are levers of inequality. First, the news must be reported in a clear and concise way. You want viewers to say, "I could understand the news better on CBS." Second, the viewers must know what to expect from the newscast. You want viewers to know that CBS has a selection of stories with more national and international reports. And finally, there must be unique news segments, like *Eye on America*, that viewers want to tune into. These segments are becoming a key lever of competition for the *Evening News*.

We're not going to promote the news by telling everyone what's happening in the world today. The audience knows that we'll do that. The news viewer is very smart and discerning. They're looking for an edge on how to be smarter, on how to be better, and on how to make choices. We go after them with the editorial product.

Poltrack believed that the *Evening News' Eye on America* segment and the use of multipart series helped draw viewership and made the CBS newscast complementary to that of its local affiliates. Multipart *Eye on America* series in early 1999 included a two-part report on sports gambling pegged to the Super Bowl, a five-part series on Internet winners and losers, and three parts on Life in the Nineties—nonagenarians who are thriving and how they got that way. Poltrack noted that the *Eye on America* series represented an attempt to increase the frequency of *Evening News* viewership.

With *Eye on America*, we usually have some kind of branded feature piece that would cover a story over a

---

[33] Peter Johnson, "CBS Nudges ABC Aside in Evening News Ratings," *USA Today*, November 19, 1997.
[34] *CBS Evening News*, December 16, 1997.

[35] *CBS Evening News*, January 19, 1998.

course of a week. Our goal is to get viewers committed to a continuity series—something more special than just the top national and international news stories and something that is more compelling than what viewers get from their local newscasts.

CBS Evening News Operations

Supported by a world-wide staff of CBS News correspondents and producers located in 9 international and 8 domestic bureaus (see Exhibit 15), the broadcast of the *Evening News* was headed up until 1998 by the program's Executive Producer Fager at the CBS Broadcast Center (see Exhibits 16a and 16b for photos of the Center). Fager, who went on in the fall of 1998 to join *60 Minutes II*, described his role:

> I'm the general. I'm responsible for the broadcast. I keep an eye on the cost and decide on the editorial direction of the show. The *Evening News* has always had a unique way of "storytelling" in its reporting—I want to maintain that tradition. The stories we broadcast are usually more analytical—we help people understand how the news will affect their lives—instead of the "play-by-play" news that you find on CNN. We look at how to report the most significant stories of the day in a 30-minute broadcast in a clear and conscientious way.

Reporting directly to the executive producer were a senior broadcast producer, and three senior producers, two in New York, and one in Washington, D.C. Supporting the senior producers were a pool of 36 producers and 26 videotape editors that supported all the hard news broadcasts. The producers were responsible for working with correspondents off-camera to put stories together, and the editors were charged with ensuring that stories were tightly presented in their allocated time-slots.

In determining what stories to develop, former executive producer Fager said that he and his senior staff looked for opportunities to present news content not found elsewhere. "When we're thinking about what stories to commission [or assign to CBS News correspondents], we are always looking for an angle that would be most interesting to our viewers—and not found anywhere else."

Rather also had a role in shaping the *Evening News* broadcast. He explained his behind-the-camera responsibilities:

> Throughout the day, I'll have been in conversation with correspondents and producers in the field and in New York. All of the staying in touch with the news and news sources, the cross-checking, the copy-editing, keeping myself available to our news team for consultation on matters large and small—this is what it means to be managing editor, and it is important to me. I believe that it is also important to viewers to know that the person on-screen presenting the news to them is directly involved in gathering the news and putting it together. A managing editor should help direct coverage, help to set standards, and keep morale up. Say what you will, this is part of my work, and I'm responsible for it. I would not want to be anchor without also being managing editor.[36]

Rather often taped a 15-second "teaser" to promote the show's upcoming stories for affiliates to broadcast during their local news shows. When the *Evening News* aired (see Exhibit 17 for a typical *Evening News* lineup), there was a reciprocal time-slot for local affiliates to promote their news shows.

The Paradox Revisited

With the decline in network evening news audiences, some TV executives questioned the value of the evening news shows. "Network news is a dinosaur," argued David Hill, president of the Fox Network.[37] While Fox had no nightly network news, it devoted all of its network news resources to creating segments for its affiliates as well as its 24-hour cable-TV Fox News Channel. Roger Ailes, Chairman and CEO of the Fox News Channel, added:

> The [network news shows] are alive for a while. I wouldn't call them dinosaurs. On the other hand, they're now a part of the news panorama. They're no longer the leading voice in America. Clearly those news shows have very little news in them. By 6:00 or 7:00 at night people can flip to CNN or Fox News Channel and get news when they walk in the door.[38]

Most CBS executives disagreed, believing that a solid evening news program helped establish a network's identity and brand. Schwartz noted:

---

[36]Dan Rather, *The Camera Never Blinks Twice*, Simon & Schuster, 1994.
[37]Tim Goodman, "Network News 'Dinosaurs' Fight to Survive," *San Francisco Examiner*, December 27, 1997.
[38]Tim Goodman, "Network News 'Dinosaurs' Fight to Survive," *San Francisco Examiner*, December 27, 1997.

There are some key building blocks that establish what it means to be a broadcasting company. One of these is how you do in prime-time—the branding and personality of that daypart. For NBC, it has been *Seinfeld* and *ER* on Thursday night, and the departure of the first, and the substantial alteration of the second, have to some extent compromised their core corporate identity. For us, it's family programming on Saturday and Sunday nights, quality made-for-television movies, comedies on Monday—that's our prime time personality. Equally important to our network's persona and perceived public role is the *CBS Evening News*, which determines the character and charter of our entire News Division. One thing that has been constant during the 50-year history of the CBS Television Network is that there has always been a *CBS Evening News*. We're the "nation's hard news broadcast of record. We've always been. And we'll continue to be."

All the network news programs come together to service a continuing, large audience looking for the last word on the events of the day. The more fragmented the world becomes, the more people need consensus, mass culture, and to some extent, tradition—their cornflakes, morning newspaper, and their evening news. So while the evening news as an entity may change with time, it will remain and thrive.

Conclusion

As Heyward prepared to leave the Broadcast Center, he mused about the night-by-night battle among the three evening news broadcasts. On that night, each led with a different story: CBS with Iraq, ABC with the Midwest storm, NBC with Elizabeth Dole's resignation from the Red Cross. It was a relief not to have led with the year-long Clinton scandal: Heyward blamed "Monica fatigue" for the loss of more than two million viewers among the three network broadcasts in the fourth quarter of 1998.

Heyward knew that some of the factors that determined ratings supremacy, like the strength of the prime time schedule and of the local news lead-in, were out of his control. But he was looking forward to the end of the scandal as a chance to recapture lost viewers and gain ground in what was still a very tight ratings race, with less than half a ratings point separating all three competitors. At stake was more than prestige: an increase in just one rating point for the *Evening News* would contribute millions of dollars in advertising revenues to the show. But over the longer term, how relevant would the network evening newscasts be to most Americans—and what else should CBS News do to reach them?

The very next week would suggest at least part of the answer. On Wednesday, January 15, 1999, *60 Minutes II* went on the air after much debate and soul-searching about the wisdom of expanding this unique magazine franchise. The program was an instant success, attracting 6 million new viewers to CBS in its Wednesday time period. Dan Rather, in addition to continuing his duties on the *Evening News* and *48 Hours*, was the principal correspondent.

Also on Wednesday, CBS Marketwatch, a financial website jointly owned by CBS and Data Broadcasting Corporation, went public. Analysts cited the CBS relationship and the promotional platform of CBS News broadcasts like the *Evening News* as a major reason to bet on CBS Marketwatch. After opening at $17, Marketwatch stock soared as high as $130 and closed at $97-1/2, making it one of the more spectacular IPOs ever.

Exhibit 1 *The CBS Evening News with Dan Rather*

Source: CBS Photo Archive

Exhibit 2 Network Evening News War (1960–present)

Season	CBS Anchor	CBS Ratings	CBS Share	NBC Anchor	NBC Ratings	NBC Share	ABC Anchor	ABC Ratings	ABC Share	Totals Ratings	Totals Share
1960–61	Douglas Edwards	15.6		John Cameron-Swayze	17.5					33.1	
1961–62	Douglas Edwards	16.7		John Cameron-Swayze	18.4		Ron Cochran	5.5		40.6	
1962–63	Walter Cronkite	16.0		Chet Huntly & David Brinkley	17.1		Ron Cochran	6.2		39.3	
1963–64	Walter Cronkite	14.5		Chet Huntly & David Brinkley	15.9		Ron Cochran	8.1		38.5	
1964–65	Walter Cronkite	15.1		Chet Huntly & David Brinkley	16.6		Ron Cochran	8.5		40.2	
1965–66	Walter Cronkite	16.0		Chet Huntly & David Brinkley	15.7		Peter Jennings	8.7		40.4	
1966–67	Walter Cronkite	15.3		Chet Huntly & David Brinkley	16.4		Peter Jennings	7.2		38.9	
1967–68	Walter Cronkite	17.5		Chet Huntly & David Brinkley	16.8		Bob Young	7.1		41.4	
1968–69	Walter Cronkite	17.4		Chet Huntly & David Brinkley	16.2		Howard K. Smith & Frank Reynolds	6.4		40.0	
1969–70	Walter Cronkite	16.8		Chet Huntly & David Brinkley	15.6		Howard K. Smith & Frank Reynolds	6.8		39.2	
1970–71	Walter Cronkite	16.4		John Chancellor	14.6		Harry Reasoner & Howard K. Smith	8.1		39.1	
1971–72	Walter Cronkite	14.7		John Chancellor	12.8		Harry Reasoner & Howard K. Smith	9.7		37.2	
1972–73	Walter Cronkite	14.6		John Chancellor	13.4		Harry Reasoner & Howard K. Smith	11.1		39.1	
1973–74	Walter Cronkite	14.3		John Chancellor	13.8		Harry Reasoner & Howard K. Smith	11.1		39.2	
1974–75	Walter Cronkite	14.7	27	John Chancellor	14.3	26	Harry Reasoner & Howard K. Smith	11.1	20	40.1	73
1975–76	Walter Cronkite	14.4	27	John Chancellor	13.6	25	Harry Reasoner & Howard K. Smith	10.0	19	38.0	71
1976–77	Walter Cronkite	16.0	30	Chancellor & Brinkley	14.0	26	Reasoner/Walters	10.0	18	40.0	74
1977–78	Walter Cronkite	15.0	29	Chancellor & Brinkley	13.4	25	Reasoner/Walters	9.9	19	38.3	73

↦ Sept. 1963: CBS and NBC expand their newscasts to 30 minutes

↦ Jan. 1967: ABC expands its newscast to 30 minutes

Ratings = % of U.S. households with television viewing programs
Share = % of viewing U.S. households at a particular time period (not available until 1974–75 season)
Note: 1995–96 and 1996–97 seasons are 35.5 averages. Prior to 1995–96, most averages represent 30 weeks

Source: Nielsen Media, CBS Research, *Newsweek* (10/11/76), *Los Angeles Times*

Exhibit 2 Network Evening News War (1960–present) (continued)

	1978–79	1979–80	1980–81	1981–82	1982–83	1983–84	1984–85	1985–86	1986–87	1987–88	1988–89	1989–90	1990–91	1991–92	1992–93	1993–94	1994–95	1995–96	1996–97	97–98
CBS	Cronkite					Dan Rather										Dan Rather & Connie Chung		Dan Rather		
Ratings	14.8	15.3	15.2	13.9	14.4	13.8	13.5	13.3	12	11.6	11.0	10.0	9.7	9.5	9.8	9.8	8.7	7.6	7.3	7.9
Share	28	28	27	24	25	24	24	23	22	21	20	19	18	18	18	18	17	15	15	16
NBC	Chancellor & Brinkley			Brokaw & Mudd						Tom Brokaw										
Ratings	12.9	13.5	12.9	12.7	11.6	11.2	11.2	12.1	12.0	10.3	10.3	9.9	9.8	9.1	9.3	9.9	8.7	8.5	8.6	8.5
Share	24	24	23	22	20	20	20	22	22	19	20	19	18	17	18	19	17	17	18	17
ABC	Reynolds, Jennings & Robinson			Reynolds & Jennings					Peter Jennings											
Ratings	10.9	13.1	12.5	12.7	12.1	11.1	11.1	11.6	10.6	10.8	10.8	10.9	11.5	10.8	11.3	10.9	10.3	9.3	8.5	8.0
Share	20	24	22	22	21	20	20	21	19	20	20	21	22	21	21	20	18	18	17	16
Totals																				
Ratings	38.6	41.9	40.6	39.3	38.1	36.1	35.8	37.0	34.6	32.7	32.1	30.8	31.0	29.4	30.4	30.6	27.7	25.4	24.4	24.4
Share	72	76	72	68	66	64	64	66	63	60	60	59	59	56	57	58	54	50	50	49

↑ June 1981: Cable News Network (CNN) first broadcast over cable

↑ Fox Network wins NFL contract; 10 CBS affiliates switch to Fox

Ratings = % of U.S. households with television viewing programs

Share = % of viewing U.S. households at a particular time period (not available until 1974–75 season)

Note: 1995–96 and 1996–97 seasons are 35.5 averages. Prior to 1995–96, most averages represent 30 weeks

Source: Nielsen Media, CBS Research, *Newsweek* (10/11/76), *Los Angeles Times*

Exhibit 3 Owned and Operated Stations, 1997

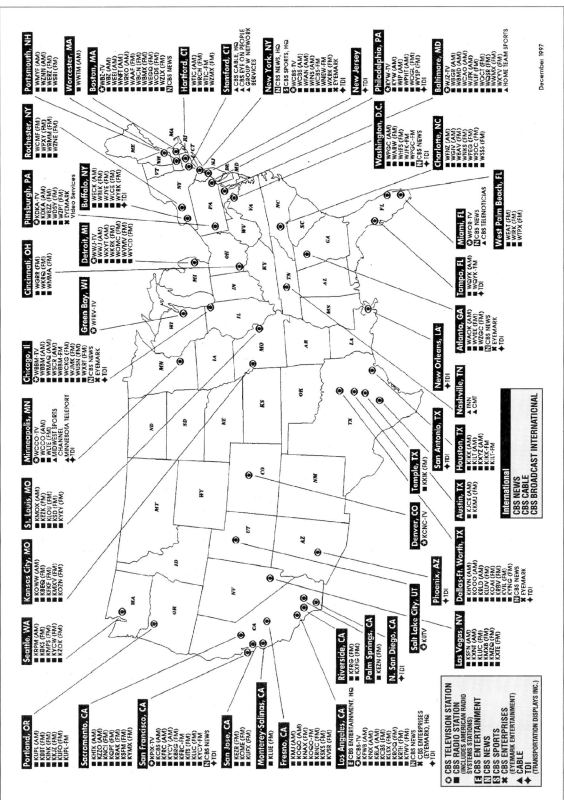

Source: CBS, Inc.

Exhibit 4 CBS Television Affiliates, 1997

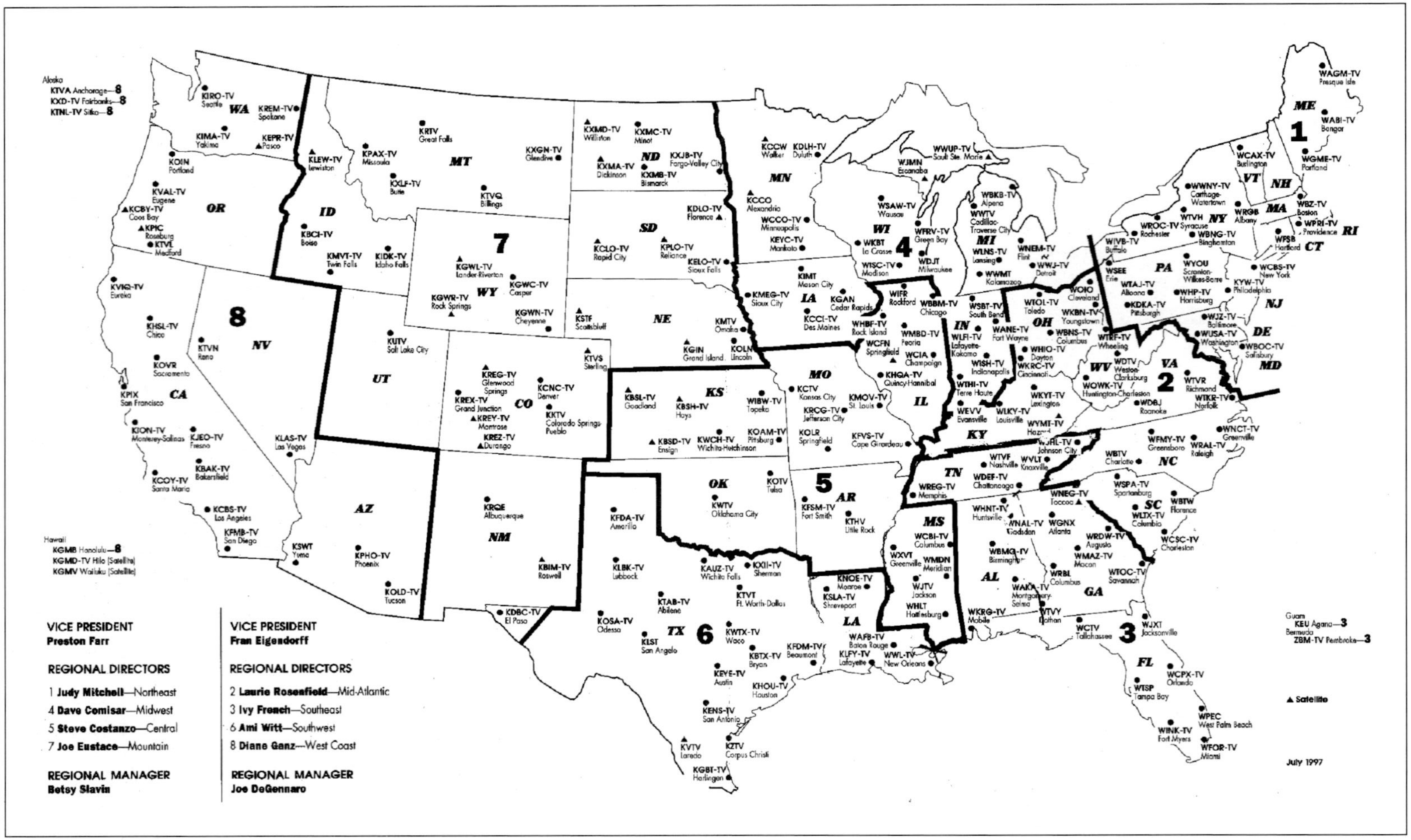

Source: CBS Affiliates Relations

Exhibit 5 CBS Corporation, 10-K, 1997 ($ millions)

	Television	Network	Radio	Cable	Other Media[a]	Total
Revenue	$836	$2,816	$1,475	$302	($66)	$5,363
Operating profit	325	(107)	390	10	(369)	249

Source: CBS Corporation, 10-K, 1997
[a]Other Media for corporate and other residual costs of discontinued businesses

Exhibit 6 Network News Programs—Morning, Late Night, and Prime-Time

Show	Description	Main Anchors	Time Aired
NBC			
The Today Show	Morning news program with international and domestic news, weather reports and interviews with newsmakers	Katie Couric Matt Lauer	Monday–Friday 7–9:00 a.m.
Meet the Press	Interviews with national and international guests followed by a roundtable discussion	Tim Russert	Sunday 9–10:00 a.m.
Nightly News	Evening news program featuring national and international news	Tom Brokaw	Monday–Friday 6:30–7:00 p.m.
Dateline	Prime-time news programming with investigative features and newsmaker profiles	Jane Pauley Stone Phillips	Monday 10–11:00 p.m. Tuesday 10–11:00 p.m. Wednesday 8–9:00 p.m. Friday 9–10:00 p.m. Sunday 8–9:00 p.m.
CBS			
CBS Morning News	Blend of local and national news	Thalia Assuras	Monday–Friday half-hour between 5–7:00 a.m.
CBS This Morning	Blend of local and national news	Jane Robelot Mark McEwen	Monday–Friday 7–9:00 a.m.
CBS Saturday Morning	Companion to CBS Sunday Morning. Segments include health, personal finance, and entertainment news	Russ Mitchell Dawn Stesland	Saturday 9–11 a.m.
CBS Sunday Morning	Featured human accomplishments in fine art, music, nature, sports, and science	Charles Osgood	Sunday 9–10:30 a.m.
Face the Nation	Public affairs program based in Washington, D.C.	Bob Schieffer	Sunday 10:30–11:00 a.m.
Evening News	Evening news program featuring national and international news	Dan Rather John Roberts	Monday–Friday 6:30–7:00 p.m. Saturday 6:30–7:00 p.m. Sunday 6–6:30 p.m.
Up to the Minute	Overnight news program	Mika Brzezinski	Monday–Friday 2–6 a.m.
60 Minutes II	Prime-time investigative journalistic magazine	Dan Rather Charlie Rose Vicki Mabrey Bob Simon Jimmy Tingle	Tuesday 9–10 p.m.
48 Hours	Prime-time news programming with investigative features and newsmaker profiles	Dan Rather Erin Moriarty Harold Dow Susan Spencer Bill Lagattuta Troy Roberts Peter van Sant	Thursday 10–11:00 p.m.
60 Minutes	Prime-time investigative journalistic magazine	Ed Bradley Steve Kroft Andy Rooney Morley Safer Lesley Stahl Mike Wallace	Sunday 7–8 p.m.
ABC			
Good Morning America	Blend of local and national news	Charles Gibson Diane Sawyer	Monday–Friday 7–9:00 a.m.
This Week	Review of week's national and international headlines	Sam Donaldson Cokie Roberts	Sunday 10:30–11:30 a.m.
World News Tonight	Nightly news program featuring national and international news	Peter Jennings	Monday–Sunday 6:30–7:00 p.m.
20/20	Prime-time news programming with investigative features and newsmaker profiles	Hugh Downs Barbara Walters Diane Sawyer Sam Donaldson Connie Chung Charles Gibson	Monday 8–9:00 p.m. Wednesday 10–11:00 p.m. Friday 10–11 p.m. Sunday 9–10:00 p.m.
Nightline	Nightly news program	Ted Koppel	Monday–Friday 11:35–12 midnight

Source: CBS Television Press Kit, NBC.com, ABC.com

Exhibit 7 Biography of Dan Rather

DAN RATHER

(Anchor and Managing Editor, CBS EVENING NEWS; Anchor, 48 HOURS)

Since 1962, when Dan Rather first joined CBS News, he has handled some of the most challenging assignments in journalism. His day-to-day commitment to substantive, fair and accurate news reporting and his tough, active style have cemented for him a position of unrivaled respect among his peers and the public.

For Rather, 1996 was a career milestone. March 9 marked the 15th anniversary of his tenure as anchor and managing editor of the CBS EVENING NEWS. Election Year '96 presented Rather at the peak of his legendary style as he covered his 11th national election campaign.

In June 1996, Rather traveled to Moscow to report on the first round of Russian elections. He made two trips to the front lines in Bosnia in late 1995, reporting on American peacekeeping troops there. The conflict in the former Yugoslavia has been a priority for Rather, who first reported from the region a quarter of a century ago. His trips since the war began have yielded unparalleled access to the political and military leaders of this bloody struggle, as well as the innocent civilians caught in the crossfire.

October 1995 literally found Rather once more in the eye of the storm, reporting on Hurricane Opal as it approached the Florida shore while two producers "anchored the anchor," clinging to his arms and legs during the ferociously high winds. In November, he reported on the assassination of Israeli Prime Minister Yitzhak Rabin from Jerusalem. Rather's reports on a stunned and mourning nation inevitably recalled his reports from Dallas in the aftermath of President John F. Kennedy's death. Rather was the only American anchor on-site at Rabin's funeral.

Author Rather's latest book is an abridgment of Mark Sullivan's landmark popular history, *Our Times: America at the Dawn of the Twentieth Century*. His memoir, *The Camera Never Blinks Twice: The Further Adventures of a Television Journalist*, has been released in paperback. Rather is also author of *The Camera Never Blinks* (1977), *I Remember* (1991) and *The Palace Guard* (1974). In June 1997, he opened another chapter in his career as a writer: weekly newspaper columnist. His column, entitled "Part of Our World," is distributed by King Features Syndicate to papers across the country, and provides additional focus on people and stories in the news. Rather also continues to be much sought after as a contributor to many of the top newspapers and magazines in the country and speaks out frequently on journalistic ethics. In October 1994, he was honored by his alma mater, Sam Houston State University in Huntsville, Texas, which named its journalism and communications building after him.

He has interviewed every United States president from Dwight D. Eisenhower to Bill Clinton and international leaders as diverse as Nelson Mandela and Boris Yeltsin. In 1990, he was the first American journalist to interview Saddam Hussein after Iraq's invasion of Kuwait.

Since the start of his career in 1950, Rather has been in the middle of America's—and the world's—defining moments. From Nov. 22, 1963 in Dallas, when Rather worked around the clock to keep the American people informed of the details of the assassination of John F. Kennedy, to the 1968 Democratic National Convention, to Beijing, Bosnia and Haiti more than two decades later, he has covered most of the major news stories in the world. Rather's reporting on the civil rights movement in the South, the White House, the wars in Vietnam, Afghanistan, the Persian Gulf and Yugoslavia and the quest for peace in South Africa and the Middle East has showcased his combination of street smarts and astute analysis.

He has received virtually every honor in broadcast journalism, including numerous Emmys and citations from critical, scholarly, professional and charitable organizations. He is regularly cited as "best anchor" in opinion surveys, and he recently received the Peabody Award for his CBS REPORTS documentary "Vietnam: A Soldier Returns."

During his 35 years with CBS News, Rather has held many prestigious positions, ranging from co-editor of 60 MINUTES to anchor of CBS REPORTS and anchor of the weekend and weeknight editions of the CBS EVENING NEWS. He has served as CBS News bureau chief in London and Saigon and as White House correspondent during the Johnson and Nixon administrations. He continues to anchor and report for 48 HOURS and is also a regular contributor to CBS News Radio, including "Dan Rather Reporting," his weekday broadcast of news and analysis which has aired on the CBS Radio network since March 9, 1981.

Rather joined CBS News in 1962 as chief of its Southwest bureau in Dallas. In 1963, he was appointed chief of the Southern bureau in New Orleans, responsible for coverage of news events in the South, Southwest, Mexico and Central America. During that time, he reported on Southern racial conflicts and the crusade of Dr. Martin Luther King Jr. On Nov. 22, 1963 in Dallas, he broke the news of the death of President John F. Kennedy.

Rather began his career in journalism in 1950 as an Associated Press reporter in Huntsville, Texas. Later, he was a reporter for United Press International (1950–52), KSAM Radio in Huntsville (1950–53), KTRH Radio in Houston and the Houston Chronicle (1954–55). He became news director of KTRH in 1956 and a reporter for KTRK-TV Houston in 1959. Prior to joining CBS News, Rather was news director for KHOU-TV, the CBS affiliate in Houston.

He was born Oct. 31, 1931 in Wharton, Texas. In 1953, he received a bachelor's degree in journalism from Sam Houston State Teachers College, where he spent the following year as a journalism instructor. He also attended the University of Houston and the South Texas School of Law.

Source: CBS Public Relations

Exhibit 8 Impact of Cable Television on Network Television Viewing

	Network Affiliates	Independent Stations	Public TV Stations	Basic Cable	Pay Cable
1985	66%	18%	3%	11%	5%
1990	55%	20%	3%	21%	6%
1991	53%	21%	3%	24%	6%
1992	54%	20%	3%	24%	6%
1993	53%	21%	4%	25%	5%
1994	52%	21%	4%	26%	5%
1995	47%	22%	3%	30%	6%
1996	46%	21%	3%	33%	6%

Source: National Cable Television Association
Note: For all television viewing Monday–Sunday, 24 hours per day. Due to multiset use and independent rounding, totals add up to more than 100%. Independent stations include the FOX network.

Exhibit 9 Percentage of Households Using Television (HUTs), Monday–Friday, Week of November 16, 1997

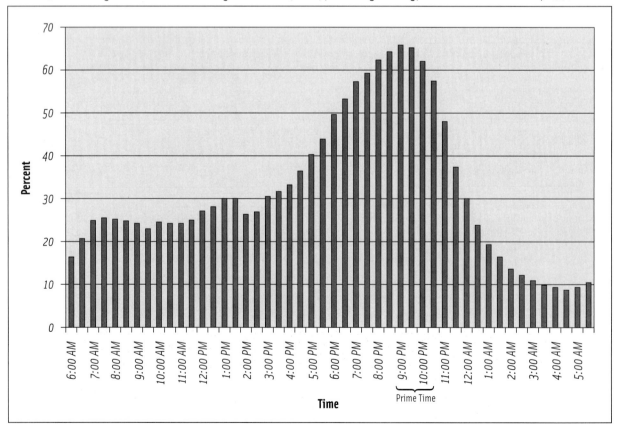

Source: NTI, S-T-D (September 21, 1988–February 14, 1999) average

Exhibit 10 Viewership Profile of Evening News Shows

	ABC **World News Tonight** **with Peter Jennings**	CBS **CBS Evening News** **with Dan Rather**	NBC **NBC Nightly News** **with Tom Brokaw**
Adults 18+	100%	100%	100%
Women 18+	59	59	57
Men 18+	41	41	43
Adults 18–34	10	9	13
Women 18–34	6	5	7
Men 18–34	4	4	6
Adults 35–54	32	31	33
Women 35–54	18	17	18
Men 35–54	14	14	15
Adults 55+	58	60	54
Women 55+	35	37	32
Men 55+	23	23	22
Median age	58.3	59.6	55.8

Sources: Nielsen Media, September 21, 1998 to February 19, 1998, CBS Research

Exhibit 11 Prime-Time Median Ages—1998/99 Season-to-Date (through 10 weeks) Programs Sorted by Ascending Median Age

CBS	NBC	ABC	FOX	WB	UPN
Nash Bridges 47.7	Friends 34.9	Sabrina–Teenage Witch 26.2	Simpsons 27.6	Dawson's Creek 20.8	Moesha Special 17.9
Chicago Hope 48.4	Jesse (N) 35.5	Boy Meets World 26.3	King of the Hill 2 28.7	Smart Guy 22.1	Clueless Special 18.0
Everybody Loves Raymond 48.6	Caroline in the City 38.2	Brother's Keeper (N) 28.4	That 70's Show (N) 28.8	Sister, Sister 24.0	Clueless 20.5
King of Queens (N) 48.7	Will & Grace (N) 38.9	Two of a Kind (NY) 30.5	Beverly Hills, 90210 29.3	Unhappily Ever After 24.0	Moesha 24.5
Maggie Winters (N) 48.9	Veronica's Closet 38.9	Wonderful World of Disney 33.7	Party of Five 29.3	Wayans Bros., The 25.6	Guys Like Us (N) 26.5
Brian Benben Show (N) 49.0	ER 39.4	Whose Line Is It Anyway? (N) 36.6	Guinness World Records 29.5	Jamie Foxx Show, The 25.8	In the House 26.7
LA Doctors (N) 49.1	Working 39.4	Two Guys, Girl & Pizza Place 37.6	King of the Hill 29.9	Buffy, the Slayer 26.2	Malcolm & Eddie–Mon 9:30P 27.1
Nanny 49.4	Just Shoot Me 39.5	Hughleys, The (N) 38.1	Costello (N) 31.4	Army Show, The (N) 26.8	In the House–Mon 9PM 27.2
Martial Law (N) 49.9	Frasier 39.9	Drew Carey Show 38.3	Melrose Place 33.5	Felicity (N) 27.0	Malcolm & Eddie 28.0
Walker Texas Ranger 50.0	Conrad Bloom (N) 39.9	Home Improvement 40.2	X-Files 34.2	Steve Harvey Show–Wed 27.5	Malcolm & Eddie 8PM 28.5
Becker (N) 50.5	Suddenly Susan 40.8	Secret Lives of Men (N) 40.3	Fox Files (N) 34.3	Charmed (N) 27.7	DiResta (N) 29.9
To Have and To Hold (N) 50.6	Made About You 42.1	Spin City 40.7	Living in Captivity (N) 34.3	For Your Love (N) 28.8	Reunited (N) 31.2
CBS Sunday Movie 50.8	News Radio 42.9	Dharma & Greg 40.8	Wrlds Wildst Police Videos 35.2	7th Heaven 28.8	Desmond Pfeffer (N) 31.3
Early Edition 51.0	Encore 'Encore (N) 43.1	Sports Night (N) 42.0	Getting Personal 35.3	Hyperion Bay (N) 31.8	America's Grtst Pets (N) 32.6
Candid Camera 51.1	NBC Sunday Night Movie 44.2	Cupid (N) 42.5	World's Funniest 35.7	7th Heaven Beginnings 32.5	Star Trek Voyager 39.5
Touched by an Angel 52.4	Pretender 44.4	Fantasy Island (N) 42.6	Ally McBeal 36.1		Mercy Point (N) 39.7
CBS Tuesday Movie (N) 52.7	Profiler 44.6	America's Funn Home Videos 43.1	Cops 41.1		7 Days (N) 41.3
Kids Say Darndest Things 53.3	3rd Rock from the Sun 45.4	NFL Monday Night Football 43.8	Cops 2 41.6		UPN Thursday Night Movie 41.4
Buddy Faro (N) 53.6	Dateline NBC Tuesday 45.7	NYPD Blue 45.1	Millennium 41.8		Legacy (N) 43.6
Cosby 54.1	Dateline NBC Monday 45.9	20/20-Sunday 45.4	Brimstone (N) 41.9		Sentinel, The 44.6
JAG 54.5	Law and Order 46.4	NFL Monday Blast 45.4	AMW America Fights Back 42.5		Love Boat: The Next Wave 46.4
48 Hours 55.2	Wind on Water (N) 46.9	ABC Thursday Night Movie 45.7			
60 Minutes 58.3	Dateline Sunday–7PM 49.2	Practice, The 45.9			
Promised Land 58.5	Homicide Life on Street 49.3	20/20–Wednesday 46.6			
Diagnosis Murder 59.1	Trinity (N) 49.7	20/20–Friday 47.3			
	Dateline Sunday–8PM 50.2	Vengeance Unlimited (N) 49.8			
	Dateline Friday–8PM 51.8				
	Dateline Wednesday–8PM 52.3				
Averages: 52.3	**42.9**	**41.6**	**34.2**	**26.4**	**37.3**

____ = The average age of the network

(N) = New to 1997/98 season

Exhibit 12 Percentage of Loyal Households by Evening Newscasts

News Program	Percentage of Loyal Households
CBS Evening News	21%
NBC Nightly News	24%
ABC World News Tonight	22%

Source: Nielsen Media Research, 1997–1998 season average

Exhibit 13 Frequency of Evening Network News Viewership—Per Evening

	1 Day	2 Days	3 Days	4 Days	5 Days
CBS Evening News	46%	19%	12%	11%	11%
NBC Nightly News	47	20	13	12	9
ABC World News Tonight	49	19	13	10	9

Source: Nielsen Media Research. Average of weeks November 10–14, 1997, December 8–12, 1997, and February 23–27, 1997

Exhibit 14 *Tyndall Report*: Top News Stories, 1997 (by minutes)

News Story	Total	ABC	CBS	NBC
Clinton sex scandal: Starr's grand jury probe, House impeachment	1,931	586	662	684
Iraq's UNSCOM weapons inspections blocked	656	191	222	244
NYSE-NASDAQ market action	389	121	119	148
Serbia cracks down on ethnic Albanian separatists in Kosovo	202	59	87	56
U.S. embassy twin bombs in East Africa: 247 killed in Nairobi	189	70	63	56
El Niño forms in Pacific Ocean, causes California storms	184	36	80	69
Tornado season kills over 100 in south and great plains	160	31	59	70
Israeli-Palestinian conflict: peace plan diplomacy meets obstacles	144	57	48	39
Sen. John Glenn returns to space on Shuttle Discovery	140	32	43	64
Clinton-Jones sexual harassment lawsuit dismissed	133	37	45	51
India-Pakistan nuclear weapons testing, arms race	120	46	30	45
Hurricane Bonnie threatens North Carolina coastline	105	38	28	39
General Motors shut down by UAW parts plant strike	103	32	42	28
Texas scorched by summer heat wave, drought	101	25	43	33
Hurricane Georges hits Dominican Republic, Florida Keys, Gulf Coast	99	31	37	30
U.S. cruise missiles attack suspected terrorists in Afghanistan, Sudan	93	41	26	25
Internal Revenue Service abuses: reform package enacted	89	27	23	40
Jonesboro Ark middle school shooting spree: two boys kill five	88	25	32	31
U.S.-PRC Beijing Summit: Bill Clinton-Jiang Zemin talks	84	35	28	21
Swissair Flight 111 crashes off Nova Scotia	84	23	27	34
Total Top 20 Stories	**5,094**	**1,543**	**1,744**	**1,807**

Source: *Tyndall Report*, ADT RESEARCH, 1999

Exhibit 15 CBS News Bureaus

Domestic Bureaus	Foreign Bureaus
New York City—Headquarters	Beijing, China
Dallas-Fort Worth	Bonn, Germany
Los Angeles	Johannesburg, South Africa
Miami	**London, England**
San Francisco	**Tokyo, Japan**
Washington, D.C.	Tel Aviv, Israel
Chicago	Moscow, Russia
Atlanta	Rome, Italy
	Paris, France

Source: CBS News
Note: Bureaus in bold

Exhibit 16a *CBS Evenings News* "Fishbowl"

Exhibit 16b *CBS Evenings News* Control Room

Exhibit 17 *CBS Evening News* Lineup (January 9, 1998)

A	correspondent/story	copy	vtime	w	orig/city
Lineup		**19:08:58**			**display 1**
The CBS Evening News with Dan Rather					**1/4/99**
	(dr/nuy)				
_a	HEADLINES	0:42			
	(PLANES/WX/REALITY)			tp	
1	Nofly W/MAP	0:33		t	
2	MARTIN/NOFLY/WALSH		2:33		LONDON
3	Saddam	0:22		t	
p4	PITTS LIVE OPEN				
4	PITTS/BAGHDAD/WHITFIELD		0:55		BAGHDAD
f4	PITTS LIVE CLOSE				
p5	Cuba	0:52		t	
5	LaNina VO MAP	0:14		p	
6	WHITAKER/WX/RNH		1:49		LA
7	Index AND VO LIDDY		0:01	j	
8	1st cml		1:32		
9	Congress	0:26		p	
p10	SCHIEFFER LIVE OPEN				
10	SCHIEFFER/HILL/WOLFE		0.29		WASHINGTON
f10	SCHIEFFER LIVE CLOSE				
11	CLINTON VO	*0:20		P	
12	Stay: Euro	1:21		t	
13	2nd cml		1:43		
14	CULT VO	0:26		t	
	Currency	0:12		t	
_	PHILLIPS/EURO/BLUFF		1:43		LONDON
17	Marketwatch (quarters, aol)	0.32		j	
18	STOCKS BUMPER	0:05			
19	3rd cml		2:12		
20	Dole	0:15		p	
21	JONES/LIDDY/DAVY		1:32		WASH
22	Minnesota	0:12		p	
23	McNAMARA/JESSE/HOOPER		1:43		MINNEAPOLIS
f23	Ahead: Eye	*0:10			
p24	BUMPER STICKER	0:02			
24	4th cml		2:01		
25	Eye on America	0:24		j	
26	HUGHES/REALITY TV @/HOOPE		3:24		LA/NY
27	Bye	0:09			
28	Credits		0:15		
29	PROMO		*0:10		
30	CBSDOTCOMEYE		0:08		
		6:47	22:00		
copy clock	00:06:47	cx+copy+vtr	00:28:47		
	—00:00:08 UNDER				

Source: CBS News

CBS MARKETWATCH

The reason we beat people like CNBC and CNNfn on the Web is because they use the Web as a way to enhance their core business [of financial cable television]. Our mission is to build a great Web site. I'm not here to be CNBC or a financial cable channel. Our audience is bigger. I have more people coming to our Web site than they have watching CNBC. The CBS relationship helps build branding, credibility and drives traffic to our site.

—Larry S. Kramer, Chairman and CEO, MarketWatch.com

As the financial markets encountered another turbulent day of heavy trading and wide fluctuations in April 2000, Larry Kramer, the 49-year-old chairman and CEO of MarketWatch.com, sat back and reflected on his company's achievements over the previous 18 months. His dot-com company had gone public in January 1999. Its sites (*http://cbs.marketwatch.com* and *www.bigcharts.com*) had become the dominant providers of financial news and information online, quickly moving ahead of a host of other competitors, including Bloomberg.com, CNBC.com, CNNfn.com, Microsoft's Money Center.com, Quicken.com, Quote.com and TheStreet.com. By March 2000, MarketWatch.com's sites had become the 40th most visited properties on the World Wide Web, averaging over 5.5 million unique visitors per month with a reach of 7.6% of Internet users in the United States,[1] up from 3.7% the year before (see Exhibit 1).[2]

Much of MarketWatch.com's early success was due to a unique partnership with CBS. In October 1997, CBS acquired 50% of MarketWatch.com through a unique non-cash transaction exchanging equity for promotion,[3] giving CBS ownership equal to that of Marketwatch.com's other key investor, Data Broadcasting Corporation (DBC). CBS branded the financial news coverage on many of its network television news programs as CBS MarketWatch, while MarketWatch.com-produced con-

tent was available for use through local news shows on many of the network's television and radio affiliates nationwide.[4]

Kramer knew that many challenges still lay ahead for MarketWatch.com, even with this partnership in place. During 1999, following the company's IPO, he moved aggressively to build market share in the financial news industry. First, MarketWatch.com acquired BigCharts.com, a provider of online financial charts to brokerage and financial media concerns, in June. In mid-September, the company launched a 30-minute syndicated television program, entitled *CBS MarketWatch Weekend*, that initially aired in 15 major markets. Finally, in late September, MarketWatch.com entered into a three-year, $21-million deal with America Online to become the primary financial news provider for its 24 million members through the AOL Personal Finance Channel.

As fast as MarketWatch.com was moving, Kramer knew the competition was not standing still. NBC Network-owned CNBC, the leading financial news channel on cable television—with an average viewership of 333,000 households[5]—was reportedly planning to revamp its Web site and more fully integrate its content with CNBC.[6] In late 1999, another competitor, TheStreet.com, moved in cooperation with *The New York Times*—one of its minority owners—to provide financial news and information on both TheStreet.com and nytimes.com sites via a joint news desk staffed by both news operations. TheStreet.com also aired a weekly program on the Fox News Channel. And CNNfn—which had just named Shelby Coffey III, the former editor of the *Los Angeles Times* and a former executive of ABC News, as its new president—was a part of the

Casewriter Dickson Louie prepared this case, with the assistance of consultant Ellie J. Kyung, under the supervision of Professor Jeffrey F. Rayport as the basis for class discussion rather than to illustrate either effective or ineffective handling of an administrative situation.

[1]"MarketWatch.com Site Climbs on Elite Media Metrix Top 50. Leading Financial Content Provider for Fourth Straight Month," PR Newswire, April 20, 2000.
[2]Media Metrix.
[3]MarketWatch.com, Proxy Statement for the 2000 Annual Meeting of stockholders, May 3, 2000.
[4]For more details about the operations of CBS News, please see the case study, "CBS Evening News," (898-086) written by Dickson L. Louie, Harvard Business School Publishing, Boston, MA.
[5]Joe Flint, "CNN Ratings Decline as Rivals Lure Away Its Viewers," *Wall Street Journal*, March 31, 2000.
[6]Kenneth Li, "CNBC Gets Serious About the Net," *Industry Standard*, October 25. 1999.

proposed AOL-TimeWarner merger announced in January 2000. In addition to these financial news sites, MarketWatch.com faced competition from personal financial planning sites, such as Microsoft's MoneyCenter.com and Quicken.com, and portal sites, such as Excite, Lycos, and Netscape, all of which provided financial news and information online.

As Kramer reflected on the competitive environment, he pondered three key questions. First, what should MarketWatch.com do to become profitable and meet Wall Street expectations? Second, how could Market-Watch.com continue to increase its dominant presence in the domestic online financial news category? And, finally, how should MarketWatch.com build its franchise globally, where the CBS brand was not as widely recognized outside of the United States?

As Kramer considered each of these questions, he knew that he faced a dilemma: While online usage was expected to continue to grow at a rapid pace in both the United States and worldwide, Wall Street was now demanding to see evidence of profitability from Internet-based start-ups like MarketWatch.com. Just four months earlier, Wall Street placed high valuations on Internet companies that pursued market share; now the emphasis was on achieving profitability. MarketWatch.com's stock price had declined over 16 months from an IPO-day high of $128 per share to $25 per share by the end of March 2000. At the same time, with an additional 17 million U.S. households expected to go online by 2003 (an increase of 51% from 1999), Kramer wondered how MarketWatch.com could afford not to aggressively attract these "newbies."[7]

These questions became increasingly relevant with additional funding. CBS and DBC announced in March that MarketWatch.com would receive an additional $56 million in cash and $30 million in trade-out promotion.

The Online Personal Finance Industry

The increasing number of financial news and information providers on the Internet reflected the growth of online trading and banking as well as the expectations of growth to come. The percentage of U.S. homes with access to the Internet was projected to grow from 32% in 2000 to 47% in 2003 (see Exhibit 2a),[8] while the number of U.S. households with online brokerage accounts was expected to double to 20 million from 2000 to 2003.[9] The number of households with online bank accounts was expected to grow from 15 million in 2000 to 24 million in 2002.[10]

Even during first quarter 2000, online trading continued to grow at a phenomenal rate. From January to March 2000, Net brokerages added more than 3 million new customer accounts, bringing the U.S. total to 15 million individual online accounts with over $1 trillion in assets. Net trades accounted for 38% of all trades executed on the New York and NASDAQ stock exchanges. The majority of these assets were held by the top five online brokerages: Charles Schwab, Fidelity, TD Waterhouse, E-Trade, and Ameritrade (see Exhibit 3).

Accompanying the burst of growth in online trading and banking was a demand for financial news and information by individual consumers. Respondents to a May 2000 *Advertising Age* survey listed "looking up financial information" as one of the five top reasons they used the Web, after general searches, news, educational resources, and travel information (see Exhibit 4).[11] To meet this demand, a variety of financial news and information providers sprang up on the Internet, including MarketWatch.com.

MarketWatch.com competed with four different types of sites providing financial news and information on the Web: niche sites, online brokers, portal sites, and traditional media companies. Niche sites such as TheStreet.com, Quote.com, and Motley Fool appealed to consumers looking for specific types of financial information. Online brokers such as Charles Schwab, Fidelity, and E-Trade included financial news as an additional service for their brokerage customers. Portal sites such as America Online, Lycos, and Yahoo! provided financial information as part of their comprehensive provider approach. Traditional media companies such as *The Wall Street Journal*'s wsj.com, CNBC's CNBC.com, and *Fortune* Magazine's Fortune.com promoted the Web as extensions of offline products (see Exhibit 5 for profiles).

Unlike *The Wall Street Journal* Interactive or TheStreet.com, which required users to pay a subscription fee to access key information, MarketWatch.com employed a business model similar to that of broadcast

---

[7]"Newbies" are defined as those individuals who have been online less than one year. "Intermediates" are those who have been online for one to two years. "A Wide Net," *Wall Street Journal*, December 6, 1999.
[8]Lanny Baker, Online Media Rules, "U.S. Penetration of Home PCs and Online Services, 1990-2003E," Salomon Smith Barney, August 1998.

[9]"Households with Brokerage Accounts to Double by 2003," *Industry Standard*, May 1, 1999.
[10]"The Number of Americans Banking Online Will Triple by 2002," *Industry Standard*, May 1, 1999.
[11]*Advertising Age*, The Interactive Future, "How Internet Use Varies from Teens to Seniors" (May 2000).

television, where most content was free and supported by paid advertising. Kramer believed that in doing so, MarketWatch.com was keeping with the "free culture of the Web." Analysts had projected that online advertising would more than triple from $5 billion to $17 billion from 2000 to 2003 (see Exhibit 2a),[12] with financial advertising as a leading category for revenue generation. Kramer believed that potential advertising revenue would continue to grow with the popularity of online banking:

> Financial transactions have now gone to the Web. We're actually accompanying, if you will, the customer to the store. His or her success is our success in a lot of ways and that will accelerate the amount of advertising on the Net. Financial advertisers are a bedrock for us. We're hugely excited because the major financial players of the world, like Merrill Lynch and Goldman Sachs, have just started on the Web.

MarketWatch.com also had the user traffic to drive advertising revenue. Traffic on MarketWatch.com sites had grown to 5.5 million unique users by March 2000 (see Exhibit 6), representing more than a three-fold increase from the 1.7 million unique users who had visited the site just 12 months earlier.[13] Page views showed a parallel increase, growing almost five-fold, from 160 million during fourth quarter 1998[14] to 771 million during first quarter 2000 (see Exhibit 7).[15] These figures outdistanced those of even the most significant competitors: Microsoft Money Central with 4.3 million unique visitors; Intuit-owned Quicken.com with 3.5 million; and Bloomberg.com with 1.5 million.[16]

By 2000, MarketWatch.com was clearly an industry leader, but the road to success had begun much earlier, in 1991.

Larry Kramer and the Birth of MarketWatch.com

Early Beginnings

Much of Larry Kramer's success with MarketWatch.com stemmed from his early experiences as a journalist and with leveraging new technology. After graduating from Harvard Business School with an MBA in 1974, Kramer began a ten-year journalism career at the *Washington Post*, where he began as a financial reporter, became a metro editor, and eventually an assistant managing editor. After leaving *The Post* in 1986,[17] Kramer served as the Executive Editor of the *San Francisco Examiner* for almost five years. At both *The Post* and *The Examiner*, Kramer's editorial staffs won Pulitzer Prizes: At *The Post*, a Pulitzer Prize for special local news reporting in 1983; at *The Examiner*, a Pulitzer Prize for spot news photography in 1987.

Kramer decided to leave daily print journalism for other media ventures, and co-founded DataSports Inc., with Ed Anderson in February 1991. DataSports was an information service that provided sports enthusiasts with up-to-the-minute game scores. The underlying concept originated with DBC, a company that provided financial market traders with real-time stock quotes that were transmitted by FM broadcast or cable signal. Kramer recalled:

> In creating DataSports, Inc., our idea was to build upon the resources of DBC that weren't being fully utilized. We came up with the idea that we could use the same infrastructure that DBC had used to provide real-time stock quotes for traders to provide real-time sports scores to fans through hand-held devices. Sporting events were usually off-cycle with market trading hours, often taking place during weekday evenings and weekends. This meant that DBC's communications system could be used for our venture when it wasn't being used for stock information transfer. We were able to create a new business by leveraging off of DBC's existing assets.

The company was a success, and over the next four years, Kramer would serve as the president of DataSports. As the company was close to achieving profitability in February 1994, DBC decided to acquire Kramer's and Anderson's shares. Following the acquisition of DataSports by DBC, Kramer remained with DBC as the company's vice president of news and sports.

Kramer's focus in the organization shifted with the activities of DBC's parent company, Infocom. As the result of an earlier bankruptcy filing, Infocom had begun selling off parts of the company, forming a new company focused around the remaining DBC quote service business, which was highly profitable.

[12]Forrester Research, August 1999.
[13]Media Metrix.
[14]MarketWatch.com, Inc., Securities and Exchange Commission, Form 10K, for year ended December 31, 1999.
[15]Steve Gelsi, CBS MarketWatch, "MarketWatch.com Revs up 300 Percent," April 25, 2000.
[16]Media Metrix, March 2000.
[17]Matt Beer, "There's Something About Larry," *Sunday San Francisco Examiner and Chronicle*, Sunday, January 24, 1999.

From DBC to DBC News Online: Moving to the Internet

Despite DBC's near monopoly on the real-time quote business, Kramer worried that other competitors would emerge, especially if they took advantage of new technologies, such as the Internet. If those efforts proved successful, DBC's proprietary broadcast, considered difficult to replicate, would be circumvented and its highly profitable core business threatened. Kramer recommended that DBC transmit headlines and news stories as a "value-added" feature for its service, in addition to quotes, to avoid becoming a commodity in the future. Realizing the potential of the Internet, DBC moved its quote services onto the Web in 1995, and DBC News Online was born.

The site carried quotes, headlines, and news stories and was supervised by Thom Calandera, a financial columnist with Kramer at the *San Francisco Examiner* who had previously worked at Bloomberg and *USA Today* Online. By 1995, the site had become quite popular with DBC service subscribers.

DBC News Online then formed alliances with several newspapers, offering to develop quote pages on their sites in exchange for a portion of advertising revenue. With the resulting exposure, DBC found its online service becoming increasingly popular. By early 1997, the site averaged a million page views per day, of which nearly 850,000 were quote searches.

Despite DBC News Online's initial success, Kramer knew it needed a major media partner to fuel expansion for its financial news site, especially if it were to sell advertising and compete against more established financial news and information providers like Dow Jones and Reuters. Most established media names were still using the Internet to protect their core businesses, and Kramer saw an opportunity for DBS to provide financial news focused primarily around the Internet with the help of an established media player.

From DBC News Online to MarketWatch.com: Developing the CBS Partnership

In early 1997, Kramer called Mike Levy, a contact from his DataSports days. Levy had founded Florida-based SportsLine, an online sports service which had recently partnered with CBS to establish CBS SportsLine. SportsLine created a non-cash partnership with CBS, exchanging equity for on-air promotion and license of the CBS brand name. The collaboration was a success, resulting in a site which rivaled the more established ESPN SportsZone in traffic within a year. Kramer hoped that a similar agreement could be reached for DBC News Online.

Levy suggested that Kramer call Derek Reisfield, then CBS Vice President of Business Development. Subsequently, in March 1997, Kramer met with Reisfield and Betsy Morgan (MBA '95), then CBS Director of Strategic Management, at the Park Hyatt Hotel in San Francisco to explore the possibility of creating a partnership similar to SportsLine's for financial news and information.

Reisfield was responsible for building CBS's new media initiatives. With little support for new media investments, he saw the value in partnering with established online entities, such as SportsLine, rather than growing CBS initiatives from the ground up. After the success of the CBS SportsLine venture, Reisfield shifted his focus to expanding CBS News' presence on the Web. Realizing the limitations of traditional television news and its declining viewership, Reisfield was attracted to the concept of real-time financial information on the Web. He was actively searching for a partner in the financial news industry.

He found an ideal partner in Kramer. With his editorial experience and top-flight journalistic staff, Kramer offered something that the scores of twentysomething Web whizzes could not—an organization that could mesh with the existing CBS News environment. Reisfield felt that a partnership with DBC News Online would allow CBS to quickly develop a footing in financial news:

> My strategy was to create new business opportunities for CBS News. Financial news had high value to its customers and high value customers. It was also a way to create additional editorial resources for CBS. At the time CBS only had one reporter [Ray Brady] covering financial news. A venture with DBC would allow CBS to beef up its coverage of the financial markets. It was really an innovation. The genius of the MarketWatch.com deal was being able to apply the CBS brand and the inherent credibility of CBS News' hard news reputation and transform it into a CBS financial news brand.

In a deal similar to the one with SportsLine, Reisfield agreed to exchange a pre-determined amount of television airtime in exchange for equity.

For Kramer, the CBS name was essential to DBC's branding efforts to differentiate itself from both established and start-up providers of financial news and information. Kramer explained:

Immediacy and credibility are the two key success factors on the Web for journalism sites. A lot of people can put news up on the Web. You don't need to buy a printing press or apply for a license with the FCC [Federal Communications Commission]. What will distinguish you on the Web, however, is the credibility of your journalism. Credibility in journalism is a big plus.

The CBS name would provide DBC with a jumpstart in the credibility game on the Web.

A few issues needed to be addressed before the deal could be finalized—mainly the way in which the two news organizations would interact. In mid-1997, Kramer met with Andrew Heyward, president of CBS News, to work out the terms of partnership. Heyward, a long-time veteran of CBS News, was in charge of the entire News Division. He arranged for Kramer to meet with his top news executives to discuss the issue. Kramer explained that he believed DBC could function as a wire service for CBS News, similar to the Dow Jones News Service's function for the *Wall Street Journal*. Recognizing CBS's weakness in financial reporting, Kramer offered journalists who could serve as additional resources—not replacements—for the CBS News staff.

While initially skeptical of an arrangement involving journalists that were not officially part of the CBS News family, CBS News executives came to see the value of the partnership. Marcy McGinnis, Vice President of CBS News, voiced these early concerns:

The very, very initial reaction was skepticism by several of the producers. It has now evolved into a very good relationship. [The producers] see MarketWatch.com as a resource—a resource for information, experts, and contacts. The MarketWatch.com organization has become a valuable research tool. As the relationship became more solid, [the producers] realized that MarketWatch.com had a wealth of information to add. With MarketWatch.com, we can ask them, "Who do you recommend?," when we need an expert to appear on a program. It's like having an extra rolodex of contacts and all you have to do is call.

McGinnis further noted the complementary nature of the two news staffs. While CBS News staff tended to be

news "story tellers," describing the effects of particular events on people, the news staff of the new venture tended to cover strictly facts of daily events. They served as resources for one another rather than competition. And with these two news staffs working together, MarketWatch.com was born.

MarketWatch.com Partnership Terms

On October 29, 1997, MarketWatch.com was formally established as a joint venture between DBC and CBS, with each partner owning approximately 50% of the new company. Under the initial partnership agreement, CBS would receive equity ownership in MarketWatch.com in exchange for $50 million of rate card promotion and advertising through October 2002 and the license of the CBS name, logo and content over the same time period.[18] CBS would also receive 30% of MarketWatch.com's banner advertising revenue and could have up to four of its executives on the company's Board of Directors.[19] Prior to the $43 million IPO in January 1999, the partnership agreement was amended.[20]

With the partnership terms solidified, MarketWatch.com began the process of creating a premiere financial information center.

Building MarketWatch.com

With a staff of over 90 reporters and editors in news bureaus located in San Francisco, New York City, Washington, D.C., Boston, Chicago, Dallas, Los Angeles, London, Hong Kong, and Tokyo, the MarketWatch.com newsroom was a 24-hour, 7-day a week news operation. During regular trading hours on Wall Street, content was updated continuously by the San Francisco editorial staff. Between 6 p.m. and 3 a.m. (ET), the trading hours of the Asian financial markets, a news editor in San Francisco updated content vetted from stories filed by MarketWatch.com correspondents in Hong Kong and Tokyo. In the remaining time the site was managed, edited, and updated by a news editor in the London bureau

[18]Rate card promotion included "mentions" (defined as each time the cbs.marketwatch.com URL was mentioned on air by a news anchor or was displayed on screen) and "scrolls" (visual display of the cbs.marketwatch.com site without the URL being mentioned).

[19]MarketWatch.com, Inc., Securities and Exchange Commission, Form 10k for year ended December 31, 1999.

[20]Under the new terms, CBS received equity ownership in exchange for $30 million of rate card promotion and advertising, instead of $50 million. The licensing agreement was extended through October 2005. CBS also would receive 6% to 8% of all gross revenue, subject to certain limitations, rather than 30% of all banner advertising. DBC received equity in MarketWatch.com for ongoing services, including the hosting of the Web site, through October 2002. (Prospectus, MarketWatch.com, January 15, 1999.)

from 3 a.m. to 6 a.m. (ET) and by a news editor in the New York bureau from 6 a.m. to 9 a.m. (ET). By 9 a.m. (ET) the cycle began again. It was a globally integrated enterprise.

MarketWatch.com reporters were organized into "beats" or regular areas of coverage, such as securities regulations, earnings, energy, commodities, mutual funds, federal agencies, software, and technology. On average, the MarketWatch.com staff generated about 600 headlines and stories a day. Seventeen online columnists, including Marshall Loeb, John F. Thoraberg, and Kathleen McBride, offered additional coverage in areas such as personal finance, sports business, and corporate executives. Personal finance features appearing on CBS.-MarketWatch.com were most popular during the weekends when the financial markets were closed. Key features of the site included:[21]

The Front Page. The MarketWatch.com Home Page (see Exhibit 8) included top stories, a market index snapshot, links to headlines, commentary stock quotes, charting, broadband features, personal finance, and a marketplace featuring MarketWatch.com e-commerce partners.

Market Data. Quotes, charts, indexes, research alerts, currencies, global market news, bonds, and market calendars provided users with data to make informed financial decisions.

Commentary. A collection of editorial commentary produced by staff and free-lance journalists. Features included Thom Calandera's StockWatch, Bazdarich on Bonds, Kellner's Forecast, Farrell on Funds, Marshall Loeb's Personal Finance Report, The Clueless Investor, and IPOnder.

Mutual Fund Center. A mutual fund expert provided "Superstar Fund" listings and edited the CBS—MarketWatch.com mutual fund section, offering Lipper Mutual Fund Profiles and providing links to other mutual fund listings, news headlines, fund rating and rankings, quotes, and charts.

Other features included specialized content areas such as Personal Finance, Tax Guide, Marketplace, and WealthClub.

MarketWatch.com did not limit its activities to the Internet alone. In addition to having an executive director for the site, David Callaway, an executive producer, Bob Leverone, supervised development of Market-Watch.com's television segments and shows. There were also four managing editors, one each in radio, news, operations, and broadband. These non-Internet activities were closely tied with MarketWatch.com's relationship with CBS.

CBS.MarketWatch.com: Leveraging the CBS Relationship

MarketWatch.com had the advantage of showcasing its content through multiple media channels due to its $30 million promotion deal with CBS. The combination of these media provided MarketWatch.com with extended reach beyond the Internet using a multimedia user interface to promote cbs.marketwatch.com.

Broadcast Television

CBS News Programs. CBS News branded existing financial news coverage on all "hard news" programs as CBS MarketWatch.[22] These programs included *The Early Show*, *The CBS Evening News with Dan Rather*, and *60 Minutes II*. In these programs, television viewers were usually prompted, visually or verbally, to go to cbs.-marketwatch.com for further financial news during a specific CBS MarketWatch.com branded segment which either previewed or summarized the day's market activities. The segments reached an estimated 2.2 to 9.3 million viewers during the 1999–2000 season depending on the program (see Exhibit 9 for television shots and Exhibit 10a, 10b, and 10c for show transcripts).[23]

Broadcast segments of MarketWatch.com also appeared on the *CBS Saturday Early Show* and *Up to the Minute*, the overnight CBS News program which aired between 2 a.m. and 4 a.m. each weekday morning.

Each time the CBS MarketWatch URL appeared on television ("scrolls") or was mentioned on the air

---

[21]CBS.MarketWatch.com section descriptions provided by Market-Watch.com, Inc. Form 10-K, for fiscal year ended December 31, 1999, Securities and Exchanges Commission.

[22]"Hard news" is defined as serious news, focused on political and foreign coverage. Typically, the network evening news programs focused on "hard news," while the news magazines in prime time focused on feature stories or "soft news."

[23]*Early Show*, 2.2 million household viewers; *CBS Evening News with Dan Rather*, 6.6 million household viewers; *60 Minutes II*, 9.3 million household viewers; (Nielsen Media, season average, from September 22, 1999, to May 28, 2000.)

("mentions"), it counted toward CBS's commitment to provide MarketWatch.com with $30 million of promotional support.[24] This was tracked monthly.

CBS Television Affiliates.

MarketWatch.com provided daily televised business news reports to over 200 CBS affiliates nationwide via CBS NewsPath, an in-house network news service that transmitted televised news stories for use by local CBS stations. All local stations subscribed to NewsPath for access to general news and sports stories that were updated when the markets opened and closed. Correspondents could also talk to local news anchors through customized news feeds.

In addition to extending its reach by providing daily business news reports to the affiliates, MarketWatch.com also produced the 30-minute weekend show, *CBS MarketWatch Weekend*, which was hosted by MarketWatch.com correspondent Susan McGinnis and aired on several CBS owned-and-operated affiliates. The show first aired on Sunday, September 19, 1999, after just six weeks in development. It featured a recap of the week's activity on Wall Street, reports by MarketWatch.com columnists, as well as features and interviews from MarketWatch.com correspondents. The show also covered many personal finance topics and was geared toward women viewers. Viewers were always reminded by McGinnis to visit the cbs.marketwatch.com site for further information.

Despite the show's limited distribution during fourth quarter 1999, it was a success. *CBS MarketWatch Weekend* had become a small profit center for MarketWatch.com, netting $345,000 in 1999 after production and programming costs. Using the CBS NewsPath studio for the show and producing it from an existing CBS facility helped contain costs.[25] Distribution for the show was expected to increase by almost three-fold, from 27 CBS affiliates in February 2000 to 70 in fall 2000.[26]

MarketWatch.com was also able to take advantage of its access to the extensive television production facilities at the CBS Broadcast Center in New York. This allowed MarketWatch.com not only to have access to premier facilities, but also to ensure that it established a physical presence with the CBS News staff and a working relationship with affiliates via CBS NewsPath.

---

[24]Effective March 2000, MarketWatch.com and CBS agreed not to count "scrolls" and "mentions" on the *CBS Evening News* against newly acquired $30 million in promotional credit.
[25]MarketWatch.com 1999 Proxy Statement to Stockholders, May 3, 2000.
[26]MarketWatch.com 1999 Proxy Statement to Stockholders, May 3, 2000.

Radio

CBS News Radio Reports.

In addition to providing content to CBS television affiliates, daily MarketWatch.com reports aired on many CBS radio affiliates as well. These reports included daily market updates by MarketWatch.com reporters during the weekdays and financial advice from MarketWatch.com columnists during the weekends.

CBS MarketWatch.com Radio Network.

Through a separate agreement in March 1999, MarketWatch.com decided to partner with Westwood One, a radio syndication business that was managed and partially owned by CBS, to create the CBS MarketWatch.com Radio Network. This network replaced CNBC Radio as the financial news provider for Westwood One and sought to provide regular financial market updates to radio stations nationwide. Revenue generated from this agreement was evenly split between Westwood One and MarketWatch.com. By Spring 2000, the CBS MarketWatch.com Radio Network was heard on nearly 90 stations in 18 out of the 20 top markets in the nation, reaching over 5.2 million unduplicated listeners.

Beyond CBS: Building a Broader User Base

Although the CBS relationship greatly increased awareness of MarketWatch.com in the offline world, MarketWatch.com needed to devise means of actually attracting consumers to the site and turning them into loyal users. This was done through adjusting media messaging, boosting features available on the site itself, and partnering with third party sites.

Attracting a Broader Audience

The average MarketWatch.com visitor was male, 35 years of age, and college educated, reflecting the typical subscriber profile of business publications such as *Fortune*, *Forbes,* and *The Wall Street Journal*. Michele Chaboudy, MarketWatch.com's vice president of marketing, was faced with the challenge of attracting the everyday financial information user—a far broader audience—in an environment where awareness for all online financial sites was relatively low.

Chaboudy believed the key to attracting this larger user base was through a savvy offline media campaign to build awareness. An *Advertising Age* survey confirmed that consumers learn about financial products and services through an evenly weighted combination of Internet, television, and newspaper channels (see Exhibit 11).[27] Utilizing a media mix including airport and billboard advertising, news/talk radio, and outdoor advertising as well as traditional print and television media, MarketWatch.com kicked off a new awareness campaign with a "Get the Story Behind the Numbers" tagline replacing the previous "Your Eye on the Market" slogan. Chaboudy explained the reason for this change:

> In our research, we discovered that people were using our site to learn more about specific financial news, and we wanted to capitalize on that fact. While I still like our original tagline, our new tagline better describes how less investor-savvy users are going to our site to find more financial news online. What we want to emphasize is our quality of journalism and that we are the best source of financial "stories" online. We also want people to know that we cover the markets 24 hours, around the clock, and that we package our information in a user-friendly way.

The new tagline was heavily promoted through radio and television campaigns in early 2000.

Keeping Users Interested

As a way to encourage visitors to make repeat visits, users could sign up for a feature offering several newsletters that were e-mailed either daily or weekly. These e-mail newsletters (see Exhibit 12) included a morning report before the start of the trading day, a mid-day report on the financial markets, and an "After-the-Bell" report providing a summary of the day's trading activities on Wall Street. All three reports provided users with hyperlinks to stories appearing on the MarketWatch.com site. A weekly newsletter that provided a summary of the week's market activity was also e-mailed to interested subscribers on Friday afternoons. Subscription to these e-mails required registration, and they were very successful in drawing users to the site. Seventy-seven percent of MarketWatch.com visitors accessed the *cbs.-marketwatch.com* site several times a day.[28]

Third Party Partnerships

In conjunction with efforts to broaden the user base, MarketWatch.com entered into a series of partnership agreements with large portal sites that would expose mass users to its services.

America Online. In October 1999, MarketWatch.com reached a three-year, $21 million agreement with America Online to serve as the "anchor tenant" for business news on its personal finance channel (Keyword: MARKETWATCH). The cbs.marketwatch.com content on America Online included daily market updates as well as features from its weekend television program, all made available to AOL's 24 million subscribers. Bill Bishop, MarketWatch.com's Executive Vice President of Development and International, explained the rationale for making a deal with AOL:

> Their personal finance channel reaches 300% to 400% more people than our Web site [prior to the AOL agreement], and from a marketing perspective it was primarily a "newbie" audience. Our research has shown that we are very effective in reaching a "newbie" audience and converting them into regular users of MarketWatch.com. And from a Wall Street perspective, it's very important to show that you have access to the masses in the online world, and frankly, without AOL, it's hard to argue that you're getting everybody in cyberspace or even having a shot at getting everybody in cyberspace.

Yahoo! and Other Distribution Partnerships. In addition to AOL, MarketWatch.com formed distribution partnerships for its editorial content with Yahoo!, Quicken.com, and NewsAlert. Under an agreement developed in August 1998 with Yahoo!, MarketWatch.com provided news headlines and placed banner advertisements in the portal's Finance section with links to the CBS.MarketWatch.com Web site for the full story.[29] At a high point in December 1999, approximately 12% of MarketWatch.com's traffic originated from Yahoo![30] The deal with Intuit made editorial content available on portions of the Quicken.com site in return for a share of advertising revenue where MarketWatch.com content appeared.[31] These additional partnerships provided exposure of the MarketWatch.com brand to a potentially huge audience of additional users.

---

[27]*Advertising Age*, The Interactive Future, "How Internet Use Varies from Teens to Seniors" (May 2000).
[28]MarketWatch.com.
[29]MarketWatch.com, Securities and Exchange Commission, Form 10K for year ended December 31, 1999.

[30]Ibid.
[31]Ibid.

Acquisition of BigCharts.com

In June 1999, MarketWatch.com acquired Minneapolis-based BigCharts.com (see Exhibit 13), a business-to-business provider of online financial charts to online brokers and other financial news providers, for $152.7 million in a combination of cash, stock, and stock options. The acquisition was a move not only to increase market share, but also to improve overall profitability.

Kramer noted that the BigCharts.com acquisition had provided MarketWatch.com with five key benefits: licensing revenue, a large unduplicated audience with MarketWatch.com, increased page views that could be sold as advertising inventory, technological capabilities, and an additional management staff. Kramer detailed the benefits of the BigCharts.com acquisition:

> The acquisition of BigCharts [in June 1999] really accelerated several things here, including our reach. We bought Big Charts for several reasons and it turned out to be a homerun for us.
>
> First, they are a licensing company. They license charts to virtually every major broker, including Ameritrade and Merrill Lynch. Their business model is that they're paid on how many customers use their site per month. So as E-Trade grows, we grow. If one of the online traders grows and another one loses, we still grow.
>
> The second reason is that it is a destination site. BigCharts.com, which had no promotion, had grown huge, and it had built a very loyal audience through word-of-mouth. When we checked with Media Metrix, three-quarters of their audience were unduplicated with MarketWatch.com, so that expanded our reach enormously for advertisers.
>
> The third reason is that they had a lot of advertising inventory and Doubleclick was not very effective [at] selling their ads—they were only half-sold. The minute we took over the operation, we doubled the advertising revenue.

With the additional revenue from advertising and licensing, MarketWatch.com was improving its potential for future profitability while extending its reach further into financial services.

Expansion Overseas

The company was also looking forward to launching a second financial Web site, FT MarketWatch.com, in June 2000. The site would bring the MarketWatch.com franchise to Europe in partnership with the Financial Times Group, which acquired 60% ownership of DBC in October 1999. Under the terms of its agreement with the *Financial Times*, concluded in January 2000, MarketWatch.com would license its trademark and technology to the new venture and provide £500,000 in exchange for 50% equity. *The Financial Times*, filling a role analogous to CBS in the CBS MarketWatch venture, would provide £15 million in rate card advertising over five years and £500,000 in cash for the remaining 50% equity. The site would have its own dedicated team of journalists with extensive links to related stories and content on both cbs.marketwatch.com and FT.com.[32] Internet usage in Europe had lagged the United States, with only 19% of all Europeans having access to the Web, but this percentage was expected to grow to 32% by 2003 (see Exhibit 2d).

MarketWatch.com Financial and Operating Results

In 1999, MarketWatch.com had an operating loss of $62.3 million on net revenue of $24.9 million. (see Exhibit 14). Excluding amortization and non-cash advertising expenses provided by CBS, MarketWatch.com had a pro forma operating loss of $17.5 million.

Approximately $18 million (72%) of MarketWatch.com's revenue was generated through advertising sales. The balance of the revenue, or the remaining $6.9 million, came from licensing revenue and other fees. Licensing revenue included fees from users of BigCharts.com, revenue derived from the sale of news content to third parties, and subscription payments from DBC for use of MarketWatch.com news content. Other fees included revenue generated by the CBS MarketWatch Radio Network partnership with Westwood One, the *CBS MarketWatch Weekend* show, and subscription fees from MarketWatch RT and MarketWatchLive[33]—two DBC

---

[32]MarketWatch.com 1999 Proxy Statement to Shareholders.
[33]MarketWatch RT was a browser-based real-time financial data service providing on demand real-time quotes from the American and New York Stock Exchanges and NASDAQ. Subscription rate was $34.95 per month. MarketWatchLIVE was a Windows-based real-time financial data service providing "streaming" real-time quotes over the Internet from all major U.S. equity and future exchanges. Subscription rate was $79 per month. MarketWatch.com took its name from the RT product.

products that provided investors with real-time stock quotes.[34]

MarketWatch.com's gross profit was $15 million, providing the company with a gross margin of 60% after a $9.9 million expense that largely reflected the cost of the news staff. Operating expenses totaled $77.3 million. This included $33.4 million for sales and marketing costs (including $14 million of CBS non-cash promotion) and a $30 million non-cash write-down related to a three-year amortization of goodwill and intangibles for the BigCharts.com acquisition.[35]

Despite the loss, the net revenue reflected a three-fold increase from that of 1998, when MarketWatch.com lost $12.2 million on revenue of approximately $7 million. The majority of this revenue was also derived from advertising.[36]

In late March 2000, DBC and CBS announced plans to invest an additional $86 million into MarketWatch.com for an additional 3% of equity ownership, increasing each partner's share from 31% to 34%. DBC would invest $43 million in cash and CBS would invest $30 million in promotion and $13 million in cash into the company.[37]

The MarketWatch.com Advantage

MarketWatch.com had two key advantages vis-à-vis its competitors: a top-flight staff capable of producing original branded content and its relationship with CBS. The worldwide news staff provided up-to-the-minute headlines 24 hours a day. The CBS relationship provided branding and credibility, distribution channels, and advertising with tremendous reach.[38]

Kramer depicted the MarketWatch advantage against its competitors through a pyramid diagram (see Exhibit 15). Against traditional media companies, such as Dow Jones, NBC, Bloomberg, and Time Warner, he knew MarketWatch.com's "Net-centric" focus was an advantage. Traditional media companies had been reluctant to use the Web to cannibalize their existing businesses in other media, such as CNBC with its cable television network or Bloomberg with its proprietary financial information system. Against portal sites, MarketWatch.com had the advantage of focus and content. In fact, MarketWatch.com was a partner more than a competitor with some, providing content similar to that of a wire service to several portals, including Yahoo! and AOL. Against online brokers such as Fidelity and E-Trade, Kramer felt that MarketWatch.com offered unbiased financial news and information to consumers because it was independent of any financial concern. And finally, against other niche financial sites on the Web, such as Motley Fool and TheStreet.com, Kramer believed that MarketWatch.com had a greater breadth of information.

Combined with its additional third party partnerships, the acquisition of BigCharts.com and the expected infusion of capital from its original investors, MarketWatch.com was strategically poised to solidify its position as the leader in online financial news.

Conclusion

With the expected infusion of additional cash and promotional commitments from both CBS and DBC, Kramer wondered which investments for Marketwatch.com would capitalize on its advantages and cement its leadership position.

He would need to consider a variety of technology investments to ensure his leadership in the market, given increased broadband (see Exhibit 2b), and wireless Internet usage (see Exhibit 2c), increased online computer usage (see Exhibit 2d) and expanded trading hours (see Exhibit 2e) just around the corner. Still, the overriding question for Kramer and his executive team remained—pursue profitability, or pursue growth?

[34]MarketWatch.com 1999 Proxy Statement to Shareholders.
[35]MarketWatch.com 1999 Proxy Statement to Shareholders.
[36]MarketWatch.com 1999 Proxy Statement to Shareholders.
[37]Bloomberg, "MarketWatch Gets $86 Million Influx," *San Francisco Examiner*, March 29, 2000.
[38]Jaime Kiggen, Marketwatch.com, Donaldson, Lufking & Jenrette, analyst report, March 19, 1999.

Exhibit 1 Top Web Sites (March 2000)

Rank	Top Web & Digital Media Properties	Unique Visitors (000)
1	America Online(a)	59,858
2	Yahoo Sites(a)	48,336
3	Microsoft Sites(a)	46,581
4	Lycos(a)	32,899
5	Excite@Home(a)	28,571
6	Go Network(a)	23,006
7	NBC Internet(a)	17,169
8	Amazon(a)	15,217
9	Time Warner Online(a)	13,636
10	Real.com Network(a)	13,482
11	Go2Net Network(a)	13,041
12	AltaVista Network(a)	12,557
13	About.com Sites(a) (b)	12,329
14	Ask Jeeves(a)	12,269
15	eBay(a)	11,155
16	LookSmart(a)	10,557
17	ZDNet Sites(a)	10,226
18	CNET Networks(a)	10,023
19	eUniverse Network(a)	9,198
20	Juno / Juno.com	9,177
21	EarthLink(a)	8,526
22	Infospace Impressions(a)	8,305
23	Viacom Online(a)	8,139
24	FortuneCity Network(a)	7,809
25	CitySearch-TicketMaster Online(a)	7,689
26	AT&T Web Sites(a)	7,610
27	Weather Channel, The(a)	7,598
28	Freelotto.com	7,365
29	Goto(a)	7,296
30	Travelocity(a)	7,218
31	Iwon.com	6,917
32	American greetings(a)	6,880
33	Snowball(a)	6,641
34	Mypoints.com	5,983
35	iVillage.com:The Women's Network(a)	5,768
36	Women.com Networks, The(a)	5,756
37	Smartbotpro.net	5,623
38	Mapquest.com	5,572
39	OnHealth(a)	5,557
40	Marketwatch.com Sites(a)	5,514
41	News corp. Online(a)	5,513
42	Sportsline.com sites(a)	5,454
43	Barnesandnoble.com	5,404
44	Theglobe.com Network(a)	5,355
45	Sony online(a)	5,283
46	Macromedia(a)	5,269
47	Lifeminders.com	5,090
48	Uproar network, the(a)	5,076
49	Priceline(a)	4,962
50	Harrispollonline.com	4,897

Note: (a) Digital Media: includes users of the World Wide Web, proprietary online services, and/or other ad-supported digital applications such as e-mail services and CD ROM.
Source: Media Metrix. "Media Metrix Releases U.S. Top 50 Web and Digital Properties for March 2000." Press Release. April 24, 2000.

Exhibit 2 Key Internet Forecasts

Exhibit 2a
U.S. Online Computer Usage

	Total U.S. Population (Millions)	Total U.S. Households (Millions)	Households with PCs (Millions)	Households Online (Millions)	Household Penetration PCs	Household Penetration Online	Online HHs Among PC HH	Online Advertising ($Millions)	% of total U.S. Advertising
1993	258	96	30	3	31%	3%	10%		
1994	260	97	33	5	34%	5%	15%		
1995	263	99	35	11	35%	11%	31%	$55	0%
1996	265	100	39	13	39%	13%	33%	$300	0%
1997	268	101	44	18	44%	18%	41%	$600	0%
1998	270	102	48	24	47%	24%	50%	$2,100	1%
1999	272	103	52	28	50%	27%	54%	$2,800	1%
2000E	274	104	55	33	53%	32%	60%	$5,400	2%
2001E	276	105	56	39	53%	37%	70%	$8,700	4%
2002E	278	106	57	45	54%	42%	79%	$12,600	5%
2003E	280	107	59	50	55%	47%	85%	$17,200	6%

Source: US Census Bureau, International Data Corporation, Smith Barney Inc./Salomon Brothers Inc. Research, Forrester Research

Exhibit 2b
U.S. Broadband Usage

	Number of Consumers (Millions)
1999	2.6
2000E	5.8
2001E	11
2002E	18.8
2003E	27.4

Source: Jupiter Communications

Exhibit 2c
Worldwide Wireless Internet Users (in Millions)

	North America	Asia Pacific	Europe	All Other	Worldwide Total
2000E	0.02	5.90	0.07	0.00	5.99
2001E	0.03	15.00	0.90	0.04	15.97
2002E	14.00	35.00	25.00	2.30	76.30
2003E	37.50	67.40	68.40	16.20	189.50
2004E	63.70	109.10	115.50	34.20	322.50
2005E	95.60	159.00	171.60	58.20	484.40

Source: OVUM, *Industry Standard*, May 29, 2000

Exhibit 2d
Europe and Asia Pacific
Online Computer Usage (Individuals, in millions)

	Europe Population	Europe PCs	Europe Online	Asia Pacific Population	Asia Pacific Online
1999	178.2	64.2	33.9	3,057.0	35.0
2000E	178.8	69.0	40.3	–	–
2001E	179.5	73.4	46.0	–	–
2002E	180.3	78.5	50.8	–	–
2003E	180.9	83.7	58.7	3,200.0	114.3

Source: Computer Economics, Forrester Research, *Industry Standard*, Feb. 14, 2000

Exhibit 2e
U.S. Trading Hours

April 2000	
All Markets	9:30 a.m. to 4:30 p.m. (ET)
Proposed	
All Markets	9:30 a.m. to 10:00 p.m. (ET)

Exhibit 3 Top Online Brokers (First Quarter 2000)

Total Online Brokerage Accounts and Assets First Quarter 2000				
	Online Customer Assets 1Q 00*	**Change from 4Q 99**	**Online Customer Accounts 1Q 00**	**Change from 4Q 99**
Schwab Online	418	20.0%	3,700,000	12.0%
Fidelity Online	328	22.0%	4,220,000	22.0%
TD Waterhouse Online	118	25.0%	1,728,000	56.0%
E-Trade	62	41.0%	2,443,416	30.0%
Ameritrade	39	23.0%	992,000	45.0%
DLJ direct	27	25.0%	402,000	16.0%
Datek	15	42.0%	456,617	34.0%
Fleet Online	13	55.0%	338,000	25.0%
National Discount Brokers	12	37.0%	207,900	17.0%
Scottrade Online	6	22.0%	201,853	17.0%
Others	21	24.0%	570,000	20.0%
Total	1060	23.0%	15,259,786	25.0%

* In Billions
Source: Salomon Smith Barney, *Industry Standard*, May 15, 2000

Exhibit 4 How Internet Usage Varies from Teens to Seniors

Top Five Future Informational Uses by Age Group				
13 to 17	**18 to 25**	**26 to 35**	**36 to 55**	**56-plus**
Looking up something using a search engine	Looking up something using a search engine	Looking up something using a search engine	Looking up something using a search engine	Looking up something using a search engine
Educational Resources	Educational Resources	News, such as current headlines, sports news or weather reports	Educational Resources	News, such as current headlines, sports news or weather reports
Information on Music	Information on Music	Educational Resources	News, such as current headlines, sports news or weather reports	Educational Resources
Information on Clothing and/or Fashion	Information on events that you might want to attend (movies . . .)	Looking up a phone number, street address or e-mail address	Travel Related Information	Travel Related Information .
Information on events that you might want to attend (movies . . .)	News, such as current headlines, sports news or weather reports	Information on events that you might want to attend (movies . . .)	Financial Information	Financial Information

Source: *Advertising Age*, The Interactive Future, "How Internet Use Varies from Teens to Seniors" (May 2000)

Exhibit 5 Profiles of Key Competitors

Site	URL	Unique Visitors Per Month (March 2000)	Business Model	Corporate Parent	Other Assets
Bloomberg.com	www.bloomberg.com	1,506,000	Wire service-type financial news free on the Web. Separate from proprietary, paid Bloomberg information system.	Bloomberg	Bloomberg Television, Bloomberg Radio, Bloomberg Magazine
CBS MarketWatch	cbs.marketwatch.com	5,514,000	Free financial information on the Web, from quotes to news stories to personal finance columns.	Joint partnership between CBS and Data Broadcasting Company.	CBS is owned by Viacom. DBC is partially owned by Pearson Group, parent of The Financial Times
CNBC.com	www.cnbc.com	1,153,000	Free financial information on the Web, usually reports and analyses from CNBC reporters.	General Electric	NBC Television NBC Television Network MSNBC Cable
CNNfn.com	www.cnnfn.com	1,422,000	Free financial information on the Web, usually wire reports and stories from CNNfn staff.	AOL–Time Warner (proposed)	CNN Cable Fortune Magazine Money Magazine America Online
Microsoft Money Center	www.moneycenter.com	4,334,000	Free. Portal for financial services, such as mortgages and investments. Uses wire service business stories from Reuters.	Microsoft	Microsoft Network Microsoft Products
Quicken.com	www.quicken.com	3,474,000	Free. Portal for financial services, such as mortgages and investments. Uses wire service business stories, including those from MarketWatch.com.	Intuit	Quicken.com Quicken products
TheStreet.com	www.thestreet.com	1,337,000	Some areas are free. Other areas, such as commentary areas, require paid subscription.	New York Times Company and NewsAmerica are minority investors.	nytimes.com, abcnews.com (distribution partnership)
Wall Street Journal Interactive	www.wsj.com	375,000 paid subscribers (Jan. 2000)	Some areas require paid subscription ($29 per year for WSJ sub- scribers; $59 for non-subscribers).	Dow Jones	Wall Street Journal Barron's Partnership with MSNBC

Sources: Individual sites; *Forbes*, "Best of the Web," May 22, 2000, March 2000 Media Metrix, *Editor and Publisher*

Exhibit 6 MarketWatch.com Number of Unique Visitors vs. Competitors
(July 1999 to March 2000)

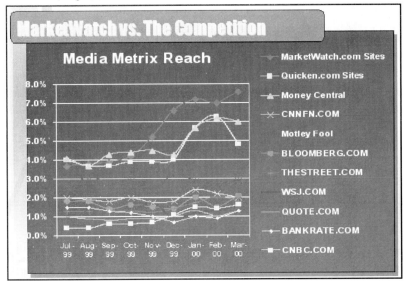

Source: MarketWatch.com, Media Metrix

Exhibit 7 MarketWatch.com Page Views by Quarter

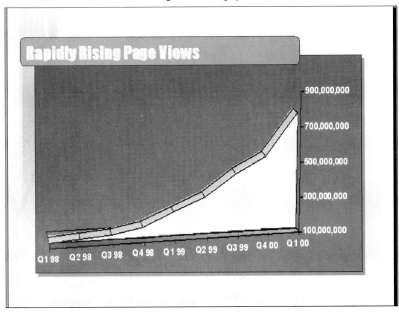

Source: MarketWatch.com

Page Views By Quarter (in thousands):			
First quarter 2000	770,000	Second quarter 1999	287,000
Fourth quarter 1999	525,000	First quarter 1999	234,000
Third quarter 1999	433,000		

Source: MarketWatch.com Press Releases

Exhibit 8 CBS MarketWatch.com Home Page

Source: *www.cbs.marketwatch.com*

Exhibit 9 CBS MarketWatch on CBS News television programs

The Early Show

The CBS Evening News with Dan Rather

60 Minutes II– CBS MarketWatch spot

Exhibit 10a Transcript of the CBS MarketWatch segment (Western States Update) which aired on *The Early Show* on Monday, May 15, 2000:

JULIE CHEN: Possible action by the Fed tops this morning's business news. CBS MarketWatch correspondent Susan McGinnis has that and the rest of today's business report. Good morning.

SUSAN MC GINNIS: Good morning Julie. We have a mixed market so far today on a trading day that will likely be driven by interest rate speculation. Tomorrow, Federal Reserve policy makers meet to make a decision on the interest rates. Wall Street expects a rate hike of one-half of one percentage point. Ahead of that report is an inflation report that is due out early tomorrow—the consumer price index for April. As long as that number and the Fed's decision bring no surprises, many expect the stock market to rally in response.

Let's check how they're doing so far for today. We have the Dow in positive territory, ahead by 41 points. The NASDAQ is down by about 40.

Lycos [LCOS] is in talks to be acquired by Spain's Telefonica Terra Networks for at least $10 billion in stock. We have Lycos up by six in response.

Phillip Morris [MO] is up as well. Said to be the favorite to acquire Nabisco's giant food unit.

Net Objects [NETO], that's a Web design software maker, has a deal with IBM to bundle its software with several of IBM's product lines. We have Net Objects ahead by one point.

Starbucks [SBUX] is under pressure from a negative comment in *Barron's*.

We follow all of these on our Web site—*CBS.MarketWatch.com*.

Exhibit 10b Transcript from the *Evening News* broadcast Tuesday, May 2, 2000:

DAN RATHER: On the CBS MarketWatch, ABC television stations are being carried once again on Time Warner cable systems in some of America's largest cities. Time Warner agreed today to restore ABC to millions of homes while it tries again to negotiate a financial compensation deal with ABC's parent company, The Walt Disney Corporation.

On Wall Street, profit-taking and a poor earnings projection of AT&T sent stock prices lower. The Dow closed down 80 points. The NASDAQ lost 172 [voiceover of slide showing Dow Jones Industrial Average down 80.66 to 10,731.12 and NASDAQ down 172.62 to 3,785.45 with *CBS.MarketWatch.com* URL shown].

Exhibit 10c Transcript of the CBS MarketWatch Update that aired during a commercial break for *60 Minutes II* on Tuesday, May 2, 2000:

NARRATOR: CBS MarketWatch Update. Sponsored by Charles Schwab.

ANTHONY MASON: Good evening. It's back. Time Warner Cable has agreed to restore ABC to millions of homes after yanking it in a financial dispute.

Stock prices closed down today as investors took profits [voiceover of slide showing Dow Jones Industrial Average down 80.66 to 10,731.12 and NASDAQ down 172.62 to 3,785.45].

And Wells Fargo Bank added movie previews to its ATM screens.

I'm Anthony Mason, CBS News.

CUT TO COMMERCIAL FOR CHARLES SCHWAB FINANCIAL SERVICES.

NARRATOR: For more business news, go to *CBS.MarketWatch.com*

Exhibit 11 Where Respondents First Heard About Web Sites That Offered . . .

			Where respondents first heard about web sites that offered:				
	Internet	Television	Magazines & Newspapers	Radio	Word of Mouth	In-Stores	Billboard
Search Engines	70%	16%	12%	6%	18%	4%	3%
Computer and computer products or information	39%	31%	33%	9%	19%	27%	4%
Financial products or services	35%	33%	31%	11%	23%	11%	6%
Travel-related products or services	47%	36%	34%	15%	21%	14%	7%
Books or magazines	30%	26%	41%	9%	20%	33%	4%
Clothing and/or fashion items	29%	34%	39%	11%	20%	32%	5%
Music	33%	38%	29%	35%	29%	19%	5%

Source: *Advertising Age*, The Interactive Future, "How Internet Use Varies from Teens to Seniors," May 2000
(Exceeds 100% due to multiple responses)

Exhibit 12 CBS.MarketWatch.com E-mail

CBS MarketWatcher After the Bell Report

http://cbs.marketwatch.com/news/newsroom.htx?dist=nwtpm

Our Sponsor

Winfreestuff.com

Today might be your lucky day! Win monthly prizes from leading online retailers in sporting goods, computers, entertainment, gourmet foods and many more! Go to: http://www.winfreestuff.com to enter today!

It's the easy way to win on the Web

Closing levels on US market indices on May 02, 2000

Last change

DJIA 10731.12 −80.66

S&P 500 1446.29 −21.96

NASDAQ 3785.45 −172.63

30-year U.S. T-Bond 6.019 +0.043

SUMMARY OF TOP STORIES FOR TUESDAY MAY 2, 2000

DOW SLUMPS ON AT&T, MICROSOFT

NEW YORK (CBS.MW)—The Nasdaq succumbed to a bout of profit-taking Tuesday, with the greatest weakness detected in the software and Internet sectors. And a tumble in shares of AT&T kept the Dow Industrials in negative territory throughout most of the session.

Weakness in Microsoft shares kept computer software shares deep in the red and put a damper on the entire tech sector. Also lower were Internet and chip stocks.

http://cbs.marketwatch.com/archive/20000502/news/current/snapshot.htx?dist=nwtpm

Exhibit 13 Big Charts.com Home Page

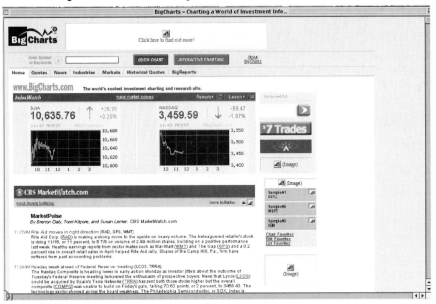

Source: *bigcharts.com*

Exhibit 14 MarketWatch.com Income Statement (1997 to 1999)

MarketWatch.com, Inc. Income Statement (in $000)			
	Year Ending December 31, 1999	**1998**	**October 29 to December 31, 1997**
Net Revenues:			
Advertising	$18,033	$5,115	$320
Licensing	5,262	1,285	210
Other	1,640	627	100
Total Revenue	$24,935	$7,027	$630
Cost of Revenue			
Advertising and News		2,398	92
Subscription		439	56
Total Cost of Revenue	$9,901	$2,837	$148
Gross Profit	$15,034	$4,190	$482
Operating Expenses:			
Product Development	$4,762	$1,468	$186
General and Administrative	8,948	3,429	248
Sales and Marketing	33,430	11,547	129
Purchased in Process R & D	200	0	0
Amortization of goodwill/intangibles	29,984	0	0
Total Operating Expenses	$77,324	$16,444	$563
Operating Loss	−$62,290	−$12,254	−$81
Interest Income (Expense)	1,412	−159	0
Loss Before Income Tax	−$60,878	−$12,413	−$81
Income Tax Benefit	0	0	0
Net Loss	−$60,878	−$12,413	−$81

Note: MarketWatch.com was incorporated on October 29, 1997, with DBC and CBS as Major Investors
Source: MarketWatch.com, Inc. Securities and Exchange Commission, Form 10K, for year ended December 31, 1999

Exhibit 15 Pyramid of MarketWatch.com's Competitive Advantages

Source: MarketWatch.com

RCA RECORDS: THE DIGITAL REVOLUTION

The music industry as it is today is a banking system; it's not about art. They'd sell a hubcap with cheese on it if they could. Who needs them . . . if you can sell music without compact disc factories, delivery trucks, radio stations, and stores?[1]
—Chuck D, Rap Artist/Online Entrepreneur

There's a whole new world out there that could open up for everybody. It's scary, it's frightening, it's exciting, but the chaos has to be managed in order for us to realize its potential. If it's not managed, it'll just be chaos. It could be totally destructive and devastating. If you can pull all this music off the Internet for free, there is no business anymore.
—Bob Jamieson, President, RCA Records

On July 21, 1999, 55 senior executives of New York City-based RCA Records gathered at the Hyatt Hotel in Greenwich, Connecticut, for the company's annual retreat. RCA President Bob Jamieson opened the meeting by announcing that Christina Aguilera, a recently signed RCA artist, had hit number one on the U.S. singles chart that week with her song "Genie in a Bottle." Financially, RCA was celebrating a fourth straight year of record performance (see Exhibit 1).

Improvement for RCA Records came on the heels of significant operating losses. Just four years earlier, the company had been considered a "tired and old music label." People in the industry had joked: "You know what the difference is between RCA and the Titanic? The Titanic at least had one good band."[2]

Since joining RCA in 1995, Jamieson and Executive Vice President/General Manager Jack Rovner had pursued a "less is more" strategy. Explained RCA CFO Neil Foster, who joined the company the same year:

> We are not an assembly line. We [do not] put out a lot of records. We [are] very selective in our signings. Hence, we'd better make sure each one counts, and

we'd better get 100% behind each one and apply maximum creativity in order to try to make each one a success. That is not the model that all other labels use. Some say, the more times I get up to bat, the higher my batting average will be. The more product I release, the more hits I'll have. That is not true. Given that this is a high fixed-cost business with tremendous operating leverage, the more releases it takes to generate a given sales figure, the far less profitable you'll be.

Although RCA managers credited this strategy with helping to turn the company around, Jamieson, Rovner, and their management team wondered whether it could continue to be successful in the face of retail and radio consolidation, "market clutter,"[3] and increasing marketing costs that were reducing net profit margins generated by physical product. Digital distribution, whereby musicians marketed and sold music direct to consumers via the Internet, posed another threat. As one industry analyst wrote: "The problem the industry faces is that the ability to ship music directly may shift the balance of economic power. If artists can deliver to fans via the [Internet], who needs labels and distributors?"[4]

The same day RCA was celebrating its previous year's success, MP3.com, described as the ultimate source of digital music downloaded from the Internet (with losses of $1.4 million on revenue of $666,785 in the first quarter of 1999), was celebrating its NASDAQ trading debut in San Diego, California. By day's end the company's stock price had climbed from $28 to $63.31. The questions facing RCA were how seriously to take new digital competitors such as MP3.com and whether to rethink aspects of its own business strategy. "Maybe the new technology is a competitor," remarked one RCA executive, "but it's so ill-defined right now and it's such a buzzword. There's no meat on the bone yet."

Research Associate Cate Reavis prepared this case under the supervision of Carin-Isabel Knoop, Director, Research and Development, Executive Education and Professor Jeffrey F. Rayport as the basis for class discussion rather than to illustrate either effective or ineffective handling of an administrative situation.

[1]Geoff Boucher, "What will be the Net effect?" *Los Angeles Times* (July 4, 1999).
[2]Bradley Bambarger, "A retooled RCA is once again a hit maker," *Billboard* (May 23, 1998).
[3]In 1998, 60,000 new albums were issued worldwide, 29,000 in the United States.
[4]Jodi Mardesich, "How the Internet hits big music," *Fortune* (May 10, 1999).

The RCA Story

Founded in 1901 as the Victor Talking Machine Company, RCA Records had signed and developed classic artists such as Elvis Presley, John Denver, and Jefferson Airplane. German media conglomerate Bertelsmann acquired RCA from General Electric in 1986 and, shortly thereafter formed the Bertelsmann Music Group (renamed BMG in 1994), which comprised RCA Records, Arista (also acquired in 1986), and Ariola. By 1999 BMG, with 200 active music labels, held 18% of the global music market through its North America and international divisions. RCA contributed sales in excess of $350 million to BMG's $4.5 billion revenue pool, making it BMG's second-largest full-service label after Arista. All BMG divisions operated as profit centers. (Exhibit 2 depicts BMG's 1998 organizational structure.)

Hitting Bottom

RCA's sales had dropped 10% between 1994 and 1995. The label's U.S. market share was 1.5% and domestic signings had enjoyed little success outside the United States. RCA's roster, according to company executives, was unfocused, with artists covering various musical genres without critical success in any one. The contemporary pop/rock roster had no platinum acts and the urban roster only one. Its waning credibility in the creative community kept RCA from attracting unsigned artists and from marketing those it did manage to sign. "There was a time at RCA," explained one 11-year veteran, "when all of us could do this job with one eye closed because the expectations were so low. We settled for C+." Employee morale was low.

BMG's other labels consistently won U.S. rights to BMG International artists over RCA. "RCA had very little credibility within the BMG distribution system," recalled one long-time executive. "We had very few viable artists. When it came time for the local BMG salesperson to go to Tower Records and say, 'I've got various projects here that we want to deal with,' it was a lot easier for them to push Kenny G or Whitney Houston from Arista than Stacy Earl or Mitch Malloy from RCA."

The Turnaround

Jamieson and Rovner hired from BMG Canada and Arista, respectively, in 1995, began to reorient RCA to be more marketing- and results-driven. They identified as the company's competitive advantages: creativity and financial commitment to artist development; genre and release focus (i.e., less is more); global orientation to artist and repertoire (A&R—those who find and sign talent) and marketing; and broad exploitation of rights through all channels. Efforts were made to improve coordination between A&R and marketing and to clarify roles and responsibilities so as to improve speed and accountability. Jamieson and Rovner introduced the concept of "cells." Consisting of one representative from A&R, marketing, media, promotion, and sales, cells were responsible for the creative and fiscal development aspects of artist development.

Between 1995 and 1999, RCA turned over 60% of its roster, exiting jazz, reggae, and heavy metal altogether to focus on rock, pop, dance, and urban. Efforts were made to repair and rebuild relationships with the artist community and BMG International. Headcount was reduced from 178 to 148 across all levels of the organization and an entire layer of management was eliminated. (By 1999, 75% of the RCA staff, including VP level and higher, were new.) Company executives described RCA as a flat organization in which "people who are creative stallions are allowed to run free," and where decisions were made quickly. "This is a partnership," Rovner explained. "You do this and I'll do this; let's not put a lot of layers in between. We lose the creative process when there's a lot of people involved." A&R staff reported to Jamieson, artist development, to Rovner. (Exhibit 3 depicts RCA's organizational structure.)

The Music Industry in 1999

Just as RCA managed to find its footing, the music industry was in turmoil. Industry consolidation, including radio and retail, together with new technology, players, distribution channels, and fickle consumers, had made the business increasingly competitive and volatile.

Although the $40 billion global music industry grew 8% in 1998 (compared to 10% per year between 1990 and 1995), the U.S. market, roughly one-third of the industry's total sales, was inching along at 2% growth and expected to remain flat through 2003. (Asia and Latin America were expected to grow 10.1% and 14.3%, respectively, between 1998 and 2003.[5]) Industry analysts attributed slow growth to increasing competition from other forms of entertainment (the video game industry

---

[5]"EMI: Time to bail out," analyst report from *Dresdner Kleinwort Benson* (November 1998).

grew 25% in the first half of 1998),[6] the end of the LP "replacement era" (the time during which consumers restocked their cassette and vinyl record collections with CDs); and radio and retail consolidation.

Government deregulation of radio in 1996 gave rise to a greater variety of radio formats (e.g., modern, adult, rhythm, Top 40, rock), making it more difficult for record companies to promote their artists, and, therefore, attain a mass appeal cross-over hit. At the same time, radio stations, becoming more risk averse to new music, focused and shortened their playlists. Moreover, the airwaves of many of the large broadcasting corporations, which were heavily in debt as a result of consolidation were dominated by "sure-fire hits."[7] After aggressive expansion during the industry's high-growth years, music retailers were also consolidating. Musicland Stores, which owned Sam Goody, Media Play, and Suncoast Motion Picture retail chains, closed 106 stores in 1997, resulting in a 10% inventory reduction. Between 1995 and 1997, the number of U.S. music retail outlets dropped 20%.[8] With general retailers accepting less new music and focusing increasingly on hits and established artists, retail promotion costs were escalating for record companies, which, responded to the effects of consolidation with more releases, thereby pushing the sales breakeven point even higher.

Although the five big label companies—Universal, Sony, Warner, EMI, and BMG—accounted for 80% of the global music market, record companies not owned by a major label, termed independents (or indies), were becoming more of a threat. (Exhibit 4 presents market share for major and independent labels.) Opportunities for the indies emerged from consolidation among the major labels and the overall slowdown in sales that reduced staff and numbers of bands represented and increased overall album releases.[9] Since 1990, the indies' market share had increased from 10% to 20%. Between 1996 and 1997, total album releases by majors and indies grew by 12.4% and 13.1%, respectively.[10]

Rock music, the biggest selling category, accounted for just under 26% of sales, down from 42% in 1989, rap and rhythm and blues (R&B) together for 23%, up from 16% in 1989. Consumers aged 30 and older bought approximately 50% of music sold, up from 34% in 1989, 15- to 29-year-olds 39%, down from 42% in 1997.[11] Meanwhile, sales of albums that were between 15 months and 3 years old dropped over 20% in 1998. One industry analyst blamed the proliferation of new acts and the many "awareness generating channels" that labels used to market artists. "There are so many ways for the listener to engage the artist and so much competition," he explained, "it accelerates the way the audience perceives the artist, the way they enjoy the artist, and, unfortunately, the way they move on to the next thing; it's often too much, too fast."[12] Major labels also, according to another industry observer, tended to jump on trends, signing hot new acts instead of developing artists on their current roster. "Artist development is now a thing of the past," he remarked. "[Labels] don't even pay lip service to it anymore."[13]

Technology

MP3,[14] the pioneer technology in digital downloading (and the most requested word on Internet search engines), enabled online consumers to download recordings, authorized and unauthorized, as computer files. (Download time for a three-minute song was approximately 20 minutes.) Downloaded songs could be played on PCs, CD players, or MP3 portable players such as Diamond Multimedia's Rio (a walkman-sized unit that played up to one hour of music), and Empeg's Empeg Player (an MP3 player for automobiles that could store up to 70 hours of music). Both retailed for roughly $200. The vast majority of the 150,000 songs available as MP3 files circulated free of charge. Forrester Research, a technology research firm, predicted that by the end of 1999 there would be one million portable downloadable music players and that by 2003 downloadable music would add $1.1 billion to U.S. music industry sales.

MP3 technology, however, was being challenged by two other major digital players.

- Liquid Audio (*www.liquidaudio.com*), positioned as the "first and only Internet company focusing exclusively on the needs of the music industry," provided a Dolby digital encoding-based streaming audio

---

[6]Ibid.

[7]David Segal, "Cost cutting has rock music all shook up," *The Washington Post* (February 20, 1999).

[8]"Time Warner," *SG Cowen Analyst Report* (March 4, 1999).

[9]Following the December 1998 $10.4 billion merger between Universal/Polygram, more than 200 acts were dropped and 15 labels consolidated into four U.S. music groups.

[10]*Dresdner Kleinwort Benson.*

[11]"Study: Music sales declining among youth. . . .," *The Atlanta Journal and Constitution* (April 2, 1999).

[12]Boucher.

[13]Glenn Gamboa, "Parallel musical universes. . . .," *The Ottawa Citizen* (April 5, 1999).

[14]MP3 was an acronym derived from the engineering term, MPEG-1, Layer 3.

system called Music-on-Demand (MOD), that yielded the highest quality digital sound possible. Registered customers received a music passport that enabled them to purchase a "liquid track," play back music on their PCs, and download the file once to a recordable CD format such as a minidisc. Liquid Audio employed "digital watermarking" technology that embedded copyright information and the identity of the original purchaser into music files.

- AT&T's a2b music enabled consumers to download CD-quality music quickly, (standard download time for a 3-minute song was reduced from 20 minutes to 9 using a 28.8K modem). Whereas songs in MP3 format could be played by anyone, a2b songs were provided with a software "key" that protected distributors, artists, record labels, and customers from electronic theft while accommodating flexible licensing for single, multiple, or shared uses of downloaded music. Consumers could download from the a2b music website (*www.a2bmusic.com*) software needed to receive and play songs on their PCs.

Other digital formats included Real Networks' Real Jukebox, Microsoft's Media Player, and Apple's Quicktime 4.0.

It was speculated that digital distribution would lessen musicians' dependency on the major labels for manufacturing and distribution and reduce the need for brick and mortar retail space.[15] (Costs related to manufacturing, packaging, distribution, artist royalty, copyright, freight, and inventory obsolescence represented 45% of wholesale revenues.) Many industry observers believed that record labels' ownership and control of music would be threatened as many new and established musicians refused label contracts, opting instead to market and sell music on their own, as had English rock legend David Bowie.

New material made available a song at a time on artists' websites could reduce demand for conventional forms of music packaging. They could also get exposure from music sites such as UBL.com, which profiled artists and their latest works and hosted chat rooms for music fans which, in turn, could reduce the need for big labels' marketing services. Finally, barriers to entry were theoretically lower for artists, enabling smaller acts to enter the industry. Digital jukeboxes such as IUMA and

MP3.com charged unsigned acts roughly $250 to "post" recordings.[16] With MP3.com, artists set the price of their CDs, received 50% of every sale, and maintained full control of master recordings. In return they agreed to "give away" one song that visitors could download for free. A number of artists, however, perceived risks in the technology presented. Explained one well-known musician: "There's a danger to making things so accessible that you devalue your own work."[17]

Most of the major labels, RCA included, viewed digital downloading as a promotional channel. Were digital distribution to become mainstream, the economic consequences for the major labels and the impact on their relationships with retailers and artists regarding copyrights and royalties were uncertain. To cushion the costs of Internet-related technology, many labels were adding to artists' contracts "technology deduction clauses" that subtracted 15%–25% from the 12%–14% royalty rate for record sales.[18] (Exhibit 5 depicts the traditional economic chain for CDs.)

Piracy posed a significant and unresolved, threat. According to industry estimates, several billion songs were downloaded for free in 1998. In late 1998 a consortium of technology companies, hardware firms, major music companies, and the Recording Industry Association of America (RIAA) formed the Secure Digital Music Initiative (SDMI) with the objective of creating an industrywide technical standard that would provide copyright protection, limit distribution of music files, and ensure royalty payments to labels and artists.[19] SDMI "blessed" the MP3 format in July 1999 under the condition that within 18 months, when a standard would be adopted that enabled piracy-protected music to be sold online, the electronics companies would make their players compliant.

Record companies, meanwhile, were partnering up with technology companies to create their own digital solutions: Sony had formed an alliance with Microsoft; Universal and BMG had partnered with InterTrust,[20] and EMI was involved with Liquid Audio.

[16]Alice Rawsthorn, "Big five shudder at digital jukeboxes," *The Financial Times* (January 13, 1999).

[17]Christopher John Farley, "Music without labels," *Time* (February 22, 1999).

[18]Neil Strauss, "A chance to break the pop stranglehold," *The New York Times* (May 9, 1999).

[19]Richard Ashton, "Pump up the volume," *Entertainment Weekly* (July 16, 1999).

[20]InterTrust developed digital rights management technologies to protect and manage artists', authors', producers', publishers', distributors', traders', brokers', enterprises', governments', and other institutions' and consumers' rights and interests in digital information.

[15]John Pareles, "Trying to get in tune with the digital age," *The New York Times* (February 9, 1999).

Distribution

The Internet was creating new, efficient, cost-effective retail and distribution opportunities for artists and labels alike. Online music retailers such as CDNow, Amazon.com, Barnesandnoble.com, and N2K sold pre-recorded music 20%–30% below traditional retail prices.[21] Brick and mortar retailer Tower Records was also selling music online (customers could download songs for $1.20 each). MP3.com, www.stereo-society.com, and musicmaker.com were the leading digital distributors, but consumers could also purchase CD versions of music. The average MP3.com CD, manufactured in-house on demand, retailed for $7.00 compared to $15.98 at a traditional retail music store.

Record labels were venturing into web-based retail as well. Getmusic.com, an April 1999 partnership between BMG and Universal, sold CDs at prices, on average, 20% higher than CDNow and Amazon.com. According to the participating companies, the most important part of the venture was not selling music *per se*, but rather generating direct communication links with customers who visited BMG-developed genre-specific music sites, including Peeps.com (for hip-hop), Bugjuice.com (for rock), and TwangThis.com (a country site). "The essence of what the companies are trying to do," remarked one industry observer, "is to use the interactive nature of the Internet to gather the names and email addresses of their customers so they can sell more music to them by artists they already like and introduce them to others."[22] The two companies together accounted for roughly 40% of all recorded music sold in the United States.

Brick and mortar retailers, however, continued to dominate music sales. In 1998, consumers' CD purchases via the Web totaled $134 million, in stores $14 million (see Table A). Industry analysts, nevertheless, predicted that online sales would exceed $3 billion by 2005.

The Balance of Power[23]

How new technology would alter "traditional" rights and contract agreements between labels and artists remained to be seen.

Copyrights. All pre-recorded music was covered by two copyrights. The record label held the copyright for the artist's recorded performance, the composer (songwriter), usually represented by a music publisher, the rights to the musical composition. U.S. copyright law permitted composers, but not copyright owners of sound recordings, to collect royalties for music played in public or private spaces (e.g., on radio and in nightclubs, concert halls, hotels, and elevators). Licensing bodies such as Broadcast Music Incorporated (BMI), the American Society of Composers, Authors, and Publishers (ASCAP), and SESAC[24] were charged with tracking all material played in these venues, live performances included.

The Digital Performance and Sound Recordings Act passed by Congress in 1995 gave copyright holders of sound recordings the right to be paid royalties equal to those paid for the sale of a pre-recorded CD for live performances digitally transferred from one person or entity to another.

Terms. There were five principal terms in a standard recording agreement.

- Advances (payments to artists), which ranged from $250,000 for new artists to several million dollars

Table A Sales Breakdown of Various Channels

	Record Store	Other Store[a]	Tape/Record Club	Mail Order	Internet
1990	69.8%	18.6%	8.9%	2.7%	NA
1995	52.2	29.2	14.3	4.3	NA
1998	51.3	35.2	9.5	2.9	1.1

Source: Recording Industry Association of America
[a]Includes mass merchants such as Wal-Mart, Best Buy

---

[21]CDNow and N2K merged in June 1999.
[22]Saul Hansell, "Labels act against online music squeeze," *Sydney Morning Herald* (April 13, 1999).

[23]Information from this section was taken from "Geffen Records," HBS case No. 898 234.
[24]SESAC is not an acronym.

for established artists, covered recording costs (which typically ranged from $175,000 to $350,000) and served as an advance on royalties. Approximately 20% of recordings recouped (recovered) their costs. Unrecouped advances were considered losses for the record company.

- Product commitments (the number of albums to be delivered to the record company) typically numbered six or seven. In the early 1990s, 10-album deals had been the norm. According to industry observers, the drop in the number of committed albums reflected artists' increased negotiating leverage.

- Royalty rate (the amount of income paid to artists), which was approximately 10% in the early 1990s, ranged from 12% to 14% of suggested retail list price (SLRP). SLRP was the royalty base of an album after a 25% CD packaging deduction fee.

Retail price of CD:	$15.98
Less packaging (25% of $15.98):	3.99
Royalty base:	$11.98[25]

- Royalty rates for music club sales were significantly less.

- Mechanical royalties (payments paid to publishers of musical compositions), were 7.5 cents per song. The rate was set by the Copyright Royalty Tribunal, a congressional agency.

- Territory referred to the countries in which a company had rights. Some artists requested a split territory deal whereby one company distributed in North America and another throughout the rest of the world.

Record labels did not own rights to tours or retail merchandise, funds from which went to artists and licensees. Among other questions being asked about how the Internet might affect rights was who should own record company-financed websites and the rights they included. Sony announced in the spring of 1999 that it would take ownership of websites previously controlled by its artists.

"Less Is More"

RCA's new strategy was to emphasize quality over quantity. "We look for artists whom we believe have something to say and who will be around for many years," explained Jamieson. RCA represented far fewer than the

[25]Donald Passman, *All You Need to Know About the Music Business,* New York: Simon & Schuster, 1997 (p. 174).

150-plus acts typical of other major labels. Of 23 albums released in 1998 across six genres, 17 were pop/rock and 6 urban (see Exhibit 6). Competitor labels typically released 40 albums per year. Observed Foster:

> One thing that will kill you in this business is high turnover in your roster. It costs you money to sign a band in the first place, more to release and market it, and more still if you drop the artist. We are very career artist oriented. We are long-term focused and we can afford to do that because we are a private company and we don't have to worry about the next quarter's results.

"Because we put out fewer records," Rovner stated, "we can focus and apply all of our muscle and passion into these records thereby making a dent in the marketplace." "We can direct the marketing efforts more specifically," added a colleague. "We can stay focused. From what I've heard at other record companies, you do things by rote. There isn't enough time to have an open discussion."

"We treat our artists as human beings, not pieces of product," remarked one executive of RCA's policy of assigning product managers to support artists' development throughout their careers. "We make every decision for their career based on what's best for them, rather than what's best for the record." On average, product managers handled six artists at one time.

Where RCA added value depended on the artist. According to Foster, other things being equal, from a content creation perspective established acts tended to be more "self-contained" than developing acts and, therefore, perhaps less reliant on the label in the making of their records. The label focused more on maximizing the creative value in imaging and marketing established artists' records. "With an established artist," explained VP of marketing Julie Bruzzone, "you have to go out of the gate with your print and TV advertising, your tie-ins, your tour. Even with a high-profile artist you need to use high-profile channels so the consumer knows you have an album out."

Typically, for new acts, the label was heavily involved in the A&R process, which included helping artists make their records, round out their bands, and refine their live performances. Developing artists relied heavily on RCA to generate awareness and introduce them to the market. "Baby bands" sometimes were opening acts for established RCA artists and new acts often performed in the same market for four consecutive weeks in what were termed "residency tours." "Sometimes the best thing is for our artists to become known in a region and grow them from there," explained Bruzzone. RCA financed the entire marketing endeavor for all artists. Whereas established acts tended to be profitable, inasmuch as subsequent releases were able to leverage the marketing investments of prior releases, with new artists, according to Foster, the company had but a 20% chance of recouping its investment. (Exhibit 7 presents a sample record company financial statement.)

A&R

The role of A&R was to scout talent, sign bands, make records, and work with marketing during the development process. At other labels, according to Jamieson, A&R's role typically ended once marketing took over. "The A&R people have a vision of where they want to lead the market," explained Foster. "They have a vision of a highly differentiated product that, combined with creative marketing, will actually create demand as opposed to react to demand in the marketplace." A&R was also familiar with defeat: "The hardest part of A&R," observed Jamieson, "is accepting that your batting average is not going to be good. If you sign 10 acts and 1 breaks, you're a hero. If you bat .300, you're in the Hall of Fame." (Exhibit 8 presents breakeven table.)

Artist Development

The development process began as soon as talent was signed. "Developing an artist," explained one executive, "entails creating mystique and creating the sense that fans are buying into something that's real. It's like chapters in a book; after each chapter is finished you start writing the next. But the good bands and the good A&R people have that book already written before the record even comes out."

RCA tailored marketing strategies for each release. It spent anywhere from four to six months determining the appropriate audience and generating awareness (creating a "buzz") for a new act both internally within RCA and externally among distributors, retailers, consumers, and the music industry as a whole. "We can't take our eye off any one of these groups when marketing a new record," Rovner stated. For some baby acts the development process began even before music was recorded.

Marketing budgets were based on such criteria as how many records were expected to ship, whether the record would be radio-friendly, how the media were expected to respond to it, whether it would get video play on MTV,

and whether or not it was a touring band. "We are in a world of marketing blitzes," Rovner explained. "In addition to radio, the consumer identifies with the artist or group through newspapers, magazines, video channels, morning and evening TV shows, commentary, touring, the Internet, and direct mail. We have to analyze every possible channel to see how we can best create awareness" (see Exhibit 9). RCA generated awareness through eight marketing departments:

- **Promotion** was responsible for identifying appropriate radio formats (e.g., R&B, adult, Top 40, mainstream rock) and ensuring that new releases were played at stations across the country. Songs were typically played for six to eight weeks on the radio prior to release of an album and were introduced first in one format and then expanded to related formats to expand the audience.

- **Publicity** ensured that RCA artists and their "feelings" about their music were heard by the general public. Among the channels it utilized were major newspapers and magazines, music-specific publications, and television (e.g., *Saturday Night Live*, specials on the Disney Channel, and other televised events).

- **Tours** were considered a natural marketing driver for an album and a way to introduce up-and-coming acts if live performance was an important element of an artist's "package." Although, like other record labels, RCA did not own its artists' touring rights, it was actively involved in the touring process.

- **Video Services** created content for local, regional, and national video outlets such as MTV and VH1.

- **Creative Services** designed album packaging and artwork. It was also responsible for distributing artists' photographs to the press and other publicity channels.

- **Product Development** was responsible for developing partnerships with consumer brand companies and creating marketing strategies that tied artists to consumer product campaigns.

- **Product Management** assumed creative leadership for artist positioning and imaging and consumer advertising campaigns as well as directed creativity and execution for the other departments.

- **Sales** was responsible for ensuring that distributors and retailers were properly stocked with RCA products and that retail displays were appropriate for conducting retail marketing.

RCA planned to add an Internet marketing capability. Website development for artists was outsourced and paid for by RCA. Consistent with BMG's corporate objective, RCA tried to obtain rights to new artists' websites. "We do this not because we want to keep control over the artist," explained one executive, "but because we want to be able to use that fan base to promote other developing artists." Established artists often managed their own sites.

Product Development, RCA's newest marketing department, was established in 1998 when the company recognized the potential cross-marketing opportunities between artists and consumer products companies. Partnering with recognized brands such as Polo, Coca-Cola, MCI, and Visa to help generate awareness of RCA artists was a win-win deal, according to Foster:

> Consider the sponsorship by Polo Jeans of one of our developing artists for a retail tour at selected Macy's stores. Aside from sponsoring some of the costs of the tour itself, Polo funds radio ads in each local market, which help support radio airplay for the artist's single; the artist's performance is seen by thousands of mall shoppers; the event is publicized in print and local TV; and coupons are distributed to bounce-back to the music retail chain in the same malls. So you can see that we can create complex and mutually reinforcing promotions, often self-liquidating from our point of view, that deliver value to all participants—the consumer, the corporate sponsor and its product, retailers, radio, and the artist development process.

The challenge with tying RCA artists to consumer products was timing, observed VP of Product Development Joe Dimuro. Big name-brand companies such as Coke could take up to two years to develop brand development strategies. "It really presents a major challenge for us because we don't know at what level the artist is going to be at that time," Dimuro explained. "We don't know if we're going to have radio play; we don't know if we're going to have video play; and we don't know if we're still going to be working that particular single."

Product development was also a way for RCA to better understand its market audience. Consumers were, for example, offered free merchandise in return for completing survey cards that asked where they heard about the artist, what type(s) of music they listened to, and where they bought their music. RCA stored this information in a database.

Marketing strategies for individual artists were discussed companywide at two weekly meetings. At "futures" meetings, which focused on the creative aspects of artist development, the questions tended to be, "What's missing? Do we need to add more? Do we need to take something away? Have we really created a buzz? Do we need to push the record back?" At "label" meetings, members of RCA's marketing departments were updated about where various artists were in the promotion and sales processes. Reports were distributed that ranked RCA artists by weekly album sales and the number of radio "spins" each song received on radio stations around the country (see Exhibit 10). "Understanding and analyzing the cause and effect between radio play and retail sales is something we watch very closely," explained SVP of Promotion Ron Geslin, "and we measure it. Radio is interested in getting good programming and good audience for their advertising rate, but that doesn't necessarily overlap with our agenda of ultimately selling records."

Employees were encouraged to challenge one another during futures and labels meetings. "We try to have a company free of politics," explained Rovner, "where people can become champions for individual projects and for the music." Added Foster: "We want our employees to be entrepreneurial. We want them to think like an owner."

Getting Product to Market

BMG's Sonopress, the world's second largest CD supplier with a daily output of 2.5 million CDs, was the primary manufacturer of RCA products. The remainder of production was outsourced to third-party suppliers. Manufacturing rates, negotiated on an annual basis, had dropped significantly since the mid-1980s due to more efficient production.

Each of BMG's nine distribution branches was staffed by marketing and sales representatives charged with selling product to retailers, overseeing in-store marketing displays, and checking inventory. RCA's marketing and sales department employed five regional directors who met weekly with BMG representatives to discuss new releases and the marketing vision for each. The directors also maintained direct contact with retail accounts. Because BMG handled distribution for several of its other labels as well as a number of third-party labels, the challenge for RCA sales representatives was to attract and hold the attention of BMG representatives.[26] "We need to

---

[26]In 1998 BMG handled 1,700 albums.

make sure that we get our piece of the pie," remarked an RCA marketing VP.

International Exploitation

RCA was able to market its artists outside the United States through BMG's International Catalogue Licensing Agreement (ICLA). This internal agreement governed exploitation rights and transfer pricing for artists owned by one and exploited by another BMG company. Its objective was to set a "fair" transfer price that encouraged repertoire owners to develop artists with international potential and affiliates to release those artists in their markets and make a profit after royalty payments to the repertoire owners. Explained Foster: "The ICLA generally addresses how we can price the repertoire in our market; what internal royalty we need to pay the repertoire owner; what reserves we can hold back against this royalty obligation; and, loosely, how marketing tools and initiatives that might benefit the marketing of the act beyond the market of exploitation are to be funded between repertoire owner and exploiter." RCA handled the U.S. rights to the band 'N SYNC, signed by BMG Germany. Foreign territories handled the foreign rights in their respective territories to RCA artists such as the Dave Matthews Band.

Challenges

RCA pondered how to retain its talent, hold the attention of its "music audience," and how seriously to take the new digital medium. Among internal challenges faced by the company were how to generate stronger synergies with BMG and Bertelsmann and ward off an attitude of complacency. Jamieson, Rovner, and their team needed to decide whether the status quo would bring continued success or if fundamental changes were needed in RCA's strategy and relationship with BMG.

Holding onto Talent. Retaining successful acts might become more challenging as more artists opted not to pursue label contracts. Part of the challenge for RCA, explained Foster, was convincing artists who were thinking of going "labelless" that to be successful they would need to replicate on their own RCA's entire marketing capability with all its creativity, judgment, expertise, skill, and relationships. Artists who chose this route would have to be willing and able to risk hundreds of

thousands of dollars before their first album unit was sold. "But," conceded Foster,

> the established artist's counter could be I have more rights than just the sound recording rights in my recorded music. I have touring rights, merchandising rights, and copyrights. Maybe what I need to do is not amortize across marketing departments, but amortize across my rights. De facto, this organization would be a hybrid of artist management, tour promotion, copyright publishing, and record company. Can such an organization be as expert in exploiting each right when it is trying to exploit all at once? Perhaps. We can't wait around to find out. What we as a record company need to do is deliver such incredible creative marketing value to established artists that they aren't inclined to test this hybrid model.

RCA needed to consider what digital distribution would mean for artist contracts. "Right now there's no model for payment of royalties for downloaded material," stated RCA's legal counsel.

> We don't know what it's going to cost per download, what we're going to be able to charge. Artists are trying right now to push us into a corner where we're agreeing to pay them 50% of our net receipts. We're trying to pay them a percentage of our receipts equal to their royalty rates for downloads. Depending on the model that develops, that may or may not work for us.

Where to Spend? Deciding how to allocate resources was becoming increasingly difficult. "We're being presented with new avenues of marketing that we could potentially tap," Foster explained. How to tie the traditional avenues of retail and radio with emerging avenues such as corporate sponsors and the Internet was one consideration. "At the same time," Foster continued, "the costs of those means are going up largely due to consolidation at radio and retail. As a result, the position of the record company relative to radio and retail has gotten weaker, making retail marketing and radio exposure more expensive than ever."

Capturing the Audience. Intriguing customers was also becoming more challenging. Wrote one industry observer: "Young people today don't feel the need to own the music they listen to. . . . They're distracted by the Internet and video games. In other words, MTV and the radio

---

[27]Jonathan Van Meter, "What's a record exec to do with Aimee Mann?" *New York Times Magazine* (July 11, 1999).

will do just fine."[27] The Internet, moreover, was creating a world of information overload. "How do people possibly absorb this overflow of information that's available to them on the Internet?" questioned Jamieson. "How do they receive it and how do they digest it? Think about it. There were 60,000 records released last year in the world; multiply that over 100 years. That's a lot of records."

Leveraging BMG. RCA was looking to enhance the exploitation of its creative content by increasing collaboration with other BMG companies. "We need to be able to balance our culture of decentralization with the global reach of the Internet," Jamieson explained. "The Internet can go all over the world instantly. As an entertainment and media company we need to figure out how to react even more on a global basis. This is a challenge since we all operate as profit centers and are compensated on our individual performance on a yearly basis." "Yet," added Rovner, "the collective bank of information at Bertelsmann is vast—between music and book clubs, record companies, and fan data. The names and purchasing habits we have collected of our customers is enormous. We need to continue to be decentralized, yet we need to manage the decentralization."

Chasing the Rabbit

Jamieson, reflecting on nearly 30 years in the music business, five at RCA, offered his vision of the future of the music industry:

A lot of these digital distribution companies won't work because, at the end of the day, you've got to have good artists. Most all of them recognize that they have to have some semblance of a traditional record company. They need the marketing. They need the sales. They need the promotion. They need all those things to get the artists the exposure to enable them to sell records on the Internet or in record stores.

And in years to come you could have all music delivered to you digitally. You could have a digital jukebox and go through your menus, pick your music, pay a fee every month. It's like the universe of music as a library. . . . You can pull down anything you want . . . play it as often as you want . . . store it in your library of music, and you'll pay a monthly maintenance fee and maybe you pay every time you play it and then you'd let it go, if you want. And we will all win: the artist gets paid; royalties get paid; publishing gets paid; record companies get paid; and it's wonderful. And you can sell so many more records so much faster. That's going to change the business.

RCA's continued success in the evolving digital world, Jamieson emphasized, largely depended on attitude:

Our biggest challenge is to never start feeling as though we've accomplished what we set out to accomplish, because the bar is always moving. We have to constantly keep ourselves out of the comfort zone, on edge, constantly improving and pushing forward, keeping motivated and focused, and seeking out new talent and new ways to expose our artists. We're no longer the underdog; we're no longer sneaking up on anybody. People take notice of what we do today and the challenge going forward is to take us to that next level. It's like a greyhound chasing a rabbit. We're chasing that rabbit and we can't ever get that rabbit because if we do, and we taste that blood, we're dead.

Exhibit 1 RCA Sales 1994–1998[a]

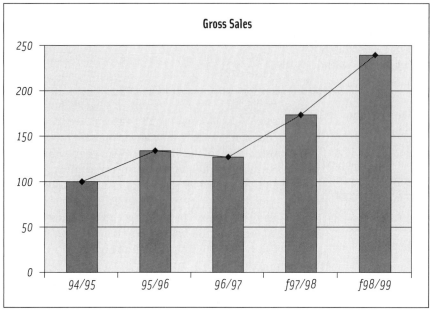

Gross Sales

Source: RCA
[a]Numbers, indexed to 100 in 1994/1995, reflect company sales growth, not sales revenue.

Exhibit 2 BMG Entertainment Organization Structure

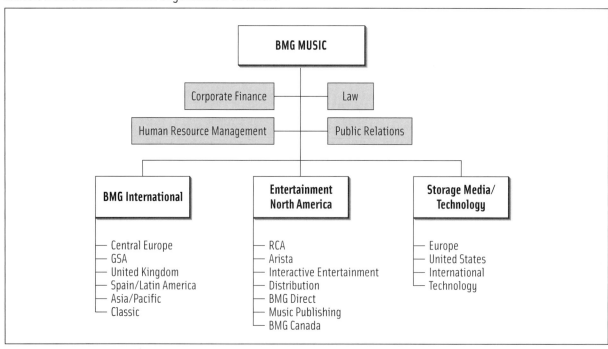

Source: BMG Annual Report, 1998

Exhibit 3 RCA Organizational Structure

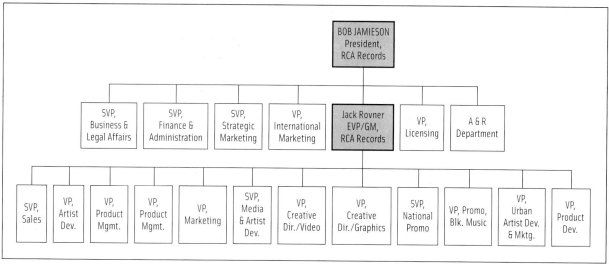

Source: RCA

Exhibit 4 1999 Global Music Market Share

Distributor	Global	U.S.
Universal/Polygram	23%	26%
Sony	16%	16%
Warner Music Group	15%	16%
EMI	14%	10%
BMG	14%	16%
Independent	18%	16%

Source: RCA

Exhibit 5 Traditional CD Value Chain

Suggested Retail List Price	$16.98[a]
Wholesale price to label after discount to retailer and distribution fee	8.80
Manufacturing, freight, obsolescence, union dues	1.00
Artist royalty	1.20
Copyright	.80
Gross margin to record label before marketing, unrecouped recording, and overhead	5.80

Source: RCA
[a]Generally, actively marketed product would be on sale for $2.00–$3.00 less than SRLP; catalog product would generally sell at full price.

Exhibit 6 RCA Records—Selected Roster by Music Type/Sales Level ('000s)

| Sales Level in Units ('000s) | Domestic | | | International |
	Pop Music	Rock	Urban	All Genres
Superstar + *2,000 +*	Christina Aguilera	Dave Matthews Band		Natalie Imbruglia 'N SYNC
Superstar *1,000–1,999*		Eve 6 The Verve Pipe Lit	Rome Tyrese	Robyn Lou Vega
Established *300–999*	Bruce Hornsby	ZZ Top		La Bouche Republica
Developing *75–299*	Jai Kristine W. Lea Andreone Wild Orchid	Robert Bradley Hum Vertical Horizon	Chantay Savage Coko Kevon Edmonds	Olive Sweetbox
New *0–74*	Andy Vargas Brenda Lesieur Danielle Brisebois David Mead Essence	Doyle Bramhall Jeremy Toback Junkster Papa Vegas Radford Thin Lizard Dawn Treble Charger Trinket	Before Dark Boy Wonder Cherokee K Star Supreme C	Innosense Jennifer Brown Kent

Source: RCA

Exhibit 7a Sample Record Company Profit & Loss Statement (illustrative only)

		1999	
Gross Sales:		**300,000**	
Return provision and distribution fee	(67,800)		
Net Sales		**232,200**	100.0%
Manufacturing cost	24,750		11.5%
Other cost of sales	2,000		
Royalty cost	63,000		27.1%
Inventory obsolescence provision	1,300		−0.6%
Costs of Goods Sold		**91,050**	39.2%
Gross Margin Before Recording Costs		**141,150**	60.8%
Gross recording costs	35,000		100.0%
Earnings recoupment	(10,000)		28.6%
Net Recording Costs		**25,000**	71.4%
Gross Margin		**116,150**	50.0%
Royalty income international	40,000		100.0%
Cost of royalty income international	(20,000)		50.0%
Net Royalty Income International		**20,000**	50.0%
Royalty income club	6,000		100.0%
Cost of royalty income club	(1,800)		30.0%
Net Royalty Income Club		**4,200**	70.0%
Royalty income outsiders	6,000		100.0%
Cost of royalty income outsiders	(2,400)		40.0%
Net Royalty Income Outsiders[a]		**3,600**	60.0%
Net Royalty Income		**27,800**	12.0%
Gross Profit		**143,950**	62.0%
Radio	14,550		6.3%
Video	6,000		2.6%
Tours	5,200		2.2%
Retail/co-op	12,200		5.3%
Publicity	3,000		1.3%
Consumer	4,500		1.9%
Artwork	3,500		1.5%
Giveaway	4,000		1.7%
Total Marketing Costs		**52,950**	22.8%
Contribution Margin		**91,000**	39.2%
Total Overhead		**63,000**	27.1%
Net Income		**28,000**	12.1%
Total Other Income/(Expense)		**2,000**	0.9%
Total Operating Income		**30,000**	12.9%

Source: RCA

[a]Licensing, synchronization in films/ads, compilations

Exhibit 7b Sample Record Company Balance Sheet, 1999 ($ in '000s) (illustrative only)

Assets		Liabilities	
Cash	10,000	Trade accounts payable	3,000
Trade accounts receivable (net reserves)	30,000	Accrued royalties payable	20,000
Other receivables	2,000	Accrued international royalties	6,000
Intercompany royalties receivable	12,000	Total operating reserves	5,500
Total Receivables	**44,000**		
		Deferred income	1,000
Finished goods inventory (net reserves)	8,000		
Component inventory (net reserves)	1,000	**Total Liabilities**	**35,500**
Total Inventory	**9,000**		
Prepaid artist advances	50,000		
Artist advance reserves	(29,000)		
Net Artist Advances	**21,000**	**Equity**	
Total Current Assets	**84,000**	Additional paid-in capital	8,000
		Prior year earnings less dividends	30,500
Total land and buildings	20,000	Current year earnings	30,000
Furniture and fixtures	10,000		
Reserve for depreciation	(10,000)	**Total Equity**	**68,500**
Net Land, Buildings, Machinery and Equipment	**20,000**		
Total Assets	**104,000**	**Total Liabilities and Equity**	**104,000**

Source: RCA

Exhibit 8 Breakeven Table

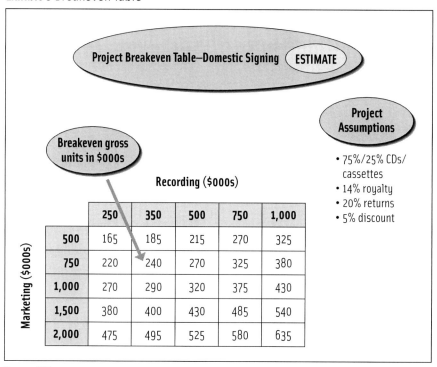

Project Breakeven Table—Domestic Signing ESTIMATE

Project Assumptions

Breakeven gross units in $000s

Recording ($000s)

Project Assumptions:
- 75%/25% CDs/cassettes
- 14% royalty
- 20% returns
- 5% discount

Marketing ($000s)	250	350	500	750	1,000
500	165	185	215	270	325
750	220	240	270	325	380
1,000	270	290	320	375	430
1,500	380	400	430	485	540
2,000	475	495	525	580	635

Source: RCA

Exhibit 9 RCA Records—Typical Marketing Spending to Launch Developing Artists ($000s)

	Description	Rap	R&B	Alternative	Mainstream
Artwork (per album)	• Package design • Photo shoots • Separations	20	25–50	25–40	25–50
Video (per single)	• Production • Promotion	100+	100–300	75–200	100–300
Radio (per single)	• Indies • Radio dates • Trade ads • Research/BDS • Airplay support	50–100	200–300	75–150	200–350
Media	• TV dates • EPKs, photos, bios • Artist receptions • Consumer ads • Outside publicists	10–30	25–50	25–50	25–75
Tour	• Tour support • Ticket buys	25–50	50–150	35–75	50–150
Retail (per month)	• Coop • Merchandising materials • Marketing services & research	50	50–100	50–100	75–150
Giveaway (total life of project)	• Promos • Promotional items (e.g., t-shirts, stickers, caps)	60	50	20	60
Total		500+	750–1,000+	500–750+	750–1,200+

Source: RCA

Exhibit 10 Soundscan Chart Summary

SOUNDSCAN — CHART SUMMARY — HIGHLIGHT SHEET

CHART SUMMARY	THIS WEEK	1 WEEK	2 WEEK	3 WEEK	%CHANGE	WEEK OF Mar 28 – Apr 3
SOUNDSCAN TOP 25 ALBUMS	2,632,677	1,942,319	2,156,863	2,280,771	36%	
SOUNDSCAN TOP 200 CHART	6,158,694	4,976,462	5,179,743	5,147,005	24%	
SOUNDSCAN SINGLES CHART	2,179,565	1,891,385	1,849,267	1,660,500	15%	
R&B CORE ALBUMS—TOP 25	402,868	430,575	483,235	489,437	-6%	

TOP 10 CURRENT ALBUMS

#	Album	TW	LW	% CHANGE
1	BRITNEY SPEARS "BABY ONE MORE TIME"	272,820	167,900	62%
2	TLC "FANMAIL"	197,482	154,285	28%
3	EMINEM "SLIM SHADY"	170,138	161,808	5%
4	ANDREA BOCELLI "SOGNO ..."	148,949	506	29,337%
5	OFFSPRING "AMERICANA"	136,520	99,849	38%
6	SHANIA TWAIN "COME ON OVER"	133,437	101,314	32%
7	VARIOUS ARTISTS "FAMILY VALUES"	121,848	144	84,517%
8	LAURYN HILL "MISEDUCATION OF ..."	120,507	108,612	11%
9	'N SYNC " 'N SYNC"	112,042	66,496	68%
10	DIXIE CHICKS "WIDE OPEN SPACES"	111,931	81,462	37%

ARTISTS/ALBUMS

ARTISTS/ALBUMS	REL. DATE	DMA DETAIL	TW	LW	THIS WK	1 WEEK	2 WEEK	3 WEEK	% CHANGE	CUM SS	NET SHIPPED	SELL-OFF %	W.VEN. SALE
'N SYNC	3/24/98	TOP 200	9*	12	112,042	66,496	67,946	68,191	68%	5,552,585	6,292,000	88%	0
		TOP 5 DMA DETAIL											
		NEW YORK	11	20	6,257	3,910	4,327	4,546	60%				
		LOS ANGELES	13	13	4,713	3,138	3,215	3,194	50%				
		CHICAGO	12	16	4,076	2,238	2,100	1,966	82%				
		PHILADELPHIA	9	12	3,295	2,115	2,095	2,172	56%				
		BOSTON	10	12	3,127	1,822	2,146	1,997	72%				
I Drive Myself Crazy		BDS: T40MSTM	2,097	1,608					CUM SPINS:	4,902			
		BDS: RHYT T40	365	290					CUM SPINS:	703			
God Must Have Spent ...		TOP SINGLES	26*	32	19,947	12,742	14,799	16,219	57%	196,938	571,900	34%	0
		TOP EXTENDED SINGLE	1	3									
		BDS: ADT CONTEMP	1,228	1,240					CUM SPINS:	9,932			
		BDS: ADT T40	475	451					CUM SPINS:	5,696			
		MTV	N/A	N/A					57%				
IN THE MIX WITH ...	11/10/98	TOP 50 MUSIC VIDEOS	2	2	11,150	6,380	7,207	6,938	75%	387,190	478,000	81%	0
HOME FOR XMAS	11/10/98	TOP 200	N/R	N/R	561	378	479	598	48%	1,420,707	1,556,000	91%	0
TYRESE													
Tyrese	9/2/98	TOP 200	36	30	43,182	41,093	48,568	51,915	5%	716,184	1,096,000	65%	0
		TOP 5 DMA DETAIL											
		NEW YORK	39	27	3,372	3,268	4,140	4,069	3%				
		LOS ANGELES	36	26	2,387	2,551	2,937	2,629	-6%				
		CHICAGO	37	25	1,963	1,900	2,285	2,264	3%				
		SAN FRANCISCO	24	22	1,507	1,378	1,767	1,692	9%				
		BOSTON	38	41	1,197	929	905	853	29%				
		R&B CORE STORE	16	18	11,072	11,885	14,831	16,181	-7%				
Sweet Lady		BDS: R&B MAINSTM	1,904	1,974					CUM SPINS:	37,142			
		BDS: T40 MSTRM	626	433					CUM SPINS:	1,378			
		BDS: T40 RHYTHM	1,486	1,574					CUM SPINS:	10,947			
		BDS: CROSSOVER	2,393	2,503					CUM SPINS:	30,825			
		MTV	N/A	N/A									
		BET											
DAVE MATTHEWS & TIM REYNOLDS													
Live at Luther College	1/19/99	TOP 200	62*	62*	58	29,845	31,624	35,033	15%	678,636	959,800	71%	0
		TOP 5 DMA DETAIL											
		NEW YORK	47	47	2,766	2,519	2,916	2,950	10%				
		CHICAGO	51	52	1,580	1,250	1,708	1,641	26%				
		PHILADELPHIA	35	33	1,492	1,286	1,554	1,735	16%				
		BOSTON	39	39	1,155	941	1,347	1,368	23%				
		LOS ANGELES	93	82	991	1,073	1,336	1,735	-8%				

Source: Soundscan

INDEX

distribution of sales of wine by price, 188 *il.*

employment distribution of consumers by wine category, 191 *il.*

income distribution of consumers by wine category, 191 *il.*

last drink taken, 193 *il.*

leading brands of domestic table wine and sales, 193 *il.*

national sales of wine by tier, 189 *il.*

on-premise *vs.* off-premise case sales of wine, 195 *il.*

percentage of persons who drink wine by category and age group, 192 *il.*

percentage of persons who drink wine by category and education level, 192 *il.*

percentage of persons who drink wine by category and employment, 189 *il.*

percentage of persons who drink wine by category and residency, 189 *il.*

percentage of wine consumers by category and gender, 190 *il.*

United States, 180–182

volume and per capita consumption trends by beverage, 188 *il.*

wireless internet service, 584 *il.*

women. *See also* iVillage.com

increase in the number of working women and dual income families, 232–233 *il.*

online women sites: timeline of key milestones, 296 *il.*

women.com, competition, 297 *il.*

Women.com, income statement, 298 *il.*

Women.com Networks, The, 583 *il.*

women's magazines, 300 *il.*

WorldCom, 477, 491, 492

World On Line, 479

World Wide Web, 471, 489, 523

World Wide Web usage, 1995-2000, projections of, 25 *il.*

www.kj.com, 182

WxWizard, 210, 212, 219 *il.*

Y

Yablon, Jill, 77

Yahoo!, 394–395, 399, 468 *il.,* 491, 515, 526t, 527, 543, 574, 580, 582, 583 *il.*

Amazon.com strategic alliances, 36, 78

Egghead.com, 166–167

strategic alliance with PlanetAll, 122–123

yearly income of web users, 177 *il.*

Z

ZDNet, BarnesandNoble.com Affiliates Network, 77

BarnesandNoble.com Affiliates Network, 37

ZDNet Sites, 583 *il.*

ZiffDavis. *See* ZDNet

ZipLock, 173

Media Convergence to a Digital Platform

	1964	1970		1980
*e*Commerce				
Television			**1975** HBO begins satellite transmission	**1980** CNN formed
Radio/Music				**1983** First CDs launched
Print				**1982** *USA Today* launched, satellite printing used **1983** *New York Times* completes conversion from letterpress to offset
Video Games		**Early 70s** Nolan Bushnell creates Pong		
Wireless				
Online Services				
Internet/Browsers	**1966** First funding to establish the Internet **1969** Internet established by U.S. Department of Defense			
Servers				
Personal Computers	**1965** IBM 360, first integrated-circuit computer & PDP-8, first minicomputer introduced by Digital	**Early 70s** Graphical User Interface developed by XEROX PARC **1970** First floppy disk created **1971** Texas Instruments creates its first pocket calculator	**1975** MIT's Altair 8800, first personal computer, introduced; Cray supercomputer created **1977** Apple II, first widely sold PC, introduced; Microsoft founded **1978** Hayes introduces first microcomputer-compatible modem	**1981** IBM introduces its personal computer **1984** Apple introduces the Macintosh **1984** Dell founded
Microprocessors		**1971** Intel introduces first microprocessor, the 4004 chip	**1973** Intel introduces the 8080 microprocessor **1978** Intel introduces the 8088 chip	**1982** Intel introduces the 80286 chip
Legal		**Mid-70s** FCC prohibits cross media ownership of newspapers and television	**1977** Federal court lifts FCC restrictions on cable television	**1984** U.S. Court orders breakup of AT&T into 8 regional "Baby Bells"